T0178422

Lecture Notes in Computer Science 14464

Founding Editors

Gerhard Goos
Juris Hartmanis

Editorial Board Members

The series Lecture Notes in Computer Science (LNCS), including its subseries Lecture Notes in Artificial Intelligence (LNAI) and Lecture Notes in Bioinformatics (LNBI), has established itself as a medium for the publication of new developments in computer science and information technology research, teaching, and education.

LNCS enjoys close cooperation with the computer science R & D community, the series counts many renowned academics among its volume editors and paper authors, and collaborates with prestigious societies. Its mission is to serve this international community by providing an invaluable service, mainly focused on the publication of conference and workshop proceedings and postproceedings. LNCS commenced publication in 1973.

Holger Hermanns · Jun Sun · Lei Bu
Editors

Dependable Software Engineering

Theories, Tools, and Applications

9th International Symposium, SETTA 2023
Nanjing, China, November 27–29, 2023
Proceedings

Editors
Holger Hermanns ⓘ
Saarland University
Saarbrücken, Germany

Jun Sun ⓘ
Singapore Management University
Singapore, Singapore

Lei Bu ⓘ
Nanjing University
Nanjing, China

ISSN 0302-9743   ISSN 1611-3349 (electronic)
Lecture Notes in Computer Science
ISBN 978-981-99-8663-7   ISBN 978-981-99-8664-4 (eBook)
https://doi.org/10.1007/978-981-99-8664-4

This Springer imprint is published by the registered company Springer Nature Singapore Pte Ltd.
The registered company address is: 152 Beach Road, #21-01/04 Gateway East, Singapore 189721, Singapore

Paper in this product is recyclable.

Preface

This volume presents the proceedings of the International Symposium on Dependable Software Engineering: Theories, Tools and Applications (SETTA) 2023, held in Nanjing on November 27–29, 2023. The purpose of the SETTA symposium series is to bring international researchers together to exchange research results and ideas on bridging the gap between formal methods and software engineering. Topics of interest to SETTA include, but are not limited to:

– Requirements specification and analysis
– Formalisms for modeling, design, and implementation
– Model checking, theorem proving, and decision procedures
– Scalable approaches to formal system analysis
– Formal approaches to simulation, run-time verification, and testing
– Integration of formal methods into software engineering practice
– Contract-based engineering of components, systems, and systems of systems
– Formal and engineering aspects of software evolution and maintenance
– Parallel and multicore programming
– Embedded, real-time, hybrid, probabilistic, and cyber-physical systems
– Mixed-critical applications and systems
– Formal aspects of service-oriented and cloud computing
– Safety, reliability, robustness, and fault-tolerance
– Dependability of smart software and systems
– Empirical analysis techniques and integration with formal methods
– Applications and industrial experience reports
– Software tools to assist the construction or analysis of software systems

This edition of the symposium received 89 submissions, out of which 9 were desk-rejected for reasons such as having a wrong format or being out of scope. Each remaining submission went through a rigorous review process with at least 3 reviews, followed by an online discussion among the PC members, overseen by the PC chairs. In the end, 24 full high-quality papers were selected for presentation at the conference.

SETTA 2023 was blessed by the presence of three internationally recognized keynote speakers, who gave talks covering current hot research topics and revealing many new interesting research directions:

– Nazareno Aguirre (Universidad Nacional de Río Cuarto, Argentina)
– Jinsong Dong (National University of Singapore, Singapore)
– Geguang Pu (East China Normal University, China)

This edition of SETTA would not have been successful without the contribution and involvement of the Program Committee members and the external reviewers who contributed to the review process. This event would not exist if authors and contributors did not submit their work. We owe our thanks to every person, reviewer, author, program committee member, and organizing committee member involved in SETTA 2023.

The local host and sponsor Nanjing University of Aeronautics and Astronautics provided financial support and tremendous help with registration and facilities. Many thanks to all the local organizers and sponsors.

November 2023   Holger Hermanns
Jun Sun
Lei Bu

Organization

General Chair

Zhiqiu Huang   Nanjing University of Aeronautics and
                                Astronautics, China

Program Co-chairs

Holger Hermanns   Saarland University, Germany
Jun Sun   Singapore Management University, Singapore
Lei Bu   Nanjing University, China

Publicity Chair

Zhibin Yang   Nanjing University of Aeronautics and
                                Astronautics, China

Local Organization Committee

Yu Zhou (Chair)   Nanjing University of Aeronautics and
                                Astronautics, China
Zhibin Yang   Nanjing University of Aeronautics and
                                Astronautics, China
Zhiyi Zhang   Nanjing University of Aeronautics and
                                Astronautics, China
Weiwei Li   Nanjing University of Aeronautics and
                                Astronautics, China
Chuanqi Tao   Nanjing University of Aeronautics and
                                Astronautics, China
Wenhua Yang   Nanjing University of Aeronautics and
                                Astronautics, China
Haiyan Chen   Nanjing University of Aeronautics and
                                Astronautics, China

Web Chairs

Zhiyi Zhang   Nanjing University of Aeronautics and
                                     Astronautics, China
Bohua Zhan   Institute of Software, Chinese Academy of
                                     Sciences, China

Program Committee

Guangdong Bai   University of Queensland, Australia
Jean-Paul Bodeveix   IRIT-UPS, France
Sudipta Chattopadhyay   Singapore University of Technology and Design,
                                     Singapore
Liqian Chen   National University of Defense Technology,
                                     China
Yuting Chen   Shanghai Jiao Tong University, China
Pedro R. D'Argenio   Universidad Nacional de Córdoba – CONICET,
                                     Argentina
Benoit Delahaye   Université de Nantes - LS2N, France
Yuxin Deng   East China Normal University, China
Rayna Dimitrova   CISPA Helmholtz Center for Information
                                     Security, Germany
Wei Dong   National University of Defense Technology,
                                     China
Clemens Dubslaff   Eindhoven University of Technology,
                                     The Netherlands
Mamoun Filali   IRIT-CNRS, France
Jan Friso Groote   Eindhoven University of Technology,
                                     The Netherlands
Nils Jansen   Radboud University, The Netherlands
Yu Jiang   Tsinghua University, China
Xiaohong Li   Tianjin University, China
Yi Li   Nanyang Technological University, Singapore
Shang-Wei Lin   Nanyang Technological University, Singapore
Yun Lin   Shanghai Jiao Tong University, China
Shuang Liu   Tianjin University, China
Malte Lochau   University of Siegen, Germany
Mohammadreza Mousavi   King's College London, UK
Thomas Noll   RWTH Aachen University, Germany
Jun Pang   University of Luxembourg, Luxembourg
Dave Parker   University of Oxford, UK

Zhiping Shi	Capital Normal University, China
Fu Song	ShanghaiTech University, China
Ting Su	East China Normal University, China
Meng Sun	Peking University, China
Jean-Pierre Talpin	Inria, France
Jingyi Wang	Zhejiang University, China
Zhilin Wu	Chinese Academy of Sciences, China
Yueling Zhang	East China Normal University, China
Yongwang Zhao	Zhejiang University, China

Additional Reviewers

André, Pascal
Ardourel, Gilles
Attiogbé, Christian
Bu, Hao
Chi, Zhiming
De Vink, Erik
Demasi, Ramiro
Dong, Yanqi
Franken, Tom
Galesloot, Maris
Holík, Lukáš
Jansen, David N.
Jantsch, Simon
Jilissen, Kevin
Kouchnarenko, Olga
Köhl, Maximilian Alexander
Laveaux, Maurice
Li, Shuo
Lime, Didier
Liu, Guanjun
Liu, Ye
Liu, Yicheng
Liu, Yixuan

Luan, Xiaokun
Ma, Feifei
Müller, Robert
Petri, Gustavo
Qi, Xiaodong
Schmidl, Christoph
Stramaglia, Anna
van Spaendonck, Flip
Wang, Junjie
Wang, Keyin
Weiß, Mathis
Wu, Xiuheng
Xu, Ming
Xu, Peng
Xu, Xiufeng
Xue, Xiaoyong
Yang, Dong
Yang, Xuqing
Zhang, Lei
Zhang, Peixin
Zhang, Teng
Zhang, Yao
Zhang, Yating

Contents

String Constraints with Regex-Counting and String-Length Solved More Efficiently

Denghang Hu[1,2] and Zhilin Wu[1,2(✉)] ⓘ

[1] State Key Laboratory of Computer Science, Institute of Software, Chinese Academy of Sciences, Beijing, China
{hudh,wuzl}@ios.ac.cn
[2] University of Chinese Academy of Sciences, Beijing, China

Abstract. Regular expressions (regex for short) and string-length function are widely used in string-manipulating programs. Counting is a frequently used feature in regexes that counts the number of matchings of sub-patterns. The state-of-the-art string solvers are incapable of solving string constraints with regex-counting and string-length efficiently, especially when the counting and length bounds are large. In this work, we propose an automata-theoretic approach for solving such class of string constraints. The main idea is to symbolically model the counting operators by registers in automata instead of unfolding them explicitly, thus alleviating the state explosion problem. Moreover, the string-length function is modeled by a register as well. As a result, the satisfiability of string constraints with regex-counting and string-length is reduced to the satisfiability of linear integer arithmetic, which the off-the-shelf SMT solvers can then solve. To improve the performance further, we also propose techniques to reduce the sizes of automata. We implement the algorithms and validate our approach on 48,843 benchmark instances. The experimental results show that our approach can solve more instances than the state-of-the-art solvers, at a comparable or faster speed, especially when the counting and length bounds are large.

1 Introduction

The string data type plays a crucial role in modern programming languages such as JavaScript, Python, Java, and PHP. String manipulations are error-prone and could even give rise to severe security vulnerabilities (e.g., cross-site scripting, aka XSS). One powerful method for identifying such bugs is *symbolic execution*, which is possibly in combination with dynamic analysis. It analyses symbolic paths in a program by viewing them as constraints checked by constraint solvers. Symbolic execution of string manipulating programs has motivated the highly active research area of *string constraint solving*, resulting in the development of numerous string solvers in the last decade, e.g., Z3seq [30], CVC4/5 [2,26], Z3str/2/3/4 [3,5,37,38], Z3str3RE [4], Z3-Trau [1,7], OSTRICH [14], Slent [35], among many others.

Regular expressions (regex for short) and the string-length function are widely used in string-manipulating programs. According to the statistics from

© The Author(s), under exclusive license to Springer Nature Singapore Pte Ltd. 2024
H. Hermanns et al. (Eds.): SETTA 2023, LNCS 14464, pp. 1–20, 2024.
https://doi.org/10.1007/978-981-99-8664-4_1

[9,17,36], regexes are used in about 30–40% of Java, JavaScript, and Python software projects. Moreover, string-length occupies 78% of the occurrences of string operations in 18 Javascript applications, according to the statistics from [31]. As a result, most of the aforementioned string constraint solvers support both regexes and string-length function. Moreover, specialized algorithms have been proposed to solve such string constraints efficiently (see e.g. [4,27]).

Counting (aka repetition) is a convenient feature in regexes that counts the number of matchings of sub-patterns. For instance, $a^{\{2,4\}}$ specifies that a occurs at least twice and at most four times, and $a^{\{2,\infty\}}$ specifies that a occurs at least twice. Note that the Kleene star and the Kleene plus operator are special cases of counting. For instance, a^* is equivalent to $a^{\{0,\infty\}}$ and a^+ is equivalent to $a^{\{1,\infty\}}$. Counting is a frequently used feature of regexes. According to the statistics from [9], Kleene star/plus occur in more than 70% of 1,204 Python projects, while other forms of counting occur in more than 20% of them. Therefore, an efficient analysis of string manipulating programs requires efficient solvers for string constraints containing regexes with counting[1] and string-length function at least.

Nevertheless, the aforementioned state-of-the-art string constraint solvers still suffer from such string constraints, especially when the counting and length bounds are large. For instance, none of the string solvers CVC5, Z3seq, Z3-Trau, Z3str3, Z3str3RE, and OSTRICH is capable of solving the following constraint within 120 s,

$$x \in (\Sigma \setminus a)^{\{1,60\}}(\Sigma \setminus b)^{\{1,60\}}(\Sigma \setminus c)^{\{0,60\}} \wedge x \in \Sigma^* c^+ \wedge |x| > 120. \quad (1)$$

Intuitively, the constraint in (1) specifies that x is a concatenation of three strings x_1, x_2, x_3 where a (resp. b, c) does not occur in x_1 (resp. x_2, x_3), moreover, x ends with a nonempty sequence of c's, and the length of x is greater than 120. It is easy to observe that this constraint is unsatisfiable since on the one hand, $|x| > 120$ and the counting upper bound 60 in both $(\Sigma \setminus a)^{\{1,60\}}$ and $(\Sigma \setminus b)^{\{1,60\}}$ imply that x must end with some character from $\Sigma \setminus c$, that is, a character different from c, and on the other hand, $x \in \Sigma^* c^+$ requires that x has to end with c.

A typical way for string constraint solvers to deal with regular expressions with counting is to unfold them into those *without* counting using the concatenation operator. For instance, $a^{\{1,4\}}$ is unfolded into $a(\varepsilon + a + aa + aaa)$ and $a^{\{2,\infty\}}$ is unfolded into aaa^*. Since the unfolding incurs an exponential blow-up on the sizes of constraints (assuming that the counting in string constraints are encoded in binary), the unfolding penalizes the performance of the solvers, especially when the length bounds are also available.

Contribution. In this work, we focus on the class of string constraints with regular membership and string-length function, where the counting operators may occur (called RECL for brevity). We make the following contributions.

---

[1] In the rest of this paper, for clarity, we use counting to denote expressions of the form $e^{\{m,n\}}$ and $e^{\{m,\infty\}}$, but not e^* or e^+.

- We propose an automata-theoretical approach for solving RECL constraints. Our main idea is to represent the counting operators by cost registers in cost-enriched finite automata (CEFA, see Sect. 5 for the definition), instead of unfolding them explicitly. The string-length function is modeled by cost registers as well. The satisfiability of RECL constraints is reduced to the nonemptiness problem of CEFA w.r.t. a linear integer arithmetic (LIA) formula. According to the results from [13], an LIA formula can be computed to represent the potential values of registers in CEFA. Thus, the nonemptiness of CEFA w.r.t. LIA formulas can be reduced to the satisfiability of LIA formulas, which is then tackled by off-the-shelf SMT solvers.
- We propose techniques to reduce the sizes (i.e. the number of states and transitions) of CEFA, in order to achieve better performance.
- Combined with the size-reduction techniques mentioned above, the register representation of regex-counting and string-length in CEFA entails an efficient algorithm for solving RECL constraints. We implement the algorithm on top of OSTRICH, resulting in a string solver called OSTRICH^{RECL}.
- Finally, we utilize a collection of benchmark suites comprising 48,843 instances in total to evaluate the performance of OSTRICH^{RECL}. The experiment results show that OSTRICH^{RECL} solves the RECL constraints more efficiently than the state-of-the-art string solvers, especially when the counting and length bounds are large (see Fig. 5b and Table 1a). For instance, on 1,969 benchmark instances where the counting bounds are greater than or equal to 50 and the string lengths are required to be beyond 200, OSTRICH^{RECL} solves at least 278 more instances than the other solvers, while spending only half or less time per instance on average.

Related Work. We discuss more related work on regexes with counting, string-length function, and automata with registers/counters. Determinism of regexes with counting was investigated in [10,19]. Real-world regexes in programming languages include features beyond classical regexes, e.g., the greedy/lazy Kleene star, capturing groups, and back references. Real-world regexes have been addressed in symbolic execution of Javascript programs [28] and string constraint solving [12]. Nevertheless, the counting operators are still unfolded explicitly in [12]. The Trau tool focuses on string constraints involving flat regular languages and string-length function and solves them by computing LIA formulas that define the Parikh images of flat regular languages [1]. The Slent tool solves the string constraints involving string-length function by encoding them into so-called length-encoded automata, then utilizing symbolic model checkers to solve their nonemptiness problem [35]. However, neither Trau nor Slent supports counting operators explicitly, in other words, counting operators in regexes should be unfolded before solved by them. Cost registers in CEFAs are different from registers in (symbolic) register automata [16,23]: In register automata, registers are used to store input values and can only be compared for equality/inequality, while in CEFAs, cost registers are used to store integer-valued costs and can be updated by adding/subtracting integer constants and constrained by the accepting conditions which are LIA formulas. Therefore, cost registers in CEFAs are more like counters in counter automata/machines [29], that is, CEFAs can be obtained from counter machines by removing transition guards and adding accepting conditions. Counting-set automata were proposed in [21,33] to quickly match a subclass of regexes with counting. Moreover, a variant of nondeterministic counter automata, called bit vector automata, was proposed recently in [25] to enable fast matching of a more expressive class of regexes with counting. Nevertheless, the nonemptiness problem of these automata was not considered, and it is unclear whether these automata models can be used for solving string constraints with regex-counting and string-length.

Organization. The rest of this paper is structured as follows: Sect. 2 gives an overview of the approach in this paper. Section 3 introduces the preliminaries. Section 4 presents the syntax and semantics of RECL. Section 5 defines CEFA. Section 6 introduces the algorithm to solve RECL constraints. Section 7 shows the experiment results. Section 8 concludes this paper.

2   Overview

In this section, we utilize the string constraint in Eq. (1) to illustrate the approach in our work.

At first, we construct a CEFA for the regular expression $(\Sigma \setminus a)^{\{1,60\}}(\Sigma \setminus b)^{\{1,60\}}(\Sigma \setminus c)^{\{0,60\}}$. Three registers are introduced, say r_1, r_2, r_3, to represent the three counting operators; the nondeterministic finite automaton (NFA) for $(\Sigma \setminus a)^*(\Sigma \setminus b)^*(\Sigma \setminus c)^*$ is constructed; the updates of registers are added to the transitions of the NFA; the counting bounds are specified by the accepting condition $1 \le r_1 \le 60 \wedge 1 \le r_2 \le 60 \wedge 0 \le r_3 \le 60$, resulting in a CEFA $\mathcal{A}_1$ illustrated in Fig. 1(a). $r_1 + +$ means that we increment the value of r_1 by one after running the transition. A string w is accepted by $\mathcal{A}_1$ if, when reading the characters in w, $\mathcal{A}_1$ applies the transitions to update the state and the values of registers, reaching a final state q in the end, and the resulting values of the three registers, say v_1, v_2, v_3, satisfy the accepting condition. In addition, we construct other two CEFAs $\mathcal{A}_2$ for $\Sigma^* c^+$ (see Fig. 1(b)) and $\mathcal{A}_3$ for string length function (see Fig. 1(c)). In $\mathcal{A}_3$, a register r_4 is used to denote the length of strings and the accepting condition is true (See Sect. 6.1 for more details about the construction of CEFA.) Note that we represent the counting operators symbolically by registers instead of unfolding them explicitly.

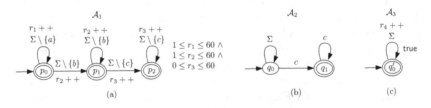

Fig. 1. CEFA for $(\Sigma \setminus a)^{\{1,60\}}(\Sigma \setminus b)^{\{1,60\}}(\Sigma \setminus c)^{\{0,60\}}$, $\Sigma^* c^+$, and $|x|$

Next, we construct $\mathcal{A}_1 \cap \mathcal{A}_2 \cap \mathcal{A}_3$, that is, the intersection (aka product) of $\mathcal{A}_1$, $\mathcal{A}_2$, and $\mathcal{A}_3$, as illustrated in Fig. 2(a), where the states can not reach the final states are removed. For technical convenience, we also think of the updates of registers in transitions as vectors (u_1, u_2, u_3, u_4), where $u_i \in \mathbb{Z}$ is the update on the register r_i for each $i \in [4]$. For instance, the transitions corresponding to the self-loop around (p_0, q_0, q_0') are thought as $((p_0, q_0, q_0'), a', (p_0, q_0, q_0'), (1, 0, 0, 1))$ with $a' \in \Sigma \setminus \{a\}$, since r_1 and r_4 are incremented by one in these transitions. After considering the updates of registers as vectors, the CEFA is like Fig. 2(b).

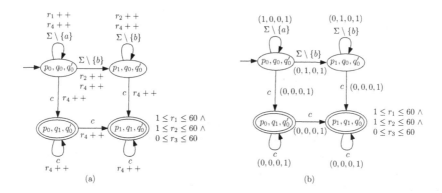

Fig. 2. $\mathcal{A}_1 \cap \mathcal{A}_2 \cap \mathcal{A}_3$: Intersection of $\mathcal{A}_1$, $\mathcal{A}_2$, and $\mathcal{A}_3$

Finally, the satisfiability of the original string constraint is reduced to the nonemptiness of the CEFA $\mathcal{A} \equiv \mathcal{A}_1 \cap \mathcal{A}_2 \cap \mathcal{A}_3$ with respect to the LIA formula $\varphi \equiv r_4 > 120$, that is, whether there exist $w \in \Sigma^*$ and $(v_1, v_2, v_3, v_4) \in \mathbb{Z}^4$ such that w is accepted by $\mathcal{A}$, so that the resulting registers values (v_1, v_2, v_3, v_4) satisfy both $1 \le v_1 \le 60 \wedge 1 \le v_2 \le 60 \wedge 0 \le v_3 \le 60$ and φ. It is not hard to observe that the nonemptiness of $\mathcal{A}$ with respect to φ is independent of the characters of $\mathcal{A}$. Therefore, the characters in $\mathcal{A}$ can be ignored, resulting into an NFA $\mathcal{B}$ over the alphabet $\mathbb{C}$, where $\mathbb{C}$ is the set of vectors from $\mathbb{Z}^4$ occurring in the transitions of $\mathcal{A}$ (see Fig. 3(a)). Then the original problem is reduced to the problem of deciding whether there exists a string $w' \in \mathbb{C}^*$ that is accepted by $\mathcal{B}$ and its Parikh image (i.e., numbers of occurrences of characters), say $\eta_{w'} : \mathbb{C} \to \mathbb{N}$, satisfies $1 \le v_1' \le 60 \wedge 1 \le v_2' \le 60 \wedge 0 \le v_3' \le 60 \wedge v_4' > 120$, where $(v_1', v_2', v_3', v_4') = \sum_{v \in \mathbb{C}} \eta_{w'}(v) v$ for each $v \in \mathbb{C}$. Intuitively, (v_1', v_2', v_3', v_4') is a weighted sum of vectors $v \in \mathbb{C}$, where the weight is the number of occurrences of v in w'. (See Sect. 6.2 for more detailed arguments).

Let $\mathbb{C} = \{v_1, \cdots, v_m\}$. From the results in [32, 34], an existential LIA formula $\psi_{\mathcal{B}}(\mathfrak{x}_1, \cdots, \mathfrak{x}_m)$ can be computed to define the Parikh image of strings that are accepted by $\mathcal{B}$, where $\mathfrak{x}_1, \cdots, \mathfrak{x}_m$ are the integer variables to denote the number of occurrences of $v_1, \cdots, v_m$. Therefore, the satisfiability of the string constraint in (1) is reduced to the satisfiability of the following existential LIA formula,

$$\psi_{\mathcal{B}}(\mathfrak{x}_1, \cdots, \mathfrak{x}_m) \wedge \bigwedge_{1 \le j \le 4} r_j = \sum_{1 \le k \le m} \mathfrak{x}_k v_{k,j} \wedge$$
$$1 \le r_1 \le 60 \wedge 1 \le r_2 \le 60 \wedge 0 \le r_3 \le 60 \wedge r_4 > 120. \tag{2}$$

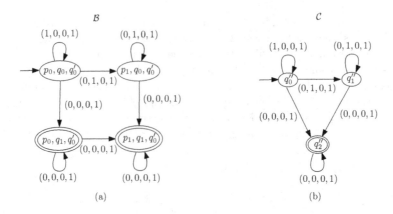

Fig. 3. Reduced automaton $\mathcal{B}$ and $\mathcal{C}$

which can be solved by the off-the-shelf SMT solvers.

Nevertheless, when the original regexes are complicated (e.g. contain occurrences of negation or intersection operators), the sizes of the NFA $\mathcal{B}$ can still be big and the sizes of the LIA formulas defining the Parikh image of $\mathcal{B}$ are also big. Since the satisfiability of LIA formulas is an NP-complete problem [20], big sizes of LIA formulas would be a bottleneck of the performance. To tackle this issue, we propose techniques to reduce the sizes of the NFA $\mathcal{B}$.

Specifically, to reduce the sizes of $\mathcal{B}$, we determinize $\mathcal{B}$, and apply the minimization algorithm to the resulting deterministic finite automaton (DFA), resulting in a DFA $\mathcal{C}$, as illustrated in Fig. 3(b). Note that $\mathcal{C}$ contains only three states q_0'', q_1'', q_2'' and six transitions, while $\mathcal{B}$ contains four states and eight transitions. Furthermore, if $\mathcal{B}$ contains **0**-labeled transitions, then we can take these transitions as ϵ-transitions and potentially reduce the sizes of automata further.

We implement all the aforementioned techniques on the top of OSTRICH, resulting in a solver OSTRICH[RECL]. It turns out that OSTRICH[RECL] is able to solve the string constraint in (1) within one second, while the state-of-the-art string solvers are incapable of solving it within 120 s.

3   Preliminaries

We write $\mathbb{N}$ and $\mathbb{Z}$ for the sets of natural and integer numbers. For $n \in \mathbb{N}$ with $n \geq 1$, $[n]$ denotes $\{1, \ldots, n\}$; for $m, n \in \mathbb{N}$ with $m \leq n$, $[m, n]$ denotes $\{i \in \mathbb{N} \mid m \leq i \leq n\}$. Throughout the paper, Σ is a finite alphabet, ranged over $a, b, \ldots$.

For a function f from X to Y and $X' \subseteq X$, we use $\mathsf{prj}_{X'}(f)$ to denote the restriction (aka projection) of f to X', that is, $\mathsf{prj}_{X'}(f)$ is the function from X' to Y, and $\mathsf{prj}_{X'}(f)(x') = f(x')$ for each $x' \in X'$.

Strings and Languages. A string over Σ is a (possibly empty) sequence of elements from Σ, denoted by $u, v, w, \ldots$. An empty string is denoted by ε. We use

Σ_ε to denote $\Sigma \cup \{\varepsilon\}$. We write Σ^* (resp., Σ^+) for the set of all (resp. nonempty) strings over Σ. For a string u, we use $|u|$ to denote the number of letters in u. In particular, $|\varepsilon| = 0$. Moreover, for $a \in \Sigma$, let $|u|_a$ denote the number of occurrences of a in u. Assume that $u = a_1 \cdots a_n$ is nonempty and $1 \le i < j \le n$. We let $u[i]$ denote a_i and $u[i,j]$ for the substring $a_i \cdots a_j$. Let u, v be two strings. We use $u \cdot v$ to denote the *concatenation* of u and v. A language L over Σ is a subset of strings. Let L_1, L_2 be two languages. Then the concatenation of L_1 and L_2, denoted by $L_1 \cdot L_2$, is defined as $\{u \cdot v \mid u \in L_1, v \in L_2\}$. The union (resp. intersection) of L_1 and L_2, denoted by $L_1 \cup L_2$ (resp. $L_1 \cap L_2$), is defined as $\{u \mid u \in L_1 \text{ or } u \in L_2\}$ (resp. $\{u \mid u \in L_1 \text{ and } u \in L_2\}$). The complement of L_1, denoted by $\overline{L_1}$, is defined as $\{u \mid u \in \Sigma^*, u \notin L_1\}$. The difference of L_1 and L_2, denoted by $L_1 \setminus L_2$, is defined as $L_1 \cap \overline{L_2}$. For a language L and $n \in \mathbb{N}$, we define L^n inductively as follows: $L^0 = \{\varepsilon\}$, $L^{n+1} = L \cdot L^n$ for every $n \in \mathbb{N}$. Finally, define $L^* = \bigcup_{n \in \mathbb{N}} L^n$.

Finite Automata. A *(nondeterministic) finite automaton* (NFA) is a tuple $\mathcal{A} = (Q, \Sigma, \delta, I, F)$, where Q is a finite set of states, Σ is a finite alphabet, $\delta \subseteq Q \times \Sigma \times Q$ is the transition relation, $I \subseteq Q$ is the set of initial states, and $F \subseteq Q$ is the set of final states. For readability, we write a transition $(q, a, q') \in \delta$ as $q \xrightarrow[\delta]{a} q'$ (or simply $q \xrightarrow{a} q'$). The *size* of an NFA $\mathcal{A}$, denoted by $|\mathcal{A}|$, is defined as the number of transitions of $\mathcal{A}$. A *run* of $\mathcal{A}$ on a string $w = a_1 \cdots a_n$ is a sequence of transitions $q_0 \xrightarrow{a_1} q_1 \cdots q_{n-1} \xrightarrow{a_n} q_n$ such that $q_0 \in I$. The run is *accepting* if $q_n \in F$. A string w is accepted by an NFA $\mathcal{A}$ if there is an accepting run of $\mathcal{A}$ on w. In particular, the empty string ε is accepted by $\mathcal{A}$ if $I \cap F \neq \emptyset$. The language of $\mathcal{A}$, denoted by $\mathcal{L}(\mathcal{A})$, is the set of strings accepted by $\mathcal{A}$. An NFA $\mathcal{A}$ is said to be *deterministic* if I is a singleton and, for every $q \in Q$ and $a \in \Sigma$, there is at most one state $q' \in Q$ such that $(q, a, q') \in \delta$. We use DFA to denote deterministic finite automata.

It is well-known that finite automata capture regular languages. Moreover, the class of regular languages is closed under union, intersection, concatenation, Kleene star, complement, and language difference [22].

Let $w \in \Sigma^*$. The *Parikh image* of w, denoted by $\mathsf{parikh}(w)$, is defined as the function $\eta : \Sigma \to \mathbb{N}$ such that $\eta(a) = |w|_a$ for each $a \in \Sigma$. The *Parikh image* of an NFA $\mathcal{A}$, denoted by $\mathsf{parikh}(\mathcal{A})$, is defined as $\{\mathsf{parikh}(w) \mid w \in \mathcal{L}(\mathcal{A})\}$.

Linear Integer Arithmetic and Parikh Images. We use standard existential *linear integer arithmetic* (LIA) formulas, which typically range over $\psi, \varphi, \Phi, \alpha$. For a set $\mathfrak{X}$ of variables, we use $\psi/\varphi/\Phi/\alpha(\mathfrak{X})$ to denote the set of existential LIA formulas whose free variables are from $\mathfrak{X}$. For example, we use $\varphi(\mathfrak{x})$ with $\mathfrak{x} = (\mathfrak{x}_1, \cdots, \mathfrak{x}_k)$ to denote an LIA formula φ whose free variables are from $\{\mathfrak{x}_1, \cdots, \mathfrak{x}_k\}$. For an LIA formula $\varphi(\mathfrak{x})$, we use $\varphi[t/\mathfrak{x}]$ to denote the formula obtained by replacing (simultaneously) $\mathfrak{x}_i$ with t_i for every $i \in [k]$ where $\mathfrak{x} = (\mathfrak{x}_1, \cdots, \mathfrak{x}_k)$ and $t = (t_1, \cdots, t_k)$ are tuples of integer terms.

At last, we recall the result about Parikh images of NFA. For each $a \in \Sigma$, let $\mathfrak{z}_a$ be an integer variable. Let $\mathfrak{z}_\Sigma$ denote the set of integer variables $\mathfrak{z}_a$ for $a \in \Sigma$. Let $\mathcal{A}$ be an NFA over the alphabet Σ. Then we say that an LIA formula

$\psi(3_\Sigma)$ defines the Parikh image of $\mathcal{A}$, if $\{\eta : \Sigma \to \mathbb{N} \mid \psi[(\eta(a)/3_a)_{a \in \Sigma}] \text{ is true}\} = \text{parikh}(\mathcal{A})$.

Theorem 1 ([32]). *Given an NFA $\mathcal{A}$, an existential LIA formula $\psi_A(3_\Sigma)$ can be computed in linear time that defines the Parikh image of $\mathcal{A}$.*

4   String Constraints with Regex-Counting and String-Length

In the sequel, we define the string constraints with regex-counting and string-length functions, i.e., **RE**gex-**C**ounting **L**ogic (abbreviated as RECL). The syntax of RECL is defined by the rules in Fig. 4, where x is a string variable, $\mathfrak{x}$ is an integer variable, a is a character from an alphabet Σ, and m, n are integer constants. A RECL formula φ is a conjunction of atomic formulas of the form $x \in e$ or $t_1 \ o \ t_2$, where e is a regular expression, t_1 and t_2 are integer terms, and $o \in \{=, \neq, \leq, \geq, <, >\}$. Atomic formulas of the form $x \in e$ are called *regular membership* constraints, and atomic formulas of the form $t_1 \ o \ t_2$ are called *length* constraints. A regular expression e is built from $\emptyset$, the empty string ϵ, and the character a by using concatenation $\cdot$, union $+$, Kleene star *, intersection $\cap$, complement $\bar{\ }$, difference $\backslash$, counting $^{\{m,n\}}$ or $^{\{m,\infty\}}$. An integer term is built from constants n, variables $\mathfrak{x}$, and string lengths $|x|$ by operators $+$ and $-$.

$$
\begin{aligned}
\varphi &::= x \in e \mid t_1 \ o \ t_2 \mid \varphi \wedge \varphi && \text{formulas} \\
e &::= \emptyset \mid \epsilon \mid a \mid e \cdot e \mid e + e \mid e^* \mid e \cap e \mid \bar{e} \mid e \backslash e \mid e^{\{m,n\}} \mid e^{\{m,\infty\}} \mid (e) && \text{regexes} \\
t &::= n \mid \mathfrak{x} \mid |x| \mid t - t \mid t + t && \text{integer terms}
\end{aligned}
$$

Fig. 4. Syntax of RECL

Moreover, for $S \subseteq \Sigma$ with $S = \{a_1, \cdots, a_k\}$, we use S as an abbreviation of $a_1 + \cdots + a_k$.

For each regular expression e, the language defined by e, denoted by $\mathcal{L}(e)$, is defined recursively. For instance, $\mathcal{L}(\emptyset) = \emptyset$, $\mathcal{L}(\varepsilon) = \{\varepsilon\}$, $\mathcal{L}(a) = \{a\}$, and $\mathcal{L}(e_1 \cdot e_2) = \mathcal{L}(e_1) \cdot \mathcal{L}(e_2)$, $\mathcal{L}(e_1 + e_2) = \mathcal{L}(e_1) \cup \mathcal{L}(e_2)$, and so on. It is well-known that regular expressions define the same class of languages as finite state automata, that is, the class of regular languages [22].

Let φ be a RECL formula and $\mathsf{SVars}(\varphi)$ (resp. $\mathsf{IVars}(\varphi)$) denote the set of string (resp. integer) variables occurring in φ. Then the semantics of φ is defined with respect to a mapping $\theta : \mathsf{SVars}(\varphi) \to \Sigma^* \uplus \mathsf{IVars}(\varphi) \to \mathbb{Z}$ (where $\uplus$ denotes the disjoint union). Note that the mapping θ can naturally extend to the set of integer terms. For instance, $\theta(|x|) = |\theta(x)|$, $\theta(t_1 + t_2) = \theta(t_1) + \theta(t_2)$. A mapping θ is said to satisfy φ, denoted by $\theta \models \varphi$, if one of the following holds: $\varphi \equiv x \in e$ and $\theta(x) \in \mathcal{L}(e)$, $\varphi \equiv t_1 \ o \ t_2$ and $\theta(t_1) \ o \ \theta(t_2)$, $\varphi \equiv \varphi_1 \wedge \varphi_2$ and $\theta \models \varphi_1$ and $\theta \models \varphi_2$. A RECL formula φ is satisfiable if there is a mapping θ such as $\theta \models \varphi$. The satisfiability problem for RECL (which is abbreviated as $\mathsf{SAT}_{\mathsf{RECL}}$) is deciding whether a given RECL formula φ is satisfiable.

5 Cost-Enriched Finite Automata

In this section, we define cost-enriched finite state automata (CEFA), which was introduced in [13] and will be used to solve the satisfiability problem of RECL later on. Intuitively, CEFA adds write-only cost registers to finite state automata. "write-only" means that the cost registers can only be written/updated but cannot be read, i.e., they cannot be used to guard the transitions.

Definition 1 (Cost-Enriched Finite Automaton). *A cost-enriched finite automaton $\mathcal{A}$ is a tuple $(R, Q, \Sigma, \delta, I, F, \alpha)$ where*

- *$R = \{r_1, \cdots, r_k\}$ is a finite set of registers,*
- *Q, Σ, I, F are as in the definition of NFA,*
- *$\delta \subseteq Q \times \Sigma \times Q \times \mathbb{Z}^R$ is a transition relation, where $\mathbb{Z}^R$ denotes the updates on the values of registers.*
- *$\alpha \in \Phi(R)$ is an LIA formula specifying an accepting condition.*

For convenience, we use $R_{\mathcal{A}}$ to denote the set of registers of $\mathcal{A}$. We assume a linear order on R and write R as a vector $(r_1, \cdots, r_k)$. Accordingly, we write an element of $\mathbb{Z}^R$ as a vector $(v_1, \cdots, v_k)$, where v_i is the update of r_i for each $i \in [k]$. We also write a transition $(q, a, q', \boldsymbol{v}) \in \delta$ as $q \xrightarrow[\boldsymbol{v}]{a} q'$.

The semantics of CEFA is defined as follows. Let $\mathcal{A} = (R, Q, \Sigma, \delta, I, F, \alpha)$ be a CEFA. A *run* of $\mathcal{A}$ on a string $w = a_1 \cdots a_n$ is a sequence $q_0 \xrightarrow[\boldsymbol{v_1}]{a_1} q_1 \cdots q_{n-1} \xrightarrow[\boldsymbol{v_n}]{a_n} q_n$ such that $q_0 \in I$ and $q_{i-1} \xrightarrow[\boldsymbol{v_i}]{a_i} q_i$ for each $i \in [n]$. A run $q_0 \xrightarrow[\boldsymbol{v_1}]{a_1} q_1 \cdots q_{n-1} \xrightarrow[\boldsymbol{v_n}]{a_n} q_n$ is *accepting* if $q_n \in F$ and $\alpha(\boldsymbol{v'}/R)$ is true, where $\boldsymbol{v'} = \sum_{j \in [n]} \boldsymbol{v_j}$. The vector $\boldsymbol{v'} = \sum_{j \in [n]} \boldsymbol{v_j}$ is called the *cost* of an accepting run $q_0 \xrightarrow[\boldsymbol{v_1}]{a_1} q_1 \cdots q_{n-1} \xrightarrow[\boldsymbol{v_n}]{a_n} q_n$.

Note that the values of all registers are initiated to zero and updated to $\sum_{j \in [n]} \boldsymbol{v_j}$ after all the transitions in the run are executed. We use $\boldsymbol{v'} \in \mathcal{A}(w)$ to denote the fact that there is an accepting run of $\mathcal{A}$ on w whose cost is $\boldsymbol{v'}$. We define the semantics of a CEFA $\mathcal{A}$, denoted by $\mathcal{L}(\mathcal{A})$, as $\{(w; \boldsymbol{v'}) \mid \boldsymbol{v'} \in \mathcal{A}(w)\}$. In particular, if $I \cap F \neq \emptyset$ and $\alpha[\boldsymbol{0}/R]$ is true, then $(\varepsilon; \boldsymbol{0}) \in \mathcal{L}(\mathcal{A})$. Moreover, we define the *output* of a CEFA $\mathcal{A}$, denoted by $\mathcal{O}(\mathcal{A})$, as $\{\boldsymbol{v'} \mid \exists w.\ \boldsymbol{v'} \in \mathcal{A}(w)\}$.

We want to remark that the definition of CEFA above is slightly different from that of [13], where CEFA did not include accepting conditions. Moreover, the accepting conditions α in CEFA are defined in a *global* fashion because the accepting condition does not distinguish final states. This technical choice is made so that the determinization and minimization of NFA can be utilized to reduce the size of CEFA in the next section.

In the sequel, we define three CEFA operations: union, intersection, and concatenation. The following section will use these three operations to solve RECL constraints. Note that the union, intersection, and concatenation operations are defined in a slightly more involved manner than register automata [23] and counter automata [19], as a result of the (additional) accepting conditions.

Let $\mathcal{A}_1 = (R_1, Q_1, \Sigma, \delta_1, q_{1,0}, F_1, \alpha_1)$ and $\mathcal{A}_2 = (R_2, Q_2, \Sigma, \delta_2, q_{2,0}, F_2, \alpha_2)$ be two CEFA that share the alphabet. Moreover, suppose that $R_1 \cap R_2 = \emptyset$ and $Q_1 \cap Q_2 = \emptyset$.

The *union* of $\mathcal{A}_1$ and $\mathcal{A}_2$ is denoted by $\mathcal{A}_1 \cup \mathcal{A}_2$. Two fresh auxiliary registers say $r_1', r_2' \notin R_1 \cup R_2$, are introduced so that the accepting condition knows whether a run is from $\mathcal{A}_1$ (or $\mathcal{A}_2$). Specifically, $\mathcal{A}_1 \cup \mathcal{A}_2 = (R', Q', \Sigma, \delta', I', F', \alpha')$ where

- $R' = R_1 \cup R_2 \cup \{r_1', r_2'\}$, $Q' = Q_1 \cup Q_2 \cup \{q_0'\}$ with $q_0' \notin Q_1 \cup Q_2$, $I' = \{q_0'\}$,
- δ' is the union of four transitions sets:
  - $\{(q_0', a, q_1', (\boldsymbol{v_1}, 0, 1, 0)) \mid \exists q_1 \in I_1. \, (q_1, a, q_1', \boldsymbol{v_1}) \in \delta_1\}$
  - $\{(q_0', a, q_2', (0, \boldsymbol{v_2}, 0, 1)) \mid \exists q_2 \in I_2. \, (q_2, a, q_2', \boldsymbol{v_2}) \in \delta_2\}$
  - $\{(q_1, a, q_1', (\boldsymbol{v_1}, 0, 0, 0)) \mid q_1 \notin I_1. \, (q_1, a, q_1', \boldsymbol{v_1}) \in \delta_1\}$
  - $\{(q_2, a, q_2', (0, \boldsymbol{v_2}, 0, 0)) \mid q_2 \notin I_2. \, (q_2, a, q_2', \boldsymbol{v_2}) \in \delta_2\}$

  where $(\boldsymbol{v_1}, 0, 1, 0)$ is a vector that updates R_1 by $\boldsymbol{v_1}$, updates R_2 by $\boldsymbol{0}$, and updates r_1', r_2' by $1, 0$ respectively. Similarly for $(\boldsymbol{0}, \boldsymbol{v_2}, 0, 1)$, and so on.
- F' and α' are defined as follows,
  - if $(\epsilon; \boldsymbol{0})$ belongs to $\mathcal{L}(\mathcal{A}_1)$ or $\mathcal{L}(\mathcal{A}_2)$, i.e., one of the two automata accepts the empty string ϵ, then $F' = F_1 \cup F_2 \cup \{q_0'\}$ and $\alpha' = (r_1' = 0 \wedge r_2' = 0) \vee (r_1' = 1 \wedge \alpha_1) \vee (r_2' = 1 \wedge \alpha_2)$,
  - otherwise, $F' = F_1 \cup F_2$ and $\alpha' = (r_1' = 1 \wedge \alpha_1) \vee (r_2' = 1 \wedge \alpha_2)$.

From the construction, we know that

$$\mathcal{L}(\mathcal{A}_1 \cup \mathcal{A}_2) = \left\{ (w; \boldsymbol{v}) \,\middle|\, \begin{array}{l} (w; \mathrm{prj}_{R_1}(\boldsymbol{v})) \in \mathcal{L}(\mathcal{A}_1) \text{ and } \mathrm{prj}_{r_1'}(\boldsymbol{v}) = 1, \text{ or} \\ (w; \mathrm{prj}_{R_2}(\boldsymbol{v})) \in \mathcal{L}(\mathcal{A}_2) \text{ and } \mathrm{prj}_{r_2'}(\boldsymbol{v}) = 1, \text{ or} \\ (w; \boldsymbol{v}) = (\epsilon, \boldsymbol{0}) \text{ if } \mathcal{A}_1 \text{ or } \mathcal{A}_2 \text{ accepts } \epsilon \end{array} \right\}.$$

Intuitively, $\mathcal{A}_1 \cup \mathcal{A}_2$ accepts the words that are accepted by one of the $\mathcal{A}_1$ and $\mathcal{A}_2$ and outputs the costs of the corresponding automaton.

The *intersection* of $\mathcal{A}_1$ and $\mathcal{A}_2$, denoted by $\mathcal{A}_1 \cap \mathcal{A}_2 = (R', Q', \Sigma, \delta', I', F', \alpha')$, is defined in the sequel.

- $R' = R_1 \cup R_2$, $Q' = Q_1 \times Q_2$, $I' = I_1 \times I_2$, $F' = F_1 \times F_2$, $\alpha' = \alpha_1 \wedge \alpha_2$,
- δ' comprises the tuples $((q_1, q_2), a, (q_1', q_2'), (\boldsymbol{v_1}, \boldsymbol{v_2}))$ such that $(q_1, a, q_1', \boldsymbol{v_1}) \in \delta_1$ and $(q_2, a, q_2', \boldsymbol{v_2}) \in \delta_2$.

From the construction,

$$\mathcal{L}(\mathcal{A}_1 \cap \mathcal{A}_2) = \{(w; \boldsymbol{v}) \mid (w; \mathrm{prj}_{R_1}(\boldsymbol{v})) \in \mathcal{L}(\mathcal{A}_1) \text{ and } (w; \mathrm{prj}_{R_2}(\boldsymbol{v})) \in \mathcal{L}(\mathcal{A}_2)\}.$$

Intuitively, $\mathcal{A}_1 \cap \mathcal{A}_2$ accepts the words that are accepted by both $\mathcal{A}_1$ and $\mathcal{A}_2$ and outputs the costs of $\mathcal{A}_1$ and $\mathcal{A}_2$.

The *concatenation* of $\mathcal{A}_1$ and $\mathcal{A}_2$, denoted by $\mathcal{A}_1 \cdot \mathcal{A}_2$, is defined similarly as that of NFA, that is, a tuple $(Q', \Sigma, \delta', I', F', \alpha')$, where $Q' = Q_1 \cup Q_2$, $I' = I_1$, $\alpha' = \alpha_1 \wedge \alpha_2$, $\delta' = \{(q_1, a, q_1', (\boldsymbol{v_1}, \boldsymbol{0})) \mid (q_1, a, q_1', \boldsymbol{v_1}) \in \delta_1\} \cup \{(q_2, a, q_2', (\boldsymbol{0}, \boldsymbol{v_2})) \mid (q_2, a, q_2', \boldsymbol{v_2}) \in \delta_2\} \cup \{(q_1, a, q_2, (\boldsymbol{0}, \boldsymbol{v_2})) \mid q_1 \in F_1, \exists q' \in I_2. \, (q', a, q_2, \boldsymbol{v_2}) \in \delta_2\}$, moreover, if $I_2 \cap F_2 \neq \emptyset$, then $F' = F_1 \cup F_2$, otherwise, $F' = F_2$. From the construction,

$$\mathcal{L}(\mathcal{A}_1 \cdot \mathcal{A}_2) = \{(w_1 w_2; \boldsymbol{v}) \mid (w_1; \mathsf{prj}_{R_1}(\boldsymbol{v})) \in \mathcal{L}(\mathcal{A}_1) \text{ and } (w_2; \mathsf{prj}_{R_2}(\boldsymbol{v})) \in \mathcal{L}(\mathcal{A}_2)\}.$$

Furthermore, the union, intersection, and concatenation operations can be extended naturally to multiple CEFA, that is, $\mathcal{A}_1 \cup \cdots \cup \mathcal{A}_n$, $\mathcal{A}_1 \cap \cdots \cap \mathcal{A}_n$, $\mathcal{A}_1 \cdots \cdots \mathcal{A}_n$. For instance, $\mathcal{A}_1 \cup \mathcal{A}_2 \cup \mathcal{A}_3 = (\mathcal{A}_1 \cup \mathcal{A}_2) \cup \mathcal{A}_3$, $\mathcal{A}_1 \cap \mathcal{A}_2 \cap \mathcal{A}_3 = (\mathcal{A}_1 \cap \mathcal{A}_2) \cap \mathcal{A}_3$, and $\mathcal{A}_1 \cdot \mathcal{A}_2 \cdot \mathcal{A}_3 = (\mathcal{A}_1 \cdot \mathcal{A}_2) \cdot \mathcal{A}_3$.

6 Solving RECL Constraints

The goal of this section is to show how to solve RECL constraints by utilizing CEFA. At first, we reduce the satisfiability of RECL constraints to a decision problem defined in the sequel. Then we propose a decision procedure for this problem.

Definition 2 (NE$_{\mathsf{LIA}}$(CEFA)). *Let $x_1, \cdots, x_n$ be string variables, $\Lambda_{x_1}, \cdots, \Lambda_{x_n}$ be nonempty sets of CEFA over the alphabet Σ with $\Lambda_{x_i} = \{\mathcal{A}_{i,1}, \cdots, \mathcal{A}_{i,l_i}\}$ for every $i \in [n]$ where the sets of registers $R_{\mathcal{A}_{1,1}}, \cdots, R_{\mathcal{A}_{1,l_1}}, \cdots, R_{\mathcal{A}_{n,1}}, \cdots, R_{\mathcal{A}_{n,l_n}}$ are mutually disjoint, moreover, let φ be an LIA formula whose free variables are from $\bigcup_{i \in [n], j \in [l_i]} R_{\mathcal{A}_{i,j}}$. Then the CEFA in $\Lambda_{x_1}, \cdots, \Lambda_{x_n}$ are said to be nonempty w.r.t. φ if there are assignments $\theta : \{x_1, \cdots, x_n\} \to \Sigma^*$ and vectors $\boldsymbol{v}_{i,j}$ such that $(\theta(x_i); \boldsymbol{v}_{i,j}) \in \mathcal{L}(\mathcal{A}_{i,j})$ and $\varphi[(\boldsymbol{v}_{i,j}/R_{\mathcal{A}_{i,j}})]$ is true, for every $i \in [n], j \in [l_i]$.*

Proposition 1 ([13]). NE$_{\mathsf{LIA}}$(CEFA) *is PSPACE-complete.*

Note that the decision procedure in [13] was only used to prove the upper bound in Proposition 1 and not implemented as a matter of fact. Instead, the symbolic model checker nuXmv [8] was used to solve NE$_{\mathsf{LIA}}$(CEFA). We do not rely on nuXmv in this work and shall propose a new algorithm for solving NE$_{\mathsf{LIA}}$(CEFA) in Sect. 6.2.

6.1 From SAT$_{\mathsf{RECL}}$ to NE$_{\mathsf{LIA}}$(CEFA)

Let φ be a RECL constraint and $x_1, \cdots, x_n$ be an enumeration of the string variables occurring in φ. Moreover, let $\varphi \equiv \varphi_1 \wedge \varphi_2$ such that φ_1 is a conjunction of regular membership constraints of φ, and φ_2 is a conjunction of length constraints of φ. We shall reduce the satisfiability of φ to an instance of NE$_{\mathsf{LIA}}$(CEFA).

At first, we show how to construct a CEFA from a regex where counting operators may occur. Let us start with register-representable regexes defined in the sequel.

Let us fix an alphabet Σ.

Let e be a regex over Σ. Then an occurrence of counting operators in e, say $(e')^{\{m,n\}}$ (or $(e')^{\{m,\infty\}}$), is said to be *register-representable* if $(e')^{\{m,n\}}$ (or

$(e')^{\{m,\infty\}}$) is not in the scope of a Kleene star, another counting operator, complement, or language difference in e. We say that e is *register-representable* if all occurrences of counting operators in e are register-representable. For instance, $a^{\{2,6\}} \cap a^{\{4,\infty\}}$ is register-representable, while $\overline{a^{\{2,6\}}}$ and $(a^{\{2,6\}})^{\{4,\infty\}}$ are not since $a^{\{2,6\}}$ is in the scope of complement and the counter operator $\{2,\infty\}$ respectively.

Let e be a register-representable regex over Σ. By the following procedure, we will construct a CEFA out of e, denoted by $\mathcal{A}_e$.

1. For each sub-expression $(e')^{\{m,n\}}$ with $m \leq n$ (resp. $(e')^{\{m,\infty\}}$) of e, we construct a CEFA $\mathcal{A}_{(e')^{\{m,n\}}}$ (resp. $\mathcal{A}_{(e')^{\{m,\infty\}}}$). Let $\mathcal{A}_{e'} = (Q, \Sigma, \delta, I, F)$. Then $\mathcal{A}_{(e')^{\{m,n\}}} = ((r'), Q', \Sigma, \delta'', I', F', \alpha')$, where r' is a new register, $Q' = Q \cup \{q_0\}$ with $q_0 \notin Q$, $I' = \{q_0\}$, $F' = F \cup \{q_0\}$, and

$$\delta'' = \{(q, a, q', (0)) \mid (q, a, q') \in \delta\} \cup$$
$$\{(q_0, a, q', (1)) \mid \exists q_0' \in I. (q_0', a, q') \in \delta\} \cup$$
$$\{(q, a, q', (1)) \mid q \in F, \exists q_0' \in I. (q_0', a, q') \in \delta\},$$

   moreover, $\alpha' = m \leq r' \leq n$ if $I \cap F = \emptyset$, otherwise $\alpha' = r' \leq n$. (Intuitively, if ε is accepted by $\mathcal{A}_{e'}$, then the value of r' can be less than m.) Moreover, $\mathcal{A}_{(e')^{\{m,\infty\}}}$ is constructed by adapting α' in $\mathcal{A}_{(e')^{\{m,n\}}}$ as follows: $\alpha' = m \leq r'$ if $I \cap F = \emptyset$ and $\alpha' = \text{true}$ otherwise.

2. For each sub-expression e' of e such that e' contains occurrences of counting operators but e' itself is not of the form $(e_1')^{\{m,n\}}$ or $(e_1')^{\{m,\infty\}}$, from the assumption that e is register-representable, we know that e' is of the form $e_1' \cdot e_2'$, $e_1' + e_2'$, $e_1' \cap e_2'$, or (e_1'). For $e' = (e_1')$, we have $\mathcal{A}_{e'} = \mathcal{A}_{e_1'}$. For $e' = e_1' \cdot e_2'$, $e' = e_1' + e_2'$, or $e' = e_1' \cap e_2'$, suppose that CEFA $\mathcal{A}_{e_1'}$ and $\mathcal{A}_{e_2'}$ have been constructed.

3. For each maximal sub-expression e' of e such that e' contains no occurrences of counting operators, an NFA $\mathcal{A}_{e'}$ can be constructed by structural induction on the syntax of e'. Then we have $\mathcal{A}_{e'} = \mathcal{A}_{e_1'} \cdot \mathcal{A}_{e_2'}$, $\mathcal{A}_{e'} = \mathcal{A}_{e_1'} \cup \mathcal{A}_{e_2'}$, or $\mathcal{A}_{e'} = \mathcal{A}_{e_1'} \cap \mathcal{A}_{e_2'}$.

For non-register-representable regexes, we first transform them into register-representable regexes by unfolding all the non-register-representable occurrences of counting operators. After that, we utilize the aforementioned procedure to construct CEFA. For instance, $(a^{\{2,6\}} \cdot b^*)^{\{2,\infty\}}$ is transformed into $(aa(\varepsilon + a + aa + aaa + aaaa) \cdot b^*)^{\{2,\infty\}}$. The unfoldings of the inner counting operators of non-register-representable regexes incur an exponential blowup in the worst case. Nevertheless, those regexes occupy only 5% of the 48,843 regexes that are collected from the practice (see Sect. 7.1). Moreover, the unfoldings are partial in the sense that the outmost counting operators are not unfolded. It turns out that our approach can solve almost all the RECL constraints involving these 48,843 regexes, except 181 of them (See Fig. 5b).

For each $i \in [n]$, let $x_i \in e_{i,1}, \cdots, x_i \in e_{i,l_i}$ be an enumeration of the regular membership constraints for x_i in φ_1. Then we can construct CEFA $\mathcal{A}_{i,j}$ from $e_{i,j}$ for each $i \in [n]$ and $j \in [l_i]$. Moreover, we construct another CEFA $\mathcal{A}_{i,0}$

for each $i \in [n]$ to model the length of x_i. Specifically, $\mathcal{A}_{i,0}$ is constructed as $((r_{i,0}), \{q_{i,0}\}, \Sigma, \delta_{i,0}, \{q_{i,0}\}, \{q_{i,0}\}, \mathtt{true})$ where $r_{i,0}$ is a fresh register and $\delta_{i,0} = \{(q_{i,0}, a, q_{i,0}, (1)) \mid a \in \Sigma\}$. Let $\Lambda_{x_i} = \{\mathcal{A}_{i,0}, \mathcal{A}_{i,1}, \cdots, \mathcal{A}_{i,l_i}\}$ for each $i \in [n]$, and $\varphi'_2 \equiv \varphi_2[r_{1,0}/|x_1|, \cdots, r_{n,0}/|x_n|]$. Then the satisfiability of φ is reduced to the nonemptiness of CEFAs in $\Lambda_{x_1}, \cdots, \Lambda_{x_n}$ w.r.t. φ'_2.

6.2   Solving $\mathsf{NE_{LIA}(CEFA)}$

In this section, we present a procedure to solve the $\mathsf{NE_{LIA}(CEFA)}$ problem: Suppose that $x_1, \cdots, x_n$ are mutually distinct string variables, $\Lambda_{x_1}, \cdots, \Lambda_{x_n}$ are nonempty sets of CEFA over the same alphabet Σ where $\Lambda_{x_i} = \{\mathcal{A}_{i,1}, \cdots, \mathcal{A}_{i,l_i}\}$ for every $i \in [n]$. Moreover, the sets of registers $R_{\mathcal{A}_{1,1}}, \cdots, R_{\mathcal{A}_{n,l_n}}$ are mutually disjoint, and φ is a LIA formula whose free variables are from $\bigcup\limits_{i \in [n], j \in [l_i]} R_{\mathcal{A}_{i,j}}$.

The procedure comprises three steps.

Step 1 (Computing intersection automata). For each $i \in [n]$, compute a CEFA $\mathcal{B}_i = \mathcal{A}_{i,1} \cap \cdots \cap \mathcal{A}_{i,l_i}$, and let $\Lambda'_{x_i} := \{\mathcal{B}_i\}$.   □

After Step 1, the nonemptiness of CEFAs in $\Lambda_{x_1}, \cdots, \Lambda_{x_n}$ w.r.t. φ is reduced to the nonemptiness of CEFAs in $\Lambda'_{x_1}, \cdots, \Lambda'_{x_n}$ w.r.t. φ.

In the following steps, we reduce the non-emptiness of CEFAs in $\Lambda'_{x_1}, \cdots, \Lambda'_{x_n}$ w.r.t. φ to the satisfiability of an LIA formula. The reduction relies on the following two observations.

Observation 1 *CEFA in $\Lambda'_{x_1} = \{\mathcal{B}_1\}, \cdots, \Lambda'_{x_n} = \{\mathcal{B}_n\}$ are nonempty w.r.t. φ iff there are $\boldsymbol{v_1} \in \mathcal{O}(\mathcal{B}_1), \cdots, \boldsymbol{v_n} \in \mathcal{O}(\mathcal{B}_n)$ such that $\varphi[\boldsymbol{v_1}/R_{\mathcal{B}_1}, \cdots, \boldsymbol{v_n}/R_{\mathcal{B}_n}]$ is true.*

Let $\mathcal{A} = (R, Q, \Sigma, \delta, I, F, \alpha)$ be a CEFA and $\mathbb{C}_\mathcal{A} = \{\boldsymbol{v} \mid \exists q, a, q'. (q, a, q', \boldsymbol{v}) \in \delta\}$. Moreover, let $\mathcal{U}_\mathcal{A} = (Q, \mathbb{C}_\mathcal{A}, \delta', I, F)$ be an NFA over the alphabet $\mathbb{C}_\mathcal{A}$ that is obtained from $\mathcal{A}$ by dropping the accepting condition and ignoring the characters, that is, δ' comprises tuples $(q, \boldsymbol{v}, q')$ such that $(q, a, q', \boldsymbol{v}) \in \delta$ for $a \in \Sigma$.

Observation 2 *For each CEFA $\mathcal{A} = (R, Q, \Sigma, \delta, I, F, \alpha)$,*

$$\mathcal{O}(\mathcal{A}) = \left\{ \sum_{\boldsymbol{v} \in \mathbb{C}_\mathcal{A}} \eta(\boldsymbol{v})\boldsymbol{v} \;\middle|\; \eta \in \mathsf{parikh}(\mathcal{U}_\mathcal{A}) \text{ and } \alpha\left[\sum_{\boldsymbol{v} \in \mathbb{C}_\mathcal{A}} \eta(\boldsymbol{v})\boldsymbol{v}/R\right] \text{ is true} \right\}.$$

For $i \in [n]$, let α_i be the accepting condition of $\mathcal{B}_i$. Then from Observation 2, we know that the following two conditions are equivalent,

- there are $\boldsymbol{v_1} \in \mathcal{O}(\mathcal{B}_1), \cdots, \boldsymbol{v_n} \in \mathcal{O}(\mathcal{B}_n)$ such that $\varphi[\boldsymbol{v_1}/R_{\mathcal{B}_1}, \cdots, \boldsymbol{v_n}/R_{\mathcal{B}_n}]$ is true,
- there are $\eta_1 \in \mathsf{parikh}(\mathcal{U}_{\mathcal{B}_1}), \cdots, \eta_n \in \mathsf{parikh}(\mathcal{U}_{\mathcal{B}_n})$ such that

$$\bigwedge_{i \in [n]} \alpha_i\left[\sum_{\boldsymbol{v} \in \mathbb{C}_{\mathcal{B}_i}} \eta_i(\boldsymbol{v})\boldsymbol{v}/R_{\mathcal{B}_i}\right] \wedge \varphi\left[\sum_{\boldsymbol{v} \in \mathbb{C}_{\mathcal{B}_1}} \eta_1(\boldsymbol{v})\boldsymbol{v}/R_{\mathcal{B}_1}, \cdots, \sum_{\boldsymbol{v} \in \mathbb{C}_{\mathcal{B}_n}} \eta_n(\boldsymbol{v})\boldsymbol{v}/R_{\mathcal{B}_n}\right]$$

is true.

Therefore, to solve the nonemptiness of CEFA in $\Lambda'_{x_1}, \cdots, \Lambda'_{x_n}$ w.r.t. φ, it is sufficient to compute the existential LIA formulas $\psi_{\mathcal{U}_{\mathcal{B}_1}}(\mathfrak{z}_{\mathbb{C}_{\mathcal{B}_1}}), \cdots, \psi_{\mathcal{U}_{\mathcal{B}_n}}(\mathfrak{z}_{\mathbb{C}_{\mathcal{B}_n}})$ to represent the Parikh images of $\mathcal{U}_{\mathcal{B}_1}, \cdots, \mathcal{U}_{\mathcal{B}_n}$ respectively, where $\mathfrak{z}_{\mathbb{C}_{\mathcal{B}_i}} = \{\mathfrak{z}_{i,v} \mid v \in \mathbb{C}_{\mathcal{B}_i}\}$ for $i \in [n]$, and solve the satisfiability of the following existential LIA formula

$$\bigwedge_{i \in [n]} \left(\psi_{\mathcal{U}_{\mathcal{B}_i}}(\mathfrak{z}_{\mathbb{C}_{\mathcal{B}_i}}) \wedge \alpha_i \left[\sum_{v \in \mathbb{C}_{\mathcal{B}_i}} \mathfrak{z}_{i,v} v / R_{\mathcal{B}_i} \right] \right) \wedge$$
$$\varphi \left[\sum_{v \in \mathbb{C}_{\mathcal{B}_1}} \mathfrak{z}_{1,v} v / R_{\mathcal{B}_1}, \cdots, \sum_{v \in \mathbb{C}_{\mathcal{B}_n}} \mathfrak{z}_{n,v} v / R_{\mathcal{B}_n} \right].$$

Intuitively, the integer variables $\mathfrak{z}_{i,v}$ represent the number of occurrences of v in the strings accepted by $\mathcal{U}_{\mathcal{B}_i}$.

Because the sizes of the LIA formulas $\psi_{\mathcal{U}_{\mathcal{B}_1}}(\mathfrak{z}_{\mathbb{C}_{\mathcal{B}_1}}), \cdots, \psi_{\mathcal{U}_{\mathcal{B}_n}}(\mathfrak{z}_{\mathbb{C}_{\mathcal{B}_n}})$ are proportional to the sizes (more precisely, the alphabet size, the number of states and transitions) of NFA $\mathcal{U}_{\mathcal{B}_1}, \cdots, \mathcal{U}_{\mathcal{B}_n}$, and the satisfiability of existential LIA formulas is NP-complete, it is vital to reduce the sizes of these NFAs to improve the performance.

Since $\sum_{v \in \mathbb{C}(\mathcal{B}_i)} \eta(v) v = \sum_{v \in \mathbb{C}(\mathcal{B}_i) \setminus \{0\}} \eta(v) v$ for each $i \in [n]$ and $\eta \in \mathsf{parikh}(\mathcal{U}_{\mathcal{B}_i})$, it turns out that the $\mathbf{0}$-labeled transitions in $\mathcal{U}_{\mathcal{B}_i}$ do not contribute to the final output $\sum_{v \in \mathbb{C}(\mathcal{B}_i)} \eta(v) v$. Therefore, we can apply the following size-reduction technique for $\mathcal{U}_{\mathcal{B}_i}$'s.

Step 2 (Reducing automata sizes). For each $i \in [n]$, we view the transitions $(q, \mathbf{0}, q')$ in $\mathcal{U}_{\mathcal{B}_i}$ as ε-transitions (q, ε, q'), and remove the ε-transitions from $\mathcal{U}_{\mathcal{B}_i}$. Then we determinize and minimize the resulting NFA.   □

For $i \in [n]$, let $\mathcal{C}_i$ denote the DFA obtained from $\mathcal{U}_{\mathcal{B}_i}$ by executing Step 2 and $\mathbb{C}_{\mathcal{C}_i} := \mathbb{C}_{\mathcal{B}_i} \setminus \{\mathbf{0}\}$. From the construction, we know that $\mathsf{parikh}(\mathcal{C}_i) = \mathsf{prj}_{\mathbb{C}_{\mathcal{C}_i}}(\mathsf{parikh}(\mathcal{U}_{\mathcal{B}_i}))$ for each $i \in [n]$. Therefore, we compute LIA formulas from $\mathcal{C}_i$'s, instead of $\mathcal{U}_{\mathcal{B}_i}$'s, to represent the Parikh images.

Step 3 (Computing Parikh images). For each $i \in [n]$, we compute an existential LIA formula $\psi_{\mathcal{C}_i}(\mathfrak{z}_{\mathbb{C}_{\mathcal{C}_i}})$ from $\mathcal{C}_i$ to represent $\mathsf{parikh}(\mathcal{C}_i)$. Then we solve the satisfiability of the following formula,

$$\bigwedge_{i \in [n]} \left(\psi_{\mathcal{C}_i}(\mathfrak{z}_{\mathbb{C}_{\mathcal{C}_i}}) \wedge \alpha_i \left[\sum_{v \in \mathbb{C}_{\mathcal{C}_i}} \mathfrak{z}_{i,v} v / R_{\mathcal{B}_i} \right] \right) \wedge$$
$$\varphi \left[\sum_{v \in \mathbb{C}_{\mathcal{C}_1}} \mathfrak{z}_{1,v} v / R_{\mathcal{B}_1}, \cdots, \sum_{v \in \mathbb{C}_{\mathcal{C}_n}} \mathfrak{z}_{n,v} v / R_{\mathcal{B}_n} \right].$$

7   Experiments

We implemented the algorithm in Sect. 6 on top of OSTRICH, resulted to a string solver called OSTRICH[RECL]. In this section, we evaluate the performance of OSTRICH[RECL] on two benchmark suites, that is, RegCoL and

AutomatArk. In the sequel, we first describe the two benchmark suites as well as the experiment setup. Then we present the experiment results. We do experiments to compare the performance of OSTRICH^{RECL} with the state-of-the-art string solvers. Moreover, in order to know whether OSTRICH^{RECL} is good at solving string constraints with large counting and length bounds, we extract 1,969 instances with large bounds out of the two benchmark suites, and compare the performance of OSTRICH^{RECL} with the other solvers on these instances. Finally, we empirically justify the technical choices made in the decision procedure of Sect. 6.2 by comparing OSTRICH^{RECL} with the following two variants of OSTRICH^{RECL}: OSTRICH$^{RECL}_{-ASR}$ and OSTRICH$^{RECL}_{NUXMV}$, where OSTRICH$^{RECL}_{-ASR}$ and OSTRICH$^{RECL}_{NUXMV}$ are obtained from OSTRICH^{RECL} by removing the automata size-reduction technique (i.e. Step 2 in Sect. 6.2) and using the nuXmv model checker to solve the nonemptiness of $NE_{LIA}(CEFA)$ respectively.

7.1 Benchmark Suites and Experiment Setup

Our experiments utilize two benchmark suites, namely, *RegCoL* and *AutomatArk*. Other industrial benchmark suites are not utilized because they contain no counting operators. There are 48,843 instances in total, and all benchmark instances are in the SMTLIB2 format. Moreover, it turns out that only 5% of regexes among the 48,843 instances are non-register-representable (see Sect. 6.1).

RegCoL Benchmark Suite. There are 40,628 RECL instances in the RegCoL suite. These instances are generated by extracting regexes with counting operators from the open source regex library [18,33] and manually constructing a RECL constraint $x \in e \land x \in e_{sani} \land |x| > 10$ for each regex e, where $e_{sani} \equiv \Sigma^*(< + > +' +'' +\&)\Sigma^*$ is a regular expression that sanitizes all occurrence of special characters $<$, $>$, $'$, $''$, or $\&$. The expression e_{sani} is introduced in view of the fact that these characters are usually sanitized in Web browsers to alleviate the XSS attacks [11,31].

AutomatArk Benchmark Suite. This benchmark suite is adapted from the AutomatArk suite [6] by picking out the string constraints containing counting operators. We also add the length constraint $|x| > 10$ for each string variable x. There are 8,215 instances in the AutomatArk suite. Note that the original AutomatArk benchmark suite [6] includes 19,979 instances, which are conjunctions of regular membership queries generated out of regular expressions in [15].

Distribution of Problem Instances w.r.t. Counting Bounds. The distribution of problem instances w.r.t. the counting bounds in RegCoL and AutomatArk suites is shown in Fig. 5a, where the x-axis represents the counting bound and the y-axis represents the number of problem instances whose maximum counting bound is equal to the value of the x-axis. From Fig. 5a, we can see that while most problem instances contain only small bounds, there are still around 2,000 (about 4%) of them using large counting bounds (i.e. greater than or equal to 50).

Experiment Setup. All experiments are conducted on CentOS Stream release 8 with 4 Intel(R) Xeon(R) Platinum 8269CY 3.10 GHz CPU cores and 190 GB memory. We use the ZALIGVINDER framework [24] to execute the experiments, with a timeout of 60 s for each instance.

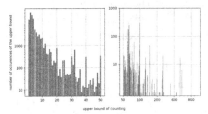

(a) Distribution of problem instances w.r.t. counting bounds

(b) Overall performance evaluation

	CVC5	Z3str3RE	Z3str3	Z3seq	OSTRICH	OSTRICH^{RECL}
sat	27813	28283	23126	27761	25975	**28360**
unsat	16941	19312	12742	18651	20291	**20302**
unknown	**8**	99	6990	98	160	28
timeout	4081	1149	5985	2333	2417	**153**
soundness error	**0**	44	44	56	**0**	**0**
solved correctly	44754	47551	35824	46356	46266	**48662**
average time (s)	5.64	**1.62**	7.63	3.59	5.94	1.93

Fig. 5. Distribution of counting bounds and performance evaluation

7.2 Performance Evaluation

We evaluate the performance of OSTRICH^{RECL} against the state-of-the-art string constraint solvers, including CVC5 [2], Z3seq [30], Z3str3 [5], Z3str3RE [4], and OSTRICH [14], on RegCoL and AutomatArk benchmark suites. The experiment results can be found in Fig. 5b. Note that we take the results of CVC5 as the ground truth[2], and the results different from the ground truth are classified as *soundness error*. We can see that OSTRICH^{RECL} solves almost all 48,843 instances, except 182 of them, that is, it solves 48,662 instances correctly. The number is 3,908/1,111/12,838/2,306/2,396 more than the number of instances solved by CVC5/Z3str3RE/Z3str3/Z3seq/OSTRICH respectively. Moreover, OSTRICH^{RECL} is the second fastest solver, whose average time on each instance is close to the fastest solver Z3str3RE (1.93 s versus 1.62 s).

7.3 Evaluation on Problem Instances with Large Bounds

We extract 1,969 problem instances with large counting bounds (greater than or equal to 50) from the RegCoL and AutomatArk benchmark suites. Moreover, in order to test the performance of the solvers on string constraints with large length bounds as well, we increase the length bound to 200, that is, $|x| > 200$.

We evaluate the performance of OSTRICH^{RECL} on the 1,969 instances. The experiment results can be found in Table 1a. We can see that OSTRICH^{RECL}

---

[2] Initially, we used the majority vote of the results of the solvers as the ground truth. Nevertheless, on some problem instances, all the results of the three solvers in the Z3 family are wrong (after manual inspection), thus failing this approach on these instances.

solves 1,873 instances correctly, which is 947/278/563/637/523 more than those solved by CVC5/Z3str3RE/Z3str3/Z3seq/OSTRICH respectively. Furthermore, OSTRICH^{RECL} is 6.79/2.88/2.61/5.27/3.95 times faster than CVC5/Z3str3RE/Z3str3/Z3seq/OSTRICH respectively. From the results, we can conclude that OSTRICH^{RECL} is much more effective and efficient to solve the problem instances with large bounds than the other solvers.

Table 1. More experiment results, where the time limit is set as 60 s

	CVC5	Z3str3RE	Z3str3	Z3seq	OSTRICH	OSTRICH^{RECL}
sat	317	827	616	346	488	**909**
unsat	609	768	694	890	862	**964**
unknown	1	11	297	11	123	14
timeout	1042	363	362	722	496	**82**
soundness error	0	0	0	0	0	0
solved correctly	926	1595	1310	1236	1350	**1873**
average time (s)	34.16	14.48	13.15	26.49	19.85	**5.03**

(a) Large bounds

	OSTRICH$^{\text{RECL}}_{\text{-ASR}}$	OSTRICH$^{\text{RECL}}_{\text{NUXMV}}$	OSTRICH^{RECL}
sat	26884	26603	**28360**
unsat	20275	20261	**20302**
unknown	48	45	**28**
timeout	1637	1935	**153**
soundness error	0	0	0
solved correctly	47159	46864	**48662**
average time (s)	4.27	6.05	**1.93**

(b) Empirical justification of the technical choices made in the decision procedure

7.4 Empirical Justification of the Technical Choices Made in the Decision Procedure

We compare OSTRICH^{RECL} with OSTRICH$^{\text{RECL}}_{\text{-ASR}}$ and OSTRICH$^{\text{RECL}}_{\text{NUXMV}}$, to justify the technical choices made in Sect. 6.2. The experiment results can be found in Table 1b. We can see that OSTRICH^{RECL} solves 1,503 more instances and is 2.21 times faster than OSTRICH$^{\text{RECL}}_{\text{-ASR}}$. Therefore, the automata size-reduction technique indeed plays an essential role in the performance improvement. Moreover, OSTRICH^{RECL} solves 1,798 more instances and is 3.13 times faster than OSTRICH$^{\text{RECL}}_{\text{NUXMV}}$. Therefore, the decision procedure in Sect. 6.2 is more efficient to solve the $\text{NE}_{\text{LIA}}(\text{CEFA})$ problem than nuXmv.

8 Conclusion

This work proposed an efficient automata-theoretical approach for solving string constraints with regex-counting and string-length. The approach is based on encoding counting operators in regular expressions by cost registers symbolically instead of unfolding them explicitly. Moreover, this work proposed automata-size reduction techniques to improve performance further. Finally, we used two benchmark suites comprising 48,843 instances in total to evaluate the performance of our approach. The experimental results show that our approach can solve more instances than the state-of-the-art best solvers, at a comparable or faster speed, especially when the counting and length bounds are large. For the future work, we plan to investigate how the symbolic approach can be extended to reason about nested counting operators.

References

1. Abdulla, P.A., et al.: Efficient handling of string-number conversion. In: Proceedings of the 41st ACM SIGPLAN Conference on Programming Language Design and Implementation, PLDI 2020, pp. 943–957. Association for Computing Machinery, New York (2020). https://doi.org/10.1145/3385412.3386034

2. Barbosa, H., et al.: CVC5: a versatile and industrial-strength SMT solver. In: TACAS 2022. LNCS, vol. 13243, pp. 415–442. Springer, Cham (2022). https://doi.org/10.1007/978-3-030-99524-9_24

3. Berzish, M.: Z3str4: a solver for theories over strings. Ph.D. thesis, University of Waterloo, Ontario, Canada (2021). https://hdl.handle.net/10012/17102

4. Berzish, M., et al.: Towards more efficient methods for solving regular-expression heavy string constraints. Theor. Comput. Sci. **943**, 50–72 (2023)

5. Berzish, M., Ganesh, V., Zheng, Y.: Z3str3: a string solver with theory-aware heuristics. In: 2017 Formal Methods in Computer Aided Design, FMCAD 2017, Vienna, Austria, 2–6 October, pp. 55–59 (2017). https://doi.org/10.23919/FMCAD.2017.8102241

6. Berzish, M., et al.: An SMT solver for regular expressions and linear arithmetic over string length. In: Silva, A., Leino, K.R.M. (eds.) CAV 2021. LNCS, vol. 12760, pp. 289–312. Springer, Cham (2021). https://doi.org/10.1007/978-3-030-81688-9_14

7. Bui, D., contributors: Z3-trau (2019). https://github.com/diepbp/z3-trau

8. Cavada, R., et al.: The NUXMV symbolic model checker. In: Biere, A., Bloem, R. (eds.) CAV 2014. LNCS, vol. 8559, pp. 334–342. Springer, Cham (2014). https://doi.org/10.1007/978-3-319-08867-9_22

9. Chapman, C., Stolee, K.T.: Exploring regular expression usage and context in Python. In: Zeller, A., Roychoudhury, A. (eds.) Proceedings of the 25th International Symposium on Software Testing and Analysis, ISSTA 2016, Saarbrücken, Germany, 18–20 July 2016, pp. 282–293. ACM (2016). https://doi.org/10.1145/2931037.2931073

10. Chen, H., Lu, P.: Checking determinism of regular expressions with counting. Inf. Comput. **241**, 302–320 (2015). https://doi.org/10.1016/j.ic.2014.12.001

11. Chen, T., Chen, Y., Hague, M., Lin, A.W., Wu, Z.: What is decidable about string constraints with the replaceall function. PACMPL **2**(POPL), 3:1–3:29 (2018). https://doi.org/10.1145/3158091

12. Chen, T., et al.: Solving string constraints with regex-dependent functions through transducers with priorities and variables. Proc. ACM Program. Lang. **6**(POPL), 1–31 (2022). https://doi.org/10.1145/3498707

13. Chen, T., et al.: A decision procedure for path feasibility of string manipulating programs with integer data type. In: Hung, D.V., Sokolsky, O. (eds.) ATVA 2020. LNCS, vol. 12302, pp. 325–342. Springer, Cham (2020). https://doi.org/10.1007/978-3-030-59152-6_18

14. Chen, T., Hague, M., Lin, A.W., Rümmer, P., Wu, Z.: Decision procedures for path feasibility of string-manipulating programs with complex operations. PACMPL **3**(POPL) (2019). https://doi.org/10.1145/3290362

15. D'Antoni, L.: Automatark: automata benchmark (2018). https://github.com/lorisdanto/automatark

16. D'Antoni, L., Ferreira, T., Sammartino, M., Silva, A.: Symbolic register automata. In: Dillig, I., Tasiran, S. (eds.) CAV 2019. LNCS, vol. 11561, pp. 3–21. Springer, Cham (2019). https://doi.org/10.1007/978-3-030-25540-4_1

17. Davis, J.C., Coghlan, C.A., Servant, F., Lee, D.: The impact of regular expression denial of service (ReDoS) in practice: an empirical study at the ecosystem scale. In: Proceedings of the 2018 26th ACM Joint Meeting on European Software Engineering Conference and Symposium on the Foundations of Software Engineering, ESEC/FSE 2018, pp. 246–256. Association for Computing Machinery, New York (2018)
18. Davis, J.C., Michael IV, L.G., Coghlan, C.A., Servant, F., Lee, D.: Why aren't regular expressions a lingua franca? An empirical study on the re-use and portability of regular expressions. In: Proceedings of the 2019 27th ACM Joint Meeting on European Software Engineering Conference and Symposium on the Foundations of Software Engineering, ESEC/FSE 2019, pp. 443–454. Association for Computing Machinery, New York (2019). https://doi.org/10.1145/3338906.3338909
19. Gelade, W., Gyssens, M., Martens, W.: Regular expressions with counting: weak versus strong determinism. SIAM J. Comput. **41**(1), 160–190 (2012). https://doi.org/10.1137/100814196
20. Haase, C.: A survival guide to Presburger arithmetic. ACM SIGLOG News **5**(3), 67–82 (2018). https://doi.org/10.1145/3242953.3242964
21. Holík, L., Síc, J., Turonová, L., Vojnar, T.: Fast matching of regular patterns with synchronizing counting. In: Kupferman, O., Sobocinski, P. (eds.) FoSSaCS 2023. LNCS, vol. 13992, pp. 392–412. Springer, Cham (2023). https://doi.org/10.1007/978-3-031-30829-1_19
22. Hopcroft, J.E., Ullman, J.D.: Introduction to Automata Theory, Languages and Computation. Addison-Wesley, Boston (1979)
23. Kaminski, M., Francez, N.: Finite-memory automata. In: Proceedings [1990] 31st Annual Symposium on Foundations of Computer Science, vol. 2, pp. 683–688 (1990). https://doi.org/10.1109/FSCS.1990.89590
24. Kulczynski, M., Manea, F., Nowotka, D., Poulsen, D.B.: ZaligVinder: a generic test framework for string solvers. J. Softw. Evol. Process **35**(4), e2400 (2023). https://doi.org/10.1002/smr.2400
25. Le Glaunec, A., Kong, L., Mamouras, K.: Regular expression matching using bit vector automata. Proc. ACM Program. Lang. **7**(OOPSLA1) (2023). https://doi.org/10.1145/3586044
26. Liang, T., Reynolds, A., Tinelli, C., Barrett, C., Deters, M.: A DPLL(T) theory solver for a theory of strings and regular expressions. In: Biere, A., Bloem, R. (eds.) CAV 2014. LNCS, vol. 8559, pp. 646–662. Springer, Cham (2014). https://doi.org/10.1007/978-3-319-08867-9_43
27. Liang, T., Tsiskaridze, N., Reynolds, A., Tinelli, C., Barrett, C.: A decision procedure for regular membership and length constraints over unbounded strings. In: Lutz, C., Ranise, S. (eds.) FroCoS 2015. LNCS (LNAI), vol. 9322, pp. 135–150. Springer, Cham (2015). https://doi.org/10.1007/978-3-319-24246-0_9
28. Loring, B., Mitchell, D., Kinder, J.: Sound regular expression semantics for dynamic symbolic execution of JavaScript. In: Proceedings of the 40th ACM SIGPLAN Conference on Programming Language Design and Implementation, PLDI 2019, Phoenix, AZ, USA, 22–26 June 2019, pp. 425–438. ACM (2019). https://doi.org/10.1145/3314221.3314645
29. Minsky, M.L.: Computation: Finite and Infinite Machines. Prentice-Hall Series in Automatic Computation. Prentice-Hall (1967)
30. de Moura, L., Bjørner, N.: Z3: an efficient SMT solver. In: Ramakrishnan, C.R., Rehof, J. (eds.) TACAS 2008. LNCS, vol. 4963, pp. 337–340. Springer, Heidelberg (2008). https://doi.org/10.1007/978-3-540-78800-3_24

31. Saxena, P., Akhawe, D., Hanna, S., Mao, F., McCamant, S., Song, D.: A symbolic execution framework for JavaScript. In: 2010 IEEE Symposium on Security and Privacy, pp. 513–528 (2010). https://doi.org/10.1109/SP.2010.38

32. Seidl, H., Schwentick, T., Muscholl, A., Habermehl, P.: Counting in trees for free. In: Díaz, J., Karhumäki, J., Lepistö, A., Sannella, D. (eds.) ICALP 2004. LNCS, vol. 3142, pp. 1136–1149. Springer, Heidelberg (2004). https://doi.org/10.1007/978-3-540-27836-8_94

33. Turoňová, L., Holík, L., Lengál, O., Saarikivi, O., Veanes, M., Vojnar, T.: Regex matching with counting-set automata. Proc. ACM Program. Lang. 4(OOPSLA) (2020). https://doi.org/10.1145/3428286

34. Verma, K.N., Seidl, H., Schwentick, T.: On the complexity of equational horn clauses. In: Nieuwenhuis, R. (ed.) CADE 2005. LNCS (LNAI), vol. 3632, pp. 337–352. Springer, Heidelberg (2005). https://doi.org/10.1007/11532231_25

35. Wang, H.E., Chen, S.Y., Yu, F., Jiang, J.H.R.: A symbolic model checking approach to the analysis of string and length constraints. In: Proceedings of the 33rd ACM/IEEE International Conference on Automated Software Engineering, ASE 2018, pp. 623–633. ACM (2018). https://doi.org/10.1145/3238147.3238189

36. Wang, P., Stolee, K.T.: How well are regular expressions tested in the wild? In: Leavens, G.T., Garcia, A., Pasareanu, C.S. (eds.) Proceedings of the 2018 ACM Joint Meeting on European Software Engineering Conference and Symposium on the Foundations of Software Engineering, ESEC/SIGSOFT FSE 2018, Lake Buena Vista, FL, USA, 04–09 November 2018, pp. 668–678. ACM (2018)

37. Zheng, Y., Ganesh, V., Subramanian, S., Tripp, O., Dolby, J., Zhang, X.: Effective search-space pruning for solvers of string equations, regular expressions and length constraints. In: Kroening, D., Păsăreanu, C.S. (eds.) CAV 2015. LNCS, vol. 9206, pp. 235–254. Springer, Cham (2015). https://doi.org/10.1007/978-3-319-21690-4_14

38. Zheng, Y., Zhang, X., Ganesh, V.: Z3-str: a Z3-based string solver for web application analysis. In: ESEC/SIGSOFT FSE, pp. 114–124 (2013). https://doi.org/10.1145/2491411.2491456

Reachability Based Uniform Controllability to Target Set with Evolution Function

Jia Geng[1], Ruiqi Hu[1], Kairong Liu[1], Zhihui Li[2], and Zhikun She[1(✉)]

[1] School of Mathematical Sciences, Beihang University, Beijing, China
{jgeng,by1809102,krliu,zhikun.she}@buaa.edu.cn
[2] China Aerodynamics Research and Development Center, Mianyang, China
zhli0097@x263.net

Abstract. In this paper, we investigate the uniform controllability to target set for dynamical systems by designing controllers such that the trajectories evolving from the initial set can enter into the target set. For this purpose, we first introduce the evolution function (EF) for exactly describing the reachable set and give an over-approximation of the reachable set with high precision using the series representation of the evolution function. Subsequently, we propose an approximation approach for Hausdorff semi-distance with a bounded rectangular grid, which can be used to guide the selection of controllers. Based on the above two approximations, we design a heuristic framework to compute a piecewise constant controller, realizing the controllability. Moreover, in order to reduce the computational load, we improve our heuristic framework by the K-arm Bandit Model in reinforcement learning. It is worth noting that both of the heuristic algorithms may suffer from the risk of local optima. To avoid the potential dilemma, we additionally propose a reference trajectory based algorithm for further improvement. Finally, we use some benchmarks with comparisons to show the efficiency of our approach.

Keywords: Controllability · Reachability · Evolution function · Reinforcement learning · Reference trajectory

1 Introduction

Control synthesis problem for reachability is a crucial issue in various realistic applications such as robotics and control communities [1–3], and has attracted attention for decades. It usually involves designing a controller such that the dynamic system will eventually reach a specific region of the state space within a finite time. How to design the explicit controllers has been intensively studied

This work is supported by the National Key R&D Program of China (2022YFA1005103) and the National Natural Science Foundation of China (12371452).

H. Hermanns et al. (Eds.): SETTA 2023, LNCS 14464, pp. 21–37, 2024.
https://doi.org/10.1007/978-981-99-8664-4_2

in the past [4–6], and can be broadly grouped into two categories: searching-based method [7] and dynamic programming-based method [8]. The searching-based method usually uses rapid and intuitive searching algorithms to obtain the controllers that meet the requirements, such as incremental sampling [9] and exploring random trees [10]; the dynamic programming-based method typically constructs an optimal control problem using the HamiltonJacobi-Bellman equation and solves the optimal controller by dynamic programming [11,12].

However, in reality, it is usually impractical to consider a single initial and final state only. For example, in robot system [13,14], the initial position obtained by the sensor is not accurate and prompt, and the specific missions of the robot are required to be completed within a specified target area. For modelling the phenomena above, it is necessary to consider the uniform controllability to target set, i.e., to design controllers such that the trajectories evolving from the initial set can enter the target set within a finite time. However, the uniform controllability problem to target set is rather challenging. First, the initial set described by a connected compact set should be considered instead of a finite number of points, thus the methods developed for points are not appropriate; second, the uniform controllability to target set usually involves the reliable computation of reachable sets and Hausdorff distance between two sets, both of which are inherently difficult; finally, most existing methods such as the Hamilton-Jacobi equation based approach usually incur in the curse of dimensionality [15,16].

In recent years, there have been many studies on theoretical approaches and engineering applications about the control synthesis of set. For example, [17] proposes an optimal control strategy for linear systems subjected to set-membership uncertainties; [18] presents approaches as a combination of Hamiltonian techniques with set-valued analysis for the problem of output feedback control under unknown but bounded disturbances. It is worth pointing out that there are some works that combine the reachability analysis with the controllability of set and have attracted much attention. For example, by combining reachability analysis with optimal control, [19] provides an approach to formally guarantee the satisfaction of constraints for disturbed linear systems; [20] presents a toolbox that automatically synthesizes verified controllers for solving reach-avoid problems using reachability analysis. Moreover, the controllability of sets has also been investigated in different application areas, such as air traffic management [21], automotive engines [22], and protein signal transduction in biology [23].

In this paper, inspired by the series representations of evolution function [24], we investigate the reachability based uniform controllability to target set. Specifically, we first introduce the concept of evolution function (EF) for exactly describing the reachable set. Due to the difficulty of solving analytic solutions of EF, we give the approximations of reachable sets with high precision by the series representation of EF. Afterwards, in virtue of the bounded rectangular grids, we propose an approximation approach for obtaining the Hausdorff semi-distance with any arbitrary precision guarantees between the reachable set and the target set. Based on the above, we develop a heuristic framework to choose an optimal piecewise constant controller from sampled candidates, in which a reachability verification condition is used as the termination criteria, realizing the controllability. However, since we take numerous candidate controllers as samples, a huge computational load is required for the computations of the corresponding reachable sets. Therefore, inspired by reinforcement learning, we improve our framework by using K-arm Bandit model. Additionally, it is notable that both heuristic frameworks are prone to a potential local optimum dilemma, which will result in the reachable set possibly missing the target set during the procedure. To overcome the possible issue, we further improve our framework by developing a reference trajectory based algorithm. Finally, we use some benchmarks with comparisons to show the effectiveness of our methods.

The paper is organized as follows. In Sect. 2, we give the problem formulation. In Sect. 3, we propose the theoretical foundations for reachability based uniform controllability to target set. Then we design a framework for searching a piecewise constant controller to realize the controllability in Sect. 4. In Sect. 5, we improve our framework by using K-arm Bandit model and reference trajectory respectively. In Sect. 6, some benchmarks are provided to show the efficiency of our approaches. We conclude the paper in Sect. 7.

2   Problem Formulation

In this paper, we consider the following dynamical system

$$\dot{\mathbf{x}} = f(\mathbf{x}, \mathbf{u}(t)), \mathbf{x} \in \mathcal{D}, t \in \mathbb{T}, \mathbf{u}(\cdot) \in \mathscr{U}(\mathbb{T}, \mathbf{U}), \tag{1}$$

where $\mathbf{x} \in \mathbb{R}^n$ is an n-dimensional vector, $\mathcal{D} \subset \mathbb{R}^n$ is a domain, time interval $\mathbb{T} = [-T, T]$, T is a given time horizon, $\mathbf{U} = \prod_{i=1}^m [a_i, b_i] \subset \mathbb{R}^m$, $\mathscr{U}(\mathbb{T}, \mathbf{U}) \triangleq$ {measurable function $\Phi | \Phi : \mathbb{T} \mapsto \mathbf{U}$}, $\mathbf{u}(t) : \mathbb{R} \mapsto \mathbb{R}^m$ is the input control in $\mathscr{U}(\mathbb{T}, \mathbf{U})$, and $f : \mathcal{D} \times \mathscr{U}(\mathbb{T}, \mathbf{U}) \mapsto \mathbb{R}^n$ is an n-dimensional analytic real function satisfying the local Lipschitz condition with respect to $\mathbf{x}$ and $\mathbf{u}(\cdot)$. Denote the trajectory starting from $\mathbf{x}_0 \in \mathbb{R}^n$ under the input control $\mathbf{u}(t)$ as $\phi_{\mathbf{u}}(\mathbf{x}_0, t)$. Note that in this paper we assume that $\mathbb{T}$ is strictly contained in the existence interval of the solution. For System (1), we define the reachable set as follows.

Definition 1. *For System* (1) *with control* $\mathbf{u}(\cdot)$ *and initial set* $\mathbb{X}_0 \subseteq \mathbb{R}^n$, *the reachable set* $Reach_{\mathbf{f}, \mathbb{X}_0}^{t,u}$ *at* $t \in \mathbb{T}$ *is defined as* $Reach_{\mathbf{f}, \mathbb{X}_0}^{t,u} = \{\phi_{\mathbf{u}}(\mathbf{x}_0, t) | \mathbf{x}_0 \in \mathbb{X}_0\}$.

To describe the reachable set, we introduce the evolution function, which is similar to the concept of advection operator in [25].

Definition 2. *Given an analytic function* $g(\mathbf{x}) : \mathbb{R}^n \to \mathbb{R}$ *and a given input control* $\mathbf{u}(\cdot)$, *the evolution function of system* (1) *with* $g(\mathbf{x})$ *is defined as*

$$Evo_{\mathbf{f},g,\mathbf{u}}(\mathbf{x}, t) = g(\phi_{\mathbf{u}}(\mathbf{x}, -t)), \forall (\mathbf{x}, t) \in \mathcal{D} \times [-T, 0]. \tag{2}$$

Then, for a given analytic function $g(\mathbf{x}) : \mathbb{R}^n \to \mathbb{R}$, we denote the *sub-level set* of $g(\mathbf{x})$ as $\mu(g) \triangleq \{\mathbf{x} \in \mathbb{R}^n | g(\mathbf{x}) \leq 0\}$. If the initial set $\mathbb{X}_0 \subseteq \mathbb{R}^n$ can be described by the sub-level set, i.e., $\mathbb{X}_0 = \mu(g)$, we use $Reach_{\mathbf{f},g}^{t,u}$ as aliases of $Reach_{\mathbf{f},\mu(g(\cdot))}^{t,u}$. With Definition 2, we directly have the following proposition, connecting evolution function $Evo_{\mathbf{f},g,\mathbf{u}}(\mathbf{x}, t)$ with reachable set $Reach_{\mathbf{f},g}^{t,u}$.

Proposition 1. *For System* (1) *and analytic function* $g(\mathbf{x}) : \mathbb{R}^n \to \mathbb{R}$, $Reach_{\mathbf{f},g}^{t,u}$
$= \mu(Evo_{\mathbf{f},g,\mathbf{u}}(\mathbf{x},t)) = \{\mathbf{x} \in \mathbb{R}^n | Evo_{\mathbf{f},g,\mathbf{u}}(\mathbf{x},t) \leq 0\}$.

From Proposition 1, computation of $Reach_{\mathbf{f},g}^{t,u}$ can be converted to computations of evolution function defined by its sub-zero level set. Then, the *reachability based uniform controllability to target set* for System (1) is defined as follows.

Definition 3. *For System* (1) *with given simply connected compact initial set* $\mathbb{G}_0 = \mu(g_0)$, *convex compact target set* $\mathbb{G}_{target} = \mu(g_{target})$ *and time horizon* $\mathbb{T}$, *the reachability based uniform controllability to target set is the problem of considering the existence of a proper input control* $u(\cdot) \in \mathscr{U}$ *such that all trajectories starting from* $\mathbb{G}_0$ *simultaneously move into* $\mathbb{G}_{target}$ *during* $[0,T]$, *that is, the existence of* $u(\cdot) \in \mathscr{U}$ *and* $t \in [0,T]$ *such that* $Reach_{\mathbf{f},g_0}^{t,u} \subseteq \mathbb{G}_{target}$ *holds.*

3   Reachability Based Theoretical Foundation

In this section, we propose the theoretical foundation for achieving reachability based uniform controllability to target set. In details, Sect. 3.1 presents an approximation of reachable set by remainder estimation-based method; Sect. 3.2 presents an approximation of the Hausdorff semi-distance by boundary grid; Sect. 3.3 presents the conditions for its reachability verification.

3.1   Approximation of Reachable Set

For reachable set computation, Proposition 1 shows that we can compute the reachable set by computing the evolution function of the system. However, the analytic solution is hard to get in general. Instead of computing the evolution function by directly using the analytic solution, following the work in [26,27], we here introduce a methodology to compute approximations of evolution functions. For the above purpose, we first define the approximations of the set as follows.

Definition 4. *For two n-dimensional scale functions* $f_1(\mathbf{x})$ *and* $f_2(\mathbf{x})$, $f_1(\mathbf{x})$ *is an* over-(or under-)approximation *of* $f_2(\mathbf{x})$ *over* S *if* $f_1(\mathbf{x}) \leq (\geq) f_2(\mathbf{x}), \forall \mathbf{x} \in S$.

Note that segmented constant value functions can approximate time-varying functions well, the segmented constant value controllers are usually considered. Due to this, we in this subsection mainly focus on the constant value controller, i.e. $\frac{d\mathbf{u}}{dt} = 0$. Based on Definition 2, the Taylor expansion of $Evo_{\mathbf{f},g,\mathbf{u}}(\mathbf{x},t)$ w.r.t. t at $t = 0$ can be expressed as

$$Evo_{\mathbf{f},g,\mathbf{u}}(\mathbf{x},t) = \sum_{i=0}^{+\infty} Evo_{\mathbf{f},g,\mathbf{u}}^{(i)}(\mathbf{x},0)\frac{t^i}{i!} = \sum_{i=0}^{+\infty} \frac{\mathcal{M}_{\mathbf{f},g,\mathbf{u}}^i(\mathbf{x})}{i!}(-t)^i, \tag{3}$$

where $\mathcal{M}_{\mathbf{f},g,\mathbf{u}}^i(\mathbf{x})$ is defined inductively as $\mathcal{M}_{\mathbf{f},g,\mathbf{u}}^0(\mathbf{x}) = g(\mathbf{x})$, and $\mathcal{M}_{\mathbf{f},g,\mathbf{u}}^{i+1}(\mathbf{x}) = \frac{\partial \mathcal{M}_{\mathbf{f},g,\mathbf{u}}^i(\mathbf{x})}{\partial \mathbf{x}} \cdot f(\mathbf{x},\mathbf{u})$ for all $\mathbf{x} \in \mathcal{D}$. Moreover, we denote $Evo_{\mathbf{f},g,\mathbf{u}}^N(\mathbf{x},t)$ as its *N*th partial sum, i.e., $Evo_{\mathbf{f},g,\mathbf{u}}^N(\mathbf{x},t) \equiv \sum_{i=0}^N \frac{(-t)^i}{i!}\mathcal{M}_{\mathbf{f},g,\mathbf{u}}^i(\mathbf{x})$.

We denote the remainder of $Evo_{\mathbf{f},g,\mathbf{u}}^N(\mathbf{x},t)$ as $Rem_{\mathbf{f},g,\mathbf{u}}^N(\mathbf{x},t) = Evo_{\mathbf{f},g,\mathbf{u}}(\mathbf{x},t) - Evo_{\mathbf{f},g,\mathbf{u}}^N(\mathbf{x},t)$. It was proved in [26] that $Rem_{\mathbf{f},g,\mathbf{u}}^N(\mathbf{x},t)$ can be represented as $\int_0^t \frac{(t-r)^N}{N!}(-1)^{N+1}\mathcal{M}_{\mathbf{f},g,\mathbf{u}}^{N+1}(\phi_\mathbf{u}(\mathbf{x},-r))dr$. Thus, if we can find proper bounds of $\mathcal{M}_{\mathbf{f},g,\mathbf{u}}^{N+1}\phi_\mathbf{u}(\mathbf{x},-r)$, then we can directly estimate remainders $Rem_{\mathbf{f},g,\mathbf{u}}^N(\mathbf{x},t)$, arriving at approximations of evolution function, as shown in Theorem 1.

Theorem 1.   *For System* (1) *with constant controller, analytic $g : \mathbb{R}^n \to \mathbb{R}$ and time bound T, assume that S is a compact set of states such that $\mathbb{D} \supseteq S \supseteq \bigcup_{t\in[0,T]} Reach_{\mathbf{f},\mathbf{u}}^{t,\mathbf{u}}$, and $S' \supseteq \bigcup_{t\in[-T,0]} Reach_{\mathbf{f},S}^{-t,\mathbf{u}}$. For any degree $N \in \mathbb{N}$, if we can have $L_{N+1} \leq (-1)^{N+1}\mathcal{M}_{\mathbf{f},g,\mathbf{u}}^{N+1}(\mathbf{x}) \leq U_{N+1}$, then for all $(\mathbf{x},t,\mathbf{u}) \in S' \times [0,T] \times \mathbf{U}$,*

1. *$Over(\mathbf{x},t,\mathbf{u}) = Evo_{\mathbf{f},g,\mathbf{u}}^N(\mathbf{x},t) + L_{N+1}\frac{t^{N+1}}{(N+1)!}$ / $Under(\mathbf{x},t,\mathbf{u}) = Evo_{\mathbf{f},g,\mathbf{u}}^N(\mathbf{x},t)$*
   $+ U_{N+1}\frac{t^{N+1}}{(N+1)!}$ is over- / under- approximation of $Evo_{\mathbf{f},g,\mathbf{u}}(\mathbf{x},t)$ over S.

2. *the precisions for approximations above is bounded by $(U_{N+1} - L_{N+1})\frac{t^{N+1}}{(N+1)!}$.*

3.2   Hausdorff Semi-distance Based Control Synthesis

After obtaining a reliable representation of the reachable set, we need to provide a metric between the reachable sets and the target set to guide the selection of controllers. For this purpose, we introduce the concept of Hausdorff semi-distance of set and give a theoretical representation of the optimal control. However, the calculation of Hausdorff semi-distance is rather difficult. Here, based on some common assumptions on sets, we present a lemma for simplification, such that the Hausdorff semi-distance between sets can be converted to the Hausdorff semi-distance between boundaries of sets. Moreover, since the Hausdorff semi-distance between connected boundaries is still difficult to obtain, we propose a rectangular grid based approximation method to give an estimate of the Hausdorff semi-distance between boundaries with a given error range, and further, give the controller selection strategy based on the above approximation.

Definition 5.   *For sets Ω_A and Ω_B, the Hausdorff semi-distance from Ω_A to Ω_B is defined by $d(\Omega_A, \Omega_B) = \sup_{a\in\Omega_A} d(a,\Omega_B)$, where $d(a,\Omega_B) = \inf_{b\in\Omega_B}\|a-b\|_2$.*

Based on the distance in Definition 5, we can use it as an important metric to assess the performance among different input control $\mathbf{u}$. Then, solving reachability based uniform controllability problem to target set can be converted to find the proper input control $\mathbf{u}^*(\cdot)$ such that

$$\mathbf{u}^*(\cdot) = \underset{\mathbf{u}\in\mathscr{U}(T,\mathbf{U})}{\operatorname{argmin}} \min_{t\in[0,T]} d(\mu(Evo_{\mathbf{f},g,\mathbf{u}}(\mathbf{x},t)), \mathbb{G}_{target}). \tag{4}$$

In general, it is difficult to directly solve (4) since accurate reachable sets are not available. Especially, as for computing accurate Hausdorff semi-distance, it usually requires comparing all points in two sets, which is obviously not possible in applications. Therefore, in order to reduce the computation cost, we propose a lemma to simplify the Hausdorff semi-distance based on the following property.

Property 1. Assume that Ω_A is a compact set and Ω_B is a convex compact set. Then there must exist $a \in \partial\Omega_A$ such that $d(a, \Omega_B) = d(\Omega_A, \Omega_B)$.

Lemma 1. *Assume that Ω_A is a compact set and Ω_B is a convex compact set. If $\partial\Omega_A \subseteq \Omega_B$, then $d(\Omega_A, \Omega_B) = 0$; else $d(\Omega_A, \Omega_B) = d((\partial\Omega_A) \cap \Omega_B^c, \partial\Omega_B)$.*

Now we consider the distance between $\mu(Evo_{f,g,u}(\mathbf{x}, t))$ and $\mathbb{G}_{target}$. Due to the continuity of $Evo_{f,g,u}(\mathbf{x}, t)$ and the compactness of the initial set, we have $\mu(Evo_{f,g,u}(\mathbf{x}, t))$ is compact. Besides, $\mathbb{G}_{target}$ is assumed to be convex and compact. Based on Lemma 1, we transform the computation of $d(\mu(Evo_{f,g,u}(\mathbf{x}, t)), \mathbb{G}_{target})$ to $d(\partial\mu(Evo_{f,g,u}(\mathbf{x}, t)) \cap \mathbb{G}_{target}^c, \partial\mathbb{G}_{target})$, reducing the complexity.

Although the distance between $\mu(Evo_{f,g,u}(\mathbf{x}, t))$ and $\mathbb{G}_{target}$ is simplified to the distance between boundaries, it is still difficult to solve the above Hausdorff semi-distances directly. This is attributed to the fact that the complexity of the evolution function will increase significantly as the system evolves, resulting in a complex sub-zero level set. Therefore, based on the general consensus that distances can be calculated numerically on a finite number of grid points [28], we propose a high-precision method to compute the distance above as follows.

Given a compact set Ω and a hypercuboid S which satisfies $\Omega \subseteq S$, we divide S and attempt to find finite grid points of S to approximate the boundary of Ω. Specifically, for a hypercuboid $S = \prod_{i=1}^{n}[\underline{a_i}, \overline{a_i}] \subseteq \mathbb{R}^n$, the rectangular bounded grid on S with k^n grid points has a spacing $(\overline{a_i} - \underline{a_i})/(k-1)$ in each of its dimensions, that is, the length of S in each dimension is divided equally into $k-1$ parts. We denote the finite set of all grid points on S by $\mathbf{N}(S, k)$, i.e.,

$$\mathbf{N}(S, k) = \{x_{i_1 \cdots i_n} \mid x_{i_1 \cdots i_n} = (\underline{a_1} + \frac{\overline{a_1} - \underline{a_1}}{k-1} * i_1, \cdots, \underline{a_n} + \frac{\overline{a_n} - \underline{a_n}}{k-1} * i_n),$$
$$i_j = 0, \cdots, k-1, j = 1, \cdots, n\},$$

and the maximum spacing of each dimension as $h = \max_{i=1,\cdots,n}\{(\overline{a_i} - \underline{a_i})/(k-1)\}$. Then we consider the grid points on S that close to the boundary of set Ω, i.e., the grid points on S for which the distance to the boundary of Ω is less than h, denoted as $N_{(\Omega)}(S, k) = \{x \in N(S, k) \mid d(x, \Omega) \leq h\}$.

However, when the set is represented by a zero sub-level set, $d(x, \Omega)$ is difficult to obtain, so we introduce a boundary determinant as follows.

$$\mathbb{N}_{(\mu(g))}(S, k) = \{\mathbf{x} = (x_{i_1,\cdots,i_j,\cdots,i_n}) \in N(S, k) \mid \exists j \in [1, n], i_j \in [1, k-1],$$
$$g(x_{i_1,\cdots,i_j-1,\cdots,i_n}) \cdot g(x_{i_1,\cdots,i_j+1,\cdots,i_n}) \leq 0\}. \tag{5}$$

Clearly, we have $\mathbb{N}_{(\mu(g))}(S, k) \subseteq N_{(\Omega)}(S, k)$, and Eq. (5) guarantees that there are points of dissimilar sign in each mesh, which means that the boundary points will be covered. To get a better visualization of (5), we use Fig. 1 for a two-dimensional example to show four boundary cases where none and four inside attributed to one case. The points on the rectangles represent the local grid points, the red lines represent the boundary $\partial(\mu(g))$, and the green circle represents $\mathbb{N}_{(\mu(g))}(S, k)$ selected to satisfy (5). Based on (5), we propose an approximation method for $d(\Omega_A, \Omega_B)$ with a given error range in Theorem 2.

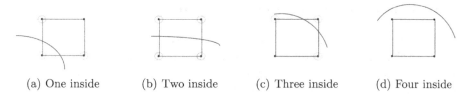

(a) One inside   (b) Two inside   (c) Three inside   (d) Four inside

Fig. 1. Schematic representation of boundary approximation grid points in (5)

Theorem 2. *Given two compact sets* $\Omega_A = \mu(g_A)$ *and* $\Omega_B = \mu(g_B)$, *then for any hypercuboids* $S_A = \prod_{i=1}^{n}[\underline{a_i}, \overline{a_i}]$ *and* $S_B = \prod_{i=1}^{n}[\underline{b_i}, \overline{b_i}]$ *satisfying* $\Omega_A \subseteq S_A$ *and* $\Omega_B \subseteq S_B$, *we define the grid distance* $\widetilde{d}(\Omega_A, \Omega_B)$ *with* k^n *grid points as*

$$\widetilde{d}(\Omega_A, \Omega_B) = \sup_{a \in \mathbb{N}_{(\mu(g_A))}(S_A, k)} \inf_{b \in \mathbb{N}_{(\mu(g_B))}(S_B, k)} \|a - b\|_2, \tag{6}$$

and the approximation error satisfies: $\|d(\Omega_A, \Omega_B) - \widetilde{d}(\Omega_A, \Omega_B)\| \leq h_A + h_B$, *where* $h_A = \max_{1 \leq i \leq n}\{\frac{(\overline{a_i} - \underline{a_i})}{k-1}\}$, *and* $h_B = \max_{1 \leq i \leq n}\{\frac{(\overline{b_i} - \underline{b_i})}{k-1}\}$.

According to Theorem 2, (4) will be converted into the following equation:
$$\mathbf{u}^*(\cdot) = \arg\min_{\mathbf{u} \in \mathscr{U}(T, \mathbf{U})} \min_{t \in [0,T]} \widetilde{d}(\mu(Over(\mathbf{x}, t, \mathbf{u})), \mathbb{G}_{target}).$$

3.3   Reachability Verification

This subsection provides a method to verify whether the current reachable set reaches the target set truly under the input control by numerical quantifier elimination. Apparently, if there exists $t^* \in [0, T]$, such that the Hausdorff semi-distance from $\mu(Evo_{\mathbf{f},g,\mathbf{u}}(\mathbf{x}, t^*))$ to $\mathbb{G}_{target}$ takes the minimal value 0, i.e., $d(\mu(Evo_{\mathbf{f},g,\mathbf{u}^*(\cdot)}(\mathbf{x}, t^*)), \mathbb{G}_{target}) = 0$, then we can obtain that $\mu(Evo_{\mathbf{f},g,\mathbf{u}}(\mathbf{x}, t)) \subseteq \mathbb{G}_{target}$. However, the grid distance $\widetilde{d}$ in Theorem 2 introduces computational errors, and thus the grid distance $\widetilde{d}(Over(\mathbf{x}, t, \mathbf{u}^*), \mathbb{G}_{target}) = 0$ can not guarantee that the reachable set at the current instant enters the target set. Therefore, we here propose an alternative approach for verification. It is worth mentioning that we only verify when the distance between the reachable set and the target set at the current moment is less than h. Specifically, based on Theorem 1 and Proposition 1, if exists $t^* \in [0, T]$, we have $Over(\mathbf{x}, t^*, \mathbf{u}) \subseteq \mathbb{G}_{target}$, then $\mu(Evo_{\mathbf{f},g,\mathbf{u}}(\mathbf{x}, t^*)) \subseteq \mathbb{G}_{target}$. Utilizing the sub-zero level set representation of the target set, we can obtain sufficient conditions for reachability as follows.

Theorem 3. *For a convex compact set* $\mathbb{G}_{target} = \{\mathbf{x} \mid g_{target} \leq 0\}$ *and the overapproximation of reachable set* $Over(\mathbf{x}, t, \mathbf{u}^*)$, *if the constraint* $\exists t \in [0, T], \forall \mathbf{x} \in S, [Over(\mathbf{x}, t, \mathbf{u}^*) \leq 0 \Rightarrow g_{target}(\mathbf{x}) \leq 0]$ *holds, then* $\mathbb{G}_{target}$ *is reachable.*

4 Reachability Based Heuristic Framework

In this section, we propose a reachability based heuristic framework for uniform controllability to target set. For this, inspired by the property that for any measurable function, there exist piecewise constant functions converging to it, we firstly propose the following sketch, attempting to search a proper piecewise constant $\mathbf{u}^*(\cdot)$ such that under $\mathbf{u}^*(\cdot)$, $Reach_{\mathbf{f},g}^{t,u^*} \subseteq \mathbb{G}_{target}$ for a certain $\mathbf{t} \in [0,T]$:

1. divide $[0,T]$ into $0 = t_0 < t_1 < \cdots < t_K = T$, and $\mathbb{G}_0 := \mu(g_0)$;
2. for each interval $[t_i, t_{i+1}]$, $0 \le i \le K - 1$,
   (a) Approximation: compute the over-approximation $\mu(Over(\mathbf{x}, t, \mathbf{u}))$ of the reachable set and a box S satisfying $S \supseteq \mu(Over(\mathbf{x}, t, \mathbf{u}))$.
   (b) Synthesis: select the optimal constant controller $\mathbf{u}_i^*$ by solving

$$\mathbf{u}_i^* = \underset{\mathbf{u} \in \mathscr{U}(T,\mathbf{U})}{\operatorname{argmin}} \; \widetilde{d}(\mu(Over(\mathbf{x}, t, \mathbf{u})), \mathbb{G}_{target}); \tag{7}$$

   (c) Verification(where $\widetilde{d}_{\mathbf{u}_i^*} \le h$): verify the constraint: $\exists t \in [t_i, t_{i+1}], \forall \mathbf{x} \in S, [Over(\mathbf{x}, t, \mathbf{u}^*) \le 0 \Rightarrow g_{target}(\mathbf{x}) \le 0]$,
      i. if the above constraint holds (reached), return $\mathbf{u}^*(\cdot)$;
      ii. else, $g_{i+1} = Over(\mathbf{x}, t_{i+1}, \mathbf{u}_i^*)$ and go to the time interval $[t_{i+1}, t_{i+2}]$.

Secondly, we design an algorithm for over-approximating reachable set in (7). That is, for given System (1), analytic function $g(\cdot)$, time horizon T and designated precision ϵ, we attempt to use Theorem 1 to compute $Over(\mathbf{x}, t, \mathbf{u})$ for any given $\mathbf{u} \in \mathbf{U}$. For this, starting from a box B containing the initial set $\mu(g)$, we first call **CORA** [29] to get an over-approximation (**Bound**) of the maximal reachable set as S and an over-approximation (**Interval**) of the backward maximal reachable set of S as S'. Then, according to S', we can iteratively increase the degree N of $Evo_{\mathbf{f},g,\mathbf{u}}^N(\mathbf{x}, t)$ and estimate the lower bound L_{N+1} and upper bound U_{N+1} of $(-1)^{N+1}M^{N+1}(\mathbf{x}, \mathbf{u})$ in $S' \times \mathbf{U}$ with interval arithmetic in **CORA** until $U_{N+1} - L_{N+1} \le \frac{\epsilon \cdot (N+1)!}{T^{N+1}}$. According to Theorem 1, all over-approximations of $Evo_{\mathbf{f},g,\mathbf{u}}(\mathbf{x}, t)$ for all $\mathbf{u} \in \mathbf{U}$ are generated with the given precision. Consequently, we have Algorithm 1 to compute over-approximations of EF with any given precision.

Thirdly, we design an algorithm to realize the verification. For this, we call **RSolver** [30] for solving the constraint $\exists t \in [t_i, t_{i+1}], \forall \mathbf{x} \in S, [Over(\mathbf{x}, t, \mathbf{u}^*) \le 0 \Rightarrow g_{target}(\mathbf{x}) \le 0]$. Note that **RSolver** can solve quantified constraints, that is, formulae in the first order predicate language over the reals, and returns 'true', 'false', and 'unknown' with corresponding intervals according to a user-provided error bound. Consequently, we design Algorithm 2 for verifying simulative reachability.

Finally, based on Algorithm 1 and 2, we can achieve our overall reachability based heuristic framework in Algorithm 3. Specifically, considering the synthesis in our framework, for given over-approximation of reachable sets $Over(\mathbf{x}, t, \mathbf{u})$, all candidates control set $[a_i, b_i]$, over-approximation of the maximal reachable set S and designated precision ϵ, we attempt to implement the selection of controllers

---

Algorithm 1. Over-approximation

Input: $f(\mathbf{x}, \mathbf{u}(t))$, $g(\mathbf{x})$, B, T, ϵ, $[a_i, b_i]$;
Output: $Over(\mathbf{x}, t, \mathbf{u}), S$.

1: Call **CORA**(f, B, T) to find **Bound** as S;
2: Call **CORA**(f, **Bound**, $-T$) to find **Interval** as S';
3: Initialize $N \leftarrow 0$, $M(\mathbf{x}, \mathbf{u}) \leftarrow g(\mathbf{x})$, $Tr(\mathbf{x}, t, \mathbf{u}) \leftarrow g(\mathbf{x})$;
4: **while** $U - L > \frac{\epsilon \cdot (N+1)!}{T^{N+1}}$ **do**
5:     $M(\mathbf{x}, \mathbf{u}) \leftarrow \frac{\partial M(\mathbf{x}, \mathbf{u})}{\partial \mathbf{x}} \cdot f(\mathbf{x}, \mathbf{u})$;
6:     $Tr(\mathbf{x}, t, \mathbf{u}) \leftarrow Tr(\mathbf{x}, t, \mathbf{u}) + \frac{(-t)^{N+1}}{(N+1)!} M(\mathbf{x}, \mathbf{u})$ and $N \leftarrow N + 1$;
7:     Compute L and U for $M(\mathbf{x}, \mathbf{u})$ in $S' \times \prod_{i=1}^{m}[a_i, b_i]$;
8: $Over(\mathbf{x}, t, \mathbf{u}) \leftarrow Tr(\mathbf{x}, t, \mathbf{u}) + L\frac{(t)^{N+1}}{(N+1)!}$;
9: **return** $Over(\mathbf{x}, t, \mathbf{u}), S$.

Algorithm 2. Verification

Input: $Over(\mathbf{x}, t, \mathbf{u}_i^*)$, S, G_{target}, η, T;
Output: $flag$.

1: Initialize $flag \leftarrow 0$;
2: **while** $flag == 0$ **do**
3:     Call **RSolver** with $(Over(\mathbf{x}, t, \mathbf{u}_i^*), S, G_{target}, \eta, T)$ for the flag in Theorem 3;
4:     **if** the interval for 'false' $\neq \emptyset$ **then**
5:         $flag \leftarrow -1$;
6:     **else if** the interval for 'unknown' $\neq \emptyset$ **then**
7:         $\eta \leftarrow 0.5\eta$;
8:     **else**
9:         $flag \leftarrow 1$;
10: **return** $flag$.

---

in step 2(a) according to Theorem 2. From Theorem 2, we generate a rectangular, bounded grid in $\mathbb{R}^n$ of k^n grid points to approximate the Hausdorff semi-distance. Grid for reachable sets is generated in the S which is found in Algorithm 1 and Grid for the target set is given by initial condition that $\mathbb{G}_{target} \subseteq S_{target}$. Then, for all candidates $\tilde{\mathbf{u}} \in [a_i, b_i]$, we try to get enough boundary points of the reachable set to compute Hausdorff semi-distance. According to Theorem 2, we use the boundary determination condition based on the sub-level set and obtain the approximate boundary points of the target set and reachable set by using the rectangular bounded grid, and then we can compute $d_{\tilde{\mathbf{u}}}$ for each candidate $\tilde{\mathbf{u}} \in [a_i, b_i]$ from a finite number of grid points. After that, we compare all approximations of $d(\mu(Evo_{\mathbf{f},g,\mathbf{u}}(\mathbf{x}, \Delta t)), \mathbb{G}_{target})$ and then select the best input control $\mathbf{u}^*$.

5 Improvements of Reachability Based Framework

In this section, we will improve our heuristic framework by K-arm Bandit Model and reference trajectory respectively. In detail, in order to reduce the computational complexity, in Subsect. 5.1 we improve our framework with less time cost

Algorithm 3. Reachability based Heuristic Framework

Input: $f(\mathbf{x}, \mathbf{u}(t))$, T, K, k, g_0, g_{target}, $\mathscr{U}(T, \mathbf{U})$, B, S_{target}, ϵ, η;
Output: $\mathbf{u}^*(\cdot)$.

1: Initialize $g(\mathbf{x}) = g_0$, $S_0 = B$, divide $[0, T]$ into $0 = t_0 < t_1 < \cdots < t_K = T$.
2: Construct T_{bounds} from the $\mathbb{N}_{(\mu(g_{target}))}(S_{target}, k)$ and get h_T in (5)
3: **for** $i = 0, \cdots, K - 1$ **do**
4:     Sampling to obtain controllers $\tilde{\mathbf{u}}_i$ in $\mathbf{U}$
5:     Call Algorithm 1 with $(f, g, S_i, t_{i+1} - t_i, \epsilon, \mathbf{U})$ for $Over(\mathbf{x}, t, \mathbf{u})$ and S_{i+1}
6:     Generate a grid in S_{i+1} of k^n grid points
7:     **for** all candidates $\tilde{\mathbf{u}}_i \in \mathbf{U}$ **do**
8:         Construct R_{bounds} from the $\mathbb{N}_{(\mu(Over(\mathbf{x}, t_{i+1}, \mathbf{u})))}(S_{i+1}, k)$ and get h_O in (5)
9:         $\tilde{d}_{\tilde{\mathbf{u}}_i} \leftarrow \max_{p_r \in R_{bounds}} \min_{p_t \in T_{bounds}} \|p_r - p_t\|_2$
10:        $\mathbf{u}_i^* = \mathrm{argmin}_{\tilde{\mathbf{u}}_i \in \mathbf{U}} \tilde{d}_{\tilde{\mathbf{u}}_i}$
11:        **if** $\tilde{d}_{\mathbf{u}_i^*} \leq h_O + h_T$ **then**
12:            Call Algorithm 2 with $(Over(\mathbf{x}, t, \mathbf{u}_i^*), S_{i+1}, G_{target}, \eta, t_{i+1} - t_i)$ for reach
               $flag$
13:            **if** $flag = 1$ **then**
14:                Let $\mathbf{u}^*(\cdot) \leftarrow \mathbf{u}_j^*$, for all $j(j = 0, \cdots, i)$
15:                **return** $\mathbf{u}^*(\cdot)$
16:        Reset $g(\mathbf{x}) \leftarrow Over(\mathbf{x}, t_{i+1}, \mathbf{u}_i^*)$
17: **return** control not found.

achieving similar results by using K-arm Bandit model in reinforcement learning. Furthermore, to avoid the possible dilemma of local optima, in Subsect. 5.2 we improve our framework based on the reference trajectory.

5.1   K-Arm Bandit Model Based Improvement

Note that for control inputs with large-scale sampling and systems of high dimensions, the number of over approximations of the reachable set and the corresponding rectangular grid points will increase exponentially, which implies the huge computational cost of Algorithm 3. In order to reduce the complexity, we propose an improved approach for selection based on K-arm Bandit model.

K-arm Bandit is a typical problem of reinforcement learning, and it describes the following task: suppose there is a slot machine with K different levers on which a positive reward is given for each pull and the goal is to maximize the total reward for a given fixed number of pulls. Inspired by the K-arm Bandit model, we abstract a similar K-arm Bandit model for solving our problem. Specifically, we regard different candidates of the controller as levers (options) of K-arm Bandit model in each $[t_i, t_{i+1}]$. Then, for each trial in the K-arm Bandit model, we select a random point $s(t_i)$ which is located in the initial set of current time interval as the test point, and the distance difference $d(s(t_i), c_{target}) - d(s(t_{i+1}), c_{target})$ is used as the reward of the current trail. Based on the reward of each trial, we can define the reward for different controllers $\tilde{\mathbf{u}}$ of the current time interval, which is defined as the average reward of each trial under $\tilde{\mathbf{u}}$.

Based on the above discussion, for given System (1), analytic $g(\mathbf{x})$, time horizon T, all candidates control set $[a, b]$, total test times M and designated precision ϵ, we attempt to design a new improved algorithm for selection of controllers. Firstly, for each time interval $[t_i, t_{i+1}]$, generate a multitude of random states $s(t_i)$ in current initial set $\mu(g(\mathbf{x}))$ and compute the state $s(t_{i+1})$ evolving from state $s(t_i)$ for each candidates $\tilde{\mathbf{u}}_i \in [a, b]$ by numerical algorithm of System (1). Then we compute return reward of the current trail as $r(\tilde{\mathbf{u}}_i) = d(s(t_i), c_{target}) - d(s(t_{i+1}), c_{target})$. For the reward of each candidate $\tilde{\mathbf{u}}_i$, after repeating M trials, we can compute the average of $r(\tilde{\mathbf{u}}_i)$, and regard it as the reward of $\tilde{\mathbf{u}}_i$, denoted as $Q(\tilde{\mathbf{u}}_i)$. We choose the candidate that maximizes the average reward as the optimal controller of current time interval $[t_i, t_{i+1}]$, and compute the $Over(\mathbf{x}, t_{i+1}, \mathbf{u}_i^*)$ under the current optimal controller $\mathbf{u}_i^*$, which can be used as the initial set for the next time interval.

As a conclusion of the above discussions, we present our overall reachability based K-armed Bandit framework in Algorithm 4. Different from Algorithm 3, we here avoid the multiple computations of over-approximations of reachable sets and their Hausdorff semi-distance, reducing the computational complexity significantly. Our benchmark (Example 1) shows that Algorithm 4 has similar performance as Algorithm 3, but with significantly lower computational cost.

Algorithm 4. K-armed Bandit Based Improved Framework

Input: $f(\mathbf{x}, \mathbf{u}(t))$, T, K, k, g_0, g_{target}, $\mathscr{U}(T, \mathbf{U})$, B, M, ϵ;
Output: $\mathbf{u}^*(\cdot)$.

1: Initialize $g(\mathbf{x}) = g_0$, $S_0 = B$, divide $[0, T]$ into $0 = t_0 < t_1 < \cdots < t_K = T$.
2: **for** $i = 0, \cdots, K - 1$ **do**
3:    $Q(\cdot) = 0$, $count = 0$, sampling to obtain controllers $\tilde{\mathbf{u}}_i$ in $\mathbf{U}$
4:    **while** count $\leq M$ **do**
5:       Generate a random point p inside $\mu(g(\mathbf{x}))$
6:       **for** all candidates $\tilde{\mathbf{u}}_i \in \mathbf{U}$ **do**
7:          $r(\tilde{\mathbf{u}}_i) \leftarrow d(s(t_i), c_{target}) - d(s(t_{i+1}), c_{target})$
8:          $Q(\tilde{\mathbf{u}}_i) \leftarrow \frac{count * Q(\tilde{\mathbf{u}}_i) + r(\tilde{\mathbf{u}}_i)}{count + 1}$, $count \leftarrow count + 1$
9:       $\mathbf{u}_i^* \leftarrow \operatorname{argmax}_{\tilde{\mathbf{u}}_i \in \mathbf{U}} Q(\tilde{\mathbf{u}}_i)$
10:      Call Algorithm 1 with $(f, g, S_i, t_{i+1} - t_i, \epsilon, \mathbf{U})$ for $Over(\mathbf{x}, t, \mathbf{u})$ and S_{i+1}
11:      **if** $d(s(t_{i+1}), c_{target}) \leq \epsilon$ **then**
12:         Call Algorithm 2 with $Over(\mathbf{x}, t, \mathbf{u}_i^*)$, S_i, G_{target}, η, $t_{i+1} - t_i$ for $flag$
13:         **if** $flag = 1$ **then**
14:            Let $\mathbf{u}^*(\cdot) \leftarrow \mathbf{u}_j^*$, for all $j(j = 0, \cdots, i)$
15:            **return** $\mathbf{u}^*(\cdot)$
16:      Reset $g(\mathbf{x}) \leftarrow Over(\mathbf{x}, t_{i+1}, \mathbf{u}_i^*)$
17: **return** control not found.

5.2 Reference Trajectory Based Further Improvement

It is worth noting that the heuristic frameworks may be subject to the risk of local optima, which means the controllers obtained by the above heuristic algorithms can not always guarantee that all trajectories will reach the target set within the time horizon. To avoid the local optimum dilemma, we further improve our algorithm using reference trajectory.

Firstly, we present the method for searching a suitable reference trajectory. The idea is to compute a feasible trajectory $\phi_u(c_0, t)$ that steers the center c_0 of the initial set $\mu(g_0)$ as close as possible to the geometric center c_{target} of the target set $\mu(g_{target})$. For this idea, one possible way is to minimize the distance between $\phi_u(c_0, t)$ and c_{target} for $t \in [0, T]$ and $u \in \mathscr{U}$. However, $\phi_{u^*}(c_0, t^*)$, where $(u^*, t^*) = \mathrm{argmin}_{t \in [0,T], \, u \in \mathscr{U}} \|\phi_u(c_0, t) - c_{target}\|$, may be very close to the center of the target set but outside of the target set; and there may exist a t such that $\phi_{u^*}(c_0, t)$ is strictly inside the target set though it might not be the closest state to c_{target}. Therefore, a better way is to search a trajectory $\phi_{u^*}(c_0, t)$ such that $\phi_{u^*}(c_0, t^*)$ is in the target set. For this, we additionally introduce an exponential function $e^{A(sgn(g_{target}(\phi_u(c_0,t)))+1)}$, where $sgn(\cdot)$ is the sign function and A is a sufficiently large positive integer, as a penalty term in the objective function, which is used to determine whether the state is inside the target set or not. Based on the above discussion, letting $R(u, t) = e^{A(sgn(g_{target}(\phi_u(c_0,t)))+1)}\|\phi_u(c_0, t) - c_{target}\|$, we can obtain the reference trajectory by minimizing $R(u, t)$ for $t \in [0, T]$ and $u \in \mathscr{U}$. However, it is difficult to solve this optimization problem since optimizing both variables directly is unrealistic. Thus, we give an alternative method for solving a reference trajectory. For this, we adopt the time splitting $0 = t_0 < t_1 < \cdots < t_K = T$, and then solve the univariate optimization problem for each time interval $[0, t_i]$ $(1 \leq i \leq K)$, i.e., $\min_{u \in \mathscr{U}} R(u, t_i)$. For each i, the optimization can be achieved by calling ACADO Toolkit [31], which is an open source framework for automatic control using multiple shooting. After obtaining the K optimal values $R(u_i^*, t_i)$ $(1 \leq i \leq K)$, where $u_i^* = \mathrm{argmin}_{u \in \mathscr{U}} R(u, t_i)$, let $j^* = \mathrm{argmin}_{1 \leq i \leq K} R(u_i^*, t_i)$ and $u_{ref} = u_j^*$. Then our reference trajectory can be given as $x_{ref}(t) = \phi_{u_{ref}}(c_0, t)$.

After obtaining the reference trajectory $x_{ref}(\cdot)$ during the interval $[0, t_j]$, we still use the concept of average reward similar to the one in Algorithm 4 as an index to measure the performance of each candidate controller for designing an improved algorithm. Specifically, for $i = 0, \cdots, j^* - 1$, instead of using the distance between $s(t_{i+1})$ and the center of the target set, we alternatively use the minus distance between $s(t_{i+1})$ and the corresponding state on the reference trajectory $x_{ref}(\cdot)$ (i.e., $-d(s(t_{i+1}), x_{ref}(t_{i+1}))$) as the new return reward. Then, we calculate the average of the above distances for each candidate controller as the average reward and choose the candidate with the largest average reward as the optimal controller of the current time interval. Thus, the selection strategy described above can ensure that the reachable set evolves almost along a predetermined reference trajectory, thereby avoiding the local optimum dilemma that usually exists in heuristic algorithms. Therefore, we can use the new reward $r(\tilde{u}_i) = -d(s(t_{i+1}), x_{ref}(t_{i+1}))$ to update lines 7 of Algorithm 4 to obtain the improved ref-trajectory-based algorithm. Note that, if $j^* < K$, then for $i = j^*, \cdots, K - 1$ we do not change the formula of $r(\tilde{u}_i)$ in Algorithm 4. The complete updated algorithm will not be listed in detail due to the space constraint, but we still refer to it as Algorithm 5 for the convenience of usage.

6 Examples and Discussions

In this section, we demonstrate our methods on three examples, where $\eta = 10^{-2}$, $\epsilon = 10^{-3}$, red lines represent the target set and green lines represent the approximations of reachable sets. Moreover, we show the performance of our methods by comparing Examples 1 and 2 with the motion primitive based control algorithms in AROC [20], setting Opts.maxIter = 20. It is worth noting that AROC aims to drive all states inside the initial set at the final time t_f as close as possible to a desired final state, whereas we aim to drive all trajectories evolving from the initial set can simultaneously enter into the target set within a time horizon. We do not compare our method with AROC for Example 3 here since it is hard to adapt AROC for this example. All examples were performed on a Laptop with 1.8GHz Intel Core i7 (4 cores) and 8 Gb of RAM.

Example 1. Consider a nonlinear multi-input control system [32]:

$$\begin{bmatrix} \dot{x}_1 \\ \dot{x}_2 \end{bmatrix} = \frac{1}{2} \begin{bmatrix} x_1^2 + x_2 \\ -x_1 x_2 \end{bmatrix} + \begin{bmatrix} 1/2 & 0 \\ 0 & 1/2 \end{bmatrix} \begin{bmatrix} u_1 \\ u_2 \end{bmatrix},$$

where $u_1 \in [-1,1]$, $u_2 \in [-1,1]$, the initial set $\mathbb{G}_0$ is $\{\mathbf{x} | (x_1 - 1)^2 + (x_2 - 2)^2 - 0.02 \leq 0\}$, the target set $\mathbb{G}_{target}$ is $\{\mathbf{x} | (x_1 - 3)^2 + (x_2 - 1)^2/4 - 0.49 \leq 0\}$ and the time horizon $T = 1$. We divide $\mathbb{T}$ into $n = 20$ parts, and take 121 samples from $[-1,1] \times [-1,1]$ as candidates of control input.

Algorithm 3 and Algorithm 4 both realize the controllability to the target set during the time segment $[0.60, 0.65]$. The time cost of Algorithm 3 is 1912 s, while Algorithm 4 is only 223 s, which shows the advantages of our K-arm Bandit Model based algorithm. The resulted over-approximations of reachable sets at $t = 0, 0.05, \cdots, 0.65$ are shown in Fig. 2(a) and Fig. 2(b) respectively. Moreover, we set the initial set to be $[0.9, 1.1] \times [1.9, 2.1]$ and the final time $t_f = 0.65$, and use the state $(2.94, 0.95)$, determined by the numerical solution at the instant $t = 0.65$ with initial state $(1, 2)$ under the controller produced by Algorithm 4, as the goal state; AROC can realize the goal of synthesizing a controller with 191 s, which makes trajectories evolving from the initial set as close as possible to the desired state $(2.94, 0.95) \in \mathbb{G}_{target}$ at the instant $t_f = 0.65$ instead of simultaneously enter into the set $\mathbb{G}_{target}$. The results of over-approximations of reachable sets obtained by AROC are listed in Fig. 2(c). However, if the goal state is reset to be $(3, 1)$ (the center of target set), AROC cannot find a feasible solution for $t_f = 0.65$ even if we set Opts.maxIter=50; and if we reset the time t_f as 0.70, AROC still cannot find a feasible solution for the goal state $(2.94, 0.95)$ even if we set Opts.maxIter = 50. These results show that AROC has a higher dependence on the final time and goal state in achieving controllability, while our approaches have relatively loose requirements on the final time and goal state.

Example 2. Consider a 4-dimensional Dubins car system [15]:

$$\begin{bmatrix} \dot{x} \\ \dot{y} \\ \dot{\theta} \\ \dot{v} \end{bmatrix} = \begin{bmatrix} vcos\theta \\ vsin\theta \\ u_1 \\ u_2 \end{bmatrix},$$

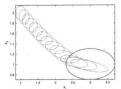

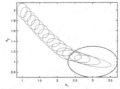

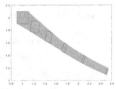

(a) Over-approximation of $Reach_{f,g}^{t,u}$ by Alg. 3.

(b) Over-approximation of $Reach_{f,g}^{t,u}$ by Alg. 4.

(c) Over-approximation of reachable set by **AROC**.

Fig. 2. Results of Example 1

where $u_1 \in [-0.4, 0.4]$, $u_2 \in [-9, 9]$, the initial set $\mathbb{G}_0$ is $\{(x, y, \theta, v) \mid x^2 + y^2 + \theta^2 + (v - 20)^2 - 0.02 \leq 0\}$, the target set $\mathbb{G}_{target}$ is $\{(x - 19.87)^2 + (y + 1.99)^2 + (\theta + 0.2)^2 - 0.25 \leq 0\}$ and time horizon $T = 1$. We divide $\mathbb{T}$ into $n = 20$ parts, and take 1369 samples from $[-0.4, 0.4] \times [-9, 9]$ as candidates of control.

Algorithm 4 and Algorithm 5 can both realize the controllability to target set during the time segment $[0.80, 0.85]$. The time cost of Algorithm 4 is 250 s, while the time cost of Algorithm 5 is 297 s, which shows that the additional use of reference trajectory in Algorithm 5 does not significantly change the time cost. The resulted over-approximations of reachable sets under the corresponding obtained controllers at $t = 0, 0.05, \cdots, 0.85$ are shown in Fig. 3(a) and Fig. 3(b) respectively. Note that this system is exactly the benchmark used in the AROC 2022 Manual [34], and we set the initial set to be $[-0.1, 0.1] \times [-0.1, 0.1] \times [-0.1, 0.1] \times [19.9, 20.1]$ and the final time $t_f = 0.85$, and use the state $((19.87, -1.99, -0.2, 25.72)$, determined by the numerical solution at the instant $t = 0.85$ with initial state $(0, 0, 0, 20)$ under the controller produced by Algorithm 5; AROC can realize the goal of synthesizing a controller with 218 s, which makes trajectories evolving from the initial set as close as possible to the desired state $(19.87, -1.99, -0.2, 25.72) \in \mathbb{G}_{target}$ at the time $t_f = 0.85$ instead of simultaneously enter into the set $\mathbb{G}_{target}$. The results of over-approximations of reachable sets obtained by AROC are listed in Fig. 2(c). Note that in addition to the dependence on the final time and goal state, AROC requires a specific target state, while our algorithms consider a specific target set that is independent on the variable v. This implies that our approach is more flexible and less restrictive.

Example 3. Consider a 6-dimensional non-polynomial system [33], which models the backflip maneuver for the quadrotor helicopter:

$$
\begin{bmatrix} \dot{p}_x \\ \dot{v}_x \\ \dot{p}_y \\ \dot{v}_y \\ \dot{\phi} \\ \dot{\omega} \end{bmatrix} = \begin{bmatrix} v_x \\ -\frac{C_D^v v_x}{m} \\ v_y \\ \frac{-mg - C_D^v v_y}{m} \\ \omega \\ -\frac{C_D^\phi \omega}{I_{yy}} \end{bmatrix} + \begin{bmatrix} 0 & 0 \\ -\frac{\sin\phi}{m} & -\frac{\sin\phi}{m} \\ 0 & 0 \\ \frac{\cos\phi}{m} & \frac{\cos\phi}{m} \\ 0 & 0 \\ \frac{l}{I_{yy}} & \frac{l}{I_{yy}} \end{bmatrix} \begin{bmatrix} u_1 \\ u_2 \end{bmatrix},
$$

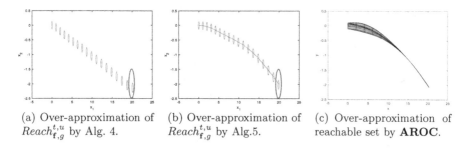

(a) Over-approximation of $Reach_{\mathbf{f},g}^{t,u}$ by Alg. 4.

(b) Over-approximation of $Reach_{\mathbf{f},g}^{t,u}$ by Alg.5.

(c) Over-approximation of reachable set by **AROC**.

Fig. 3. Results of Example 2

where p_x, p_y, and ϕ represent the horizontal, vertical, rotational positions, v_x, v_y, and ω represent the corresponding velocities, $u_1 \in [-20, 20]$ and $u_2 \in [-20, 20]$ are thrusts exerted on either end of the quadrotor. For the coefficients, $C_D^v = 0.1$ for translational drag, $m = 5$ for mass, $g = 9.8$ for gravity, $C_D^\phi = 0.1$, for rotational drag, $I_{yy} = 10$ for the moment of inertia and $l = 0.5$. The initial set $\mathbb{G}_0$ is $\{p_x^2 + (v_x - 2)^2 + p_y^2 + (v_y - 1)^2 + (\phi - \pi/6)^2 + (\omega - 0.1)^2 - 0.01 \leq 0\}$, the target set $\mathbb{G}_{target}$ is $\{(p_x - 2.29)^2 + (p_y + 4.425)^2 - 0.25^2 \leq 0\}$ and time horizon $T = 2$. We divide $\mathbb{T}$ into $n = 40$ parts, and take 1681 samples from $[-20, 20] \times [-20, 20]$ as candidates of control input.

Note that Algorithm 4 can terminate within 237 s, but Fig. 4(a) shows that Algorithm 4 cannot control the initial set into the target set within the given time horizon $T = 2$. Fortunately, by using Algorithm 5, we can realize the controllability to target set during the time segment $[1.00, 1.05]$ within 397 s. Figure 4(c) shows the resulted over-approximations of reachable sets obtained by Algorithm 5. This demonstrates the advantage of our reference trajectory-based Algorithm 5 over Algorithm 4. Note that we also use $n = 80$ and sampled 40,401 candidate inputs, but Algorithm 4 still failed to realize the controllability to the target (see Fig. 4(b)). This is because for this example, Algorithm 4 falls into the local optimum.

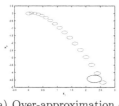 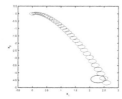 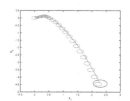

(a) Over-approximation of $Reach_{\mathbf{f},g}^{t,u}$ with 1681 input candidates by Alg. 4.

(b) Over-approximation of $Reach_{\mathbf{f},g}^{t,u}$ with 40401 input candidates by Alg. 4.

(c) Over-approximation of $Reach_{\mathbf{f},g}^{t,u}$ with 1681 input candidates by Alg.5.

Fig. 4. Results of Example 3

7 Conclusion

In this paper, we study the uniform controllability to target set such that the trajectories evolving from the initial set under designed controllers can enter into the target set. Firstly, we provide an over-approximation of the reachable set by using the series representation of EF. Subsequently, we propose an approximation approach for Hausdorff semi-distance with a bounded rectangular grid to measure the distance between reachable sets and the target set. Then, we design a heuristic framework to compute a piecewise constant controller, realizing the controllability. Moreover, to reduce the complexity, we improve our framework by K-arm Bandit Model in reinforcement learning. Since the heuristic algorithms may suffer from the local optima, we additionally use the reference trajectory for further improvement. Finally, some benchmarks with comparisons are presented to show the efficiency of our approaches. In the future, we will investigate the reachability based uniform controllability for avoidance-guaranteed problem.

References

1. Dolgov, D., Thrun, S., Montemerlo, M., Diebel, J.: Practical search techniques in path planning for autonomous driving. Ann Arbor **1001**(48105), 18–80 (2008)
2. Stefanovski, J.: Fault tolerant control of descriptor systems with disturbances. IEEE TAC **64**(3), 976–988 (2019)
3. Kurzhanski, A.B., Mesyats, A.I.: The Hamiltonian formalism for problems of group control under obstacles. IEEE TAC **49**(18), 570–575 (2016)
4. Fisac, J.F., Akametalu, A.K., et al.: A general safety framework for learning-based control in uncertain robotic systems. IEEE TAC **64**(7), 2737–2752 (2018)
5. Ornik, M., Broucke, M.E.: Chattering in the reach control problem. Automatica **89**(1), 201–211 (2018)
6. Broucke, M.E.: Reach control on simplices by continuous state feedback. SIAM J. Control. Optim. **48**(5), 3482–3500 (2010)
7. Kavralu, L.E., Svestka, P., Latombe, J.C., Overmars, M.H.: Probabilistic roadmaps for path planning in high-dimensional configuration spaces. IEEE Trans. Robot. Autom. **12**(4), 566–580 (1994)
8. Nevistic, V., Primbs, J.A.: Constrained nonlinear optimal control: a converse HJB approach. Technical Memorandum, No. CIT-CDS 96-021 (1996)
9. Bekris, K.E., Chen, B.Y., Ladd, A.M., Plaku, E., Kavraki, L.E.: Multiple query probabilistic roadmap planning using single query planning primitives. In: IEEE IROS, pp. 656–661 (2003)
10. Xu, J., Duindam, V., Alterovitz, R., Goldberg, K.: Nonlinear Systems Analysis, Stability and Control. Springer, New York (1999). https://doi.org/10.1007/978-1-4757-3108-8
11. Klamka, J.: Controllability of dynamical systems. A survey. Bull. Pol. Acad. Sci.: Tech. Sci. **61**(2), 335–342 (2013)
12. Khalaf, M.A., Lewis, F.L.: Nearly optimal control laws for nonlinear systems with saturating actuators using a neural network HJB approach. Automatica **41**(5), 779–791 (2005)
13. Wang, L., Ames, A.D., Egerstedt, M.: Safety barrier certificates for collisions-free multirobot systems. IEEE Trans. Robot. **33**(3), 661–674 (2017)

14. Fisac, J.F., Akametalu, A.K., Zeilinger, M.N., Kaynama, S., Gillula, J., Tomlin, C.J.: A general safety framework for learning-based control in uncertain robotic systems. IEEE TAC **64**(7), 2737–2752 (2019)
15. Bansal, S., Chen, M., Herbert, S., et al.: Hamilton-Jacobi reachability: a brief overview and recent advance. In: IEEE CDC, pp. 2242–2253 (2017)
16. Chen, M., Tomlin, C.J.: Exact and efficient Hamilton-Jacobi reachability for decoupled systems. In: IEEE CDC, pp. 1297–1303 (2015)
17. Dmitruk, N., Findeisen, R., Allgower, F.: Optimal measurement feedback control of finite-time continuous linear systems. IFAC Proc. Vol. **41**(2), 15339–15344 (2008)
18. Kurzhanski, A.B., Varaiya, P.: Optimization of output feedback control under set-membership uncertainty. J. Optim. Theory Appl. **151**(1), 11–32 (2011)
19. Schurmann, B., Althoff, M.: Optimal control of sets of solutions to formally guarantee constraints of disturbed linear systems. In: American Control Conference, pp. 2522–2529 (2017)
20. Kochdumper, N., Gruber, F., Schürmann, B., et al.: AROC: a toolbox for automated reachset optimal controller synthesis. In: HSCC, pp. 1–6 (2021)
21. Tomlin, C.J., Pappas, G.J., Sastry, S.S.: Conflict resolution for air traffic management: a study in multiagent hybrid systems. IEEE TAC **43**(4), 509–521 (2002)
22. Koo, T.J., Pappas, G.J., Sastry, S.: Mode switching synthesis for reachability specifications. In: HSCC, pp. 333–346 (2004)
23. Lincoln, P., Tiwari, A.: Symbolic systems biology: hybrid modeling and analysis of biological networks. In: HSCC, pp. 660–672 (2004)
24. Li, M., She, Z.: Over- and under-approximations of reachable sets with series representations of evolution functions. IEEE TAC **66**(3), 1414–1421 (2021)
25. Wang, T.C., Lall, S., West, M.: Polynomial level-set method for polynomial system reachable set estimation. IEEE TAC **58**(10), 2508–2521 (2013)
26. Hu, R., Liu, K., She, Z.: Evolution function based reach-avoid verification for time-varying systems with disturbances. ACM Trans. Embed. Comput. Syst. (2023). https://doi.org/10.1145/3626099
27. Hu, R., She, Z.: OURS: over- and under-approximating reachable sets for analytic time-invariant differential equations. J. Syst. Architect. **128**, 102580 (2022)
28. Kraft, D.: Computing the Hausdorff distance of two sets from their distance functions. J. Comput. Geom. Appl. **30**(1), 19–49 (2020)
29. https://tumcps.github.io/CORA/
30. Ratschan, S.: Efficient solving of quantified inequality constraints over the real numbers. ACM Trans. Comput. Log. **7**, 723–748 (2006)
31. Houska, B., Ferreau, H., Diehl, M.: ACADO toolkit - an open source framework for automatic control and dynamic optimization. Optimal Control Appl. Methods **32**(3), 298–312 (2011)
32. Slotine, J.E., Li, W.: Applied Nonlinear Control. Prentice-Hall, Englewood Cliffs (1991)
33. Chen, M., Herbert, S.L., Vashishtha, M.S., Bansal, S., Tomlin, C.J.: Decomposition of reachable sets and tubes for a class of nonlinear systems. IEEE TAC **63**(11), 3675–3688 (2018)
34. https://tumcps.github.io/AROC/

Enhancing Branch and Bound for Robustness Verification of Neural Networks via an Effective Branching Strategy

Shaocong Han[1]([✉]) [iD] and Yi Zhang[1,2] [iD]

[1] Department of Automation, Tsinghua University, Beijing 100084, China
hsc20@mails.tsinghua.edu.cn, zhyi@mail.tsinghua.edu.cn
[2] Beijing National Research Center for Information Science and Technology
(BNRist), Beijing 100084, China

Abstract. The existence of adversarial examples highlights the vulnerability of neural networks and brings much interest to the formal verification of neural network robustness. To improve the scalability of neural network verification while approaching completeness, researchers have adopted the branch-and-bound (BaB) framework. Better branching can reduce the number of branches to explore and plays an important role in BaB verification methods. In this paper, we propose a new branching strategy. It utilizes a low-cost metric to make splitting decisions and supports branching on ReLU activation functions. We conduct experiments on widely used benchmarks to evaluate its performance. Simulation results demonstrate that this branching strategy effectively improves the verification efficiency and is better than the state-of-the-art strategies in overall performance.

Keywords: Robustness verification · Neural network · Branching strategy · Branch and bound

1 Introduction

Neural networks have accomplished significant success in a variety of applications [1,2] such as image recognition [3], object detection [4], and so on [5]. It provides a new way to develop software systems by training neural networks on a finite set of samples to tackle more unseen inputs correctly [6]. Despite their success, the finding of adversarial examples implies the vulnerability of neural networks [7] and brings concerns about their application in safety-critical tasks [8]. It is shown that small and imperceptible perturbations to the input can lead to unexpected behavior of the neural network [9–11]. To guarantee reliability, formal verification of neural networks has received much more attention in recent years. Approaches based on satisfiability modulo theory (SMT) [12,13], interval propagation [14], and reachability analysis [15] are developed to rigorously prove the property of neural networks satisfies some given specifications.

H. Hermanns et al. (Eds.): SETTA 2023, LNCS 14464, pp. 38–54, 2024.
https://doi.org/10.1007/978-981-99-8664-4_3

Completeness and scalability are two major concerns of formal verification methods for neural networks [16]. To reach high scalability, methods based on over-approximation are devised. Such approaches transform the verification task into solving relaxed convex optimization problems [17]. These approaches are highly scalable and sound, but can only verify certain specifications due to the relaxation error raised [18], i.e., they are incomplete. To overcome incompleteness, the branch and bound (BaB) framework was applied by some researchers, which incorporates fast bounding approaches with splitting procedures to eliminate approximation error iteratively. BaB methods can finally approach complete verification [19,20].

There are two approaches to improving the efficiency of BaB methods: better bounding and better branching. Better branching can enhance efficiency by reducing the number of sub-problems needed to be explored [20,21] and save verification time. In this paper, we investigate and propose a new branching strategy, which supports splitting over ReLU nonlinear activation functions. This strategy utilizes a computationally inexpensive metric to sort and choose splitting actions. It can be incorporated with various off-the-shelf sound bounding methods to build verifiers. Experiments are set up to evaluate the performance of this strategy and compare against baselines including two state-of-the-art ones on MNIST [22] and CIFAR [23] image classification tasks. Experiment results show that this strategy is more efficient than others in the verification benchmarks.

In summary, the main contributions of this paper are as follows:

- We investigate the branch and bound framework for neural network verification and propose a new branching strategy that supports splitting over ReLU nonlinear activation function and can be integrated with various off-the-shelf sound bounding methods to build complete verifiers.
- We combine the new branching strategy with a sound bounding method to form a new type of BaB method and implement the method in Python.
- We design and conduct some experiments to evaluate the performance of the strategy and compare it against three baselines to show its efficacy.

The rest of this paper is structured as follows. Section 2 presents some preliminaries, including the task of neural network verification and the formal formulation of a verification problem. In Sect. 3, we propose a new branching scheme that can be applied within the branch and bound verification framework. Section 4 describes the setup of experiments and presents the results. We conclude the paper and picture the future work in Sect. 5.

2   Preliminaries

In this section, we review some background on neural network verification problems and present terminologies and notations applied throughout this paper.

2.1　Neural Network Verification

Notation of Neural Network. A k-layer feed-forward neural network denoted by $f : \mathbb{R}^{n_0} \to \mathbb{R}^{n_k}$ can be expressed as [24]

$$
\begin{aligned}
\hat{z}_i &= W_i z_{i-1} + b_i, && \text{for } i = 1, \ldots, k \\
z_i &= \text{ReLU}(\hat{z}_i), && \text{for } i = 1, \ldots, k-1
\end{aligned}
\tag{1}
$$

Here $z_0 \equiv x \in \mathbb{R}^{n_0}$ denotes the input vector variable and $\hat{z}_k \in \mathbb{R}^{n_k}$ refers to the output of the neural network. ReLU refers to the element-wise non-linear activation function which is defined as $\text{ReLU}(x) = \max\{0, x\}$. We refer to n_i as the number of neurons of the i-th layer, $W_i \in \mathbb{R}^{n_i \times n_{i-1}}$ as the weight matrix, and $b_i \in \mathbb{R}^{n_i}$ as the bias vector. $\hat{z}_{i,j}$ and $z_{i,j}$ are defined as the pre-activation value and post-activation value of the j-th neuron of the i-th layer respectively.

Verification Problem. We now specify the problem of formal verification of neural networks. Given a neural network $f : \mathbb{R}^{n_0} \to \mathbb{R}^{n_k}$, the input x in a bounded domain $\mathcal{C}$, and some property P of the output, the formal verification problem denoted by $(f, \mathcal{C}, P)$ can be expressed as [19]

$$
\forall x \in \mathcal{C} \wedge y = f(x) \Rightarrow P(y).
\tag{2}
$$

As most properties examined, such as the robustness to adversarial example, usually can be expressed as a combination of certain linear inequalities of the output value [17,18], for instance, $c^T y - \theta > 0$, the property P can be merged into the last layer of the network as [20,25]:

$$
c^T \hat{z}_k - \theta = c^T (W_k z_{k-1} + b_k) - \theta = \underbrace{c^T W_k}_{W_k{}'} z_{k-1} + \underbrace{c^T b_k - \theta}_{b_k{}'}.
\tag{3}
$$

The merged $f_P : \mathbb{R}^{n_0} \to \mathbb{R}$ is called the canonical form [19]. The verification problem can be reformulated as proving or disproving the specification

$$
\forall x \in \mathcal{C}, f_P(x) = \hat{z}_k \geq 0.
\tag{4}
$$

One typical approach to tackle Eq. (4) is to build an optimization model [26] and determine the sign of its optimal value:

$$
\begin{aligned}
\min_{\hat{z}, z} \quad & f_P(x) \equiv \hat{z}_k \\
\text{s.t.} \quad & z_0 = x \in \mathcal{C} \\
& \hat{z}_i = W_i z_{i-1} + b_i, && \text{for } i = 1, \ldots, k \\
& z_i = \text{ReLU}(\hat{z}_i), && \text{for } i = 1, \ldots, k-1
\end{aligned}
\tag{5}
$$

Since ReLU is a nonlinear function, the model in Eq. (5) is a non-convex optimization problem [27]. It is an NP-hard problem and very difficult to find the global optimal solution, so researchers turn to compute a lower bound of the minimum value of $f_P(x)$, denoted by $\underline{f}_P(x)$, which is relatively easy to obtain. If $\underline{f}_P(x) \geq 0$, then the property can be proved. Based on this idea, several efficient sound verification methods have been developed [17,24].

2.2 Branch and Bound

Although sound methods are computationally efficient, they are not complete: some properties can not be proved since the bounds calculated are not tight enough. To improve the tightness of the lower bound of the optimal value, the BaB framework was introduced and adopted by Bunel et al. [19]. BaB is an iterative process, it performs two steps in each iteration: branching and bounding.

In the branching step, the bounded input domain $\mathcal{C}$ is divided into some disjoint domains $\mathcal{C}_j$, such that $\mathcal{C} = \cup \mathcal{C}_j$, and the original problem can be substituted by several sub-problems:

$$\min_{\hat{z}, z} f_{P, \mathcal{C}_j}(x), x \in \mathcal{C}_j \ (j = 1, \dots).$$

In the bounding step, BaB uses a certain approximation method to estimate a lower bound $\underline{f}_{P, \mathcal{C}_j}(x)$ and an upper bound $\bar{f}_{P, \mathcal{C}_j}(x)$ for the minima of each sub-problem. Taking the minimum of all lower bounds as

$$\underline{f}'_P(x) = \min_j \underline{f}_{P, \mathcal{C}_j}(x)$$

and the minimum of all upper bounds as

$$\bar{f}'_P(x) = \min_j \bar{f}_{P, \mathcal{C}_j}(x),$$

tighter global lower and upper bounds for $\min f_P(x)$ over $\mathcal{C}$ can be obtained. If $\underline{f}'_P(x) > 0$, then the property is proved; if $\bar{f}'_P(x) < 0$, then the property is disproved or falsified; otherwise, the domain $\mathcal{C}_j$ in which $\bar{f}_{P, \mathcal{C}_j}(x) > 0 > \underline{f}_{P, \mathcal{C}_j}(x)$ will be further partitioned into subdomains and the iteration continues to tighten the global lower bound until the property is proved or disproved [18, 21].

The efficiency of branch and bound highly depends on the bounding algorithm and the branching strategy. A lot of effort has been committed to revising sound and fast bounding methods that can be used in BaB. As far as we know, linear programming (LP) bounding procedure [28] and linear relaxation based perturbation analysis (LiPRA) [29] are two of the most representative methods. Both methods perform some kind of linear relaxations on the non-convex equality constraints in Eq. (5) as follows.

Linear Programming Bounding. The linear programming bounding method constructs a linear program by relaxing the non-linear ReLU equality constraint $z_{i,j} = \text{ReLU}(\hat{z}_{i,j})$ to a group of linear equality or inequality constraints [28]:

$$
\begin{aligned}
z_{i,j} &= 0 && \text{if } u_{i,j} < 0 \\
z_{i,j} &= \hat{z}_{i,j} && \text{if } l_{i,j} > 0 \\
\left.
\begin{aligned}
z_{i,j} &\geq \hat{z}_{i,j} \\
z_{i,j} &\geq 0 \\
z_{i,j} &\leq \frac{(\hat{z}_{i,j} - l_{i,j})}{(u_{i,j} - l_{i,j})} u_{i,j}
\end{aligned}
\right\} && \text{if } u_{i,j} > 0 > l_{i,j}
\end{aligned}
\tag{6}
$$

where $u_{i,j}$ denotes the upper bound of $\hat{z}_{i,j}$ and $l_{i,j}$ denotes the lower bound of $\hat{z}_{i,j}$, as shown in Fig. 1.

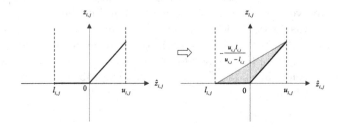

Fig. 1. The trilateral convex envelope for the ReLU equality constraint. The points along the black bold folded line in the left part form a non-convex set. The shaded area in the right part represents the relaxed linear region which is convex [28].

Under the assumption $x \in \mathcal{C}$ can be expressed as some linear constraints, a lower bound of the optimal value of Eq. (5) can be acquired by solving the linear program in Eq. (7), subject to Eq. (6).

$$
\begin{aligned}
\min_{\hat{z},z} \quad & f_P(x) \equiv \hat{z}_k, \\
\text{s. t.} \quad & z_0 = x \in \mathcal{C} \\
& \hat{z}_i = W_i z_{i-1} + b_i \quad \text{for } i = 1, \dots, k
\end{aligned}
\tag{7}
$$

There are also other types of linear relaxation for ReLU equality constraints. For example, LiPRA [18] substitutes the ReLU equation constraints with

$$
z_{i,j} = \mathrm{ReLU}(\hat{z}_{i,j}) \Rightarrow
\begin{aligned}
& z_{i,j} = 0 && \text{if } u_{i,j} < 0 \\
& z_{i,j} = \hat{z}_{i,j} && \text{if } l_{i,j} > 0 \\
& \left.
\begin{aligned}
& z_{i,j} \geq \alpha \hat{z}_{i,j} \\
& z_{i,j} \leq \frac{(\hat{z}_{i,j} - l_{i,j})}{(u_{i,j} - l_{i,j})} u_{i,j}
\end{aligned}
\right\} && \text{if } u_{i,j} > 0 > l_{i,j}
\end{aligned}
\tag{8}
$$

where α can be any value that belongs to the interval $[0, 1]$.

Domain Splitting. In addition to the bounding algorithm, branch strategy also influences the efficiency of BaB [19]. If the bounded domain is divided properly, branches and running time can be saved. For ReLU-based networks, a typical approach for dividing a domain $\mathcal{C}$ is splitting an unfixed ReLU unit $z_{i,j} = \mathrm{ReLU}(\hat{z}_{i,j})$ to be in active and inactive states, resulting in two independent subdomains [21]

$$
\begin{aligned}
\mathcal{C}_1 &= \{x | x \in \mathcal{C}, \hat{z}_{i,j} \geq 0\} \\
\mathcal{C}_2 &= \{x | x \in \mathcal{C}, \hat{z}_{i,j} < 0\}
\end{aligned}
\tag{9}
$$

Within $\mathcal{C}_1$ and $\mathcal{C}_2$, the convex envelop in Eq. (6) will be replaced by the linear equality constraint $z_{i,j} = \hat{z}_{i,j}$ and $z_{i,j} = 0$ respectively. This reduces the size of the feasible region for each sub-problem. So, the global lower bound can be tightened by taking the minimum of the lower bounds of sub-problems.

The crucial issue for branching is to decide which unfixed ReLU unit to split. Two of the state-of-the-art are **BaBSR** [19] and **Filtered Smart Branching (FSB)** [20]. BaBSR estimates the effect of splitting each unfixed ReLU unit on tightening the lower bound with a score $s_{i,j}$ calculated by

$$s_{i,j} = \left| \max(v_{i,j} b_{i-1,j} - \frac{u_{i,j} l_{i,j}}{u_{i,j} - l_{i,j}} [\mu_{i,j}]_+, \right.$$
$$\left. -\mu_{i,j} b_{i-1,j} + v_{i,j} b_{i-1,j} - \frac{u_{i,j} l_{i,j}}{u_{i,j} - l_{i,j}} [\mu_{i,j}]_+) \right| (10)$$

where $v_{i,j}$ and $\mu_{i,j}$ are defined as [24]:

$$v_k = -1$$
$$\mu_i = W_{i+1}^T v_{i+1}, \text{for } i = k-1, \ldots 0$$
$$v_{i,j} = \begin{cases} 0, & \text{if } u_{i,j} < 0 \\ \mu_{i,j}, & \text{if } l_{i,j} > 0 \\ \frac{u_{i,j}}{u_{i,j} - l_{i,j}} [\mu_{i,j}]_+ + \alpha_{i,j} [\mu_{i,j}]_-, & \text{if } l_{i,j} \le 0 \le u_{i,j} \end{cases} \quad (11)$$
$$\text{for } i = k-1, \ldots 1$$

Then BaBSR takes the ReLU unit with the highest $s_{i,j}$ value to split on.

Inspired by mimicking strong branching, FSB [20] defines another metric $t_{i,j}$ called the backup score as

$$t_{i,j} = \frac{u_{i,j} l_{i,j}}{u_{i,j} - l_{i,j}} [\mu_{i,j}]_+. \quad (12)$$

FSB employs $s_{i,j}$ and $t_{i,j}$ to choose a subset of splitting decision candidates D_{FSB} in each hidden layer by

$$D_{FSB} = \bigcup_{i=1}^{k-1} \left\{ \left(i, \underset{j \in \mathcal{I}_i}{\arg\max} \, s_{i,j} \right), \left(i, \underset{j \in \mathcal{I}_i}{\arg\max} \, t_{i,j} \right) \right\} \quad (13)$$

where $\mathcal{I}_i = \{j | u_{i,j} > 0 > l_{i,j}\}$ denotes the index set of unfixed ReLU units in the i-th layer. Then it applies the fast dual bounding method proposed in [17,24] to evaluate and choose the splitting decision

$$d_{FSB} = \arg\max_{d \in D_{FSB}} \left(\min_{h \in \{1,2\}} \{l_A(p_{d,[h]})\} \right) \quad (14)$$

where $l_A(p_{d,[h]})$ denotes the lower bound acquired by bounding algorithm A for the h-th subproblem of p with applying splitting decision d.

3   Enhancing BaB with a Better Branching Strategy

In this section, we investigate the effect of tightening the lower bound through splitting on an unfixed ReLU unit and define a new type of metric to indicate the effect. Based on this metric, we propose a branching strategy, which is computationally low-cost and can be applied in BaB for neural network verification.

3.1   Improvement to Lower Bound by Splitting

According to the weak duality theorem, the best lower bound of the linear program in Eq. (7) can be obtained by solving its Lagrange dual problem [17,21,24]. The bound can be computed by

$$\underline{f}_p = -\sum_{i=1}^{k} v_i^T b_i + \sum_{i=1}^{k-1}\sum_{j\in\mathcal{I}} \frac{u_{i,j}l_{i,j}}{u_{i,j}-l_{i,j}}[\mu_{i,j}]_+ - \mu_0^T x_0 - \varepsilon\|\mu_0\| \qquad (15)$$

with

$$v_k = -1$$

$$\mu_i = W_{i+1}v_{i+1}, \text{ for } i = k-1,...0$$

$$v_{i,j} = \begin{cases} 0, & \text{if } u_{i,j} < 0 \\ \mu_{i,j}, & \text{if } l_{i,j} > 0 \\ \frac{u_{i,j}}{u_{i,j}-l_{i,j}}[\mu_{i,j}]_+ + \alpha_{i,j}[\mu_{i,j}]_-, & \text{if } l_{i,j} \le 0 \le u_{i,j} \end{cases}$$

$$\text{for } i = k-1,...1$$

when $x \in \mathcal{C} = \{x | x - x_0 \ge -\varepsilon, x \le x_0 + \varepsilon\}$. Here, $[a]_+ = \max(a,0)$ denotes the positive part of a and $[a]_- = \min(a,0)$ denotes its negative part.

When we split an unfixed ReLU unit $z_{i,j} = \text{ReLU}(\hat{z}_{i,j})$ with additional domain constrains $\{x \in \mathcal{C} | \hat{z}_{i,j} \ge 0\}$ and $\{x \in \mathcal{C} | \hat{z}_{i,j} < 0\}$, the state of the unit $z_{i,j}$ in subproblems will be turned into positive and negative. According to Eq. (15), the item $v_{i,j}$ will change from $v_{i,j}$ to 0 in positive state, or from $v_{i,j}$ to $\mu_{i,j}$ in negative state respectively. Assuming other terms in Eq. (15) remain unchanged [19,20], the improvement to the lower bound of each sub-problem can be approximated by

$$l(p_{s\in\{1,2\}}) - l(p)$$
$$= \begin{cases} v_{i,j}b_{i-1,j} - \frac{u_{i,j}l_{i,j}}{u_{i,j}-l_{i,j}}[\mu_{i,j}]_+, & \text{for } v_{i,j} \to 0 \\ -\mu_{i,j}b_{i-1,j} + v_{i,j}b_{i-1,j} - \frac{u_{i,j}l_{i,j}}{u_{i,j}-l_{i,j}}[\mu_{i,j}]_+, & \text{for } v_{i,j} \to \mu_{i,j} \end{cases} \qquad (16)$$

An immediate idea is to use the maximum or minimum of the two items in Eq. (16) to select the best potential ReLU unit to split on, as which is applied in BaBSR and FSB [19,20].

3.2   Better Splitting Decision

Inspect the value of the items by Eq. (16), we can draw three key observations:

1. For each subproblem $p_s(s = 1, 2)$, the item $-u_{i,j}l_{i,j}[\mu_{i,j}]_+/(u_{i,j} - l_{i,j})$ is always greater than or equal to zero since $-u_{i,j}l_{i,j}/(u_{i,j} - l_{i,j})$ and $[\mu_{i,j}]_+$ are both non-negative for any unfixed ReLU unit, while the other items such as $v_{i,j}b_{i-1,j}$, $-\mu_{i,j}b_{i-1,j} + v_{i,j}b_{i-1,j}$ can be positive or negative. So $-u_{i,j}l_{i,j}[\mu_{i,j}]_+/(u_{i,j} - l_{i,j})$ may be used to indicate the extent of the improvement for lower bound.

2. $-u_{i,j}l_{i,j}/(u_{i,j} - l_{i,j})$ is the intercept of the upper bound line of the trilateral convex envelope for the ReLU equality constraint, as shown in Fig. 1. It depicts the maximum deviation of the points in the convex region from the corresponding points in the original non-convex set. The smaller $-u_{i,j}l_{i,j}/(u_{i,j} - l_{i,j})$ is, the less deviation incurred by relaxation.

3. In certain situations, there may be a fraction of unfixed ReLU units that have $[\mu_{i,j}]_+$ equal to zero. Another metric is needed to prioritize these units as soon as all the ones with $-u_{i,j}l_{i,j}[\mu_{i,j}]_+/(u_{i,j} - l_{i,j}) \neq 0$ have been split while the lower bound is still not tight enough to prove the specification.

Based on those observations stated above, we can use $-u_{i,j}l_{i,j}[\mu_{i,j}]_+/(u_{i,j} - l_{i,j})$ to approximately measure the effect of splitting the unfixed units and pick up the one that may bring the most significant improvement to the lower bound to split on. Once all unfixed ones with $-u_{i,j}l_{i,j}[\mu_{i,j}]_+/(u_{i,j} - l_{i,j}) \neq 0$ have been split, we then turn to choose among those which have $v_{i,j}b_{i-1,j} \geq 0$ or $-\mu_{i,j}b_{i-1,j} + v_{i,j}b_{i-1,j} \geq 0$.

In implementation, we evaluate the choice of splitting on an unfixed ReLU unit $z_{i,j}$ by the metric

$$h(z_{i,j}) = \begin{cases} \frac{-u_{i,j}l_{i,j}[\mu_{i,j}]_+}{u_{i,j} - l_{i,j}}\eta + ([v_{i,j}b_{i-1,j}]_+ + [-\mu_{i,j}b_{i-1,j}]_+)(1 - \eta), & j \in \mathcal{I}_i \\ 0, & j \notin \mathcal{I}_i \end{cases}$$
(17)

where $\mathcal{I}_i$ denotes the index set of unfixed ReLU units in the i-th layer as in Eq. (13). Here, η is a hyperparameter that belongs to the interval $(0, 1)$ and can be determined through experiments; $[\cdot]_+$ is an operator that takes the positive part of the operand. Then among all unfixed ReLU units, we select the one with the largest score $h(z_{i,j})$ to split on

$$z^*_{i,j} = \operatorname*{argmax}_{z_{i,j}} h(z_{i,j}).$$
(18)

We name this branching strategy relaxation loss minimization (RLM). This strategy is computationally efficient given that: 1) all $v_{i,j}$ and $\mu_{i,j}$ can be computed by one single backward pass with Eq. (15); 2) the intermediate bounds $u_{i,j}$ and $l_{i,j}$ needed for the calculation in Eq. (17) are the outputs of the previous bounding step so they are ready for use; 3) the branching strategy just commits a very little overhead by computing $h(z_{i,j})$ for those unfixed ReLU units and picking out the maximal one. In addition, this branching strategy is very general and can be applied in combination with a variety of off-the-shelf bounding algorithms such as LP [19] and CROWN [18,21] within the BaB framework.

4   Experimental Evaluation

In this section, we set up experiments to evaluate the effectiveness of our proposed branching strategy and compare it against three baseline strategies: One trivial strategy denoted by Random Choice (RC), which randomly selects an unfixed node to split, and two state-of-the-art strategies: BaBSR devised by Bunel et al. [19] and FSB by Palma et al. [20].

4.1   Benchmarks

To conduct a fair comparison, we use one fixed sound bounding algorithm that is based on CROWN [21,30] in the bounding phase. We then combine the bounding algorithm with those four branching strategies respectively, resulting in four BaB verification methods denoted as BaB-RC, BaB-SR, BaB-FSB, and BaB-RLM. We use the identical bounding algorithm in all the BaB methods to make sure only the branching strategies contribute to the difference in the verification performance.

We assess these verification methods on a set of widely used benchmark tasks. In detail, we use four types of pre-trained robust neural networks in our evaluation. These networks are trained for image classification on MNIST [22] dataset and CIFAR [23] dataset and are used in previous research works [17,18, 21,30,31]. The networks are denoted by MNIST-6-100, MNIST-9-200, CIFAR-A-Adv, and CIFAR-B-Adv respectively. MNIST-6-100 is a 6-layer and MNIST-9-200 is a 9-layer fully-connected feed-forward neural network; CIFAR-A-Adv is a 4-layer convolutional neural network and CIFAR-B-Adv is also a 4-layer convolutional network but with wider layers.

We intend to certify the adversarial robustness of the networks on a set of images: for each image x_i, provided that the network $f(x)$ can correctly predict its true label y_i, the task is to verify the property that every x in the region $\{x| \|x - x_i\|_\infty \leq \varepsilon\}$ can be assigned the same label as x_i. This problem can be formulated as proving the specifications shown in Eq. (19).

$$\forall x \in \{x \,|\, \|x - x_i\|_\infty \leq \varepsilon\} \mapsto f(x)_i - f(x)_j > 0, \forall j \neq i. \qquad (19)$$

With MNIST-6-100 and MNIST-9-200, an image from the MNIST dataset could be predicted to one of ten labels. Assuming its true label is y_i, then we need to verify nine specifications for one image, i.e. $f(x)_i > f(x)_j, j \in \{0, 1, \ldots, i - 1, i + 1, 9\}$. With CIFAR-A-Adv and CIFAR-B-Adv, one image taken from the CIFAR dataset also has ten possible labels, so there are also nine specifications to verify for each correctly-predicted image.

In the experiments, we use N images from the dataset and use some specific ε-values as the L_∞-norm of adversarial perturbation noise. We evaluate BaB-RLM and other baseline verification methods on MNIST-6-100, MNIST-9-200, CIFAR-A-Adv, and CIFAR-B-Adv respectively and compare their performance. Those ε-values are intentionally chosen to make the verification tasks not trivial since too small values (without any noise) will cause 100% verification and too big ones will lead to 100% falsification with a small number of iterations or even a single bounding operation. To force the program to end within a limited time, we set a timeout for verifying a specification for each method in the experiment.

All the experiments were conducted on a workstation with an AMD EPYC 7742 CPU, 4 NVIDIA GeForce RTX 3080 GPUs, and 512 GB of RAM. Our program was developed using Python 3.10 and PyTorch 1.12.0.

4.2 Experiment Results

Results on the Feed-Forward Network MNIST-6-100. In this experiment, the L_∞-norm of adversarial noise is set to various ε-values taken from the interval [0.01, 0.04]. In each round, $N = 100$ images randomly taken from the MNIST dataset are used and the timeout value is set to 200s for verifying one specification. The hyperparameter η of BaB-RLM is determined by a bisection search and is set to 0.99. We measured the percentage of the successfully verified specifications and calculated the average runtime for verifying one image [30]. The numerical experiment results are given in Table 1. To visually compare the performance of the four methods, we also plot the data in Fig. 2.

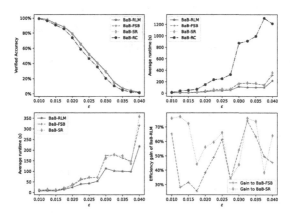

Fig. 2. Comparison of verified accuracy, average runtime and verification efficiency for BaB-FSB, BaB-RLM, BaB-SR, and BaB-RC on the neural network MNIST-6-100. The lower part depicts the comparison without BaB-RC for illustrative purposes.

Table 1. The percentage of verified specifications and the average runtime for verifying one image by each method on MNIST-6-100 with various values of ε. The best-performing values are highlighted in bold and the second-best are underlined. The gains of average verification efficiency by BaB-RLM relative to the second-best method are presented in the lower part of the table.

ε	Verified accuracy			
	BaB-RLM	BaB-FSB	BaB-SR	BaB-RC
0.0100	**99.89%**	99.43%	99.43%	99.32%
0.0125	**98.30%**	**98.30%**	97.96%	96.49%
c.0150	**93.08%**	**93.08%**	92.74%	90.82%
0.0175	**88.55%**	**88.55%**	88.10%	85.60%
0.0200	**79.71%**	79.25%	78.80%	74.04%
0.0225	**66.21%**	65.65%	65.08%	58.73%
0.0250	**52.61%**	51.70%	51.47%	46.49%
0.0275	**41.27%**	40.93%	40.36%	35.60%
0.0300	**29.93%**	29.14%	29.02%	20.41%
0.0325	**15.42%**	14.97%	14.74%	10.54%
0.0350	**7.48%**	7.26%	7.26%	4.88%
0.0375	**4.42%**	4.20%	4.20%	2.61%
0.0400	**2.27%**	2.04%	1.93%	1.36%
ε	Average runtime (s)			
	BaB-RLM (Efficiency gain)	BaB-FSB	BaB-SR	BaB-RC
0.0100	**7.05(+65.14%)**	11.64	12.41	13.48
0.0125	**8.87(+28.09%)**	11.36	15.72	40.17
0.0150	**7.96(+31.60%)**	10.48	13.73	51.38
0.0175	**14.90(+25.49%)**	18.70	21.50	69.22
0.0200	**24.83(+38.27%)**	34.33	38.75	149.48
0.0225	**40.00(+48.93%)**	59.57	63.80	236.51
0.0250	**43.16(+61.36%)**	69.65	71.68	252.82
0.0275	**53.52(+33.09%)**	71.22	71.71	324.56
0.0300	**113.54(+54.11%)**	174.98	163.29	872.64
0.0325	**101.92(+74.31%)**	177.65	179.46	909.53
0.0350	**100.14(+63.43%)**	163.65	174.11	993.24
0.0375	**98.75(+49.57%)**	147.71	136.64	1309.39
0.0400	**218.39(+45.27%)**	317.27	358.21	1213.64

From Table 1 and Fig. 2, we can see that BaB-RLM achieves the highest verified accuracy among all methods in each round of the experiment. It also takes the least amount of average runtime to do the verification. The other three methods can occasionally get the same high verification rate as BaB-RLM with certain specific ε-values while they all require more average runtime. Based on the Pareto principle, we can see that the overall performance of the four methods is ranked as: **BaB-RLM>BaB-FSB>BaB-SR>BaB-RC**.

It is important to note that BaB verification methods are theoretically complete, which means if sufficient runtime is provided, the verified accuracy of all methods will be almost the same. However, the average runtime can be different for each method. The average runtime can indicate the efficiency of the verification method: the less average runtime implies the higher efficiency, provided the experiment is conducted on the same dataset.

In terms of verification efficiency (defined as the reciprocal of average verification time), it is clear that BaB-RLM outperforms BaB-FSB, BaB-SR, and BaB-RC under each condition. We calculate the gain of verification efficiency by BaB-RLM to the second-best method by Eq. (20)

$$gain = \frac{\frac{1}{t_{RLM}} - \frac{1}{t_{2nd}}}{\frac{1}{t_{2nd}}} = \frac{t_{2nd} - t_{RLM}}{t_{RLM}} \times 100\% \qquad (20)$$

where t_{RLM} denotes the average runtime of BaB-RLM and t_{2nd} refers to the average runtime of second-best method. From Table 1 and Fig. 2, it can be seen that BaB-RLM improves the verification efficiency by **25%–74%** relative to the second-best-performing method. The gain of efficiency by BaB-RLM to the other two methods is even larger.

Results on the Convolutional Network CIFAR-A-Adv. In this experiment, the L_∞-norm of adversarial noise is set to various ε-values taken from the interval [0.009,0.025], making the property not too easy to verify without any branching. In each round, $N = 100$ images randomly taken from the CIFAR dataset are utilized and the timeout value is set to 25 s for verifying one specification. The hyperparameter η for BaB-RLM remains 0.99 as previously. We record the percentage of the successfully verified specifications and the average runtime in verifying one image. The numerical experiment results are given in Table 2. To make a visual comparison, we also plot the results in Fig. 3.

According to Table 2, we can see that BaB-RC constantly achieves the lowest verification accuracy under all conditions while consuming the most amount of average runtime, so it is no doubt the worst one. Similar to the results in Table 1, BaB-SR and BaB-FSB can occasionally reach the same high verification accuracy as BaB-RLM under a certain level of adversarial noise, so they are better than BaB-RC. Above all, BaB-RLM steadily gets the highest verification accuracy among all methods and always requires the least average runtime in all cases.

Given the results in Table 2 and Fig. 3, it is clear that the overall efficiency of BaB-RLM is superior to the other three methods. According to the Pareto comparison principle, the overall performance of the four methods is **BaB-RLM>BaB-FSB>BaB-SR>BaB-RC**. This also conforms to the results in Table 1 and Fig. 2. In terms of the verification efficiency, BaB-RLM improves

Table 2. Percentage of verified specifications and average runtime for verifying one image by each method on CIFAR-A-Adv with various values of ε. All the best-performing values are highlighted in bold, and the second-best underlined. The gains of average verification efficiency by BaB-RLM relative to the second-best method are also presented in the table.

ε	Verified accuracy			
	BaB-RLM	BaB-FSB	BaB-SR	BaB-RC
0.009	**92.42%**	**92.42%**	91.25%	88.38%
0.011	**89.06%**	88.89%	86.53%	77.10%
0.013	**83.33%**	**83.33%**	79.29%	61.62%
0.015	**74.92%**	74.75%	68.01%	39.73%
0.017	**63.13%**	62.29%	54.55%	18.52%
0.019	**46.30%**	45.29%	39.73%	6.90%
0.021	**30.13%**	28.79%	23.57%	1.68%
0.023	**13.13%**	11.78%	10.61%	0.34%
0.025	**5.22%**	4.71%	4.38%	0.00%
ε	Average runtime (s)			
	BaB-RLM (Efficiency gain)	BaB-FSB	BaB-SR	BaB-RC
0.009	**6.27(+5.52%)**	6.61	8.86	15.87
0.011	**8.25(+10.71%)**	9.13	14.82	40.02
0.013	**10.72(+21.83%)**	13.05	22.06	84.77
0.015	**15.54(+22.78%)**	19.09	37.76	204.55
0.017	**25.21(+33.11%)**	33.56	60.79	550.22
0.019	**32.26(+38.70%)**	44.75	70.66	1289.14
0.021	**41.70(+51.64%)**	63.23	104.26	3806.76
0.023	**67.55(+44.59%)**	97.68	125.11	8555.99
0.025	**83.03(+41.77%)**	117.72	121.32	inf

by **5%–51%** relative to the second-best method (i.e., BaB-FSB) as shown in the lower part of Table 2. Besides BaB-FSB, the gain of efficiency by BaB-RLM to the other two methods will be even larger as shown in Fig. 3. To clearly demonstrate the comparison with BaB-FSB and BaB-SR, the plot for BaB-RC is omitted in the lower part of Fig. 3.

Results on MNIST-9-200 and CIFAR-B-Adv. For MNIST-9-200, the L_∞-norm of adversarial noise is set to various ε-values in the interval [0.006,0.019] and $N = 100$ images randomly taken from the MNIST are utilized in each round. The timeout value is set to 200 s for verifying one specification and the hyperparameter η is assigned to 0.99 as before. We record and compare the percentage of the successfully verified specifications and the average runtime in

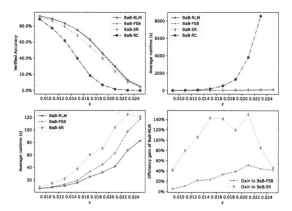

Fig. 3. Comparison of verified accuracy, average runtime and verification efficiency for BaB-FSB, BaB-RLM, BaB-SR, and BaB-RC on the convolutional neural network CIFAR-A-Adv. The lower part depicts the comparison without BaB-RC for clarity.

verifying one image. The numerical results show that the overall efficiency of BaB-RLM is superior to the other three methods and BaB-RLM improves the verification efficiency by **1%–26%** compared to the second-best method.

For CIFAR-B-Adv, the L_∞-norm of adversarial noise is set to various ε-values in the interval [0.007,0.017] and $N = 100$ images randomly taken from the CIFAR are utilized. The timeout value is set to 25 s for verifying one specification and the hyperparameter η for RLM is also set to 0.99. Experiment results confirm that BaB-RLM is superior to the other three methods in term of the overall efficiency, i.e. it verifies more specifications than or as many as other three methods and always takes less average runtime, and BaB-RLM gains the verification efficiency by **14%–40%** relative to the second-best method.

Here we omit the details of the results due to the limitation on the length of the paper and to avoid redundancy. Interested readers can contact the authors for more information about the experiments.

As we know, all the verification methods involved in the comparison adopt the same bounding algorithm. The evaluation experiments were performed in the same hardware environment with the identical parameter configuration for each method, so the only difference lies in the branching strategy. Based on the results of the simulation experiments, it is reasonable for us to claim that the RLM strategy can effectively enhance the performance of BaB in neural network verification. In summary, our branching strategy is very competitive and can outperform the baseline strategies, including the state-of-the-art ones, in promoting the efficiency of the verification method.

5   Conclusion

In this paper, we investigate the BaB framework for neural network verification and propose a new branching strategy that is general and can be easily integrated with other bounding algorithms. The branching approach uses a computationally inexpensive metric to make the appropriate splitting decision to quickly tighten the global lower bound and avoid exploring unnecessary branches. We design and conduct several simulation experiments to evaluate the performance of our strategy and compare it with state-of-the-art baselines on some widely used verification benchmarks. Experiment results show that the overall performance of our strategy can outperform all other baselines in terms of the verified accuracy and the average runtime of the verification process. It can significantly enhance the efficiency of the BaB method in neural network verification.

In the future, we will engage in research on reducing the computational cost of the bounding algorithm to further enhance the efficiency of the BaB verification method.

Acknowledgements. This research was supported in part by the National Natural Science Foundation of China under Grant 62133002 and the National Key Research and Development Program of China under Grant 2021YFB2501200.

References

1. Lecun, Y., Bengio, Y., Hinton, G.: Deep learning. Nature **521**(7553), 436–444 (2015). https://doi.org/10.1038/nature14539
2. Goodfellow, I., Bengio, Y., Courville, A.: Deep Learning. MIT Press, Cambridge (2016)
3. He, K., Zhang, X., Ren, S., Sun, J.: Deep residual learning for image recognition. In: 2016 IEEE Conference on Computer Vision and Pattern Recognition, CVPR 2016, Las Vegas, NV, USA, 27–30 June 2016, pp. 770–778. IEEE Computer Society (2016). https://doi.org/10.1109/CVPR.2016.90
4. Bochkovskiy, A., Wang, C.Y., Liao, H.Y.M.: YOLOv4: optimal speed and accuracy of object detection. ArXiv abs/2004.10934 (2020)
5. Kuutti, S., Bowden, R., Jin, Y., Barber, P., Fallah, S.: A survey of deep learning applications to autonomous vehicle control. IEEE Trans. Intell. Transp. Syst. **22**(2), 712–733 (2021)
6. Katz, G., et al.: The Marabou framework for verification and analysis of deep neural networks. In: Dillig, I., Tasiran, S. (eds.) CAV 2019. LNCS, vol. 11561, pp. 443–452. Springer, Cham (2019). https://doi.org/10.1007/978-3-030-25540-4_26
7. Szegedy, C., et al.: Intriguing properties of neural networks. In: 2nd International Conference on Learning Representations, ICLR 2014, Banff, AB, Canada, April 14–16, 2014, Conference Track Proceedings. OpenReview.net (2014)
8. Meng, M.H., et al.: Adversarial robustness of deep neural networks: a survey from a formal verification perspective. IEEE Trans. Dependable Secur. Comput. 1 (2022)
9. Gnanasambandam, A., Sherman, A.M., Chan, S.H.: Optical adversarial attack. In: IEEE/CVF International Conference on Computer Vision Workshops, ICCVW 2021, Montreal, BC, Canada, 11–17 October 2021, pp. 92–101. IEEE (2021)
10. Finlayson, S.G., Bowers, J.D., Ito, J., Zittrain, J.L., Beam, A.L., Kohane, I.S.: Adversarial attacks on medical machine learning. Science **363**(6433), 1287–1289 (2019). https://doi.org/10.1126/science.aaw4399
11. Chakraborty, A., Alam, M., Dey, V., Chattopadhyay, A., Mukhopadhyay, D.: A survey on adversarial attacks and defences. CAAI Trans. Intell. Technol. **6**(1), 25–45 (2021). https://doi.org/10.1049/cit2.12028

12. Katz, G., Barrett, C., Dill, D.L., Julian, K., Kochenderfer, M.J.: Reluplex: an efficient SMT solver for verifying deep neural networks. In: Majumdar, R., Kunčak, V. (eds.) CAV 2017. LNCS, vol. 10426, pp. 97–117. Springer, Cham (2017). https://doi.org/10.1007/978-3-319-63387-9_5

13. Zhang, Y., Wei, Z., Zhang, X., Sun, M.: Using Z3 for formal modeling and verification of FNN global robustness (S). In: Chang, S. (ed.) The 35th International Conference on Software Engineering and Knowledge Engineering, SEKE 2023, KSIR Virtual Conference Center, USA, 1–10 July 2023, pp. 110–113. KSI Research Inc. (2023). https://doi.org/10.18293/SEKE2023-110

14. Weng, T., et al.: Towards fast computation of certified robustness for ReLu networks. In: Dy, J.G., Krause, A. (eds.) Proceedings of the 35th International Conference on Machine Learning, ICML 2018, Stockholmsmässan, Stockholm, Sweden, 10–15 July 2018. Proceedings of Machine Learning Research, vol. 80, pp. 5273–5282. PMLR (2018)

15. Tran, H., et al.: Parallelizable reachability analysis algorithms for feed-forward neural networks. In: Gnesi, S., Plat, N., Day, N.A., Rossi, M. (eds.) Proceedings of the 7th International Workshop on Formal Methods in Software Engineering, FormaliSE@ICSE 2019, Montreal, QC, Canada, 27 May 2019, pp. 51–60. IEEE/ACM (2019). https://doi.org/10.1109/FormaliSE.2019.00012

16. Leucker, M.: Formal verification of neural networks? In: Carvalho, G., Stolz, V. (eds.) SBMF 2020. LNCS, vol. 12475, pp. 3–7. Springer, Cham (2020). https://doi.org/10.1007/978-3-030-63882-5_1

17. Zhang, H., Weng, T.W., Chen, P.Y., Hsieh, C.J., Daniel, L.: Efficient neural network robustness certification with general activation functions. In: Proceedings of the 32nd International Conference on Neural Information Processing Systems, pp. 4944–4953. NIPS'18, Curran Associates Inc., Red Hook, NY, USA (2018)

18. Xu, K., et al.: Fast and complete: Enabling complete neural network verification with rapid and massively parallel incomplete verifiers. In: 9th International Conference on Learning Representations, ICLR 2021, Virtual Event, Austria, 3–7 May 2021. OpenReview.net (2021)

19. Bunel, R., Turkaslan, I., Torr, P.H.S., Kumar, M.P., Lu, J., Kohli, P.: Branch and bound for piecewise linear neural network verification. J. Mach. Learn. Res. 21(42), 1–39 (2020)

20. Palma, A.D., et al.: Improved branch and bound for neural network verification via lagrangian decomposition. ArXiv abs/2104.06718 (2021)

21. Wang, S., et al.: Beta-crown: efficient bound propagation with per-neuron split constraints for neural network robustness verification. In: Ranzato, M., Beygelzimer, A., Dauphin, Y., Liang, P., Vaughan, J.W. (eds.) Advances in Neural Information Processing Systems. vol. 34, pp. 29909–29921. Curran Associates, Inc. (2021)

22. Deng, L.: The MNIST database of handwritten digit images for machine learning research. IEEE Signal Process. Mag. 29(6), 141–142 (2012)

23. Krizhevsky, A.: Learning multiple layers of features from tiny images (2009)

24. Wong, E., Kolter, J.Z.: Provable defenses against adversarial examples via the convex outer adversarial polytope. In: Dy, J.G., Krause, A. (eds.) Proceedings of the 35th International Conference on Machine Learning, ICML 2018, Stockholmsmässan, Stockholm, Sweden, 10–15 July 2018. Proceedings of Machine Learning Research, vol. 80, pp. 5283–5292. PMLR (2018)

25. Bunel, R., Turkaslan, I., Torr, P.H., Kohli, P., Kumar, M.P.: A unified view of piecewise linear neural network verification. In: Proceedings of the 32nd International Conference on Neural Information Processing Systems, pp. 4795–4804. Curran Associates Inc., Red Hook, NY, USA (2018)

26. Tjeng, V., Xiao, K.Y., Tedrake, R.: Evaluating robustness of neural networks with mixed integer programming. In: 7th International Conference on Learning Representations, ICLR 2019, New Orleans, LA, USA, 6–9 May 2019. OpenReview.net (2019)
27. Boyd, S., Vandenberghe, L.: Convex Optimization. Cambridge University Press, Cambridge (2004). https://doi.org/10.1017/cbo9780511804441
28. Ehlers, R.: Formal verification of piece-wise linear feed-forward neural networks. In: D'Souza, D., Narayan Kumar, K. (eds.) ATVA 2017. LNCS, vol. 10482, pp. 269–286. Springer, Cham (2017). https://doi.org/10.1007/978-3-319-68167-2_19
29. Xu, K., et al.: Automatic perturbation analysis for scalable certified robustness and beyond. In: Proceedings of the 34th International Conference on Neural Information Processing Systems, pp. 1129–1141. Curran Associates Inc., Red Hook, NY, USA (2020)
30. Singh, G., Ganvir, R., Püschel, M., Vechev, M.: Beyond the single neuron convex barrier for neural network certification. In: Proceedings of the 33rd International Conference on Neural Information Processing Systems, pp. 15098–15109. Curran Associates Inc., Red Hook, NY, USA (2019)
31. Zhang, H., et al.: Towards stable and efficient training of verifiably robust neural networks. In: 8th International Conference on Learning Representations, ICLR 2020, Addis Ababa, Ethiopia, 26–30 April 2020. OpenReview.net (2020)

Graph-Based Log Anomaly Detection via Adversarial Training

Zhangyue He[1], Yanni Tang[2], Kaiqi Zhao[2], Jiamou Liu[2], and Wu Chen[1,3(✉)]

[1] College of Computer and Information Science, Southwest University,
Chongqing, China
hezhangyue@email.swu.edu.cn
[2] University of Auckland, Auckland, New Zealand
ytan370@aucklanduni.ac.nz, {kaiqi.zhao,jiamou.liu}@auckland.ac.nz
[3] School of Software, Southwest University, Chongqing, China
chenwu@swu.edu.cn

Abstract. Log analysis can diagnose software system issues. Log anomaly detection always faces the challenge of class distribution imbalance and data noise. In addition, existing methods often overlook log event structural relationships, causing instability. In this work, we propose AdvGraLog, a Generative Adversarial Network (GAN) model based on log graph representation, to detect anomalies when the reconstruction error of discriminator is terrible. We construct log graphs and employ Graph Neural Network (GNN) to obtain a comprehensive graph representation. We use a GAN generator to transform original negative logs into adversarial samples. Discriminator adopts an AutoEncoder (AE) to detect anomalies by comparing reconstruction error to a threshold. Adversarial training enhances adversarial sample quality and boosts the discriminator's anomaly recognition. Experimental results demonstrate the superiority of our proposed method over baseline approaches in real-world datasets. Supplementary experiments further validate the effectiveness of our model in handling imbalanced log data and augmenting model robustness.

Keywords: Log analysis · Anomaly detection · Graph representation learning · Generative adversarial network · Adversarial sample

1 Introduction

System logs contain essential information about system operations, event interactions, and status [20,30]. They provide a trackable record of system activities, aiding in understanding how the system works, diagnosing issues, and troubleshooting. Thus, log-based anomaly detection is critical for maintaining proper system operations.

Imbalanced data challenges anomaly detection and hinders machine learning's ability to spot anomalies within numerous logs. Skewed fault distributions are frequently observed in large software systems [6,36,37], with anomalous logs

H. Hermanns et al. (Eds.): SETTA 2023, LNCS 14464, pp. 55–71, 2024.
https://doi.org/10.1007/978-981-99-8664-4_4

typically comprising a small fraction of datasets (e.g., 2.93% in HDFS). Research on software defect models demonstrates that imbalanced data can lead to unsatisfactory predictions [38]. In addition, common public datasets (e.g., HDFS and BGL) are manually inspected and labeled by engineers, but this process can introduce erroneous labels, leading to model misinterpretations and reduced anomaly detection accuracy. Despite being a small portion of the logs, data noise significantly degrades existing model performance.

Many approaches exist for log-based anomaly detection. As systems grow in capacity and complexity, the volume and intricacy of log data increase, making manual analysis challenging and time-consuming [18]. Therefore, the need for automated anomaly detection in system logs has become increasingly urgent. Conventional machine learning methods like PCA [29] and LogCluster [14] use statistical models for anomaly detection, leading to unstable performance across diverse datasets. Existing deep learning-based methods (e.g., DeepLog [5], LogRobust [39], and NeuralLog [12]) utilize Long Short-Term Memory (LSTM) to learn log sequence patterns to detect anomalies. However, these methods cannot fully utilize structural information among log events.

To overcome these limitations, we propose *AdvGraLog*, a weakly supervised approach for anomaly detection based on log graph embeddings using generative adversarial networks. First, a graph neural network is employed to create a graph-level representation for logs. Moreover, rare anomalies provide valuable information for log anomaly detection. The generator in AdvGraLog is used to modify the original negatives to generate adversarial samples. Meanwhile, based on the idea of sample reconstruction [22], we adopt an autoencoder model discriminator for log anomaly detection tasks, where the discriminator reconstructs the input samples. In addition, we adopt state-of-the-art techniques [19] to improve the encoder in the discriminator to stabilize the training of the model. The main contributions of this work are summarized as follows:

(1) We propose a novel log anomaly detection method based on graph representation learning through adversarial training.
(2) GAN-based system log anomaly detection improves the detection capability and further addresses the problem of data imbalance in real-world datasets.
(3) We conduct extensive experiments using two real-world log datasets to show significant improvement and the robustness of AdvGraLog over baselines.

2   Related Work

2.1   Log-Based Anomaly Detection

Log-based anomaly detection involves creating algorithms to automate the detection of anomalies in log data. Three main approaches are covered: rule-based, sequence-based, and graph-based approaches. Rule-based methods rely on predefined rules developed by experts [23,32], which can identify known anomalies but struggle with new or complex logs. Sequence-based approaches (e.g., DeepLog [5], NLSALOG [31], and LogAnomaly [17]) treat logs as sequences and use deep learning methods, Recurrent Neural Network or LSTM, to detect anomalies. Recently GNN-based log anomaly detection methods have been proposed. Graph-based approaches (e.g., GLAD-PAW [26] and LogGD [28]) employ graph neural networks to capture log dependencies, enhancing anomaly detection by considering intricate log data relationships [3]. DeepTraLog [35], a deep learning-based approach for microservice anomaly detection, uses a unified graph representation to capture complex trace structures and log events.

Log anomaly detection can be categorized in another way. Supervised models, represented by LogRobust [39], depend on labeled data for precision but require high-quality labels, while unsupervised models (e.g., PCA [29], LogCluster [14], LogTAD [7]) may not be able to cover all anomaly types . Semi-supervised models (e.g., LogAnomaly [17]) minimize label reliance but can lead to false alarms.

2.2 Generative Adversarial Network for Anomaly Detection

Generative Adversarial Networks have gained recognition for their ability to model data distributions, offering a fresh approach to anomaly detection. Recent studies [2,9,24] have successfully applied GANs to various anomaly detection tasks. AnoGAN [21] initiated GAN integration in image anomaly detection but required parameter updates during testing. EGBAD [33] addressed this issue with improved efficiency. GANomaly [1], a GAN-autoencoder hybrid, outperformed EGBAD in metrics and speed. In the field of log anomaly detection, LogGAN [27] applies GAN principles to discern anomalies from normal events in log sequences using generators.

In summary, our approach introduces log graph embedding based on generative adversarial networks for log anomaly detection. We utilize graph neural networks for graph representation learning. In addition, we employ a generative adversarial network that utilizes a small amount of anomaly data to generate high-quality adversarial samples, addressing the challenge of sparse anomaly samples. A high-quality discriminator is obtained through adversarial training to determine anomalies by log sample reconstruction loss.

3 Framework

Figure 1 illustrates the proposed log anomaly detection algorithm based on graph representation learning and generative adversarial networks. It involves five main steps: Log Processing, Graph Construction, Graph Representation Learning, Adversarial Training Model, and Anomaly Detection. This chapter details log graph representation learning and the training of anomaly detection models within the framework.

3.1 Problem Statement

This work tackles the problem of graph-level log anomaly detection. Given a log graph embedding $h_\mathcal{G}$, the target of the anomaly detection model is to learn a mapping mechanism to calculate the anomaly score $A(\cdot)$, which describes the abnormal degree of the $\mathcal{G}$. Consequently, when evaluating the anomaly score $A(x)$ of a specific sample x against a threshold λ, it determines whether x is anomalous or not.

3.2   Log Preprocessing

The log preprocessing mainly includes log parsing, log partition, and log template feature extraction.

Log Parsing. Log parsing is the process of converting semi-structured raw log messages into organized log templates. Several log text extraction methods exist, including SLCT [25], IPLoM [16], Spell [4], Drain [8], etc. Experimental valuation [40] confirms the superior performance of Drain compared to mainstream parsing methods since its independence from additional information. In this paper, we adopt Drain to extract log templates from collected messages. For instance, an initial log message *"Receiving block blk_-1608999687919862906 src: 10.250.19.102:54106 dest: 10.250.19.102:50010"* is parsed into the corresponding log event *"Receiving block ∗ "*.

Log Partition. The parsed log events are partitioned into distinct log sequences. Specifically, in the context of system logs containing identifiers, log events can be segmented into separate sequences based on identifiers found in the original log message, such as *"block_id"* in HDFS logs, represented as *"blk_-"* in

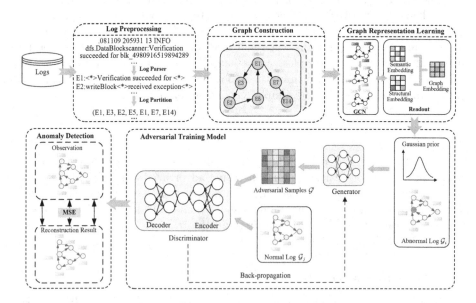

Fig. 1. The overall architecture of AdvGraLog.

the aforementioned log message "1608999687919862906". In cases where system logs lack such identifiers, a fixed window or sliding window approach is adopted for log sequence division. We adopt a fixed window for logs without identifiers to group logs.

Semantic Feature Extraction. Converting unstructured text data to numbers is crucial for machine learning, as many models can't handle strings. We extract semantic information from log templates, turning them into structured vectors for computations. Specifically, we generate a vector representation for each log event in the following steps: (1) *Preprocessing*: Considering log entry as a natural language sentence, we remove non-characters and decompose compound symbols for analysis. (2) *Word Embedding*: We utilize a pre-trained FastText [10] model to extract the d-dimensional semantic vector for each word embedded in log templates where d = 300. (3) *Template Embedding*: Calculate TF-IDF (Term Frequency-Inverse Document Frequency) for each word, followed by generating vector representations for each template. The resulting embeddings have the advantage of being much less dimensional and also incorporate information about the word contexts.

3.3   Graph Construction

All logs are categorized into different groups based on sessions or predefined windows, each representing a distinct directed graph.

A log graph structure consisting of log events can be described as follows. Given a log graph $\mathcal{G} = (\mathcal{V}, \mathcal{E}, \mathbf{X})$, where $\mathcal{V}$ denotes the set of unique log events $\{v_1, v_2, \ldots, v_n\}$ and $\mathcal{E}$ indicates the sequence of events $\{e_1, e_2, \ldots, e_m\}$. For example, the directed graph in Fig. 1 is constituted by a sequence of log events $(E1, E3, E2, E5, E1, E7, E14)$. The d-dimensional log template semantic vectors obtained in Sect. 3.2 are denoted by $\mathbf{X} = [\mathbf{x}_1, \mathbf{x}_2, \ldots, \mathbf{x}_n] \in \mathbb{R}^{n \times d}$. The attributed graph can also be represented as $\mathcal{G} = (\mathbf{X}, \mathbf{A})$ for simplicity. Here $\mathbf{A} = \{0, 1\}^{n \times n}$ is an adjacency matrix where $\mathbf{A}_{i,j} = 1$ indicates that there is an edge between node v_i and node v_j, otherwise, $\mathbf{A}_{i,j} = 0$.

3.4   Graph Representation Learning

GNN Module. The aim of the Graph Representation Learning module is to aggregate node information and obtain comprehensive structural and semantic embedding of a log graph. The log graph $\mathcal{G}$ is fed into a GNN with three stacked layers, where a single layer can be written as:

$$\mathbf{H}^{(\ell)} = GNN\left(\mathbf{A}, \mathbf{H}^{(\ell-1)}; \mathbf{W}^{(\ell-1)}\right), \tag{1}$$

where $\mathbf{H}^{(\ell-1)}$ and $\mathbf{H}^{(\ell)}$ are the hidden representation matrices learned by the $(\ell - 1)$-th layer and ℓ-th layer respectively, guided by weight matrix $\mathbf{W}^{(\ell-1)}$ of the $(\ell - 1)$-th layer, and $\mathbf{A}$ is an adjacency matrix of a directed log graph. The input representation $\mathbf{H}^{(0)}$ is defined as the log template semantic attribute $\mathbf{X}$ obtained from Sect. 3.4. $GNN(\cdot)$ can be set to any type of mainstream GNN. In practice, we adopt GCN [11] due to its high efficiency. Then Eq. 1 can be specifically written as:

$$\mathbf{H}^{(\ell)} = \phi \left(\widetilde{\mathbf{D}}^{-\frac{1}{2}} \widetilde{\mathbf{A}} \widetilde{\mathbf{D}}^{-\frac{1}{2}} \mathbf{H}^{(\ell-1)} \mathbf{W}^{(\ell-1)} \right), \tag{2}$$

where $\widetilde{\mathbf{A}} = \mathbf{A} + \mathbf{I}$ is the adjacency matrix with self-loop, $\widetilde{\mathbf{D}}^{-\frac{1}{2}}$ is the inverted square root of the diagonal degree matrix for normalizing the adjacency matrix, and $\phi(\cdot)$ is the activation function such as ReLU. Through multi-layer iteration, nodes gradually capture more graph structure information to form the structural embedding of the graph, while node representations are updated at each layer to synthesize the structure and feature information of the whole graph.

Readout Module. Next, a READOUT operation is applied to the node representations to obtain the graph-level log representation for $\mathcal{G}$. To detect anomalies, we aggregate extreme features through max-pooling in the READOUT operation. Thus, the idea of our readout function is that each log node plays a role in the graph and key nodes should contribute more explicitly:

$$\mathbf{h}_{\mathcal{G}} = \frac{1}{|\mathcal{V}|} \sum_{v \in \mathcal{V}} \mathbf{h}_v + \text{Maxpooling} \left(\mathbf{h}_1 \ldots \mathbf{h}_\nu \right). \tag{3}$$

Through the readout function, the semantic embedding and structural embedding of the log graph are fused to obtain a comprehensive graph representation.

3.5   Adversarial Training Model

This module focuses on learning good mapping mechanisms in GAN to detect anomalies. Adversarial training enhances model strength by capturing genuine and representative features. Further insights into the generator and discriminator are presented subsequently.

Generator Network. The generator acts as a competitor in adversarial learning. We aim to enhance performance and robustness by training the generator to choose diverse and high-quality negative samples. The architecture of the generator is defined as follows:

$$G\left(z_i\right) = R\left(\tanh\left(f\left(z_i\right)\right)\right). \tag{4}$$

Generator employs a three-layer fully-connected network and combines noise with anomalous graph embeddings to craft these adversarial samples. The ReLU function $F = \max(0, x)$ activates the first two linear layer outputs. The final generator layer employs $tanh()$ for [0,1] normalization. The function R adapts data to inputs of the first layer discriminator.

Discriminator Network. The discriminator is an autoencoder consisting of a standard encoder-decoder. Given an input feature vector $\mathbf{x}$, a typical AE can be defined as:

$$\mathbf{x}' = \text{AE}(\mathbf{x}) = f_{\text{dec}}\left(f_{\text{enc}}\left(\mathbf{x}\right)\right), \tag{5}$$

where $\mathbf{x}' = f_{\text{dec}}\left(\mathbf{h}\right)$ and $\mathbf{h} = f_{\text{enc}}\left(\mathbf{x}\right)$ are deep decoder and encoder, respectively. In the above equation, $\mathbf{x}'$ is the reconstructed feature vector, and $\mathbf{h}$ denotes the latent representation of $\mathbf{x}$. The encoder and decoder structures in the autoencoder also use fully connected neural networks, the specific parameters of which we will clearly describe in the experimental setup.

Adversarial Training. The main idea of adversarial training is to add the adversarial samples to the training set together with the original samples, which is an effective regularization technique to improve the accuracy of the model and the robustness of the anomaly detection model.

For the loss function of the generator, we introduce the Pull-away Term [34] to encourage the generator to generate more diverse samples in the latent space.

$$\mathcal{L}_{pt} = \frac{1}{N(N-1)} \sum_{i=1}^{N} \sum_{j \neq i} \left(\frac{f\left(x_i\right)^{\text{T}} f\left(x_j\right)}{\|f\left(x_i\right)\| \, \|f\left(x_j\right)\|} \right)^2, \tag{6}$$

where N is the batch size, x_i and x_j represent different generated adversarial samples from the same batch, $f(x_i)$ and $f(x_j)$ represent the corresponding feature vector. The total loss function of the generator is defined as:

$$\mathcal{L}_G\left(\text{G}, \text{D}, z_i\right) = \frac{1}{N} \sum_{i=1}^{N} \log\left(\left|\alpha - \text{D}\left(\text{G}\left(z_i\right)\right)\right|\right) + \lambda_0 \mathcal{L}_{pt}, \tag{7}$$

where α in the front part of the generator loss function ensures the high quality of the adversarial samples, λ_0 is a hyperparameter used to balance the two losses, which is set to 1 in the experiment, and G and D refer to the generator and discriminator, respectively.

The discriminator attempts to discriminate generated negative samples as 0 and the real samples as 1. We can define the loss of the discriminator D as:

$$\mathcal{L}_D\left(\text{G}\left(z_i\right), x_i, \text{D}\right) = \frac{1}{N} \sum_{i=1}^{N} \left[-\log\left(\text{D}\left(x_i\right)\right)\right] - \mu \times \log\left(1 - \text{D}\left(\text{G}\left(z_i\right)\right)\right), \tag{8}$$

where μ is a parameter by which the discriminator weighs generated samples against anomalous samples.

In each training epoch, we iterate the training set in small batches to train the generator while the discriminator parameters are fixed. Then, with the generator parameters fixed, we iterate the training set again to train the discriminator. This training process can also be seen as a way to make the generator search for high-quality adversarial samples, filter out some useless information, and then use it to challenge the discriminator. We also use Spectral Normalization (SN) [19] in discriminator encoder training to enhance stability and overcome pattern collapse. SN controls the Lipschitz constant by normalizing weight matrices or convolutional layer's spectral norms.

3.6 Anomaly Detection

Anomaly detection aims to identify patterns that deviate from the majority. In the experiment, we use a proportion-based approach to set the threshold of anomaly scores. The thresholds are determined based on the distribution of anomaly samples across various datasets. When fewer anomalies exist, a lower threshold is chosen to detect them effectively. Specifically, given a test graph sample $\mathcal{G}$, we use the Mean Squared Error (MSE) between the reconstructed output $\hat{\mathbf{h}}_\mathcal{G}$ and the observed data $\mathbf{h}_\mathcal{G}$:

$$A(\mathcal{G}) = \frac{1}{|h_\mathcal{G}|} \sum_{i=1}^{|h_\mathcal{G}|} \left(\mathbf{h}_\mathcal{G} - \hat{\mathbf{h}}_\mathcal{G} \right)^2. \tag{9}$$

An input sample is classified as abnormal if its anomaly score $A(\cdot)$ surpasses a predefined threshold λ.

4 Experiments and Results

In this section, we perform empirical evaluations to demonstrate the effectiveness of our proposed framework AdvGraLog. Specifically, we aim to answer the following research questions:

- **RQ1**: How effective is the AdvGraLog approach in detecting graph-level log anomalies with different imbalanced data ratios?
- **RQ2**: How much does the performance of AdvGraLog change by providing different levels of data noise contamination?
- **RQ3**: How does the component of AdvGraLog (i.e., negative sample generator and spectral normalization) contribute to the final detection performance?

4.1 Datasets and Evaluation Metrics

Datasets. In this section, we evaluate the performance of AdvGraLog with two real-world datasets HDFS and BGL. Details of these datasets are as follows:

HDFS (Hadoop Distributed File System) dataset is produced by executing Hadoop-based MapReduce jobs on a cluster of over 200 Amazon EC2 nodes and annotated by Hadoop domain experts. The HDFS dataset contains a total of 11,175,629 log messages, approximately 2.9% of blocks are abnormal.

BGL (Blue Gene/L) dataset, collected by Lawrence Livermore National Labs (LLNL), comprises 4,747,963 manually labeled supercomputing system log

Table 1. Dataset Statistics.

Dataset	Time Span	Data Size	#Messages	#Templates	Window	%Anomalies
HDFS	38.7 h	1.47 GB	11,175,629	48	session	2.93%
BGL	214.7 days	708.76 MB	4,747,963	1848	100logs	10.24%

messages. One log with an abnormal label in the same group, group is considered an anomaly (Table 1).

In subsequent experiments, we utilize the first 80% of the dataset for training and the remaining 20% for testing based on timestamps, which is done to prevent potential data leakage. In addition, since the provided dataset is manually labeled, we consider these annotations as the definitive reference for evaluation.

Metrics. The goal of anomaly detection is to identify unusual points. Therefore, anomalies are treated as positive samples to measure the ability to detect anomalous situations. Log anomaly detection studies commonly employ standard classification evaluation metrics: precision, recall, and F1-score, as follows:

$$precision = \frac{TP}{TP + FP} \tag{10}$$

Precision measures the proportion of correctly predicted anomalies among all instances classified as anomalies.

$$recall = \frac{TP}{TP + FN} \tag{11}$$

Recall calculates the proportion of correctly predicted anomalies from all actual anomalies.

$$F1 - score = 2 \times \frac{precision \times recall}{precision + recall} \tag{12}$$

The F1-score is the harmonic mean of precision and recall. TP (true positive) is the number of anomaly logs correctly detected as anomalies. FP (false positive) denotes the number of normal logs incorrectly detected as abnormal. FN (false positive) represents the number of abnormal logs incorrectly detected as normal.

4.2 Baselines and Implementation Details

Baseline Methods. We compared AdvGraLog with five representative log anomaly detection methods. Specifically, there are two unsupervised learning methods PCA [29] and LogCluster [14], a supervised learning method LogRobust [39], a semi-supervised learning method DeepLog [5], and a graph-based semi-supervised method GLAD-PAW [26]. For the baseline method used for comparison, we use the implementations in the studies [13, 15]. For models whose hyperparameter settings are reported in their paper, we use the same hyperparameter values. Otherwise, we tune their hyperparameters empirically.

Experimental Setup. In this paper, experiments are conducted on a server with Intel Xeon Platinum 8255C CPU @ 2.50 GHz CPU and NVIDIA RTX 2080TI GPU running Python 3.8 and PyTorch 1.11.0. A fixed-window grouping approach is chosen for efficient storage of log sequences in the BGL dataset. A 3-layer GCN network with a hidden layer dimension of 128 is used in the AdvGra-Log model for graph representation learning. The generator and discriminator employ 3-layer and 5-layer fully connected neural networks, respectively, with LeakyReLU as the activation function. The generator's hidden layer has 256 and 128 nodes, while the discriminator's hidden layer has 128, 256, 128, and 64 nodes. Training consists of 100 epochs with early stopping, using Adam as the optimizer, a learning rate of 0.0002, and a batch size of 64.

In our experiments, we varied the proportion of anomalies in HDFS and BGL datasets from 0.1% to 10% (i.e., 0.1%, 0.5%, 1%, 5%, and 10% respectively). We introduced noise by modifying log labels, simulating noise proportions spanning from 0.1% to 15% (specifically, 0.1%, 0.5%, 1%, 5%, 10%, and 15% respectively). Each method was run three times on different datasets, and the averages were reported to reduce randomness in the results.

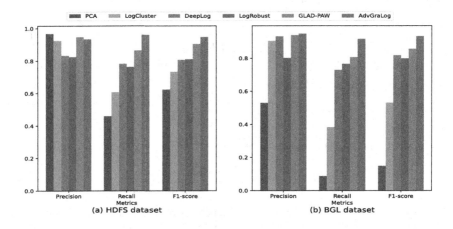

Fig. 2. Algorithm performance with various clean log sets.

4.3   RQ1: Comparison with Baseline Models

Overall Comparison. In the experiments, we evaluate the performance of AdvGraLog compared with the included baseline methods. We present the evaluation results (based on the original imbalance ratio) w.r.t. precision, recall, and F1-score in Fig. 2. Accordingly, we have the following observations: (1) Our proposed method AdvGraLog outperforms other compared methods on two datasets in the original anomaly ratio. (2) PCA and LogCluster rely on log data statistics for anomaly detection but exhibit unstable performance. LSTM-based

Table 2. Model performance with different anomaly ratios. In the table, the best F1 values at different scales are **bolded**, and all the second-best are <u>underlined</u>.

Model		HDFS					BGL				
		0.1%	0.5%	1%	5%	10%	0.1%	0.5%	1%	5%	10%
PCA	Precision	0.990	0.993	0.993	0.996	0.995	0.541	0.504	0.528	0.532	0.524
	Recall	0.421	0.473	0.459	0.461	0.443	0.081	0.090	0.082	0.081	0.082
	F1-score	0.591	0.641	0.628	0.631	0.613	0.141	0.153	0.142	0.141	0.142
LogCluster	Precision	0.972	0.975	0.971	0.970	0.978	0.987	0.985	0.982	0.991	0.986
	Recall	0.711	0.711	0.708	0.711	0.711	0.349	0.341	0.337	0.351	0.355
	F1-score	<u>0.821</u>	<u>0.823</u>	<u>0.819</u>	0.821	0.823	0.516	0.507	0.502	0.519	0.522
DeepLog	Precision	0.963	0.957	0.961	0.968	0.968	0.926	0.923	0.925	0.967	0.969
	Recall	0.483	0.489	0.529	0.825	0.863	0.402	0.437	0.562	0.748	0.834
	F1-score	0.643	0.648	0.682	0.891	0.912	0.560	0.593	0.699	0.844	0.897
LogRobust	Precision	0.667	0.698	0.750	0.933	0.949	0.433	0.499	0.759	0.804	0.825
	Recall	0.433	0.553	0.740	0.902	0.927	0.358	0.403	0.647	0.870	0.922
	F1-score	0.525	0.617	0.745	<u>0.917</u>	0.937	0.392	0.446	<u>0.699</u>	0.836	0.871
GLAD-PAW	Precision	0.952	0.950	0.942	0.948	0.969	0.924	0.924	0.925	0.942	0.948
	Recall	0.564	0.609	0.673	0.873	0.925	0.518	0.526	0.562	0.823	0.864
	F1-score	0.708	0.742	0.785	0.909	<u>0.946</u>	<u>0.664</u>	<u>0.670</u>	<u>0.699</u>	<u>0.878</u>	<u>0.904</u>
AdvGraLog	Precision	0.966	0.964	0.967	0.958	0.981	0.956	0.952	0.962	0.961	0.966
	Recall	0.824	0.850	0.871	0.944	0.968	0.805	0.815	0.838	0.907	0.940
	F1-score	**0.890**	**0.903**	**0.917**	**0.951**	**0.975**	**0.874**	**0.878**	**0.896**	**0.933**	**0.953**

models like DeepLog and LogRobust excel on simple data but face challenges with diverse templates in complex datasets like BGL. In contrast, graph-based methods, AdvGraLog and GLAD-PAW, outperform statistical and sequential approaches in log anomaly detection. This reaffirms the superiority of graph-based log anomaly detection methods. (3) AdvGraLog surpasses GLAD-PAW on both datasets, affirming its superiority and GAN-based approach for training effective graph-based log anomaly detection models. Adversarial training mitigates anomaly sample scarcity, enhancing anomaly detection tasks.

Generalization Evaluation. To evaluate the generalization ability of AdvGraLog for anomaly detection with limited abnormal data, we evaluate it by simulating different data imbalance scenarios. We test AdvGraLog's performance using log data with different percentages of anomalies (0.1%, 0.5%, 1%, 5%, 10%) on two different datasets. As shown in Table 2, the supervised and semi-supervised models get better as the proportion of anomalous data increases, while the performance of the unsupervised model does not fluctuate much. Furthermore, for anomaly rates lower than 1% in HDFS data, unsupervised models achieve the second-highest F1 scores, suggesting the possible utilization of inherent data structure and patterns independent of anomaly labels. Specifically, AdvGraLog demonstrates exceptional performance with highly imbalanced data (0.1% anomalies), surpassing all baseline methods and showcasing its remarkable

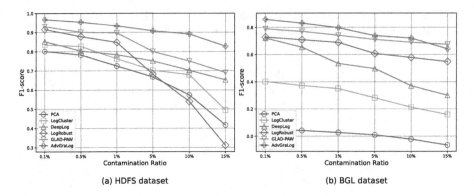

Fig. 3. F1-score performance of models w.r.t. different contamination levels.

adaptability and robustness. For instance, at 0.1% anomaly rate, GLAD-PAW gets F1 scores of 70.8% and 66.4% on HDFS and BGL data, respectively. This surpasses DeepLog (64.3%, 56.0%), yet AdvGraLog excels further with F1 of 89.0% and 87.4% on both datasets, respectively.

4.4   RQ2: Robustness w.r.t. Data Contamination

We often utilize assumed-normal training data for spotting anomalies. Yet, real-world data may be noisy due to human labeling errors. We examine how AdvGra-Log copes with this challenge by introducing noise to training data. Specifically, we add anomalous data in semi-supervised scenarios, while in supervised scenarios, we randomize anomaly labels. Contamination ratios range from 0.1% to 15%.

In Fig. 3, we present the evaluation results of AdvGraLog and baseline models. The charts illustrate that increased log noise affects all models, especially supervised learning. AdvGraLog, trained on anomalous and adversarial data,

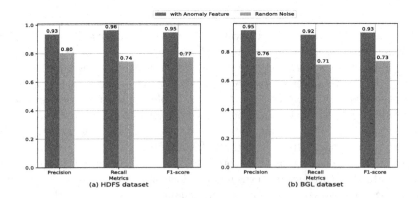

Fig. 4. The performance of the generator.

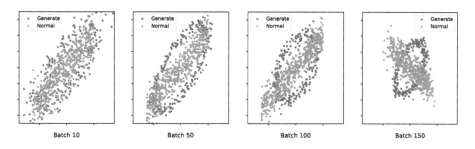

Fig. 5. t-SNE visualization of the reconstruct samples process.

exhibits resilience and maintains high performance even with 10% noise, with a slight drop at 15%, but F1-scores remain fairly stable. Its ability to adapt to diverse data distributions and recognize noisy and genuine patterns leads to good generalization, minimizing the impact of training data noise and enhancing performance on test data.

4.5   RQ3: Ablation Study

In this section, we performed a series of studies to understand AdvGraLog.

Adversarial Training. AdvGraLog utilizes adversarial training, we conducted an ablation study on its generator, which is responsible for creating adversarial negative samples to enhance anomaly detection by the discriminator. We assessed the impact of using both random noise vectors and original anomaly sample features as input for the generator, comparing it with using solely random noise vectors as input while keeping other experimental settings constant.

Figure 4 illustrates the experimental results. It shows a significant difference between our model and the baseline. In HDFS, AdvGraLog exceeds the random noise model by 12.9% in precision, 21.9% in recall, and 17.5% in F1-score. Similarly, in the BGL dataset, AdvGraLog also improves these metrics by 18.6%, 20.6%, and 19.7%, respectively. This is because AdvGraLog including anomalous features can learn diverse and unique anomaly representations from the small number of anomalous samples encountered during training, thus generating more valuable negative sample information. This results in adversarial samples that enhance the discriminator's ability to detect anomalies, thereby significantly improving anomaly detection performance.

In Fig. 5, we used t-SNE to visualize anomaly scores of 200 random samples. As the model training progresses, normal and anomalous sample distributions become more focused, the anomalous samples distinctly separate from the normal ones, and the generated samples cluster near real sample boundaries. This shows the generator effectively achieves the goal of generating diverse and high-quality negative samples, thus confirming the validity of the model.

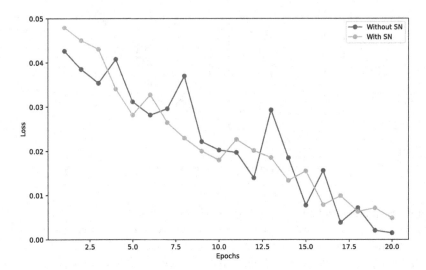

Fig. 6. Effect of SN on discriminator training.

Evaluation of Spectral Normalization. We expanded our approach by adding Spectral Normalization to AdvGra-Log's discriminator encoder to assess its impact on anomaly detection. We observed the discriminator's loss during training and noted reduced fluctuations after introducing SN, as Fig. 6.

5   Conclusion

This paper presents AdvGraLog, an anomaly detection approach using adversarial learning to represent log data as graphs. Log events are transformed into directed graphs, and graph neural networks generate log graph embeddings, framing log anomaly detection as graph-level classification. Adversarial samples, created from original anomalies, enhance the discriminator's understanding of diverse anomaly patterns. Adversarial training helps the discriminator accurately reconstruct normal samples, resulting in higher reconstruction loss for anomalies. The loss is compared to a threshold to identify abnormalities, and the model's effectiveness and robustness are evaluated using public log datasets.

References

1. Akcay, S., Atapour-Abarghouei, A., Breckon, T.P.: GANomaly: semi-supervised anomaly detection via adversarial training. In: Jawahar, C.V., Li, H., Mori, G., Schindler, K. (eds.) ACCV 2018. LNCS, vol. 11363, pp. 622–637. Springer, Cham (2019). https://doi.org/10.1007/978-3-030-20893-6_39

2. Avola, D., et al.: A novel GAN-based anomaly detection and localization method for aerial video surveillance at low altitude. Remote Sens. **14**(16), 4110 (2022)
3. Capra, L.: Graph transformation systems: a semantics based on (stochastic) symmetric nets. In: Pang, J., Zhang, L. (eds.) SETTA 2020. LNCS, vol. 12153, pp. 35–51. Springer, Cham (2020). https://doi.org/10.1007/978-3-030-62822-2_3
4. Du, M., Li, F.: Spell: streaming parsing of system event logs. In: 2016 IEEE 16th International Conference on Data Mining (ICDM), pp. 859–864. IEEE (2016)
5. Du, M., Li, F., Zheng, G., Srikumar, V.: DeepLog: anomaly detection and diagnosis from system logs through deep learning. In: Proceedings of the 2017 ACM SIGSAC Conference on Computer and Communications Security, pp. 1285–1298 (2017)
6. Fenton, N.E., Ohlsson, N.: Quantitative analysis of faults and failures in a complex software system. IEEE Trans. Softw. Eng. **26**(8), 797–814 (2000)
7. Han, X., Yuan, S.: Unsupervised cross-system log anomaly detection via domain adaptation. In: Proceedings of the 30th ACM International Conference on Information & Knowledge Management, pp. 3068–3072 (2021)
8. He, P., Zhu, J., Zheng, Z., Lyu, M.R.: Drain: an online log parsing approach with fixed depth tree. In: 2017 IEEE International Conference on Web Services (ICWS), pp. 33–40. IEEE (2017)
9. Jiang, W., Hong, Y., Zhou, B., He, X., Cheng, C.: A GAN-based anomaly detection approach for imbalanced industrial time series. IEEE Access **7**, 143608–143619 (2019)
10. Joulin, A., Grave, E., Bojanowski, P., Mikolov, T.: Bag of tricks for efficient text classification. arXiv preprint arXiv:1607.01759 (2016)
11. Kipf, T.N., Welling, M.: Semi-supervised classification with graph convolutional networks. arXiv preprint arXiv:1609.02907 (2016)
12. Le, V.H., Zhang, H.: Log-based anomaly detection without log parsing. In: 2021 36th IEEE/ACM International Conference on Automated Software Engineering (ASE), pp. 492–504. IEEE (2021)
13. Le, V.H., Zhang, H.: Log-based anomaly detection with deep learning: How far are we? In: Proceedings of the 44th International Conference on Software Engineering, pp. 1356–1367 (2022)
14. Lin, Q., Zhang, H., Lou, J.G., Zhang, Y., Chen, X.: Log clustering based problem identification for online service systems. In: Proceedings of the 38th International Conference on Software Engineering Companion, pp. 102–111 (2016)
15. Liu, Z., Xia, X., Lo, D., Xing, Z., Hassan, A.E., Li, S.: Which variables should i log? IEEE Trans. Softw. Eng. **47**(9), 2012–2031 (2019)
16. Makanju, A.A., Zincir-Heywood, A.N., Milios, E.E.: Clustering event logs using iterative partitioning. In: Proceedings of the 15th ACM SIGKDD International Conference on Knowledge Discovery and Data Mining, pp. 1255–1264 (2009)
17. Meng, W., et al.: LogAnomaly: unsupervised detection of sequential and quantitative anomalies in unstructured logs. In: IJCAI, vol. 19, pp. 4739–4745 (2019)
18. Mi, H., Wang, H., Zhou, Y., Lyu, M.R.T., Cai, H.: Toward fine-grained, unsupervised, scalable performance diagnosis for production cloud computing systems. IEEE Trans. Parallel Distrib. Syst. **24**(6), 1245–1255 (2013)
19. Miyato, T., Kataoka, T., Koyama, M., Yoshida, Y.: Spectral normalization for generative adversarial networks. arXiv preprint arXiv:1802.05957 (2018)
20. Oliner, A.J., Aiken, A., Stearley, J.: Alert detection in system logs. In: 2008 Eighth IEEE International Conference on Data Mining, pp. 959–964. IEEE (2008)
21. Park, S., Lee, K.H., Ko, B., Kim, N.: Unsupervised anomaly detection with generative adversarial networks in mammography. Sci. Rep. **13**(1), 2925 (2023)

22. Pimentel, M.A., Clifton, D.A., Clifton, L., Tarassenko, L.: A review of novelty detection. Signal Process. **99**, 215–249 (2014)
23. Rouillard, J.P.: Real-time log file analysis using the simple event correlator (SEC). In: LISA, vol. 4, pp. 133–150 (2004)
24. Sagar, B., Manjul, M., et al.: Anomaly detection in wireless sensor network using generative adversarial network (GAN). In: Automation and Computation, pp. 45–49 (2023)
25. Vaarandi, R.: Mining event logs with SLCT and LogHound. In: NOMS 2008–2008 IEEE Network Operations and Management Symposium, pp. 1071–1074. IEEE (2008)
26. Wan, Y., Liu, Y., Wang, D., Wen, Y.: GLAD-PAW: graph-based log anomaly detection by position aware weighted graph attention network. In: Karlapalem, K., et al. (eds.) PAKDD 2021. LNCS (LNAI), vol. 12712, pp. 66–77. Springer, Cham (2021). https://doi.org/10.1007/978-3-030-75762-5_6
27. Xia, B., Yin, J., Xu, J., Li, Y.: LogGAN: a sequence-based generative adversarial network for anomaly detection based on system logs. In: Liu, F., Xu, J., Xu, S., Yung, M. (eds.) SciSec 2019. LNCS, vol. 11933, pp. 61–76. Springer, Cham (2019). https://doi.org/10.1007/978-3-030-34637-9_5
28. Xie, Y., Zhang, H., Babar, M.A.: LogGD: detecting anomalies from system logs with graph neural networks. In: 2022 IEEE 22nd International Conference on Software Quality, Reliability and Security (QRS), pp. 299–310. IEEE (2022)
29. Xu, W., Huang, L., Fox, A., Patterson, D., Jordan, M.I.: Detecting large-scale system problems by mining console logs. In: Proceedings of the ACM SIGOPS 22nd Symposium on Operating Systems Principles, pp. 117–132 (2009)
30. Yan, Y., Jiang, S., Zhang, S., Huang, Y.: CSFL: fault localization on real software bugs based on the combination of context and spectrum. In: Qin, S., Woodcock, J., Zhang, W. (eds.) SETTA 2021. LNCS, vol. 13071, pp. 219–238. Springer, Cham (2021). https://doi.org/10.1007/978-3-030-91265-9_12
31. Yang, R., Qu, D., Gao, Y., Qian, Y., Tang, Y.: nLSALog: an anomaly detection framework for log sequence in security management. IEEE Access **7**, 181152–181164 (2019)
32. Yen, T.F., et al.: Beehive: large-scale log analysis for detecting suspicious activity in enterprise networks. In: Proceedings of the 29th Annual Computer Security Applications Conference, pp. 199–208 (2013)
33. Zenati, H., Foo, C.S., Lecouat, B., Manek, G., Chandrasekhar, V.R.: Efficient GAN-based anomaly detection. arXiv preprint arXiv:1802.06222 (2018)
34. Zenati, H., Romain, M., Foo, C.S., Lecouat, B., Chandrasekhar, V.: Adversarially learned anomaly detection. In: 2018 IEEE International Conference on Data Mining (ICDM), pp. 727–736. IEEE (2018)
35. Zhang, C., et al.: DeepTraLog: trace-log combined microservice anomaly detection through graph-based deep learning. In: Proceedings of the 44th International Conference on Software Engineering, pp. 623–634 (2022)
36. Zhang, H.: On the distribution of software faults. IEEE Trans. Softw. Eng. **34**(2), 301–302 (2008)
37. Zhang, H.: An investigation of the relationships between lines of code and defects. In: 2009 IEEE International Conference on Software Maintenance, pp. 274–283. IEEE (2009)
38. Zhang, H., Zhang, X.: Comments on "data mining static code attributes to learn defect predictors". IEEE Trans. Softw. Eng. **33**(9), 635–637 (2007)

39. Zhang, X., et al.: Robust log-based anomaly detection on unstable log data. In: Proceedings of the 2019 27th ACM Joint Meeting on European Software Engineering Conference and Symposium on the Foundations of Software Engineering, pp. 807–817 (2019)
40. Zhu, J., He, S., Liu, J., He, P., Xie, Q., Zheng, Z., Lyu, M.R.: Tools and benchmarks for automated log parsing. In: 2019 IEEE/ACM 41st International Conference on Software Engineering: Software Engineering in Practice (ICSE-SEIP), pp. 121–130 (2019)

Formal Verification Based Synthesis for Behavior Trees

Weijiang Hong[1,2,3], Zhenbang Chen[1,2(✉)] (iD), Minglong Li[1,3], Yuhan Li[1],
Peishan Huang[1,2,3], and Ji Wang[1,2,3(✉)] (iD)

[1] College of Computer, National University of Defense Technology, Changsha, China
{hongweijiang17,zbchen,liminglong10,liyuhan,Huang_ps,wj}@nudt.edu.cn
[2] Key Laboratory of Software Engineering for Complex Systems, National University
of Defense Technology, Changsha, China
[3] Institute for Quantum Information & State Key Laboratory of High Performance
Computing, National University of Defense Technology, Changsha, China

Abstract. Behavior trees (BTs) have been extensively applied in the
area of both computer games and robotics, as the control architectures.
However, the construction of BTs is labor-expensive, time-consuming,
and even impossible as the complexity of task increases. In this work,
we propose a formal verification based synthesis method to automatically construct BTs whose behaviors satisfy the given Linear Temporal
Logic (LTL) specifications. Our method first explores candidate BTs by
a grammar-based Monte Carlo Tree Search (MCTS), then the explored
BTs are transformed into Communicating Sequential Processes (CSP)
models. After that, we invoke the verifier to check the models' correctness *w.r.t.* specifications, and provide feedback based on the verification
result for guiding the search process. The application of our method on
several representative robotic missions indicates its promising.

Keywords: Behavior Trees · MCTS · CSP · Synthesis

1 Introduction

Behavior Trees (BTs) [15] are models that control the agent's decision-making
behavior through a hierarchical tree structure. The development of BTs can be
traced back to their applications in the field of computer games, wherein BTs
are initially used to facilitate the design and control of non-player characters
[18,20,26]. Afterwards, BTs' application is gradually extended to the area of
robotics, like mobile ground robots [7,19], unmanned aerial vehicles [17,28], to
name a few. It's incontestable that BTs play a more and more important role in
the area of both computer games and robotics, as the control architectures.

Compared with other control architectures, like Decision Trees (DTs) [27],
Teleo-reactive Programs (TRs) [22] and Finite State Machines (FSMs) [14], the

H. Hermanns et al. (Eds.): SETTA 2023, LNCS 14464, pp. 72–91, 2024.
https://doi.org/10.1007/978-981-99-8664-4_5

reactivity and *modularity* of BTs make it more applicable and flexible to accomplish tasks in unpredictable environments [8]. The support for *reactivity* means the agent can interrupt an ongoing task to execute another task for reacting to the environment changes, while the support of *modularity* means we can naturally combine several individually designed BTs into a more complex BT without providing any auxiliary glue-codes. Although BTs are being adopted and developed due to their promising features, their construction is still problematic especially when dealing with complex robotic tasks in unpredictable environments. Manually designing BTs usually becomes labor-expensive, time-consuming, and even impossible as the task involves more and more objects and subtasks. Therefore, it's expected that the construction of BTs can be automatic.

In this work, we propose a formal verification based synthesis method to automatically construct BTs whose behaviors satisfy the given Linear Temporal Logic (LTL) specifications. Our method first explores candidate BTs by a grammar-based Monte Carlo Tree Search (MCTS). Considering that BTs are not suitable formal models for formal verification *w.r.t.* properties, the explored BTs are transformed into Communicating Sequential Processes (CSP [13]) models. After that, we invoke the verifier to check the models' correctness *w.r.t.* specifications, and provide feedback based on the verification result for guiding the search process. The main contributions of this work are as follows:

- We proposed a formal verification based synthesis method for BTs. To the best of our knowledge, the combination of the verification method and the synthesis method for BTs hasn't been investigated before.
- We designed a CSP modelling method for BTs to capture their behaviors. The correctness of BTs' behaviors thereby can be checked by verifying the CSP model *w.r.t.* LTL specifications.
- We provided a method to evaluate the verification result and utilized this evaluation feedback to guide the search process, which improved the search efficiency.
- We successfully synthesized the expected BTs for several representative robotic missions within 1 h, which indicates the effectiveness of our method.

This paper is organized as follows. Some backgrounds are provided in Sect. 2. The problem formulation and the proposed approach are presented in Sect. 3 and Sect. 4, respectively. The demonstration result is shown in Sect. 5. The overview for the existing work is given in Sect. 6. Finally, Sect. 7 concludes the paper.

2   Background

This section first briefly introduces Behavior Trees with an example that used throughout the paper. Then, we provide some necessary prerequisite knowledge about Linear Temporal Logic and Communicating Sequential Processes.

2.1 Behavior Trees

Behavior Trees (BTs) [15] are the hierarchical trees that control the agent's decision-making behavior. Figure 1 shows a BT example that controls the robot to pick up a cube from a specific position. The leaf nodes of BTs are execution nodes that can be classified into *action nodes* and *condition nodes*. Apart from those execution nodes, there are four types of control flow nodes that include *sequences nodes, fallbacks nodes, parallel nodes*, and *decorator nodes*. In this work, we mainly focus on the usage of *sequences nodes* and *fallbacks nodes*. More details about them can be found below:

- *action nodes*: The gray and rectangle-shaped ones, like GotoPos, Pickup. It may return one of the three statuses: success (the action is completed), failure (the action is impossible to complete), running (the action is not completed yet).
- *condition nodes*: The ellipse-shaped ones, like Picked, AtPos. It may only return success (the condition holds) or failure (the condition does not hold).
- *sequences nodes*: It is represented as the symbol →. It returns success when all of its children return success in an order from left to right; returns failure/running as soon as one of its children returns failure/running.
- *fallbacks nodes*: It is represented as the symbol ?. It returns failure when all of its children return failure in an order from left to right; returns success/running as soon as one of its children returns success/running.

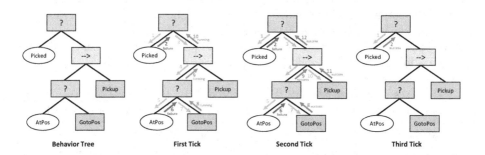

Fig. 1. BT example.

The execution of BTs starts from the root and infinitely delivers *ticks* to its children at a particular frequency. *Ticks* can be seen as a signal to identify which node is executable. We take one possible execution of the BT example for illustrations, which requires that the robot firstly goes to the specific position, then picks up a cube. The node's execution order *w.r.t. ticks* is labeled, as shown in Fig. 1. We assume that the conditions Picked and AtPos don't hold initially. In the first tick, the condition node Picked is ticked but returns failure, then the condition node AtPos is ticked due to the functionality of these control flow nodes. AtPos also returns failure and the action node GotoPos is ticked and returns running. The status running is propagated to the root since all the control flow nodes will return running if one of its children returns running. Similar to the first tick, the action node GotoPos is ticked again but returns success in the second tick. During the second tick, the action node Pickup is also ticked since the first child of the sequences node returns success and Pickup returns success. The success of Pickup means the condition Picked holds. Therefore, the condition node Picked always returns success in the third and following ticks.

2.2   Linear Temporal Logic

Linear Temporal Logic (LTL) is widely used to describe specifications about long-term goals, like safety and liveness. It can be used to specify the BTs' behaviors [3]. The basic elements of LTL include a set of atomic proposition $p \in P$, the propositional logic operators $\neg$ (negation), $\vee$ (disjunction), and $\wedge$ (conjunction), and several temporal logic operators $\mathcal{X}$ (next), $\mathcal{U}$ (until), $\mathcal{G}$ (always), and $\mathcal{F}$ (eventually).

$$\varphi ::= p \mid \neg p \mid \varphi \vee \varphi \mid \varphi \wedge \varphi \mid \mathcal{X}\varphi \mid \varphi \, \mathcal{U} \, \varphi \mid \mathcal{G}\varphi \mid \mathcal{F}\varphi$$

For example, the previous BT example controls the robot to finally pick up a cube can be expressed as the LTL specification $\mathcal{F} \, p$, wherein p denotes "*Picked holds*". We only mentioned those notions used in this paper, and more details about LTL can be found in [1].

2.3   Communicating Sequential Processes

Communicating Sequential Processes, or CSP [13] is a kind of language for describing an interaction system consisting of processes. For convenience, we use the lower case letters $(a, b, ...)$ to represent events in the process and the upper case letters $(P, Q, ...)$ to represent processes. The following provides part of the standard semantics, and more details about the completed semantics can be found in [13].

$$P ::= \text{Skip} \mid a \to P \mid P; P \mid P \,\square\, P$$

We take some expressions used in this paper as examples:

- Skip is a normal terminated process that does nothing.
- $a \to P$ executes the event a then behaves like the process P. If a is additionally decorated by [Guard] a {Program}, it requires that a can only be executed when the condition Guard satisfies and the effect of executing a is represented by Program.
- P_1 ; P_2 executes the process P_1 first, then executes the process P_2.
- $P_1 \,\square\, P_2$ executes the process P_1 or P_2, wherein which process executed depends on the external environment.

The following CSP model represents all executions in the form of a^*b. The whole process may continuously executes the event a due to the process P's recursive behavior or executes the event b once and terminates immediately due to Skip.

$$P = (a \rightarrow P) \;\square\; (b \rightarrow Skip);$$

There are many verifiers to support the verification of CSP model *w.r.t.* the LTL specification φ, like PAT [24] and FDR [11], to name a few.

3   Problem Formulation

Before carrying out our formal verification based synthesis method, there are some prerequisites: the BTs' construction grammar, the action nodes' function descriptions and the LTL specification. The BTs' construction grammar is shown in Fig. 2, wherein the action nodes $\{act_1, .., act_N\}$ and the condition nodes $\{cond_1, .., cond_M\}$ are regarded as the terminal symbols. The grammar will be used to carry a grammar-based MCTS to generate plenty of candidate BTs.

$$
\begin{aligned}
Root ::=\ & (\ ?\ Root\ Root\ )\ |\ (\ \rightarrow\ Root\ Root\ ) \\
& |\ (\ ?\ C\ Root\ )\ |\ (\ \rightarrow\ C\ Root\ )\ |\ A \\
A ::=\ & act_1\ |\ act_2\ |\ ...\ |\ act_N \\
C ::=\ & cond_1\ |\ cond_2\ |\ ...\ |\ cond_M
\end{aligned}
$$

Fig. 2. The BTs' construction grammar.

As for the action nodes' function descriptions, we noticed that the interaction between BTs and unpredictable environments is actually reflected in the effect of actions $\{act_1, .., act_N\}$ on conditions $\{cond_1, .., cond_M\}$. Therefore, we regard the condition set as a proposition set Σ, and represent the interaction snapshot between BTs and environments as a state set $\mathcal{S} = 2^\Sigma$. The function of an action can be represented in the form of $s_1 \xrightarrow{a} s_2$, wherein $s_1, s_2 \in \mathcal{S}$ and $a \in \{act_1, .., act_N\}$. For each action node, we clarify its function as shown in Table 1, which will be used to facilitate the CSP modelling for BTs.

Table 1. The function descriptions of action nodes.

Action	Requirement	Result
..	. . .	. . .
act_i	$cond_j, \ldots, \neg cond_k$	$cond_p, \ldots, \neg cond_q$
..	. . .	. . .
GotoPos	\	AtPos
Pickup	AtPos, ¬Picked	Picked

We use cond and ¬cond to represent whether the condition holds or not, respectively. For each action node act_i, **Requirement** is the pre-condition needed to be satisfied before executing act_i, *i.e.*, $s_1 \models cond_j \wedge ... \wedge \neg cond_k$; while **Result** is the post-condition caused by successfully executing act_i, *i.e.*, $s_2 \models cond_p \wedge ... \wedge \neg cond_q$. For example, the execution of GotoPos is without any requirements, but results in AtPos to be hold; the execution of Pickup requires that AtPos holds while Picked does not hold, but Picked will hold after the success execution of Pickup.

Goal: Given the BTs' construction grammar, the function descriptions of action nodes, and the LTL specification φ, our goal is to synthesize the expected BT whose behavior satisfies the specification φ.

4   Proposed Approach

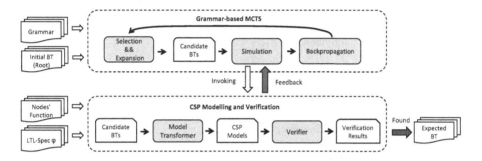

Fig. 3. The formal verification based synthesis framework.

The formal verification based synthesis framework is presented in Fig. 3, which consists of two modules: Grammar-based MCTS and CSP Modelling and Verification. In this framework, we conduct a Monte Carlo Tree Search process based on the grammar rules shown in Fig. 2, which starts from the non-terminal symbol Root and continually expands non-terminal symbols to obtain the candidate BTs. During the simulation phase, the candidate BT will be transformed into CSP model with the nodes' function embedding, then the model *w.r.t.* LTL specification φ will be checked by the verifier. The verification result will be utilized to provide feedback for guiding the search process. This search process will repeat until the expected BT has been found or the time is running out. In the following subsections, we will first focus on the verification module, then combine it with the search module.

4.1   CSP Modelling and Verification

Given the candidate BT $\mathcal{B}$ and the nodes' function $\mathcal{F}$, we construct the corresponded CSP model $\mathcal{M}$ in a bottom-up manner as shown in Algorithm 1. Considering that each node with its children in a BT is corresponded to a sub-BT, we use a mapping to store the corresponding CSP model for each node/sub-BT (line 1). During the modelling process, we first construct CSP model for each leaf node *w.r.t.* $\mathcal{F}$ (line 2–5), then focus on the structure building for the control node (line 6–14). For each control node whose CSP model is not defined but its child nodes are defined (line 8), we compose these child nodes together based on the type of control nodes to construct the control node's CSP model (line 9–13). Finally, we select the root's CSP model to return (line 15–17). The corresponding CSP model for the BT in Fig. 1 is presented in Fig. 4. We next describe the Function Embedding and the Structure Building for Fig. 4 in detail.

Algorithm 1: Modelling($\mathcal{B}$, $\mathcal{F}$)

Require: The candidate behavior tree $\mathcal{B}$ and the function information of action nodes $\mathcal{F} = \{(require_1, action_1, result_1), ..., (require_n, action_n, result_n)\}$.
Ensure: The corresponding CSP model $\mathcal{M}$ for $\mathcal{B}$.
 1: $\mathcal{E} \leftarrow \{\}$ // Mapping each node to a CSP model
 2: // Function Embedding
 3: **for** each *leaf* node n in $\mathcal{B}$ **do**
 4:    $\mathcal{E}[n] \leftarrow$ functionEmbedding$(n, \mathcal{F})$
 5: **end for**
 6: // Structure Building
 7: **while** exist undefined *control* node in $\mathcal{B}$ *w.r.t.* $\mathcal{E}$ **do**
 8:    $(n_1, n_2, n) \leftarrow$ select$(\mathcal{B}, \mathcal{E})$ // n_1, n_2 are defined, while the parent n is not.
 9:    **if** n is $\rightarrow$ **then**
10:       $\mathcal{E}[n] \leftarrow$ composeSequence(n_1, n_2)
11:    **else**
12:       $\mathcal{E}[n] \leftarrow$ composeFallback(n_1, n_2)
13:    **end if**
14: **end while**
15: // The Final Model *w.r.t.* Root
16: $\mathcal{M} \leftarrow \mathcal{E}[$selectRoot$(\mathcal{B})]$
17: **return** $\mathcal{M}$

Function Embedding. First, we present CSP model without the function embedding for each leaf node. Note that, a single leaf node can be also regarded as a BT. For example, the model for a condition node $cond_i$ is like

$$BT = (cond_i\_f \rightarrow BT) \ \square \ (cond_i\_s \rightarrow BT)$$

It captures the two possible return statuses of $cond_i$ by the external choice operator $\square$, wherein $cond_i\_f$ and $cond_i\_s$ are the events that mean the node returns failure and success, respectively. Besides, this node will be infinitely ticked at a particular frequency, which has been depicted as the recursion structure. The action node act_i can be constructed in the similar way by adding act_i_r for the status running as shown below.

$$BT = (act_i\_r \rightarrow BT) \ \square \ (act_i\_f \rightarrow BT) \ \square \ (act_i\_s \rightarrow BT)$$

```
1  var a1, a2;        // a1/a2 represents whether GotoPos/Pickup returns success
2  var c1, c2;        // c1/c2 represents whether Picked/AtPos returns success
3  var n1=0, n2=0;    // n1/n2 records the number of running times an action keeps
4  #define N 2;        // N times running must eventually leads to success
5
6  BT = ([c1==0] picked_f -> ([c2==0] atpos_f ->
7              (([n1<N] gotopos_r {n1++;a1=0;c2=0} -> BT)
8              []
9              ([n1==0] gotopos_f {n1=0;a1=0;c2=0} -> BT)
10             []
11             ([n1<=N] gotopos_s {n1=0;a1=1;c2=1} ->
12                 // ---------- the modelling for terminals ---------- //
13                 ([n2<N&&c1==0&&c2==1] pickup_r {n2++;a2=0;c1=0} -> BT
14                 []
15                 [n2==0&&(c1==1||c2==0)] pickup_f {n2=0;a2=0;c1=0} -> BT
16                 []
17                 [n2<=N&&c1==0&&c2==1] pickup_s {n2=0;a2=1;c1=1} -> BT)
18                 // -------- the modelling for non-terminals -------- //
19                 // Unknown -> BT
20             ))) []
21             ([c2==1] atpos_s ->
22                 ([n2<N&&c1==0&&c2==1] pickup_r {n2++;a2=0;c1=0} -> BT
23                 []
24                 [n2==0&&(c1==1||c2==0)] pickup_f {n2=0;a2=0;c1=0} -> BT
25                 []
26                 [n2<=N&&c1==0&&c2==1] pickup_s {n2=0;a2=1;c1=1} -> BT)
27                 // Unknown -> BT
28             )) []
29         ([c1==1] picked_s -> BT);
30
31  P = (set_c1_0{c1=0} -> set_c2_0{c2=0} -> Skip); BT;
32
33  #assert P |= F pickup_s; // check whether the cube is finally picked up?
```

Fig. 4. The CSP model for the BT example in Fig. 1, wherein [] represents the external choice □ and // represents comments. (1) if picked holds, the process is re-executed (line 29); (2) if picked doesn't hold but atpos holds, pickup is executed (line 22–26); (3) if both picked and atpos don't hold, gotopos and pickup are executed (line 7–17).

Second, we consider to add the function embedding into the model. The key point is using a flag (c_i for $cond_i$ and a_i for act_i) to indicate which status the execution node returns (1 for success and 0 for others), which will be further used to guide other nodes' executions. The function embedding of events in CSP model is presented in the following form

$$\underbrace{[\ldots \ldots \ldots]}_{\text{Guard}} \textbf{Event} \underbrace{\{\ldots \ldots \ldots\}}_{\text{Program}}$$

, wherein Guard is a boolean expression to represent the pre-condition needed for Event to take, and Program is the detailed description for the effect of Event taken. For each condition node $cond_i$, its related events will be depicted by

$$|c_i==0| \; \textbf{cond}_i\_\textbf{f} \; \{ \; \} \qquad |c_i==1| \; \textbf{cond}_i\_\textbf{s} \; \{ \; \}$$

The value of c_i depends on the environment initialization as shown in line 31 of Fig. 4 that assumes there is no condition holds initially. Besides, the value of c_i can be also altered by the execution of action nodes as shown below.

For illustrations, we assume the requirement for act_i is $cond_j \wedge \neg cond_k$, and the result for act_i is $cond_p$, its related events will be depicted by

$$[c_j==1 \text{ \&\& } c_k==0] \text{ act}_i\_r \{c_p=0; a_i=0\}$$

$$[c_j==0 \text{ || } c_k==1] \text{ act}_i\_f \{c_p=0; a_i=0\}$$

$$[c_j==1 \text{ \&\& } c_k==0] \text{ act}_i\_s \{c_p=1; a_i=1\}$$

Besides, we require N times running of an action eventually leads to the status success and use n_i to record the number of running times an action has kept. Therefore, the events above will be additionally decorated by

$$[(c_j==1 \text{ \&\& } c_k==0) \text{ \&\& } n_i < N] \text{ act}_i\_r \{(c_p=0; a_i=0) ; n_i++\}$$

$$[(c_j==0 \text{ || } c_k==1) \text{ \&\& } n_i==0] \text{ act}_i\_f \{(c_p=0; a_i=0)\}$$

$$[(c_j==1 \text{ \&\& } c_k==0) \text{ \&\& } n_i \leq N] \text{ act}_i\_s \{(c_p=1; a_i=1) ; n_i=0\}$$

After the function embedding for each leaf node, we next focus on the structure building for control nodes.

Structure Building. We consider more complex BTs that contain control nodes (Fallbacks or Sequences) other than the single node. We construct CSP model in a bottom-up manner by considering the functionality of control nodes described in Sect. 2.1. We take the BT in Fig. 1 as an example for the whole modelling process. We first construct the model for each leaf node as shown below and ignore those details of Guard and Program for clarity.

$$BT_1 = ([...] \text{ picked\_f } \{...\} \rightarrow BT_1) \square ([...] \text{ picked\_s } \{...\} \rightarrow BT_1)$$

$$BT_2 = ([...] \text{ atpos\_f } \{...\} \rightarrow BT_2) \square ([...] \text{ atpos\_s } \{...\} \rightarrow BT_2)$$

$$BT_3 = ([...] \text{ gotopos\_r } \{...\} \rightarrow BT_3) \square ([...] \text{ gotopos\_f } \{...\} \rightarrow BT_3)$$
$$\square ([...] \text{ gotopos\_s } \{...\} \rightarrow BT_3)$$

$$BT_4 = ([...] \text{ pickup\_r } \{...\} \rightarrow BT_4) \square ([...] \text{ pickup\_f } \{...\} \rightarrow BT_4)$$
$$\square ([...] \text{ pickup\_s } \{...\} \rightarrow BT_4)$$

Next, we consider the node ? associated with AtPos and GotoPos, which requires that the execution of GotoPos only happened when AtPos doesn't hold. Therefore, we deconstruct BT_3 and compose it with BT_2 to reconstruct a new model BT_{23}. BT_{23} consists with the modelling shown in line 6–11 of Fig. 4.

$$BT_{23} = ([...] \text{ atpos\_f } \{...\} \rightarrow (([...] \text{ gotopos\_r } \{...\} \rightarrow BT_{23})$$
$$\square ([...] \text{ gotopos\_f } \{...\} \rightarrow BT_{23})$$
$$\square ([...] \text{ gotopos\_s } \{...\} \rightarrow BT_{23}))$$
$$) \square ([...] \text{ atpos\_s } \{...\} \rightarrow BT_{23})$$

After that, we consider the node $\rightarrow$ associated with the left subtree and Pickup. It required that the execution of Pickup only happened under two cases: (1) atpos_s of the left subtree taken (corresponded to line 21–26 of Fig. 4); (2)

both `atpos_f` and `gotopos_s` of the left subtree taken (corresponded to line 11–17). The model's construction process is similar to the previous one described. Finally, we tackle with the modelling of the node ? associated with `Picked` and the right subtree based on the functionality of Fallbacks, as shown in Fig. 4. Intuitively, we automatically construct CSP model in a bottom-up manner based on the type of control nodes and the event each child nodes takes.

Verification. After the scene-customized function embedding for leaf nodes and the structure building for control nodes, we construct a CSP model from the given BT. Then, we can verify the correctness of CSP model *w.r.t.* specifications (line 33, *i.e.* the robot finally picks up a cube) by the verifier PAT [24]. The final verification result shows this CSP model is truly valid *w.r.t.* specifications, which implies the behavior of BT satisfies such specification. The verifier can also provide a counter-example trace if the final verification result shows *invalid*. For example, let the specification be that the robot never picks up a cube, *i.e.*, $\mathcal{G} \neg$`pickup_s`, the verifier may return a counter-example trace like `picked_f`; `atpos_f`; `gotopos_s`; `pickup_s`. The counter-example provided by the verifier will be useful in the following search process.

4.2 Grammar-Based MCTS

We instantiate the grammar-based search as a Monte Carlo Tree Search (MCTS) process. Starting from the non-terminal symbol `Root` as the initial candidate BT, MCTS consists of four phases:

- selection phase: it selects the most promising candidate BT based on the current exploration.
- expansion phase: it expands the selected BT based on the given grammar shown in Fig. 2 to generate more candidate BTs.
- simulation phase: it evaluates the candidate BT based on the feedback provided by the verifier.
- backpropagation phase: it updates the information of BTs that have been explored. After backpropagation phase, a new round of search begins.

The whole process is presented in Fig. 5. The search process will repeat until the expected BT has been found or the time is running out.

Instead of applying simulators to do the simulation phase, our method utilizes the verifier to evaluate the BT and provides feedback. The main consideration is that, the feedback provided by robotic simulators is not timely enough since the dynamic interaction and reaction with environments is time-consuming. Compared with robotic simulators, the verifier can provide timely feedback in a static manner without the interaction. Therefore, we invoke the verifier to check the candidate BT and calculate its value as shown in Fig. 6.

We first classify candidate BTs' models into two categories: determined one and non-determined one, based on the existence and reachability of non-terminals. After that, we invoke the verifier to check the model's correctness

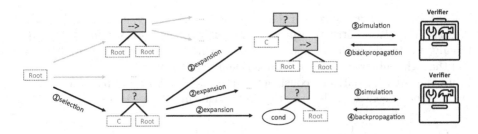

Fig. 5. Grammar-based MCTS.

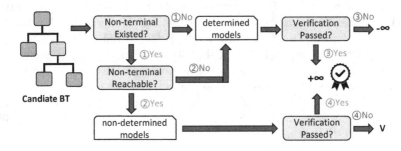

Fig. 6. The evaluation of candidate BTs.

w.r.t. specifications and assign different values for candidate BTs according to the verification result: (1) the value is $-\infty$ when the determined model failed to pass the verification; (2) the value is calculated as v when the non-determined model failed to pass the verification; (3) the value is ∞ when the model passed the verification, which means the expected BT is found. We next describe them in detail.

Type Classification. During the grammar-based search process, we may get plenty of candidate BTs with or without non-terminals. For the candidate BT without non-terminals, it's undoubtedly classified into the category of determined models; while for the candidate BT with non-terminals, its category depends on the reachability of non-terminals.

For example, the BT in Fig. 1 might be derived from a candidate BT with non-terminals that only has difference in the rightmost as shown in Fig. 7, wherein A is a non-terminal symbol. For modelling candidate BTs with non-terminals, we treat all the non-terminal symbols as the symbol Unknown, which represents the behavior of this node is unknown and full of possibility. Then, the corresponding CSP model can be obtained by replacing the whole part of Pickup in Fig. 4 with Unknown → BT (line 19 and line 27 of Fig. 4). Intuitively, the reachable of Unknown in CSP model, *i.e.*, $\mathcal{G} \neg$ Unknown is not valid, means there exist the possibility to satisfy any specifications, even it doesn't yet. Conversely, the unreachable means that the behavior of BT has been determined. Therefore, we

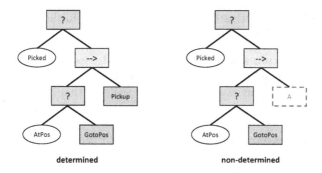

Fig. 7. The candidate BTs.

classify those candidate BTs with non-terminals into different categories based on the reachability checking.

The Verification for Determined Models. For the model without Unknown, or the model wherein Unknown is unreachable, we invoke the verifier to check whether it satisfies specifications. If the verifier returns *valid*, then we found the expected BT and stopped the search; otherwise, the value of this model's corresponding candidate BT is set as $-\infty$, which implies this candidate BT will never be explored again, and we abandon it to prune the search space.

The Verification for Non-determined Models. For the model wherein Unknown is reachable, we also invoke the verifier to check the model's correctness *w.r.t.* specification φ. If the verifier returns *valid*, then we found the expected BT and stopped the search; otherwise, we got a counter-example like $event_1$; $event_2$; ...; $event_N$. Next we evaluate the value in the following four aspects, wherein the first two focus on the BT itself, the last two focus on the specification.

- V_1: we evaluated the ratio of terminal symbols in the candidate BT to investigate the model's determinacy.
- V_2: we evaluated the expansion way that results in the current candidate BT to investigate its influence.
- V_3: we evaluated the relevance between the specification and the candidate BT from the perspective of literal comparison.
- V_4: we evaluated the relevance between the specification and the candidate BT from the perspective of verification result.

Given the action nodes {GotoPos, Pickup}, the condition nodes {Picked, AtPos}, the function descriptions shown in Table 1, and the specification $\varphi = \mathcal{F}$ picked_s, we take the candidate BT with non-terminals in Fig. 7 as an example. We depict those values one by one: V_1 is calculated as the ratio of the already existing terminals to all symbols in the BT like $\frac{3}{4} = 0.75$, while V_2

evaluates the influence of this BT's expansion manners in the expansion phase, which can be classified into three different cases:

- **key terminal expansion**: the BT is expanded based on a non-terminal to terminal rules, wherein the new terminal symbol is related to the existing terminals *w.r.t.* nodes' function. For example, the case that (? AtPos GotoPos) is derived from (? AtPos A), wherein AtPos is entangled in the function of GotoPos as shown in Table 1.
- **non-terminal expansion**: the BT is expanded based on a non-terminal to non-terminal rules like Root → A.
- **other terminal expansion**: the BT is expanded based on a non-terminal to terminal rules that the new symbol is not related to the existing terminals *w.r.t.* nodes' function.

We prefer **key terminal expansion**, followed by **non-terminal expansion**, and finally **other terminal expansion**. The $\mathbf{V}_2$ value of three cases is set as 0.9, 0.6, 0.3, respectively.

As for the other two values, the literal relevance value $\mathbf{V}_3$ is calculated as the proportion of the current occurring terminals in φ like $\frac{1}{1} = 1$ (here φ only contains Picked and Picked exists); while the verification relevance value $\mathbf{V}_4$ measures the complexity of counter-example. It's worth noting that the longer the counter-example trace generated, the closer the behavior of the candidate BT may be likely to φ. For convenience, we project the length of counter-example (event$_1$; event$_2$; ...; event$_N$) to a value by the formula $\mathbf{V}_4 = \ln N/(\ln N + 2)$. The final value $\mathbf{V}$ is the sum of those four values. Based on the value feedback, we continue advance the later backpropagation phase and search in a new round.

Optimizations. To improve the efficiency, we optimize the search process in two aspects. The first one is to make MCTS parallelizing. Note that, for the candidate BTs collected by the expansion phase, we usually do the simulation phase for each candidate BT at a time. However, the simulation phase can be parallelizing. Here we take a leaf parallelization method [23], which invokes multiple threads to deal with those candidate BTs generated by the expansion phase in parallel, then collects all simulation values to propagate backwards through the tree by one single thread. This parallelization can effectively reduce the time required for the simulation phase. The second one is to utilize the nodes' function to make an early checking for the candidate BTs before invoking the verifier. For example, the candidate BT (? Picked (→ AtPos GotoPos) Root) can be pruned in advance although the non-terminal Root is reachable. The reason is that the success of AtPos relies on GotoPos under the function descriptions shown in Table 1. However, in this case, the failure of AtPos will skip the execution of AtPos, which makes the status of AtPos to be always failure. Therefore, we can deduct that there exists a redundant structure in view of BT's execution and we can prune it for the simplicity of the expected synthesized BT. This pruning can effectively reduce the search space without invoking the verifier.

5   Demonstration

We have implemented our method as a prototype in Python and applied it on several representative robotic missions. To demonstrate its effectiveness and efficiency, we have conducted the following experiments: (1) the comparison experiment between our framework (MCTS with verifier) and the framework instantiated as MCTS with a simple simulator used by [16] (MCTS with simulator); (2) the ablation experiment for the value designed in Sect. 4.2.

5.1   Experimental Setup

We collect several representative robotic missions which are shown in Table 3, wherein the first column shows the names of missions and the second column gives a short description for missions. The detailed information about those missions is provided in the website[1]. The time threshold for synthesis is 1 h. All the experiments were carried out on a machine with an Intel Core i9 processor (3.6 GHz, 8 cores) and 8 GB of RAM, and the operating system is Ubuntu 22.04.

5.2   Comparison Experiment

Case Study. We take the mission **Alarm** as an example. The mission requires the robot to react with the unpredictable environment factor Alarm. The robot may navigate to the position A (GotoA) to complete TaskA (DoTaskA) if the alarm occurs or navigate to the position B (GotoB) to complete TaskB (DoTaskB) otherwise. Given the action nodes {GotoA, GotoB, DoTaskA, DoTaskB} and the condition ndoes {Alarm, AtA, AtB, TaskFinishedA, TaskFinishedB}, the semantics for each action node is provided in Table 2.

Table 2. Nodes' function for mission Alarm.

Action	Requirement	Result
GotoA	\	AtA, ¬AtB
GotoB	\	¬AtA, AtB
DoTaskA	AtA, Alarm, ¬TaskFinishedA	TaskFinishedA
DoTaskB	AtB, ¬Alarm, ¬TaskFinishedB	TaskFinishedB

The specification φ is presented as follows. The first part declares the existence of an alarm and specifies that the robot needs to complete at least one of the two tasks. The second part specifies that whenever the alarm occurs, the robot is forbidden to complete TaskB until the alarm frees. The third one is similar.

---

[1] https://github.com/FM4BT/Synthesizer4BT.

$$\mathcal{F}\,(\texttt{Alarm\_s} \lor \texttt{Alarm\_f}) \ \land \ \mathcal{F}\,(\texttt{DoTaskA\_s} \lor \texttt{DoTaskB\_s})$$

$$\land\,\mathcal{G}\,(\texttt{Alarm\_s} \rightarrow ((\lnot\texttt{DoTaskB\_s}\,\mathcal{U}\,\texttt{Alarm\_f}) \lor \mathcal{G}\,\lnot\texttt{DoTaskB\_s}))$$

$$\land\,\mathcal{G}\,(\texttt{Alarm\_f} \rightarrow ((\lnot\texttt{DoTaskA\_s}\,\mathcal{U}\,\texttt{Alarm\_s}) \lor \mathcal{G}\,\lnot\texttt{DoTaskA\_s}))$$

Our method (MCTS with verifier) successfully synthesized the expected BT as shown in the left of Fig. 8, while MCTS with simulator didn't. After an hour of learning, it obtained the synthesized BT as presented in the right of Fig. 8. The result BT failed to complete the mission.

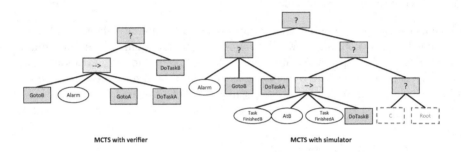

Fig. 8. The synthesis result for the mission **Alarm**.

Overall Results. The full experimental results are presented in Table 3. The third column records the time-cost of our method (MCTS with verifier) to synthesize the expected BT (✔) for each mission. The fifth column represents that no expected BT is synthesized by MCTS with simulator in one hour (✖ 3600 s). The latter lacks the evaluation and pruning of non-determined models, as well as the timely feedback from simulators. The detailed synthesis information can be found in the aforementioned website. Note that, compared with the other missions, the significant time overhead increase for the mission **Alarm** is mainly due to the difficulty of determining the position where the node Alarm should locate. The forth column represents the number of pruned candidate BTs by the verifier, and the corresponding proportion of these pruned ones in the total verified ones is labeled. There is about 11.6% of the candidate BTs are pruned in average, whose number of leaf nodes is mostly no more than 3. The result implies that we avoid a plenty of meaningless expansions in the early stage.

5.3 Ablation Experiment

Besides, we also investigate the rationality of the value design (V_1, V_2, V_3 and V_4) in Sect. 4.2. By disabling the four values individually, we found that the final synthesis time-cost increased to some extent, or even timed out in 16 cases out of 20, as shown in Fig. 9. The result implies that the rationality of the value design in guiding the search process.

Table 3. The description and experimental result of missions.

Mission	Description	MCTS with verifier		MCTS with simulator
		Result	#Pruned	Result
Charge	recharge when the battery is low	✅ 174s	79(15.3%)	❌ 3600s
Patrol$_1$	visit pos$_A$, pos$_B$, pos$_C$ without an order	✅ 124s	57(14.8%)	❌ 3600s
Patrol$_2$	visit pos$_A$, pos$_B$, pos$_C$ in order	✅ 182s	78(14.0%)	❌ 3600s
Pickup	pick up a cube from pos$_A$ and place it at pos$_B$	✅ 1102s	313(9.1%)	❌ 3600s
Alarm	do different tasks depending on the status of alarm	✅ 2535s	353(4.9%)	❌ 3600s

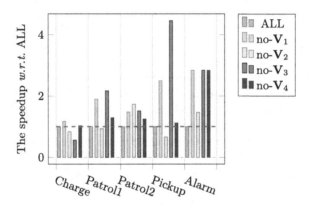

Fig. 9. The speedup *w.r.t.* ALL for each mission and ALL includes all four values.

5.4 Discussion

We are currently primarily focused on BTs composed of only *action, condition, sequences,* and *fallbacks* nodes. The main bottleneck of our method lies in two aspects. (1) How to design the suitable formal specification to depict the behavior of BTs? This problem can be relieved by utilizing large language models to translate natural language to temporal logics as [9] does. This is not a focal point of our work. (2) How to improve the efficiency of finding the expected BT? This problem can be relieved by designing more effective heuristic search strategy, which is better to customize the heuristic search based on the specific scenario. In this work, we design a general search strategy and demonstrated its effectiveness in the experiment.

6   Related Work

There are many works dedicated to automatically designing and constructing BTs [15]. For example, QL-BT [10] applied reinforcement learning (RL) methods to decide the child nodes' execution order and further optimize early behavior tree prototypes. Banerjee [2] used RL methods to obtain control policies, then converted it into the expected BTs, while Scheide *et al.* [29] utilized Monte Carlo DAG Search to learn BTs based on the formal grammar. Besides, the evolution-inspired learning is another choice for synthesizing BTs [16,18,21,25], which evolves BTs by the generic programming. However, for the above methods, the burden of simulation time for learning and evolving are usually intractable and the synthesized BT just tends to rather than guarantees to meet the specification.

Apart from those learning-based synthesis methods, there also exist some planning-based ones. Colledanchise *et al.* [5] and Cai *et al.* [4] synthesized BTs based on the idea of back chaining, which iteratively extended the action to meet the goal condition. Starting from the formal specifications, Tumova *et al.* [32] constructed an I/O automaton that is the maximally satisfying discrete control strategy *w.r.t.* State/Event Linear Temporal Logic, then converted it into BTs. Colledanchise *et al.* [6] and Tadewos [31] *et al.* taken a divide-and-conquer way to synthesize BTs whose missions are expressed in Fragmented-Linear Temporal Logic. For the method's effectiveness, the expressiveness of those synthesized BTs is usually sacrificed by the limited form of specifications. Compared with that, this work does not impose any restrictions on the specification form.

As regards the verification method for BTs, Biggar *et al.* [3] provided a framework for checking whether the given BT's behavior satisfies LTL specifications. Henn *et al.* [12] utilized Linear Constrained Horn Clauses to verify the BT's safety properties. Serbinowski *et al.* [30] translated BTs into nuXmv models for verification. In this work, we model the behavior of BTs as CSP models and utilize the verifier to check its correctness.

7   Conclusion

In this paper, we proposed a formal verification based synthesis method to automatically construct BTs, which combines Monte Carlo Tree Search with a CSP modelling and verification method. In this method, we innovatively utilized the verifier to complete the simulation phase in MCTS and make the search space pruning based on verification results. The application of our method on several representative robotic missions indicates its promising.

The future work lies in several directions: (1) further exploiting the counter-example traces provided by the verifier, like analyzing the invalidness reason, to guide the search and facilitate the pruning; (2) supporting the modelling for more control node types, like *Parallel, Decorator, Memorized Sequences, Memorized Fallbacks*, and so on; (3) utilizing the concurrence feature of CSP models to verify the robotic mission involved with multi-BTs.

Acknowledgement. This research was supported by National Key R&D Program of China (No. 2022YFB4501903) and the NSFC Programs (No. 62172429 and 62032024).

References

1. Baier, C., Katoen, J.: Principles of model checking (2008)
2. Banerjee, B.: Autonomous acquisition of behavior trees for robot control. In: 2018 IEEE/RSJ International Conference on Intelligent Robots and Systems, IROS 2018, Madrid, Spain, 1–5 October 2018, pp. 3460–3467. IEEE (2018)
3. Biggar, O., Zamani, M.: A framework for formal verification of behavior trees with linear temporal logic. IEEE Robot. Autom. Lett. **5**(2), 2341–2348 (2020)
4. Cai, Z., Li, M., Huang, W., Yang, W.: BT expansion: a sound and complete algorithm for behavior planning of intelligent robots with behavior trees. In: Thirty-Fifth AAAI Conference on Artificial Intelligence, AAAI 2021, Virtual Event, pp. 6058–6065 (2021)
5. Colledanchise, M., Almeida, D., Ögren, P.: Towards blended reactive planning and acting using behavior trees. In: International Conference on Robotics and Automation, ICRA 2019, Montreal, QC, Canada, 20–24 May 2019, pp. 8839–8845. IEEE (2019)
6. Colledanchise, M., Murray, R.M., Ögren, P.: Synthesis of correct-by-construction behavior trees. In: 2017 IEEE/RSJ International Conference on Intelligent Robots and Systems, IROS 2017, Vancouver, BC, Canada, 24–28 September 2017, pp. 6039–6046. IEEE (2017)
7. Colledanchise, M., Ögren, P.: How behavior trees modularize robustness and safety in hybrid systems. In: 2014 IEEE/RSJ International Conference on Intelligent Robots and Systems, Chicago, IL, USA, 14–18 September 2014, pp. 1482–1488. IEEE (2014)
8. Colledanchise, M., Ögren, P.: Behavior trees in robotics and AI: an introduction. CoRR abs/1709.00084 (2017)
9. Cosler, M., Hahn, C., Mendoza, D., Schmitt, F., Trippel, C.: nl2spec: interactively translating unstructured natural language to temporal logics with large language models. In: Enea, C., Lal, A. (eds.) Computer Aided Verification. CAV 2023. LNCS, vol. 13965, pp. 383–396. Springer, Cham (2023). https://doi.org/10.1007/978-3-031-37703-7_18
10. Dey, R., Child, C.: QL-BT: enhancing behaviour tree design and implementation with q-learning. In: 2013 IEEE Conference on Computational Intelligence in Games (CIG), Niagara Falls, ON, Canada, 11–13 August 2013, pp. 1–8. IEEE (2013)
11. Gibson-Robinson, T., Armstrong, P., Boulgakov, A., Roscoe, A.W.: FDR3 — a modern refinement checker for CSP. In: Ábrahám, E., Havelund, K. (eds.) TACAS 2014. LNCS, vol. 8413, pp. 187–201. Springer, Heidelberg (2014). https://doi.org/10.1007/978-3-642-54862-8_13
12. Henn, T., Völker, M., Kowalewski, S., Trinh, M., Petrovic, O., Brecher, C.: Verification of behavior trees using linear constrained horn clauses. In: Groote, J.F., Huisman, M. (eds.) Formal Methods for Industrial Critical Systems. FMICS 2022. LNCS, vol. 13487, pp. 211–225. Springer, Cham (2022). https://doi.org/10.1007/978-3-031-15008-1_14
13. Hoare, C.A.R.: Communicating Sequential Processes (1985)
14. Hopcroft, J.E., Motwani, R., Ullman, J.D.: Introduction to Automata Theory, Languages, and Computation, 3rd edn. Pearson international edition. Addison-Wesley, Boston (2007)

15. Iovino, M., Scukins, E., Styrud, J., Ögren, P., Smith, C.: A survey of behavior trees in robotics and AI. Robot. Auton. Syst. **154**, 104096 (2022)
16. Iovino, M., Styrud, J., Falco, P., Smith, C.: Learning behavior trees with genetic programming in unpredictable environments. In: IEEE International Conference on Robotics and Automation, ICRA 2021, Xi'an, China, 30 May–5 June 2021, pp. 4591–4597. IEEE (2021)
17. Lan, M., Xu, Y., Lai, S., Chen, B.M.: A modular mission management system for micro aerial vehicles. In: 14th IEEE International Conference on Control and Automation, ICCA 2018, Anchorage, AK, USA, 12–15 June 2018, pp. 293–299. IEEE (2018)
18. Lim, C.-U., Baumgarten, R., Colton, S.: Evolving behaviour trees for the commercial game DEFCON. In: Di Chio, C., et al. (eds.) EvoApplications 2010. LNCS, vol. 6024, pp. 100–110. Springer, Heidelberg (2010). https://doi.org/10.1007/978-3-642-12239-2_11
19. Marzinotto, A., Colledanchise, M., Smith, C., Ögren, P.: Towards a unified behavior trees framework for robot control. In: 2014 IEEE International Conference on Robotics and Automation, ICRA 2014, Hong Kong, China, May 31–7 June 2014, pp. 5420–5427 (2014)
20. Mateas, M., Stern, A.: A behavior language for story-based believable agents. IEEE Intell. Syst. **17**(4), 39–47 (2002)
21. Neupane, A., Goodrich, M.A.: Learning swarm behaviors using grammatical evolution and behavior trees. In: Proceedings of the Twenty-Eighth International Joint Conference on Artificial Intelligence, IJCAI 2019, Macao, China, 10–16 August 2019, pp. 513–520 (2019)
22. Nilsson, N.J.: Teleo-reactive programs for agent control. J. Artif. Intell. Res. **1**, 139–158 (1994)
23. Papakonstantinou, G.K., Andronikos, T., Drositis, I.: On parallelization of UET/UET-UCT loops. Neural Parallel Sci. Comput. **9**(3–4), 279–318 (2001)
24. PAT Website. http://pat.comp.nus.edu.sg
25. Perez, D., Nicolau, M., O'Neill, M., Brabazon, A.: Evolving behaviour trees for the Mario AI competition using grammatical evolution. In: Di Chio, C., et al. (eds.) EvoApplications 2011. LNCS, vol. 6624, pp. 123–132. Springer, Heidelberg (2011). https://doi.org/10.1007/978-3-642-20525-5_13
26. Puga, G.F., Gómez-Martín, M.A., Gómez-Martín, P.P., Díaz-Agudo, B., González-Calero, P.A.: Query-enabled behavior trees. IEEE Trans. Comput. Intell. AI Games **1**(4), 298–308 (2009)
27. Quinlan, J.R.: Induction of decision trees. Mach. Learn. **1**(1), 81–106 (1986)
28. Ramírez, M., et al.: Integrated hybrid planning and programmed control for real time UAV maneuvering. In: Proceedings of the 17th International Conference on Autonomous Agents and MultiAgent Systems, AAMAS 2018, Stockholm, Sweden, 10–15 July 2018, pp. 1318–1326 (2018)
29. Scheide, E., Best, G., Hollinger, G.A.: Behavior tree learning for robotic task planning through Monte Carlo DAG search over a formal grammar. In: IEEE International Conference on Robotics and Automation, ICRA 2021, Xi'an, China, 2021, pp. 4837–4843 (2021)
30. Serbinowski, B., Johnson, T.T.: BehaVerify: verifying temporal logic specifications for behavior trees. In: Schlingloff, B.H., Chai, M. (eds.) Software Engineering and Formal Methods. SEFM 2022. LNCS, vol. 13550, pp. 307–323. Springer, Cham (2022). https://doi.org/10.1007/978-3-031-17108-6_19

31. Tadewos, T.G., Newaz, A.A.R., Karimoddini, A.: Specification-guided behavior tree synthesis and execution for coordination of autonomous systems. Expert Syst. Appl. **201**, 117022 (2022)
32. Tumova, J., Marzinotto, A., Dimarogonas, D.V., Kragic, D.: Maximally satisfying LTL action planning. In: 2014 IEEE/RSJ International Conference on Intelligent Robots and Systems, Chicago, IL, USA, 14–18 September 2014, pp. 1503–1510. IEEE (2014)

SeHBPL: Behavioral Semantics-Based Patch Presence Test for Binaries

Jintao Huang[1,2], Gaosheng Wang[1,2], Zhiqiang Shi[1(✉)], Fei Lv[1],
Weidong Zhang[1], and Shichao Lv[1]

[1] Institute of Information Engineering, CAS, Beijing, China
{huangjintao,wanggaosheng,shizhiqiang,lvfei,zhangweidong,
lvshichao}@iie.ac.cn
[2] University of Chinese Academy of Sciences, Beijing, China

Abstract. Patch presence testing is a critical component of risk and loss assessment for software vulnerabilities. By determining whether a patch has been applied to their software, organizations can better understand their exposure to potential threats. Many schemes for patch presence testing have be proposed. However, they did not consider the challenges brought about by various compilation options, they are not practical when testing patch presence for binaries compiled with complex compilation configurations.

To address the issue, we propose a new semantic-level feature named "behavioral semantics" to represent fixing patches precisely and stably. Behavioral semantics is a high-level abstraction of functions within binaries and is not affected by compilation differences. It consists of the behavior performed by the function and the path constraints for the behavior. We implement a system named *SeHBPL* based on behavioral semantics, and test patch presence by generating a behavioral semantics signature of the patch and searching for it in the target binary.

SeHBPL is tested with 6,912 binaries corresponding to 91 vulnerabilities and achieves high accuracy and precision, outperforming the state-of-the-art tool. This paper presents a novel approach to patch presence testing that overcomes the limitations of current methods and has the potential to significantly improve risk and loss assessment.

Keywords: Patch presence testing · Behavioral semantics · Risk assessment

1 Introduction

Open-source software is popular now. According to Synopsys [1], which examined over 2400 codebases across 17 industries, 97% of codebases contain open-source code, with 78% of code being open-source. However, such popularity facilitates the widespread dissemination of vulnerabilities that exist in open-source code [2–4]. In 2014, a critical vulnerability named "*Heartbleed*"[1] occurred in the popular *OpenSSL* cryptographic software library, allowing for the theft of protected

---

[1] https://cve.mitre.org/cgi-bin/cvename.cgi?name=cve-2014-0160.

H. Hermanns et al. (Eds.): SETTA 2023, LNCS 14464, pp. 92–111, 2024.
https://doi.org/10.1007/978-981-99-8664-4_6

information [5]. As *OpenSSL* is a fundamental component used for SSL/TLS encryption, this vulnerability affected around 17% of SSL web servers using certificates issued by trusted certificate authorities [6].

To mitigate the large-scale impact caused by such vulnerabilities, which can impede production and daily life, downstream application users must conduct patch presence testing on software using the affected component. Patch presence testing aims to determine whether a patch for a specific vulnerability has been applied to a target binary. In terms of the techniques used, there are three main approaches to conducting patch presence testing: (1) proof-of-concept (PoC) based penetration testing for the target binary; (2) identifying the version of the component used in the binary and checking if it falls within the scope of the vulnerability (e.g., OSSPolice [7]); and (3) deriving signatures from the patch and then determining the patching status of the target binary by signature searching (e.g., BINXRAY [8]).

However, the PoC program for a specific vulnerability is not always available. Additionally, the conditions for a PoC program to successfully trigger a vulnerability are strict, and the design of the software and the environment in which it is running can all affect the effectiveness of triggering. For methods based on version identification, they are not fine-grained enough. Developers can customize code according to their needs and partially use the library code, which can result in inaccurate patch existence test results. For signature search-based approaches, the features they currently use are not robust enough. These features differ greatly in binaries compiled with different compilation configurations. The schemes proposed by previous researches are not applicable to the binaries compiled with complex compilation options, this has created a large gap between existing approaches and real-world programs. In short, patch presence testing across compilation configurations remains an open problem in practice [9,10].

To bridge the gap, we introduce behavioral semantics, which is defined as a combination of behavior and path constraints on the behavior, and is described with a tuple "*<Behavior, Constraints>*". Based on behavioral semantics, we have developed a system named *SeHBPL* which determines patch presence in three steps: (1) parsing source code to obtain function definitions and data structures; (2) extracting behavioral semantics from binaries; and (3) comparing behavioral semantics sets of two reference binaries to derive patch signatures and then searching for these signatures in target binaries.

SeHBPL has been tested with 6,912 binaries those are compiled with different compilation configurations. The results show that *SeHBPL* achieves high accuracy and precision and is highly tolerant to diverse compilation settings, outperforming the state-of-the-art approach.

The contributions are summarized as follows:

– **The concept of behavioral semantics.** This paper proposes the concept of behavioral semantics, a high-level abstraction of functions with high tolerance for various compilation options.

- **A new approach for patch presence testing.** This paper presents the design and implementation of *SeHBPL*, a system for accurate and precise patch presence testing using behavioral semantics. *SeHBPL* is highly tolerant to various compilation options, making it more practical.
- **Comprehensive evaluation.** *SeHBPL* is tested with a large corpus of test cases to evaluate its effectiveness and efficiency. Evaluations show that *SeHBPL* achieves high accuracy (>88%) and precision (>86%), outperforming the state-of-the-art tool.

2   Overview

The patch presence testing addressed in this paper targets open source components utilized in software. Given a target binary and specific vulnerability information, the goal is to determine whether the patch fixing the vulnerability has been applied to the target binary. To perform patch presence testing, the following assumptions are made:

(1) Target binaries are not obfuscated. As obfuscation schemes will change the code executed by CPUs and result in differences in behavior, they are outside the scope of *SeHBPL*.
(2) Source code for the binary is available. As the focus is on open source software, their source code is readily accessible to the public. It requires only engineering effort to download the related source code from the Internet.
(3) Addresses of functions related to the patch can be obtained in target binary. *SeHBPL* requires the entry point of a function to hook it for the parameters passed in. To determine the location of functions, researches on binary code search [11–14] can be used.

2.1   Challenges

The challenges of patch presence testing are summarized as follows:

(1) Subtleness of a change in patch. Patches typically result in modest modifications [15]. The security patch for CVE-2018-18557[2], an "out-of-bounds write" vulnerability in the library *LibTIFF*, is shown in Fig. 1. The patch only changes the arguments of a function call, and does not affect the control flow. Such minor changes are difficult to handle with code similarity-based approaches since these methods require certain tolerances for code variations.
(2) Various compilation options. When a component is released in binary, its code is usually optimized using multiple compilation optimization options. Different options enable compilers to employ different optimization algorithms. The compilation optimization option '-Os', for example, allows the compiler to reduce the size of the generated binary files as much as possible during compilation [16]. As a result, control flows and instructions vary significantly in binaries produced with different compilation configurations.

---

[2] https://gitlab.com/libtiff/libtiff/-/commit/681748ec.

2.2 Behavioral Semantics

Considering these challenges, we summarize the characteristics that practical patch signatures should possess. These characteristics include uniqueness, sensitivity, and stability.

(1) **Uniqueness**: In signature search-based schemes, the uniqueness of the signature is crucial. Patch features should not be easily duplicated to avoid misjudgments and a high false positive rate.

(2) **Sensitivity**: Changes introduced by a patch can be subtle and only involve minor updates. This requires patch features to be sensitive enough to detect such slight differences.

(3) **Stability**: Good signatures should remain consistent under various compilation options. This is necessary as different compilation settings are used in practical development.

To construct patch signatures that conform to these principles, the concept of behavioral semantics is proposed. The behavioral semantics of a function are defined as the behavior in the function and the path constraints on the behavior. In *SeHBPL*, behavior includes function calls, memory reads, and memory writes. Function calls consist of the name of the called function and the arguments passed to it. Memory reads consist of the target address, the data read, and the size of the data. Memory writes are similar to memory reads. Path constraints in *SeHBPL* are restrictions on variables along paths from the function entry to the behavior position.

Taking the patch shown in Fig. 1 as an example. The line in red is to be removed while the line in green is to be added. The changes introduced by the patch are too subtle to change the Control Flow Graph (CFG). However, the changes in behavioral semantics are significant. Since the data involved in the behavior is part of the behavioral semantics, the changes in the arguments of function *TIFFReverseBits* will result in completely new behavioral semantics. This demonstrates the sensitivity of behavioral semantics to subtle changes.

```
01 static int JBIGDecode(
02     TIFF* tif, uint8* buffer,
03     tmsize_t size, uint16 s) {
04     // ......
05     if (isFillOrder(tif, tif->tif_dir.td_fillorder))
06     {
07 -       TIFFReverseBits(tif->tif_rawdata,
08 -                       tif->tif_rawdatasize);
09 +       TIFFReverseBits(tif->tif_rawcp,
10 +                       tif->tif_rawcc);
11     }
12     // ......
13 }
```

Fig. 1. The source code of CVE-2018-18557

The path constraint in behavioral semantics consists of a series of branching conditions along the execution path from the function entry to the associated

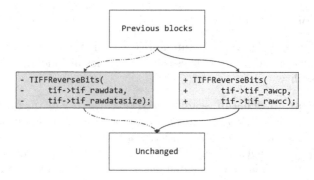

Fig. 2. The CFG of CVE-2018-18557

behavior. Executions that conform to these constraints will reach the behavior no matter where they end up. Furthermore, the data involved in a behavior differentiates it from other behaviors subject to the same path constraints, ensuring that each behavioral semantics is unique.

Behavioral semantics are defined in source code written by developers and will not be altered by compilers or compilation settings. The comparison of behavioral semantics is based on semantic equality, making them unaffected by changes to control flow and instruction sequence that do not change semantics. As a result, behavioral semantics are more robust to various compilation options compared to other features and are more reliable.

2.3 Insights

Behavioral semantics is based on the following insights:

(1) The behavior of a function remains invariant to compilation settings. Regardless of the compiler or compilation options used, the intended behavior of a function cannot be altered. For instance, if a function *func* in the source code is designed to output the sum of its inputs, the binary program generated from that source code will not output the result of the subtraction of its inputs.

(2) The constraints that must be satisfied when performing an action are unchanged. Suppose that two binaries Bin_a and Bin_b are generated from the same source code with different compilation settings. If a memory write action M_w in binary Bin_a can only be conducted when "$len>0,\ n>32$", then M_w cannot be performed within binary Bin_b when "$len=0,\ n=3$", i.e., both the action itself and its path constraints remain constant.

2.4 Running Example

The CFG of the function *JBIGDecode* related to CVE-2018-18557 is shown in Fig. 2. As can be seen, the CFG remains unchanged after the patch is applied. This means that the approaches which rely on analyzing changes of the CFG to test patch presence, like researches proposed by Sun et al. [10], will not be effective in this case. As for PDiff [9], which utilizes code semantics as well, it also records memory operation in functions. However, it uses the name of the called function to represent a function call, changes like this will be ignored by it. Moreover, in most binaries, symbol tables are unavailable, thus it's difficult to know the name of callee functions, let alone to use the name to represent function calls.

SeHBPL tests patch presence in target binary in 3 steps:

Step 1: Parsing the source code. *SeHBPL* first identifies the function affected by the vulnerability (i.e. *JBIGDecode* in this case), and then parses the source code to obtain the definition of the function as well as the arguments of the function. If an argument is of a composite data type, such as *struct* in C language, *SeHBPL* will parse each field of the type recursively. In addition to the definition of *JBIGDecode* itself, *SeHBPL* also extracts the definition of each function called by *JBIGDecode*.

Step 2: Behavioral semantics extraction. At first, *SeHBPL* constructs symbolic data with with definitions extracted from the source code. Then it sets memory content with symbolic data, and sets hooks for function calls. Finally, *SeHBPL* extracts behavioral semantics with symbolic execution powered by *angr*. For CVE-2018-18557 that shown in Fig. 1, before the patch is applied, the behavioral semantics for the function call in lines *07* and *08* is "< *TIFFReverseBits(tif->tif_rawdata, tif->tif_rawdatasize), isFillOrder(tif, tif-> tif_dir.td_fillorder)$\neq$0>*". After the patch being applied, the behavioral semantics is "< *TIFFReverseBits(tif->tif_rawcp, tif->tif_rawcc), isFillOrder(tif, tif-> tif_dir.td_fillorder)$\neq$0>*".

Step 3: Patch presence testing. The differences in behavioral semantics brought about by a patch are regarded as the signatures of the patch. *SeHBPL* searches for the data that satisfies the constraints existing in patch signatures, and then sets memory space of the target binary. After that, *SeHBPL* performs symbolic execution on the target binary, and extracts behavioral semantics from it. In the case for CVE-2018-18557, *SeHBPL* searches for possible values of *tif* and *tif->tif_dir.td_fillorder* that satisfy the constraint "*isFillOrder(tif, tif->tif_dir.td_fillorder)$\neq$0*". As for arguments that are not involved in these constraints, their values do not affect the extraction of target behavioral semantics, so their values are randomly chosen according to their constraints. *SeHBPL* sets the memory space for the target binary with these values, and performs symbolic execution on the related function in the target binary. Finally, *SeHBPL* checks the behavioral semantics set BS_t of the target binary. If BS_t contains the behavioral semantics "< *TIFFReverseBits(tif->tif_rawcp, tif->tif_rawcc), isFillOrder(tif, tif->tif_dir.td_fillorder)$\neq$0>*" and does not contain "< *TIFFReverseBits(tif->tif_rawdata, tif->tif_rawdatasize), isFillOrder(tif, tif->tif_dir.td_fillorder)$\neq$0 >*", then the binary is thought to be patched.

3   Approach Design

The overview of *SeHBPL* is presented with Fig. 3. *SeHBPL* tests patch presence based on related vulnerability information and source code. Then *SeHBPL* determines if a target binary is patched in three steps, namely "source code parsing", "behavioral semantics extracting" and "behavioral semantics matching".

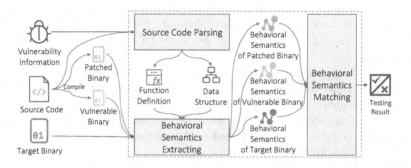

Fig. 3. Workflow of *SeHBPL*. Dashed line framed part is *SeHBPL*.

3.1 Source Code Parsing

When parsing source code for function definitions, *SeHBPL* extracts function names, argument names, argument data types, and returned data types.

Considering the source code shown in Fig. 4(a) and suppose that the target function is *Func*. At first, *SeHBPL* extracts the definition for function *Func* from the source code, including the function name "Func", the returned data type *void* and the definitions for arguments. Then, *SeHBPL* extracts definitions for function *setName*, which is called by *Func*. Similar to function *JBIGDecode*, *SeHBPL* extracts argument definitions for *setName*.

Data structures consist of basic data types (e.g., *char*) and composite data types (e.g., *struct*). During source code parsing, *SeHBPL* recursively parses the data type to which each data field in a composite data type belongs.

3.2 Behavioral Semantics Extracting

SeHBPL relies on *angr* for symbolic execution. For normal binaries, *SeHBPL* loads them with the base addresses declared in their ELF headers. For PIE and shared libraries, they are loaded with the base address 0x0.

Figure 4 shows the behavioral semantics extraction process. *SeHBPL* symbolizes memory space and registers with the names of the variables stored within them. Suppose that the target function in Fig. 4(a) is *Func*. *SeHBPL* first initializes memory for it with its definition as if it were called. To simplify the illustration, it is assumed that the arguments for *Func* are passed on the stack. *SeHBPL* creates two pieces of symbolic data, Sym_a and Sym_p, with the names of the arguments in *Func*, and stores them in the correct place in *Func*'s stack. As argument p is a pointer to type *Person*, which is a structure type, *SeHBPL* allocates a memory space Mem_{person} of size *sizeof(Person)* for it and replaces

Sym_p in the stack with the address of Mem_{person}. For Mem_{person}, $SeHBPL$ initializes it with symbolic data created with the name of each data field in $Person$. Furthermore, as the field $name$ in $Person$ belongs to type $char^*$, $SeHBPL$ allocates a new memory area of 256 bytes, namely Mem_{name}, and fills it with the symbolic data named by $Mem_{name[idx]}$, one for each byte, where idx ranges from 0 to 255. Finally, $SeHBPL$ replaces $name$ in Mem_{person} with the address of Mem_{name}.

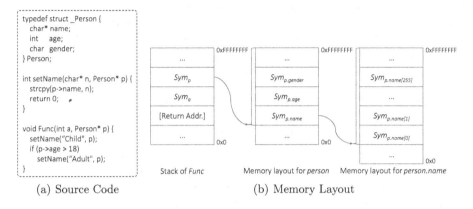

(a) Source Code   (b) Memory Layout

Fig. 4. Behavioral Semantics Extraction.

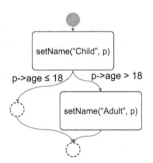

Fig. 5. Behavior Graph

After initializing the memory for $Func$, $SeHBPL$ catches behaviors using symbolic execution. $SeHBPL$ sets hooks for each function call and memory operation. If the behavior is performed by $Func$ itself, $SeHBPL$ records it and extracts the involved data as well as the path constraints on the behavior. For a memory operation, $SeHBPL$ records it in the same way as other works do, namely by recording the operating address, operated data, and data size. For a function call, however, $SeHBPL$ not only records the name of the called function but also the arguments passed within the call. This level of detail makes *SeHBPL* more sensitive than approaches that only record function names when a patch changes the arguments of function calls.

SeHBPL relies on behavior graph to construct behavioral semantics after all the behavior be captured. The source code of the function *Func* in Fig. 4(a) can be transformed into the behavior graph shown with Fig. 5. In a behavior graph, an edge e connecting node v with node t indicates that to perform actions in node t after node v occurs, the constraint on edge e must be satisfied. The path constraints for each behavior in rectangle r consist of a series of branch conditions represented by edges connecting the entrance node (dashed-line circle in red) to r. A rectangle node in the behavior graph represents a set of behaviors under the same path constraints.

The extraction is not easy, it faces some challenges:

(1) Function pointers. Function pointers can be used as arguments in function calls and fields in composite data types. The uncertainty of a function pointer's value makes it difficult to determine the function to which the pointer points.

To address this issue, *SeHBPL* sets the value of a variable of function pointer type to a pseudo function entry. Then, *SeHBPL* hooks all function calls that target at the faked addresses and records all involved data. As for the function name in the call, *SeHBPL* generates a patterned name based on the definition of the type for it. For example, if there is a call to a variable of the function pointer type "HandleResultCb" with two arguments named "result" and "error" respectively, the name generated will be "FAKE_FUNC_HandleResultCb_result_error".

(2) Path explosion. *SeHBPL* extracts behavioral semantics based on symbolic execution. However, symbolic execution faces the problem of path explosion, which can consume a lot of resources and time during analysis. To alleviate the problem of path explosion, loops in functions are expanded only twice and constrained symbolic execution is used to avoid unnecessary explorations.

3.3   Behavioral Semantics Matching

Data is stored in memory and registers during the runtime of a program, so references to this data are actually to related memory units and registers. However, the same data can be stored at different memory addresses in different memory layout models, this makes the forms of behavior using this data vary and further make it difficult to compare behavioral semantics. For example, the variable v is stored at $addr_a$ and $addr_b$ in binary A and B respectively. When $addr_a$ is not equal to $addr_b$, the function calls that utilize v are $func(addr_a)$ and $func(addr_b)$, thus it it difficult to determine if the two behaviors utilize the same data.

To address the problem, *SeHBPL* symbolizes memory areas and registers with the names of the variables stored in them. Then it converts the references to these memory areas and registers to the references to corresponding symbolic data. As a result, all the references to the same variable have same forms, regardless of the exact addresses where the variable is stored. That means the function calls in binaries A and B that utilize v are now both transformed into *func(v)*.

Regarding behavior comparison, *SeHBPL* considers the behavior types and the data involved in the behavior, it deems two pieces of behavior identical only if they possess same behavior types and data. Meanwhile, *SeHBPL* employs semantic equality to compare the two path constraints. If a path constraint PC_1 has the same variable set V as another path constraint PC_2, and for each variable v in V, the constraints on it in both PC_1 and PC_2 are semantically equal, then PC_1 is regarded equal to PC_2. Furthermore, two pieces of behavioral semantics are only identical if they possess the same behavior and equal path constraints.

Assume that two behavioral semantics sets $BS_{patched}$ and BS_{vul} are extracted from reference binaries (i.e., patched and vulnerable ones) respectively, then the patch signature is represented as (BS_{add}, BS_{del}). Here,

$$\begin{aligned} BS_{add} &= BS_{patched} \setminus BS_{vul} \quad, \\ BS_{del} &= BS_{vul} \setminus BS_{patched} \end{aligned} \tag{1}$$

For each behavioral semantics in sets BS_{add} and BS_{del}, *SeHBPL* solves its constraints with *angr* [17] and then selects satisfied data to set the memory space of target binary. After performing symbolic execution on the target binary, *SeHBPL* obtains the behavioral semantics set BS_t of the target binary. If $BS_{add} \subset BS_t$ and $BS_{del} \cap BS_t = \emptyset$, the target binary is regarded to be patched by *SeHBPL*.

4   Evaluation

A prototype system, *SeHBPL*, has been implemented on top of *angr* with 5119 lines of Python code. And a set of evaluations were performed to address the following questions:

- Q1: Can *SeHBPL* reliably determine patch presence?
- Q2: Can *SeHBPL* tolerate diversities in compilation configurations?
- Q3: How does *SeHBPL*'s efficiency compare to that of state-of-the-art tools?
- Q4: Can behavioral semantics precisely reflect the changes in a patch?

4.1   Testing Data Setup

All the vulnerabilities that used in the evaluation are selected based on the following criteria:

- The fixing patch does not change the definition of vulnerable functions, including their names and arguments;
- The fixing patch does not change the definition of data structures involved in the arguments of vulnerable functions;
- The source code could be successfully parsed by current implementation of *SeHBPL*.

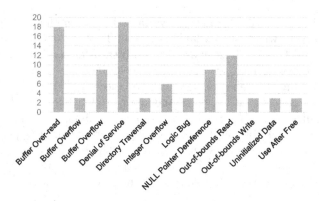

Fig. 6. Quantity of different CVE types.

Ultimately, 91 vulnerabilities were chosen, and their corresponding patches were collected. Detailed information on vulnerability types of these vulnerabilities are shown in Fig. 6. As the figure demonstrates, the collected vulnerabilities encompasses multiple common vulnerability types.

The source code associated with these vulnerabilities was obtained from their official repositories. To assess *SeHBPL*'s tolerance to varying compilation settings, the code was compiled using a combination of different compilers and optimization levels. For each vulnerability, two code releases were selected, one before and one after the introduction of the patch, to create target binaries. If the vulnerable function was present in multiple executable binaries after compilation, up to three binaries were chosen. In total, 6,912 binaries were generated, with details provided in Table 1.

For each of the 91 vulnerabilities, the most neighboring commits of code respectively before and after the patch was introduced were chosen to build reference binary pairs for it, with each pair including a patched version and a vulnerable version. In addition to compilation options composed of a combination of compilers and optimization levels, the code was compiled with various compilers and the default compilation options to create another part of reference binaries. In the end, 2,187 reference binary pairs were obtained.

4.2   Evaluation Setup

The evaluation setup is described below, and all evaluations were conducted on a workstation with an Intel Core i9-9880H CPU and 64 GB memory. Only one thread was used for testings on each binary.

Evaluation 1. This evaluation was conducted to evaluate the ability of *SeHBPL* to test for patch presence when confronted with binaries compiled using different compilers or optimization levels. When testing *SeHBPL*'s ability to perform patch presence testing across compilers, we use the reference binaries that are compiled with the compiler C and optimization level O, and then test the binaries that are compiled with the same optimization level O but different compilers, vice versa.

Table 1. Binaries in the dataset

The compiler	Optimization level	Targets[a]	Reference pair
gcc	O0	507	126
	O1	483	111
	O2	474	111
	O3	459	111
	Os	471	111
	default[b]	-	192
icc	O0	444	102
	O1	447	105
	O2	423	105
	O3	423	105
	Os	447	105
	default	–	168
clang-10	O0	486	120
	O1	486	120
	O2	471	105
	O3	438	105
	Os	453	105
	default	–	180

[a] Some binaries are lost due to compilation failure.
[b] Compiled with default configuration predefined by developers.

Evaluation 2. In practice, it can be difficult to reliably determine which compiler and optimization level were used to compile the target binary. Therefore, this evaluation was designed to assess whether *SeHBPL* is capable of testing patch presence across compilers and optimization levels simultaneously. The source code was compiled using different compilers and default compilation options preset by developers to create reference binary pairs, and the testing is then performed on target binaries that are compiled with all other compilers and optimization levels.

Evaluation 3. This evaluation was conducted to test whether behavioral semantics can express the changes introduced by a patch. The patches were manually compared with the patch signatures generated by *SeHBPL*. Within the current capability scope of *SeHBPL*, The judgment criteria for the effective extraction of patch features by *SeHBPL* are introduced as follows:

- The patch introduces new behavior - new behavioral semantics should be included in BS_{add};
- The patch deletes original behavior - original behavioral semantics should be included in BS_{del};
- The patch changes constraints - behavioral semantics constrained by the original constraints should be included in BS_{del}, and those constrained by the new constraints should be included in BS_{add}.

4.3   Evaluation on Effectiveness

SeHBPL was evaluated with 22,872 (reference binaries, target binary) pairs to seek answers to *Q1* and *Q2*, And BINXRAY was used for comparison.

Different Compiler or Optimization Level. Table 2 summarizes the performance of *SeHBPL* as well as the comparison between *SeHBPL* and BINXRAY. The statistics listed in the *Supported* column show a low support rate for BINXRAY on the test cases, slightly higher than 10%. This is due to BINXRAY's inability to output exact results for most cases, instead returning "NT no trace" and "NA too much diff".

Table 2. Evaluation on tolerance of *SeHBPL* to diverse compiling configurations.

Stage	Tool	Targets	Supported[a]	Intersection[b]			Overall[c]		
				Acc.	*Pre.*	$F_{0.5}$	*Acc.*	*Pre.*	$F_{0.5}$
AC[d]	BINXRAY	8,445	870 (10.30%)	0.86	0.72	0.75	0.60	0.72	0.29
	SeHBPL	8,445	8,445 (100.00%)	**0.95**	**0.91**	**0.92**	**0.89**	**0.87**	**0.87**
AO	BINXRAY	14,427	1,452 (10.06%)	**0.86**	0.71	**0.74**	0.60	0.71	0.28
	SeHBPL	14,427	14,427 (100.00%)	0.85	**0.73**	**0.74**	**0.90**	**0.87**	**0.88**

* Some binaries are not counted due to errors occur during the analysis.
[a] The amount and the ratio of the testing targets supported by each tool.
[b] Metrics for targets that can be analyzed by both the two tools.
[c] Cases where BINXRAY fails to output results are treated as if the binary is considered unpatched.
[d] Short for "Across Compiler" and "Across Optimization Level".

As Table 2 illustrates, *SeHBPL* consistently outperforms BINXRAY in three key metrics. When evaluating patch presence in binaries compiled with different compilers, *SeHBPL* achieves superior performance, with improvements of 10-28%, 15–20%, and 0.17-0.58 in accuracy, precision, and $F_{0.5}$ score, respectively. The great gaps in these metrics indicate the greater robustness of *SeHBPL*. When testing patch presence in binaries compiled with different optimization levels, BINXRAY achieves close performance when faced with target binaries which it can process. However, among 14,427 target binaries, BINXRAY is only able to output concrete result for 1,452 binaries, for only 10.06%. Considering the overall metrics in both across-compiler evaluation and across-optimization level evaluation, *SeHBPL* is regarded as more reliable and more practical.

An analysis of the false negatives of *SeHBPL* was conducted and it was concluded that the majority of them were caused by incomplete path explorations by *angr*. The incomplete explorations resulted in *SeHBPL* not reaching the instruction position to which the patches brought changes. If this occurs when *SeHBPL* extracts behavioral semantics for reference binaries, *SeHBPL* will be unable to derive patch signatures, causing the subsequent patch presence testing to fail.

Among the remaining false negatives, most were incurred by function inlining. In these cases, the behavior of the callee functions is integrated into that of the caller, and both the behavior and path constraints in the caller function are greatly changed. Currently, *SeHBPL* tolerates function inlinings that occur in reference binaries, but when a callee function within the target binary is inlined, *SeHBPL* will fail to match its behavioral semantics with patch signatures, ultimately causing the patch presence testing to fail.

Answer to Q1: *SeHBPL* can reliably perform patch presence testing, even when the reference binaries and the target binary differ in compilation options.

Different Compiler and Different Optimization Level. The results of evaluation 2 are presented in Table 3. Both *SeHBPL* and BINXRAY face challenges when conducting patch existence tests on binaries generated with varying compilers and optimization levels, resulting in a slight decrease in accuracy and precision for both tools. The most significant changes for both *SeHBPL* and BINXRAY are observed in their precision, which decrease from over 86% to less than 70% and from over 70% to around 60% respectively. Among all the 7,074 binaries, BINXRAY still can only output concrete results for a small portion (14.76%) of target binaries, showing inability of processing complex targets.

In comparison to its counterpart, *SeHBPL* outperforms BINXRAY in all metrics. Even when analyzing binaries that both tools can handle, BINXRAY falls short in terms of accuracy and precision. Given that the reference binaries are compiled using default settings, these results suggest that *SeHBPL* is more reliable and practical in practice.

Table 3. Evaluation on *SeHBPL* with reference binaries compiled with default configuration.

Tool	Targets	# of Supported	Supported			Overall		
			Acc.	*Pre.*	$F_{0.5}$	*Acc.*	*Pre.*	$F_{0.5}$
BINXRAY	7,074	1,044 (14.76%)	0.72	0.60	0.61	0.58	0.61	0.15
SeHBPL	7,074	7,074 (100.00%)	**0.80**	**0.71**	**0.74**	**0.76**	**0.68**	**0.71**

Answer to Q2: *SeHBPL* can accurately and precisely test patch presence with reference binaries generated using the default compilation setting, indicating that *SeHBPL* is practical.

4.4 Evaluation of Efficiency

The efficiency comparison of *SeHBPL* and BINXRAY is summarized in Table 4. Overall, *SeHBPL* takes an average of 94.464 s to perform patch presence testing on a binary. In many cases, such as the test on CVE-2016-8884, *SeHBPL* completes the testing within one second. However, in a few cases, such as the test on CVE-2019-20387, *SeHBPL* takes more than 400 min. In these cases, the vulnerability-related functions contain excessive branches and loops, resulting in a dramatic increase in the number of execution paths waiting to be explored. As a result, *SeHBPL* spends more time extracting behavioral semantics for these cases than it does for others. For the most of other targets (>90%), *SeHBPL* finishes patch presence testing on them within 120 s.

The detailed distribution of time costs for patch presence tests by *SeHBPL* is shown in Fig. 7. As the figure shows, for most target binaries, no matter they are compiled across compilers or across optimization levels, *SeHBPL* finishes testing patch presence on them with 10 to 100 s. More specifically, *SeHBPL* tests patch presence on 32.22% of targets within less than 10 s.

Compared to BINXRAY, *SeHBPL* takes longer to perform tests due to the use of symbolic execution. To precisely extract changed behavioral semantics, *SeHBPL* must explore many execution paths. Due to the relatively low efficiency of symbolic execution, these explorations are time-consuming. However, considering that many symbolic execution efficiency improvement techniques [18,19] and engineering efforts can be introduced into *SeHBPL* in the future, this time consumption is considered acceptable.

Table 4. Time cost of BINXRAY and *SeHBPL* (in seconds).

Tool	Minimum	Average	Median	Maximum	Done In 120 s
BINXRAY	0.002	2.10	0.07	270.04	99.72%
SeHBPL	0.32	94.46	17.68	28567.00	92.87%

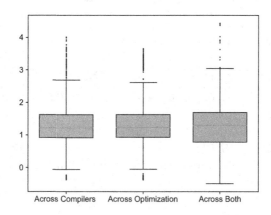

Fig. 7. Time Cost Distribution For *SeHBPL*. Values on Y-axis are in log scale.

Answer to Q3: *SeHBPL* can conduct patch presence tests with high efficiency. It completes the analysis for most binaries within an acceptable time frame.

4.5   Performance of Behavioral Semantics

The efficiency of extracting behavioral semantics signatures was tested and the results are summarized in Table 5. A signature is extracted in two steps: source code parsing and signature generation. As the table shows, signature generation takes much more time than source code parsing due to the symbolic execution it involves. On average, it takes *SeHBPL* 426.01 s to generate patch signatures. Although this is time costing, behavioral semantics extraction for patch signature generation only needs to be performed once due to the tolerance of *SeHBPL* to various compilation options. This means that the behavioral semantics signature for a patch only needs to be generated once, and can then be used for patch presence testing on target binaries compiled with various compilation settings. As demonstrated earlier, *SeHBPL* outperforms its adversary in terms of both accuracy and precision, indicating the usefulness of patch signatures based on behavioral semantics. Therefore, it is considered worthwhile to spend this long time to derive high-quality signatures.

Table 5. Time cost on source code parsing and patch signature generating (in seconds).

Stage	Min.	Ave.	Med.	In 120 s
Source Code Parsing	1.56	19.95	5.22	95.87%
Signature Generation	2.85	426.01	84.16	71.49%
Overall	7.78	445.96	85.95	69.01%

Second, the capability of behavioral semantics to capture changes introduced by patches was measured. Among 91 vulnerabilities, source code changes introduced by patches for 80 vulnerabilities were faithfully included in patch signatures based on behavioral semantics. For other 11 vulnerabilities, errors occurred in *angr* when *SeHBPL* extracted behavioral semantics, resulting in incomplete symbolic executions and behavioral semantics extraction.

Answer to Q4: Behavioral semantics reliably reflects the changes in patches.

5   Discussion

Path Explosion. *SeHBPL* employs symbolic execution, which is susceptible to path explosion. Path explosion has greatly affected the efficiency of *SeHBPL*. To mitigate this issue, loops are currently expanded only twice and constraints are applied during symbolic execution. In the future, additional approaches [18,19] could be implemented to enhance execution efficiency.

Availability of Symbols. *SeHBPL* depends on symbol tables in target binaries to locate relevant functions. However, symbol tables may not always be present, particularly in commercial off-the-shelf (COTS) products. This can hinder *SeHBPL*'s ability to test patch presence in these products. To overcome this limitation, code search techniques [11,12,20] could be utilized.

6 Related Work

Binary-Level Code Search. Previous research utilized many characteristics as features, including control flow [12–14], data constants [11,14], and call graphs [20,21]. For instance, Andreas et al. [22] employs mnemonics for instructions and normalized operands to detect code copying in Windows XP and the Linux kernel. Works that use control flows as features, such as BinDiff [23], BinSlayer [24], and discovRE [12], focus on the structure of the control flow graph, while Genius [13] and Gemini [25] encode the control flow for efficiency. As natural language processing techniques have advanced, they have been applied in Asm2vec [26], Deepbindiff [27], and Yu et al. [28].

Identification of Component Versions. Version identification aims to ascertain the specific version of a component used in a target binary. OSSPolice [7] and B2SMatcher [29] extract features from different versions of components, such as strings and names of exported functions, to create signatures for specific versions. LibScout [30], which targets third-party components in Android applications, constructs a variant of Merkle trees [31] based on package hierarchical structures and uses it as a signature. Libradar [32] performs version identification based on the frequency of function calls to the Android API.

Testing for Patch Presence. Brahmastra [33] seeks to trigger vulnerabilities through dynamic driving. However, the triggering results are heavily influenced by the quality of the inputs generated for the target binary. FIBER [34] extracts syntactic and semantic changes in source code and attempts to match these changes in target binaries. PDiff [9] converts execution paths affected by patches into formulas and performs similarity calculations on these formulas between reference binaries and the target binary to determine patch presence.

7 Conclusion

This paper presents two key challenges in patch presence testing for binaries: the subtlety of changes introduced by patches and the diversity of compilation configurations. To address these challenges, the concept of behavioral semantics is introduced and *SeHBPL*, a patch presence testing system based on behavioral semantics, is implemented. *SeHBPL* accurately captures changes introduced by patches and exhibits high tolerance to different compilation options. Evaluation results demonstrate that *SeHBPL* achieves high accuracy and precision, outperforming state-of-the-art tools.

Acknowledgment. This work was supported by National Key R&D Program of the Ministry of Science and Technology of China (No. 2020YFB2010902), Youth Science Fund Project of China (No. 62002342) and Projects from the Ministry of Industry and Information Technology of China (No. TC220H055). In addition, Siyi Zheng deserves thanks for her work on beautifying the figures.

References

1. Synopsys, I.: 2022 open source security and analysis report (2022). https://www.synopsys.com/software-integrity/resources/analyst-reports/open-source-security-risk-analysis.html. Accessed 15 Apr 2022
2. Jang, J., Agrawal, A., Brumley, D.: Redebug: finding unpatched code clones in entire OS distributions. In: IEEE Symposium on Security and Privacy, pp. 48–62. IEEE (2012)
3. Kim, S., Woo, S., Lee, H., Oh, H.: Vuddy: a scalable approach for vulnerable code clone discovery. In: IEEE Symposium on Security and Privacy (SP), pp. 595–614. IEEE (2017)
4. Li, Z., Zou, D., Xu, S., Jin, H., Qi, H., Hu, J.: Vulpecker: an automated vulnerability detection system based on code similarity analysis. In: Proceedings of the 32nd Annual Conference on Computer Security Applications, pp. 201–213 (2016)
5. Synopsys, I.: The heartbleed bug (2020). https://heartbleed.com/. Accessed 8 Apr 2022
6. Ltd. N. Half a million widely trusted websites vulnerable to heartbleed bug (2014). https://news.netcraft.com/archives/2014/04/08/half-a-million-widely-trusted-websites-vulnerable-to-heartbleed-bug.html. Accessed 8 Apr 2022
7. Duan, R., Bijlani, A., Xu, M., Kim, T., Lee, W.: Identifying open-source license violation and 1-day security risk at large scale. In: Proceedings of the 2017 ACM SIGSAC Conference on Computer and Communications Security, pp. 2169–2185 (2017)
8. Xu, Y., Xu, Z., Chen, B., Song, F., Liu, Y., Liu, T.: Patch based vulnerability matching for binary programs. In: Proceedings of the 29th ACM SIGSOFT International Symposium on Software Testing and Analysis, pp. 376–387 (2020)
9. Jiang, Z., et al.: PDiff: semantic-based patch presence testing for downstream kernels. In; Proceedings of the 2020 ACM SIGSAC Conference on Computer and Communications Security, pp. 1149–1163 (2020)
10. Sun, P., Yan, Q., Zhou, H., Li, J.: Osprey: a fast and accurate patch presence test framework for binaries. Comput. Commun. **173**, 95–106, 2021. https://www.sciencedirect.com/science/article/pii/S0140366421001079
11. Costin, A., Zaddach, J., Francillon, A., Balzarotti, D.: {Large-Scale} analysis of the security of embedded firmwares. In: 23rd USENIX Security Symposium (USENIX Security 14), pp. 95–110 (2014)
12. Eschweiler, S., Yakdan, K., Gerhards-Padilla, E.: discovRE: efficient cross-architecture identification of bugs in binary code. In: NDSS, vol. 52, pp. 58–79 (2016)
13. Feng, Q., Zhou, R., Xu, C., Cheng, Y., Testa, B., Yin, H.: Scalable graph-based bug search for firmware images. In: Proceedings of the 2016 ACM SIGSAC Conference on Computer and Communications Security, pp. 480–491 (2016)
14. Khoo, W.M., Mycroft, A., Anderson, R.: Rendezvous: a search engine for binary code. In: 2013 10th Working Conference on Mining Software Repositories (MSR), pp. 329–338. IEEE (2013)

15. Tian, Y., Lawall, J., Lo, D.: Identifying Linux bug fixing patches. In: 34th International Conference on Software Engineering (ICSE), pp. 386–396. IEEE (2012)
16. GNU, "Optimize options for GCC" (2022). https://gcc.gnu.org/onlinedocs/gcc/Optimize-Options.html. Accessed 8 Apr 2022
17. Shoshitaishvili, Y., et al.: SoK: (State of) the art of war: offensive techniques in binary analysis. In: IEEE Symposium on Security and Privacy (2016)
18. Chen, J., Hu, W., Zhang, L., Hao, D., Khurshid, S., Zhang, L.: Learning to accelerate symbolic execution via code transformation. In: 32nd European Conference on Object-Oriented Programming (ECOOP 2018). Schloss Dagstuhl-Leibniz-Zentrum fuer Informatik (2018)
19. Zhang, C., Groce, A., Alipour, M. A.: Using test case reduction and prioritization to improve symbolic execution. In: Proceedings of the 2014 International Symposium on Software Testing and Analysis, pp. 160–170 (2014)
20. Liu, B., et al.: αdiff: cross-version binary code similarity detection with DNN. In: Proceedings of the 33rd ACM/IEEE International Conference on Automated Software Engineering, pp. 667–678 (2018)
21. Wang, X., Jhi, Y.-C., Zhu, S., Liu, P.: Detecting software theft via system call based birthmarks. In: Annual Computer Security Applications Conference, pp. 149–158. IEEE (2009)
22. Sæbjørnsen, A., Willcock, J., Panas, T., Quinlan, D., Su, Z.: Detecting code clones in binary executables. In: Proceedings of the Eighteenth International Symposium on Software Testing and Analysis, pp. 117–128 (2009)
23. zynamics, "Bindiff" (2004). https://www.zynamics.com/bindiff.html. Accessed 15 Apr 2022
24. Bourquin, M., King, A., Robbins, E.: Binslayer: accurate comparison of binary executables. In: Proceedings of the 2nd ACM SIGPLAN Program Protection and Reverse Engineering Workshop, pp. 1–10 (2013)
25. Xu, X., Liu, C., Feng, Q., Yin, H., Song, L., Song, D.: Neural network-based graph embedding for cross-platform binary code similarity detection. In: Proceedings of the 2017 ACM SIGSAC Conference on Computer and Communications Security, pp. 363–376 (2017)
26. Ding, S.H., Fung, B.C., Charland, P.: Asm2vec: boosting static representation robustness for binary clone search against code obfuscation and compiler optimization. In: IEEE Symposium on Security and Privacy (SP), pp. 472–489. IEEE (2019)
27. Duan, Y., Li, X., Wang, J., Yin, H.: DeepBinDiff: learning program-wide code representations for binary diffing. In: Network and Distributed System Security Symposium (2020)
28. Yu, Z., Cao, R., Tang, Q., Nie, S., Huang, J., Wu, S.: Order matters: semantic-aware neural networks for binary code similarity detection. In: AAAI Conference on Artificial Intelligence (2020)
29. Ban, G., Xu, L., Xiao, Y., Li, X., Yuan, Z., Huo, W.: B2smatcher: fine-grained version identification of open-source software in binary files. Cybersecurity 4(1), 1–21 (2021)
30. Backes, M., Bugiel, S., Derr, E.: Reliable third-party library detection in android and its security applications. In: Proceedings of the 2016 ACM SIGSAC Conference on Computer and Communications Security, pp. 356–367 (2016)
31. Merkle, R.C.: A digital signature based on a conventional encryption function. In: Pomerance, C. (ed.) CRYPTO 1987. LNCS, vol. 293, pp. 369–378. Springer, Heidelberg (1988). https://doi.org/10.1007/3-540-48184-2_32

32. Ma, Z., Wang, H., Guo, Y., Chen, X.: LibRadar: fast and accurate detection of third-party libraries in android apps. In: Proceedings of the 38th International Conference on Software Engineering Companion, pp. 653–656 (2016)
33. Bhoraskar, R., et al.: Brahmastra: driving apps to test the security of third-party components. In: 23rd USENIX Security Symposium (USENIX Security 14), pp. 1021–1036 (2014)
34. Zhang, H., Qian, Z.: Precise and accurate patch presence test for binaries. In: 27th USENIX Security Symposium (USENIX Security 18), pp. 887–902 (2018)

Session Types with Multiple Senders Single Receiver

Zekun Ji[1,2], Shuling Wang[1(✉)], and Xiong Xu[1]

[1] State Key Laboratory of Computer Science, Institute of Software, Chinese
Academy of Sciences, Beijing, China
{jizk,wangsl,xux}@ios.ac.cn
[2] University of Chinese Academy of Sciences, Beijing, China

Abstract. Message passing is a fundamental element in software development, ranging from concurrent and mobile computing to distributed services, but it suffers from communication errors such as deadlocks. Session types are a typing discipline for enforcing safe structured interactions between multiple participants. However, each typed interaction is restricted to having one fixed sender and one fixed receiver. In this paper, we extend session types with existential branching types, to handle a common interaction pattern with multiple senders and a single receiver in a synchronized setting, i.e. a receiver is available to receive messages from multiple senders, and which sender actually participates in the interaction cannot be determined till execution. We build the type system with existential branching types, which retain the important properties induced by standard session types: type safety, progress (i.e. deadlock-freedom), and fidelity. We further provide a novel communication type system to guarantee progress of dynamically interleaved multiparty sessions, by abandoning the strong restrictions of existing type systems. Finally, we encode Rust multi-thread primitives in the extended session types to show its expressivity, which can be considered as an attempt to check the deadlock-freedom of Rust multi-thread programs.

Keywords: Communications · Session types · Type system · Deadlock-freedom

1 Introduction

Distributed and concurrent programming plays an increasingly important role due to the high demand for distributed applications and services across networks. Message passing is one fundamental element in these areas and its correctness is very crucial. Many existing programming languages provide communication primitives, but still leave to the programmers the responsibility of guaranteeing safety [26]. Concurrent and distributed programming suffers from communication errors such as deadlocks, and how to guarantee the correctness of communication behaviors is challenging.

Supported by NSFC under grant No. 61972385, 62032024, and 62192732.

H. Hermanns et al. (Eds.): SETTA 2023, LNCS 14464, pp. 112–131, 2024.
https://doi.org/10.1007/978-981-99-8664-4_7

There have been many academic studies on the specification and verification of communicating behaviors. Session types [9,10] are a type theory for describing structured communications between multiple end-point participants to statically ensure safe interactions of them. It has been studied extensively in the context of process calculi [1,2,5,7,24,28] and also in many programming languages [3, 13,17,18]. A variety of interaction patterns can be captured by session types, via sequencing, branching, recursion, and channel mobility, however, each interaction is typed with one fixed sender and one fixed receiver. In reality, a receiver may be available to receive messages from a set of senders, and which sender actually synchronizes with the receiver to complete the interaction is not determined till execution, e.g. Rust multiple-producer, single-consumer channels. Existing session types are not expressive enough to handle such communication behaviors.

This paper extends session types with an *existential branching* type that allows to specify interactions with multiple senders and one receiver, enforcing that at execution one among a set of senders synchronizes with the receiver each time. With the addition of the existential branching type, we need to first re-establish the whole type theory, which should retain the critical properties of session types including type safety, progress (deadlock-freedom), and session fidelity (type adherence). These properties guarantee that communications of all the end-point processes together realize the global interaction protocol specified by a session global type. However, same as existing works based on global types [1,23], the latter two properties put very strong restrictions on processes, e.g. each process plays only one role in the protocol. Other alternative approaches on guaranteeing deadlock-freedom loose these restrictions, but instead they must obey strong order structures for nested channels [2,5], or require heavy syntax annotations on the usage of channels [15,16]. In our approach, we present a novel communication type system that records the execution orders between communication events over different channels, and checks the existence of dependence loops in the transition closure of all the orders. In particular, in order to deal with the dynamic mobility of channels, we define a unification process to transfer the channel to be moved and its communication history to the target receiver.

At the end, to show the expressivity of the extended session types, we encode concurrent primitives of Rust, including multiple-producer, single-consumer channels, mutex, and read-write locks, in the extended session calculus. As a result, a Rust multi-thread program can be encoded as a process that can be checked by the type systems presented in this paper. In summary, the contribution of this paper includes the following three aspects:

- We extend session type with an existential branching type to specify the interactions that allow multiple senders and one receiver, and establish the type system to ensure type safety, deadlock-freedom, and session fidelity;
- We further propose a communication type system for checking deadlock-freedom of concurrent processes, by dropping strong restrictions of existing approaches;

- We encode concurrent primitives of Rust as processes in the extended session calculus, which shows the possibility of checking the communication behaviors of Rust using our approach in the future.

After presenting the related work, the paper is organized as follows: Sect. 2 gives a motivating example to illustrate our approach; Sect. 3 presents the extended session calculus and session types with existential branching resp.; Sect. 4 defines the new type system and proves the theorems corresponding to type safety, progress, and fidelity, and Sect. 5 proposes the communication type system for ensuring progress without restrictions. Section 6 encodes Rust multi-thread primitives in the extended session calculus, and Sect. 7 concludes the paper and addresses future work.

1.1 Related Work

Session types were introduced by Honda [9,10] initially for describing and validating interactions between binary parties, and then extended to more generalized multiparties [2,11]. Session types, either follow a top-down approach to require the communications between multiple participants conform to a global type via projections [2,8,11,29], or check local session types of communicating systems directly, by requiring them to be compatible [10], satisfy behavioural predicates corresponding to safety, liveness, etc [23], or by rely-guarantee reasoning [22]. Session types have been extended for various purposes. Dynamic multirole session type introduces a universal polling operator to describe that an arbitrary number of participants share common interaction behaviors and they can dynamically join and leave [5]. The more general parameterized multiparty session types integrate session types with indexed dependent types, to specify the number of participants and messages as parameters that can dynamically change [28]. Both of them focus on specifying communication topologies with arbitrary number of participants and universally quantified interactions. Dependent types are integrated into session types to specify and verify the dependency and safety of data that are exchanged among multiple participants [24,25,27]. There are also extensions of session types on specifying crash-stop failures [1] and continuous time motion behaviors [20]. However, all these works remain the interaction patterns of original session types unchanged, with no support to existential branching interactions considered in this paper.

The progress property, also called deadlock-freedom, has been studied a lot for channel-based communicating systems. The types of channels in [15,16] were decorated explicitly with capabilities/obligations to specify the relations on channel-wise usages, thus they need heavy syntax annotations. The type systems for ensuring progress in session types were studied in [2,4], avoiding any tagging of channels or names in syntax. However, the typing rules of [2,4] put strong restrictions on nested channels in order to keep the correct orders between different parties, and moreover, the output is assumed to be asynchronous. Our communication type system was inspired by [2,4], but abandons the restrictions and moreover both input and output are synchronous. There is also work on verifying progress by checking multiparty compatibility of endpoint communications [12,19], via model checking or other verification techniques.

Session types have also been embedded in mainstream programming languages to guarantee the correctness of communication behaviors [3,6,13,17,18]. For more details, readers are referred to a recent survey [26]. The commonality of them is to define session channels as enriched types to express the sequences of messages that are expected to occur along the channels, the ordering of messages, or the synchronization between inputs and outputs, to guarantee deadlock-freedom or other safety properties. However, none of these efforts focus on how the native parallel programs can be directly checked for communication correctness, and the strong-typed session channels may be not user-friendly to use and only generate code for fixed patterns.

2   A Motivating Example

Figure 1 shows a motivating example of a satellite control system, which includes three parts: the controller **Ctrl**, the ground control **Grd**, and the gyroscope **Gys**. The controller receives data from the gyroscope periodically, then calculates the control command based on the received data and sends it to the gyroscope to obey in the next period; meanwhile, the ground control also needs to communicate with the controller to request current data or manually modify a certain control parameter of the controller. Therefore, the controller should be always ready to handle the requests from both the ground and the gyroscope. However, the ground and the gyroscope cannot play one role due to their different responsibilities. Session types cannot specify the interactions of this example.

Figure 1 shows how to specify this example using our approach. G defines the global type for the interactions between the controller, the ground control and the gyroscope from a global perspective. Let p_r denote the ground control, p_y the gyroscope, and p_c the controller. The controller p_c first receives a message from ground p_r or gyroscope p_y and then takes further actions according to the source of this message. If the message is from p_r, then p_r continues to send a query request inq and receive a response from p_c, or send a modification request mod to modify the control parameter and further send the value to be changed. If the message is from p_y, then the controller receives $data$ from p_y and sends a new control command $comm$ back. Local types $s[p_c]$ and $s[A]$, where $A = \{p_i\}_{i \in \{r,y\}}$, are projections from G to the three roles resp., to define the types of communications they participate in from their local view. Especially, $s[p_c]$ defines the local type for p_c, while $s[A]$ defines the local types for p_r and p_y as a whole, as it is not determined statically which among p_r and p_y interacts with p_c at each time.

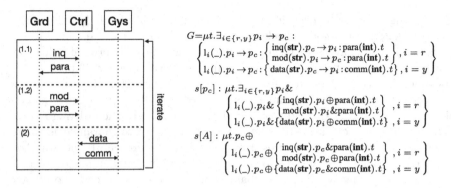

Fig. 1. Example of Attitude Control of Satellite

3   MSSR Session Types

This section introduces the extended session π-calculus, and the corresponding session types for typing the calculus. We call the session calculus and types extended with multiple senders single receiver *MSSR session calculus* and *MSSR session types* resp.

3.1   Session π-Calculus

As an extension of [1, 23], MSSR session calculus is used to model processes interacting via multiparty channels. The syntax is given below, where c stands for channels, d for data that can be transmitted during communication, including both basic values and channels, P, Q for processes, and D for function declarations. The sessions s in restriction, and variables $x_i, y_i, \tilde{x}$ in branching and function declaration are bounded. We adopt the Barendregt convention that bounded sessions and variables, and free ones are assumed pairwise distinct.

$$
\begin{aligned}
c &::= x \mid s[p] & \text{variable, session with roles} \\
d &::= x \mid a \mid s[p] & \text{variable, constant, session with roles} \\
P, Q &::= \mathbf{0} \mid (\nu s)P \mid P|Q & \text{inaction, restriction, parallel composition} \\
& \mid c[q] \oplus \mathrm{l}\langle d\rangle.P & \text{selection towards } q \\
& \mid c[q]\&\{\mathrm{l}_i(x_i).P_i\}_{i\in I} & \text{branching from } q \text{ with } I \neq \emptyset \\
& \mid \exists_{i\in I}c[q_i]\&\{\mathrm{l}_i(y_i).P_i\} & \text{existential branching from } \{q_i\}_{i\in I} \\
& \mid \mathbf{def}\ D\ \mathbf{in}\ P \mid X(\tilde{d}) & \text{process definition, call} \\
D &::= X(\tilde{x}) = P & \text{function declaration}
\end{aligned}
$$

Channels can be a variable, or $s[p]$ representing the channel of participant p (called role p interchangeably) in session s. Restriction $(\nu s)P$ declares a new session s with the scope limited to process P. Parallel composition $P|Q$ executes

P and Q concurrently, with communication actions between two roles synchronized. Selection $c[q] \oplus l\langle d \rangle.P$ sends value d labelled by l to role q, using channel c, and then continues as P. In contrary, branching $c[q]\&\{l_i(x_i).P_i\}_{i \in I}$ expects to receive a value from role q using channel c, and if a value d_k with label l_k is received for some $k \in I$, x_k will be replaced by received value and the execution continues as the corresponding P_k. The l_is must be pairwise distinct, and the scopes of x_is are limited to P_is. Existential branching $\exists_{i \in I} c[q_i]\&\{l_i(y_i).P_i\}$ is the newly added construct, which expects to receive a value from senders $\{q_i\}_{i \in I}$, and if some q_k sends a value, y_k will be replaced by the received value and the execution continues as P_k. Note the difference between branching and existential branching: the former waits for a message from a single role that may provide multiple messages, while the latter waits for a message from a set of different roles. For the above three kinds of prefix communications, we call c their *subject*.

$X(\tilde{x}) = P$ declares the definition for process variable X, which can be called by $X(\tilde{d})$ with actual parameters $\tilde{d}$. Recursive processes can be modelled using it. **def** D **in** P introduces the process definitions in D and proceeds as P. To make sure that a recursive process has a unique solution, we assume P in $X(\tilde{x}) = P$ is guarded [23], i.e. before the occurrence of X in P, a prefix communication event occurs. For example, $P = x_1[q] \oplus l\langle d \rangle.X(-)$ is guarded, while $P = X(-)$ is not.

Semantics. Before presenting the semantics, we define the reduction context $\mathbb{C}$ as follows:

$$\mathbb{C} := \mathbb{C}|P \mid (\nu s)\mathbb{C} \mid \textbf{def } D \textbf{ in } \mathbb{C} \mid [\ ]$$

$\mathbb{C}$ is defined with a hole $[\ ]$ and for any process P, $\mathbb{C}[P]$ represents the process reached by substituting P for $[\ ]$ in $\mathbb{C}$. The execution of $\mathbb{C}[P]$ can always start with executing P. The semantics of the calculus are then defined by a set of reduction rules, denoted by $P \to P'$, meaning that P can execute to P' in one step. We define $P \to^* P'$ to represent that P executes to P' via zero or more steps of reductions, and $P \to$ to represent that there exists P' such that $P \to P'$, and $P \nrightarrow$ otherwise. The semantics are given below:

$$
\begin{aligned}
[\&\oplus] \quad & s[p][q]\&\{l_i(x_i).P_i\}_{i \in I} | s[q][p] \oplus l_k\langle w \rangle.Q \ \to \ P_k[w/x_k]|Q \qquad \text{if } k \in I \\
[\exists\oplus] \quad & \exists_{i \in I} s[p][q_i]\&\{l_i(y_i).P_i\} | s[q_k][p] \oplus l_k\langle w \rangle.Q \ \to \ P_k[w/x_k]|Q \quad \text{if } k \in I \\
[X] \quad & \textbf{def } X(x_1, ..., x_n) = P \textbf{ in } (X(w_1, ..., w_n)|Q) \\
& \quad \to \textbf{def } X(x_1, ..., x_n) = P \textbf{ in } (P[w_1/x_1, ..., w_n/x_n]|Q) \\
[Ctx] \quad & P \to P' \text{ implies } \mathbb{C}[P] \to \mathbb{C}[P'] \\
[\equiv] \quad & P' \equiv P \text{ and } P \to Q \text{ and } Q \equiv Q' \text{ implies } P' \to Q'
\end{aligned}
$$

Rule $[\&\oplus]$ defines the synchronized communication between roles p (receiver) and q (sender), matched by label l_k, resulting in the substitution of w for x_k in continuation P_k, where w is a constant a or a session channel, say $s'[r]$. Rule $[\exists\oplus]$ defines the synchronized communication between receiver p and a sender among $\{q_i\}_{i \in I}$, with the sender q_k determined (externally from the sender side) for the communication. Rule $[X]$ replaces the occurrences of call $X(w_1, ..., w_n)$

by rolling its definition P after substituting w_is for corresponding parameters x_is. Rule $[Ctx]$ defines that, if P reduces to P', then context $\mathbb{C}[P]$ reduces to $\mathbb{C}[P']$. Rule $[\equiv]$ defines that reduction is closed with respect to the structural equivalence. Here $P \equiv P'$ holds if P can be reconstructed to P' by α-conversion for bounded variable renaming, or the commutativity and associativity laws of parallel composition operator.

3.2 Global and Local Session Types

Session types define the use of channels in π-calculus. A global type specifies the interactions of all the participants from a global view, and on the contrary a local type specifies the interactions of each participant from its local view. The projection of a global type upon a specific role produces the local type of the corresponding participant. Below we define the MSSR global and local types, denoted by G and T resp.

$$
\begin{aligned}
S &::= \mathbf{int} \mid \mathbf{bool} \mid \mathbf{real} \mid \langle G \rangle & B &::= S \mid T \\
G &::= p \to q : \{l_i(B_i).G_i\}_{i \in I} & T &::= p \oplus \{l_i(B_i).T_i\}_{i \in I} \mid p\&\{l_i(B_i).T_i\}_{i \in I} \\
&\mid \exists_{i \in I} q_i \to p : \{l_i(B_i).G_i\} & &\mid \exists_{i \in I} p_i \& \{l_i(B_i).T_i\} \\
&\mid \mu t.G \mid t \mid \mathbf{end} & &\mid \mu t.T \mid t \mid \mathbf{end}
\end{aligned}
$$

Sort types S for values include basic types and global types. B defines types of messages exchanged over channels, which can be sort types and channel types (denoted by T). The global interaction type $p \to q : \{l_i(B_i).G_i\}_{i \in I}$ describes an interaction between role p and q, saying that p sends to q one of the messages labelled by l_i, with payload type B_i for some $i \in I$, and then continues according to the continuation type G_i. The global existential interaction type $\exists_{i \in I} q_i \to p : \{l_i(B_i).G_i\}$ specifies that there exists $i \in I$ such that role q_i sends to role p a message, labelled by l_i with payload type B_i and then continues according to G_i. We call $\{q_i\}_{i \in I}$ the *domain* of the existential type. $\mu t.G$ defines a recursive global type and t represents a type variable. Type variables t are assumed to be guarded in the standard way. **end** represents that no more communication will occur.

Local types T define the types of end-point channels. The first three are corresponding to the selection, branching and existential branching processes in session π-calculus. The selection type (or internal choice) $p \oplus \{l_i(B_i).T_i\}_{i \in I}$ specifies a channel that acts as a sender and sends a message among $\{l_i(B_i)\}_{i \in I}$ to receiver p, and in contrary, the branching type (or external choice) $p\&\{l_i(B_i).T_i\}_{i \in I}$ specifies a channel that acts as a receiver and expects to receive from sender p a message among $\{l_i(B_i)\}_{i \in I}$, and for both of them, the corresponding continuations are specified as types T_i. The existential branching type (or existential external choice) $\exists_{i \in I} p_i \& \{l_i(B_i).T_i\}$ defines a receiving channel that expects to receive from a sender among $\{p_i\}_{i \in I}$ with corresponding message and continuation.

Example 1. We use a simpler running example to explain the notations and definitions throughout this paper. The global type G given below specifies a protocol between seller r_s, buyer r_b, and distributor r_d:

$G = \exists_{i \in \{b,d\}} r_i \to r_s :$
$$\left\{ \begin{array}{ll} \text{purchase}.r_s \to r_i : \text{price}(\textbf{int}).r_i \to r_s\{\text{ok}.\textbf{end}, \text{quit}.\textbf{end}\}, & i = b \\ \text{deliver}.r_s \to r_i : \text{restock}(\textbf{str}).\textbf{end}, & i = d \end{array} \right\}$$

At first, the seller expects to receive either a purchase message from the buyer or a delivery message from the distributor. If the former occurs, the seller sends the price to the buyer, who in turn sends the seller its decision on whether or not to purchase; if the latter occurs, the seller sends a message to the distributor about what it wants to restock.

Below presents the process, associated with G, for the three roles r_s, r_b, r_d in the syntax of MSSR session calculus (we omit irrelevant message payloads). The buyer sends a purchase request to start a conversation with the seller, while the distributor not.

$(\nu s)(P_{r_s} | P_{r_b} | P_{r_d})$, where
$$\left\{ \begin{array}{l} P_{r_s} : \exists_{i \in \{b,d\}} s[r_s][r_i] \& \left\{ \begin{array}{ll} \text{purchase}.s[r_s][r_i] \oplus \text{price}(100) & i = b \\ \quad .s[r_s][r_i] \& \{\text{ok}.\textbf{0}, \text{quit}.\textbf{0}\}, & \\ \text{deliver}.s[r_s][r_i] \oplus \text{restock}(\text{"bread"}).\textbf{0}, & i = d \end{array} \right\} \\ P_{r_b} : s[r_b][r_s] \oplus \text{purchase}.s[r_b][r_s] \& \text{price}(x).s[r_b][r_s] \oplus \text{ok}.\textbf{0} \\ P_{r_d} : \textbf{0} \end{array} \right.$$

3.3 Projection and Well-Formed Global Types

The projection of a global type G to a role p is denoted by $G \upharpoonright_p$, which maps G to the local type corresponding to p. Before defining $G \upharpoonright_p$, consider the projection of the existential branching type $\exists_{i \in I} q_i \to p : \{l_i(B_i).G_i\}$ to each q_i. At execution, there must exist one $i_0 \in I$, such that q_{i_0} sends to p while others in $\{q_i\}_{i \neq i_0, i \in I}$ do not. The choice of q_{i_0} is not determined statically, and meanwhile unique, i.e. there are not two q_k, q_j with $k \neq j$ such that they both send to p. Due to this reason, we define the projection of the existential branching type to all q_is as a whole. Instead of $G \upharpoonright_p$, we define $G \upharpoonright_A$, where A is a set of roles, that can be a singleton as before, or contains multiple roles corresponding to the domain of some existential type occurring in G. When A is a singleton $\{r\}$, we write $G \upharpoonright_r$ for simplicity. $G \upharpoonright_A$ is defined as follows:

$$(\mu t.G) \upharpoonright_A \triangleq \left\{ \begin{array}{ll} \mu t.G \upharpoonright_A & \text{if } G \upharpoonright_A \neq t' \text{ for all } t' \\ \textbf{end} & \text{otherwise} \end{array} \right. \qquad t \upharpoonright_A = t \qquad \textbf{end} \upharpoonright_A = \textbf{end}$$

$$(p \to q : \{l_i(B_i).G_i\}_{i \in I}) \upharpoonright_A \triangleq \left\{ \begin{array}{ll} q \oplus \{l_i(B_i).G_i \upharpoonright_A\}_{i \in I} & \text{if } A = \{p\} \\ p \& \{l_i(B_i).G_i \upharpoonright_A\}_{i \in I} & \text{if } A = \{q\} \\ \sqcap \{G_i \upharpoonright_A\}_{i \in I} & \text{otherwise} \end{array} \right.$$

$$(\exists_{i \in I} q_i \to p : \{l_i(B_i).G_i\}) \upharpoonright_A \triangleq \left\{ \begin{array}{ll} \exists_{i \in I} q_i \& \{l_i(B_i).G_i \upharpoonright_A\} & \text{if } A = \{p\} \\ p \oplus \{l_i(B_i).G_i \upharpoonright_{q_i}\}_{i \in I} & \text{if } A = \{q_i\}_{i \in I} \\ \sqcap \{G_i \upharpoonright_A\}_{i \in I} & \text{otherwise} \end{array} \right.$$

For global type $p \to q : \{l_i(B_i).G_i\}_{i \in I}$, the projection to sender p or receiver q results in the corresponding selection and branching local types; while the projection to A that is neither $\{p\}$ nor $\{q\}$, is defined to be the merge of the projections of continuation types G_i (denoted by $\sqcap$, to be explained below). The third case indicates that, from the eye of any role rather than p and q, it is not known which case among I is chosen thus all the continuations in I need to be merged to include all possible choices. The projection of $\exists_{i \in I} q_i \to p : \{l_i(B_i).G_i\}$ to receiver p results in the existential branching type on the set of senders, while the projection to the set of senders $\{q_i\}_{i \in I}$ is defined as the selection type on receiver p. The projection of $\mu t.G$ to r is defined inductively.

Now we define the merge operator $\sqcap$ for two local types, presented below:

$$p \& \{l_i(B_i).T_i\}_{i \in I} \sqcap p \& \{l_j(B_j).S_j\}_{j \in J} \qquad \exists_{i \in I} p_i \& \{l_i(B_i).T_i\} \sqcap \exists_{j \in J} p_j \& \{l_j(B_j).S_j\}$$
$$= p \& \{l_k(B_k).(T_k \sqcap S_k)\}_{k \in I \cap J} \ \& \qquad = \exists_{k \in I \cap J} p_k \& \{l_k(B_k).(T_k \sqcap S_k)\} \ \&$$
$$p \& \{l_i(B_i).T_i\}_{i \in I \setminus J} \ \& \qquad\qquad \exists_{i \in I \setminus J} p_i \& \{l_i(B_i).T_i\} \ \&$$
$$p \& \{l_j(B_j).S_j\}_{j \in J \setminus I} \qquad\qquad \exists_{j \in J \setminus I} p_j \& \{l_j(B_j).S_j\}$$

$$p \oplus \{l_i(B_i).T_i\}_{i \in I} \sqcap p \oplus \{l_i(B_i).T_i\}_{i \in I} = p \oplus \{l_i(B_i).T_i\}_{i \in I}$$

$$\mu t.T \sqcap \mu t.S = \mu t.(T \sqcap S) \quad t \sqcap t = t \quad \mathbf{end} \sqcap \mathbf{end} = \mathbf{end}$$

The merge of two branching types $\&$ combines together to form a larger branching type to allow to receive more messages. However, two selection types $\oplus$ can only be merged when they have exactly the same choices. Otherwise, a selection type with more (internal) choices will produce unexpected behaviors than the global type as specified.

A global type G is *well-formed*, if $G \upharpoonright_A$ is defined for each $A \in roles(G) \cup exdom(G)$, where $roles(G)$ returns the set of roles occurring in G and $exdom(G)$ returns the set of domains of all existential branching types occurring in G. From now on, we only consider well-formed global types.

Example 2. The projection of G presented in Example 1 upon each role returns the corresponding local type. Let $R = \{r_i\}_{i \in \{b,d\}}$, then:

$$s[r_s] : G \upharpoonright_{r_s} = \exists_{i \in \{b,d\}} r_i \& \begin{cases} \text{purchase}.r_i \oplus \text{price}(\mathbf{int}).r_i \& \{\text{ok}.\mathbf{end}, \text{quit}.\mathbf{end}\}, & i = b \\ \text{deliver}.r_i \oplus \text{restock}(\mathbf{str}).\mathbf{end}, & i = d \end{cases}$$

$$s[R] : G \upharpoonright_R = r_i \oplus \begin{cases} \text{purchase}.r_s \& \text{price}(\mathbf{int}).r_s \oplus \{\text{ok}.\mathbf{end}, \text{quit}.\mathbf{end}\}, & i = b \\ \text{deliver}.r_s \& \text{restock}(\mathbf{str}).\mathbf{end}, & i = d \end{cases}$$

3.4 Consistency of Global Types and Local Types

The transition semantics of types abstract the communications that might occur over typed channels. They can also be used to investigate the consistency between a global type and its projections. First, we define the typing context for channels:

Definition 1 (Typing context for channels). *The channel typing context* Γ *maps a channel (e.g.* $x, s[p]$*) or a set of channels (e.g.* $s[A]$*) to local types, defined as:*

$$\Gamma \triangleq \emptyset \mid \Gamma, s[p] : T \mid \Gamma, s[A] : T \mid \Gamma, x : T$$

The *domain* of each Γ denotes the set of channels of the form $s[p]$ or $s[A]$. We write Γ_1, Γ_2 to denote the union of Γ_1 and Γ_2, when they have disjoint domains.

The transition semantics for global and local type is defined by transition relations $G \xrightarrow{\alpha}_G G'$ and $\Gamma \xrightarrow{\alpha'}_L \Gamma'$ resp. We select some of the rules shown below and the full semantics can be found in [14]. Here α represents a communication, while α' can be an input, output or a communication, as shown in the following rules.

$$\exists_{i \in I} q_i \to p : \{l_i(B_i).G_i\} \xrightarrow{q_k \to p:l_k(B_k)}_G G_k \quad \forall k \in I \qquad \text{(G-exist)}$$

$$\frac{\forall i \in I.G_i \xrightarrow{\alpha}_G G'_i \quad \{p, q_i\}_{i \in I} \cap roles(\alpha) = \emptyset}{\exists_{i \in I} q_i \to p : \{l_i(B_i).G_i\} \xrightarrow{\alpha}_G \exists_{i \in I} q_i \to p : \{l_i(B_i).G'_i\}} \qquad \text{(G-exist')}$$

$$s[p] : \exists_{i \in I} q_i \& \{l_i(B_i).T_i\} \xrightarrow{p:q_k \& l_k(B_k)}_L s[p] : T_k \ \forall k \in I \qquad \text{(L-exist)}$$

$$s[\{p_i\}_{i \in I}] : q \oplus \{l_i(B_i).T_i\}_{i \in I} \xrightarrow{p_k:q \oplus l_k(B_k)}_L s[p_k] : T_k \ \forall k \in I \qquad \text{(L-select')}$$

$$\frac{\Gamma_1 \xrightarrow{p:q \oplus l(B)}_L \Gamma'_1 \quad \Gamma_2 \xrightarrow{q:p \& l(B)}_L \Gamma_2}{\Gamma_1, \Gamma_2 \xrightarrow{p \to q:l(B)}_L \Gamma'_1, \Gamma'_2} \qquad \text{(L-par)}$$

Rule (G-exist) performs a global interaction from a sender among $\{q_i\}_{i \in I}$ to p, while rule (G-exist') defines the case which permutes the order of two actions that are causally unrelated. The action to be executed for (G-exist') is required to be available no matter what choice is made for the prefix interaction. For local types, rules (L-exist) and (L-select') define the input and output resp., and rule (L-par) defines the synchronization between an input and a compatible output.

Consistency of Projection. Suppose G is a global type with roles $\{p_1, ..., p_k\}$ and domain sets $\{A_1, ..., A_l\}$. Let $\{s[p_1] : T_1, ..., s[p_k] : T_k; s[A_1] : T'_1, ..., s[A_l] : T'_l\}$ be the local types obtained from the projection of G towards the roles, denoted by $proj(G)$ below. We give the definition of *consistent* global type and local types below.

Definition 2 (Consistency). *A global type* G *and a set of local types* Γ *are consistent, if the following conditions hold: if* $G \xrightarrow{p \to q:l(B)} G'$*, then there must exist* Γ_1, Γ_2 *in* Γ *with* $\Gamma = \Gamma_1, \Gamma_2, \Gamma_3$*, such that* $\Gamma_1, \Gamma_2 \xrightarrow{p \to q:l(B)} \Gamma'_1, \Gamma'_2$*, and let* $\Gamma' = \Gamma'_1, \Gamma'_2, \Gamma_3$*,* G' *and* Γ' *are consistent; and vice versa.*

Theorem 1. *Let* G *be a well-formed global type, then* G *and its projection* $proj(G)$ *are consistent.*

The proof of this theorem, plus the ones for the following theorems, are all given in [14].

4   Type System

The type system is defined under two typing contexts: the one for channels Γ defined in Definition 1, and Θ mapping variables to basic types and process variables to a list of types.

$$\Theta \triangleq \emptyset \mid \Theta, X : T_1, ..., T_n$$

The typing judgment $\Theta \cdot \Gamma \vdash P$ states that under the typing contexts Θ and Γ, process P is well-typed. Figure 2 presents a selection of typing rules for MSSR π-calculus, to mainly show the difference from the standard session types [2, 23].

$$\frac{\Gamma_1 \vdash c : q \& \{l_i(B_i).T_i\}_{i \in I} \quad \forall i \in I. \Theta \cdot \Gamma, y_i : B_i, c : T_i \vdash P_i \quad I \subseteq J}{\Theta \cdot \Gamma, \Gamma_1 \vdash c[q] \& \{l_i(y_i).P_i\}_{i \in J}} \text{T-branch}$$

$$\frac{\Gamma_1 \vdash c : \exists_{i \in I} q_i \& \{l_i(B_i).T_i\}_{i \in I} \quad \forall i \in I. \Theta \cdot \Gamma, y_i : B_i, c : T_i \vdash P_i \quad I \subseteq J}{\Theta \cdot \Gamma, \Gamma_1 \vdash \exists_{i \in I} c[q_i] \& \{l_i(y_i).P_i\}_{i \in J}} \text{T-exist}$$

$$\frac{\Gamma_1 \vdash c : q \oplus \{l_i(B_i).T_i\}_{i \in I} \quad \Gamma_2 \vdash d_k : B_k \quad \Theta \cdot \Gamma, c : T_k \vdash P_k \quad k \in I}{\Theta \cdot \Gamma, \Gamma_1, \Gamma_2 \vdash c[q] \oplus \{l_k\langle d_k\rangle.P_k\}} \text{T-select}$$

$$\frac{\Gamma_1 \vdash c : \textbf{end} \quad \Gamma_2 \vdash s[A] : q \oplus \{l_i(B_i).T_i\}_{i \in I}}{\Gamma_3 \vdash d_k : B_k \quad \Theta \cdot \Gamma, c : T_k \vdash P_k \quad k \in I \quad c = s[p] \Rightarrow p \in A}{\Theta \cdot \Gamma, \Gamma_1, \Gamma_2, \Gamma_3 \vdash c[q] \oplus \{l_k\langle d_k\rangle.P_k\}} \text{T-select'}$$

$$\frac{s \notin \Gamma \quad \Gamma_1 = \{s[p] : G \restriction_p\}_{p \in roles(G)} \quad \Theta \cdot \Gamma, \Gamma_1 \vdash P}{\Theta \cdot \Gamma \vdash (\nu s)P} \text{T-new}$$

Fig. 2. Selection of Typing Rules for Processes (see [14] for the full version)

The rules are explained as follows:

- Rule (T-branch): $c[q] \& \{l_i(y_i).P_i\}_{i \in J}$ is typed under Γ and Γ_1, if under Γ_1, c has a type that is an external choice from q with a smaller label set $I \subseteq J$, and for each $i \in I$, P_i is typed under the channel typing context composed of Γ, the typing for bounded variable y_i that occurs in P_i and the continuation type T_i of c.
- Rule (T-exist): $\exists_{i \in I} c[q_i] \& \{l_i(y_i).P_i\}_{i \in J}$ is typed, if c has a type that is an existential external choice from the senders in $\{q_i\}_{i \in I}$ satisfying $I \subseteq J$, and for each $i \in I$, P_i is typed under Γ, the typing for y_i and the continuation type T_i of c.
  Both of the above rules indicate that processes allow more external choices.
- Rule (T-select): $c[q] \oplus \{l_k\langle d_k\rangle.P_k\}$ is typed, if c has a type that is an internal choice towards q, with a label set containing l_k inside.

- Rule (T-select'): $c[q] \oplus \{l_k \langle d_k \rangle . P_k\}$ is also typed, if the typing context corresponding to c is **end**, but the typing context for some $s[A]$ exists such that c corresponds to some role in A and c is fixed for performing the communications specified by $s[A]$. A must be the domain of some existential branching, and the role of c is among it.
- Rule (T-new): $(\nu s)P$ is typed under Γ, if P is typed under the typing context composed of Γ and the one for session s (i.e. Γ_1). Γ_1 guarantees that there exists a global type G such that each role of s has exactly the local type projected from G.

Example 3. We have the following typing derivation for the running example:

$$
\cfrac{
\cfrac{\cdots}{s[R] : G \upharpoonright_R \vdash P_{r_b} | P_{r_d}}\text{(T-select')}
\quad
\cfrac{\cdots}{s[r_s] : G \upharpoonright_{r_s} \vdash P_{r_s}}\text{(T- exist)}
}{
\cfrac{s[R] : G \upharpoonright_R, s[r_s] : G \upharpoonright_{r_s} \vdash P_{r_s} | P_{r_b} | P_{r_d}}{\emptyset \vdash (\nu s)(P_{r_s} | P_{r_b} | P_{r_d})}\text{(T-new)}
}\text{(T-Par)}
$$

The above derivation result shows that the processes are typed with the corresponding local types projected from global type G.

Subject Reduction and Progress. There are two important properties for evaluating a type system: subject reduction (also called type safety) and progress.

Theorem 2 (Subject reduction). *Assume $\Theta \cdot \Gamma \vdash P$ is derived according to the type system in Fig. 2. Then, $P \to P'$ implies $\exists\, \Gamma'$ such that $\Gamma \to_L^* \Gamma'$ and $\Theta \cdot \Gamma' \vdash P'$.*

The subject reduction guarantees that if a typed process takes a step of evaluation, then the resulting process is also typed. However, it does not guarantee that a well-typed process can always take one further step of execution if it is not terminated: it could be stuck in a deadlock while waiting for dual actions. The deadlock freedom is usually called *progress* in some literature [21]. We prove the following theorem on progress.

Theorem 3 (Progress). *Let P be $(\nu s)(\Pi_{i \in I} P_i)$, with $|roles(P_i)| = 1$ and $roles(P_i) \cap roles(P_j) = \emptyset$ for any $i, j \in I, i \neq j$. Then $\Theta, \emptyset \vdash (\nu s)P$ and $P \to^* P' \nrightarrow$ implies $P' = 0$. Here $roles(P_i)$ returns the roles of P_i.*

However, the above theorem has a strong restriction by requiring that each sequential process plays only one role. If a process plays multiple roles in a session, deadlock might occur. The reason is that the projection from a global type to local types loses the orders of actions occurring over different roles. See the example below.

Example 4. Define $P = (\nu s)P_1|P_2$, where $P_1 = s[p][r]\&\{l_1(x_1).s[p][q] \oplus \{l_2(a_2).\mathbf{0}\}\}$ and $P_2 = s[q][p]\&\{l_2(x_2).s[r][p]\oplus\{l_1(a_1).\mathbf{0}\}\}$, where P_1 plays one role p, and P_2 plays two roles q and r. Let $G = r \rightarrow p : \{l_1(B_1).p \rightarrow q : \{l_2(B_2).\mathbf{end}\}\}$, $\Gamma \vdash a_1 : B_1, a_2 : B_2$, we have

$$G \restriction_r = p \oplus l_1(B_1).\mathbf{end} \quad G \restriction_q = p\&l_2(B_2).\mathbf{end} \quad G \restriction_p = r\&l_1(B_1).q \oplus l_2(B_2).\mathbf{end}$$

By the type system, $\emptyset \cdot \Gamma \vdash P$. However, P leads to a deadlock. In next section, we will define a communication type system by abandoning the restriction on a single role.

Session Fidelity. The session fidelity connects process reductions to typing context reductions. It says that the interactions of a typed process follow the transitions of corresponding local types, thus eventually follow the protocol defined by the global type.

Theorem 4 (Session Fidelity). *Let P be $\Pi_{i \in I}P_i$, with $|roles(P_i)| = 1$ and $roles(P_i) \cap roles(P_j) = \emptyset$ for any $i, j \in I, i \neq j$. If $\Theta, \Gamma \vdash P$, $\Gamma = \{s[p] : G \restriction_p \}_{p \in roles(G)}$ for some global type G, and $\Gamma \rightarrow_L$, then there exist Γ' and P' such that $\Gamma \rightarrow_L \Gamma'$, $P \rightarrow P'$ and $\Theta \cdot \Gamma' \vdash P'$.*

5   A Communication Type System for Progress

This section defines a communication type system for guaranteeing the progress of processes in MSSR π-calculus, especially for the cases when one sequential process plays multiple roles. This is achieved by recording the execution orders of communication events for processes and then checking if there exists a dependence loop indicating that all processes are on waiting status and cannot proceed.

Notations. First of all, we introduce the notion of *directed events*:

- A *directed event* $(c[r], 1, i)$, where c is a channel, r a role, 1 a label and $i > 0$ a time index, representing that this event is the i-th communication action of $c[r]$ and the label is 1. The event is *directed* from the role of c to r, e.g. if $c = s[p]$, it means that p sends to or receives from r at this event.
- A *directed event with channel mobility* $(c[r], 1, i, c', A)$, where c' is the channel exchanged over this event and A is a set recording the communication history of c' till this event occurs. Each element of A has form $(c'[p], k)$, where p is a role and $k > 0$, indicating that k times of communications on $c'[p]$ have occurred before c' is moved by this event.

Below we denote the sets of these two kinds of events by $\mathcal{E}$ and $\mathcal{E}_M$, and for simplicity, call them *events* and *mobility events* resp. For any e in $\mathcal{E}$ or $\mathcal{E}_M$, we will use $e.i$ to represent the i-th sub-component.

Each communication typing rule takes the form $\Delta \vdash P \triangleright U, M, R$, where P is the process to be typed, $U \subseteq \mathcal{E}$ is the set of the least events of P such that no event has occurred prior to them, M is the set of mobility events that have occurred in P, $R \subseteq \mathcal{E} \times \mathcal{E}$ is a set of relations describing the execution order of events, and Δ is the communication context for functions, of the form $\{X(\tilde{y}) \triangleright U_X, M_X, R_X\}_{X \in P}$, for any function X called in P. $(e_1, e_2) \in R$ means that e_1 occurs strictly before e_2 in P, and we will write $e_1 \prec_R e_2$ as an abbreviation (R omitted without confusion). The addition of M is mainly to transfer the history information of each channel to be moved to the corresponding target receiver.

Before presenting the typing rules, we introduce some notations (all symbols are defined as before). $U \setminus c[r]$ removes all events of $c[r]$ from U, i.e. $\{e \mid e \in U \wedge e.1 \neq c[r]\}$; $pre(x, U)$ is defined as $\{x \prec y \mid y \in U\}$, to represent that x occurs prior to all events in U; $\mathcal{C}(d)$ is a boolean condition judging whether d is a channel value; $M_1 \triangleleft b \triangleright M_2$ returns M_2 if b is true, otherwise M_1; events $(s[p][q], 1, i)$ and $(s[q][p], 1, i)$ are said to be *dual*, and we use $\bar{e}$ to represent the dual event of e. At the end, we define the *k-th index increase* of events with respect to a fixed pair of sender and receiver α, which has the form $c[q]$ for some c and q. Let e be an event $(c[r], l, i)$ and me be a mobility event $(c[r], l, i, c', A)$:

$$e \uparrow_k^\alpha \triangleq \begin{cases} (c[r], l, i + k) & \text{if } \alpha = c[r] \\ e & \text{otherwise} \end{cases} \qquad A \uparrow_k^\alpha \triangleq \begin{cases} A \setminus (\alpha, i) \cup \{(\alpha, i + k)\} & \text{if } (\alpha, i) \in A \\ A \cup \{(\alpha, k)\} & \text{otherwise} \end{cases}$$

$$me \uparrow_k^\alpha \triangleq \begin{cases} (c[r], l, i + k, c', A) & \text{if } \alpha = c[r] \\ (c[r], l, i, c', A \uparrow_k^{c'[p]}) & \text{if } \alpha = c'[p] \text{ for some } p \\ me & \text{otherwise} \end{cases}$$

$$R \uparrow_k^{c[q]} \triangleq \{e \uparrow_k^{c[q]} \prec e' \uparrow_k^{c[q]} \mid e \prec e' \in R\} \qquad M \uparrow_k^{c[q]} \triangleq \{me \uparrow_k^{c[q]} \mid me \in M\}$$

$$R \uparrow^A \triangleq \bigcup_{(c[q], k) \in A} R \uparrow_k^{c[q]} \qquad M \uparrow^A \triangleq \bigcup_{(c[q], k) \in A} M \uparrow_k^{c[q]}$$

$e \uparrow_k^\alpha$ says, when e is occurring on α, its time index is increased by k, otherwise not changed. $me \uparrow_k^\alpha$ not only promotes the event itself with respect to α (the first case), but also the communication history of c' (the second case). As defined by $A \uparrow_k^\alpha$, the pair corresponding to α is increased by k, or added if it is not in A. $R \uparrow_k^{c[q]}$ and $M \uparrow_k^{c[q]}$ perform the pointwise k-th index increase with respect to $c[q]$ to all events in them, $R \uparrow^A$ and $M \uparrow^A$ perform the index increase of events in R and M with respect to A. For simplicity, we omit the subscript k of all the above definitions when $k = 1$.

$$\frac{\Delta \vdash P \triangleright U, M, R \quad M' = (\emptyset \triangleleft \mathcal{C}(d) \triangleright \{(c[q], 1, 1, d, \emptyset)\})}{\Delta \vdash c[q] \oplus \{l\langle d\rangle.P\} \triangleright \{(c[q], 1, 1)\}, M \uparrow^{c[q]} \cup M',}$$ C-select
$$R \uparrow^{c[q]} \cup \{pre((c[q], 1, 1), U \backslash c[q])\}$$

$$\frac{\forall i \in I \quad \Delta \vdash P_i \triangleright U_i, M_i, R_i \quad M_i' = (\emptyset \triangleleft \mathcal{C}(y_i) \triangleright \{(c[q], l_i, 1, y_i, \emptyset)\})}{\Delta \vdash c[q] \& \{l_i(y_i).P_i\}_{i \in I} \triangleright \bigcup_{i \in I}\{(c[q], l_i, 1)\}, \bigcup_{i \in I}(M_i \uparrow^{c[q]} \cup M_i'),}$$ C-bran
$$\bigcup_{i \in I}(R_i \uparrow^{c[q]} \cup \{pre((c[q], l_i, 1), U_i \backslash c[q])\})$$

$$\frac{\forall i \in I \quad \Delta \vdash P_i \triangleright U_i, M_i, R_i \quad M_i' = (\emptyset \triangleleft \mathcal{C}(y_i) \triangleright \{(c[q_i], l_i, 1, y_i, \emptyset)\})}{\Delta \vdash \exists_{i \in I} c[q_i] \& \{l_i(y_i).P_i\} \triangleright \bigcup_{i \in I}\{(c[q_i], l_i, 1)\}, \bigcup_{i \in I}(M_i \uparrow^{c[q_i]} \cup M_i'),}$$ C-exist
$$\bigcup_{i \in I}(R_i \uparrow^{c[q_i]} \cup \{pre((c[q], l_i, 1), U_i \backslash c[q_i])\})$$

$$\frac{}{\Delta \vdash \mathbf{0} \triangleright \emptyset, \emptyset, \emptyset}$$ C-0 $$\frac{\Delta \vdash P \triangleright U, M, R \quad \Delta \vdash Q \triangleright U', M', R'}{\Delta \vdash P|Q \triangleright U \cup U', M \cup M', R \cup R'}$$ C-par

$$\frac{}{\Delta, X(\tilde{x}) \triangleright U, M, R \vdash X(\tilde{d}) \triangleright U[\tilde{d}/\tilde{x}], M[\tilde{d}/\tilde{x}], R[\tilde{d}/\tilde{x}]}$$ C-call

$$\frac{\Delta \vdash P[0/X] \triangleright U, M, R \quad \Delta, X(\tilde{x}) \triangleright U, M, R \vdash Q \triangleright U', M', R'}{\Delta \vdash \mathbf{def}\, X(\tilde{x}) = P \,\mathbf{in}\, Q \triangleright U', M', R'}$$ C-def

$$\frac{\Delta \vdash P \triangleright U, M, R \quad M, R \Rightarrow_u M', R'}{\Delta \vdash P \triangleright U, M', R'}$$ C-unify $$\frac{\Delta \vdash P \triangleright U, M, R \quad R \Rightarrow_t R'}{\Delta \vdash P \triangleright U, M, R'}$$ C-trans

$$\frac{B = A[x/s[m]]}{M \cup (s[p][q], 1, i, s[m], A) \cup (s[q][p], 1, i, x, \emptyset), R \Rightarrow_u (M \uparrow^B)[s[m]/x], (R \uparrow^B)[s[m]/x]}$$ Unify

$$\frac{}{\{e_1 \prec e_2, \overline{e_2} \prec e_3\} \Rightarrow_t \{e_1 \prec e_3\}}$$ Trans-1 $$\frac{R' \subseteq R \quad R' \Rightarrow_t R''}{R \Rightarrow_t R \cup R''}$$ Trans-2

Fig. 3. A Communication Type System for Processes and Auxiliary Definitions

5.1 Typing Rules

Figure 3 presents the communication type system for MSSR session calculus and the auxiliary rules for unification and transitivity of relations, with explanations below:

- Rule (C-select): The prefix selection produces event $(c[q], 1, 1)$, which becomes the (only) least event of the current process. If d is a channel value, $(c[q], 1, 1, d, \emptyset)$ is added to M, especially $\emptyset$ indicating no communication along d has occurred till now. The occurrence of $(c[q], 1, 1)$ promotes the time indexes of events of $c[q]$ in both R and M by 1. The precedence from $(c[q], 1, 1)$ to all events of non-$c[q]$ channels in U holds and the corresponding relations are added to the R-set.
- Rule (C-bran): The prefix branch process produces a set of least events $(c[q], l_i, 1)$ for $i \in I$. When y_i is a channel, $(c[q], l_i, 1, y_i, \emptyset)$ is added to M_i. The M_i, R_i-sets are joined together, and furthermore, they promote all events with respect to $c[q]$. The precedence from $(c[q], l_i, 1)$ to non-$c[q]$ events in U_i are added to each R_i-set.
- Rule (C-exist): Each existential branch from q_i for $i \in I$ is handled similarly as in (C-bran) to update the three sets.

- Rule (C-par): The three communication typing sets corresponding to P and Q are joined together for $P|Q$.
- Rules (C-call) and (C-def): Function call $X(\tilde{d})$ instantiates the communication typing sets for $X(\tilde{x})$ by substituting $\tilde{d}$ for $\tilde{x}$. Function declaration $X(\tilde{x})$ unfolds the function body P once by replacing the (possibly recursive) occurrence of X in P by $\mathbf{0}$ to compute the communication typing sets of $X(\tilde{x})$. This is adequate, because by the type system of Fig. 2, each process is typed with the corresponding projection of a global type, thus all end-point processes conform to the same recursive structure as specified by the global type and one time unfolding is enough for representing all cases of communication orders between events.
- Rule (C-unify): It defines the unification of M and R according to rule (Unify). Rule (Unify) transfers the channel value $s[m]$ and its communication history recorded by A from sender p to receiver q, by first promoting the events on x with respect to the history $A[x/s[m]]$ and then substituting all occurrences of x for $s[m]$. Through unification, all variable channels in R are instantiated to constant channels and the events of them have the correct time indexes (globally).
- Rule (C-trans): It defines the transitivity of R according to rules (Trans-1) and (Trans-2), based on the synchronization of an event and its dual.

A relation R is *safe*, if $e \prec \bar{e} \notin R$ for any e, i.e. there does not exist an event e such that e and its dual event $\bar{e}$ (that are expected to be synchronized) are in a strict order.

Theorem 5 (Progress). *Suppose* $\Theta, \emptyset \vdash (\nu s)P$ *and* $\Delta \vdash P \triangleright U, M, R$, *if both* *(C-unify) and (C-trans) cannot be applied anymore to M and R, and if R is safe, then $P \rightarrow^* P' \nrightarrow$ implies $P' = \mathbf{0}$.*

Example 5. We show how to use the communication type system to type the processes in Example 4. In particular, P_2 produces a relation between $s[q][p]$ and $s[r][p]$, which is absent in the previous type system.

$$\frac{\dfrac{\Delta \vdash \mathbf{0} \triangleright \emptyset, \emptyset, \emptyset}{\Delta \vdash s[p][q] \oplus \{l_2(a_2).\mathbf{0}\} \triangleright \{(s[p][q], l_2, 1)\}, \emptyset, \emptyset}[\text{C-select}]}{\begin{array}{l}\Delta \vdash s[p][r]\&\{l_1(x_1).s[p][q] \oplus \{l_2(a_2).\mathbf{0}\}\} \triangleright \{(s[p][r], l_1, 1)\}, \emptyset, \\ \qquad\qquad\qquad\qquad\qquad\qquad\qquad\qquad \{(s[p][r], l_1, 1) \prec (s[p][q], l_2, 1)\}\end{array}}[\text{C-bran}]$$

$$\frac{\dfrac{\Delta \vdash \mathbf{0} \triangleright \emptyset, \emptyset, \emptyset}{\Delta \vdash s[r][p] \oplus \{l_1(a_1).\mathbf{0}\} \triangleright \{(s[r][p], l_1, 1)\}, \emptyset, \emptyset}[\text{C-select}]}{\begin{array}{l}\Delta \vdash s[q][p]\&\{l_2(x_2).s[r][p] \oplus \{l_1(a_1).\mathbf{0}\}\} \triangleright \{(s[q][p], l_2, 1)\}, \emptyset, \\ \qquad\qquad\qquad\qquad\qquad\qquad\qquad\qquad \{(s[q][p], l_2, 1) \prec (s[r][p], l_1, 1)\}\end{array}}[\text{C-bran}]$$

By [C-par], (Trans-1) and (C-Trans), $P_1|P_2$ produces a relation set containing $(s[p][r], l_1, 1) \prec (s[r][p], l_1, 1)$, which is not *safe*.

6   Modelling Rust Multi-threads in MSSR Session Types

Rust offers both message-passing and shared-state mechanisms for concurrent programming. This section presents how to model these different concurrency primitives using MSSR session types.

Channel. Rust library provides communication primitives for handling multi-producer, single-consumer communications. A channel x contains two parts (tx, rx), with tx standing for the transmitter and rx for the receiver. The channel can be synchronous or asynchronous, and allows a buffer to store the values. Let s be the session created for (tx, rx), p and q the owner threads of tx and rx respectively. If the channel is synchronous with buffer size 0, it is consistent with synchronous communication in session types. The Rust primitives $tx.\mathsf{send}(val)$ and $a = rx.\mathsf{recv}()$, representing that tx sends val and rx receives the value and assigns it to a, are encoded as the processes resp. below:

$$tx.\mathsf{send}(val) : s[p][q] \oplus \mathrm{x}(val) \qquad a = rx.\mathsf{recv}() : s[q][p] \& \mathrm{x}(a)$$

where the threads of tx and rx (i.e. p and q) are translated as roles, and the channel name x is translated as the message label. Through this way, each thread plays one role, which satisfies the condition of progress property of the type system of Fig. 2.

The transmitter can be cloned to multiple copies, denoted by $tx_i, i \in I$, each of which communicates with the same receiver rx. The existential branching process models this case. Suppose $x_i = (tx_i, rx)$, and the threads of tx_i are p_i for $i \in I$, then

$$tx_i.\mathsf{send}(val) : c[p_i][q] \oplus \mathrm{x}_i(val) \qquad a = rx.\mathsf{recv}() : \exists_{i \in I} c[q][p_i] \& \{\mathrm{x}_i(a)\}$$

If the channel has a buffer with size $n > 0$, the transmitter can send without waiting for the first n times. We model this case in the extended report [14].

Mutex. For shared state concurrency, Rust provides mutex to allow only one thread to access the shared data at one time. Assume threads $t_i, i \in I$ want to access shared data d, protected by the mutex lock m. Each thread can call lock, $\mathsf{try\_lock}$, unlock[1] to acquire, try to acquire and release the lock resp. They are encoded as follows:

$$m.\mathsf{lock}() : \qquad m[t_i][s_m] \oplus l_i(\_).m[t_i][s_m] \oplus \mathsf{lock}(\_).m[t_i][s_m] \& \mathrm{ok}(d)$$
$$m.\mathsf{try\_lock}() : m[t_i][s_m] \oplus l_i(\_).m[t_i][s_m] \oplus \mathsf{try\_lock}(\_).m[t_i][s_m] \& \{\mathrm{ok}(d), \mathrm{block}(\_)\}$$
$$\mathsf{unlock}(m) : \qquad m[t_i][s_m] \oplus l_i(\_).m[t_i][s_m] \oplus \mathsf{unlock}(d)$$

---

[1] Rust releases locks implicitly, but we treat unlock explicitly for illustrating our approach.

For each method, thread t_i first sends a message to server s_m to build the connection, followed by the lock/try_lock/unlock requests resp. Message ok received from s_m indicates that t_i acquires the lock successfully, while message block means that the lock is occupied by another thread and t_i fails to get it.

A server thread s_m is defined to coordinate the access of the shared data from different threads as follows. P models the initial state, expects to receive a message from $t_i, i \in I$, and for either lock or try_lock request, sends ok to t_i. The process continues as P_i, which is available to receive messages from either P_i to release the lock and go back to P again, or from another P_j to try to acquire the lock but it is denied and goes back to P_i.

$$P = \exists_{i \in I} m[s_m][t_i] \& \{l_i(\_).m[s_m][t_i] \& \left\{ \begin{array}{l} \mathrm{lock}(\_).m[s_m][t_i] \oplus \mathrm{ok}(d).P_i, \\ \mathrm{try\_lock}(\_).m[s_m][t_i] \oplus \mathrm{ok}(d).P_i \end{array} \right\}$$

$$P_i = \exists_{j \in I} m[s_m][t_j] \& \{l_j(\_).P_{ij}\}, i \in I$$

$$P_{ij} = \left\{ \begin{array}{ll} m[s_m][t_i] \& \mathrm{unlock}(d).P & , i = j, i, j \in I \\ m[s_m][t_j] \& \mathrm{try\_lock}(\_).m[s_m][t_j] \oplus \mathrm{block}(\_).P_i & , i \neq j, i, j \in I \end{array} \right.$$

Except for the above channels and mutex, we also model Rust Read-Write Lock in [14].

Discussion on Rust Programs. With the help of the encoding of concurrency primitives, we can represent a whole Rust multi-threaded program as an MSSR process. Some details such as assignments are neglected (similar to most static analysis approaches), while concurrency primitives and control flow such as sequential composition, if-else, loop, and (recursive) functions, are supported by MSSR calculus directly. After a Rust program is translated to an MSSR process, it can be typed according to the type systems defined in this paper, to check whether it is type-safe and deadlock-free. A Rust program that passes the type checking is guaranteed to be type-safe and deadlock-free, but the inverse does not hold, i.e. programs that fail in the check might be safe in execution, mainly due to abstraction of the encoding from Rust to session calculus.

7   Conclusion and Future Work

This work introduced an extension of session types with existential branching type for specifying and validating more flexible interactions with multiple senders and a single receiver. This extension can represent many communication protocols, such as Rust multi-thread primitives as encoded in the paper. We established the type system for the extended session types based on projection and global types, to ensure type safety, progress and fidelity. We proposed a more general communication type system for guaranteeing progress without restrictions of existing approaches, by studying the execution orders between communication events among different participants.

To make full use of the extended session types, several future works can be considered. First, the type systems presented in this paper follow a top-down approach based on end-point projections, which might be restrictive to reject some valid processes when the corresponding global types do not exist. To avoid this, we will consider to define the type systems by checking local session types directly instead, as in [23]. Second, as an important application, we are considering to implement the translation from Rust multi-threaded programs to the extended session types for safety checking; Third, we will apply our approach to model and check more practical protocols and applications.

References

1. Barwell, A.D., Scalas, A., Yoshida, N., Zhou, F.: Generalised multiparty session types with crash-stop failures. In: CONCUR 2022, volume 243 of LIPIcs, pp. 1–25. Schloss Dagstuhl - Leibniz-Zentrum für Informatik (2022)
2. Bettini, L., Coppo, M., D'Antoni, L., De Luca, M., Dezani-Ciancaglini, M., Yoshida, N.: Global progress in dynamically interleaved multiparty sessions. In: van Breugel, F., Chechik, M. (eds.) CONCUR 2008. LNCS, vol. 5201, pp. 418–433. Springer, Heidelberg (2008). https://doi.org/10.1007/978-3-540-85361-9_33
3. Chen, R., Balzer, S., Toninho, B.: Ferrite: a judgmental embedding of session types in Rust. In: ECOOP 2022, volume 222 of LIPIcs, pp. 1–28. Schloss Dagstuhl - Leibniz-Zentrum für Informatik (2022)
4. Dezani-Ciancaglini, M., de'Liguoro, U., Yoshida, N.: On progress for structured communications. In: Barthe, G., Fournet, C. (eds.) TGC 2007. LNCS, vol. 4912, pp. 257–275. Springer, Heidelberg (2008). https://doi.org/10.1007/978-3-540-78663-4_18
5. Deniélou, P.-M., Yoshida, N.: Dynamic multirole session types. In: POPL 2011, pp. 435–446. ACM (2011)
6. Fowler, S., Lindley, S., Morris, J.G., Decova, S.: Exceptional asynchronous session types: session types without tiers. In: POPL 2019, pp. 1–29. ACM (2019)
7. Gheri, L., Lanese, I., Sayers, N., Tuosto, E., Yoshida, N.: Design-by-contract for flexible multiparty session protocols. In: ECOOP 2022, volume 222 of LIPIcs, pp. 1–28. Schloss Dagstuhl - Leibniz-Zentrum für Informatik (2022)
8. Ghilezan, S., Jaksic, S., Pantovic, J., Scalas, A., Yoshida, N.: Precise subtyping for synchronous multiparty sessions. J. Log. Algebraic Methods Program. **104**, 127–173 (2019)
9. Honda, K.: Types for dyadic interaction. In: Best, E. (ed.) CONCUR 1993. LNCS, vol. 715, pp. 509–523. Springer, Heidelberg (1993). https://doi.org/10.1007/3-540-57208-2_35
10. Honda, K., Vasconcelos, V.T., Kubo, M.: Language primitives and type discipline for structured communication-based programming. In: Hankin, C. (ed.) ESOP 1998. LNCS, vol. 1381, pp. 122–138. Springer, Heidelberg (1998). https://doi.org/10.1007/BFb0053567
11. Honda, K., Yoshida, N., Carbone, M.: Multiparty asynchronous session types. In: POPL 2008, pp. 273–284. ACM (2008)
12. Imai, K., Lange, J., Neykova, R.: Kmclib: automated inference and verification of session types from OCaml programs. In: TACAS 2022. LNCS, vol. 13243, pp. 379–386. Springer, Cham (2022). https://doi.org/10.1007/978-3-030-99524-9_20

13. Jespersen, T.B.L., Munksgaard, P., Larsen, K.F.: Session types for rust. In: WGP@ICFP 2015, pp. 13–22. ACM (2015)
14. Ji, Z., Wang, S., Xu, X.: Session types with multiple senders single receiver (report version). https://arxiv.org/abs/2310.12187 (2023). arxiv CoRR (2023)
15. Kobayashi, N.: Type-based information flow analysis for the pi-calculus. Acta Informatica **42**(4–5), 291–347 (2005)
16. Kobayashi, N.: A new type system for deadlock-free processes. In: Baier, C., Hermanns, H. (eds.) CONCUR 2006. LNCS, vol. 4137, pp. 233–247. Springer, Heidelberg (2006). https://doi.org/10.1007/11817949_16
17. Kokke, W.: Rusty variation: deadlock-free sessions with failure in rust. In: ICE 2019, volume 304 of EPTCS, pp. 48–60 (2019)
18. Lagaillardie, N., Neykova, R., Yoshida, N.: Implementing multiparty session types in rust. In: Bliudze, S., Bocchi, L. (eds.) COORDINATION 2020. LNCS, vol. 12134, pp. 127–136. Springer, Cham (2020). https://doi.org/10.1007/978-3-030-50029-0_8
19. Lange, J., Yoshida, N.: Verifying asynchronous interactions via communicating session automata. In: Dillig, I., Tasiran, S. (eds.) CAV 2019. LNCS, vol. 11561, pp. 97–117. Springer, Cham (2019). https://doi.org/10.1007/978-3-030-25540-4_6
20. Majumdar, R., Yoshida, N., Zufferey, D.: Multiparty motion coordination: From choreographies to robotics programs. Proc. ACM Program. Lang. **4**(OOPSLA), 1–30 (2020)
21. Pierce, B.C.: Types and Programming Languages. MIT Press, Cambridge (2002)
22. Scalas, A., Yoshida, N.: Multiparty session types, beyond duality. J. Log. Algebraic Methods Program. **97**, 55–84 (2018)
23. Scalas, A., Yoshida, N.: Less is more: multiparty session types revisited. In: POPL 2019, pp. 1–29 (2019)
24. Toninho, B., Yoshida, N.: Certifying data in multiparty session types. J. Log. Algebraic Methods Program. **90**, 61–83 (2017)
25. Toninho, B., Yoshida, N.: Depending on session-typed processes. In: Baier, C., Dal Lago, U. (eds.) FoSSaCS 2018. LNCS, vol. 10803, pp. 128–145. Springer, Cham (2018). https://doi.org/10.1007/978-3-319-89366-2_7
26. Tu, T., Liu, X., Song, L., Zhang, Y.: Understanding real-world concurrency bugs in go. In: ASPLOS 2019, pp. 865–878. ACM (2019)
27. Wu, H., Xi, H.: Dependent session types. https://arxiv.org/abs/1704.07004. arXiv CoRR. (2017)
28. Yoshida, N., Deniélou, P.-M., Bejleri, A., Hu, R.: Parameterised multiparty session types. In: Ong, L. (ed.) FoSSaCS 2010. LNCS, vol. 6014, pp. 128–145. Springer, Heidelberg (2010). https://doi.org/10.1007/978-3-642-12032-9_10
29. Yoshida, N., Gheri, L.: A very gentle introduction to multiparty session types. In: Hung, D.V., D'Souza, M. (eds.) ICDCIT 2020. LNCS, vol. 11969, pp. 73–93. Springer, Cham (2020). https://doi.org/10.1007/978-3-030-36987-3_5

Understanding the Reproducibility Issues
of Monkey for GUI Testing

Huiyu Liu[1], Qichao Kong[1], Jue Wang[2(✉)], Ting Su[1], and Haiying Sun[1(✉)]

[1] Shanghai Key Laboratory of Trustworthy Computing,
East China Normal University, Shanghai, China
hysun@sei.ecnu.edu.cn
[2] Nanjing University, Nanjing, China
juewang591@gmail.com

Abstract. Automated GUI testing is an essential activity in developing Android apps. MONKEY is a widely used representative automated input generation (AIG) tool to efficiently and effectively detect crash bugs in Android apps. However, it faces challenges in reproducing the crash bugs it detects. To deeply understand the symptoms and root causes of these challenges, we conducted a comprehensive study on the reproducibility issues of MONKEY with Android apps. We focused on MONKEY's capability to reproduce crash bugs using its built-in replay functionality and explored the root causes of its failures. Specifically, we selected six popular open-source apps and conducted automated instrumentation on them to monitor the invocations of event handlers within the apps. Subsequently, we performed GUI testing with MONKEY on these instrumented apps for 6,000 test cases and collected 56 unique crash bugs. For each bug, we replayed it 200 times using MONKEY's replay function and calculated the success rate. Through manual analysis of screen recording files, log files of event handlers, and the source code of the apps, we pinpointed five root causes contributing to MONKEY's reproducibility issues: Injection Failure, Event Ambiguity, Data Loading, Widget Loading, and Dynamic Content. Our research showed that only 36.6% of the replays successfully reproduced the crash bugs, shedding light on MONKEY's limitations in consistently reproducing detected crash bugs. Additionally, we delved deep into the unsuccessfully reproduced replays to discern the root causes behind the reproducibility issues and offered insights for developing future AIG tools.

Keywords: Reproducibility · Empirical Study · Android GUI Testing

1 Introduction

The Android apps have become increasingly widespread [2]. In Android app development, GUI (Graphical User Interface) testing is crucial for ensuring the stability and reliability of Android apps. It aims to mitigate the risk of software failures, data breaches, and other potentially expensive issues. To support

H. Hermanns et al. (Eds.): SETTA 2023, LNCS 14464, pp. 132–151, 2024.
https://doi.org/10.1007/978-981-99-8664-4_8

efficient and robust GUI testing, numerous AIG (Automated Input Generation) tools have been developed [1,6,16–18,20,29,31–33]. By sending GUI events automatically to the app under test and monitoring its performance, these AIG tools effectively detect and report crash bugs in Android apps.

Despite the success of AIG tools in detecting crash bugs, the primary challenge in addressing these bugs is reproducing them. Most existing AIG tools lack replay functionality. As a result, testers must manually attempt to reproduce any reported crash bugs, which can be both challenging and labor-intensive. Even for AIG tools that offer replay functionalities (e.g., MONKEY [23], APE [11], DROID-BOT [16]), they cannot guarantee reliable reproduction due to varying runtime contexts [30], which brings challenges for testers to diagnose and fix these crash bugs. Flakiness in Android testing refers to the inconsistent results of automated tests. Most of the existing studies about flakiness in Android testing primarily focus on flaky tests in UI testing frameworks like ESPRESSO. A few works have also studied the reproducibility issues associated with AIG tools [28,30]. However, these studies reproduce the buggy trace only a few times, which might not be comprehensive or systematic. We believe that a deep understanding of the reproducibility issues of AIG tools is crucial. Such insight can pinpoint the limitations of these tools and suggest directions for improvement.

Therefore, we conducted an in-depth study of the reproducibility issues of AIG tools. Specifically, we focus on MONKEY [23], a widely adopted AIG tool for Android apps in industry [26,34]. MONKEY provides the capability to simulate user interactions by generating random events such as clicks, touches, or gestures, as well as some system-level events. Moreover, it has a built-in functionality to replay the event sequences it generated. Google has officially integrated MONKEY into the Android SDK (Software Development Kit) [24], highlighting the representativeness and significance of MONKEY for Android GUI testing. To get insights on the reproducibility of MONKEY, in this work, we primarily focus on the following two research questions:

- **RQ1**: How reliably can MONKEY reproduce the crash bugs it detects?
- **RQ2**: What are the root causes of the reproducibility issues of MONKEY?

To answer the two research questions, we selected six real-world, open-source Android apps, and conducted GUI testing on them with MONKEY. When a crash bug was detected, we replayed it with MONKEY's built-in functionality. Specifically, to get further information about the execution status of each replay, we implemented an instrumentation tool in the form of a Gradle Plugin using a Java bytecode manipulation and analysis framework - ASM [5]. Applying the plugin to our subject apps can help us observe how the app reacts to input events from the event handler level. We recorded the execution information of each replay, including the event sequence, screen recording, and the event handler invocations recorded by our instrumentation. Finally, we conducted a manual analysis of the unsuccessfully-reproduced replays and identified the root causes.

According to our experimental results, only 36.6% of the replays can successfully reproduce the crash bugs detected by MONKEY on average. We categorized the root causes of the reproducibility issues into five types, namely *Injection*

Failure, Event Ambiguity, Data Loading, Widget Loading and *Dynamic Content*. The most prevalent cause, *Injection Failure*, stems from MONKEY's event generation mechanism, accounting for 54.4% of the 7,100 unsuccessful replays. *Event Ambiguity, Data Loading, Widget Loading,* and *Dynamic Content* account for 20.9%, 15.1%, 9.2%, and 0.4%, respectively. Our study reveals the limitation of MONKEY in reliably reproducing the crash bugs it detects, which can also be generalized to AIG tools implemented based on the principles of MONKEY. For researchers, understanding these limitations can guide the enhancement of existing AIG tools and the future development of the coming AIG tools. For developers, understanding these limitations can help to interpret the bug reports and assess whether the AIG tool's inputs truly represent the user interactions that led to the crash. It also allows developers to distinguish between genuine bugs and false positives (reporting a bug that doesn't exist) or false negatives (not detecting an actual bug) caused by the tool's inaccuracies.

Overall, the main contributions of this paper can be summarized as follows:

- To our knowledge, we conducted the first systematic and in-depth study to investigate MONKEY's reproducibility issues.
- To study the reproducibility issues of MONKEY, we implemented an instrumentation tool that can help observe the runtime behavior of the apps from the event handler level.
- We identified five root causes of MONKEY's reproducibility issues from different perspectives (e.g., MONKEY's self unreliability, app's feature), and some of these root causes (e.g., *Injection Failure, Event Ambiguity*) were not identified previously.
- We have publicly released our tool and dataset at https://github.com/ InstrumentDroid/InstrumentDroid.

2 Empirical Study Methodology

This section presents our methodology for investigating the reproducibility rate of crash bugs detected by MONKEY and analyzing the root causes of the reproducibility issues of MONKEY. Figure 1 shows the methodology of our study.

2.1 Notations and Definitions

An Android app is a GUI-based event-driven program P. A crash bug r can be described as a type of fault in P that triggers a runtime exception resulting in an app crash or hang. A MONKEY event e is an event generated by MONKEY to simulate various user interactions, such as touch events, key events, and system events. Note that MONKEY is coordinate-sensitive rather than widget-sensitive, so not event MONKEY event interacts with UI elements. We denote these MONKEY events as blank events. When finished a MONKEY testing, P responds to a sequence of MONKEY events $E = [e_1, e_2, ..., e_n]$ and yields an execution trace $\tau = \langle E, I \rangle$, where E denotes the MONKEY event sequence and I denotes the event handler invocation sequence.

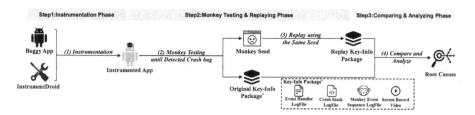

Fig. 1. Overview of our methodology including three major phases

2.2 Experimental Method

Step 1: Instrumentation Phase. To monitor the real-time execution sequence of GUI events during MONKEY testing, we crafted an instrumentation tool, INSTRUMENTDROID, which was capable of capturing the invocations of event handlers in the app. Event handlers are responsible for responding to the events generated by UI widgets when interacting with them. Therefore, INSTRUMENT-DROID hook into the event handlers corresponding to the UI widgets to get the GUI event sequences. Specifically, we first used a bytecode manipulation framework ASM to collect all the event handlers as an *Event Handler List*. Next, we developed the Gradle plugin INSTRUMENTDROID. When applying INSTRUMENT-DROID to the apps, it can automatically scan all the event handlers in the app's source code and insert a piece of code into these event handlers to get runtime information about these event handlers. In this way, when users interact with a specific UI widget, its corresponding event handler is invoked, then the log information of this event handler is output to a designated file so that we can know which UI widget users are interacting with. Figure 2 shows the workflow of instrumentation.

Step 2: Monkey Testing & Replaying Phase. In this phase, we aim to conduct automated random GUI testing with MONKEY on the instrumented apps until we get a series of unique crash bugs, and replay them with MONKEY's built-in functionality.

Key-Info Package. To quantify app execution status, we recorded data termed *Key-Info Package*. A *Key-Info Package* consists of four components: *Event Handler LogFile*, *Crash Stack LogFile*, *Monkey Event Sequence LogFile* and *Screen Record Video*. The *Event Handler LogFile* is the output from INSTRUMENT-DROID, which documents the invocation state of event handlers. When an event handler is triggered, the *Event Handler LogFile* logs its invocation time, the related UI widget information, and its fully qualified name. For example, in Fig. 3, lines 1-3 show the logs for *onOptionsItemSelected* invocation. Line 1 indicates the invocation time of *onOptionsItemSelected*. Line 2 indicates its UI widget details (with the resourceId of this Option Menu as '2131296485' and the Menu Option labeled 'History'). Line 3 gives its fully qualified name. The *Crash Stack LogFile* and *Monkey Event Sequence LogFile* are both outputs from MONKEY. *Crash Stack LogFile* details crash events, including the crash location, exception information, etc. *Monkey Event Sequence LogFile* records events and actions performed by MONKEY, including action types, coordinates, etc. Finally, *Screen Record Video* captures the real-time Android device display during the MONKEY test, showcasing all visual actions during the MONKEY testing process. It is obtained by the built-in screen recording functionality *screenrecord* of Android ADB.

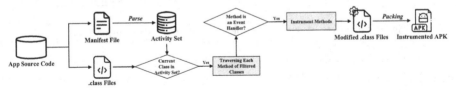

Fig. 2. Workflow of our instrumentation approach

Monkey Testing. We aim to use MONKEY for random GUI testing to collect unique crash bugs and their corresponding *Key-Info Package*. For each app, we set up 1,000 test cases, and each test case is a single MONKEY test. We customize the command-line parameters for each test, including throttle and event count. For off-line apps, half of the test cases have a throttle of 200 ms and the other half 500 ms. On-line apps have throttles set at 500 ms and 1000 ms, based on empirical findings from other automated testing studies [4, 22]. We set an event count limit of 5,000 MONKEY events per test. If a crash happens within this limit, MONKEY stops and outputs the test's *Key-Info Package*. We use a shell script to manage the processes, from starting the emulator to extracting the *Key-Info Package*. Finally, we can get the execution traces and *Key-Info Packages* of these crash bugs. We denote the execution trace of a crash bug as τ_O, representing the original execution trace.

```
1   18:34:50.364/
2   131296485/History
3   com/amaze/filemanager/activities/MainActivity/onOptionsItemSelected
```

Fig. 3. Example of the output log of INSTRUMENTDROID

Replaying. A key feature of MONKEY is its capability to generate identical pseudo-random event sequences using a *Seed*. Leveraging this, we replay each τ_O 200 times with consistent seed and throttle settings, collecting the replay execution traces and their *Key-Info Packages*. The replay execution trace is denoted as τ_R.

Step 3: Comparing & Analyzing Phase. In this stage, our goals are (1) comparing each pair of τ_O and τ_R, determining how many replays successfully reproduced the crash bugs, and computing the reproducibility rate of each crash bug, and (2) for the failed replays, analyzing the possible reasons for the reproducibility issues of these replays.

To achieve the first goal, given $\tau_O = \langle E_O, I_O \rangle$ and $\tau_R = \langle E_R, I_R \rangle$ with $E_O = [e_1, e_2, ..., e_m]$ and $E_R = [e_1, e_2, ..., e_n]$, we use two metrics to evaluate whether τ_R is successfully reproduced τ_O: (1) the index of MONKEY event causing the crash, and (2) exception information. The crash-causing event index refers to the last MONKEY event's index when the crash bug occurs. Specifically, if $m = n$, τ_O and τ_R crashed at the same event index. Exception information refers to the runtime exception when the crash occurs. Specifically, if τ_O and τ_R have the same exception type (e.g., *NullPointerException*) and description, they triggered the same runtime exception. If τ_R matches the event index and runtime exception of τ_O, we denote that τ_R successfully reproduced τ_O. Finally, for each crash bug, we calculated the percentage of successfully-reproduced replays out of all 200 replays as the reproducibility rate of this crash bug.

To achieve the second goal, we analyzed the *Event Handler LogFile* and the *Screen Record Video* of each pair of τ_O and τ_R. First, we preprocessed the *Event Handler LogFile*, abstracting each event handler's invocation as a GUI event, forming a GUI event sequence. Next, we compared the GUI event sequences of τ_O and τ_R, pinpointing differences. For the first divergent GUI event, we used the event execution times from the *Event Handler LogFile* to locate positions in the *Screen Record Video*. We compared frames around the divergence in both videos and manually determined the discrepancy's root causes. Specifically, for all the unsuccessfully-reproduced replays, two co-authors independently analyzed the root causes based on their knowledge and understanding. Then, the co-authors conducted cross-validation and discussion, reaching a consensus on the discrepancies. When they could not reach a consensus, the other three co-authors participated and helped make the final decision together. Manual analysis of all the unsuccessfully-reproduced replays was time-consuming, spanning about three months to complete. This analysis extended beyond *Key-Info Package*'s information to include specific bug lines in the source code. This makes the results more accurate and convincing.

2.3   Experimental Setup

Selecting Subject Apps. We selected six Android apps as the test subjects of our study. We focus on the open-source Android apps from GitHub so that we can monitor their execution to identify and analyze the root causes of the reproducibility issues. Our app selection was based on three criteria: popularity as indicated by GitHub stars, diversity of app categories for experimental validity, and feature variety. Specifically, we included both on-line (internet-required) and off-line apps, covering a wide range of app categories to enhance the validity of our experiment. We sourced all apps from Themis [30] and the app subjects of the recent empirical study conducted by Xiong *et al.* [35], because both of these datasets are recent studies of real-world bugs, meaning they are suitable for testing. From the intersection of these datasets, we initially picked three apps including two off-line and one on-line. Since MONKEY lacks auto-login capabilities, our subsequent selections were non-login apps, ensuring diverse category representation. Ultimately, we selected four off-line and two on-line apps. The specifics of these six apps are detailed in Table 1.

Table 1. Six popular open-source and representative Android apps used in our study (K = 1,000), '#Stars' indicates the number of GitHub Stars, '#LOC' indicates the number of lines of app source code.

App Name	App Category	#Stars	#LOC	Type
AmazeFileManager	File Manager	4.6K	94,768	Off-Line
AnkiDroid	Flashcard Learning	6.5K	218,558	Off-Line
ActivityDiary	Personal Diary	68	2,011	Off-Line
Sunflower	Gallery App	16.9K	1,687	Off-Line
AntennaPod	Podcast Manager	5K	90,427	On-Line
NewPipe	Video Player	24.2K	94,245	On-Line

Execution Environment. We conducted experiments on a physical machine with 128 GB RAM and a 64-cores AMD 3995WX CPU, running a 64-bit Ubuntu 20.04 operating system. To run the apps, we used a set of Android x86 emulators, where each emulator was configured with 4 CPU cores, 2 GB of RAM, 1 GB of SD card, and the version of Android OS 8.0 (API level 26). For each test case, the Android emulator is initialized to a fresh state at the beginning to provide a clean testing environment.

3   Experimental Results Analysis

During automated GUI testing, we ran 6,000 test cases across the six apps, collecting 56 unique crash bugs. After replaying each crash-triggering test case 200 times, we obtained 11,200 replays. Of these, 4,100 were successfully-reproduced replays, while 7,100 were not. In this section, RQ1 studied MONKEY's reproducibility rates, while RQ2 explores the root causes of its reproducibility issues.

3.1   RQ1: REPRODUCIBILITY RATE

Through a systematic analysis of 11,200 replays across six apps (four offline and two online), only 36.6% successfully reproduced the crash bug, indicating MONKEY's limitation in reliably reproducing the crash bugs it detected. Table 2 details the reproducibility rates for the 56 identified bugs, segmented into four categories: (1) "Same eid and Same Crash" where tau_R and tau_O have matching MONKEY event indexes leading to the crash and identical exception information, indicating successfully-reproduced replays; (2) "Different eid and Same Crash" where tau_R crash at differing event indexes but share tau_O's runtime exception;

Table 2. List of the reproducibility rate of MONKEY on the six subject apps. '#Activities' indicates the number of activities in this app.

App Name	#Activities	Type	Throttle	Crash Bug Id	Same Eid Same Crash	Different Eid Same Crash	Different Eid Different Crash	No Crash
AmazeFileManager	10	Off-Line	200 ms	Crash#1	178	4	0	18
				Crash#2	0	0	107	93
				Crash#3	5	1	1	193
				Crash#4	43	118	29	10
				Crash#5	163	0	6	31
			500 ms	Crash#1	143	45	10	2
				Crash#2	161	14	21	4
				Crash#3	8	0	10	182
				Crash#4	1	1	12	186
				Crash#5	11	0	0	189
AnkiDroid	21	Off-Line	200 ms	Crash#1	0	1	173	26
				Crash#2	96	1	1	102
				Crash#3	39	0	133	28
				Crash#4	0	0	0	200
				Crash#5	7	0	12	181
				Crash#6	0	0	194	6
			500 ms	Crash#1	39	1	3	157
				Crash#2	0	64	134	2
				Crash#3	108	4	38	50
				Crash#4	98	0	90	12
				Crash#5	110	0	0	90
				Crash#6	91	0	71	38
				Crash#7	59	0	55	86
Sunflower	1	Off-Line	200 ms	Crash#1	20	0	0	180
				Crash#2	177	23	0	0
				Crash#3	60	6	2	132
				Crash#4	121	15	1	63
				Crash#5	95	11	1	93
			500 ms	Crash#1	0	0	0	200
				Crash#2	200	0	0	0
				Crash#3	196	0	0	4
				Crash#4	132	0	0	68
				Crash#5	134	0	0	66
ActivityDiary	7	Off-Line	200 ms	Crash#1	1	0	0	199
				Crash#2	97	3	47	53
				Crash#3	89	0	28	83
				Crash#4	114	0	2	84
			500 ms	Crash#1	45	0	0	155
				Crash#2	65	0	0	135
				Crash#3	0	0	5	195
				Crash#4	0	0	2	198
				Crash#5	180	0	13	7
AntennaPod	10	On-Line	500 ms	Crash#1	200	0	0	0
				Crash#2	19	0	181	0
				Crash#3	46	0	0	154
				Crash#4	136	0	44	20
				Crash#5	0	0	21	179
				Crash#6	0	0	9	191
				Crash#7	18	0	4	178
			1000 ms	Crash#1	200	0	0	0
				Crash#2	1	0	105	94
				Crash#3	18	0	0	182
				Crash#4	189	1	0	10
NewPipe	14	On-Line	500 ms	Crash#1	174	0	3	23
			1000 ms	Crash#1	3	0	53	144
				Crash#2	10	36	30	124
#Total					4100	349	1651	5100
#Proportion					36.6%	3.1%	14.7%	45.5%

(3) "Different eid and Different Crash" where tau_R have a distinct event index and trigger a different bug; and (4) "No Crash" where no crash occurs within the 5,000 MONKEY events span.

. Based on the experimental results, we have two interesting findings. First, the reproducibility rate of MONKEY is not significantly correlated with the runtime exception type. We conducted a statistical one-way ANOVA [9] of variance on the reproducibility rates of different exceptions using SPSS [13]. We first categorized the runtime exceptions of the 56 crash bugs and excluded exception types with sample sizes less than 3 due to their potential random occurrences that could affect experimental results. In the end, we obtained eight groups of exception types, including *NullPointerException, ClassCastException*, etc. Next, we employed the homogeneity of variance test and set the null hypothesis (H0) as follows: the reproducibility rates of crash bugs with different exception types are equal, indicating that reproducibility rates are independent of exception types. The results of the variance analysis showed a significance level (P-value) of 0.412, which is greater than 0.05. This implies that there is no significant correlation between the reproducibility rate and the exception types of crash bugs.

Second, the reproducibility rate of MONKEY is not significantly correlated with the app's complexity. Generally, apps with more complex features usually have more components in their activities, and different actions on these components may correspond to different functionalities, increasing the likelihood of executing error events. Apps with simpler features typically have simpler activity designs with more blank pages, resulting in a relatively higher probability of executing blank events. We conducted a similar ANOVA analysis between app features and the reproducibility rates, yielding a P-value of 0.441. This indicates that there is no significant correlation between them.

3.2   RQ2: ROOT CAUSE

By manually analyzing 7,100 unsuccessfully-reproduced replays' *Key-Info Packages*, we finally identified five root causes of the reproducibility issues in MONKEY: Injection Failure, Event Ambiguity, Data Loading, Widget Loading and Dynamic content. Table 3 shows the detailed proportion.

Injection Failure. "Injection failure" describes situations where MONKEY experiences issues while inserting events into the *InputManager*, causing the event to not be added. Ideally, with the same *Seed*, MONKEY should generate consistent event sequences. However, our experiments revealed occasional event execution failures by the Android framework due to injection issues, denoted in the *Monkey Event Sequence LogFile* by "//Injection Failed". This results in inconsistencies between the original and replay execution traces, contributing to MONKEY's reproducibility challenges. In our study, 3,864 of the 7,100 problematic replays (or 54.4%) suffered from injection failure.

To understand the reasons behind injection failure, we conducted an in-depth analysis of MONKEY's source code. MONKEY has two types of event: KeyEvent, which corresponds to a physical button, and MotionEvent, such as click and long press. For KeyEvent, if the action code of the KeyEvent is not a valid key action such as *UP* and *DOWN*, it will fail to be injected into the InputManager. For MotionEvent, if the pointer count (the multitouch number on the screen) of the MotionEvent is less than 1 or greater than 16, or any individual pointer ID in the MotionEvent is less than 0 or greater than the maximum allowed pointer ID, the MotionEvent will fail to be injected to the InputManager. A common case of Injection Failure is that the pointer count equals 0 when injecting MotionEvents due to the rapid event execution speed of MONKEY.

> **Finding 1**: *Injection Failure* affects 54.4% of the reproducibility issues, which is the most common root causes.

Event Ambiguity. When recognizing actions, Android framework typically utilizes algorithms and rules to determine the type of action based on properties like pointer speed, distance, direction, and so on. Event ambiguity refers to the situation where the Android framework identifies the same MONKEY event as different UI events, leading to a disparity between the original execution trace and the replay execution trace. This discrepancy contributes to the reproducibility issues of MONKEY. In our experiment, 1483 out of 7100 replays with reproducibility issues (accounting for 20.9%) were attributed to event ambiguity.

For example, in the case of *Anki-Android*, the component *deck* has registered two different event handlers, which is shown in Fig. 4. When clicking on a certain deck, *onClick* will be executed, while when long-clicking this deck, *onLongClick* will be executed. During GUI testing with MONKEY, for the same MONKEY event, the Android framework identified it in the original execution trace as a click event, but in the replay execution trace as a long-click event. Then this discrepancy led to the reproducibility issues. Figure 5 shows the real scenario of this example.

> **Finding 2**: *Event Ambiguity* affects 20.9% of the reproducibility issues, which is an important factor affecting the reproducibility rate.

Data Loading. Data loading refers to the situation where MONKEY interacted with a partially loaded page or component, resulting in an empty event execution. Specifically, when switching to a new page, the app needs a period to fully load the content, and there will be a loading icon or some skeleton images on the page usually. Because MONKEY is not widget-sensitive but coordinate-sensitive, when MONKEY generates a click event, it may hit an area where the data is not yet available. That will possibly miss a pivot event. In our experiments, 1071 out of 7100 replays with reproducibility issues (accounting for 15.1%) are related to data loading. The reproducibility issues in MONKEY caused by data loading can be fundamentally categorized into two types: database loading and network loading. Database loading refers to the situation where loading a new page or component requires retrieving information from a local or remote database. Such

```
holder.rl.setOnClickListener(            holder.rl.setOnLongClickListener(
  new View.OnClickListener() {            new View.OnLongClickListener() {
    @Override                               @Override
    public void onClick(View v) {           public boolean onLongClick(View p1) {
      //Handle events                         //Handle events
    }                                       }
});                                      });
            (a)                                      (b)
```

Fig. 4. Source Code of Event Ambiguity

query operations typically take some time to complete. Network loading refers to the situation where loading a new page or component requires some time to retrieve information from a remote server or certain APIs. This can lead to failures in reproducing actions accurately due to variations in network speed or connectivity, causing discrepancies between the original and replayed events. For instance, in *AmazeFileManager*, showcased in Fig. 5(c) and (d), there's a noticeable difference in the file list display attributable to database loading speed. In Fig. 5(c), while the file list was still populating, MONKEY clicked an empty space, maintaining the app's state. Conversely, in Fig. 5(d), the app had efficiently fetched and displayed file data, leading MONKEY to click on the 'gr' folder and transition to a new page. Such inconsistencies, stemming from varied database loading rates, amplify MONKEY's reproducibility challenges.

Widget Loading. Widget loading refers to the situation where the widget with animated effects is clicked before all the menu options have been fully displayed, leading to clicking the incorrect menu option during the replay process. In our experiments, 653 out of 7100 replays with reproducibility issues (accounting for 9.2%) are related to widget loading.

For example, in the case of *AmazeFileManager* illustrated in Fig. 5(e) and (f), in the original execution trace, the click event landed on the *'GridView'* option within the Options Menu. However, in the replay execution trace, the dropdown speed of the Options Menu was slower, causing MONKEY not to click on any option within the Options Menu. As a result, the original execution trace and replay execution trace ended up on different pages.

Specifically, for further investigating widget loading, we manually analyzed the *Screen Record Video* and found that specific widgets like Drawer Menu and Options Menu typically require 60 ms to 150 ms (according to our video frame-by-frame statistics) to load completely to respond accurately to click events. In one particular experiment, we observed that when setting the throttle of MONKEY to 200 ms, if a MONKEY event e_i triggered a pop-up of Options Menu, e_{i+1} had a 63% probability of being unable to select the well-prepared menu options. In addition, in a broader analysis encompassing four offline apps, when setting the throttle of MONKEY to 200 ms, 58% of the pivot GUI events were missed or affected due to clicking on partially loaded widgets. This highlights the

Table 3. List of the root causes of the reproducibility issues of MONKEY that we identified. A '-' in the 'Dynamic Content' column indicates that the off-line apps do not have this situation.

App Name	Type	Throttle	Injection Failure	Event Ambiguity	Data Loading	Widget Loading	Dynamic Content	Exception Type Of Crash Bug
AmazeFileManager	Off-Line	200 ms	20	0	2	0	-	NullPointerException
			79	68	48	5	-	ClassCastException
			161	13	13	8	-	ClassCastException
			123	24	9	1	-	StringIndexOutOfBoundsException
			22	5	8	2	-	IllegalArgumentException
		500 ms	28	26	0	3	-	NullPointerException
			28	6	4	1	-	StringIndexOutOfBoundsException
			151	36	1	4	-	ClassCastException
			175	12	11	1	-	StringIndexOutOfBoundsException
			175	3	10	1	-	NullPointerException
AnkiDroid	Off-Line	200 ms	68	9	123	0	-	NullPointerException
			69	34	1	0	-	NullPointerException
			38	95	28	0	-	NullPointerException
			102	90	4	4	-	NullPointerException
			182	8	2	1	-	RuntimeException
			39	158	2	1	-	ArrayIndexOutOfBoundsException
		500 ms	126	30	5	0	-	NullPointerException
			4	193	3	0	-	NullPointerException
			51	41	0	0	-	ActivityNotFoundException
			70	4	28	0	-	ArrayIndexOutOfBoundsException
			53	13	24	0	-	NullPointerException
			96	13	0	0	-	FileOutputStreamError
			117	17	7	0	-	IllegalArgumentException
Sunflower	Off-Line	200 ms	77	8	0	95	-	IllegalArgumentException
			19	0	0	4	-	IllegalArgumentException
			97	1	0	42	-	IllegalArgumentException
			47	2	0	30	-	IllegalArgumentException
			65	3	0	37	-	IllegalArgumentException
		500 ms	0	20	0	180	-	IllegalArgumentException
			0	0	0	0	-	IllegalArgumentException
			0	0	0	4	-	IllegalArgumentException
			0	7	0	61	-	IllegalArgumentException
			0	46	0	20	-	IllegalArgumentException
ActivityDiary	Off-Line	200 ms	199	0	0	0	-	NullPointerException
			101	0	2	0	-	IndexOutOfBoundsException
			85	1	23	2	-	IndexOutOfBoundsException
			59	7	9	11	-	SQLException
		500 ms	131	6	17	1	-	SQLException
			121	4	10	0	-	SQLException
			14	12	173	1	-	SQLException
			198	0	2	0	-	IndexOutOfBoundsException
			6	0	13	1	-	IndexOutOfBoundsException
AntennaPod	On-Line	500 ms	0	0	0	0	0	VerifyError
			7	75	0	94	5	VerifyError
			61	0	91	0	2	VerifyError
			8	0	55	0	1	VerifyError
			27	12	145	8	8	libcoreError
			49	132	12	5	2	Ioexception
			48	87	33	9	5	InterruptedIOException
		1000 ms	0	0	0	0	0	VerifyError
			37	93	59	8	2	IllegalArgumentException
			64	37	73	6	2	VerifyError
			0	8	0	2	1	VerifyError
NewPipe	On-Line	500 ms	13	5	7	0	1	NullPointerException
		1000 ms	187	4	6	0	0	RemoteServiceException
			167	15	8	0	0	NullPointerException
#Total			3864	1483	1071	653	29	
#Proportion			54.4%	20.9%	15.1%	9.2%	0.4%	

significance of timing and synchronization between click events and the loading of interactive widgets.

Dynamic Content. Dynamic content refers to the situation where some specific app dynamic contents may change (e.g., recommended items, pop-up advertisements), leading to the different execution traces in replays from those in the original execution traces, thus resulting in the reproducibility issues of MONKEY. In our experiments, 29 out of 7100 replays with reproducibility issues (accounting for 0.4%) are related to dynamic content.

In certain specific on-line apps, the presence of dynamic content introduces significant challenges to reproducing crashes. For example, in the case of *AntennaPod* illustrated in Fig. 5(g) and (h), the continuous changes in the recommendation list primarily arise from the app's reliance on fetching and updating data from remote sources. User interactions and time-dependent factors trigger these data updates, resulting in constant changes in the recommendation list. Consequently, even though we use the read-only mode to ensure that the app starts from the same state every time, for apps with recommendation lists, the content of the recommendation list may change when run at different times. The dynamic nature of the recommendation lists may lead to discrepancies between the events executed in tau_O and tau_R.

4   Discussions and Implications

4.1   How Does Throttle Affect MONKEY's Reproducibility Rate?

A recent study by Feng *et al.* [8] proposed a lightweight image-based approach ADAT to dynamically adjust the inter-event time based on GUI rendering state. ADAT can infer the rendering state and synchronize with the testing tool to schedule the next event when the GUI is fully rendered, which can improve the testing effectiveness. Another study by Behrang *et al.* [3] also indicated that for UI-based flaky tests, the typical root causes behind flaky UI tests include issues like async wait and resource rendering due to improper configuration of time intervals between two events, leading to the flakiness of UI tests. According to our experimental results, we are curious about the impact of throttle on the reproducibility rate of MONKEY. To investigate the relationship between the throttle and the reproducibility rate, we randomly chose 19 τ_O, both increased and decreased the throttle of each τ_O, and replayed them 200 times with the new throttle to get their corresponding new τ_R, then computed the new reproducibility rate. Then we similarly conducted the ANOVA analysis, and the results revealed the P-value of 0.280. This indicates that altering the throttle, whether increased or decreased, did not significantly improve the reproducibility rate. When the throttle is increased, the app gets a longer GUI loading time, but the reproducibility rate of the crash bug has not been significantly improved. One potential explanation for this phenomenon is that triggering a crash bug usually requires dozens of MONKEY events to reach a specific state that leads

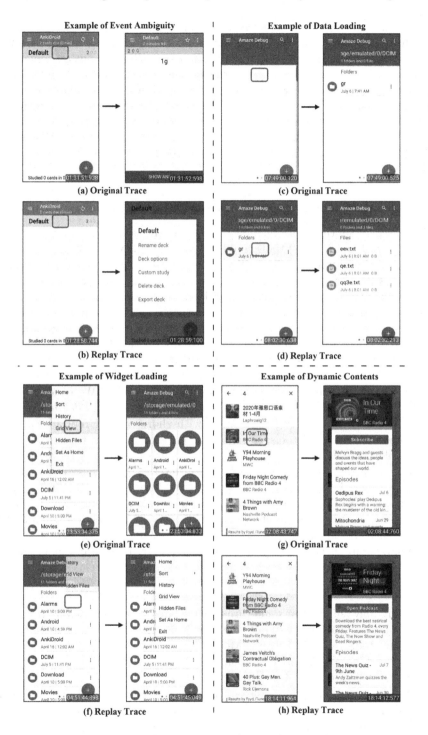

Fig. 5. Illustrative examples of root causes. The red boxes indicate the click area. (Color figure online)

to a crash. Some of the pivot events need to be executed rapidly, while others need to be executed after the app is fully rendered. So a uniform adjustment of throttle (whether increase or decrease) may potentially miss out on some pivot events, making the app cannot reach the specific state to crash. Therefore, during testing, if each event waits until the GUI is fully loaded before execution, there's a possibility of missing some bugs which are triggered only when user events are executed during the partial rendering state of the GUI. Our experimental results indicate that a larger throttle isn't necessarily better. The better selection of intervals between events in automated GUI testing remains a topic worthy of discussion.

4.2 Can R&R Tools Improve MONKEY's Reproducibility Rate?

After discovering the reproducibility issues of MONKEY, we wondered if the R&R (Record and Replay) tools could improve MONKEY's reproducibility rate. To validate this assumption, we initially selected three recent and representative R&R tools - RERAN[10], Rx[14] and SARA[12]. Then we use MONKEY's built-in functionality to replay existing crash bugs, and record them with the R&R tools at the same time. However, we found that RERAN was unable to capture the events executed by MONKEY. This is because RERAN records events from the system file /dev/input/event. Only events captured by *InputReader* are logged into /dev/input/event. Consequently, the events generated by MONKEY cannot be recorded by RERAN. After that, we replayed the sequences recorded by Rx and SARA and assessed their reproducibility rate. We conducted our small-scale experiments on two off-line apps namely *AmazeFileManager* and *AnkiDroid*, and selected two crash bugs with short τ_O and reproduced them five times with the R&R tools. According to our experimental results, we found that employing R&R tools to reproduce crash bugs yields a lower reproducibility rate than that of MONKEY. This is because MONKEY generates events quickly, and most of the R&R tools record events in the form of scripts, which is time-consuming. Secondly, the R&R tools can only record certain event types, so they cannot record all the events executed by MONKEY, which leads to a failure to reproduce the crash bug. This also highlights that for R&R tools, recording speed and comprehensive recording of event types are crucial and important.

4.3 Threats to Validity

Our study may suffer from some threats to validity. First, our research focused exclusively on MONKEY without assessing the reproducibility capabilities of other AIG tools. This is because MONKEY is a widely used AIG tool in the industry and is representative of commonly applied testing tools. Additionally, MONKEY itself provides self-replay capabilities, which eliminates the impact of additional record and replay tools on the experimental results. Moreover, many AIG tools (e.g., APE, FASTBOT) are designed upon MONKEY. Therefore, studying the reproducibility issues of MONKEY is a meaningful work and can provide insights to other AIG tools. Specifically, *Injection Failure* may apply to AIG tools that inject events into *InputManager*. *Data Loading* and *Widget Loading* may apply to AIG tools that are coordinate-sensitive but not widget-sensitive. *Event Ambiguity* may not apply to widget-sensitive AIG tools, because they directly perform corresponding actions on the widgets. In the future, we plan to expand our research to investigate the reproducibility capabilities of other AIG tools as well. Second, our study involves some manual analysis, which may bring some potential biases in the results. To mitigate this threat, two co-authors independently conducted the analysis and then reached a consensus to derive the final results. When they could not reach a consensus, the other three co-authors participated and helped make the final decision together. This approach helps ensure a more objective and reliable assessment of the findings and minimizes the influence of individual biases.

Additionally, we have introduced INSTRUMENTDROID, which may cause some potential problems. First, we detect bugs based on the instrumented app, which makes τ_O and τ_R unified. Second, INSTRUMENTDROID only inserts a snippet of log code to the event handlers, which is a lightweight implant and will not have a big impact on the performance of the program. Moreover, we've verified INSTRUMENTDROID's accuracy in event recognition, ensuring that the same UI controls don't produce duplicate content in *Event Handler LogFile*. Nevertheless, our tool does have its limitations. While it can cover most widgets, widgets without corresponding event handlers require special actions. Yet, this limitation minimally affects the reproducibility issues, as the behavior between the original and replay traces remains consistent.

5   Related Work

Flakiness in Android GUI Testing. Flaky tests refer to software tests that produce inconsistent or unreliable results. Different from the reproducibility issues, in the literature, flakiness usually refers to the uncertainty of test results. A flaky test does not necessarily trigger a crash bug. However, the reproducibility issues focus on a known bug and study whether the bug can be reliably reproduced. There are many works about the flakiness in UI tests and unit tests. Romano *et al.* [25] investigated flaky UI tests, identifying common causes such as Async Wait, Environment, Test Runner API, and Test Script Logic issues. SHAKER [27] offers a technique to improve test rerun effectiveness for spotting flaky tests. Both our study and previous ones found that UI rendering and asynchronous data loading contribute to flakiness. Our work uniquely introduces Injection Failure and Event Ambiguity as causes. Conversely, other studies highlight concurrency and thread competition as sources of flakiness.

Some works also researched the topic of reproducibility. Su *et al.* conducted a study about the reproducibility of exception bugs [28]. They chose two Android GUI Testing tools, i.e., STOAT [29] and SAPIENZ [19], and utilized MONKEY and UIAUTOMATOR scripts for test recording and replay. If an app crashed, they recorded the exception trace and the crash-triggering test, rerunning each test five times to determine reproducibility. They identified three challenges for testing tools in reliably reproducing exceptions: test dependency, timing of events, and specific running environment. Our work differs in several respects. First, our tool choice was MONKEY due to its widespread industry use and built-in replay functionality, negating the need for extra scripts. Notably, Su *et al.* mentioned the flakiness of MONKEY tests so they didn't choose it. Second, we replayed crash bugs 200 times for reproducibility, as opposed to their five times. Third, the 56 crash bugs in our work were discovered through random GUI testing using MONKEY in a unified environment. These bugs are all independent of each other, so there is no correlation between them, and they are not affected by the testing environment. We also addressed event timing via *Data Loading* and *Widget Loading*. Compared to their work, our work is more systematic and comprehensive.

Deterministic Replay in Other Systems. Deterministic replay, often referred to as reproducibility, is less studied in the Android field than in non-smartphone platforms where it has been widely explored and implemented. In hardware, FDR [36] offers a low-overhead solution for reproducible execution in cache-coherent multiprocessors. Conversely, BugNet [21] is designed to record information continuously for deterministic bug replay and resolution. In virtual machines, ReVirt [7] enhances intrusion analysis by using logging and replay techniques, minimizing interference from the target OS. LoRe [15] serves a similar purpose, but is tailored for the popular full virtualization solution, KVM.

6   Conclusion and Future Work

In this paper, we conducted an in-depth empirical study on the reproducibility issues of MONKEY about how effectively can it reproduce the crash bugs it detected and the root causes of its reproducibility issues. Specifically, we studied 56 unique crash bugs detected by MONKEY from six popular open-source Android apps to understand the reproducibility issues. Our results show that only 36.6% of the crashes could be reproduced on average. Through the manual analysis, we categorized five types of root causes of the reproducibility issues of MONKEY: *Injection Failure*, *Event Ambiguity*, *Data Loading*, *Widget Loading* and *Dynamic Content*. The corresponding proportions of them are 54.4%, 20.9%, 15.1%, 9.2%, and 0.4% on average. In the future, we plan to come up with some solutions to improve the reproducibility issues of MONKEY and research the reproducibility issues of other AIG tools.

Acknowledgements. We thank the SETTA reviewers for their valuable feedback, Yiheng Xiong and Shan Huang from East China Normal University for their insightful comments, and Cong Li from Nanjing University for the mechanism of Rx. This work was supported in part by National Key Research and Development Program (Grant 2022YFB3104002), NSFC Grant 62072178, "Digital Silk Road" Shanghai International Joint Lab of Trustworthy Intelligent Software under Grant 22510750100, and the Shanghai Collaborative Innovation Center of Trusted Industry Internet Software.

References

1. Arnatovich, Y., Wang, L., Ngo, N., Soh, C.: Mobolic: an automated approach to exercising mobile application GUIs using symbiosis of online testing technique and customated input generation. Softw. Pract. Exp. **48**, 1107–1142 (2018). https://doi.org/10.1002/spe.2564

2. Ash Turner: The Rise of Android: Why is Android Successful? (2023). https://www.bankmycell.com/blog/how-many-android-users-are-there

3. Behrang, F., Orso, A.: Seven reasons why: an in-depth study of the limitations of random test input generation for android. In: Proceedings of the 35th IEEE/ACM International Conference on Automated Software Engineering, pp. 1066–1077. ASE 2020, Association for Computing Machinery, New York, NY, USA (2021). https://doi.org/10.1145/3324884.3416567

4. Bläsing, T., Batyuk, L., Schmidt, A.D., Camtepe, S.A., Albayrak, S.: An android application sandbox system for suspicious software detection. In: 2010 5th International Conference on Malicious and Unwanted Software, pp. 55–62 (2010). https://doi.org/10.1109/MALWARE.2010.5665792

5. Bruneton, E., Lenglet, R., Coupaye, T.: ASM: a code manipulation tool to implement adaptable systems. Adapt. Extensible Compon. Syst. **30**(19) (2002)

6. Chen, S., Fan, L., Su, T., Ma, L., Liu, Y., Xu, L.: Automated cross-platform GUI code generation for mobile apps. In: 2019 IEEE 1st International Workshop on Artificial Intelligence for Mobile (AI4Mobile), pp. 13–16 (2019). https://doi.org/10.1109/AI4Mobile.2019.8672718

7. Dunlap, G.W., King, S.T., Cinar, S., Basrai, M.A., Chen, P.M.: ReVirt: enabling intrusion analysis through virtual-machine logging and replay **36**(SI), 211–224 (2003). https://doi.org/10.1145/844128.844148

8. Feng, S., Xie, M., Chen, C.: Efficiency matters: Speeding up automated testing with GUI rendering inference. In: Proceedings of the 45th International Conference on Software Engineering, pp. 906–918. ICSE 2023 (2023). https://doi.org/10.1109/ICSE48619.2023.00084

9. Girden, E.R.: ANOVA: Repeated measures. No. 84, Sage (1992)

10. Gomez, L., Neamtiu, I., Azim, T., Millstein, T.: Reran: timing- and touch-sensitive record and replay for android. In: 2013 35th International Conference on Software Engineering (ICSE), pp. 72–81. IEEE Computer Society, Los Alamitos, CA, USA (2013). https://doi.org/10.1109/ICSE.2013.6606553

11. Gu, T., et al.: Practical GUI testing of android applications via model abstraction and refinement. In: 2019 IEEE/ACM 41st International Conference on Software Engineering (ICSE), pp. 269–280 (2019). https://doi.org/10.1109/ICSE.2019.00042

12. Guo, J., Li, S., Lou, J.G., Yang, Z., Liu, T.: Sara: self-replay augmented record and replay for android in industrial cases. In: ISSTA 2019, Association for Computing Machinery, New York, NY, USA (2019). https://doi.org/10.1145/3293882.3330557

13. IBM Corp.: IBM SPSS statistics for windows. https://hadoop.apache.org

14. Li, C., Jiang, Y., Xu, C.: Cross-device record and replay for android apps. In: ESEC/FSE 2022, Association for Computing Machinery, pp. 395–407. New York, NY, USA (2022). https://doi.org/10.1145/3540250.3549083

15. Li, J., Si, S., Li, B., Cui, L., Zheng, J.: Lore: supporting non-deterministic events logging and replay for KVM virtual machines. In: 2013 IEEE 10th International Conference on High Performance Computing and Communications, vol. 1, pp. 442–449 (2013). https://doi.org/10.1109/HPCC.and.EUC.2013.70

16. Li, Y., Yang, Z., Guo, Y., Chen, X.: DroidBot: a lightweight UI-guided test input generator for android. In: 2017 IEEE/ACM 39th International Conference on Software Engineering Companion (ICSE-C), pp. 23–26 (2017). https://doi.org/10.1109/ICSE-C.2017.8

17. Li, Y., Yang, Z., Guo, Y., Chen, X.: Humanoid: a deep learning-based approach to automated black-box android app testing. In: 2019 34th IEEE/ACM International Conference on Automated Software Engineering (ASE), pp. 1070–1073 (2019). https://doi.org/10.1109/ASE.2019.00104

18. Lv, Z., Peng, C., Zhang, Z., Su, T., Liu, K., Yang, P.: Fastbot2: reusable automated model-based GUI testing for android enhanced by reinforcement learning. In: Proceedings of the 37th IEEE/ACM International Conference on Automated Software Engineering. ASE 2022 (2023). https://doi.org/10.1145/3551349.3559505

19. Mao, K., Harman, M., Jia, Y.: Sapienz: multi-objective automated testing for android applications. In: Proceedings of the 25th International Symposium on Software Testing and Analysis. ISSTA 2016 (2016). https://doi.org/10.1145/2931037.2931054

20. Moran, K., Linares-Vásquez, M., Bernal-Cárdenas, C., Vendome, C., Poshyvanyk, D.: Automatically discovering, reporting and reproducing android application crashes. In: 2016 IEEE International Conference on Software Testing, Verification and Validation (ICST), pp. 33–44 (2016). https://doi.org/10.1109/ICST.2016.34

21. Narayanasamy, S., Pokam, G., Calder, B.: BugNet: continuously recording program execution for deterministic replay debugging. In: ISCA 2005, IEEE Computer Society, pp. 284–295. USA (2005). https://doi.org/10.1109/ISCA.2005.16

22. Patel, P., Srinivasan, G., Rahaman, S., Neamtiu, I.: On the effectiveness of random testing for android: or how i learned to stop worrying and love the monkey. In: Proceedings of the 13th International Workshop on Automation of Software Test, pp. 34–37 (2018). https://doi.org/10.1145/3194733.3194742

23. Project, A.O.S.: Monkey - android developers (2023). https://developer.android.com/studio/test/other-testing-tools/monkey

24. Project, A.O.S.: SDK platform tools release notes (2023). https://developer.android.com/tools/releases/platform-tools

25. Romano, A., Song, Z., Grandhi, S., Yang, W., Wang, W.: An empirical analysis of UI-based flaky tests. In: 2021 IEEE/ACM 43rd International Conference on Software Engineering (ICSE), pp. 1585–1597 (2021). https://doi.org/10.1109/ICSE43902.2021.00141

26. Roy Choudhary, S., Gorla, A., Orso, A.: Automated test input generation for android: are we there yet? (e), pp. 429–440 (2015). https://doi.org/10.1109/ASE.2015.89

27. Silva, D., Teixeira, L., d'Amorim, M.: Shake it! detecting flaky tests caused by concurrency with shaker. In: 2020 IEEE International Conference on Software Maintenance and Evolution (ICSME), pp. 301–311 (2020). https://doi.org/10.1109/ICSME46990.2020.00037

28. Su, T., et al.: Why my app crashes? Understanding and benchmarking framework-specific exceptions of android apps. IEEE Trans. Softw. Eng. 48(4), 1115–1137 (2022). https://doi.org/10.1109/TSE.2020.3013438

29. Su, T., et al.: Guided, stochastic model-based GUI testing of android apps. In: Proceedings of the 2017 11th Joint Meeting on Foundations of Software Engineering, pp. 245–256. ESEC/FSE 2017 (2017). https://doi.org/10.1145/3106237.3106298

30. Su, T., Wang, J., Su, Z.: Benchmarking automated GUI testing for android against real-world bugs. In: Proceedings of 29th ACM Joint European Software Engi-

neering Conference and Symposium on the Foundations of Software Engineering (ESEC/FSE), pp. 119–130 (2021). https://doi.org/10.1145/3468264.3468620

31. Su, T., et al.: Fully automated functional fuzzing of android apps for detecting non-crashing logic bugs 5(OOPSLA) (2021). https://doi.org/10.1145/3485533

32. Sun, J., et al.: Understanding and finding system setting-related defects in android apps. In: Proceedings of the 30th ACM SIGSOFT International Symposium on Software Testing and Analysis, pp. 204–215 (2021). https://doi.org/10.1145/3460319.3464806

33. Wang, J., Jiang, Y., Xu, C., Cao, C., Ma, X., Lu, J.: ComboDroid: generating high-quality test inputs for android apps via use case combinations. In: Proceedings of the ACM/IEEE 42nd International Conference on Software Engineering, pp. 469–480. ICSE 2020 (2020). https://doi.org/10.1145/3377811.3380382

34. Wang, W., et al.: An empirical study of android test generation tools in industrial cases. In: Proceedings of the 33rd ACM/IEEE International Conference on Automated Software Engineering, pp. 738–748. ASE 2018, Association for Computing Machinery, New York, NY, USA (2018). https://doi.org/10.1145/3238147.3240465

35. Xiong, Y., et al.: An empirical study of functional bugs in android apps, pp. 1319–1331 (2023). https://doi.org/10.1145/3597926.3598138

36. Xu, M., Bodik, R., Hill, M.D.: A "flight data recorder" for enabling full-system multiprocessor deterministic replay, pp. 122–135. ISCA 2003, Association for Computing Machinery, New York, NY, USA (2003). https://doi.org/10.1145/859618.859633

Multi-dimensional Abstraction and Decomposition for Separation of Concerns

Zhiming Liu(✉)⬚, Jiadong Teng(✉), and Bo Liu(✉)⬚

School of Computer and Information Science, Southwest University, Chongqing, China
{zhimingliu88,liubocq}@swu.edu.cn, swu20201518@email.swu.edu.cn

Abstract. Model-driven engineering (MDE) or model-driven architecture (MDA) holds significant appeal for the software industry. Its primary aim is to address software complexity by enabling automated model creation and transformation. Consequently, many software development firms are actively seeking integrated development platforms (IDP) to enhance automation within their software production processes. However, the adoption of MDE and the utilisation of IDPs remain low, with doubts surrounding their success. To tackle this issue, this paper uses the formal refinement of component and object systems (rCOS) as a framework to identify different types of requirements and their relationships, with the goal of supporting MDE. We emphasise the necessity for families of formal languages and transformations among them, as well as the indispensability of architecture modelling and refinement in MDE. Furthermore, to enhance the handling of changes during the development and operation of systems, there is a paramount need for formal methods that facilitate abstractions and decompositions, leading to a multi-dimensional separation of concerns.

Keywords: Abstraction · Refinement · Decomposition · Separation of Concerns · Architecture modelling · Software Complexity

1 Introduction

Software engineering has focused on the development, study, and practice of methods for mastering inherent complexity [6–8] in the software development activities of requirements analysis, development processes, design and implementation (also called software construction), verification and validation, respectively. The goal has been to improve software comprehensibility, support reuse, enable evolution, and increase automation of development. In this paper, a *method* mainly consists of its *underlying theory*, a suite of *sound techniques*, and related *tool supports* (also called a platform) to the use of these techniques. Furthermore, a *formal method* (FM) refers to a method whose underlying theory is a *formal theory* consisting of a *formal language*, a *proof system*, and *model theory*, essentially constituting a *formal logic system* [48].

Supported by the Chinese National NSF grant (No. 62032019) and the Southwest University Research Development grant (No. SWU116007).

Some formal methods (FMs) offer languages for modelling specific aspects and their properties, while others provide languages for specifying various types of requirements. An aspect represents concerns related to particular types of requirements, including data, functionality, concurrency, communication, and more.

Separation of Concerns by Abstractions. An abstraction allows developers to simplify complex or domain-specific realities, focusing only what is essential. It introduces a layer of indirection between a general idea and specific implementations. By showcasing the core attributes of a problem, abstractions make problem clearer. This clarity aids in managing complexity, letting developers concentrate on a single aspect without being bogged down by intricate details. Such a method promotes a step-by-step approach to understanding and problem-solving. It also enhances reusability, as either the high-level problem or its solution can be reused in various scenarios, given that their connection is traceable. Automating tasks becomes feasible, especially when translating from an abstract to a concrete representation. Examples of these layers of indirection in software include pointers, APIs, the symbolic assembler that transform assembly programs to programs in machine language, the interpreter or compiler which translates a program in a high-level programming language to an machine language program, as well as concepts like super- and sub- class in object-oriented programming and super- and sub- type in type theory.

Separation of Concerns by Decompositions. Decompositions are essential strategies for mastering software complexity, involving the process of breaking down software into smaller, more manageable, clear, and well-defined components. Decomposition allows developers to focus on understanding and perfecting individual parts rather than being overwhelmed by the entire system. This not only improves software comprehensibility, as each part becomes self-contained with a specific responsibility, but also supports reuse. These components can be designed in a way that enables their use in multiple places within the same application or even across different projects, eliminating the need to recreate the same functionality. In terms of software evolution, decompositions allow for easier scalability and adaptability. If a single component needs to be updated or replaced, it can be done without disrupting the entire system. Finally, decompositions lend themselves well to the automation of development processes. Tools can be better designed for the automatic construction and testing of smaller and simpler components, as well as for hierarchical components and system integration with clearly defined interfaces.

Process of Decomposition and Refinements. A *top-down development (sub)process* is a sequence of decompositions and implementation mechanisms or representations of abstractions, which are termed *refinements* of abstractions. Conversely, a the bottom-up (sub)process involves a sequence of activities centred around the integration of subcomponents, each of which has been developed through refinements. For large-scale systems, the vast design space encompasses the processes of decompositions, refinements, and compositions. Moreover, the requirements for decomposition and refinement are intricate [40,47]. Accordingly, it is essential to incorporate large-scale reusable components, ensure low coupling and high cohesion, and to facilitate potent, non-invasive adaptation and customisation capabilities. It is also crucial to maintain traceability of refinements and decompositions throughout the software lifecycle to minimise the impact of changes and substitutability.

Existing Approaches. To address the above challenges and requirements, substantial research has been made in the areas of decomposition and abstraction. Notably, *modularisation* is an important technique for partitioning a system into modules, premised on related functional units [14,41]. This approach is also referred to as algorithm-based decomposition. On the other hand, *object-oriented decomposition* adopts a distinct philosophical stance, envisioning a system as an ensemble of interacting objects [3,6]. These objects are software representations congruent with those discerned in the application domain. In light of their promising potential to enhance reusability, enable independent development, and facilitate standalone deployment, *component-based development* (CBD) [46] and *service-oriented architecture* (SOA) [5] are increasingly gaining prominence in contemporary academic and industry discussions.

Aims and Objectives of the Paper. Despite advancements in software engineering research, significant challenges persist in current model-driven engineering (MDE) frameworks to abstraction and decomposition. Many of these challenges arise from the inability of these approaches to effectively separate concerns as highlighted in previous literature [16,24,47]. These deficiencies have caused them to fall short of achieving the primary objectives of MDE as described in the referenced article [16]. We identify the following limitations in the current modelling approaches:

(1) Insufficient tool support for life-cycle management. Changes in the generated models or some constructed models often lead to round-trip issues.
(2) Ineffectiveness in reducing the sensitivity of primary artefacts to various changes, such as personnel adjustments, requirement updates including those in the development platform, and changes in deployment platforms.
(3) Limited flexibility to accommodate development team members with diverse methodological expertise due to each approach's adherence to fixed theories, techniques, and tools.
(4) Constrained dimensions for abstractions and decompositions in modelling approaches. For instance, MDA only emphasises on abstractions which move from platform-independent models to platform-specific ones. Decompositions, on the other hand, primarily focus on modules, objects, components, or services, neglecting the separation of different aspects.

Several of these challenges have been identified and discussed in existing literature [16,24,40,47]. Notably, these references represent early explorations in this field. The discussions in [16,24] offer broad conceptual discussions, without proposing concrete technical solutions. The work presented in [40] discusses the importance of these challenges, demonstrating with examples that decomposing a program into modules differs fundamentally from decomposing it based on its flowchart steps. The research in [47] introduces an approach to decomposition by presenting the concept of hyperslices, which capture concerns that cross cut various modules or methods across different classes. However, this approach is primarily presented within the context of programming languages, and it appears to lack a formal definition of what constitutes "concerns". Importantly, formal methods are not the primary focus of these studies.

In this paper, we utilise the modelling methodology of the Refinement Calculus of Object and Component Systems (rCOS) as a formal framework to further investigate these issues. Our objective is to showcase how a multi-dimensional architectural modelling technique can be devised to rectify and surpass the limitations found in mainstream approaches. It is our believe that to improve the limitations discussed above, MDA requires an IDPs to support consistent integration of models of different FMs.

2   Linking Formal Methods

As mentioned in Sect. 1, an FM consists of the techniques and tools developed underpinned the formal theory. These include

- Techniques and tools for constructing models and specifying the properties of software systems using the formal language of the theory.
- Theorem proving techniques and tools for proving the required properties and laws of refinements of software systems within the proof system.
- Techniques, algorithms, and tools for model checking and solving constraint satisfaction problems.

The research on FMs actually started with beginning of computer science, and it experienced a period of rapid development. There are now a large number FMs have been developed. There are a number of well-known classifications, including

(a) *By formalism*: model-based methods (e.g. those based on state transition systems), deductive methods which focus on the derivation of correct systems using formal logic, and process algebras (e.g. CCS, CSP, and the π-calculus).
(b) *By Phase of Application*: specification method, development (correct by construction) method, verification methods and validation methods.
(c) *By Verification Technique*: model checking, theorem proving, and type systems.
(d) *By level of formalisation*: lightweight formal methods and full/heavyweight formal methods.

FMs are also typically classified into *operational methods* or *denotational methods*, according to the semantics of their languages. For the purpose of this paper, we describe a classification of FMs according to the aspects of software they model, or *classification for separation of concerns*.

2.1   Formal Theories of Different Aspects

We primarily focus on discussing mechanisms of abstraction (vs. refinement) and decomposition (vs. composition) to achieve the purpose of separation of concerns. Consequently, we classify FMs based on the aspects their languages are designed to express. These aspects are determined by the viewpoints from which developers observe the system. They can be orthogonal but are often interrelated. Different aspects are typically modelled using different formal theories, and there are various theories for modelling the same aspect. A complete model of a system is the integration of models from different aspects.

Typically, an FM's language is defined with a specific set of symbols known as the *signature*, which is often finite and nonempty. This signature is commonly partitioned into disjoint subsets termed *sorts* (borrowed from algebras). Using this signature, expressions and statements are formed using symbols of *operations* following specific *grammatical rules*. For tool development in the FM, the grammatical correctness (also called *well-formedness*) of these expressions and statements needs to be machine-checkable. As a result, the language's design adheres to automata theory principles, making the language a set of symbol strings produced by a certain type of automaton.

The signature and grammatically rules of an FM's language are designed based one the aspect to be specified by the language. The signature and grammatical rules represents what relevant to the aspect the modeller need to observe in the system behaviour. We present the important aspects and give examples of their modelling theories below.

Data Types. All software systems require to process data of different types. Their representation, operations and implementations can be separated from controls flow and data flows of programs. Abstract data types (ADTs) are a formal theory for data types, in which each ADT is modelled by an abstract (or formal) algebra. In object-oriented programming paradigms, an ADT is implemented as class and a general class is also regarded as an ADT. In rCOS, the theory of semantics and refinement of class declarations (also represented by UML class diagrams) serves the purpose of *theory of data model* [18,32].

Local Functionality. Theories like Hoare Logic [20] and Calculus of Predicate Transformers [12] are used to specify and verify sequential programs, possibly with non-determinism. We also include in this class those theories, such as VDM [23], Z [45] and B [1], which are based these and have mechanisms for modularity. Object-Z [44], rCOS theory of semantics and refinement for OO programs [18] and Java Modeling Language (JML) [28] can be regarded as OO extensions, and the latest VDM also treats object-orientation. These theories do not explicitly deal with concurrency and synchronisation.

Communication and Concurrency. Process algebras, such as CSP [21,43] and CCS [38,39], are event-based and abstract local computation away and explicitly treat concurrency and synchronisation. Petri Net [42] is another popular even-based formalism for concurrency. The the theory of input-output automata is control state and event based theory for communication and synchronisation.

Communication and Concurrency with Data Functionality. There are formalisms which combine local functionality with concurrency and synchronisation, where local computations are represented as atomic actions and specified in away like that in Hoare-Logic. Among them, we have logic systems like Temporal Logic of Actions (TLA) [25, 26] and UNITY [9], Action Systems [4], and Event-B [2]. A formal theory of this kind are more power than the above event-based theories in that they can specify properties of shared states. The apparently disadvantage they do not explicitly describe concurrency and synchronisation activities.

Performance and Quantity Aspects. A formalism for dealing with performance, such as timing, spacial aspects and energy consumption, can be defined by extending the signatures of an existing formal theory in the above list. In theory, security and privacy requirements can be treated without the need of fundamentally new formalism [35], neither does fault-tolerance [33].

The list of formal theories referenced earlier is by no means exhaustive. We believe that there is no single FM that is sufficient for addressing all issues across every aspect of a system's lifecycle. In particular, the development of modern, complex software systems requires a family of FMs to build models for different aspects of the artefacts, which can then be analysed and verified. Moreover, for 2 and 3 outlined in the paragraph of aims and objectives in Sect. 1, an integrated model-driven development environment should support the utilisation and transformation of models, proofs, verification algorithms, and verified theorems from various formal methods for the same aspect. Thus, from both educational and industrial adoption perspectives of Model-Driven Engineering (MDE), understanding the interrelationships between different FMs is crucial.

2.2 UTP for Linking Formal Theories

he Unifying Theories of Programming (UTP) [22], developed by Tony Hoare and He Jifeng, presents a unified approach to defining formal programming theories. A theory $\mathbf{T}$ of programming in a specific paradigm aims to characterise the behaviour of programs using a set of alphabetised predicates. In $\mathbf{T}$, a predicate contains free variables from a designated set known as the alphabet of the predicate. The set of predicates, also denoted as $\mathbf{T}$, is subject to constraints defined by a set of axioms known as *healthiness conditions*.

The theory also establishes a set of symbols representing operations on the set $\mathbf{T}$. These symbols, along with the alphabets, collectively form the *signature* of $\mathbf{T}$. The connection between different theories is established based on the theory of complete lattices and Galois connections

As an example, we define a relational theory $\mathbf{R}$ for imperative sequential programming. In this theory, observables are represented by a given set X of input variables, along with their decorated versions $X' = x'|x \in X$ as output variables. The set $\alpha = X \cup X'$ is referred to as the *input alphabet*, *output alphabet*, and *alphabet* of $\mathbf{R}$.

In theory $\mathbf{R}$, a program (or specification) is expressed as a first-order logic formula P, associated with a subset αP of α in such a way that P only mentions variables in αP, which is known as the alphabet of P. Thus, a relation is written in the form $(\alpha P, P)$, and αP is the union of the input and output alphabets of P, denoted as $in\alpha P \cup out\alpha P$. We always assume that $in\alpha P \subseteq X$ and $out\alpha P = in\alpha' P = \{x \mid x \in in\alpha P\}$.

It is easy to define the meaning of operations symbols in sequential programming

$$(\alpha, \mathbf{skip}) \stackrel{def}{=} \bigwedge_{x \in in\alpha} x' = x, \ (\alpha, x := e) \stackrel{def}{=} x' = e \wedge \bigwedge_{x \in in\alpha - \{x\}} x' = x$$

The sequential composition is defined as for given relations D_1 and D_2 and conditional choice $D_1 \lhd b \rhd D_2$, where b is a Boolean expression

$$D_1; D_2 \overset{def}{=} \exists v_0. D_1[v_0/out\alpha D_1] \wedge D_2[v_0/inD_2], \text{ provided } out\alpha D_1 = in\alpha D_2$$

$$in\alpha(D_1; D_2) \overset{def}{=} in\alpha(D_1), \qquad\qquad out(D_1; D_2) \overset{def}{=} out\alpha(D_1)$$

$$D_1 \lhd b \rhd D_2 \overset{def}{=} b \wedge D_1 \vee \neg b \wedge D_2 \qquad\qquad \text{provided } \alpha b \subset in\alpha D_1 = in\alpha D_2$$

$$\alpha(D_1 \lhd b \rhd D_2) = \alpha(D_1) = \alpha(D_2)$$

We say that a predicate D_2 is refinement of predicate D_1 in theory **R**, denoted as $D_1 \sqsubseteq_{\mathbf{R}} D_2$, if the implication $D_2 \rightarrow D_1$ is valid, i.e. the *universal closure* $[D_2 \rightarrow D_1]$ of $D_2 \rightarrow D_1$ holds. The refinement relation is a partial order, and *true* and *false* are the bottom and top elements. The formulas of **R** then forms a complete lattice and thus, according to Tarski's fixed point theorem, the least fixed-point $\mu X.(D; X) \lhd b \rhd \mathbf{skip}$ exists and it is defined to be loop state $b * D$. If we want to have nondeterministic choice $D_1 \sqcap D_2$, it is defined to be the disjunction $D_2 \vee D_2$.

We can readily observe that neither *true*; $D = true$ nor D; *true* = *true* holds for an arbitrary relation D in **R**. However, in all practical programming paradigms, they should both hold for an arbitrary program D if we use *true* to define the chaotic program $\bot$. Therefore, these *healthiness conditions* are imposed as axioms of **R**.

Theory **R** is for specification and verification of partial correctness reasoning as it is not concerned *termination* of programs. When termination becomes an aspect of concern, it is necessary to extend **R** to a theory, denoted by **D**, for specification and reasoning about total correctness of programs. To this end, we introduce two fresh observables ok and ok' which are Boolean variables. **D** contains the specifications of the form $P \vdash Q$ called *designs*, where P and Q are predicates in **R**. The meaning of $P \vdash Q$, is however defined by the formulation $(P \wedge ok) \rightarrow (Q \wedge ok')$. We still use input alphabet, output alphabet and alphabet of P and Q as those of the design $P \vdash Q$.

We can then refine the meaning of operations on programs, where we omit the alphabets for simplicity:

$$\mathbf{skip} \overset{def}{=} true \vdash x' = x \text{ for all } x \in \alpha$$

$$\bot \overset{def}{=} false \vdash true = \mathtt{true}$$

$$\top \overset{def}{=} \neg ok$$

$$x := e \overset{def}{=} defined(e) \vdash x' = e \text{ and } \forall y \in (\alpha - \{x\}).y' = y$$

$$D_1 \lhd b \rhd D_2 \overset{def}{=} defined(b) \rightarrow (b \wedge D_1 \vee \neg b \wedge D_2)$$

$$b * D \overset{def}{=} \mu X.(D; X) \lhd b \rhd \mathbf{skip}$$

Latter we allow to write **true** $\vdash Q$ as $\vdash Q$. The least fixed-point of loop statement is defined for the refinement relation on **D** which is still implication, $\bot$ and $\top$ defined above.

It is easy to prove that both *true*; $D = true$ and D; *true* = *true* hold in **D**. Likewise, the left zero law $(\bot; D) = D$ and the left unit law $(\mathbf{skip}; D) = D$ also hold in **D**. However, neither the right zero law $(D; \bot) = \bot$ nor the right unit law $(D; \mathbf{skip}) = D$ holds in **D**. In UTP, healthiness conditions were imposed to ensure that they hold.

In either $\mathbf{R}$ or $\mathbf{D}$, we can encode Hoare logic and Dijkstra's calculus predicate transformer. Given a predicate D in $\mathbf{R}$ or $\mathbf{D}$, and two state properties p and q, we define the Hoare triple as $\{p\}P\{q\} \overset{def}{=} P \to (p \to q')$. where p' is the predicate obtained from p by replacing all free variables in p with their dashed version. Then, the axioms and inference rule hold in $\mathbf{D}$ and $\mathbf{R}$. Given a predicate D of $\mathbf{R}$ or $\mathbf{D}$ and a state property r, we define the *weakest precondition* of D for the postcondition r as $wp(D, r) \overset{def}{=} \neg(D; \neg r)$. Then, the rules in the wp calculus are valid in $\mathbf{D}$ and $\mathbf{R}$.

The above definitions show that the theories of Hoare logic and calculus of predicate transformers can be mapped into the theory $\mathbf{D}$ and $\mathbf{R}$ and used consistently. Furthermore, we can treat $\mathbf{D}$ as *sub-theory* of $\mathbf{R}$ with alphabet $X \cup X' \cup \{ok, ok'\}$ by the translation mapping $\mathcal{T} : \mathbf{D} \to \mathbf{R}$ such that $\mathcal{T}(P \vdash Q) = (P \to Q)$ for each design $(P \vdash Q)$ in $\mathcal{D}$. It is important to note the differences and relations between the languages, proof systems and models (i.e. semantics) of $\mathbf{R}$, $\mathcal{D}$, Hoare logic and the calculus of predicate transformers.

Another important theory for unifying or linking formalisms is the theory of *institution* [15] by Goguen and Burstall. The theory is based category theory and using a group of related mappings to define *meaning serving* translations between formal languages, and their associated mappings between specifications, theorems, proofs, and models. It is an interesting research problem to establish the formal relation of UTP and the theory of institution. It is important to say that the the purpose of unification is actually for consistent use to support separation of concerns.

3   rCOS Theory for Component-Based Architecture

The formal theory of rCOS is an extension to the design calculus $\mathbf{D}$ introduced in the previous section for modelling and refinement of OO and component-based software systems [17,18,31]. It has the advantage of supporting modelling and refinement of continuously evolving architectures that accommodate open design [36].Here, open design means that the architecture allows the use of subsystems that are designed and operated by different organisations.

3.1   rCOS Theory of Semantics and Refinement of OO Programming

The theory defined an abstract OO programming language (OPL). A normal form of an OO program P is *Classes* • *Main*, where

- *Classes* is a finite (possibly empty) class declarations $C_1; \ldots; C_n$.
- A class declaration C has a name N; a list of typed attributes and a list of methods $m_1(in_1; out_1)\{c_1\}; \ldots; m_k(in_k; out_k)\{c_k\}$, where a method $m(in, out)\{c\}$ has a name m, a list *in* of input parameters and *out* of output parameters with their types, a body c which is a command written in OPL.
- *Main* is the main class which it has a list of attributes and its main method *main*$\{c\}$.
- The syntax of the OPL is defined as:

$$c ::= P \vdash Q \mid \mathbf{skip} \mid \mathbf{chaos} \mid \mathbf{var}\ x := e \mid \mathbf{end}\ x \mid le := e \mid C.New(x, e) \mid$$
$$(c; c) \mid c \lhd b \rhd c \mid le.m(e)$$

The type of an attribute or a program vairaible can be either a primitive type or or a class, and the order of the methods in a class is not essential.

Notably, we allow to use a design as a command, and *le* is called an assignable expression defined by $le ::= x \mid a \mid le.a \mid slef$, i.e. it is either a simply variable name x, an attribute name, a trace of attributes names or *self*. An expression e, which can appear on the right hand side of assignment symbol $:=$, is defined as $e ::= x \mid slef \mid null \mid e.a \mid f(e)$. Here $f(e)$ is an expression constructed using operations of primitive types. The full language also include in encapsulations of class attributes, and commands of type casting and type testing, but we omit them here as they are not particularly discussed.

The rCOS theory on OO programming is presented in the paper [18]. There, an object of class is formally defined and the state space of the a program is all the objects of the *Main* class. For intuitive explanation, we use graphs as follows.

- An object of a class C is represented as a directed graph with a root that represents the object. From the root, each edge points to a node, which can be an object of the class of an attribute or a node that represents a value in the type of an attribute with a primitive type. The edges are labelled with the names of attributes. Nodes that represent values of primitive types or null objects are considered leaves. Non-leaf nodes represent objects and are recursively defined as sub-graphs.
- A state of a program is an object of the *Main* class.
- An execution of the program is to change the initialised object to a final object, each step of the execution may create a new object, modify the values of an attribute of primitive type, replace an edge with another one (swings an edge, say by executing $le.a := self.b$).

The formal definition of an object is by finite paths by the graph, thus having ruled out infinitely looping in the graph. Therefore, a design $P \vdash Q$ in the OO theory specifies a relation on state graphs. The refinement relation is also defined as logic implication. In the paper [50], an operational semantics for the OO language is actually defined using graphs, and a set sound and relative complete refinement rules are proven to actually form a refinement calculus of OO programs.

It is easy to realise that the class declarations of an OPL program can be represented as a UML class diagram. On the other hand, a UML class diagram also represents a list of OPL class declarations plus constraints, such as those specified by association multiplicities and textual comments. There is no difficulty in extending the OPL syntax to allow the specification of these constraints on classes and attributes, which can be written in the *Object Constraint Language* (OCL) or formal predicate logic.

We refer to UML diagrams and OPL class declaration sections with object constraints as *class models*. Therefore, a class model defines a set of UML object diagrams, with each object in an object diagram corresponding to an object graph. This enables us to utilise the rCOS object-oriented semantic theory as a formal semantics for UML class models, as well we the type system of rCOS OPL programs.

3.2 Model of Interface Contracts of Components

According to Szyperski [46], 'A software component is a unit of composition with contractually specified interfaces and explicit context dependencies only. A software component can be deployed independently and is subject to composition by third parties.' In the semantic theory, we specifically focus on 'contractually specified interfaces and explicit context dependencies only' and the idea of being 'subject to composition by third parties.' Therefore, *interfaces* are considered first-class syntactic model elements, and *interface contracts* represent the first-class semantic modelling concept.

Interfaces. An *interface* $\mathcal{I} = \langle \mathcal{T}, \mathcal{V}, \mathcal{M} \rangle$ consists of a list $\mathcal{T}$ of type declarations, a list $\mathcal{V}$ of state variables (or attributes) with types defined in $\mathcal{T}$, and a list $\mathcal{M}$ of method declarations with parameters having types from $\mathcal{T}$. $\mathcal{T}$ can include class declarations, and both $\mathcal{V}$ and $\mathcal{M}$ follow the syntax of the rCOS OPL language. The state variables in $\mathcal{V}$ are encapsulated within the component and can only be accessed from outside the component through specified methods. The implementation details of the interface methods are hidden inside the component, but their functionalities must be specified and published to enable proper use.

Example 1 (Interface of Memory). A memory provides services for writing values to it and reading values from it from it with an interface

$$M.I = \langle \{int, array[int]\}\{array[int] \; m\}, \{w(int \; v), r(; int \; u)\} \rangle$$

where m is a variable for the content of memory. Later we simply omit the types in example when they are clear, and use a program template to write interfaces.

Reactive Designs. Components in component-based systems are distributedly deployed and run concurrently, often requiring to be reactive. To specify the reactive behaviour of components, we introduce the concept of *reactive designs*. Similar to the approach in Sect. 3, where the relational theory **R** is extended to the design theory **D**, we extend the theory **D** to the theory **C** by introducing two new Boolean observables, $wait, wait'$, and defining that a design D is considered *reactive* if it is a fixed point of the lifting mapping $\mathcal{W}$, i.e., $\mathcal{D}(D) = D$, where $\mathcal{W}$ is defined as follows:

$$\mathcal{W}(D) \stackrel{def}{=} (true \vdash (wait' \wedge (in\alpha' = in\alpha) \wedge (ok' = ok)) \triangleleft wait \triangleright D$$

Here $in\alpha$ is the input alphabet of D without ok and $wait$ being in it. Hence, when $wait$ is true the execution of D is blocked.

To specify both the functionality and synchronisation conditions of interface methods, we introduce the concept of 'guarded design' in the form $g\&D$, where g is a Boolean expression based on program variables (namely, ok and $wait$), and D is a reactive design in **C**. The meaning of $g\&D$ is defined as:

$$D \triangleleft g \triangleright (\mathbf{true} \vdash (in\alpha' = in\alpha) \wedge (ok' = ok))$$

It can be easily proven that $\mathcal{W}$ is monotonic with respect to implication, thus the set **C** of reactive designs. forms a complete lattice. This, along with the following two theorems, is necessary for **C** to be used as a theory of reactive programming.

Theorem 1. *For any designs D, D_1 and D_2 of **D**, we have*

(1) W is idempotent $W^2(D) = W(D)$;
(2) W is nearly closed for sequencing: $(W(D_1); W(D-2)) = W(D_1, W(D_2))$;
(3) W is closed for non-deterministic choice: $(W(D_1) \vee W(D_2)) = W(D_1 \vee D_2)$;
(4) W is closed for conditional choice: $(W(D_1) \lhd b \rhd W(D_2)) = W(D_1 \lhd b \rhd D_2)$.

Here, "=" denotes logical equivalence, and the following properties hold for guarded designs, which ensure that they can be used as commands in reactive programming.

Theorem 2. *For any react designs D, D_1 and D_2 of $\mathbf{D}$, we have*

(1) $g\&D$ is reactive;
(2) $(g\&D_1 \vee g\&D_2) = g\&(D_1 \vee D_2)$
(3) $(g_1\&D_1 \lhd b \rhd g_2\&D_2) = (g_1 \lhd bg2)\&(D1 \lhd B \rhd D_2)$;
(4) $(g_1\&D_1; g_2\&D_2) = g_1\&(D_1; g_2\&D_2)$.

It is important to note that from Theorem 1(1) a(1), D in a guarded design $g\&D$ can be a design in $\mathbf{D}$ too, and the top level interface specification only uses guarded designs of this kind. We need to define programs in a programming language, such as one in Subsect. 2.2 and the OPL in Subsect. 3.1, as reactive designs. The way to do this is to define the primitive commands directly as reactive design and the apply the above two theorems for composite composite commands. We take the following primitive commands as examples.

$$\mathbf{skip} \overset{def}{=} W(true \vdash \neg wait' \wedge in\alpha' = in\alpha), \quad \mathbf{choas} \overset{def}{=} W(false \vdash true)$$
$$\mathbf{stop} \overset{def}{=} W(true \vdash wait' \wedge in\alpha' = in\alpha)$$
$$x := e \overset{def}{=} W(true \vdash (x' = e) \wedge \neg wait' \wedge (in\alpha - \{x\})' = (in\alpha - \{x\})$$

We will write $true\&D$ as D.

Contracts of Interfaces. An *interface* of a component is a point through which the component interact with its environment, that is to provide services or require services. Therefore, a component can have a number of interfaces, some of them are *provided* and some *required services*, but their semantics is defined in the same way, as *contracts*.

Definition 1 (Contract of Interface). *Given an interface $\mathcal{I} = \langle \mathcal{T}, \mathcal{V}, \mathcal{M} \rangle$, a **contract** $\mathcal{C}$ for $\mathcal{I}$ is a pair (θ, Φ), where*

- *θ is a predicate with free variables in $\mathcal{V}$, called the initial condition;*
- *and θ is a mapping from $\mathcal{M}$ to $\mathbf{C}$ such that each $m(in; out)$ is assigned with a guarded design $g\&D$ over input variables $\mathcal{V} \cup in$ and output variables $\mathcal{V}' \cup out'$.*

A contract $\mathcal{C}$ is denoted by a tripe $\mathcal{C} = \langle \mathcal{I}, \theta, \Phi \rangle$.

Example 2 (Contracts for memory interface). We give two contracts for *M.I*. The first $\mathcal{C}_1 = \langle M.I, true, \Phi_1 \rangle$, where Φ_1 is defined by giving the designs as bodies of the corresponding methods as follows

$$w(int\ v)\{\neg isFull(m) \vdash m' = append(a, m)\};$$
$$r(; int\ u)\{\neg isEmpty(m) \vdash (u' = head(m) \wedge m' = tail(m))\}$$

Here, operations on data *isEmpty, isFull, append*(), *head*(), and *tail*() are supposed to have been defined in the definitions of the types.

The second contracts $C_2 = \langle M.I, isEmpty = false, \Phi_2 \rangle$ imposes controls to the invocations to the interface methods with gourds, where

$$w(int\ v)\{\neg isFull(m)\&(\neg isFull(m) \vdash m' = append(a, m))\};$$
$$r(; int\ u)\{\neg isEmpty\&(\neg isEmpty(m) \vdash u' = head(m) \wedge m' = tail(m))\}$$

Thus, the first invocation must be write, and then the user cal write into the memory as long it is not full, and can read from it as long as it is not not empty.

Dynamic Behaviours of Contracts. In an operational view, a contract defines the behaviour of an *labelled state transition system* (LSTS) in such a way that its states include elements from $V \cup ok, wait$, where the labels of transitions represent invocations $?m(v)$ and returns $!m(u)$ with actual input parameters v and actual output parameters u. An execution of the LSTS diverges once it enters a state in which ok is *false*, and it deadlocks when it reaches a state where *wait* is *true*. However, when we define the 'refinement relation' between contracts, a denotational model becomes more convenient. The dynamic behaviour of a contract $C = \langle \mathcal{I}, \theta, \Phi \rangle$ is defined in terms of its *divergences*, *failures*, and *traces*, which captures the key characteristics of concurrent programs.

Definition 2 (Divergences). *For a contract $C = \langle \mathcal{I}, \theta, \Phi \rangle$, the set $Div(C)$ of **divergences** of C consists of sequences of invocations and returns of methods from the interface $\langle ?m_1(v_1)!m_1(u_1) \ldots ?m_k(v_k)!m_k(u_k) \rangle$ whose executions end in a divergent state. In other words, the execution of $\theta; m_1(v_1; u_1); \ldots; m_j(v_j; u_j)$ as a prefix of the sequence, starting from an initial state, results in ok' being false, where v_i and u_i are the actual input and output parameters of the invocation $m_i()$.*

Definition 3 (Failures). *Given a contract C, a **failure** of C is pair (tr, M), where tr is a finite trace of method invocations and returns $\langle ?m_1(v_1)!m_1(u_1) \ldots \rangle$ of the interface, and M a set of method invocations, such that one of the following conditions holds*

(1) tr is the empty sequence, and M is the set of invocations $?m(v)$ with their guards being false in the initial states;

(2) tr is a trace $\langle ?m_1(v_1)!m_1(u_1) \ldots ?m_k(v_k)!m_k(u_k) \rangle$ and M consists of the invocations $?m(v)$ that after the executions of the invocations $m_1(x_1, y_1) \ldots m_k(x_k, y_k)$ from an initial state the guard of $m(v)$ is false;

(3) tr is a trace $\langle ?m_1(x_1)!m_1(y_1) \ldots ?m_k(x_k) \rangle$ and the execution of the invocation $m_k(v)$ is yet to deliver an output, and M contains all invocations;

(4) tr is a trace $\langle ?m_1(x_1)!m_1(y_1) \ldots ?m_k(x_k) \rangle$ and the execution of the invocation $m_k(v)$ has entered a wait state, and M contains all invocations; or

(5) tr is a divergence in $\mathcal{D}_C$, and M contains all invocations (all invocations can be refused after the execution diverges).

We use $Fail(C)$ to represent set of failures of contract C.

It is worth noting that some guards are more complex than others, depending on whether they involve only control states, both control and data states, or a combination of input parameters, control, and data states. For example, consider to change the guard of $r()$ in Example 2 to $\neg isEmpty \wedge Even(v) \wedge count(m) \le 4$. In general, changing preconditions of designs affects the divergence set and failures. Similarly, altering guards influences failures and divergences, potentially leading to invocations that violate the design's precondition. These properties are characterised by the concept of contract refinement and its associated theorem.

Definition 4 (Contract refinement). *A contract C_1 is refined by a contract C_2, denoted as $C_1 \sqsubseteq C_2$, if they have same interface, and*

(1) C_2 is not more likely to diverge, i.e. $Div(C_2) \subseteq Div(C_1)$; and
(2) C_2 is not more likely to block the environment, i.e. $Fail(C_2) \subseteq Fail(C_1)$.

The effective way to establish contract refinement is by *upward simulation* and *downward simulation* [17].

The above discussion shows how we can extract models of failures and divergences from the models of contracts defined by reactive designs. This establishes a connection between the theory of input and automata, action systems, and process calculi. It is often simpler to specify communication requirements in terms of communication traces or protocols. We first define the set of traces for a contract C from its failures

$$Trace(C) \stackrel{def}{=} \{tr | \text{there exists an } M \text{ such that } (tr, M) \in Fail(C)\}$$

Then, a protocol $\mathcal{P}$ is a subset of $Prot(C) \stackrel{def}{=} \{tr \downarrow_? | tr \in Trace(C)\}$.

Definition 5 (Consistency of Protocol with Contract). *A protocol T is consistent with $(D_C, \mathcal{F}_C)$ (thus with contract C), if the execution of any prefix of any invocation sequence sq in T does not enter a state in which all invocations to the provided services are refused, i.e. for any $sq \in T$ and any $(tr, M) \in \mathcal{F}_C$ such that $sq = tr \downarrow_?$, $M \ne \{m(v) \mid m() \in O\}$ if $tr \downarrow_?$.*

We have the following theorem for the consistency between protocols and contracts.

Theorem 3. *Given a contract C and its protocols T_1 and T_2, we have*

(1) If T_1 is consistent with C and $T_2 \subseteq T_1$, T_2 is consistent with C.
(2) If both T_1 and T_2 are consistent with C, so is $T_1 \cup T_2$.
(3) If $C_1 = (I, \theta_1, \Phi_1)$ is another contract of interface I and $\theta \sqsubseteq \theta_1$ and $\Phi(m()) \sqsubseteq \Phi_1(m())$ for any operation $m()$ of the interface, T_1 is consistent with C_1 if it is consistent with C.

The concept and theorems discussed above regarding consistency are essential for the correct use of components in different interaction environments. It also enables the separation of designing functional aspects from tailoring communication protocols. In an incremental development process, the specification of a component's interface can first be provided as a pair $(D, \mathcal{P})$ of designs in OPL (not guarded designs) along with a protocol $\mathcal{P}$. This initial specification can then be further developed into a fully specified contract as required. Another advantage of separating the specification of functionality using designs and interaction protocols is that, as shown in Example 2, it allows for different interaction protocols for the same functionality specification, and vice versa.

4   rCOS Support to Separation of Concerns in MDE

We have developed an understanding of the unification of data, local functionality, and dynamic behaviour. However, the purpose of this unification is to ensure consistent integration of models of these different aspects. This is particularly crucial for Model-Driven Engineering (MDE) and integrated development platforms. Now, let us discuss how this is put into practice in MDE. In rCOS, we propose to support a use-case-driven incremental development process, also known as the Rational Unified Process (RUP). However, we place a strong emphasis on component-based architectural models and refinement.

4.1   Use Case Driven Requirements Model Building

A requirements model consists of a set of interrelated use cases identified from the application domain. Each use case is modelled as an interface contract of a component in the following steps:

1. The operations provided by the component's interface corresponding to a use case consist of the interactions with the actors.
2. The classes are represented in conceptual class diagrams that the use case involves, and the state variables are names for objects that the use case needs to know (i.e., to record, check, modify, and communicate).
3. The interaction protocol of the use case represents the possible events of the interactions between the actors and the system to carry out the use case, and they are modelled by sequence diagrams.
4. The dynamic behaviour of a use case is modelled by a state diagram of the use case.
5. The functionalities of interface operations are specified by designs (pre- and post-conditions), focusing on what new objects are created, which attributes are modified, and the new links of objects that are formed.
6. The requirements architecture is modelled by UML component-based diagrams that reflect the relations among use cases in the use case diagram.

The models of above aspects of a component for a use case consisting of interactions, dynamic behaviour, types and functionality. More systematic presentation of the method can be found in [11,13], but with less formal support.

4.2   Component Development Process

A OO design process for components consists of the following modelling steps as shown in Fig. 1:

1. It takes each use-case component and designs each of its provided operations according to its pre- and post-conditions using the object-oriented refinement rules, with a focus on the four patterns of GRASP, in particular [11,27].
2. This decomposes the functionality of each use case operation into internal object interactions and computations, refining the use case sequence diagram into an object sequence diagram of the use case [11].

3. During the decomposition of the functionality of use-case operations into internal object interactions and computations, the requirements class model is refined into a design class model by adding methods and visibilities in classes based on responsibility assignments and method invocation directions [11].
4. Select some of the objects in an object sequence diagram and consider them as candidate component controllers if they satisfy six given invariant properties through automatic checks. Then, transform the design sequence diagram into a component-sequence diagram [30].
5. Generate a component diagram for each use case from the component sequence diagram obtained in the previous step, automatically decomposing the use-case component in the requirements model into a composition of sub-components. This leads to the decomposition of the entire component-based architecture model at the requirements level into a component-based design architecture model [30].
6. The coding from the design architecture model is not particularly difficult and can largely be automated [37, 49].

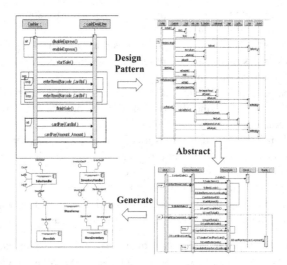

Fig. 1. Transformations from requirements to design of a component

4.3   System Development

For a given application domain, we assume a repository of implemented components for 'plenty' of use cases, their contract specifications, information on context dependencies, and (possibly) their sub-components[1].

Roughly speaking, the system development begins with the development of a requirements model in the form of use case contracts. The use case contracts are then

---

[1] We do not know such as an existing repository.

refined and/or decomposed into compositions of components to create a model of the system architecture. Subsequently, we search for candidate components in the repository that match a component in the architecture and check if their contracts are refinements of those in the architecture. The verification of functional requirements and synchronisation requirements can be conducted separately, and they can be refined independently by adding connectors and coordinators, respectively.

It is possible that for some contracts of components in the architecture, there are no appropriate components that can be easily adapted for implementation. In such cases, we have to develop them using the component development method discussed in the previous subsection. The main features of component and system development in rCOS are shown in Fig. 2.

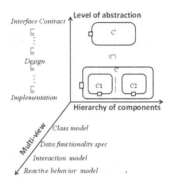

Fig. 2. Features of the rCOS modelling and development

To gain a deeper understanding of the processes described above, we recommend referring to the paper in [10], which reports the application of rCOS to the CoCoMe common case study [19]. Please note that domain knowledge is essential for providing the requirements model in terms of use cases, for designing the architecture, and for mapping them to components in the repository. The primary challenge in formalizing the mapping and developing tool support lies in the different naming schemes used in the requirements models, the architecture design, and the representations of the models of the components in the repository. In our opinion, significant effort is required in this area.

5 Conclusions

Abstractions and decompositions with respect different aspects are, which are essential for reuse and modification. We are skeptical that there exists a tool capable of automatic modelling and decomposition that can seamlessly achieve this separation of concerns. It predominantly requires human intelligence and effort. Nonetheless, a formal modelling method should offer multi-dimensional decomposition beyond just component-based methods, and multi-dimensional abstraction surpassing mere focus on a single aspect of the system. Additionally, when it comes to model refinement, there should be a broader spectrum of transformation options than just those transitioning from platform-independent models (PIMs) to platform-specific models (PSMs).

We have highlighted the significance and challenges associated with the development and application of formal methods that systematically aid in addressing abstraction and decomposition. We have introduced the rCOS framework to delineate the dimensions of models for different aspects and to discuss issues related to their decomposition, refinement, and consistent composition. While our discussion primarily centres on the formalisms and their capabilities, we acknowledge that there is limited coverage of tool implementation and support. However, for rCOS tools, we refer to the work in [29,34,49], though they are still in the form of proof of concepts.

References

1. Abrial, J.R.: The B-Book: Assigning Programs to Meanings. Cambridge University Press, Cambridge (1996)
2. Abrial, J.R.: Modeling in Event-B: System and Software Engineering. Cambridge University Press, Cambridge (2010)
3. Andersen, E.P., Reenskaug, T.: System design by composing structures of interacting objects. In: Madsen, O.L. (ed.) ECOOP 1992. LNCS, vol. 615, pp. 133–152. Springer, Heidelberg (1992). https://doi.org/10.1007/BFb0053034
4. Back, R.J.R., von Wright, J.: Trace refinement of action systems. In: Jonsson, B., Parrow, J. (eds.) CONCUR 1994. LNCS, vol. 836, pp. 367–384. Springer, Heidelberg (1994). https://doi.org/10.1007/978-3-540-48654-1_28
5. Bell, M.: Service-Oriented Modeling: Service Analysis, Design, and Architecture. Wiley, Hoboken (2008)
6. Booch, G.: Object-Oriented Analysis and Design with Applications. Addison-Wesley, Boston (1994)
7. Brooks, F.P.: No silver bullet: essence and accidents of software engineering. IEEE Comput. **20**(4), 10–19 (1987)
8. Brooks, F.P.: The mythical man-month: after 20 years. IEEE Softw. **12**(5), 57–60 (1995)
9. Chandy, K.M., Misra, J.: Parallel Program Design: A Foundation. Addison-Wesley, Reading (1988)
10. Chen, Z., et al.: Modelling with relational calculus of object and component systems - rCOS. In: Rausch, A., Reussner, R., Mirandola, R., Plášil, F. (eds.) The Common Component Modeling Example. LNCS, vol. 5153, pp. 116–145. Springer, Heidelberg (2008). https://doi.org/10.1007/978-3-540-85289-6_6
11. Chen, Z., Liu, Z., Ravn, A.P., Stolz, V., Zhan, N.: Refinement and verification in component-based model driven design. Sci. Comput. Program. **74**(4), 168–196 (2009)
12. Dijkstra, E.W.: A Discipline of Programming. Prentice-Hall, Englewood Cliffs (1976)
13. Dong, J.S., Woodcock, J. (eds.): Formal Methods and Software Engineering, 5th International Conference on Formal Engineering Methods, ICFEM 2003, Singapore, November 5–7, 2003, Proceedings. Lecture Notes in Computer Science, vol. 2885. Springer, Heidelberg (2003). https://doi.org/10.1007/b94115
14. Gauthier, R., Pont, S.: Designing Systems Programs. Prentice-Hall, Englewood Cliffs (1970)
15. Goguen, A.J., Burstall, R.M.: Institutions: abstract model theory for specification and programming. J. ACM **39**(1), 95–146 (1992)
16. Haan, J.D.: 8 reasons why model-driven approaches (will) fail, infoQ. https://www.infoq.com/articles/8-reasons-why-MDE-fails/

17. He, J., Li, X., Liu, Z.: A theory of reactive components. Electr. Notes Theor. Comput. Sci. **160**, 173–195 (2006)

18. He, J., Liu, Z., Li, X.: rCOS: a refinement calculus of object systems. Theoret. Comput. Sci. **365**(1–2), 109–142 (2006)

19. Herold, S., et al.: The common component modeling example. In: Rausch, A., Reussner, R., Mirandola, R., Plášil, F. (eds.) The Common Component Modeling Example. Lecture Notes in Computer Science, chap. 1, , vol. 5153, pp. 16–53. Springer, Heidelberg (2008)

20. Hoare, C.A.R.: An axiomatic basis for computer programming. Commun. ACM **12**(10), 576–580 (1969)

21. Hoare, C.A.R.: Communicating sequential processes. Commun. ACM **21**(8), 666–677 (1978)

22. Hoare, C.A.R., He, J.: Unifying Theories of Programming. Prentice-Hall, Upper Saddle River (1998)

23. Jones, C.B.: Systematic Software Development using VDM. Prentice Hall, Upper Saddle River (1990)

24. Kent, S.: Model driven engineering. In: Butler, M., Petre, L., Sere, K. (eds.) IFM 2002. LNCS, vol. 2335, pp. 286–298. Springer, Heidelberg (2002). https://doi.org/10.1007/3-540-47884-1_16

25. Lamport, L.: The temporal logic of actions. ACM Trans. Program. Lang. Syst. **16**(3), 872–923 (1994)

26. Lamport, L.: Specifying Systems: The TLA+ Language and Tools for Hardware and Software Engineers. Addison-Wesley, Boston (2002)

27. Larman, C.: Applying UML and Patterns: An Introduction to Object-Oriented Analysis and Design and the Unified Process, 2nd edn. Prentice-Hall, Upper Saddle River (2001)

28. Leavens, G.T., Baker, A.L.: Enhancing the pre- and postcondition technique for more expressive specifications. In: Wing, J.M., Woodcock, J., Davies, J. (eds.) FM 1999. LNCS, vol. 1709, pp. 1087–1106. Springer, Heidelberg (1999). https://doi.org/10.1007/3-540-48118-4_8

29. Li, D., Li, X., Liu, J., Liu, Z.: Validation of requirements models by automatic prototyping. J. Innov. Syst. Softw. Eng. **4**(3), 241–248 (2008)

30. Li, D., Li, X., Liu, Z., Stolz, V.: Interactive transformations from object-oriented models to component-based models. In: Arbab, F., Ölveczky, P.C. (eds.) FACS 2011. LNCS, vol. 7253, pp. 97–114. Springer, Heidelberg (2012). https://doi.org/10.1007/978-3-642-35743-5_7

31. Liu, Z.: Linking formal methods in software development - a reflection on the development of rCOS. In: Bowen, J.P., Li, Q., Xu, Q. (eds.) Theories of Programming and Formal Methods. LNCS, vol. 14080, pp. 52–84. Springer, Cham (2023). https://doi.org/10.1007/978-3-031-40436-8_3

32. Liu, Z., Jifeng, H., Li, X., Chen, Y.: A relational model for formal object-oriented requirement analysis in UML. In: Dong, J.S., Woodcock, J. (eds.) ICFEM 2003. LNCS, vol. 2885, pp. 641–664. Springer, Heidelberg (2003). https://doi.org/10.1007/978-3-540-39893-6_36

33. Liu, Z., Joseph, M.: Specification and verification of fault-tolerance, timing, and scheduling. ACM Trans. Program. Lang. Syst. **21**(1), 46–89 (1999)

34. Liu, Z., Mencl, V., Ravn, A.P., Yang, L.: Harnessing theories for tool support. In: Proceedings of the Second International Symposium on Leveraging Applications of Formal Methods, Verification and Validation (ISoLA 2006), pp. 371–382. IEEE Computer Society (2006)

35. Liu, Z., Morisset, C., Stolz, V.: A component-based access control monitor. In: Margaria, T., Steffen, B. (eds.) ISoLA 2008. CCIS, vol. 17, pp. 339–353. Springer, Heidelberg (2008). https://doi.org/10.1007/978-3-540-88479-8_24

36. Liu, Z., Wang, J.: Human-cyber-physical systems: concepts, challenges, and research opportunities. Frontiers Inf. Technol. Electron. Eng. **21**(11), 1535–1553 (2020)

37. Long, Q., Liu, Z., Li, X., He, J.: Consistent code generation from UML models. In: 16th Australian Software Engineering Conference (ASWEC 2005), 31 March–1 April 2005, Brisbane, Australia, pp. 23–30. IEEE Computer Society (2005). https://doi.org/10.1109/ASWEC.2005.17

38. Milner, R.: Communication and Concurrency. Prentice-Hall Inc., Upper Saddle River (1989)

39. Milner, R.: A Calculus of Communicating Systems. Springer, Heidelberg (1980). https://doi.org/10.1007/3-540-10235-3

40. Parnas, D.L.: On the criteria to be used in decomposing systems into modules. Commun. ACM **15**(12), 1053–1058 (1972)

41. Parnas, D.L.: A technique for software module specification with examples. Commun. ACM **15**, 330–336 (1972)

42. Petri, C.A., Reisig, W.: Petri net. Scholarpedia **3**(4) (2008)

43. Roscoe, A.W.: Theory and Practice of Concurrency. Prentice-Hall, Upper Saddle River (1997)

44. Smith, G.: The Object-Z Specification Language. Springer, Heidelberg (2000). https://doi.org/10.1007/978-1-4615-5265-9

45. Spivey, J.M.: The Z Notation, A Reference Manual. International Series in Computer Science, 2nd edn. Prentice Hall, Upper Saddle River (1992)

46. Szyperski, C.: Component Software: Beyond Object-Oriented Programming, 2nd edn. Addison-Wesley Longman Publishing Co., Inc., Boston (2002)

47. Tarr, P., Ossher, H., Harrison, W., Sutton, S.M.: N degrees of separation: multi-dimensional separation of concerns. In: Proceedings of the 1999 International Conference on Software Engineering, pp. 107–119. IEEE (1999)

48. Wang, J., Zhan, N., Feng, X., Feng, Liu, Z.: Overview of formal methods (in Chinese). Ruan Jian Xue Bao/J. Softw. **30**(1), 33–61 (2019)

49. Yang, Y., Li, X., Ke, W., Liu, Z.: Automated prototype generation from formal requirements model. IEEE Trans. Reliab. **69**(2), 632–656 (2020)

50. Zhao, L., Liu, X., Liu, Z., Qiu, Z.: Graph transformations for object-oriented refinement. Formal Aspects Comput. **21**(1–2), 103–131 (2009)

Solving SMT over Non-linear Real Arithmetic via Numerical Sampling and Symbolic Verification

Xinpeng Ni[ID], Yulun Wu[ID], and Bican Xia[(✉)][ID]

School of Mathematical Sciences, Peking University, Beijing, China
nxp@stu.pku.edu.cn, yulunwu@pku.edu.cn, xbc@math.pku.edu.cn

Abstract. Popular SMT solvers have achieved great success in tackling Nonlinear Real Arithmetic (NRA) problems, but they struggle when dealing with literals involving highly nonlinear polynomials. Current symbolic-numerical algorithms can efficiently handle the conjunction of highly nonlinear literals but are limited in addressing complex logical structures in satisfiability problems. This paper proposes a new algorithm for SMT(NRA), providing an efficient solution to satisfiability problems with highly nonlinear literals. When given an NRA formula, the new algorithm employs a random sampling algorithm first to obtain a floating-point sample that approximates formula satisfaction. Then, based on this sample, the formula is simplified according to some strategies. We apply a DPLL(T)-based process to all equalities in the formula, decomposing them into several groups of equalities. A fast symbolic algorithm is then used to obtain symbolic samples from the equality sets and verify whether the samples also satisfy the inequalities. It is important to note that we adopt a sampling and rapid verification approach instead of the sampling and conflict analysis steps in some complete algorithms. Consequently, if our algorithm fails to verify the satisfiability, it terminates and returns 'unknown'. We validated the effectiveness of our algorithm on instances from SMTLIB and the literature. The results indicate that our algorithm exhibits significant advantages on SMT(NRA) formulas with high-degree polynomials, and thus can be a good complement to popular SMT solvers as well as other symbolic-numerical algorithms.

Keywords: SMT · Nonlinear real arithmetic · Random sampling

1 Introduction

The Satisfiability Modulo Theories (SMT) aims to solve the problem of determining the satisfiability of logical formulas with respect to certain background theories, efficiently tackling complex real-world problems in various domains through a dedicated decision procedure. In this paper, we focus on Nonlinear Real Arithmetic (NRA), in which each literal of the logical formula is a polynomial formula in real variables.

H. Hermanns et al. (Eds.): SETTA 2023, LNCS 14464, pp. 171–188, 2024.
https://doi.org/10.1007/978-981-99-8664-4_10

A famous and widely used complete algorithm for solving polynomial formulas is the Cylindrical Algebraic Decomposition (CAD) algorithm [1], which, for a given formula, divides the space $\mathbb{R}^n$ into finitely many disjoint cells, guaranteeing that the satisfiability of the formula is invariant in each cell. Therefore, one sample point selected from each cell is enough for satisfiability checking. Suppose there are n variables involved and the highest degree of polynomials is d. An upper bound, $O(2^{2^n} d^{2^n})$, of cell number is given in [2]. That means in the worst case there are numerous cells must be computed and checked. To accelerate the solving process, the MCSAT framework, making use of the CAD algorithm for conflict analysis and clause learning, has been proposed, introducing single-cell projections instead of decomposing the space into cells [3,4]. In this method, the space is sampled first, followed by calculating the single-cell projection of CAD if conflicts occur. Notably, the computational complexity of individual cells is much smaller than that of the entire space decomposition. If a sample point satisfies the formula, the algorithm terminates early. This approach is widely used in popular SMT solvers, $e.g.$ Z3 [5], CVC5 [6], Yices2 [7], and MathSAT5 [8], bringing significant improvements to solving these types of problems. However, when the formula is unsatisfiable, a number of sampling and single-cell computations are needed by exhaustive search. There is another decision procedure, called δ-complete decision procedure [9], for non-linear formulas, which may answer unsat or δ-sat on input formulas for an error bound δ given by the users.

One point worth noting is that for most satisfiable SMT problems, an appropriate sampling method may prove satisfiability with just a few times of sampling. Therefore, some solvers are dedicated to quickly sampling specific instances. For example, Li $et\ al.$ [10] proposed a local searching method to solve inequality constraints and Li and Cai [11] introduced a method for multilinear constraints. Another approach was proposed by Cimatti $et\ al.$ to combine optimization and topological test [12], which uses optimization algorithms to obtain an initial numerical sample, followed by topological testing to verify if there is a true solution within a small box near the numerical solution.

In the field of symbolic computation, polynomial constraint systems are widely studied. Compared to general nonlinear formulas, there is a much simpler class of problems: zero-dimensional systems (equation systems with only a finite number of complex zeros). Various works focus on finding solutions to these systems. Techniques such as triangular decomposition [13] and Gröbner bases [14,15] have been used to symbolically find all solutions of zero-dimensional systems, while the homotopy continuation method [16] and moment matrix completion method [17] have been employed to compute numerical solutions. Existing algorithms perform significantly better in handling zero-dimensional systems than CAD-based methods. Efficient methods for handling zero-dimensional systems have also led to some work on symbolic-numerical methods to prove the satisfiability of polynomial constraints (see $e.g.$ [18,19]). In fact, through our experiments, five degree 3 and 5-variable constraints conjunctions randomly generated are beyond the capability of all popular SMT solvers, while specialized algorithms that are designed specifically for managing zero-dimensional systems can verify points on special polynomial systems of significantly larger sizes [18,19]. However, these symbolic computation algorithms are limited to accepting conjunctive forms and fall short when it comes to handling formulas in conjunction normal form.

The main motivation of our work is to design an algorithm which may efficiently solve NRA satisfiability problems with complicated logical structures and highly nonlinear literals so that it can be a good complement to popular SMT solvers as well as existing symbolic-numerical methods. The key of our idea is to replace the exhaustive search and conflict analysis in the complete algorithms with more efficient sampling and quick verification methods for faster problem-solving. Our method is straightforward: we first obtain a numerical sample point through a numerical algorithm and simplify the formula by discarding constraints in the formula that have a high cost (see Sect. 5.2). Then, a DPLL(T)-based splitting algorithm is utilized for equality constraints in the formula. The formula is transformed into several equation systems, and we obtain symbolic sample points for each equation system. Finally, we verify if the inequality constraints in the formula are satisfied by the symbolic samples.

Example 1. The following instance, originating from a modified P3P problem [20], is satisfiable. The degrees of all the polynomials contained within it do not exceed 3, but all mainstream solvers failed to prove its satisfiability in 1000 s. Our algorithm can find a satisfactory point in less than 0.1 s.

$$
\begin{aligned}
&((x^2 + y^2 - xy - 1 \leq 0) \vee ((z^2 + x^2 - zx - b^2)x > 0)) \\
&\wedge\ ((y^2 + z^2 - yz - a^2 \leq 0) \vee (a + b < x) \vee (z^2 - x^2 - 2 = 0)) \\
&\wedge\ z^2 + x^2 - zx - b^2 = 0\ \wedge\ a^2 - 1 + b - b^2 \leq 0 \\
&\wedge\ x > 0\ \wedge\ y > 0\ \wedge\ z > 0\ \wedge\ a > 5/4\ \wedge\ b \geq a.
\end{aligned} \tag{1}
$$

We conduct experiments on SMTLIB and examples collected from the literature and find that our approach achieves competitive results with existing solvers on all satisfiable problems. For those instances containing highly nonlinear literals, our performance is significantly better. Moreover, we demonstrate the characteristics of our method for different difficulty levels using random examples.

The organization of this paper is as follows: Sect. 2 introduces the basic concepts, notation, and essential functions for handling zero-dimensional systems. Section 3 explains how we obtain a numerical sample point and use it to simplify formulas. Section 4.5 discusses how we utilize a symbolic sample point to verify whether an inequality formula is satisfied. Section 4 presents the main algorithm. In Sect. 5, several experiments are conducted to validate the effectiveness of the algorithm. Finally, Sect. 6 concludes the paper.

2　Preliminaries

2.1　Real Arithmetic Formula

Let $\bar{x} = (x_1, \ldots, x_n)$ be n variables taking real values. We use $\mathbb{Q}$ and $\mathbb{R}$ to denote the sets of rational and real numbers, respectively. The ring of polynomials in the variables $x_1, \ldots, x_n$ with coefficients in $\mathbb{Q}$ is denoted by $\mathbb{Q}[\bar{x}]$. A polynomial constraint is a polynomial equation or inequality, which may also be referred to as a constraint or literal in this paper. A formula in Nonlinear Real Arithmetic (NRA) consists of a logical composition of polynomial constraints. Furthermore, we make sure that the formula includes only $<$ and $=$ symbols because other symbols can be readily replaced in CNF.

Example 2. Formula 1 is converted to

$$(\ (x^2 + y^2 - xy - 1 < 0) \vee (x^2 + y^2 - xy - 1 = 0) \vee (-(z^2 + x^2 - zx - b^2)x < 0) \ )$$
$$\wedge \ (\ (y^2 + z^2 - yz - a^2 < 0) \vee (y^2 + z^2 - yz - a^2 = 0)$$
$$\vee \ (a + b - x < 0) \vee (z^2 - x^2 - 2 = 0) \ )$$
$$\wedge \ (z^2 + x^2 - zx - b^2 = 0) \ \wedge \ (\ (a^2 - 1 + b - b^2 < 0) \vee (a^2 - 1 + b - b^2 = 0) \ )$$
$$\wedge \ (-x < 0) \ \wedge \ (-y < 0) \ \wedge \ (-z < 0) \ \wedge \ (-a + 5/4 < 0)$$
$$\wedge \ (\ (-(b - a) < 0) \vee (-(b - a) = 0) \ ).$$

Let $\Lambda = \{P_1, \ldots, P_m\}$, where every P_i corresponds to a finite subset of $\mathbb{Q}[\bar{x}]$. Consider the formula: $F = \bigwedge_{P_i \in \Lambda} \bigvee_{p_{ij} \in P_i} p_{ij}(x_1, \ldots, x_n) \lhd_{ij} 0$, where $\lhd_{ij} \in \{<, =\}$. We refer to F as a *formula*, $p_{ij}(x_1, \ldots, x_n) \lhd_{ij} 0$ as an *atomic formula*, and $\bigvee_{p_{ij} \in P_i} p_{ij}(x_1, \ldots, x_n) \lhd_{ij} 0$ as a *clause*.

SMT(NRA) problems can be formulated as the decision problem of determining the satisfiability of the formula F: Is F satisfiable?

2.2　Zero-Dimensional Systems and Real Zeros

During our symbolic sampling process, zero-dimensional systems play a key role in our algorithm. In general, multivariate polynomial equality constraint systems are difficult to handle, as it is often challenging to represent the set of real zeros. However, zero-dimensional systems, *i.e.* systems with only finitely many complex solutions, can be effectively managed.

Definition 1. *A finite polynomial set $T \subseteq \mathbb{Q}[\bar{x}]$ is a zero-dimensional system if the zeros of T, $\{\bar{x} \in \mathbb{C}^n | f(\bar{x}) = 0, \forall f \in T\}$, form a finite set.*

Definition 2. *Let $T \subseteq \mathbb{Q}[\bar{x}]$ be a zero-dimensional system. A real zero cube or an isolating cube of T consists of a list of intervals $([a_1, b_1], \ldots, [a_n, b_n])$ such that T has exactly one root $(x_1, ..., x_n)$ with $x_i \in [a_i, b_i]$ for $i = 1, \ldots, n$. We denote the precision of this isolating cube as $\max_i\{b_i - a_i\}$.*

As discussed in the introduction, some algorithms can efficiently obtain real zero cubes of a zero-dimensional system. In our method, we use triangular decomposition to do this, which is able to calculate all real zero cubes of any zero-dimensional system. Although it costs an exponential time for a zero-dimensional system [21] and is not the fastest in practice among those algorithms, it can handle problems of a much bigger size than CAD.

In this paper, the triangular decomposition is only a solver for computing the set of zero cubes, and we don't explain its details. The algorithms we used are from [21,22]. Also, the triangular decomposition algorithm can be used for determining whether a given polynomial set is a zero-dimensional system.

For ease of understanding, we describe the specifications of four functions about real zero calculating progress mentioned above:

- `RealZero`(equations): Calculating all real zeros of a zero-dimensional system. The input is an equation system and the output is a list containing all real zero cubes of the system if it is zero-dimensional.
- `IsZeroDimension`(equations): Whether an equation set is zero-dimensional. The input is a list of equations and the output is true or false.
- `IsConsistent`(equations): Whether an equation set has at least one real zero. The input is a list of equations and the output is true or false.
- `IncreasePrecison`(cube, equations): Increase the precision of a real zero cube. The input is a list of equations and a given zero cube. The output is a new cube with higher precision containing the same zero. If the context is clear, we use `IncreasePrecison`(cube) for brevity.

Note that `IsZeroDimension` and `IsConsistent` are actually sub-processes of `RealZero`. And `IncreasePrecison` can be done efficiently with any precision [22]. Now, we give an example to show a zero-dimensional system and the real zero cubes of it.

Example 3. Suppose we collect a list T_0 of some polynomials appearing in Formula 1 (see Example 2): $T_0 = [x^2 + y^2 - xy - 1, y^2 + z^2 - yz - a^2, z^2 + x^2 - zx - b^2, a^2 - 1 + b - b^2]$. We have `IsZeroDimension`$(T_0) =$ false.

Substituting $a = 1$ and $b = 2$, we get a new system $T_1 = [x^2 + y^2 - xy - 1, y^2 + z^2 - yz - 1, z^2 + x^2 - zx - 4, -2]$, which is a zero-dimensional system. `IsConsistent`$(T_1) =$ false, which means T_1 has no real zeros.

Substituting $a = 0$ in T_0, we get a square system $T_2 = [x^2 + y^2 - xy - 1, y^2 + z^2 - yz, z^2 + x^2 - zx - b^2, b - b^2 - 1]$. `IsConsistent`$(T_2)$ is still false. Substituting $a = 2$ in T_0, a zero-dimensional system T_3 is obtained, where $T_3 = [x^2 + y^2 - xy - 1, y^2 + z^2 - yz, z^2 + x^2 - zx - b^2, b - b^2 - 1]$. It has 8 real zeros, which are represented as real zero cubes:

$$\texttt{RealZero}(T_3) = \{ \ [\ [0,0],[1,1],[\frac{1179}{512}, \frac{2361}{1024}], [\frac{77266941}{33554432}, \frac{38682627}{16777216}] \ ] \ ],...\}.$$

The intervals in every cube correspond to the variables x, y, z, and b in sequence. We can call `IncreasePrecison`(*cube*) to increase the precision of these cubes, where *cube* is a zero cube in `RealZero`(T_3).

3   Numeric Sampling via Random Global Optimization

In this section, we provide details on encoding an SMT formula into an objective function for an unconstrained optimization problem. Several samples are generated using a Markov chain Monte Carlo algorithm. Actually, a CNF formula inherently corresponds to an optimization objective function.

Definition 3. *For any polynomial constraint* $p_{ij}(x_1, \ldots, x_n) \lhd_{ij} 0$, *where* $p_{ij} \in \mathbb{Q}[\bar{x}]$ *and* $\lhd_{ij} \in \{<, =\}$, *the "distance" function, which measures how far it is to be satisfied, is defined as:* $\text{distance}(p_{ij}(\bar{x}) < 0) := p_{ij}(\bar{x}) < 0 \: ? \: 0 : p_{ij}(\bar{x})^2$ *and* $\text{distance}(p_{ij}(\bar{x}) = 0) := p_{ij}(\bar{x})^2$.

For a polynomial formula $F = \bigwedge_{P_i \in \Lambda} \bigvee_{p_{ij} \in P_i} p_{ij}(x_1, \ldots, x_n) \lhd_{ij} 0$, *where* Λ *is a set of finite subsets* $P_i \subseteq \mathbb{Q}[\bar{x}]$ *and* $\lhd_{ij} \in \{<, =\}$, *the corresponding optimization goal is:* $\text{Obj}[F](\bar{x}) = \sum_{P_i \in \Lambda} \min_{p_{ij} \in P_i} \text{distance}(p_{ij}(\bar{x}) \lhd_{ij} 0)$.

It is easy to see that a constraint is satisfiable if and only if its distance is equal to zero and the formula is satisfiable if and only if the minimum value of its corresponding optimization goal is equal to 0.

However, we cannot claim that F is satisfiable if a sample makes the optimization goal very close to zero. If a CNF formula is satisfied, at least one constraint in each clause needs to be satisfied. As the optimization goal approaches zero, based on its construction, it implies that the distances for those satisfied constraints are also close to 0. Nonetheless, having a distance close to or equal to 0 does not necessarily mean that a constraint is satisfied. Firstly, a floating-point number is highly unlikely to satisfy an equation precisely. Secondly, if the distance of an inequality constraint is near or even equal to zero, it does not guarantee that the polynomial of the inequality is genuinely less than 0. Due to numerical errors, a function that is always greater than or equal to zero may also be evaluated as being less than zero numerically at certain points.

Example 4. Consider the formula: $F = (x^2 - 1 = 0) \wedge [(x^2 - 1 < 0) \vee (x < 0)]$ and two points $x_1 = 0.9998$ and $x_2 = -1.0002$. By Definition 3, we have $\text{Obj}[F](x) = (x^2 - 1)^2 + \min(x^2 - 1 < 0 \: ? \: 0 : (x^2 - 1)^2, x < 0 \: ? \: 0 : x^2)$ and $\text{Obj}[F](x_1) = \text{Obj}[F](x_2) = 4 \times 10^{-7}$, which means the two points are equally good.

To avoid such a situation, we modify the "distance" of inequalities. Let $d > 0$ be a constant. Define $\text{distance}(p_{ij}(\bar{x}) < 0) = p_{ij}(\bar{x}) + d < 0 \: ? \: 0 : (p_{ij}(\bar{x}) + d)^2$.

It is sufficient for d to be several orders of magnitude larger than the precision of the numerical algorithm. It is set to 10^{-2} in our implementation[1]. By this change, $\text{Obj}[F](x_1)$ is several orders of magnitude larger than $\text{Obj}(F)(x_2)$ and the numeric sampling process can obtain that x_2 is better than x_1.

---

[1] $d = 10^{-2}$ has nothing special. In our experiment, the numbers between 10^{-1} and 10^{-5} make no significant difference. We just need a number several orders of magnitude larger than the precision of the numerical algorithm here.

4   The Main Algorithm

Now, we begin to explain the details of our algorithm. Our main algorithm is provided in **Main** (see Algorithm 1). It accepts an SMT formula as input and encodes it into an optimization function, as described in Sect. 3. The algorithm then calls an MCMC method to obtain several numeric samples for the formula. Next, in **SimplifyFormula** (see Algorithm 2), we discard some literals from the formula to streamline its logical structure. Then, **EquationSplit** (see Algorithm 3) attempts to divide the original formula into several sub-problems. Finally, **ModelObtain**(see Algorithm 4) is used to obtain a symbolic sample that satisfies the formula, guided by the points obtained throughout the process.

Algorithm 1. Main

Input : formula F, δ
Output: sat or **unknown**

$Samples \leftarrow$ MCMC(F)
for $sample$ in $Samples$ **do**
    $F_1 \leftarrow$ SimplifyFormula($F, sample, \delta$)
    $Problems \leftarrow$ EquationSplit($F_1, \{\}, \{\}, sample$)
    for $problem$ in $Problems$ **do**
        $equations \leftarrow problem[1]$
        $formula \leftarrow problem[2]$
        if ModelObtain$(equations, formula, sample)$ = **true then**
            ∟ **return sat**

return unknown

4.1   Using Numeric Samples to Simplify the Formula

Our goal is to obtain a symbolic sample that satisfies the formula by taking use of a floating-point sample. A constraint with a smaller distance is more likely to be satisfied through certain adjustments. Based on these ideas, we use the algorithm **SimplifyFormula** to simplify the formula. It takes an NRA formula, a (numerical) sample, and a threshold δ as input, and it ignores the constraints if its distance is greater than the threshold δ.

    This algorithm yields a formula that is expected to be satisfied by the sample. Furthermore, the satisfiability of this simplified formula inherits the satisfiability of the original formula. In our implementation, δ is set to 1. This selection might seem arbitrary but is actually based on empirical evidence and does not carry any special meaning.

Example 5. We use the CNF formula in Example 2 to explain Algorithm 2. Suppose that we obtain the following sample point (For ease of presentation, here we retain four decimal places after the decimal point.): $a = 1.3996, b = 1.5995, x = 1.1547, y = 0.5773, z = 1.8257$. By setting $\delta = 1$, we get the following

Algorithm 2. SimplyFormula

Input   : formula F, sample s, δ
Output: simplified NRA formula

for *constraint* **in** F **do**
$\quad$ **if** distance*(constraint)* $>= \delta$ **then**
$\quad\quad$ $F \leftarrow F \setminus \{constraint\}$
return F

---

simplified formula, named $formula_1$, where every constraint has a distance less than δ:

$$((x^2 + y^2 - xy - 1 < 0) \vee (x^2 + y^2 - xy - 1 = 0) \vee (-(z^2 + x^2 - zx - b^2)x < 0))$$
$$\wedge ((y^2 + z^2 - yz - a^2 = 0) \vee (z^2 - x^2 - 2 = 0)) \wedge (z^2 + x^2 - zx - b^2 = 0)$$
$$\wedge ((a^2 - 1 + b - b^2 < 0) \vee (a^2 - 1 + b - b^2 = 0)) \wedge (-x < 0) \wedge (-y < 0)$$
$$\wedge (-z < 0) \wedge (-a + 5/4 < 0) \wedge ((-(b - a) < 0) \vee (-(b - a) = 0)).$$

4.2 DPLL-Based Splitting Procedure

Our main progress for symbolic verification is a modified version of the DPLL algorithm, considering that NRA formulas together with a numeric sample. If the formula is not satisfied under this sample, we try to adjust it to fit some equations. Therefore, our first step is to select a set of equations in the formula.

In the `EquationSplit` algorithm, we solely focus on determining the truth value of each equation. It takes in a $formula$. $TrueEqs$ and $FalseEqs$ are sets of equations, representing equations assigned true and false, respectively. On each invocation of this process, we select an equation (`SelectEquation`) from the formula and add it to both $TrueEqs$ and $FalseEqs$. Once we have determined the truth value of all equations in the formula, we retain all remaining inequalities in $formula$, and $[TrueEqs, F]$ will be a subproblem to be solved. In the `main` algorithm, we use `ModelObtain` to adjust the sample to $TrueEqs$ and verify whether the system can be satisfied.

In the `UnitPropagation` process, in addition to propagating through single-literal clauses, we simultaneously apply the following two rules to infer the truth value of equations or inequalities: $p_1 \in TrueEqs \wedge p_1 \mid p_2 \Rightarrow \neg p2 < 0$ and $p_1 \in FalseEqs \wedge p_2 \mid p_1 \Rightarrow \neg p2 = 0$, where $A \mid B$ denotes A divides B.

Example 6. We perform `EquationSplit` on the simplified formula (see Example 5). There are 6 equations in this formula.

On the first invocation of this process, `UnitPropagation`$(z^2 + x^2 - zx - b^2 = 0)$ is true since it is the only literal in some clause. Furthermore, we have $(z^2 + x^2 - zx - b^2) \mid -(z^2 + x^2 - zx - b^2)x \Rightarrow \neg(-(z^2 + x^2 - zx - b^2)x < 0)$. So, $-(z^2 + x^2 - zx - b^2)x < 0$ is dropped from the formula. Then, we select an equation $-b + a = 0$ and assign it to true, invoke `ModelObtain` again. Now we have $TrueEqs_2 = [z^2 + x^2 - zx - b^2, -b + a], FalseEqs_2 = [\ ]$, and $formula_2 = ((x^2 + y^2 - xy - 1 < 0) \vee (x^2 + y^2 - xy - 1 = 0)) \wedge ((y^2 + z^2 - yz - a^2 =$

Algorithm 3. EquationSplit

Input   : formula F, $TrueEqs$, $FalseEqs$, sample s
Output: a list of problems

$F \leftarrow$ UnitPropagation$(F, TrueEqs, FalseEqs)$
$ProblemList \leftarrow [\,]$
if ExistEquation(F) **then**
  $equation \leftarrow$ SelectEquation(F)
  for $problem$ **in** EquationSplit$(F, TrueEqs \cup \{equation\}, FalseEqs, s)$ **do**
    add $problem$ to $ProblemList$
  for $problem$ **in** EquationSplit$(F, TrueEqs, FalseEqs \cup \{equation\}, s)$ **do**
    add $problem$ to $ProblemList$
  return $ProblemList$
else
  $problem \leftarrow [TrueEqs, F]$
  return $[problem]$

$0) \vee (z^2 - x^2 - 2 = 0)\,) \wedge (\,(a^2 - 1 + b - b^2 < 0) \vee (a^2 - 1 + b - b^2 = 0)\,) \wedge (-x < 0) \wedge (-y < 0) \wedge (-z < 0) \wedge (-a + \frac{5}{4} < 0)$.

We sequentially assign $x^2 + y^2 - xy - 1 = 0$, $a^2 - 1 + b - b^2 = 0$ and $y^2 + z^2 - yz - a^2 = 0$ to true. Eventually, we obtain a sub-problem: $TrueEqs_3 = [z^2 + x^2 - zx - b^2, -b + a, x^2 + y^2 - xy - 1, a^2 - 1 + b - b^2, y^2 + z^2 - yz - a^2]$ and $formula_3 = (-x < 0) \wedge (-y < 0) \wedge (-z < 0) \wedge (-a + \frac{5}{4} < 0)$. If we assign $-b + a = 0$ and $x^2 + y^2 - xy - 1 = 0$ to false while set $z^2 - x^2 - 2 = 0$ and $a^2 - 1 + b - b^2 = 0$ to true, another sub-problem is obtained: $TrueEqs_4 = [z^2 + x^2 - zx - b^2, a^2 - 1 + b - b^2, z^2 - x^2 - 2]$, and $formula_4 = (\,(x^2 + y^2 - xy - 1 < 0) \vee (-(z^2 + x^2 - zx - b^2)x < 0)\,) \wedge (-x < 0) \wedge (-y < 0) \wedge (-z < 0) \wedge (-a + \frac{5}{4} < 0) \wedge (-(b - a) < 0)$. By considering different assignments, we obtain a total of 24 sub-problems.

4.3   Model Generation and Verification

Now, we explain a sub-process of computing the model of a formula. Suppose we have a set of *equations*, and a *formula* containing only inequalities, we consider the satisfiability of $(\wedge_{p \in equations} p = 0) \wedge formula$. Furthermore, suppose we have a *sample* that assigns a rational value for each variable. We attempt to adapt the sample to fit the equations and obtain a symbolic sample satisfying this formula using ModelObtain.

First, we reduce the equations to a zero-dimensional system by assigning some variables to their value in *sample*. Then, we perform RealZero and calculate the zero cubes. Finally, we invoke CheckInequality (Algorithm 6) to check if the formula is satisfiable using interval arithmetic. For those variables whose values are not given in cubes, we just use the values in *sample*.

Example 7. Continue with Example 6 to explain Algorithm 4. Suppose the sub-problem is $TrueEqs_4$, $formula_4$ in Example 6. We first take $x = 1.15$, and obtain

---

Algorithm 4. ModelObtain

Input : equations Eqs, formula F, sample s
Output: true or **false**

$equations \leftarrow$ `ReduceToZeroDimension`(Eqs, s)
$cubes \leftarrow$ `RealZero`(Eqs)
for $cube$ **in** $cubes$ **do**
  | **if** `CheckInequality`$(F, cube, s)$ **then**
  | └ **return true**
return false

---

a consistent zero-dimensional system $[b^2+z^2-1.15z+1.33, a^2-b^2+b-1, z^2-3.33]$. (All the numbers used in the algorithm are actually represented as rational numbers, but for the sake of presentation, we uniformly display them here with two decimal places.) Then, `RealZero` calculated 8 real zero cubes of it. One of them is $z \in [1.82\ldots, 1.82\ldots], b \in [1.59\ldots, 1.59\ldots], a \in [1.39\ldots, 1.39\ldots]$ together with $x = 1.15\ldots, y = 0.57\ldots$. `CheckInequality` confirms that this sample satisfies the formula symbolically.

4.4   Reducing the Equation Set to Zero-Dimensional System

It is essential to note that the input equation set for the `RealZero` process requires a zero-dimensional system. If the equation set input to the `ModelObtain` process is not a zero-dimensional system, we need to reduce it to a zero-dimensional system first.

Algorithm 5. ReduceToZeroDimension

Input : equations Eqs, formula F, sample s
Output: equations Eqs or **false**

$Eqs \leftarrow$ `AssignAllVariables`(Eqs, s)
while *not* `IsConsistent`*(equations)* **do**
  | $variable \leftarrow$ `ChooseOneVariable`(Eqs)
  | **if** $variable =$ **false then**
  | └ **break**
  | $Eqs \leftarrow$ `BacktrackOneVariable`$(Eqs, variable)$
if `IsZeroDimension`*(Eqs)* *and* `IsConsistent`*(Eqs)* **then**
  | **return** Eqs
else
  └ **return false**

In the `ReduceToZeroDimension` procedure, we assign variables with the sample value, hoping that when some variables are substituted, a consistent zero-dimensional system will emerge. We choose to substitute all variables (`AssignAllVariables`) first and backtrack one assignment each time if the system is not consistent (`ChooseOneVariable` and then `BacktrackOneVariable`).

The main reason is the time cost of inputs in the `IsZeroDimension` procedure is considerably more for non-zero-dimensional systems than that for zero-dimensional systems. During `ChooseOneVariabe`, in order to avoid the system having no real zeros, we always choose variables in the polynomials assigned to a constant first.

Example 8. Consider a list of polynomials $[z^2 + x^2 - zx - b^2, a^2 - 1 + b - b^2, z^2 - x^2 - 2]$. First, substituting $a = 1.39, b = 1.59, x = 1.15, z = 1.82$, we get a non-consistent system containing 3 constants. Then, backtrack z to reduce constants in this system. After that, since $a^2 - 1 + b - b^2$ is still a constant. We backtrack a. Finally, b is backtracked. And a consistent zero-dimensional system is obtained.

4.5   Determine Satisfiability of Inequality

In this subsection, we address a sub-problem of solving SMT problems. Given a CNF formula with only inequalities, suppose we have a complete symbolic assignment for all variables. Our goal is to check whether the formula is satisfied under this assignment.

More precisely, we consider a formula in the form $F = \wedge_{P_i \in \Lambda} \vee_{p_{ij} \in P_i}$ $p_{ij}(x_1, ..., x_n) < 0$. The set of variables is divided into two parts: one part is assigned rational values, and the other part is assigned by a real zero cube of a certain zero-dimensional system. We aim to determine whether the formula F is ture or false under this assignment.

It is important to note that although cubes formally appear as a series of interval-defined cubes, they actually represent a single point. Moreover, as stated in Sect. 2, we can increase the precision of cubes to any value small enough using the function `IncreasePrecision`(cube) with a low cost.

Before showing how to solve this problem, we give a brief introduction to interval arithmetic. All the concepts of interval arithmetic are classic. A subset X of $\mathbb{R}$ is called an interval if X has one of the forms from the following list: $[a, b], [a, +\infty), (-\infty, b], (-\infty, +\infty)$, where $a, b \in \mathbb{R}$. Letting $a, b \in \mathbb{R} \cup \{+\infty, -\infty\}$, we use $[a, b]$ to unify all the forms of an interval. We also use a list of intervals to denote a cube, which represents a cube in a multidimensional space.

Definition 4. *For an interval $X = [a, b]$, the sign of X is defined as follows: $\text{Sign}(X)$ is -1 if $b < 0$; 0 if $a \le 0 \le b$; and 1 if $a > 0$. For two intervals X, Y and an operation $\circ \in \{+, -, \cdot\}$, we define $X \circ Y = \{x \circ y \mid x \in X, y \in Y\}$.*

A multivariate polynomial p is actually a combination of operations from $\{+, -, \cdot\}$, and we can get an interval evaluation of its value in a cube using the operations on intervals. This is denoted as $\text{Subs}(p, cube)$. Additionally, when the cube shrinks to a point $\bar{x}$, $\text{Subs}(p, cube)$ will approach $p(\bar{x})$.

Example 9. Suppose we have $x \in [-1, 1], y \in [1, 3/2]$ and a polynomial $p = x^2 + y^2 - xy - 1$. Using interval arithmetic, we get an evaluation of p as $\text{Subs}(p, [[-1, 1], [1, 3/2]]) = [-5/2, 15/4]$ and $\text{Sign}(\text{Subs}(p, [[-1, 1], [1, 3/2]])) = 0$.

As shown in Algorithm 6, we are given a CNF formula with only $<$ constraints, rational assignments for part of the variables, and a real zero cube assignment for the other variables. And the algorithm returns the Boolean value (true or false) of the formula under this assignment. In each loop, we use interval arithmetic to determine the sign of each constraint and infer the Boolean value of each clause. In case we cannot determine the value of the formula after one loop, *i.e.* there is some sign of constraint that cannot be determined by the cube precision, we increase the precision of the cube and repeat this progress.

Algorithm 6. CheckInequality

Input : $formula, cube, x$ (where $formula$ has only inequality constraints)
Output: true or **false**

for i from 1 to 5 **do**
    $newformula \leftarrow [\ ]$
    forall the *clause* **in** *formula* **do**
        $newclause \leftarrow [\ ]$
        forall the *constraint* **in** *clause* **do**
            if $\text{Sign}(constraint, x \cup cube) = -1$ **then**
                $newclause \leftarrow [true]$
                break
            else
                if $\text{Sign}(constraint, x \cup cube) = 0$ **then**
                    $newclause \leftarrow newclause \cup \{constraint\}$
        if $newclause = [true]$ **then**
            break
        else
            if $newclause = [\ ]$ **then**
                return false
            else
                $newformula \leftarrow newformula \cup \{newclause\}$
    if $newclause = [\ ]$ **then**
        return true
    else
        $cube \leftarrow \text{IncreasePrecision}(cube)$
return false

Note that no matter how many times we increase the precision, we may always get $\text{Sign}(p) = 0$ if the assignment is a zero of a certain constant $p < 0$. Therefore, we restrict the precision adjustment to a maximum of five increases[2]. Beyond these increases, any remaining constraints are considered as "$=0$" for this assignment, and subsequently yield a result of false.

---

[2] The function, IncreasePrecision, escalates the precision level of the cube by a factor of 2^{-8}. After 5 iterations, the precision ascends by a factor of 2^{-40}, which, as per our judgment, is deemed adequate.

5   Experiment

We conducted experiments to evaluate the performance of our algorithm on three classes of instances. The first one is NRA from SMTLIB, the second one is collected from the literature and is partially manually created, and the last one is composed of randomly generated instances. We compare our tool with state-of-the-art SMT(NRA) solvers.

5.1   Experiment Preparation

Implementation: We use the basinhopping package from the Python Scipy library as the implementation tool for our optimization program, and implemented the subsequent algorithm with Maple2021 as a tool, which is named ET.

Experiment Setup: All experiments were conducted on 8-Core Intel Core i7-11700K with 64GB of memory and Ubuntu 22.04.2 LINUX SYSTEM. We compare our tool with 4 state-of-the-art SMT(NRA) solvers, namely Z3(4.12.1), CVC5(1.0.5), Yices2(2.6.4) and MathSAT5(5.6.9). Each solver is executed with a cutoff time of 90 s for each instance.

5.2   Instances

We prepare three classes of instances. The first dataset is QF-NRA comes from SMTLIB[3]. It contains all the 12134 instances, among which 5248 are satisfiable, 5534 are unsatisfiable, and 1352 unknown. The second class of instances named SC contains **two subsets**, with a total of 147 instances[4]. RW is taken from a book on symbolic computation [23], and all cases in Vers are from Verschelde's test suite[5]. The third class is random instances. The method used to generate those instances is almost identical to the method in [10], with the only difference being that we modify it to allow "=" with a certain probability.

After conducting extensive experiments, some parameters that can determine the structure of the formula are reasonably fixed in a certain interval, and the remaining parameters are used to adjust the difficulty of the formula to illustrate the experimental effect. Let $\mathbf{rdn}(down,up)$ denote a random integer between two integers $down$ and up. All randomly generated formulas have a structure that is defined by a set of parameters following these criteria: vn is the number of possible variables with a value of $\mathbf{rdn}(10,15)$, pn is the number of polynomials that may appear in formulas with a value of $\mathbf{rdn}(20,40)$, pvn is the number of variables that each polynomial may have with a value of $\mathbf{rdn}(4,6)$, pl is the size of a polynomial with a value of $\mathbf{rdn}(10,30)$, cl is the length of clauses in the formula with a value of $\mathbf{rdn}(3,5)$. The other two parameters are used to adjust the difficulty of the formula in two different aspects, namely pd which decides the degree of each polynomial, and cn which is the clause num of the formula.

---

[3] https://clc-gitlab.cs.uiowa.edu:2443/SMT-LIB-benchmarks/QF_NRA.

[4] https://gitee.com/wuyulunPM/etsolver.

[5] https://www.math.uic.edu/~jan.

5.3 Comparison to Symbolic Computation Tools

symbolic computation tools can handle the conjunction of polynomial constraints, yet lack the ability to manage logical formulas. Our method transforms non-linear SMT problems into problems that can be solved by symbolic computation tools, effectively augmenting the reach of such tools. For this reason, a comparison with symbolic computation tools is not necessary.

5.4 Comparison to State-of-the-Art SMT Solvers

Our tool can only respond with 'sat' and 'unknown', whereas the state-of-the-art SMT solvers deliver answers in the form of 'sat' or 'unsat'. We run our algorithm three times on every example to mitigate random effects and only count those instances where the response of our tool is 'sat'. It's crucial to note that a majority of state-of-the-art SMT solvers integrate a combination of strategies, both complete and incomplete. Our intention, via these experiments, is to demonstrate that our approach can handle a class of problems that these integrated methods struggle with, that is, highly non-linear cases.

We run our algorithm together with state-of-the-art SMT solvers on all instances with satisfiable or unknown status and discard the instances with Boolean variables. The results are presented in Tables 1 and 2. The tables show that for each solver, the number of instances they solve successfully and give a sat answer. The first column on the left is the overall, and the remaining ones correspond to each benchmark family. The best results corresponding to each benchmark family are highlighted in boldface.

For QF-NRA, we have observed that our performance in solving instances with high nonlinearity, specifically in Sturm-MBO and Geogebra, exceeds that of other solvers. However, our performance on instances that exhibit nearly linear behavior falls short, and these instances make up the majority of the QF-NRA. Although we solve fewer instances compared to Z3, CVC5, and Yices2, we have successfully solved 55 unique instances that other solvers could not handle. It is worth considering that our algorithm, despite employing a single strategy unlike state-of-the-art solvers, demonstrates a competitive advantage.

For the SCs manually collected from the literature, formulas in RW are structured with the conjunction of polynomial constants, while formulas in Vers only contain equations. The instance in both of them don't have a complex logical structure, but the degree of polynomials is relatively high. The performance on these instances being better than all state-of-the-art solvers is as expected, as shown in Table 2. However, we observed that there are still some cases that we can not solved. As mentioned earlier, in our framework, triangular decomposition is used in handling zero-dimensional systems, which can calculate all real roots of any zero-dimensional system. However, it is slower than many incomplete algorithms for zero-dimensional systems. Our tool is also weaker than many other algorithms for handling zero-dimensional systems in the instances of Vers. Other solvers may be added to overcome this in the future.

Table 1. Summary of results for cases without Boolean variables in QF-NRA. The data in the table represents the number of instances where the solver returned 'sat' as the result.

	Total	Sturm-MBO	Sturm-MGC	UltimateInv	Economics-M	Pine	Geogebra	Uncu	kissing	LassoRanker	meti-tarski	UltimateAut	zankl
ET	4683	**43**	0	0	58	189	**111**	66	24	0	4155	0	37
z3	**5257**	0	**2**	44	**93**	**235**	109	69	**32**	173	**4391**	**44**	**65**
cvc5	5152	0	0	34	89	199	91	62	16	232	4335	34	60
yices	5112	0	0	39	90	**235**	98	69	20	96	4368	39	58
mathsat	2677	0	0	34	84	11	0	45	18	**266**	2159	34	26
Unique	55	43	0	0	7	0	3	0	1	0	1	0	0

On randomly generated examples, by the specific fixed parameter mentioned above (except *pd* and *cn*), we compare our algorithm with popular solvers in different equality possibilities (*ep* represents the possibilities a constraint is an equation). The result is shown in Fig. 1. In each row, the value of *ep* is set to different values, specifically 0.15, 0.3, and 0.5. In each column, the complexity of the random formulas is changed from different dimensions. In the first column, we fix the number of clauses(*cn*) as rnd(15,25) and increase the polynomial degree *pd* from 1 to 100, *i.e.* changing the nonlinearity degree of the formulas. We find that under the three equality probabilities, the curves have the same trend. Besides, ET is weaker than the popular SMT solvers in the linear case, similar to their capabilities in the quadratic case, and much better than them when the polynomial degree is greater than 3.

Table 2. Summary of results for SC without Boolean variables. The data in the table represents the number of instances where the solver returned 'sat' as the result.

	Total	RW	Vers
ET	**75**	**22**	**53**
z3	44	11	33
cvc5	30	10	20
yices	32	5	27
mathsat	36	7	29

To further clarify the comparison of solver capabilities when the polynomial degree reaches 3, the second column of the chart is drawn. In these three sets of experiments, we fix the polynomial degree(*pd*) at 3 and increase the number of clauses(*cn*) from 10 to 100 (recall the clause length(*cl*) value as rdn(3,5)), that is, changing the complexity of the logical structure of the formula. We can see that under the three equality probabilities, regardless of how *cn* changes, we always outperform existing solvers. Therefore, we conclude that our algorithm has an absolute advantage over the popular solvers when the polynomial degree is greater than or equal to 3.

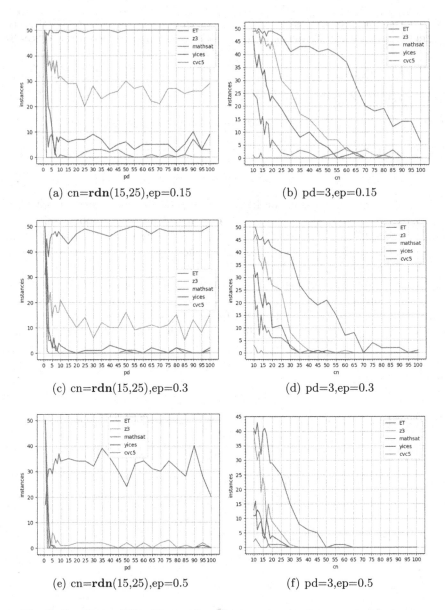

(a) cn=**rdn**(15,25),ep=0.15   (b) pd=3,ep=0.15

(c) cn=**rdn**(15,25),ep=0.3   (d) pd=3,ep=0.3

(e) cn=**rdn**(15,25),ep=0.5   (f) pd=3,ep=0.5

Fig. 1. Comparing ET with popular solvers on randomly generated instances.

6   Conclusion and Future Work

In this paper, we presented a new approach for proving satisfiability in NRA, utilizing a sampling and verification process as its foundation. Our algorithm, referred to as ET, was implemented and evaluated on three sets of benchmark problems. Though our algorithm may not be able to respond to cases marked as "unsat" and its sampling heuristics do not provide a guarantee for a "sat" response in all satisfiable instances, the results clearly demonstrate the competitiveness of our method on all satisfiable instances. It also showcases a significant improvement over state-of-the-art techniques, particularly for highly nonlinear problems involving more than 10 variables and polynomial degrees greater than 2. However, our approach faces challenges when dealing with cases that are almost linear or consist of large equation systems. Moving forward, we plan to integrate more heuristics, such as local search, to enhance sampling capabilities and incorporate some incomplete but rapid solvers for zero-dimensional systems.

Acknowledgements. This work was supported by the National Key R & D Program of China (No. 2022YFA1005102).

References

1. Collins, G.E.: Quantifier elimination for real closed fields by cylindrical algebraic decomposition: a synopsis. ACM SIGSAM Bull. **10**(1), 10–12 (1976)
2. Mouraford, R., Davenport, J.H., England, M., McCallum, S., Wilson, D.: Truth table invariant cylindrical algebraic decomposition. J. Symb. Comput. **76**, 1–35 (2016)
3. de Moura, L., Jovanović, D.: A model-constructing satisfiability calculus. In: Giacobazzi, R., Berdine, J., Mastroeni, I. (eds.) Verification, Model Checking, and Abstract Interpretation, pp. 1–12 (2013)
4. Jovanović, D., de Moura, L.: Solving non-linear arithmetic. In: Gramlich, B., Miller, D., Sattler, U. (eds.) Automated Reasoning, pp. 339–354 (2012)
5. De Moura, L., Bjørner, N.: Z3: an efficient SMT solver. In: TACAS, pp. 337–340 (2008)
6. Barbosa, H., et al.: CVC5: a versatile and industrial-strength SMT solver. In: TACAS, pp. 415–442 (2022)
7. Dutertre, B.: Yices 2.2. In: CAV, pp. 737–744 (2014)
8. Cimatti, A., Griggio, A., Schaafsma, B.J., Sebastiani, R.: The MathSAT5 SMT solver. In: Piterman, N., Smolka, S.A. (eds.) TACAS 2013. LNCS, vol. 7795, pp. 93–107. Springer, Heidelberg (2013). https://doi.org/10.1007/978-3-642-36742-7_7
9. Gao, S., Kong, S., Clarke, E.M.: dReal: an SMT solver for nonlinear theories over the reals. In: Bonacina, M.P. (ed.) CADE 2013. LNCS (LNAI), vol. 7898, pp. 208–214. Springer, Heidelberg (2013). https://doi.org/10.1007/978-3-642-38574-2_14
10. Li, H., Xia, B., Zhao, T.: Local search for solving satisfiability of polynomial formulas. In: Enea, C., Lal, A. (eds.) CAV, pp. 87–109 (2023)
11. Li, B., Cai, S.: Local search for SMT on linear and multilinear real arithmetic, arXiv preprint arXiv:2303.06676 (2023)
12. Cimatti, A., Griggio, A., Lipparini, E., Sebastiani, R.: Handling polynomial and transcendental functions in SMT via unconstrained optimisation and topological degree test. In: Bouajjani, A., Holík, L., Wu, Z. (eds.) ATVA 2022. LNCS, vol. 13505, pp. 137–153. Springer, Cham (2022). https://doi.org/10.1007/978-3-031-19992-9_9
13. Wu, W.-T.: On the decision problem and the mechanization of theorem proving in elementary geometry. Sci. Sinica **21**(2), 159–172 (1978)

14. Buchberger, B.: Ein Algorithmus zum Auffinden der Basiselemente des Restklassenringes nach einem nulldimensionalen Polynomideal. Ph.D. thesis, Math. Inst., University of Innsbruck (1965)
15. Bose, N.K.: Gröbner bases: an algorithmic method in polynomial ideal theory. In: Buchberger, B. (ed.) Multidimensional Systems Theory and Applications, pp. 89–127. Springer, Dordrecht (1985). https://doi.org/10.1007/978-94-017-0275-1_4
16. Li, T.-Y.: Numerical solution of multivariate polynomial systems by homotopy continuation methods. Acta Numerica **6**, 399–436 (1997)
17. Lasserre, J.B., Laurent, M., Rostalski, P.: Semidefinite characterization and computation of zero-dimensional real radical ideals. Found. Comput. Math. **8**, 607–647 (2008)
18. Yang, Z., Zhi, L., Zhu, Y.: Verified error bounds for real solutions of positive-dimensional polynomial systems. In: Proceedings of ISSAC, pp. 371–378 (2013)
19. Yang, Z., Zhao, H., Zhi, L.: Verifyrealroots: a matlab package for computing verified real solutions of polynomials systems of equations and inequalities. J. Syst. Sci. Compl. **36**(2), 866–883 (2023)
20. Eriksson, F.: Which triangles are plane sections of regular tetrahedra? Amer. Math. Monthly **101**(8), 788–789 (1994)
21. Li, H., Xia, B., Zhao, T.: Square-free pure triangular decomposition of zero-dimensional polynomial systems. J. Syst. Sci. Compl. (2023)
22. Xia, B., Zhang, T.: Real solution isolation using interval arithmetic. Comput. Math. Appl. **52**(6), 853–860 (2006)
23. Xia, B., Yang, L.: Automated Inequality Proving and Discovering. World Scientific (2016)

Leveraging TLA$^+$ Specifications to Improve the Reliability of the ZooKeeperCoordination Service

Lingzhi Ouyang⬥, Yu Huang$^{(\boxtimes)}$⬥, Binyu Huang⬥, and Xiaoxing Ma⬥

State Key Laboratory for Novel Software Technology, Nanjing 210023, China
{lingzhi.ouyang,binyuhuang}@smail.nju.edu.cn, {yuhuang,xxm}@nju.edu.cn

Abstract. ZooKeeper is a coordination service, widely used as a backbone of various distributed systems. Though its reliability is of critical importance, testing is insufficient for an industrial-strength system of the size and complexity of ZooKeeper, and deep bugs can still be found. To this end, we resort to formal TLA$^+$ specifications to further improve the reliability of ZooKeeper. Our primary objective is usability and automation, rather than full verification. We incrementally develop three levels of specifications for ZooKeeper. We first obtain the *protocol specification*, which unambiguously specifies the Zab protocol behind ZooKeeper. We then proceed to a finer grain and obtain the *system specification*, which serves as the super-doc for system development. In order to further leverage the model-level specification to improve the reliability of the code-level implementation, we develop the *test specification*, which guides the explorative testing of the ZooKeeper implementation. The formal specifications help eliminate the ambiguities in the protocol design and provide comprehensive system documentation. They also help find critical deep bugs in system implementation, which are beyond the reach of state-of-the-art testing techniques. Our specifications have been merged into the official Apache ZooKeeper project.

Keywords: TLA$^+$ · ZooKeeper · Zab · Specification · Model checking

1 Introduction

ZooKeeper is a distributed coordination service for highly reliable synchronization of cloud applications [23]. ZooKeeper essentially offers a hierarchical key-value store, which is used to provide a distributed configuration service, synchronization service, and naming registry for large distributed systems. Its intended

This work is supported by the National Natural Science Foundation of China (62372222), the CCF-Huawei Populus Grove Fund (CCF-HuaweiFM202304), the Cooperation Fund of Huawei-Nanjing University Next Generation Programming Innovation Lab (YBN2019105178SW38), the Fundamental Research Funds for the Central Universities (020214912222) and the Collaborative Innovation Center of Novel Software Technology and Industrialization.

H. Hermanns et al. (Eds.): SETTA 2023, LNCS 14464, pp. 189–205, 2024.
https://doi.org/10.1007/978-981-99-8664-4_11

usage requires Zookeeper to provide strong consistency guarantees, which it does by running a distributed consensus protocol called Zab [25].

Consensus protocols are notoriously difficult to get right. The complex failure recovery logic results in an astronomically large state space, and deep "Heisenbugs" still often escape from intensive testing [31,32]. Toward this challenge, we resort to formal methods to improve the reliability of ZooKeeper. We do not aim to achieve full verification, but instead emphasize a high degree of automation and practical usability. Moreover, our primary goal is to improve the reliability of both the model-level design and the code-level implementation.

We adopt TLA$^+$ as our specification language. TLA$^+$ has been successful in verifying distributed concurrent systems, especially consensus protocols. Many consensus protocols, including Paxos, Raft and their derivatives, have their TLA$^+$ specifications published along with the protocol design and implementation [8,10,18,30]. However, the current usage of TLA$^+$ is mainly restricted to verification of the protocol design. Considering code-level implementation, model checking-driven test case generation is used to ensure the equivalence between two different implementations in MongoDB Realm Sync [16].

Our primary objective is to improve the reliability of ZooKeeper. We incrementally obtain three levels of specifications in TLA$^+$. We first obtain the *protocol specification*, which unambiguously specifies the Zab protocol behind ZooKeeper. We then proceed to a finer grain and obtain the *system specification*, which serves as the super-doc[1] for ZooKeeper development. In order to leverage the model-level specification to improve the reliability of the code-level implementation, we further develop the *test specification*, which guides the explorative testing of the ZooKeeper implementation. The formal specifications help eliminate the ambiguities in the protocol design and provide comprehensive system documentation. They also help find critical deep bugs in system implementation, which are beyond the reach of state-of-the-art testing techniques. Our specifications are available in the online repository [6]. Writing TLA$^+$ specifications for ZooKeeper was raised as an issue [3]. Our specifications have addressed this issue and been accepted by the Apache ZooKeeper project [11].

We start in Sect. 2 by introducing the basics of ZooKeeper and TLA$^+$. We present our three levels of specifications in Sects. 3, 4 and 5. In Sect. 6, we discuss the related work. Finally, Sect. 7 concludes with a discussion on the benefits of and the potential extensions to our formal specification practices.

2   ZooKeeper and TLA$^+$

2.1   ZooKeeper and Zab

ZooKeeper is a fault-tolerant distributed coordination service used by a variety of distributed systems [14,23,35]. These systems often consist of a large number of processes and rely upon ZooKeeper to perform essential coordination tasks, such

---

[1]   Super-doc refers to the precise, concise and testable documentation of the system implementation, which can be explored and experimented on with tools [37].

as maintaining configuration information, storing status of running processes and group membership, providing distributed synchronization and managing failure recovery.

Due to the significant reliance of large applications on ZooKeeper, the service must maintain a high level of availability and possess the ability to mask and recover from failures. ZooKeeper achieves availability and reliability through replication and utilizes a primary-backup scheme to maintain the states of replica processes consistent [13, 24, 25]. Upon receiving client requests, the primary generates a sequence of non-commutative state changes and propagates them as transactions to the backup replicas using *Zab*, the ZooKeeper atomic broadcast protocol. The protocol consists of three phases: DISCOVERY, SYNC and BROADCAST. Its primary duties include agreeing on a leader in the ensemble, synchronizing the replicas, managing the broadcast of transactions, and recovering from failures.

To ensure progress, ZooKeeper requires that a majority (or more generally a quorum) of processes have not crashed. Any minority of processes may crash at any moment. Crashed processes are able to recover and rejoin the ensemble. For a process to perform the primary role, it must have the support of a quorum of processes.

2.2   TLA$^+$ Basics

TLA$^+$ (Temporal Logic of Actions) is a lightweight formal specification language that is particularly suitable for designing distributed and concurrent systems [7]. In contrast to programming languages, TLA$^+$ employs simple mathematics to express concepts in a more elegant and precise manner. In TLA$^+$, a system is specified as a state machine by defining the possible initial *states* and the allowed *actions*, i.e., state transitions. Each state represents a global state of the system. Whenever all *enabling conditions* of a state transition are satisfied in a given *current* state, the system can transfer to the *next* state by applying the action.

One of the notable advantages of TLA$^+$ is its ability to handle different levels of abstraction. Correctness properties and system designs can be regarded as steps on a ladder of abstraction, with correctness properties occupying higher levels, system designs and algorithms in the middle, and executable code at the lower levels [37]. The flexibility to choose and adjust levels of abstraction makes TLA$^+$ a versatile tool suited to a wide range of needs.

TLA$^+$ provides the TLC model checker, which builds a finite state model from the specifications for checking invariant safety properties (in this work, we mainly focus on safety properties and do not consider liveness properties). TLC first generates a set of initial states that satisfy the specification, and then traverses all possible state transitions. If TLC discovers a state violating an invariant property, it halts and provides the trace leading to the violation. Otherwise, the system is verified to satisfy the invariant property. With TLC, we are able to explore every possible behavior of our specifications without additional human effort. As a result, we can identify subtle bugs and edge cases that may not be exposed through other testing or debugging techniques.

3   Protocol Specification

We first develop the *protocol specification*, i.e., specification of the Zab protocol based on its informal description [23,25]. The protocol specification aims at precise description and automatic model checking of the protocol design. It also serves as the basis for further refinements, as detailed in Sects. 4 and 5.

3.1   Development of Protocol Specification

The protocol specification necessitates a comprehensive description of the design of Zab, along with the corresponding correctness conditions that must be upheld. In the following, we present our practice of developing the TLA$^+$ specifications for both aspects.

Specification of Zab. The "upon-do clauses" in the Zab pseudocode can be readily transformed to the enabling conditions and actions in TLA$^+$. This feature greatly simplifies the task of obtaining the initial skeleton of the protocol specification. The real obstacle lies in handling the ambiguities and omissions in the informal design. We have three challenges to address, as detailed below.

First, we need to cope with the ambiguities concerning the abstract mathematical notion of *quorum*. ZooKeeper is a leader-based replicated service. The leader requires certain forms of acknowledgements from a quorum of followers to proceed. Though the notion of quorum greatly simplifies presentation of the basic rationale of Zab, it introduces subtle ambiguities in the design. Specifically, the set Q, which denotes the quorum of followers in the Zab pseudocode, is severely overloaded in the informal design. It refers to different sets of followers in different cases, as shown in Fig. 1. In the TLA$^+$ specification, we must use separate variables for different quorums in different situations, e.g., variable cepochRecv for the quorum acknowledging the CEPOCH message and ackeRecv for the quorum acknowledging the ACKEPOCH message.

Second, the design of Zab mainly describes the "happy case", in which the follower successfully contacts the leader and the leader proceeds with support from a quorum of followers. In our TLA$^+$ specification, we must precisely describe the unhappy case where the leader has not yet received sufficient acknowledgements from the followers. We must also explicitly model failures in the execution environment, enabling the TLC model checker to exhaustively exercise the fault-tolerance logic in Zab. Moreover, Zab is a highly concurrent protocol. Actions of ZooKeeper processes and environment failures can interleave. The complex interleavings are not covered in the protocol design, and we supplement the detailed handling of the interleavings in our TLA$^+$ specification.

Third, the Zab protocol does not implement leader election, but relies on an assumed leader oracle. In our TLA$^+$ specification, we use a variable called leaderOracle to denote the leader oracle. The leader oracle exposes two actions UpdateLeader and FollowLeader to update the leader and to find who is the leader, respectively.

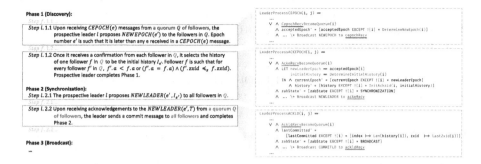

Fig. 1. From informal design to formal specification. In the informal design (Left), the set Q, which denotes the quorum of followers, is ambiguous and overloaded. In the TLA⁺ specification (Right), the set Q is specified with different variables (cepochRecv, ackeRecv and ackldRecv) for different quorums in different situations.

The details of protocol design we supplement in the TLA⁺ specification are verified by model checking. It is also confirmed by our development of the system specification (see Sect. 4).

Specification of Correctness Conditions. We specify two types of correctness conditions, the *core correctness conditions* and the *invariant properties* (with a focus on safety properties in this work). The Zab protocol [25] prescribes six core correctness conditions, namely *integrity, total order, agreement, local primary order, global primary order* and *primary integrity*. These properties are extracted from the requirement analysis of the ZooKeeper coordination service. They constrain the externally observable behavior from the user client's perspective.

Designers usually do not directly guarantee the core correctness conditions when designing a complex protocol like Zab. Rather, they decompose the core correctness conditions into a collection of invariant properties. In principle, the invariants maintained in different parts of the protocol can collectively ensure the core correctness conditions. Model checking against the invariants can also accelerate the detection of bugs in protocol design. We extract the invariant properties based on our understanding of the Zab protocol. We are also inspired by the invariants specified for Paxos, Raft and their derivatives [8,10,30,38].

3.2 Ensuring Quality of Protocol Specification

Upon completing the development of the protocol specification, we perform model checking to ensure its quality. The protocol specification is amenable to automatic exploration by the TLC model checker. We utilize TLC in two modes: the standard *model-checking mode*, in which TLC traverses the state space in a BFS manner, and the *simulation mode*, where TLC keeps sampling execution paths of a predefined length until it uses up the testing budget.

In this work, we perform model checking on a PC equipped with an Intel I5-9500 quad-core CPU (3.00 GHz) and 16 GB RAM, running Windows 10 Enterprise. The software used is TLA$^+$ Toolbox v1.7.0. We first tame the state explosion problem for the model checking and identify subtle bugs resulting from ambiguities in the informal design. Then we conduct further model checking to verify the correctness of the protocol specification.

Taming State Explosion. Model checking suffers from the state explosion problem, making it impractical to fully check models of arbitrary scales. To mitigate this issue, we prune the state space by tuning the enabling conditions of key actions in the protocol specification. The basic rationale behind this is to constrain the scheduling of meaningless events. For example, too many failure events are meaningless when the leader does not even contact the followers, and such scheduling should be ruled out during the checking process.

Furthermore, we directly limit the state space based on the small-scope hypothesis, which suggests that analyzing small system instances suffices in practice [34]. Specifically, we control the scale of the model by restricting the following configuration parameters: the number of servers, the maximum number of transactions, the maximum number of timeouts, and the maximum number of restarts. The server count is confined to a maximum of 5, as it is sufficient to trigger most invariant violations in most cases according to ZooKeeper's bug tracking system [1]. Similarly, the number of transactions is limited to a small value, as it already suffices to cause log differences among servers.

It is also worth noting that in the protocol specification, we model failures as Timeout and Restart mainly for state space reduction. These two actions can effectively describe the effects of multiple failures in the execution environment.

Finding Ambiguities in the Informal Design. Following the above techniques to mitigate the state explosion, we perform model checking and find two invariant violations in the preliminary version of our protocol specification. One is due to the misuse of the quorum of followers. The other concerns how the leader responds to a recovering follower in between logging a transaction and broadcasting it to the followers. The paths to the violations help us find the root cause and fix the bugs in the protocol specification. Our fixes are also in accordance with the system implementation (see Sect. 4), though the implementation contains more details.

Verifying Correctness. After resolving the aforementioned bugs in the protocol specification, we proceed with model checking to ensure its correctness. We adjust the scale of the model using the parameters specified in the model configuration mentioned earlier. For each configuration, we record the checking mode, the number of explored states, and the checking time cost. For the model checking mode, we also record the diameter of the state space graph generated by the TLC model checker. For the simulation mode, we set the maximum length of the trace to 100. We restrict the model checking time to 24 h and the disk space used to 100 GB.

Table 1. Model checking results of the protocol specification.

Config*	Checking mode	Diameter	Num of states	Time cost
$(2,2,2,0)$	Model-checking	38	$19,980$	$00:00:03$
$(2,2,0,2)$	Model-checking	38	$25,959$	$00:00:04$
$(2,2,1,1)$	Model-checking	38	$26,865$	$00:00:04$
$(2,3,2,2)$	Model-checking	60	$10,370,967$	$00:06:58$
$(3,2,1,0)$	Model-checking	43	$610,035$	$00:00:28$
$(3,2,0,1)$	Model-checking	50	$1,902,139$	$00:02:36$
$(3,2,2,0)$	Model-checking	54	$26,126,204$	$00:17:07$
$(3,2,0,2)$	Model-checking	68	$245,606,642$	$03:41:23$
$(3,2,1,1)$	Model-checking	61	$84,543,312$	$01:00:18$
$(3,2,2,1)$	Model-checking	50	$1,721,643,089$	$>24:00:00$
$(3,2,1,2)$	Model-checking	46	$1,825,094,679$	$>24:00:00$
$(3,3,3,3)$	Simulation	–	$1,194,558,650$	$>24:00:00$
$(4,2,1,0)$	Model-checking	64	$21,393,294$	$00:23:29$
$(4,2,0,1)$	Model-checking	71	$79,475,010$	$01:37:31$
$(4,2,2,0)$	Model-checking	57	$1,599,588,210$	$>24:00:00$
$(5,2,3,3)$	Simulation	–	$1,044,870,264$	$>24:00:00$
$(5,3,2,2)$	Simulation	–	$817,181,422$	$>24:00:00$

* In the protocol specification, the **Config** parameters represent the number of servers, the maximum number of transactions, the maximum number of timeouts, and the maximum number of restarts.

Table 1 presents statistics regarding the model checking of the protocol specification. The explorations shown in the table cover a variety of configurations, with the server count ranging from 2 to 5, and the maximum number of transactions, timeouts, and restarts up to 3. Within the time limit of 24 h, the explorations of all configurations do not exceed the space limit. When limiting the model to a relatively small scale, the model-checking mode can exhaustively explore all possible interleavings of actions. In contrast, the simulation mode tends to explore deeper states. All specified correctness conditions are met without violation during the explorations in models of diverse configurations. Based on the results and the small-scope hypothesis [34], we have achieved a high level of confidence in the correctness of our protocol specification.

Moreover, we further tweak the specification a little and see if the model checker can find the planted errors. For instance, in one trial, we modified the definition of the constant Quorums in the specification, which originally denotes a set of all majority sets of servers, to include server sets that comprise no less than half of all servers. In expectation, the modification will lead to invariant violations only when the number of servers is even. We executed model checking on the modified specification, and as anticipated, no violations occurred when the server number was 3 or 5. However, in the case of 2 or 4 servers, invariant violations emerged, such as two established leaders appearing in the same epoch. Such trials illustrate the effectiveness of the specified correctness conditions and further indicate the correctness of the protocol specification. More details about the verification of the protocol specification can be found in [6].

4   System Specification

Given the protocol specification, we further develop the system specification, which serves as the super-doc supplementing detailed system documentation of Zab implementation for the ZooKeeper developers. In the following, we first discuss the essentials of a system specification written in TLA$^+$. Then, we present the practice of developing the system specification and the approach to ensuring its quality.

4.1   Essentials of a Super-Doc in TLA$^+$

To develop the system specification, we first need to decide which should and should not be included in the specification. We fathom out the right level of abstraction from two complementary perspectives, namely what the system developers need from a super-doc and what the TLA$^+$ specification language can express.

As a super-doc, the system specification should reconcile accuracy with simplicity. When we submitted the preliminary version of the system specification to the ZooKeeper community [22], a basic principle the community suggests is that "whether or not an action should be retained in the specification depends on whether it is critical to reveal important details of the protocol". Further suggestions include "implement the minimum required" and "keep things simpler". These suggestions guide us to calibrate the level of abstraction. In principle, the system specification should cover every aspect of the ZooKeeper system. Meanwhile, low-level details, e.g. the leader-follower heartbeat interactions and internal request queues for blocked threads, can be omitted. We also inherit the modularity of the system implementation in our specification.

The precision of the specifications written in TLA$^+$ is intended to uncover design flaws. TLA$^+$ specifications mostly consist of ordinary non-temporal mathematics, e.g., basic set theory, which is less cumbersome than a purely temporal specification. A major advantage of TLA$^+$ is that it frees us from complex programming considerations like multi-threading and object encapsulation. When enjoying the simplicity of TLA$^+$, we inevitably need to handle the gap in expressiveness between TLA$^+$ and the programming language (Java in the ZooKeeper case). In ZooKeeper, the block-and-wakeup style multi-thread programming is heavily used, while in TLA⁺, actions are executed in an asynchronous style. We decompose the block-and-wakeup thread logic into two conditional branches in one TLA⁺ action. The timing of scheduling the wakeup logic is encoded in the entry conditions of the branches. Moreover, we combine the wakeup logic of multiple threads in one conditional branch in the TLA⁺ action. This not only improves specification readability, but also helps mitigate the state explosion.

4.2 Development of the Super-Doc

The system specification is in principle a refinement of the protocol specification. Details in the system specification are supplemented based on the source code, as shown in Fig. 2. ZooKeeper inherits the basic architecture of Zab, and we discuss each of its modules in turn.

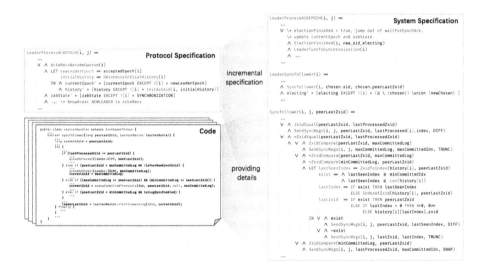

Fig. 2. Incremental development of the system specification. The system specification is in principle a refinement of the protocol specification, with supplementary details derived from the source code.

ZooKeeper implements its own Fast Leader Election (FLE) algorithm [35], which is omitted in Zab. FLE elects a leader which has the most up-to-date history. We also extract the invariant properties FLE should maintain from its design. Moreover, to conduct "unit test" on the FLE design, i.e., to model check the FLE module alone, we simulate the interaction between FLE and its outside world, e.g., actions updating the epoch or the transaction ID (zxid).

Compared with Zab, the DISCOVERY module in ZooKeeper is simplified, since the leader already has the most up-to-date history. We reuse most part of this module in the protocol specification, and make several revisions according to the implementation. Specifically, the follower does not need to send its full history to the leader, and only needs to send the latest zxid it has. The leader checks the validity of each follower's state rather than updates its history based on all histories received from the followers.

In Zab, the leader sends its full history to the followers in the SYNC phase. This is obviously a simplification for better illustration of the design rationale. In the implementation, the SYNC module is significantly optimized for better performance. We rewrite the system specification for this module based on the implementation. Specifically, NEWLEADER acts as a signaling message without carrying concrete history data. The leader's history will be synchronized to the followers in one of three modes, namely DIFF, TRUNC, and SNAP. The leader will select the right mode based on the differences between its history and the follower's latest zxid. The follower may update its log or snapshot according to the sync mode. These supplemented details in the system specification are confirmed by the system implementation. The BROADCAST module is basically inherited from the protocol specification.

In order to facilitate conformance checking (see Sect. 4.3), we also refine the failure modeling of the protocol specification. Specifically, we model environment failures as node crash/rejoin events and network partition/reconnection events in the system specification. These failure events are more fundamental and can generate the failures modeled in the protocol specification.

Correctness conditions, including core correctness conditions and invariant properties, are mainly inherited from the protocol specification. Table 2 presents the model checking results of the system specification under certain configuration parameters. No violation of correctness conditions is found during the checking.

Table 2. Model checking results of the system specification.

Config *	Checking mode	Diameter	Num of states	Time cost
$(3, 2, 3, 3)$	Model-checking	24	$3,322,996,126$	$> 24 : 00 : 00$
$(5, 2, 3, 3)$	Model-checking	16	$693,381,547$	$> 24 : 00 : 00$
$(3, 5, 5, 5)$	Simulation	–	$1,139,420,778$	$> 24 : 00 : 00$
$(5, 5, 5, 5)$	Simulation	–	$1,358,120,544$	$> 24 : 00 : 00$
$(3, 5, 0, 10)$	Simulation	–	$1,463,314,104$	$> 24 : 00 : 00$
$(3, 5, 10, 0)$	Simulation	–	$1,211,089,513$	$> 24 : 00 : 00$

* In the system specification, the **Config** parameters represent the number of servers, the maximum number of transactions, the maximum number of node crashes, and the maximum number of network partitions.

4.3 Ensuring Quality of the Super-Doc

The quality of the super-doc primarily depends on whether the doc precisely reflects the system implementation, with unimportant details omitted. Note that model checking can only ensure that the specification satisfies the correctness conditions. It cannot tell whether the specification precisely reflects the system implementation.

We conduct conformance checking between the system specification and the system implementation to ensure the quality of the specification, as shown in Fig. 3. We first let the TLC model checker execute the system specification and obtain the model-level execution traces. We extract the event schedule from the model checking trace, and then control the system execution to follow the event schedule.

The controlled system execution is enabled by the Model Checking-driven Explorative Testing (MET) framework [5]. We first instrument the ZooKeeper system, which enables the test execution environment to intercept the communication between the ZooKeeper nodes, as well as local events of interest, e.g., logging transactions. The intercepted events are dispatched according to the event schedule extracted from the model checking trace. In this way, we control the system execution to "replay" the model checking trace, and check the conformance between these two levels of executions.

Once the conformance checking fails, discrepancies between the specification and the implementation are detected. The specification developer checks the discrepancies and revises the specification based on the implementation. After multiple rounds of conformance checking, the system specification obtains sufficient accuracy. This process is analogous to the regression testing [15].

During our practice, we discovered several discrepancies between the specification and the implementation. For example, in the initial version of the system specification, it was assumed that whenever the leader processes a write request, the client session has already been successfully established. However, client session creation is also considered a transaction in ZooKeeper and requires confirmation by a quorum of servers. This discrepancy was identified during conformance checking, and the specification was subsequently revised to address it. Further details about the system specification can be found in [6].

5   Test Specification

Given the protocol and system specifications, we further develop the test specification, in order to guide the explorative testing of ZooKeeper. The basic workflow of explorative testing following the MET framework is shown in Fig. 3. We detail the three core parts of the framework below.

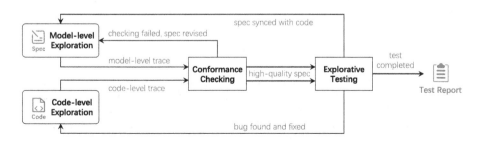

Fig. 3. Model checking-driven explorative testing.

5.1 Obtaining the Test Specification

In the explorative testing, we mainly focus on the recovery logic of ZooKeeper in its SYNC phase (though MET can be applied to each module of ZooKeeper). This module is heavily optimized in practice. It is under continual revision and deep bugs can still be found, according to ZooKeeper's bug tracking system [1].

The test specification is in principle a refinement of the system specification toward the source code. The test specification first inherits the system specification. The part of the specification to be refined, which corresponds to the part of the system under test, can be obtained by copy-pasting the ZooKeeper source code and manually updating the syntax to be valid TLA$^+$ specification [16]. Due to the inherent gap in the expressiveness, certain details are inevitably omitted or transformed in the test specification, including low-level programming considerations like multi-threading. The developer can also intentionally omit certain details if they deem such details irrelevant to the potential deep bugs. For example, we do not explicitly model the client and "pack" the workload generation logic inside the leader.

Due to the state explosion, we cannot model check the test specification of the whole ZooKeeper system. In practice, we follow the Interaction-Preserving Abstraction (IPA) framework [19]. We refine one single module to its test specification, while keeping other modules as abstract as possible, with the interactions between modules preserved. As we conduct MET on the SYNC module, we abstract all other modules. For example, we combine ELECTION and DISCOVERY into one action, while their interactions with the SYNC module are preserved.

5.2 Improving the Accuracy of Specification

The quality of the testing specification is also incrementally improved by multiple rounds of conformance checking (see Sect. 4). Typically, we find a number of discrepancies. The developer may need to fine-tune the test specification to better conform to the code. He may also neglect the discrepancy if he confirms that the discrepancy is due to the inherent differences in expressiveness and is irrelevant to the potential deep bug we try to find. The conformance checking keeps going like the regression testing until no discrepancy can be found. This means that the test specification is (sufficiently) accurate to guide the explorative testing.

5.3 Test Specification in Action

With the help of our test specification and the MET framework, we stably trigger and reproduce several critical deep bugs in ZooKeeper [6]. Here, we use ZK-2845 [2] and ZK-3911 [4] as examples to demonstrate the effectiveness and efficiency of this approach. These two bugs will result in the inconsistency of accepted logs or the loss of committed logs, which can be particularly severe for a coordination service like ZooKeeper. However, similar to other deep bugs, they are difficult to uncover and reproduce. Triggering these bugs typically requires numerous steps, and the timing of failures is subtle. The space of all possible bug-triggering patterns is so vast that it is beyond human reasoning. We can only find the bugs by explorative search guided by model checking.

Table 3 lists the statistics related to the invariant violations of ZK-2845 and ZK-3911. As indicated, we can obtain the traces of these two bugs within a short time by model checking against the invariants. The high efficiency is mainly attributed to the test specification, which abstracts irrelevant details while preserving the necessary information.

Table 3. Invariant violations of ZK-2845 and ZK-3911.

Bug	Invariant violation *	Simulation mode		Model-checking mode	
		Len.	Time cost	Len.	Time cost
ZK-2845	ProcessConsistency	23	00 : 00 : 02	10	00 : 00 : 12
	ProposalConsistency	20	00 : 00 : 03	11	00 : 00 : 18
ZK-3911	LeaderLogCompleteness	25	00 : 01 : 29	14	00 : 00 : 42
	MonotonicRead	39	00 : 01 : 35	18	00 : 13 : 13

* The column **Invariant violation** lists the violated invariants of the bugs. The definitions of these invariants can be found in the test specification. The results in the table are obtained using the configuration of 3 servers, 2 transactions in max, 4 node crashes in max, and 4 network partitions in max.

Trace analysis reveals that a bug may violate multiple invariants that represent different aspects of the system's requirements. For instance, for the two invariants violated by ZK-3911, LeaderLogCompleteness constrains the internal behavior from the developer's perspective, while MonotonicRead constrains the externally observable behavior from the user client's perspective. The quality of the invariants specified in the test specification significantly affects the efficiency of bug detection. Typically, invariants that constrain internal behaviors can expedite the bug-triggering process compared to the invariants that constrain external behaviors.

The two checking modes of TLC exhibit different capabilities in triggering invariant violations. In most cases, the simulation mode is typically faster and more effective in detecting deeper bugs since it tends to explore deeper states. Conversely, the model-checking mode is better suited for searching for the shortest trace that leads to an invariant violation.

It is worth noting that exposing these bugs through model checking on the system specification can be challenging (see Table 2). The human knowledge behind the development of the test specification plays a crucial role in pruning the state space and accelerating the bug-triggering process. With the flexibility to adjust levels of abstraction in TLA$^+$, one can generate the test specification from the system specification at a low cost. Besides, TLC enables efficient explorations without additional human effort, and MET allows us to replay the traces of invariant violations in the system to validate their authenticity. More bugs exposed by our approach are detailed in [6].

6   Related Work

Specification in TLA⁺. TLA⁺ is widely used for the specification and verification of distributed protocols in both academia and industry. Lamport *et al.* utilized TLA⁺ to specify the original Paxos protocol [30], as well as various Paxos variants, including Disk Paxos [18], Fast Paxos [28], and Byzantine Paxos [29]. These protocols were also verified to be correct using TLC. Diego Ongaro provided a TLA⁺ specification for the Raft consensus algorithm and further verified its correctness through model checking [10]. Yin *et al.* employed TLA⁺ to specify and verify three properties of the Zab protocol [42]. Moraru *et al.* utilized TLA⁺ to specify EPaxos when first introducing the protocol [36].

In industry, Amazon Web Services (AWS) extensively employs TLA⁺ to help solve subtle design problems in critical systems [37]. Microsoft's cloud service Azure leverages TLA⁺ to detect deeply-hidden bugs in the logical design and reduce risk in their system [12]. PolarFS also uses TLA⁺ to precisely document the design of its ParallelRaft protocol, effectively ensuring the reliability and maintainability of the protocol design and implementation [20]. WeChat's storage system PaxosStore specifies its consensus algorithm TPaxos in TLA⁺ and verifies its correctness using TLC to increase confidence in the design [9].

The practices mentioned above utilize TLA⁺ to specify and verify distributed protocols with the goal of identifying design flaws and increasing confidence in the core protocol design. However, they do not address the code-level implementation and cannot guarantee that the specification accurately reflects the system implementation. Discrepancies between the specification and the implementation can result from transcription errors, and model checking is solely responsible for verifying the specification. Our TLA⁺ specifications for ZooKeeper focus on both the protocol design and the system implementation. Based on the source code and the protocol specification, we incrementally develop the system specification that serves as the super-doc for the ZooKeeper developers. Additionally, we conduct conformance checking between the system specification and the system implementation to eliminate discrepancies between them and ensure the quality of the specification.

Model Checking-Driven Testing on ZooKeeper. Model checking-driven testing has been extensively employed in distributed systems such as ZooKeeper. The FATE and DESTINI framework systematically exercises multiple combinations of failures in cloud systems and utilizes declarative testing specifications to support the checking of expected behaviors [21]. This framework has been effectively used to reproduce several bugs in ZooKeeper. SAMC incorporates semantic information into state-space reduction policies to trigger deep bugs in ZooKeeper [32]. FlyMC introduces state symmetry and event independence to reduce the state-space explosion [33]. PCTCP employs a randomized scheduling algorithm for testing distributed message-passing systems [39], while taPCT integrates partial order reduction techniques into random testing [40]. Both approaches have been utilized to detect bugs in ZooKeeper's leader election module. Modulo utilizes divergence resync models to systematically explore divergence failure bugs in ZooKeeper [26]. The aforementioned works explore ZooKeeper based on implementation-level model checkers.

In contrast, inspired by the practice of eXtreme Modelling [16] and other test case generation techniques with TLA$^+$[17,27], we leverage the TLA$^+$ specification and the TLC model checker to guide the explorative testing of ZooKeeper. TLC is highly efficient at exploring long traces and uncovering subtle deep bugs that require multiple steps to trigger, making it a powerful tool for test case generation. Similarly, Mocket uses TLC to guide the testing and reproduces bugs in ZooKeeper [41]. We further reduce the state space by taking advantage of the flexibility of the TLA$^+$ specification, which can be integrated with human knowledge at a low cost. We develop a test specification that efficiently triggers bugs in ZooKeeper, further enhancing the effectiveness of our model checking-driven explorative testing framework.

7 Conclusion and Future Work

In this work, we use TLA$^+$ to present precise design of and provide detailed documentation for ZooKeeper. We also use model checking to guide explorative testing of ZooKeeper. The formal specifications well complement state-of-the-art testing techniques and further improve the reliability of ZooKeeper.

In our future work, we will use TLA$^+$ specifications in more distributed systems, e.g., cloud-native databases and distributed streaming systems. Enabling techniques, such as taming of state explosion and deterministic simulation of system execution, also need to be strengthened.

References

1. Apache ZooKeeper's issue tracking system. https://issues.apache.org/jira/projects/ZOOKEEPER/issues
2. Issue: ZK-2845. https://issues.apache.org/jira/browse/ZOOKEEPER-2845
3. Issue: ZK-3615. https://issues.apache.org/jira/browse/ZOOKEEPER-3615
4. Issue: ZK-3911. https://issues.apache.org/jira/browse/ZOOKEEPER-3911
5. MET. https://github.com/Lingzhi-Ouyang/MET
6. Three levels of TLA$^+$ specifications for ZooKeeper. https://github.com/Disalg-ICS-NJU/zookeeper-tla-spec
7. TLA$^+$ home page. https://lamport.azurewebsites.net/tla/tla.html
8. TLA$^+$ specification for Paxos. https://github.com/tlaplus/Examples/blob/master/specifications/PaxosHowToWinATuringAward/Paxos.tla
9. TLA$^+$ specification for PaxosStore. https://github.com/Starydark/PaxosStore-tla
10. TLA$^+$ specification for Raft. https://github.com/ongardie/raft.tla
11. TLA$^+$ specifications for the Apache ZooKeeper project. https://github.com/apache/zookeeper/tree/master/zookeeper-specifications

12. The use of TLA$^+$ in industry. https://lamport.azurewebsites.net/tla/industrial-use.html

13. Zab's wiki. https://cwiki.apache.org/confluence/display/ZOOKEEPER/Zab1.0

14. ZooKeeper home page. https://zookeeper.apache.org/

15. Bourque, P., Fairley, R.E., Society, I.C.: Guide to the Software Engineering Body of Knowledge (SWEBOK(R)): Version 3.0, 3rd edn. IEEE Computer Society Press, Washington, DC, USA (2014)

16. Davis, A.J.J., Hirschhorn, M., Schvimer, J.: eXtreme modelling in practice. Proc. VLDB Endow. **13**(9), 1346–1358 (2020). https://doi.org/10.14778/3397230.3397233

17. Dorminey, S.: Kayfabe: model-based program testing with TLA$^+$/TLC. Technical report, Microsoft Azure WAN (2020). https://conf.tlapl.us/2020/11-Star_Dorminey-Kayfabe_Model_based_program_testing_with_TLC.pdf

18. Gafni, E., Lamport, L.: Disk Paxos. Distrib. Comput. **16**(1), 1–20 (2003). https://doi.org/10.1007/s00446-002-0070-8

19. Gu, X., Cao, W., Zhu, Y., Song, X., Huang, Y., Ma, X.: Compositional model checking of consensus protocols specified in TLA$^+$ via interaction-preserving abstraction. In: Proceedings of International Symposium on Reliable Distributed Systems (SRDS 2022). IEEE (2022). https://doi.org/10.1109/srds55811.2022.00018

20. Gu, X., Wei, H., Qiao, L., Huang, Y.: Raft with out-of-order executions. Int. J. Softw. Informatics **11**(4), 473–503 (2021). https://doi.org/10.21655/ijsi.1673-7288.00257

21. Gunawi, H.S., et al.: FATE and DESTINI: a framework for cloud recovery testing. In: Proceedings of the 8th USENIX conference on Networked Systems Design and Implementation. p. 239 (2011). https://dl.acm.org/doi/10.5555/1972457.1972482

22. Huang, B., Ouyang, L.: Pull request for ZOOKEEPER-3615: provide formal specification and verification using TLA$^+$ for Zab #1690. https://github.com/apache/zookeeper/pull/1690

23. Hunt, P., Konar, M., Junqueira, F.P., Reed, B.: ZooKeeper: wait-free coordination for internet-scale systems. In: Proceedings of ATC 2010, USENIX Annual Technical Conference, pp. 145–158. USENIX (2010). https://dl.acm.org/doi/10.5555/1855840.1855851

24. Junqueira, F.P., Reed, B.C., Serafini, M.: Dissecting Zab. Technical report, YL-2010-007, Yahoo! Research, Sunnyvale, CA, USA (2010). https://cwiki.apache.org/confluence/download/attachments/24193444/yl-2010-007.pdf

25. Junqueira, F.P., Reed, B.C., Serafini, M.: Zab: high-performance broadcast for primary-backup systems. In: Proceedings of DSN 2011, IEEE/IFIP Conference on Dependable Systems and Networks, pp. 245–256. IEEE (2011). https://doi.org/10.1109/DSN.2011.5958223

26. Kim, B.H., Kim, T., Lie, D.: Modulo: finding convergence failure bugs in distributed systems with divergence resync models. https://www.usenix.org/conference/atc22/presentation/kim-beom-heyn

27. Kuprianov, A., Konnov, I.: Model-based testing with TLA$^+$ and Apalache. Technical report, Informal Systems (2020). https://conf.tlapl.us/2020/09-Kuprianov_and_Konnov-Model-based_testing_with_TLA_+_and_Apalache.pdf

28. Lamport, L.: Fast Paxos. Distrib. Comput. **19**(2), 79–103 (2006). https://doi.org/10.1007/s00446-006-0005-x

29. Lamport, L.: The PlusCal Code for Byzantizing Paxos by Refinement. TechReport, Microsoft Research (2011)

30. Lamport, L., Merz, S., D, D.: A TLA$^+$ specification of Paxos and its refinement (2019). https://github.com/tlaplus/Examples/tree/master/specifications/Paxos

31. Leesatapornwongsa, T., Gunawi, H.S.: SAMC: a fast model checker for finding Heisenbugs in distributed systems (demo). In: Proceedings of the 2015 International Symposium on Software Testing and Analysis, ISSTA 2015, pp. 423–427. Association for Computing Machinery, New York (2015). https://doi.org/10.1145/2771783.2784771

32. Leesatapornwongsa, T., Hao, M., Joshi, P., Lukman, J.F., Gunawi, H.S.: SAMC: semantic-aware model checking for fast discovery of deep bugs in cloud systems. In: Proceedings of the 11th USENIX Conference on Operating Systems Design and Implementation, OSDI 2014, pp. 399–414. USENIX Association, Berkeley (2014). https://dl.acm.org/doi/10.5555/2685048.2685080

33. Lukman, J.F., et al.: Flymc: highly scalable testing of complex interleavings in distributed systems. In: Proceedings of the Fourteenth EuroSys Conference 2019, pp. 1–16 (2019). https://doi.org/10.1145/3302424.3303986

34. Marić, O., Sprenger, C., Basin, D.: Cutoff bounds for consensus algorithms. In: Majumdar, R., Kunčak, V. (eds.) CAV 2017. LNCS, vol. 10427, pp. 217–237. Springer, Cham (2017). https://doi.org/10.1007/978-3-319-63390-9_12

35. Medeiros, A.: ZooKeeper's atomic broadcast protocol: theory and practice (2012). https://www.tcs.hut.fi/Studies/T-79.5001/reports/2012-deSouzaMedeiros.pdf

36. Moraru, I., Andersen, D.G., Kaminsky, M.: There is more consensus in egalitarian parliaments. In: Proceedings of the Twenty-Fourth ACM Symposium on Operating Systems Principles, pp. 358–372 (2013). https://doi.org/10.1145/2517349.2517350

37. Newcombe, C., Rath, T., Zhang, F., Munteanu, B., Brooker, M., Deardeuff, M.: How amazon web services uses formal methods. Commun. ACM **58**(4), 66–73 (2015). https://doi.org/10.1145/2699417

38. Ongaro, D., Ousterhout, J.: In search of an understandable consensus algorithm. In: Proceedings of the 2014 USENIX Conference on USENIX Annual Technical Conference, USENIX ATC 2014, pp. 305–320. USENIX Association, Berkeley (2014). https://dl.acm.org/doi/10.5555/2643634.2643666

39. Ozkan, B.K., Majumdar, R., Niksic, F., Befrouei, M.T., Weissenbacher, G.: Randomized testing of distributed systems with probabilistic guarantees. Proc. ACM Program. Lang. **2**(OOPSLA), 1–28 (2018). https://doi.org/10.1145/3276530

40. Ozkan, B.K., Majumdar, R., Oraee, S.: Trace aware random testing for distributed systems. Proc. ACM Program. Lang. **3**(OOPSLA), 1–29 (2019). https://doi.org/10.1145/3360606

41. Wang, D., Dou, W., Gao, Y., Wu, C., Wei, J., Huang, T.: Model checking guided testing for distributed systems. In: Proceedings of the Eighteenth European Conference on Computer Systems, pp. 127–143 (2023). https://doi.org/10.1145/3552326.3587442

42. Yin, J.Q., Zhu, H.B., Fei, Y.: Specification and verification of the Zab protocol with TLA$^+$. J. Comput. Sci. Technol. **35**, 1312–1323 (2020). https://doi.org/10.1007/s11390-020-0538-7

Modeling Regex Operators for Solving Regex Crossword Puzzles

Weihao Su[1,2], Haiming Chen[1(✉)], Rongchen Li[1,2], and Zixuan Chen[1,2]

[1] State Key Laboratory of Computer Science, Institute of Software, Chinese Academy of Sciences, Beijing 100190, China
{suwh,chm,lirc,chenzx}@ios.ac.cn
[2] University of Chinese Academy of Sciences, Beijing 101400, China

Abstract. Modeling regular expressions (regexes) has been applied in abundant scenes, but at present, there is a lack of comprehensive modeling for extended operators, which limits their usage in related scenes. To address the problem, we comprehensively model the operators of regexes and apply the modeling method to solve regex crossword puzzles. Firstly, to solve the challenges of comprehensive modeling of regexes, we propose an over-approximate modeling method for regex operators according to their languages or semantics, and use a counterexample-guided abstraction refinement scheme to strengthen constraints, thereby eliminating spurious solutions and ensuring the correctness of our modeling. Then, based on our modeling method, we present a novel algorithm for solving regex crossword puzzles. We collect 803 rectangular puzzles and 95 hexagonal puzzles from the most popular regex crossword puzzles website, and compare our algorithm with five state-of-the-art tools. Experiment results show that our algorithm can solve 97.76% rectangular puzzles and 98.95% hexagonal puzzles in an acceptable running time, which are 19.06% and 65.27% higher than the highest success rates of other methods respectively.

Keywords: modeling regex operators · regex crossword puzzles · SMT constraints

1 Introduction

As a string processing tool, regular expressions (regexes) are widely used in various fields of computer science and software, such as software engineering [13,15,42,47], network security [4,32,56], natural language processing [5,11,23,27,34,40], database [8,36,39], etc. Because they are so common, modeling regexes have been applied in plenty of scenarios, such as program analysis [41,42], regular expression denial of service (ReDoS) detection [37], regex synthesis and repair [14,17,38,45], regex testing [54], regex crossword puzzle solving [33], and so on. However, there is a lack of comprehensive modeling for extended operators—many extended operators are usually ignored or imprecisely

---

Zixuan Chen is currently employed at Kuaishou Technology.

H. Hermanns et al. (Eds.): SETTA 2023, LNCS 14464, pp. 206–225, 2024.
https://doi.org/10.1007/978-981-99-8664-4_12

approximated (we show this by an example shortly). This lack of support can lead to limited usage in various scenarios, such as the loss of test code coverage, the omission of ReDoS detection, the failure of expression synthesis or repair, the incomplete test, and the failure of solving puzzles. There are further complexity results on the hardness of dealing with regexes where lookarounds and backreferences are involved, e.g. in [18] authors proved the constraint solving problem of [42] is undecidable.

Now let us consider the problem of solving regex crossword puzzles. Traditional crossword puzzles [3], as typical satisfaction problems, have received attention from constraint programming [6,31]. As a new form of a crossword puzzle, regex crossword puzzles enjoyed popularity in several programmers' communities [9,52] and appeared in Capture-the-Flag (CTF) competitions [22] and MIT's puzzle-based scavenger hunting [43].

A regex crossword puzzle contains a blank grid and constraints. In a basic regex crossword puzzle, we are given two non-empty regex lists labeling the m rows and n columns of an $m \times n$ empty grid, respectively. The challenge of basic puzzles is to fill the grid with characters such that each row reading left to right forms a string matching the corresponding regex, and the same as each column reading top to bottom. For details see Sect. 4.1. For example, Fig. 1(a) shows a 2×2 basic puzzle[1], which has a unique solution. There are two variants of the basic regex crossword puzzle. One is rectangular regex crossword puzzles (R-rcps) which has two

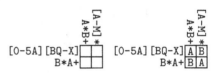

(a) A R-rcp (left) and its solution (right).

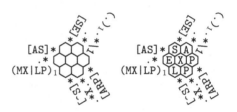

(b) A H-rcp (left) and its solution (right).

Fig. 1. Examples of R-rcp and H-rcp.

regexes in each row and column, and the string must match the two regexes simultaneously. Another is hexagonal regex crossword puzzles (H-rcps), which are composed of hexagonal cells, and contain regexes in three independent directions, an example[2] is shown in Fig. 1(b).

Some complexity results of regex crossword puzzles have been obtained [25,26], for example, the complexity of a restricted regex crossword puzzle (i.e., an R-rcp where all the row regexes are equal to one another and similarly the column regexes) is NP-complete. On the other hand, for solving regex crossword puzzles in practice, the state-of-the-art techniques are based on different methods: string constraint solving (e.g. Jeong [33]), heuristic algorithms (e.g. Trux [53] and Shcherban [51]), backtracking algorithm (e.g. Abolofia [1] and Schaaf [49]). But experimentally we found that among the existing tools, the highest success rate

---

[1] http://regexcrossword.com/playerpuzzles/28c1c678-b94d-4a54-bcbb-ac09beab3876.

[2] http://regexcrossword.com/playerpuzzles/59e76811836a3.

in rectangular puzzles is 78.70%, while in hexagonal puzzles is only 33.68% (see Sect. 5), which is undoubtedly very limited for users to solve puzzles automatically.

This motivated us to design a comprehensive model for regex operators, and apply it to solve regex crossword puzzles. As we have mentioned above, modeling for extended operators is not comprehensive at present. In detail, the modeling of regexes usually supports regexes in the language-theoretical sense, while either ignoring or imprecisely approximating the irregular or semantically different parts of regexes. For example, regex $r = $ `<img>\s[^>]*?(?<=\s)src\s*=\s*(["` `']?)`$_1$`(.*?)`$_2$`\1` parses img tags in html files, which defines a context-sensitive language, where the same string matched in `(["']?)`$_1$ has to be matched twice in `\1`. In this example, the lookbehind (the `(?<=\s)` which is used for restricting the matching content before it), the capturing groups (the parentheses ( )$_1$, ( )$_2$ (see further in Sect. 2)), the backreference (the `\1` referring to the first capturing group), and the non-greedy matching precedence (the `*?` which is non-greedy) are usually ignored or imprecisely approximated, owing to the difficulty of precise modeling of these extended operators. This in turn may lead to, for example, the failure of solving puzzles. Furthermore, Loring et al. [42] point out that extended operators, such as backreferences, etc., are widely used.

To address the challenges above, in this paper, we first propose an over-approximate method for comprehensively modeling regex operators. Our model translates a regex r into a first-order logic formula φ which is used as constraints for Satisfiability Modulo Theories (SMT) solvers, such that the solution s satisfies $s \in \mathcal{L}(r)$, where $\mathcal{L}(r)$ stands for the language of r. We also deploy a counterexample-guided abstraction refinement (CEGAR) [19] scheme to ensure the correctness of our modeling.

Then, based on our modeling method, we propose RCPS, a novel algorithm for solving regex crossword puzzles. In detail, the algorithm first initializes the variable matrix according to the puzzle. Then it generates constraints based on our modelings. Finally, it solves the constraints with an SMT solver. Note that for some extended operators, the generated constraints are over-approximated. In this case it eliminates possible spurious solutions generated by our model by a CEGAR scheme. Experimental results show that our algorithm is significantly more effective than existing methods.

The contributions of this paper are listed as follows.

- We propose an over-approximate modeling method for regex operators according to their languages or semantics, and use a CEGAR scheme to ensure the correctness of our modeling (Sect. 3).
- We present a novel algorithm RCPS to solve R-rcps and H-rcps, which assigns bounded length variables to cells of the puzzles according to coordinates, solves string constraints by an SMT solver and eliminates spurious solutions by the CEGAR scheme (Sect. 4).
- We collect 803 R-rcps and 95 H-rcps from the most popular regex crossword puzzle website, and compare our algorithm with five state-of-the-art tools. The evaluation results show that our algorithm can solve 97.76% R-rcps and 98.95% H-rcps in an acceptable running time, which are 19.06% and 65.27% higher than the highest success rates of other methods respectively (Sect. 5).

2   Preliminaries

Let Σ be an alphabet of all printable symbols except each of the following symbols is written with an escape character \ in front of it: (,), {, }, [,], ^, \$, |, \, ., ?, *, and +. The set of all strings over Σ is denoted by Σ^*. Let $\mathbb{N} = \{0,1,2,\ldots\}$ and $\mathbb{N}_+ = \mathbb{N} \setminus \{0\}$. $|K|$ stands for the size of a set K or the length of a string K. For a string $s = s_0 \ldots s_{n-1}$ ($n \in \mathbb{N}$), when $n \geq 1$, we write $s[i:j]$ ($0 \leq i \leq j < n$) to represent a sub-string $s_i \ldots s_j$ of s, or an empty string ε otherwise. Regex, the regular expression used in practice, is defined as follows.

A regex r on Σ is a well-formed parenthesized formula that extends the following operators on the basis of standard regular expressions [57]: (i) character class $[C]$ (or $[\hat{} C]$), where $C \subseteq \Sigma$; (ii) capturing group[3] $(r)_i$; (iii) non-capturing group $(?:r)$; (iv) backreference \\$i$, where $i \in \mathbb{N}_+$; (v) lookarounds: positive lookahead $(?=r)$, negative lookahead $(?!r)$, positive lookbehind $(?<=r)$, and negative lookbehind $(?<!r)$; (vi) anchors: start-of-line anchor ^, end-of-line anchor \$, word boundary \b, and non-word boundary \B; (vii) quantifiers: greedy quantifier $r\{\mathtt{m},\mathtt{n}\}$, lazy quantifier $r\{\mathtt{m},\mathtt{n}\}?$, where $\mathtt{m} \in \mathbb{N}$, $\mathtt{n} \in \mathbb{N} \cup \{+\infty\}$, and $\mathtt{m} \leqslant \mathtt{n}$.

The *language* $L(r)$ of a regex r is the set of all strings accepted by r. For a subexpression r_k of r we define $\mathcal{L}(r_k) = \{s[k,k] \mid s \in \mathcal{L}(r), |s| \geq k, k > 0\}$. For *quantifiers* in the form of $r\{\mathtt{m},\mathtt{n}\}$ [30], we have the following abbreviations: (i) $r\{\mathtt{m}\} = r\{\mathtt{m},\mathtt{m}\}$; (ii) $r\{\mathtt{m},\} = r\{\mathtt{m},+\infty\}$; (iii) $\varepsilon = r\{0,0\}$; (iv) $r? = r\{0,1\}$; (v) $r* = r\{0,\}$; (vi) $r+ = r\{1,\}$.

Next, we informally illustrate the semantics of these extended operators. A *character class* $[C]$ (or $[\hat{} C]$) matches a character in (or not in) set C. There are some abbreviations of character class: \w represents [a-zA-Z0-9_], and . matches any symbol except \n (a newline character). Note that for any $[\hat{} C]$, there is always a set $C' = \Sigma \setminus C$ satisfying $\mathcal{L}([C']) = \mathcal{L}([\hat{} C])$. In the following, we use $[C]$ to uniformly represent $[C]$ and $[\hat{} C]$. In regexes, quantifiers include *greedy quantifier* $r\{\mathtt{m},\mathtt{n}\}$ and *lazy quantifier* $r\{\mathtt{m},\mathtt{n}\}?$. A greedy quantifier is repeated as many times as possible while a lazy quantifier is repeated as few times as possible. A *capturing group* $(r)_i$ matches r, and stores the matched substring in the memorizer $\mathcal{M}_i$ identified by the index i. A *non-capturing group* $(?:r)$ matches r without storing the matched substring. A *backreference* \\$i$ matches the content stored in $\mathcal{M}_i$. In addition, the number i of the backreference \\$i$ cannot exceed the maximum number of capturing groups in a regex r. We call the backreference \\$i$ as *uninstantiated backreference* when $\mathcal{M}_i = \varnothing$. According to [7], there are ε-semantic [10,28,29,42,50] or $\varnothing$-semantic [2,12] for uninstantiated backreferences. In this paper, we follow the ECMAScript standard [24] and set the value of uninstantiated backreferences to ε. *Lookarounds* are zero-length assertions, and search for strings that satisfy certain contexts. Specifically, it includes *lookahead* and *lookbehind*, specifying the context after and before the searching strings, respectively. *Anchors* are also zero-length assertions, which specify the non-character context. A *start-of-line anchor* ^ denotes the start of a line, while an *end-of-line anchor* \$ denotes the end. A *word boundary anchor* \b

---

[3] Capturing group in the real world do not have the subscript i ($i \in \mathbb{N}_+$), we write it here for readability.

matches the position where one side is a word and the other side is not a word. A *non-word boundary anchor* \B, the negation of \b, matches at any position between two-word characters as well as at any position between two non-word characters.

3   Modeling Regex Operators

In this section, we introduce our modeling of regex operators, which is the basis of our algorithm RCPS. As mentioned in Sect. 1, for a given regex r, the output of the modeling is a formula in first-order logic, such that its solution s satisfies $s \in \mathcal{L}(r)$. We introduce our modeling for regex operators (Sect. 3.1) and explain how to eliminate spurious solutions by refinement (Sect. 3.2).

In this paper, we parse regexes according to the grammar[4]: $r \rightarrow \varepsilon \mid a \mid [C]$ $\mid r|r \mid rr \mid$ ^$r \mid r$\$ $\mid r$\br$\mid r$\Br$\mid (r)_i \mid$ (?:r) $\mid r${m,n}? $\mid r${m,n} $\mid$ (?=r)$r \mid$ (?!r)$r \mid r$(?<=r) $\mid r$(?<!r) $\mid$ \$i$, where $a \in \Sigma$, $C \subseteq \Sigma$, $i \in \mathbb{N}_+$, m $\in \mathbb{N}$, n $\in \mathbb{N} \cup \{+\infty\}$, and m $\leqslant$ n.

3.1   The Function $\Phi(r, p, l)$

For a regex r, we define the function $\Phi(r, 0, k)$ for generating the constraint such that its solution is a fixed-length string s ($|s| = k$) that satisfies $s = s_0 s_1 \ldots s_{k-1} \in \mathcal{L}(r)$. The constraint is generated by recursively traversing the nodes on the abstract syntax tree (AST) of r. For each sub-regex r_i in r, the function $\Phi(r_i, p_i, l_i)$ generates the constraint such that the sub-string $s[p_i : p_i + l_i - 1]$ of s satisfies $s[p_i : p_i + l_i - 1] = s_{p_i} s_{p_i+1} \ldots s_{p_i+l_i-1} \in \mathcal{L}(r_i)$. Next, we use the variable sequence $V = \langle x_0, x_1, \ldots, x_{k-1} \rangle$ to represent the string $s = s_0 s_1 \ldots s_{k-1}$, where x_i corresponds to s_i ($0 \leq i < k$). We first define function $\text{len}(r, k)$ to calculate all the possible lengths of string s satisfying $s \in \mathcal{L}(r) \wedge |s| \leq k$, see Fig. 2.

Algorithm 1: $\Phi(r, p, l)$

Input: a regex r, two integers $p \in \mathbb{N}$ and $l \in \mathbb{N}$, where p represents the starting subscript of variable x_p in variable sequence V, and l is the number of variables assigned to this modeling.

Output: a formula φ in first-order logic.

1 **if** $l \notin \text{len}(r, k)$ **or** $p + l > k$ **then**
2 $\quad \mid \quad \varphi \leftarrow$ **False**;   // k is a global constant value.
3 **else**
4 $\quad \lfloor \quad \varphi \leftarrow$ calculate $\Phi(r, p, l)$ through Eq. (17) – Eq. (34);

5 **return** φ;

---

[4] We refer to ECMAScript® 2022 language specification [24] which summarizes the grammar used in this paper.

The recursive calculation of $\Phi(r, p, l)$ is shown in Algorithm 1. Note that throughout the constraint modeling, k is a global constant value. For any regex r, if $l \notin \text{len}(r, k)$ or $p + l > k$, then

$$\Phi(r, p, l) = \textbf{False}. \tag{1}$$

Otherwise, the calculation of $\Phi(r, p, l)$ is shown in Fig. 3. Intuitively, Eq. (1) indicates that (i) the length l of the sub-string which matches r should satisfy the restriction of $\text{len}(r, k)$; (ii) for the length p of matched sub-string and the length l of to-be-matched sub-string, $p + l$ cannot exceed k.

$$\text{len}(\varepsilon, k) = \{0\} \tag{2}$$

$$\text{len}(a, k) = \text{len}([C], k) = \{1\} \quad (a \in \Sigma) \tag{3}$$

$$\text{len}(r_1 r_2, k) = \text{sum}(\text{len}(r_1, k), \text{len}(r_2, k), k) \tag{4}$$

$$\text{len}(r_1 | r_2, k) = \text{len}(r_1, k) \cup \text{len}(r_2, k) \tag{5}$$

$$\text{len}(r\{m,n\}, k) = \begin{cases} \{0\} \cup \text{len}(r, k) \cup \ell(2, n) & m = 0 \\ \text{len}(r, k) \cup \ell(2, n) & m = 1 \\ \ell(m, n) & m \geqslant 2 \end{cases} \tag{6}$$

$$\text{len}(r\{m,n\}?, k) = \text{len}(r\{m,n\}, k) \tag{7}$$

$$\text{len}((?=r_1)r_2, k) = \{x \mid x \in \text{len}(r_2, k), x \geq \min\{\text{len}(r_1, k)\}\} \tag{8}$$

$$\text{len}((?!r_1)r_2, k) = \text{len}(r_2, k) \tag{9}$$

$$\text{len}(r_1(?<=r_2), k) = \{x \mid x \in \text{len}(r_1, k), x \geq \min\{\text{len}(r_2, k)\}\} \tag{10}$$

$$\text{len}(r_1(?<!r_2), k) = \text{len}(r_1, k) \tag{11}$$

$$\text{len}(\hat{}r, k) = \text{len}(r\$, k) = \text{len}(r, k) \tag{12}$$

$$\text{len}(r_1 \backslash b r_2, k) = \text{sum}(\text{len}(r_1, k), \text{len}(r_2, k), k) - \{0\} \tag{13}$$

$$\text{len}(r_1 \backslash B r_2, k) = \text{sum}(\text{len}(r_1, k), \text{len}(r_2, k), k) \tag{14}$$

$$\text{len}((r)_i, k) = \text{len}((?:r), k) = \text{len}(r, k) \tag{15}$$

$$\text{len}(\backslash i, k) = \text{len}((r)_i, k) \cup \{0\} \tag{16}$$

Fig. 2. The calculation of the function $\text{len}(r, k)$, where the functions $\text{sum}(N_1, N_2, k) = \{x + y \mid x \in N_1, y \in N_2, x + y \leq k\}$, and $\ell(m, n) = \bigcup_{m-1 \leqslant t \leqslant n-1} \text{sum}^t(\text{len}(r, k), \text{len}(r, k), k)$, the symbol sum^t represents calling the function sum t times recursively.

Modeling of Standard Operators. For an empty string ε, when $l \in \text{len}(\varepsilon, k) = \{0\}$, there are no variables assigned to the modeling of it. Obviously, this is always **True**, hence we have Eq. (17). For a character $a \in \Sigma$, $\mathcal{L}(a) = \{a\}$, when l and p satisfy $l \in \text{len}(a, k) = \{1\}$ and $p + l \leq k$, we assign a variable x_p to a in Eq. (18). Character class $[C]$ consumes only one character, thus x_p may be any character in C, so we have Eq. (19).

For alternation $r_1 | r_2$, $\mathcal{L}(r_1 | r_2) = \mathcal{L}(r_1) \cup \mathcal{L}(r_2)$. We assign the variable sequence $\langle x_p, x_{p+1}, \ldots, x_{p+l-1} \rangle$ to $\Phi(r_1, p, l)$ and $\Phi(r_2, p, l)$ at the same time to generate the constraints of $s \in \mathcal{L}(r_1)$ and $s \in \mathcal{L}(r_2)$, respectively. Therefore, we have Eq. (20).

For concatenation $r_1 r_2$, $\mathcal{L}(r_1 r_2) = \mathcal{L}(r_1)\mathcal{L}(r_2)$. We split the string s into two parts (s_1 and s_2), the first l' characters are used to match r_1 (i.e., $\Phi(r_1, p, l')$

$$\Phi(\varepsilon, p, l) = \textbf{True}. \tag{17}$$

$$\Phi(a, p, l) = (\boldsymbol{x_p} = a). \tag{18}$$

$$\Phi([C], p, l) = \bigvee_{a \in [C]} (\boldsymbol{x_p} = a). \tag{19}$$

$$\Phi(r_1 | r_2, p, l) = \Phi(r_1, p, l) \vee \Phi(r_2, p, l). \tag{20}$$

$$\Phi(r_1 r_2, p, l) = \bigvee_{l' \in \texttt{len}(r_1, k)} \big(\Phi(r_1, p, l') \wedge \Phi(r_2, p + l', l - l') \big). \tag{21}$$

$$\Phi(r\{\texttt{m,n}\}, p, l) = \begin{cases} \bigvee_{l' \in \texttt{len}(r\{\texttt{m}\}, k)} \big(\Phi(r\{\texttt{0,n-m}\}, p + l', l - l') \\ \wedge \Phi(\underbrace{rr \cdots r}_{m}, p, l') \big), & \texttt{m} > 0 \\ \bigvee_{i=n}^{0} \big(\Phi(\underbrace{rr \cdots r}_{i}, p, l) \big), & \texttt{m} = 0, \ l > 0 \\ \textbf{True}. & \texttt{m} = 0, \ l = 0 \end{cases} \tag{22}$$

$$\Phi(r\{\texttt{m,n}\}?, p, l) = \Phi(r\{\texttt{m,n}\}, p, l). \tag{23}$$

$$\Phi((?=r_1) r_2, p, l) = \Phi(r_1 \Sigma^*, p, l) \wedge \Phi(r_2, p, l). \tag{24}$$

$$\Phi((?!r_1) r_2, p, l) = \neg\Phi(r_1 \Sigma^*, p, l) \wedge \Phi(r_2, p, l). \tag{25}$$

$$\Phi(r_1 (?<=r_2), p, l) = \Phi(r_1, p, l) \wedge \Phi(\Sigma^* r_2, p, l). \tag{26}$$

$$\Phi(r_1 (?<!r_2), p, l) = \Phi(r_1, p, l) \wedge \neg\Phi(\Sigma^* r_2, p, l). \tag{27}$$

$$\Phi(\hat{\ }r, p, l) = \begin{cases} \Phi(r, p, l), & p = 0 \\ \textbf{False}. & p > 0 \end{cases} \tag{28}$$

$$\Phi(r\$, p, l) = \begin{cases} \Phi(r, p, l), & p + l = k \\ \textbf{False}. & p + l < k \end{cases} \tag{29}$$

$$\Phi(r_1 \backslash br_2, p, l) = \bigvee_{l' \in \texttt{len}(r_1, k)} \big(\Phi(r_1, p, l') \wedge \Phi(r_2, p + l', l - l') \wedge \hbar(p, l') \big). \tag{30}$$

$$\Phi(r_1 \backslash Br_2, p, l) = \bigvee_{l' \in \texttt{len}(r_1, k)} \big(\Phi(r_1, p, l') \wedge \Phi(r_2, p + l', l - l') \wedge \neg\hbar(p, l') \big). \tag{31}$$

$$\text{where } \hbar(p, l') = \begin{cases} \bigvee_{c \in \backslash w} (\boldsymbol{x_{p+l'}} = c), & p + l' = 0 \\ \bigvee_{c \in \backslash w} (\boldsymbol{x_{p+l'-1}} = c), & l - l' = 0 \\ \big(\bigvee_{c \in \backslash w} (\boldsymbol{x_{p+l'-1}} = c) \wedge \bigvee_{c \in \backslash w} (\boldsymbol{x_{p+l'}} = c) \big) \vee \\ \big(\bigvee_{c \in \backslash w} (\boldsymbol{x_{p+l'-1}} = c) \wedge \bigvee_{c \in \backslash w} (\boldsymbol{x_{p+l'}} = c) \big). & p + l' > 0 \wedge l - l' > 0 \end{cases}$$

$$\Phi((r)_i, p, l) = \Phi(r, p, l). \qquad \text{// meanwhile, let } p_i' \leftarrow p \tag{32}$$

$$\Phi((?:r), p, l) = \Phi(r, p, l). \tag{33}$$

$$\Phi(\backslash i, p, l) = \begin{cases} \textbf{True}, & p_i' \text{ is undefined} \\ \phi(p, p_i', l). & \text{otherwise} \end{cases} \tag{34}$$

$$\text{where } \phi(p, p_i', l) = \begin{cases} \textbf{False}, & p_i' = p \vee p_i' + l > k \vee l = 0 \\ \bigwedge_{0 \leqslant m < l} (\boldsymbol{x_{p+m}} = \boldsymbol{x_{p_i'+m}}). & \text{otherwise} \end{cases}$$

Fig. 3. The calculation of the function $\Phi(r, p, l)$ according to regex operators.

for $s_1 \in \mathcal{L}(r_1)$), and the remaining $l - l'$ characters are used to match r_2 (i.e., $\Phi(r_2, p + l', l - l')$ for $s_2 \in \mathcal{L}(r_2)$), where $l' \in \texttt{len}(r_1, k)$. $\texttt{len}(r_1, k)$ calculates the length of the sub-string that regex r_1 matched. So, we have Eq. (21).

Modeling on Quantifiers. For greedy quantifier $r\{\texttt{m,n}\}$, when $\texttt{m} > 0$, $\mathcal{L}(r\{\texttt{m,n}\}) = \mathcal{L}(r\{\texttt{0,n-m}\}) \mathcal{L}(\underbrace{rr \cdots r}_{m})$, we utilize Eq. (21) to model this case. Let $r_1 = r\{0,n-m\}$, $r_2 = \underbrace{rr\cdots r}_{m}$, so we infer that $\Phi(r\{m,n\}) = \bigvee_{l'\in\text{len}(r\{m\},k)} \left(\Phi(r\{0,n-m\}, p + l', l - l') \wedge \Phi(\underbrace{rr\cdots r}_{m}, p, l')\right)$. When $m = 0$, $\mathcal{L}(r\{m,n\}) = \mathcal{L}(\underbrace{rr\cdots r}_{n}) \cup \cdots \cup \mathcal{L}(rr) \cup \mathcal{L}(r) \cup \mathcal{L}(\varepsilon)$. According to different values of l, we further divide constraints for $L(\varepsilon)$ into (i) $l > 0, \Phi(\varepsilon, p, l) =$ **False**, $\Phi(r\{m,n\}, p, l) = \Phi_1 \vee$ **False** $= \Phi_1$; and (ii) $l = 0, \Phi(\varepsilon, p, l) =$ **True**, $\Phi(r\{m,n\}, p, l) = \Phi_1 \vee$ **True** $=$ **True**. In summary, we have Eq. (22).

Lazy quantifier $r\{m,n\}$? mainly affects the content matched by capturing groups rather than membership [20]. We give an over-approximate modeling by reusing the modeling for the greedy quantifier $r\{m,n\}$ in Eq. (23), and ensure the correctness by the refinement strategy introduced in Sect. 3.2. Notice that the capturing groups decorated by quantifiers have the same subscript when modeled as $\Phi(r, p, l)$ functions.

Modeling on Zero-Length Assertions. For lookarounds (e.g., $(?=r_1)r_2$, $(?!r_1)r_2$, $r_1(?<=r_2)$ and $r_1(?<!r_2)$), we give approximate definitions of their languages. Taking positive lookahead $(?=r_1)r_2$ as an example, $\mathcal{L}((?=r_1)r_2) = \{s \mid s \in \mathcal{L}(r_1\Sigma^*) \wedge s \in \mathcal{L}(r_2)\}$, the condition $s \in \mathcal{L}(r_1\Sigma^*)$ is modeled as $\Phi(r_1\Sigma^*, p, l)$, and the condition $s \in \mathcal{L}(r_2)$ is modeled as $\Phi(r_2, p, l)$. So we have Eq. (24). Also, we model the condition $s \notin \mathcal{L}(r_1\Sigma^*)$ as $\neg\Phi(r_1\Sigma^*)$. Therefore, we have Eq. (25–27). We model start-of-line anchor $\hat{\ }r$ and end-of-line anchor $r\$$ according to the starting (or ending) position of the sub-string, as shown in Eq. (28) and Eq. (29), respectively.

We model word boundary $r_1\backslash br_2$ and non-word boundary $r_1\backslash Br_2$ according to their semantics. The matching positions of $r = r_1\backslash br_2$ are shown in Fig. 4. \b restricts the form of the last character of s_1 and the first character of

①$\hat{\ }$⋮\w   ②\w⋮\$ ③\W⋮\w   ④\w⋮\W

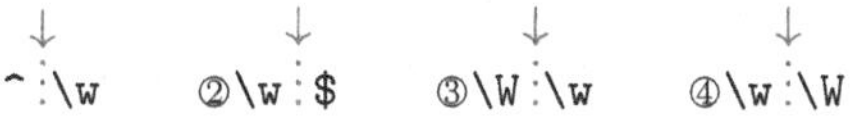

Fig. 4. The matching positions of \b.

s_2 in the string $s = s_1 s_2 \in \mathcal{L}(r)$, where $s_1 \in \mathcal{L}(r_1)$, $s_2 \in \mathcal{L}(r_2)$. The modeling of $r_1\backslash br_2$ should satisfy Eq. (21) and the matching position constraint, then we have Eq. (30). Similarly, we model $s \in \mathcal{L}(r_1\backslash Br_2)$ as Eq. (31).

Modeling on Capturing Group and Backreference. Next, we propose an over-approximate modeling for backreference. The correctness is guaranteed by the refinement strategy introduced in Sect. 3.2.

Capturing group $(r)_i$ matches the same string as r, which is stored in the memorizer $\mathcal{M}_i$ labeled by the index i. We use an extra variable p'_i to record the starting position p when calculating the constraint $\Phi((r)_i, p, l)$. The variable p'_i and the memorizer $\mathcal{M}_i$ are overwritten each time $(r)_i$ is matched. Therefore, we have Eq. (32). The non-capturing group $(?:r)$ does not affect the membership of r, then we have Eq. (33).

Backreference \i matches the content stored in $\mathcal{M}_i$. The function $\Phi(\backslash i, p, l)$ generates the constraint satisfying $x_p x_{p+1} \cdots x_{p+l-1} = x_{p'_i} x_{p'_i+1} \cdots x_{p'_i+l-1}$ through the variable p'_i, when p, p'_i and l are valid. When p'_i is undefined (uninstantiated), we set $\Phi(\backslash i, p, l)$ to $True$, the same as an empty string. To sum up we have Eq. (34).

3.2 Refinement

As we mentioned in Sect. 3.1, our modeling of regex for some extended operators is over-approximated. For example, our modeling cannot guarantee the number of variables used for matching $(r)_i$ is equal to that used for matching $\backslash i$. For the regex $r = ([ab]+)_1 \backslash 1$, when $k = 4$ (the length of the matching string s is $|s| = 4$), the constraint generated by our models is $\varphi = \Phi(r, 0, 4) = \left(\bigvee_{a \in [ab]} (x_0 = a) \wedge \bigwedge_{0 \leqslant m < 3} (x_{1+m} = x_m) \right) \vee \left(\bigvee_{a \in [ab]} (x_0 = a) \wedge \bigvee_{a \in [ab]} (x_1 = a) \wedge \bigwedge_{0 \leqslant m < 2} (x_{2+m} = x_m) \right) \vee \left(\bigvee_{a \in [ab]} (x_0 = a) \wedge \bigvee_{a \in [ab]} (x_1 = a) \wedge \bigvee_{a \in [ab]} (x_2 = a) \wedge (x_3 = x_0) \right)$. Through an SMT solver, a solution $s_\varphi = \{x_0 = \mathtt{a}, x_1 = \mathtt{a}, x_2 = \mathtt{b}, x_3 = \mathtt{a}\}$ is obtained. But obviously, the string composed by the values of the variables in s_φ is $s = x_0 x_1 x_2 x_3 = \mathtt{aaba} \notin \mathcal{L}(r)$. We call this kind of solutions that satisfy the constraint φ but $s \notin \mathcal{L}(r)$ *spurious solutions*.

To address this problem, we use a *counterexample-guided abstraction refinement (CEGAR)* scheme that validates candidate strings with a concrete matcher (e.g., an ECMAScript-compliant matcher [24]). If the matching validation fails, then we refine the constraint as $\varphi \leftarrow \varphi \wedge s \neq s_\varphi$. In this example, the string $s = \mathtt{aaba}$ is rejected by running the concrete matcher. Therefore, we refine the constraint φ by adding the counterexample s_φ, e.g., $\varphi \leftarrow \varphi \wedge s \neq aaba$. We then solve and validate a new solution (string) and repeat the refinement scheme until the string is matched by the concrete matcher or terminate when an iteration bound is reached to avoid non-termination [19].

4 Solving Regex Crossword Puzzles

In this section, we present our algorithm RCPS to solve regex crossword puzzles. We first introduce the definition of regex crossword puzzles (Sect. 4.1), then we present our algorithm RCPS (Sect. 4.2), including the major technical details and an example in Fig. 1(a) (left).

4.1 The Definitions

First, we formally define rectangular and hexagonal regex crossword puzzles.

Definition 1. *Rectangular Regex Crossword Puzzle, R-rcp.* *A rectangular regex crossword puzzle T (see Fig. 5(a) ①) is represented as a 7-tuple $(n_1, n_2, \Gamma_1, \Gamma_2, \Gamma_1', \Gamma_2', G_T)$, where:*

- *G_T is an empty grid consisted of n_1 rows and n_2 columns of square cells;*
- *for $i = 1, 2$, Γ_i and Γ_i' are different regex lists, where $|\Gamma_i| = n_i$ ($\Gamma_i = \langle r_{i,1}, \ldots, r_{i,n_i} \rangle$), $|\Gamma_i'|$ is either n_i ($\Gamma_i' = \langle r_{i,1}', \ldots, r_{i,n_i}' \rangle$) or 0 ($\Gamma_i' = \varnothing$).*

Rule. *Players can fill a square cell with a character.*
Challenge. *Players fill G_T such that:*

- *Reading left to right (called direction d_1, see Fig. 5(a) ②), the string s_i is composed of all square cells on line l_i, satisfying $s_i \in \mathcal{L}(r_{1,i})$ (and $s_i \in \mathcal{L}(r_{1,i}')$, if $\Gamma_1' \neq \varnothing$), where $i \in [1, n_1]$.*

– *Similar for reading top to bottom (called direction d_2, see Fig. 5(a) ③).*

Solution. *If the challenge is successful, the filled grid G_T is a solution of T.*

Definition 2. Hexagonal Regex Crossword Puzzle, H-rcp. *A hexagonal regex crossword puzzle T (see Fig. 5(b) ①) is represented as a 7-tuple $(n_1, n_2, n_3, \Gamma_1, \Gamma_2, \Gamma_3, G_T)$ where:*

– *G_T is an empty grid composed of hexagonal cells.*
– *for $i = 1, 2, 3$, Γ_i represents a regex list, where $|\Gamma_i| = n_i$ ($\Gamma_i = \langle r_{i,1}, \dots, r_{i,n_i} \rangle$).*

Rule. *Players can fill a hexagonal cell with a character.*
Challenge. *Players fill G_T such that:*

– *Reading left to right (called direction d_1, see Fig. 5(b) ②), the string s_i is composed by all hexagonal cells on the line l_i, satisfying $s_i \in \mathcal{L}(r_{1,i})$, where $i \in [1, n_1]$.*
– *Similar to reading top right to bottom left (called direction d_2, see Fig. 5(b) ③) and bottom right to top left (called direction d_3, see Fig. 5(b) ④).*

Solution. *Same as the Solution in Definition 1.*

In addition, it should be noted that any puzzle belongs to one of the following three cases: (1) no solution; (2) a unique solution; (3) more than one solution. We call the first case *unsolvable* and the other cases *solvable*. In particular, a puzzle with more than one solution is called *ambiguous*.

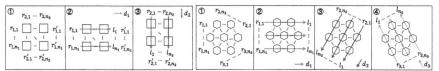

(a) Rectangular regex crossword puzzles   (b) Hexagonal regex crossword puzzles

Fig. 5. Modeling of rectangular and hexagonal regex crossword puzzles.

4.2   RCPS: Regex Crossword Puzzle Solver

Algorithm 2 shows the details of our algorithm RCPS. The input of RCPS is a regex crossword puzzle T, including the grid G_T, and the regex lists on each edge of G_T. The output of RCPS is one of the following three forms: (1) a character-filled grid G_S, which has the same shape and size as the grid G_T; (2) $\varnothing$, indicating that the puzzle T is *unsolvable*; (3) *failed*, indicating that the algorithm cannot determine whether T has a solution G_S. Generally speaking, our algorithm includes four processes:

Initialize the Variable-Marked Grid. We first initialize the constraint Ψ as **True**. (line 1). To model the regex crossword puzzle T, we need to mark each cell in G_T with a unique variable x_i, via the function MARKVAR(G_T). The input of MARKVAR(G_T) is an empty grid G_T, and the output is a variable-marked grid G_{MT} with the same shape and size as G_T.

For rectangular grids, we uniquely identify the cells by their row and column indexes. For hexagonal grids, we use the cubic coordinates[5] to uniquely mark each cell. (line 2). For example, for the grid G_T in Fig. 1(a) (left), the variable-marked grid G_{MT} is shown in Fig. 6 ①.

Select Variables to Form Variable Sequences. Notice that a cell in the puzzle T is constrained by more than one regex simultaneously (e.g., the variable $x_{1,1}$ in G_S (Fig. 6 ①) is constrained by both the regex r_1 of the first row and the regex r_3 of the first column at the same time). Therefore we need to select the variables in G_S to form the variable sequence V. That is, the function SELECTVARS(G_{MT}, T) is used to select the variables by

---

Algorithm 2: RCPS

Input: a regex crossword puzzle T
Output: a character-filled grid G_S, or ∅, or *failed*

1 $\Psi \leftarrow$ **True**;
2 $G_{MT} \leftarrow$ MARKVAR(G_T);
3 **foreach** regex r in T **do**
4     $V \leftarrow$ SELECTVARS(G_{MT}, T);
5     $\Psi \leftarrow \Psi \wedge$ the constraint $\Phi(r, 0, |V|)$ encoded by V;
6 $i \leftarrow 0$;
7 **while** $i <$ ITER_MAX **do**
8     $S \leftarrow$ solve Ψ by an solver;
9   **if** Ψ is satisfiable **then**
10        $G_S \leftarrow$ FILLCHARS(G_{MT}, S);
11   **if** VERIFY(G_S, T) $= true$ **then** return G_S **else** $\Psi \leftarrow \Psi \wedge G_S \neq S$
12   **else return** ∅
13     $i \leftarrow i + 1$;
14 **return** *failed*;

---

reading all cells on line l in direction d to form a variable sequence V. (line 4). Let's continue with the example in Fig. 1(a). Reading left to right (see Fig. 6 ②), we get $V_1 = \langle x_{1,1}, x_{1,2} \rangle$ and $V_2 = \langle x_{2,1}, x_{2,2} \rangle$ for regex r_1 and r_2, respectively. Reading top to bottom (see Fig. 6 ③), we get $V_3 = \langle x_{1,1}, x_{2,1} \rangle$ (for r_3), and $V_4 = \langle x_{1,2}, x_{2,2} \rangle$ (for r_4) similarly.

Generate the Constraint on the Puzzle. Using V and r from the last step, we have the constraint $\Phi(r, 0, |V|)$ on a regex r (line 5). The constraint Ψ on the puzzle T is $\Psi = \bigwedge_{1 \leqslant i \leqslant n} \Phi(r_i, 0, |V_i|)$, where n is the number of regexes in T. At line 8 we solve Ψ by the solver to find a solution.

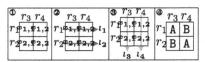

Fig. 6. The solving process of the R-rcp in Fig. 1(a) (left), where $r_1 = $ [0-5A][BQ-X], $r_2 = $ B*A+, $r_3 = $ A*B+, and $r_4 = $ [A-M]*.

Likewise, let us consider the example in Fig. 1(a) (left). The constraint encoded by V_1 is $\Phi(r_1, 0, |V_1|) = \bigvee_{a \in [0\text{-}5A]}(x_{1,1} = a) \wedge \bigvee_{a \in [BQ\text{-}X]}(x_{1,2} = a)$. Similarly, we have: $\Phi(r_2, 0, |V_2|) = (x_{2,1} = $ B$) \wedge (x_{2,2} = $ A$)$; $\Phi(r_3, 0, |V_3|) = (x_{1,1} = $ A$) \wedge (x_{2,1} = $ B$)$; $\Phi(r_4, 0, |V_4|) = \bigvee_{a \in [A\text{-}M]}(x_{1,2} = a) \wedge \bigvee_{a \in [A\text{-}M]}(x_{2,2} = a)$. Therefore, the constraint Ψ on T is $\Psi = \bigwedge_{1 \leqslant i \leqslant 4} \Phi(r_i, 0, |V_i|)$.

CEGAR for Solving Regex Crossword Puzzles. After filling the solution we obtained from the solver, we fill the satisfiable solution into G_S in line 10. At

---

[5] https://www.redblobgames.com/grids/hexagons/.

line 11 of Algorithm 2, we utilize the function VERIFY(G_S, T) to judge whether the challenge (see Definition 1 and Definition 2) is successful, since the modeling is over-approximate. The function VERIFY(G_S, T) takes a character-filled grid G_S and a puzzle T as input, and it returns *true* if and only if each regex r in T is matched by the corresponding string s in the grid G_S, or *false* otherwise. If the function VERIFY(G_S, T) returns *false*, at line 12 of Algorithm 2 we add the counterexample $G_S \neq S$ to the constraint Ψ. In the constraint solving process, the CEGAR scheme iterates until the condition VERIFY(G_S, T) = *true* or i = ITER_MAX is reached, and RCPS returns G_S or *failed*.

Let us further consider the example in Fig. 1(a) (left). By using an SMT solver to solve Ψ, we get a solution $S = \{x_{1,1} = \text{A}, x_{1,2} = \text{B}, x_{2,1} = \text{B}, x_{2,2} = \text{A}\}$. We call function FILLCHARS(G_{MT}, S) to replace the variables in G_{MT} with the corresponding values in S, and get a character-filled grid G_S (as shown in Fig. 6 ④). We call function VERIFY(G_S, T) to judge whether (i) AB $\in \mathcal{L}(r_1)$, (ii) BA $\in \mathcal{L}(r_2)$, (iii) AB $\in \mathcal{L}(r_3)$, and (iv) BA $\in \mathcal{L}(r_4)$ are satisfied. The function VERIFY(G_S, T) returns *true*, so our algorithm returns G_S (Fig. 6 ④).

5   Experiments

In the experiments, we evaluate the effectiveness and efficiency of RCPS on large-scale regex crossword puzzle datasets. We first introduce the benchmark datasets, tools for comparison, and experimental configurations (Sect. 5.1), then analyze our experimental results (Sect. 5.2).

5.1   Experiment Setup

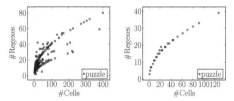

(a) Distribution of #Cells & #Regexes in R-rcps.

(b) Distribution of #Cells & #Regexes in H-rcps.

Benchmark Datasets. We collected puzzles from the most popular regex crossword puzzle website[6], which allows players to upload solvable rectangular or hexagonal regex crossword puzzles with solutions. We obtained 803 R-rcps and 95 H-rcps, as shown in Fig. 7. We counted the number of cells (#Cells) and regexes (#Regexes) for each puzzle. Figure 7(a) and Fig. 7(b) show the distribution of #Cells and #Regexes in R-rcps and H-rcps respectively. Figure 7(c) summarizes the minimum, maximum and average values of #Cells and #Regexes in R-rcp and H-rcp respectively.

Furthermore, we also analyze the usage of each extended operator in the

Type	#Puzzles	#Cells			#Regexes		
		Min.	Max.	Avg.	Min.	Max.	Avg.
R-rcp	803	1	400	24.84	2	80	13.77
H-rcp	95	1	127	26.53	3	39	15.61

(c) Minimum, maximum and average values of #Cells and #Regexes in R-rcps and H-rcps.

Fig. 7. The benchmark datasets for evaluation.

---

[6] https://regexcrossword.com/.

regexes extracted from all puzzles. Table 1 shows statistics on the number and proportion of regexes, where RE stands for the standard regular expressions which do not contain any extended operator.

In general, both Loring et al. [42] and our statistics confirm that regexes usually contain complex features, which also indicates it is necessary to study the modeling of regex extended operators. Specifically, character class and greedy quantifier are the two most popular operators, while negative lookbehind is the least.

Baselines. To evaluate the effectiveness and efficiency of RCPS, we selected five state-of-the-art tools for comparison: Jeong [33], Trux [53], Shcherban [51], Abolofia [1], and Schaaf [49]. We list extended operators supported by each tool in Table 2. In the tables and figures below, the abbreviations JE, TR, SH, AB and SC represent Jeong [33], Trux [53], Shcherban [51], Abolofia [1], Schaaf [49], respectively.

Table 1. Usage of regex operators in datasets.

Operator	Total	%	Unique	%
Total Regex	12,538	100.00%	10,872	100.00%
RE	381	3.04%	306	2.81%
Character Class	10,398	82.93%	9,883	90.90%
Capturing Group	5,079	40.51%	4,519	51.57%
Non-Capturing Group	195	1.56%	145	1.33%
Backreference	2,773	22.12%	2,288	21.04%
Lookarounds	1,582	12.62%	1,305	12.00%
Positive Lookahead	781	6.23%	675	6.21%
Negative Lookahead	1,094	8.73%	846	7.78%
Positive Lookbehind	26	0.21%	26	0.24%
Negative Lookbehind	6	0.05%	6	0.06%
Anchors	658	5.25%	570	5.24%
Start-of-line Anchor	388	3.09%	346	3.18%
End-of-line Anchor	471	3.76%	396	3.64%
Word Boundary	24	0.19%	23	0.21%
Non-word Boundary	20	0.16%	20	0.18%
Quantifiers	13,366	82.68%	8,979	82.59%
Greedy Quantifier	13,346	82.52%	8,961	82.42%
Lazy Quantifier	95	0.76%	78	0.72%

* The unique version is deduplicated, while the total version retains the duplicates.

Configurations. We implemented the prototype of RCPS in Python 3 where the SMT solver we used is Z3 solver [44]. Our experiments were run on a machine with 2.20 GHz Intel Xeon(R) Silver processor and 128G RAM, running Windows 10. We used the parameter configuration ITER_MAX = 5,000 in our algorithms for all experiments. All baselines were configured in the same settings as reported in their original documents.

Table 2. Extended operators supported by each tool.

	JE	TR	SH	AB	SC	RCPS
Character Class	✓	✓	✓	✓	✓	✓
Capturing Group	✓	✓	✓	✓	✓	✓
Non-Capturing Group	✗	✓	✓	✓	✓	✓
Backreference	✓	✓	✓	✓	✗	✓
Positive Lookahead	✗	✓	✓	✓	✗	✓
Negative Lookahead	✗	✗	✓	✓	✗	✓
Positive Lookbehind	✗	✗	✓	✓	✗	✓
Negative Lookbehind	✗	✗	✓	✓	✗	✓
Start-of-line Anchor	✓	✓	✓	✓	✓	✓
End-of-line Anchors	✓	✓	✓	✓	✓	✓
Word Boundary	✗	✓	✓	✓	✓	✓
Non-word Boundary	✗	✓	✓	✓	✓	✓
Greedy Quantifier	✓	✓	✓	✓	✓	✓
Lazy Quantifier	✗	✗	✓	✓	✓	✓

* ✓ means the operator is supported; ✗ indicates the operator is not supported.

5.2 Effectiveness and Efficiency of RCPS

Table 3 gives the overall evaluation results on the benchmark datasets. According to Table 3, RCPS outperforms all baseline techniques in success rate, which successfully solved 97.76% R-rcps and 98.95% H-rcps. According to Algorithm 2, our algorithm may output *failed* (e.g., RCPS cannot determine whether the puzzle

Table 3. Comparison of the effectiveness and efficiency on the benchmarks.

Tools	R-rcps					H-rcps				
	#Sol.	%	Min. T.(s)	Max. T.(s)	Avg. T.(s)	#Sol.	%	Min. T.(s)	Max. T.(s)	Avg. T.(s)
JE [33]	398	49.56%	0.01	128.40	1.27	—	—	—	—	—
TR [53]	632	78.70%	0.01	3.79	0.04	32	33.68%	0.02	0.05	0.03
SH [51]	93	11.58%	0.14	38.04	2.49	17	2.49%	0.13	16.83	1.51
AB [1]	229	28.52%	0.00	1205.50	11.02	—	—	—	—	—
SC [49]	138	17.19%	0.00	1511.78	11.01	—	—	—	—	—
RCPS	**785**	**97.76%**	**0.02**	**252.25**	**6.65**	**94**	**98.95%**	**0.02**	**497.57**	**3.20**

* The symbol "—" indicates that the corresponding tools cannot solve the H-rcps.

has a solution), mainly because the CEGAR-scheme is still not refined successfully within ITER_MAX times. In order to balance the success rate and efficiency, we kept ITER_MAX = 5,000.

Effectiveness. Jeong [33] is also based on Z3 [44]. Among the 5 baselines, it supports the least number of extended operators (see Table 1 and Table 2). Furthermore, its modeling of operators is incomplete, e.g., it neither supports negated character classes such as [^\w], nor generates constraints for regex $((A)_2\backslash 2)_1\backslash 1$. Due to the incomplete modeling of the extended operators, the success rate is only 49.56% on the R-rcps, which is nearly $\frac{1}{2}$ of ours.

Trux [53] employs a heuristic algorithm to recursively calculate the possible characters of each cell, and supports most of the extended operators in Table 2. Trux has limited support for lookarounds and its constraint propagation strategy for backreferences may prune the correct answer. It solved 78.70% R-rcps, which performed best among all baselines but nearly 18% lower than RCPS, while on the H-rcps, its success rate is 33.68%, which is only close to $\frac{1}{3}$ of ours.

Shcherban [51] is based on a genetic algorithm, evolving strings using crossover and mutation operators. The genetic algorithm does not consider the structure of regexes or the semantics of regex operators. Therefore Shcherban supports all extended operators in Table 2. However, in the experiment, its success rate is the lowest, whether on the R-rcps (11.58%) or H-rcps (2.49%). This also shows that the analysis of the structures and semantics of regexes is essential for solving regex crossword puzzles.

Abolofia [1] is based on a backtracking regex engine[7] which supports all extended operators in Table 2. Abolofia uses a backtracking algorithm to continuously extend s such that its length $|s|$ is equal to the number of cells corresponding to r. However, due to the size of the search space, it is difficult to solve puzzles with large alphabets. In the experiments, it only solved 28.52% of R-rcps, which is 68.49% less than ours.

Schaaf [49] obtains the automaton compiled by the regex engine of Go[8]. The tool maintains states compiled by the engine according to the positions of the puzzle and uses a backtracking algorithm to fill the puzzle. Go's regex engine

---

[7] https://pypi.org/project/regex/.
[8] https://pkg.go.dev/regexp.

follows Re2's [21] syntax, which does not include backreferences or lookarounds. Additionally, the size of the search space also affects its performance. In the experiments, the tool has a low success rate on the R-rcps (17.19%) due to incomplete support for regex operators.

In addition, we analyze the puzzles commonly solved by each tool to further evaluate the effectiveness of RCPS. In Fig. 8, the Venn plot shows the relationship of puzzle sets solved by each tool on R-rcps. The number of puzzles solved by each baseline is less than that of RCPS, and the puzzles they solved are subsets of RCPS. In the UpSet plot, the upper vertical bar chart represents the intersection size of puzzles solved by one or more

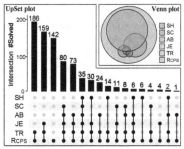

Fig. 8. An illustration of effectiveness of RCPS on R-rcps datasets.

tools, and the lower dot-line chart represents the corresponding tools, e.g., the value of the first vertical bar is 186, and the corresponding tools are Trux and RCPS, which means that among all the solved R-rcps, 186 puzzles can only be solved by Trux and RCPS, but not by the other four tools. The UpSet plot shows RCPS can solve 142 R-rcps that the other tools cannot. Similarly, on the H-rcps, RCPS covers all the puzzles solved by the baselines, and there are 51 H-rcps uniquely solved by ours. These results demonstrate that RCPS is significantly more effective than all baselines in solving regex crossword puzzles.

Efficiency. Compared with Jeong [33], RCPS is only 5.38(s) slower on R-rcps, which is acceptable because we consider the modeling of complex extended operators, and our success rate (97.76%) is nearly doubled that of Jeong (49.56%). From Table 3, RCPS achieved a much higher success rate than that achieved by Trux [53], taking only around 6 and 3 more seconds running time on R-rcps and H-rcps respectively. Shcherban [51] has a lower average time than ours, meanwhile, their success rate is low (11.58%). RCPS also has speedups (1.66x and 1.66x on average) and much higher success rates (69.2% and 80.5%) over Abolofia [1] and Schaaf [49] respectively on R-rcps. To sum up, RCPS can solve more puzzles in an acceptable running time.

Summary. First, RCPS has a higher success rate than all baselines, which is 97.76% on the R-rcps and 98.95% on the H-rcps, which are 19.06% and 65.27% higher than the highest success rates of existing methods, respectively. The solutions of all baselines are subsets of RCPS. Besides, there are 142 R-rcps and 51 H-rcps uniquely solved by ours. Second, RCPS can solve regex crossword puzzles efficiently, RCPS takes an average of 6.65 s to achieve around 20% more success rate on the R-rcps, and achieves 65% more success rate at the cost of 3 more seconds on the H-rcps.

Limitations. There are also limitations to the efficiency of our algorithm. In the experiments, we found following regex structures caused our model generation time-consuming.

Continuous quantifiers such as $r_1^* r_2^* \ldots r_n^*$. Suppose all r_i are identical, and $\text{len}(r_i, k) = \{0, 1, \ldots, k\}$, there are about $\sum_{i=1}^{\min\{k,n\}} \binom{k-1}{i-1} \binom{n}{i}$ variable allocation schemes; Nested quantifiers such as $((r_1*)* \ldots)*$. Assuming the quantifiers are nested n layers and $\text{len}(r_1, k) = \{0, 1, \ldots, k\}$, there are about k^n variable allocation schemes; Negative lookarounds and backreferences, e.g., expression $(?!.*(r_2)_1.*\backslash 1) r_1$ limits the form of string $s_1 \in \mathcal{L}(r_1)$ not to be $s_1 = \ldots s_2 \ldots s_2 \ldots$, where string $s_2 \in \mathcal{L}(r_2)$ appears discontinuously.

Structures we mentioned above need to be further optimized in the future.

6 Related Work

Modeling Regex Operators. In 2004, G. Peasant introduced a global constraint to model complex sequencing rules using DFA [46]. Their model did not consider extended features. Saxena et al. [48] proposed the first scheme to encode the capturing groups through string constraints. Li and Ghosh [35] described a string constraint solver, which supports most JavaScript string operations and partially supports ECMAScript regex but it does not support backreferences or lookaheads. Loring et al. [41] introduced the partial support for encoding JavaScript regex in terms of classical regular language membership and string constraints. In their follow-up work [42], they supplemented the modeling of lookaheads and anchors, and solved the challenge of matching precedence through a CEGAR scheme. However, they do not support lookbehinds. Chen et al. [16] proposed a transducer model PSST combining priorities to capture greedy/lazy semantics, and support for lookarounds and backreferences are in their future work. This paper and [55] both propose novel methods for modeling regexes. However, they develop different techniques because the problems they solve are different. The algorithmic difference between this paper and [55] are listed as follows: firstly our implementation is based on SMT solver Z3 [44] instead of the induction system to generate a solution. Secondly since regex crossword puzzles has fixed number of cells, we introduced the $\text{len}(r, k)$ function in fine-grained modeling of regex operators, which is not considered in [55]. Thirdly because regex crossword puzzles do not specify the matching functions, we have not considered the semantic difference between full matching and partial matching. However the matching functions for regexes are ubiquitous in practical programs, thus the authors modeled them in [55]. Another difference is that we rely on CEGAR strategy to eliminate spurious solutions, which makes our algorithm sound, yet incomplete, while in [55], authors constrained the expressive power of the input regex by induction rules to ensure the completeness of their algorithm within the subclass of regexes that they support.

Regex Crossword Puzzles. In [25,26], authors have shown the complexity of a number of variants and restrictions of regex crossword puzzles. In practice, the state-of-the-art tools for solving regex crossword puzzles include Jeong [33],

Trux [53], Abolofia [1], Shcherban [51], and Schaaf [49], which are based on different algorithms (see Sect. 1), we also analysis their pros and cons (see Sect. 5.2). In this paper, we provide more comprehensive regex operator modeling for solving regex crossword puzzles.

7   Conclusion

In this paper, we propose an over-approximate modeling method for regex operators. For a given regex r, the output of the modeling is a formula φ in first-order logic, such that the solution s satisfies $s \in \mathcal{L}(r)$. We deploy a CEGAR scheme to strengthen φ and ensure the correctness of our modeling. We also apply the modeling to solve regex crossword puzzles and develop a novel algorithm RCPS. We compare our algorithm with five state-of-the-art tools in 803 R-rcps and 95 H-rcps. Experiment results show that, due to the comprehensive modeling, our algorithm can solve 97.76% R-rcps and 98.95% H-rcps in an acceptable running time, which are 19.06% and 65.27% higher than the highest success rates of other methods respectively.

Acknowledgements. The authors would like to thank the anonymous reviewers for their helpful comments and suggestions. Work supported by the Natural Science Foundation of Beijing, China (Grant No. 4232038) and the National Natural Science Foundation of China (Grant No. 62372439).

References

1. Abolofia, R.: regex-crossword-solver (2015). https://github.com/purple4reina/regex-crossword-solver
2. Alfred, V.: Algorithms for finding patterns in strings. Algorithms Complex. **1**, 255 (2014)
3. Anderson, R., Kolko, J.: Crossword puzzle: clues and solutions. Interactions **15**(3), 35 (2008)
4. Appelt, D., Panichella, A., Briand, L.: Automatically repairing web application firewalls based on successful SQL injection attacks. In: ISSRE 2017, pp. 339–350 (2017)
5. Bartoli, A., De Lorenzo, A., Medvet, E., Tarlao, F.: Active learning of predefined models for information extraction: selecting regular expressions from examples. In: FSDM 2019, pp. 645–651 (2019)
6. Beacham, A., Chen, X., Sillito, J., van Beek, P.: Constraint programming lessons learned from crossword puzzles. In: AI 2001, pp. 78–87 (2001)
7. Berglund, M., van der Merwe, B.: Re-examining regular expressions with backreferences. Theor. Comput. Sci. **940**, 66–80 (2022)
8. Björklund, H., Martens, W., Schwentick, T.: Conjunctive query containment over trees using schema information. Acta Informatica **55**(1), 17–56 (2018)
9. Black, L.: Can You Do the Regular Expression Crossword (2014). https://www.i-programmer.info/news/144-graphics-and-games/5450-can-youdo-the-regular-expression-crossword.html

10. Câmpeanu, C., Salomaa, K., Yu, S.: A formal study of practical regular expressions. Int. J. Found. Comput. Sci. **14**(06), 1007–1018 (2003)

11. Cao, J., Li, M., Li, Y., Wen, M., Cheung, S.C., Chen, H.: SemMT: a semantic-based testing approach for machine translation systems. In: TOSEM 2022, pp. 1–36 (2022)

12. Carle, B., Narendran, P.: On extended regular expressions. In: LATA 2009, pp. 279–289 (2009)

13. Caruccio, L., Cirillo, S., Deufemia, V., Polese, G.: Efficient validation of functional dependencies during incremental discovery. In: SEBD 2021, pp. 5–9 (2021)

14. Chen, Q., Wang, X., Ye, X., Durrett, G., Dillig, I.: Multi-modal synthesis of regular expressions. In: PLDI 2020, pp. 487–502 (2020)

15. Chen, T., et al.: Solving string constraints with regex-dependent functions through transducers with priorities and variables. POPL **2022**(6), 1–31 (2022)

16. Chen, T., et al.: Solving string constraints with regex-dependent functions through transducers with priorities and variables. In: POPL 2022, vol. 6, pp. 1–31 (2022)

17. Chida, N., Terauchi, T.: Repairing DoS vulnerability of real-world regexes. In: S&P 2022, pp. 1049–1066 (2022)

18. Chida, N., Terauchi, T.: On lookaheads in regular expressions with backreferences. In: FSCD 2022, vol. 228, pp. 15:1–15:18 (2022)

19. Clarke, E., Grumberg, O., Jha, S., Lu, Y., Veith, H.: Counterexample-guided abstraction refinement. In: CAV 2000, pp. 154–169 (2000)

20. Cox, R.: Regular Expression Matching Can Be Simple And Fast (2007). https://swtch.com/~rsc/regexp/regexp1.html

21. Cox, R.: Regular Expression Matching in the Wild (2010). https://swtch.com/~rsc/regexp/regexp3.html

22. CTFtime.org: CTFtime.org/HackPack CTF 2021/Regex World (2021). https://ctftime.org/task/15582

23. Doleschal, J., Kimelfeld, B., Martens, W.: Database principles and challenges in text analysis. ACM SIGMOD Rec. **50**(2), 6–17 (2021)

24. ECMA-262: ECMAScript® 2022 Language Specification (2022). https://tc39.es/ecma262/multipage/

25. Fenner, S.: The complexity of some regex crossword problems (2014)

26. Fenner, S., Padé, D., Thierauf, T.: The complexity of regex crosswords. Inf. Comput. **286**, 104777 (2021)

27. Florenzano, F., Riveros, C., Ugarte, M., Vansummeren, S., Vrgoč, D.: Efficient enumeration algorithms for regular document spanners. ACM Trans. Database Syst. **45**(1), 1–42 (2020)

28. Freydenberger, D.D.: Extended regular expressions: succinctness and decidability. Theory Comput. Syst. **53**(2), 159–193 (2013)

29. Freydenberger, D.D., Schmid, M.L.: Deterministic regular expressions with backreferences. J. Comput. Syst. Sci. **105**, 1–39 (2019)

30. Gelade, W., Gyssens, M., Martens, W.: Regular expressions with counting: weak versus strong determinism. SIAM J. Comput. **41**(1), 160–190 (2012)

31. Ginsberg, M.L., Frank, M.C., Halpin, M.P., Torrance, M.C.: Search lessons learned from crossword puzzles. In: AAAI-1990 (1990)

32. Gu, H., et al.: DIAVA: a traffic-based framework for detection of SQL injection attacks and vulnerability analysis of leaked data. IEEE Trans. Reliab. **69**(1), 188–202 (2019)

33. Jeong, Y.: regex-crossword-solver (2018). https://github.com/blukat29/regex-crossword-solver

34. Jiang, C., Zhao, Y., Chu, S., Shen, L., Tu, K.: Cold-start and interpretability: turning regular expressions into trainable recurrent neural networks. In: EMNLP 2020, pp. 3193–3207 (2020)
35. Li, G., Ghosh, I.: PASS: string solving with parameterized array and interval automaton. In: HVC 2013, pp. 15–31 (2013)
36. Li, Y., Cao, J., Chen, H., Ge, T., Xu, Z., Peng, Q.: FlashSchema: achieving high quality XML schemas with powerful inference algorithms and large-scale schema data. In: ICDE 2020, pp. 1962–1965 (2020)
37. Li, Y., et al.: ReDoSHunter: a combined static and dynamic approach for regular expression DoS detection. In: USENIX Security 2021, pp. 3847–3864 (2021)
38. Li, Y., et al.: FlashRegex: deducing anti-ReDoS regexes from examples. In: ASE 2020, pp. 659–671 (2020)
39. Libkin, L., Martens, W., Vrgoč, D.: Querying graphs with data. J. ACM **63**(2), 1–53 (2016)
40. Liu, J., Bai, R., Lu, Z., Ge, P., Aickelin, U., Liu, D.: Data-driven regular expressions evolution for medical text classification using genetic programming. In: CEC 2020, pp. 1–8 (2020)
41. Loring, B., Mitchell, D., Kinder, J.: ExpoSE: practical symbolic execution of standalone JavaScript. In: SPIN 2017, pp. 196–199 (2017)
42. Loring, B., Mitchell, D., Kinder, J.: Sound regular expression semantics for dynamic symbolic execution of JavaScript. In: PLDI 2019, pp. 425–438 (2019)
43. MIT: A Regular Crossword (Solution) (2013). http://www.mit.edu/activities/puzzle/2013/coinheist.com/rubik/a_regular_crossword/answer/index.html
44. de Moura, L., Bjørner, N.: Z3: an efficient SMT solver. In: TACAS 2008, pp. 337–340 (2008)
45. Pan, R., Hu, Q., Xu, G., D'Antoni, L.: Automatic repair of regular expressions. In: OOPSLA 2019, vol. 3, pp. 1–29 (2019)
46. Pesant, G.: A regular language membership constraint for finite sequences of variables. In: CP 2004, pp. 482–495 (2004)
47. Polo, M., Pedreira, O., S. Places, Á., Garcia Rodriguez de Guzman, I.: Automated generation of oracled test cases with regular expressions and combinatorial techniques. J. Softw. Evol. Process **32**(12), e2273 (2020)
48. Saxena, P., Akhawe, D., Hanna, S., Mao, F., McCamant, S., Song, D.: A symbolic execution framework for JavaScript. In: S&P 2010, pp. 513–528 (2010)
49. Schaaf, H.: regex-crossword-solver (2014). https://github.com/hermanschaaf/regex-crossword-solver
50. Schmid, M.L.: Characterising REGEX languages by regular languages equipped with factor-referencing. Inf. Comput. **249**, 1–17 (2016)
51. Shcherban, M.: GP-crossword-solver (2019). https://github.com/maxymczech/gp-regex-crossword
52. Slashdot: Can You Do the Regular Expression Crossword (2013). https://games.slashdot.org/story/13/02/13/2346253/canyou-do-the-regular-expression-crossword
53. Trux, A.: Regex-crossword-solver (2017). https://github.com/antoine-trux/regex-crossword-solver
54. Veanes, M., De Halleux, P., Tillmann, N.: Rex: symbolic regular expression explorer. In: ICST 2010, pp. 498–507 (2010)
55. Yan, Y., et al.: Deducing matching strings for real-world regular expressions. In: SETTA 2023 (2023, accepted)

56. Yu, F., Shueh, C.Y., Lin, C.H., Chen, Y.F., Wang, B.Y., Bultan, T.: Optimal sanitization synthesis for web application vulnerability repair. In: ISSTA 2016, pp. 189–200 (2016)
57. Yu, S.: Regular languages. In: Handbook of Formal Languages, Vol. 1: Word, Language, Grammar, pp. 41–110 (1997)

Software Vulnerability Detection Using an Enhanced Generalization Strategy

Hao Sun[1,2], Zhe Bu[3], Yang Xiao[1], Chengsheng Zhou[3], Zhiyu Hao[4],
and Hongsong Zhu[1(✉)]

[1] Institute of Information Engineering, Chinese Academy of Sciences, Beijing, China
{sunhao,xiaoyang,zhuhongsong}@iie.ac.cn
[2] School of Cyber Security, University of Chinese Academy of Sciences,
Beijing, China
[3] Institute of Security, China Academy of Information and Communications
Technology, Beijing, China
[4] Zhongguancun Laboratory, Beijing, China
haozy@zgclab.edu.cn

Abstract. Detecting vulnerabilities in software is crucial for preventing cybersecurity attacks, and current machine learning-based methods rely on large amounts of labeled data to train detection models. On the one hand, a major assumption is that the training and test data follow an identical distribution. However, vulnerabilities in different software projects may exhibit various distributions due to their application scenarios, coding habits, and other factors. On the other hand, when detecting vulnerabilities in new projects, it is time-consuming to retrain and test the models. Especially for new projects being developed, it has few or no instances of vulnerabilities. Therefore, how to leverage previous learning experience to learn new projects faster is important. To address these issues, we propose VulGML, a vulnerability detection approach using graph embedding and meta-learning. The goal is to establish a model with enhanced generalization, so that the model trained on multiple known projects can detect vulnerabilities in new projects. To further illustrate the strong generalization of VulGML, we also choose multiple known vulnerability types to train the meta-learning model and a new vulnerability type for vulnerability detection. Experimental results show that VulGML outperforms the state-of-the-art methods by 6.44–39.61% in detecting new projects, achieves an accuracy higher than 77.80% when detecting vulnerabilities in new vulnerability types, and its modules have greatly improved detection performance, demonstrating that VulGML is potentially valuable in practical usage.

Keywords: Cybersecurity attacks · Vulnerability detection · Enhanced generalization · Graph embedding · Meta-learning

H. Hermanns et al. (Eds.): SETTA 2023, LNCS 14464, pp. 226–242, 2024.
https://doi.org/10.1007/978-981-99-8664-4_13

1 Introduction

According to the CVEDetails report [3], a total of 25,227 vulnerabilities are reported in 2022, 25.1% over the previous year and the most ever recorded of any year since the website began. Software vulnerabilities are security flaws, glitches, or weaknesses found in software systems that could be exploited by attackers to undertake malicious activities [16]. In particular, criminal groups may make use of unresolved security vulnerabilities in software to attack and damage a system to steal confidential information or extort assets, resulting in severe economic damage [6]. Therefore, it is essential and indispensable to detect the software vulnerabilities as soon as possible.

Current research mainly focuses on in-domain vulnerability detection based on supervised machine learning models [7,15,18,19,23]. As shown in Fig. 1(a), they divides the sufficient labeled data from multiple projects into two parts: one part for training and another part for testing, i.e. assuming that the training data and test data come from the same distribution. When a new project needs to be detected, the model requires multiple retraining iterations after incorporating the data from the new project to update parameters, especially those that simulate high-complexity problems. If there is only a small amount of training data in the new project, even the timely machine learning algorithm using gradient descent is not very effective [22]. In fact, due to factors such as coding style and application scenarios, the vulnerability features in different software projects may obey different probability distributions. In addition, the in-domain vulnerability detection relies on large amounts of labeled data to train detection models. However, there is no known publicly available large-scale software vulnerability database that directly provides real vulnerability data with code and label pairs [11]. Real-world software projects, particularly those in the early stages of development, have few or no instances of vulnerabilities. Constructing the new training dataset based on the vulnerabilities of new projects is also prohibitively expensive.

As shown in Fig. 1(b), to address the above issues, detection models need to leverage previous learning experience to learn new projects faster, rather than retraining the detection model for new projects. In other words, the trained vulnerability detection model should exhibit enhanced generalization capabilities. For example, a vulnerability detection model trained on project1 and project2 can also be applied to the other projects.

In this paper, we present VulGML, an enhanced generalization method using graph embedding and meta-learning. VulGML treats the existing multiple projects as multiple meta-tasks, and the goal is to use multiple meta-tasks to train a vulnerability detection model with strong generalization ability, so that it can also detect vulnerabilities in a new project. Specifically, we take the following steps: **First**, Data preparation. We crawl the source codes of five projects to obtain vulnerability functions and their fixed functions, which avoids the impact of highly normative synthetic datasets on model generalization and meets the needs of real-world vulnerability detection. Each function is constructed into a program dependency graph (PDG) to obtain graph embedding, which can

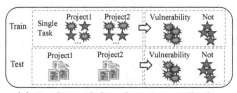

(a) Traditional deep learning methods.

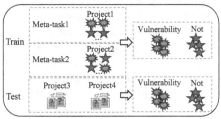

(b) Our approach.

Fig. 1. Comparison of traditional DNN approach and our approach.

not only represent rich dependency semantic information in the function, but also reduce the error in randomly initialized the graph embedding in meta-learning model. **Second**, A meta-learning model. It involves basic network and meta-learner. We utilize the basic network to learn the vulnerability features of functions in each meta-task, and the meta-learner to enhance the generalization ability of the basic network across various vulnerability features through learning multiple meta-tasks. The trained meta-learning model can learn accurate generalization representations for different vulnerability features of multiple meta-tasks. **Third**, Detection vulnerabilities for the new projects. The trained meta-learning model can obtain a generalized representation of vulnerability feature, we use a portion of the samples in the new project fine-tune the trained meta-learning model, and then detect vulnerabilities for the remaining samples. It avoids the time consumption caused by retraining on new projects. The results demonstrate that our method outperforms the state-of-the-art model, which enables us to accurately judge whether the samples is a vulnerability.

To summarize, this paper makes the following contributions:

(1) We propose a novel approach VulGML that better enhances the generalization of the vulnerability detection model. VulGML utilizes the graph embedding and meta-learning to enable faster learning of new projects by leveraging previous learning experience.
(2) Data preparation that adopts the graph embedding of the PDG for each function, successfully obtaining the dependency semantic information of the source code, and reducing the impact of meta-learning random initialization of vulnerability features on detection results.
(3) A meta-learning method that represents the general vulnerability features of multiple meta-tasks using basic network and meta-learner, achieving a strong generalization capability across different projects.

(4) A fine-tuning-based detection method involves utilizing the new project to fine-tune the trained meta-learning model and subsequently detecting vulnerabilities in the new project, which avoids the time consumption caused by retraining on new projects. The results demonstrate our method outperforms state-of-the-art methods on detecting the vulnerability.

The remainder of this paper can be organized as follows. Section 2 provides the state-of-the-art related work and advantages of our method. Section 3 presents the design of VulGML. Section 4 evaluates the experimental results. In Sect. 5, we conclude the paper and discuss its limitations and future work.

2 Related Works

Machine learning does not rely on human experts to identify vulnerability patterns, and automatically detects potential vulnerabilities through model training. We review the work related to machine learning from two directions: in-domain and cross-domain vulnerability detection methods.

2.1 In-Domain Vulnerability Detection Methods

In-domain vulnerability detection methods assume that the sufficient labeled training data and test data in multiple projects come from the same distribution. The main tasks include serialization-based methods [1,10,11] and graph-based methods [2,17,24].

Serialization-based methods. They input the source code into the model as serialized tokens for learning. For example, VulDeePecker [11] generates code gadgets which is represented by a set of semantically related lines of C/C+ code, and then uses BiLSTM to convert them into vectors in a serialized form for training. SySeVR [10], based on syntax and semantics of source code, fully exploits data dependencies and control dependencies. BGNN4VD [1] extracts the syntax and semantic information of source code through AST, CFG, and DFG, and learn the different features using BGNN.

Graph-based methods. The source code is transformed into graph structures, and graph models are utilized to learn the syntax and semantic information within the graph. For example, Devign [24] utilizes various components of GNN to learn the rich semantic information in Code Property Graph, which enables GNN to better learn node representations and thus achieve graph-level classification. FUNDED [17] shows how a multi-relational, gated graph neural network can be developed for vulnerability detection and exploit transfer learning to port vulnerability detection models across programming languages.

Compared with serialization-based vulnerability detection, graph-based models fully integrate richer semantic information. Therefore, in this paper, we represent source code as the PDG and use a graph neural network to learn its graph embedding as initial input for meta-learning.

2.2   Cross-Domain Vulnerability Detection Methods

For the in-domain methods, the prerequisite for detecting new projects is to retrain the model with the new project added to the dataset. This operation overlooks the fact that due to application scenarios, coding habits, and other factors, vulnerability features of different software projects may obey different probability distributions.

In order to apply a detection model trained on limited training data to new projects, there have been some recent studies on cross-domain methods [9,12,14]. They involve training models in one domain and applying them to a different domain, aiming to generalize knowledge and transfer it across domains. For example, Literature [14] uses migration component analysis to map software metrics in the source and target domains to the same feature space. VulGDA [9] uses GRU [4] for code encoding and implements cross domain vulnerability detection based on Maximum Mean Discrepancy. CD-VulD [12] uses a metric transfer learning framework (MTLF) [20] to bridge the gap between different domains' distribution.

Cross-domain approaches for software vulnerability detection are limited to one source domain (i.e., training on a single source project, and assessing the generalization performance on another project). However, the vulnerability features covered by a single source project are limited, and the ability to generate general vulnerability features across multiple source projects needs improvement. Our method treats multiple source projects as multiple meta-tasks, combining accurate vulnerability features representing each meta-task to generate generalized vulnerability features for all source projects. Finally, when detecting the model on other projects, it exhibits significantly improved generalization performance compared to cross-domain methods.

3   Approach

The overview architecture of VulGML is illustrated in Fig. 2. As can be seen, it is composed of three modules, i.e., Data preparation, Meta-learning model and Detection model.

Data Preparation. We crawl the vulnerability functions and their fixed functions for multiple projects, which avoids the impact of highly normative synthetic datasets on model generalization and meets the needs of real-world vulnerability detection. In addition, we construct the PDG for each function, and obtain graph embedding using the graph neural network, which can not only represent dependency semantic information for the function, but also reduce the error in randomly initialized the graph embedding in meta-learning model.

Meta-learning Model. Given M projects as multiple meta-tasks, the dataset of each meta-task is divided into support set and query set. We use support set of each meta-task to train the meta-learning model, i.e., utilizing the basic network to learn the vulnerability features of functions in each meta-task, and the meta-learner to minimize the sum of generalization losses of overall multiple meta-tasks. The query set is used to test the performance of the meta-learning model.

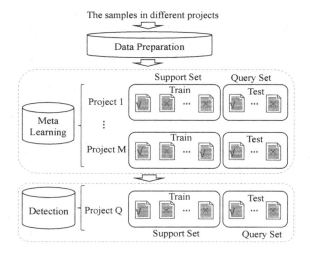

Fig. 2. Overview of VulGML.

Detection Model. Given that a trained meta-learning model can represent the general vulnerability features of multiple meta-tasks, so when a new project needs to be detected, instead of in-domain machine learning methods to retrain the model, we only need to utilize this prior knowledge to better train specific detection tasks and obtain accurate detection results. Specifically, the samples in each new project are divided into support set and query set, of which support set is used to fine-tune the trained meta-learning model, and query set is used to evaluate the generalization ability.

3.1 Data Preparation

This section is used to obtain the dependency semantic information of each function and input it into the meta-learning model, which can reduce the detection error caused by the random initialization code embedding in meta-learning model. As shown in Fig. 3, data preparation includes obtaining the PDG by parsing source code and graph embedding by GPT-GNN.

Given the function of source code as the input, we first apply a robust parser Joern [21] to parse each function, and generate PDG of the function. The PDG of function f is denoted by $G = (V, E)$, where $V = \{v_1, \ldots, v_k\}$ is a set of nodes with each node representing a statement or control predicate, $E = \{e_1, \ldots, e_n\}$ is a set of direct edges with each edge representing a data dependency (DDG) or control dependency (CDG) between a pair of nodes.

Then, we get graph embedding using GPT-GNN. The set of node embeddings is referred to as graph embeddings, where embedding of each node fuses the dependency semantic information of adjacent nodes. GPT-GNN [8] introduces a self-supervised attributed graph generation task to pre-train a GNN, which not only avoids relying on large amounts of labeled data, but also captures the

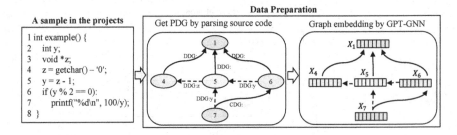

Fig. 3. The structure of data preparation for VulGML (DDG and CDG represent data and control dependencies between nodes, respectively).

inherent dependency between node attributes and graph structure for each node in the PDG. GPT-GNN calculates the attribute and edge generation for each node simultaneously. The attribute generation nodes is masked out by replacing their attributes with a dummy token and learn a shared vector to represent it. The attribute generation loss is as follows.

$$\mathcal{L}_i^{\text{Attr}} = \text{Distance}\left(Dec^{\text{Attr}}\left(h_i^{\text{Attr}}\right), X_i\right) \tag{1}$$

where h^{Attr} represents the output embeddings of attribute generation node, $Dec^{\text{Attr}}(\cdot)$ is its decoder. Its goal is to minimize the distance between the generated and masked attributes, and can capture the semantic of this PDG for nodes.

The edge generation nodes can keep their attributes and put them as input to the GNN. After getting the edge generation node representation h^{Edge}, GPT-GNN model the likelihood that node i is connected with node j by $Dec^{Edge}(\cdot)$, where Dec^{Edge} is a pairwise score function, j^+ is the linked node and S_i^- is the unconnected nodes, the loss is as follows.

$$\mathcal{L}_i^{\text{Edge}} = -\sum_{j^+ \in E_{i,-o}} L \tag{2}$$

$$L = \log \frac{\exp\left(Dec^{Edge}\left(h_i^{\text{Edge}}, h_{j^+}^{Edge}\right)\right)}{\sum_{j \in S_i^- \cup \{j^+\}} \exp\left(Dec^{Edge}\left(h_i^{\text{Edge}}, h_j^{\text{Edge}}\right)\right)} \tag{3}$$

By optimizing $\mathcal{L}^{\text{Edge}}$, it is equivalent to maximizing the likelihood of generating all the edges, and thus the pre-trained model is able to capture the intrinsic structure of the graph. By minimizing $\mathcal{L}^{\text{Attr}}$ and $\mathcal{L}^{\text{Edge}}$, GPT-GNN is optimal.

3.2   Meta Learning Model

To generalize a vulnerability detection model trained on multiple meta-tasks to new projects, we propose a meta-learning method, which involves basic network and meta-learner. Basic network is utilized to learn the vulnerability features of functions. Meta-learner is a framework that improves the generalization ability of the basic network to various vulnerability features via multiple meta-tasks. Figure 2 shows the overall structure of meta-learning. We regard each project as a task T_i, and divide the data of each task D_{T_i} into support data (defined as $D_{T_i}^{support}$) and query data (defined as $D_{T_i}^{query}$), where $D_{T_i}^{support}$ is used to train the meta-learning model, and $D_{T_i}^{query}$ is used to test the meta-learning model.

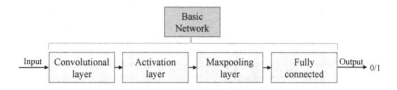

Fig. 4. Composition of the basic network.

1) Basic network. Software vulnerability detection treats source code as text processing. Text-CNN is considered effective in text classification [5], we use it as basic network for vulnerability detection. As shown in Fig. 4, the basic network includes convolutional layer, activation layer, maxpooling layer, fully connected layer. The basic network is able to automatically learn the graph embedding initialized by GPT-GNN, which can be very useful in identifying patterns and dependency semantic information within the graph.

2) Meta-learner. In this part, we aim to minimize the sum of generalization losses of overall multiple meta-tasks and optimize the model parameters with a small number of gradient steps on each meta-task. As shown in Fig. 5, the meta-learner consists of inner-learner and outer-learner.

The inner-learner is utilized to improve the ability of the basic network to capture the vulnerability features of functions in a single meta-task. It is trained with $D_{T_i}^{support}$ and feedback from corresponding loss, and then tested on $D_{T_i}^{query}$. Suppose there is a parametrized function f_θ with parameters θ. We update the parameters θ to θ^* when adapting to a new project T_i. Using one gradient update as an example, the parameters of inner-learner are updated as follows:

$$\theta_i^* = \theta - \alpha \nabla_\theta L_{T_i}(f_\theta) \tag{4}$$

where α is the learning rate of the inner-learner, and ∇ represents the operation of gradient descent.

The outer-learner enables the basic network to obtain superior generalization performance to various tasks. The updating process of the outer-learner is by optimizing the performance of $f_{\theta_i^*}$ with respect to θ across all tasks sampled from $p(T)$. The learning process is presented in the form of parameter iterative updates, i.e.,

$$\min_\theta \sum_{T_i \sim p(T)} L_{T_i}(f_{\theta_i^*}) = \sum_{T_i \sim p(T)} L_{T_i}(f_\theta - \alpha \nabla_\theta L_{T_i}(f_\theta)) \tag{5}$$

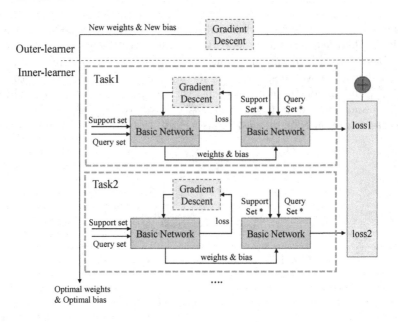

Fig. 5. Composition of meta-learner.

The optimization across tasks of outer-learner is performed via stochastic gradient descent, then the updating process for outer-learner would be simplified as follow:

$$\theta \leftarrow \theta - \beta \nabla_\theta \sum_{T_i \sim p(T)} L_{T_i}\left(f_{\theta_i^*}\right) \qquad (6)$$

where β is the learning rate of the outer-learner.

Our work can be viewed as a binary classification task to determine whether the source code is a vulnerability (labeled as 1) or a normal sample (labeled as 0). We use a cross entropy loss for the input/output pair $x^{(j)}$, $y^{(j)}$ sampled from task T_i, the loss takes the form:

$$\begin{aligned} L_{T_i}\left(f_\phi\right) = \sum_{x^{(j)},y^{(j)} \sim T_i} & y^{(j)} \log f_\phi\left(x^{(j)}\right) \\ & + \left(1 - y^{(j)}\right) \log \left(1 - f_\phi\left(x^{(j)}\right)\right) \end{aligned} \qquad (7)$$

3.3   Detection Model

This section is to apply the learned knowledge by meta-learning model to detect new projects. Figure 6 shows the vulnerability detection process. Note that the basic network used for detection in new projects is the same as shown in Fig. 4.

The new project is divided into the support set and query set, as illustrated in Fig. 2. To improve the detection performance in new projects, we utilize the optimal prior knowledge θ_0 as initialization parameters for fine-tuning in support

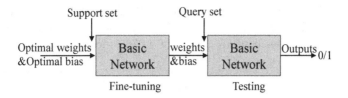

Fig. 6. The vulnerability detection process (vulnerabilities labeled 1).

set. This process yields updated weights and bias denoted as θ_{t_n}. Then, we utilize θ_{t_n} as the parameters of the detection model to assess whether samples in query set have vulnerabilities. One gradient update process is taken as an example:

$$\theta_{t_n} = \theta - \gamma \nabla_{\theta_0} L_{t_n} (f_{\theta_0}) \tag{8}$$

where L_{t_n} is the loss function in the new projects for detection, θ_0 is defined as the optimal trained parameters of the meta-learning model.

4   Evaluation

4.1   Experimental Setup

1) DataSet. The dataset is a C/C++ open source project, and other programming languages will also be considered in the future. We first crawl the vulnerabilities and its fixed functions of five projects from Cvedetails and Github websites. The application domain includes network packet analyzer, operating system kernel, software library providing safe communication, network analysis tool, and multimedia file operators, which exhibit different security concerns. The dataset and usage of five projects are shown in Table 1.

Table 1. The number of vulnerable and fixed functions in five projects

Projects (Tasks)	Vulnerabilities	Patch	Total	Usage
Wireshark	3,123	6,013	9,136	Meta-learning
Linux	473	654	1,127	Meta-learning
Openssl	57	221	278	Detection
Tcpdump	64	64	128	Detection
Ffmpeg	59	59	118	Detection

In order to measure the detection generalization of VulGML to other vulnerability types, we also collect four different vulnerability types from Cvedetails and Github websites, namely improper input validation (CWE20), improper restriction of operations within the bounds of a memory buffer (CWE119), numeric errors (CWE189) and resource management errors (CWE399). Each vulnerability type includes vulnerabilities and its fixed functions with the same ratio. Four vulnerability types contain a total of 4,676 functions. Figure 7 shows the proportion of functions.

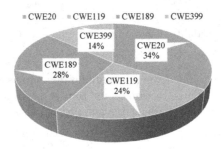

Fig. 7. The proportion of functions in four vulnerability types.

2) Metrics and setting. We measure the performance in terms of *Accuracy, Precision, Recall,* and *F1-Score.* In VulGML, the output dimension of GPT-GNN for each node embedding is 64. During training the meta-learning model, the number of Text-CNN layers in basic network is 3. The learning rate of inner-learners and outer-learner is 0.001, the optimizer is Adam, and the training batch size for each meta-iteration is 16. During the detecting procedure of the new projects, we set the learning rate as 0.001, and the fine-tuning batch size for each iteration is 16.

4.2   Experiment Results

1) Generalization of detecting vulnerabilities in new projects. In order to study the improvement of generalization in detecting vulnerabilities within new projects, we compare VulGML with five state-of-the-art baselines, including three in-domain methods (i.e. BGNN4VD [1], VulDeePecker [11] and SySeVR [10]) and two cross-domain methods (i.e. VulGDA [9] and CD-VulD [12]).

The emergence of new projects often contains potential vulnerabilities, and the number of vulnerability samples available for training in new projects is very small. We train on Wireshark and Linux (called Wireshark-Linux), which have a sufficient number of vulnerable (labeled 1) and fixed functions (labeled 0) for training. In addition, we use Openssl, Tcpdump, and Ffmpeg, which have fewer vulnerable and fixed functions, as detection tasks to evaluate the generalization of the different models. The following is the processing of the three types of methods: in-domain method, cross-domain method, and meta-learning method.

In-Domain Method. We integrate Wireshark-Linux for training the model, and use Openssl, Tcpdump, and Ffmpeg respectively to detect the generalization of the trained model. Note that when training the model, we use 80% of the

Wireshark-Linux as the training dataset and perform 5-fold cross-validation to train the models, and use the remaining 20% as the testing dataset.

Cross-Domain Method. We use Wireshark-Linux as source domain, and Openssl, Tcpdump, and Ffmpeg as the target domain respectively. The dataset in the target domain is divided into two subsets. In the case of the Openssl, we hold out 80% as labeled data of Openssl and use it with Wireshark-Linux to train the cross-domain model. Then the remaining 20% is used to detect the generalization of the model.

Meta-learning Method. We consider Wireshark-Linux as two tasks to train meta-learning model, and Openssl, Tcpdump, and Ffmpeg as new projects to evaluate the generalization of trained meta-learning model. The following describes the specific details.

During training the meta-learning model, first, we consider Wireshark-Linux as two meta-tasks and split their datasets into 80% for training (support data) and 20% for testing (query data). Second, we construct the PDG for each sample, and use GPT-GNN to generate the graph embedding. The graph embedding as input for the model training below. Third, we design Text-CNN as basic network in the inner-learner to determine whether the samples of each meta-task have vulnerabilities. Finally, we minimize the sum of generalization losses of overall meta-tasks in outer-learner, and update all the parameters in the inner-learner.

During detection stage, we evaluate the generalization performance of the trained meta-learning model on new projects, namely Tcpdump, Ffmpeg, and Rdesktop. First, we split the dataset for each new project into 90% for training (support data) and 10% for testing (query data). Second, we extract the graph embedding for each sample in the new projects (using the same method with training the meta-learning model), and use them as input for the following process. Third, the support data is used to fine-tune the trained meta-learning model. Finally, the query data is used to evaluate the generalization performance of VulGML.

Table 2 shows the performance measures when Wireshark-Linux is used for training the model and Openssl is used for detection. Here are our findings.

Table 2. Wireshark+Linux→Openssl

Approach type	Approach	Acc(%)	P(%)	R(%)	F1(%)
In-domain	BGNN4VD	50.32	47.91	54.53	52.34
	VulDeePecker	61.28	63.36	70.14	65.41
	SySeVR	67.14	65.33	69.25	68.18
Cross-domain	VulGDA	75.29	79.37	68.67	71.83
	CD-VulD	77.49	80.19	76.84	77.16
Meta-learning	VulGML	83.93	82.50	80.86	82.38

First, the generalization performance of in-domain methods is poor because new projects are not retrained and directly tested, resulting in no vulnerability features of new projects in the trained model. For example, the *Accuracy* of BGNN4VD is only 50.32%. Specifically, BGNN4VD lacks preprocessing operations on graph information, and the convolution operation on the state vectors matrix causes some important graph structure information to be lost, which may be the main reason affecting it. In addition, SySeVR-enabled BGRU is 3.12% higher than VulDeePecker in *F1-Score*. Because VulDeePecker cannot accommodate semantic information induced by control dependency.

Second, cross-domain methods outperform in-domain methods. Because domain adaptation in cross-domain methods promotes the emergence of features that are both discriminative for vulnerability detection and invariant to the shift between domains. For example, compared with SySeVR, CD-VulD achieves 8.98% improvement in *F1-Score*, showing a great improvement in reducing distribution differences between different domains. In addition, CD-VulD is 5.33% higher than VulGDA in *F1-Score*, we think that the metric transfer learning framework in CD-VulD is better than Maximum Mean Discrepancy in VulGDA in minimizing the distribution divergence between the source domain and the target domain.

Finally, our method outperforms cross-domain methods. Because cross-domain approaches for software vulnerability detection are limited to one source domain (i.e., train on a single project, and detect on another project). For multiple projects, the ability to generate general vulnerability features between multiple tasks needs to be improved. Our approach VulGML achieves 6.44%, 2.31%, 4.02% and 5.22% improvement in *Accuracy, Precision, Recall* and *F1-Score* respectively, showing the strong generalization in software vulnerability detection.

Table 3. Wireshark+Linux→Tcpdump

Approach type	Approach	Acc(%)	P(%)	R(%)	F1(%)
In-domain	BGNN4VD	51.01	48.15	54.41	52.62
	VulDeePecker	61.46	63.57	70.97	65.15
	SySeVR	66.19	66.76	70.84	68.27
Cross-domain	VulGDA	75.11	79.23	69.41	73.00
	CD-VulD	79.97	81.77	77.59	78.75
Meta-learning	VulGML	83.29	82.95	81.18	82.22

To further illustrate the generalization of VulGML to other new projects besides Openssl, we detect Tcpdump and Ffmpeg in Table 3 and Table 4, respectively. Compared with the best method on Tcpdump in Table 3, VulGML achieves 3.47% improvement in *F1-Score*. Similarly, for detecting the Ffmpeg in Table 4, VulGML achieves 3.55% improvement in *F1-Score*. These detection

Table 4. Wireshark+Linux→Ffmpeg

Approach type	Approach	Acc(%)	P(%)	R(%)	F1(%)
In-domain	BGNN4VD	50.09	48.80	53.72	51.84
	VulDeePecker	62.70	62.08	71.90	66.99
	SySeVR	67.75	65.65	68.38	68.06
Cross-domain	VulGDA	74.20	78.63	69.55	71.80
	CD-VulD	79.11	80.60	77.89	78.50
Meta-learning	VulGML	83.01	82.11	81.14	82.05

results show that our method can also generalize to other new projects. Additionally, we also found that the results of VulGDA and CD-VulD in our experiments are higher than those shown in the original paper [9,12]. This is mainly because the vulnerabilities types present in the detection projects (i.e., e Openssl, Tcpdump, and Ffmpeg) are also encompassed in the meta-learning projects (i.e., Wireshark and Linux).

2) Generalization of detecting vulnerabilities with new vulnerability types. To further illustrate the strong generalization to vulnerabilities with new vulnerability types, we use the vulnerabilities with CWE20 and CWE189 for training the meta-learning model, and CWE119 and CWE399 for detection, respectively. The experiments indicate that this work is more challenging than *1)*.

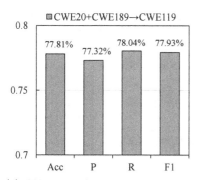

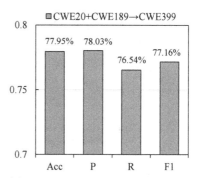

(a) CWE20 and CWE189 for meta-learning, and CWE119 for detection.

(b) CWE20 and CWE189 for meta-learning and CWE399 for detection.

Fig. 8. Generalization of detecting vulnerabilities with new vulnerability types.

Figure 8(a) shows the performance measures when using CWE119 to detect generalization. The *F1-Score* of it is 77.93%, lower than detecting a new project Ffmpeg which is 82.05%. Similarly, The *F1-Score* of CWE399 in Fig. 8(b) is 4.89% lower than detecting a new project Ffmpeg. Because different projects might have varying distributions due to factors like application scenarios and coding styles. However, vulnerabilities in different projects might belong to the same vulnerability type. For example, both Wireshark and Tcpdump may have vulnerabilities of the CWE119, which results in similar aspects of vulnerability features across different projects. But different vulnerability types come from different projects and represent different vulnerability features, so the common features that meta-learning can learn will be less. In addition, the detection generalization effect of CWE119 is slightly better than that of CWE399. We think that the reason may be that the data of CWE119 is 10% more than that of CWE399, so the fine-tune is more powerful.

Overall, despite the distinct features of different vulnerability types, VulGML still demonstrates strong generalization performance in detecting vulnerabilities with different vulnerability types. For instance, As shown in Fig. 8(a), after training on vulnerabilities with CWE20 and CWE189 and detecting on vulnerabilities with CWE119, the values of *Accuracy, Precision, Recall,* and *F1-Score* achieve 77.81%, 77.32%, 78.04%, and 77.93%, respectively.

3) Gain of Proposed Methods. To measure the effect gain of using graph embedding and meta-learning, we evaluate the detection generalization of VulGML with a single method, i.e., word2vec [13] instead of GPT-GNN to represent the initial graph embedding of each sample, or Text-CNN instead of meta-learning to train the vulnerability detection model. The results show that the effect is much lower than that of VulGML.

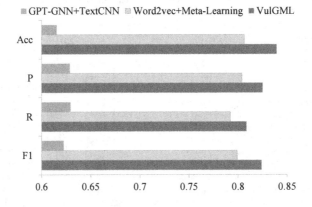

Fig. 9. The gain of proposed methods.

Figure 9 shows the detection results on Openssl using trained model by Wireshark-Linux. We found that the effect gain of using graph embedding is up to 3.28%, 2.10%, 1.63%, 2.45% in *Accuracy, Precision, Recall,* and *F1-Score* respectively, which means that graph structured information can better represent dependency semantic information. In addition, the effect gain of using meta-learning is up to 22.39%, 19.63%, 17.93%, 20.15% in *Accuracy, Precision, Recall,* and *F1-Score* respectively, which shows that our meta-learning model can detect new projects based on existing multiple meta-tasks. In conclusion, VulGML uses graph embedding and meta-learning to effectively enhance the generalization of the model and improve the vulnerability detection ability.

5 Conclusion

To leverage previous learning experience to learn new projects faster, this paper presents VulGML, a vulnerability detection approach using graph embedding and meta-learning. The goal is to establish a model with strong generalization, so that the model trained on multiple meta-tasks can detect vulnerabilities in new projects. To illustrate the strong generalization to new projects, we choose two projects as two meta-tasks for training the meta-learning model and a new project for vulnerability detection. Furthermore, we also analyze the generalization effect of the model learned based on existing vulnerability types to new vulnerabilities with new vulnerability types. The experimental results show that VulGML outperforms state-of-the-art in-domain and cross-domain methods when multiple meta-tasks as input, and its modules have greatly improved detection performance. However, VulGML is not a perfect vulnerability detection method, and the following are its limitations as well as our future work.

This paper focuses on training and detecting C/C++ programs. VulGML is a generic solution, and exploring vulnerability detection in other programming languages will be an interesting work for future research. Additionally, the effectiveness of VulGML on datasets beyond those used in this paper remains to be validated. In the experiments, neural network parameters are set to default values or widely used values within the deep learning community. Adjusting these parameters in the future may lead to improved experimental results.

Acknowledgement. This work is supported by the National Natural Science Foundation of China under Grant 61972392, Grant 62072453 and Grant 62202462.

References

1. Cao, S., Sun, X., Bo, L., Wei, Y., Li, B.: BGNN4VD: constructing bidirectional graph neural-network for vulnerability detection. Inf. Softw. Technol. **136**, 106576 (2021)
2. Chakraborty, S., Krishna, R., Ding, Y., Ray, B.: Deep learning based vulnerability detection: are we there yet. IEEE Trans. Softw. Eng. (2021)
3. CVEDetails. https://www.cvedetails.com/
4. Dey, R., Salem, F.M.: Gate-variants of gated recurrent unit (GRU) neural networks. In: 2017 IEEE 60th International Midwest Symposium on Circuits and Systems (MWSCAS), pp. 1597–1600. IEEE (2017)
5. Dharma, E.M., Gaol, F.L., Warnars, H., Soewito, B.: The accuracy comparison among word2vec, glove, and fasttext towards convolution neural network (CNN) text classification. J. Theor. Appl. Inf. Technol. **100**(2), 31 (2022)
6. Dowd, M., McDonald, J., Schuh, J.: The Art of Software Security Assessment: Identifying and Preventing Software Vulnerabilities. Pearson Education (2006)

7. Guo, W., Fang, Y., Huang, C., Ou, H., Lin, C., Guo, Y.: HyVulDect: a hybrid semantic vulnerability mining system based on graph neural network. Comput. Secur. 102823 (2022)
8. Hu, Z., Dong, Y., Wang, K., Chang, K.W., Sun, Y.: GPT-GNN: generative pre-training of graph neural networks. In: Proceedings of the 26th ACM SIGKDD International Conference on Knowledge Discovery & Data Mining, pp. 1857–1867 (2020)
9. Li, X., Xin, Y., Zhu, H., Yang, Y., Chen, Y.: Cross-domain vulnerability detection using graph embedding and domain adaptation. Comput. Secur. 125, 103017 (2023)
10. Li, Z., Zou, D., Xu, S., Jin, H., Zhu, Y., Chen, Z.: SySeVR: a framework for using deep learning to detect software vulnerabilities. IEEE Trans. Dependable Secure Comput. 19(4), 2244–2258 (2021)
11. Li, Z., et al.: VulDeePecker: a deep learning-based system for vulnerability detection. arXiv preprint arXiv:1801.01681 (2018)
12. Liu, S., et al.: CD-VulD: cross-domain vulnerability discovery based on deep domain adaptation. IEEE Trans. Dependable Secure Comput. 19(1), 438–451 (2020)
13. Mikolov, T., Chen, K., Corrado, G., Dean, J.: Efficient estimation of word representations in vector space. arXiv preprint arXiv:1301.3781 (2013)
14. Nam, J., Pan, S.J., Kim, S.: Transfer defect learning. In: 2013 35th International Conference on Software Engineering (ICSE), pp. 382–391. IEEE (2013)
15. Nguyen, V.A., Nguyen, D.Q., Nguyen, V., Le, T., Tran, Q.H., Phung, D.: ReGVD: revisiting graph neural networks for vulnerability detection. In: Proceedings of the ACM/IEEE 44th International Conference on Software Engineering: Companion Proceedings, pp. 178–182 (2022)
16. NVD. https://nvd.nist.gov/
17. Wang, H., et al.: Combining graph-based learning with automated data collection for code vulnerability detection. IEEE Trans. Inf. Forensics Secur. 16, 1943–1958 (2020)
18. Wartschinski, L., Noller, Y., Vogel, T., Kehrer, T., Grunske, L.: VUDENC: vulnerability detection with deep learning on a natural codebase for Python. Inf. Softw. Technol. 144, 106809 (2022)
19. Wu, Y., Zou, D., Dou, S., Yang, W., Xu, D., Jin, H.: VulCNN: an image-inspired scalable vulnerability detection system. In: Proceedings of the 44th International Conference on Software Engineering, pp. 2365–2376 (2022)
20. Xu, Y., et al.: A unified framework for metric transfer learning. IEEE Trans. Knowl. Data Eng. 29(6), 1158–1171 (2017)
21. Yamaguchi, F., Golde, N., Arp, D., Rieck, K.: Modeling and discovering vulnerabilities with code property graphs. In: 2014 IEEE Symposium on Security and Privacy, pp. 590–604. IEEE (2014)
22. Zha, D., Lai, K.H., Wan, M., Hu, X.: Meta-AAD: active anomaly detection with deep reinforcement learning. In: 2020 IEEE International Conference on Data Mining (ICDM), pp. 771–780. IEEE (2020)
23. Zhang, L., et al.: CBGRU: a detection method of smart contract vulnerability based on a hybrid model. Sensors 22(9), 3577 (2022)
24. Zhou, Y., Liu, S., Siow, J., Du, X., Liu, Y.: Devign: effective vulnerability identification by learning comprehensive program semantics via graph neural networks. In: Advances in Neural Information Processing Systems, vol. 32 (2019)

HeatC: A Variable-Grained Coverage Criterion for Deep Learning Systems

Weidi Sun, Yuteng Lu, Xiaokun Luan, and Meng Sun[✉]

School of Mathematical Sciences, Peking University, Beijing, China
{weidisun,luyuteng,lxk_5826,sunm}@pku.edu.cn

Abstract. Deep learning (DL) systems have achieved significant success in numerous cutting-edge fields. However, the deployment of DL systems in safety-critical areas has raised public concerns about their correctness and robustness. To provide testing evidence for the dependable behavior of Deep Neural Networks (DNNs), various DL coverage criteria have been proposed. These coverage criteria are often "ad-hoc" in terms of granularity for different tasks, but designing appropriate criteria for every possible usage scenario is infeasible and will make the coverage testing lack of uniform standards. In this paper, we proposes a variable-grained DL coverage criterion named HeatC as a common solution for different coverage testing tasks. HeatC leverages class-activation-map-based features from neural networks and clusters these features to generate test targets. Experiments demonstrate that HeatC outperforms existing mainstream coverage criteria in assessing the adequacy of test suites and selecting high-value test samples from unlabeled datasets.

Keywords: Neural networks · HeatC · Testing · Coverage criteria

1 Introduction

Deep Neural Networks (DNNs) are increasingly becoming popular for their ability to handle a wide range of tasks in various domains, such as autonomous driving [5], natural language processing [23], and climate science [8]. However, the growing applications of DNNs have set higher demands on their behavior reliability. Recent accidents involving autonomous vehicles [10] have further emphasized the urgent need for improved assurance evaluation practices for DNN systems. The efforts made to guarantee the trustworthiness of DNNs mainly focus on five aspects: verification [6], testing [21,29], adversarial attack [14,22], defense [4,9], and interpretability [2,18]. Among these aspects, testing is one of the best ways to ensure the adequacy of DNNs, considering the balance between completeness and efficiency. However, quantifying DNNs' test adequacy is challenging as their behavior cannot be explicitly encoded into control flow structures [24].

To address this challenge, various coverage criteria have been proposed to evaluate the adequacy of a test suite for a DNN. The first coverage criterion, Neuron Coverage (NC) [20], is inspired by code coverage in software testing and

H. Hermanns et al. (Eds.): SETTA 2023, LNCS 14464, pp. 243–261, 2024.
https://doi.org/10.1007/978-981-99-8664-4_14

calculates the ratio of activated neurons during test execution. The follow-up studies are IDC [7], NBC, SNAC, KMNC [17], which partition the output value range of neurons into buckets and calculate the activated bucket ratio, and 2-way coverage [16], MC/DC neuron coverage [28], 3-way coverage [25], INC [27], which analyze interactions between neurons in adjacent layers or all neurons. Additionally, TKNC [17] evaluates the ratio of top-k neurons, while SC [11] measures the relative novelty of test inputs with respect to the training set. These coverage criteria are crucial in assessing the adequacy of test suites for DNNs, enabling better reliability of these systems in industrial domains.

However, these existing coverage criteria are "ad-hoc" in terms of granularity. For example, NC is designed to guide the gradient optimization in DeepXplore whitebox testing framework [21]. It underachieves in test adequacy evaluation due to its coarse granularity. The coarse-grained coverage criteria have a small number of "test targets" which makes them easy to satisfy and cannot capture the subtle differences between different test suites. DeepCT [16] and 3-way coverage [25] are designed for test adequacy evaluation, they are too fine-grained to select a small number of high-value test inputs. Since fine-grained coverage criteria have a large number of test targets, they cannot determine the exploration priorities of uncovered cases. In the case of selecting a small number of samples, each input covers a large number of targets, that makes it difficult to decide which input is more valuable. Different application fields require coverage criteria with different levels of granularity. However, designing appropriate criteria for every possible usage is complicated and difficult, which needs a huge amount of manual labor and will make the coverage testing lack of uniform standards.

In this paper, we present a variable-grained DL coverage criterion named HeatC. To provide a common solution for different coverage testing tasks, HeatC generates variable-grained test targets from benchmark datasets (usually the training set). These class activation mapping based test targets are named *heat feature buckets*, which combine the attention of the neural networks and the features of inputs to reflect the behaviors of DNNs. HeatC computes the covered ratio of heat feature buckets to evaluate the test adequacy and utilizes the representative samples from heat feature buckets to form high-quality test suites. We evaluate HeatC and other mainstream coverage criteria comprehensively to show that HeatC performs better than existing works in assessing test adequacy and test sample selection. The evaluation is based on two publicly available datasets (Fashion-MNIST [31] and CIFAR-10 [13]) and 10 representative DNNs.

The main contributions of this paper are as follows:

- We propose the variable-grained coverage criterion HeatC to provide a common solution for different coverage testing tasks.
- We design the test adequacy evaluation and test sample selection methods for HeatC.
- We analyze HeatC and other mainstream criteria on 2 public datasets and 10 representative DNNs. The experiments show that HeatC is superior to existing works in test adequacy evaluation and test sample selection.

The rest of this paper is organized as follows. Section 2 introduces the class activation mapping which is the foundation of HeatC. Then we present the workflow of HeatC in Sect. 3. Section 4 evaluates HeatC and other mainstream coverage criteria in two aspects: test adequacy evaluation and test sample selection. Finally, Sect. 5 summarizes this paper.

2   Class Activation Mapping

Class Activation Mapping (CAM) indicates the features contributing to neural networks' prediction. It is a vector with values ranging from 0 to 1 at each position, which is also known as class heat map, saliency map, etc. A high score in CAM means that the corresponding feature has a high response and contribution to the network's prediction (Fig. 1).

Fig. 1. CAM shows the main prediction basis of DL systems

The first CAM is proposed by Zhou et al. in [33] based on the global average pooling (GAP) of neural networks. GAP [15] is a pooling operation commonly used in deep learning architectures which computes the average value of each feature map across its spatial dimensions to capture global context and spatial relationships while preserving spatial invariance. Zhou et al. define the CAM by the equation:

$$M(x,y) = \sum_k w_k f_k(x,y)$$

where $M(x,y)$ is the value of CAM at position (x,y), w_k is the weight connecting GAP's k-th output channel and the neuron of the predicted class, f_k is the k-th input channel of GAP. This CAM generation method requires GAP layer in the network architecture, but not all models are equipped with GAP layer.

To overcome this defect, Selvaraju et al. [26] present Grad-CAM which replaces the weight in CAM with the average gradients of the target channels. The workflow of Grad-CAM can be divided into two steps. In the first step,

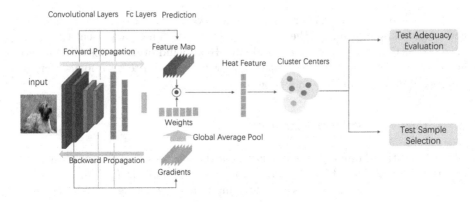

Fig. 2. Overview of HeatC coverage criterion

Grad-CAM calculates the gradients of given channels via back-propagation and obtains the importance weights by using the equation:

$$\alpha_k^c = \frac{1}{Z} \sum_i \sum_j \frac{\partial y^c}{\partial A_{i,j}^k}$$

where α_k^c is the weight corresponding to channel k and prediction class c, Z is the number of neurons in the channel k, $\frac{\partial y^c}{\partial A_{i,j}^k}$ is the gradient of class c's score with respect to each neuron in channel k. Grad-CAM applies global average pooling to gradients instead of channels. In the second step, Grad-CAM multiplies weights with corresponding channels and follow it with a ReLU function:

$$L_{Grad-CAM}^c = ReLU(\sum_k \alpha_k^c A^k)$$

Chattopadhay et al. [1] and Omeiza et al. [19] propose Grad-CAM++ and Smooth Grad-CAM++, respectively, to improve the calculation of weights in Grad-CAM. Some other CAM generation methods do not rely on gradients. For example, Wang et al. [30] present Score-CAM based on Channel-wise Increase of Confidence (CIC) and Desai et al. [3] propose Ablation-CAM based on ablation study. In this paper, we extract the features based on CAM to reflect the behaviors of DL systems for specific inputs, especially the subtle behaviors that are vulnerable to adversarial attacks.

3   HeatC Coverage Criterion

In this section, we present our HeatC coverage criterion. To provide a common solution for different tasks, HeatC generates variable-grained test targets from benchmark datasets (usually the training set). The workflow of HeatC is shown in Fig. 2, which can be divided into two parts:

Algorithm 1. Algorithm for generating heat feature

1: **Input:** set of activation results D
2: **Output:** heat features $HeatF$
3: $HeatF = \varnothing$
4: **for** each A in D **do**
5:     $A = A.\text{reshape}(A.\text{batch\_size},-1)$
6:     $HeatF.\text{connect}(A)$
7: **end for**
8: **Return** $HeatF$

- extracting the heat features and clustering them to generate the heat feature buckets,
- using the heat feature buckets to evaluate test adequacy or selecting high-value test samples from the unlabeled dataset.

We introduce these two parts in the following subsections.

3.1 Generation of Heat Feature Buckets

Heat feature buckets are the test targets of HeatC. A heat feature bucket can be denoted as a tuple (O, r) where O is a cluster center of heat features and r is the given radius of the bucket. One heat feature bucket (O, r) is covered by an input set when there exists at least one sample whose feature f falls into (O, r). In other words, the distance between f and O is less than r. The generation of heat feature buckets can be divided into three steps.

The first step is to extract heat features. For each sample in a given dataset, HeatC extracts the specified intermediate results from different layers of DNNs. It then calculates the gradients of these results with respect to the prediction results via backward propagation. The intermediate results and the corresponding gradients are denoted as vector R and G in shape $B \times C \times W \times H$ where B is the batch size, C is the number of channels, W and H are the width and height of channels. We apply the global average pool to G to get the channel weights ω by the following equation.

$$\omega_{b,k} = \frac{1}{W \times H} \sum_i \sum_j G_{b,k,i,j}$$

Then we merge ω and R linearly to get the activation result A.

$$A_{b,k,i,j} = \omega_{b,k} R_{b,k,i,j}$$

Finally, we flatten the activation results and connect them to get the one-dimensional heat features for each input as shown in Algorithm 1.

The distance of the heat feature is defined as follows.

Definition 1 (Distance of heat feature). *Each heat feature $HeatF$ can be divided into slices $HeatF_k = HeatF[i_k : j_k]$ which come from different intermediate results of a DNN. In this paper, we treat each layer's heat feature as a slice*

Algorithm 2. Algorithm for heat feature cluster

1: **Input:** heat feature bucket radius θ, benchmark dataset D, neural network N, convergence parameters ϵ
2: **Output:** heat feature cluster centers C
3: $A_D = N(D).\text{heat\_feature}$
4: $Buckets = \varnothing$
5: $Selected = \varnothing$
6: **while** $(A_D \setminus Selected) \neq \varnothing$ **do**
7: 　　$center = $ select one feature from $A_D \setminus Selected$ randomly
8: 　　**while** True **do**
9: 　　　　$temp\_dis = \text{Dis}(center, A_D)$
10: 　　　　$candidate = \varnothing$
11: 　　　　**for** each $d \in temp\_dis$ and the corresponding $A \in A_D$ **do**
12: 　　　　　　**if** $d < \theta$ **then**
13: 　　　　　　　　$candidate.\text{add}(A)$
14: 　　　　　　**end if**
15: 　　　　**end for**
16: 　　　　$new\_center = \dfrac{\sum_{A' \in candidate} A'}{|candidate|}$
17: 　　　　**if** $(\exists c \in Buckets : \text{Dis}(c, new\_center) < \frac{\theta}{2}) \vee (\text{Dis}(center, new\_center) < \epsilon)$
　　then
18: 　　　　　　$Selected.\text{add}(candidate)$
19: 　　　　　　$Buckets.\text{add}(center)$
20: 　　　　　　break
21: 　　　　**else**
22: 　　　　　　$center = new\_center$
23: 　　　　**end if**
24: 　　**end while**
25: **end while**
26: **Return** $Buckets$

---

of the whole heat feature. Given two heat features $HeatF_1$, $HeatF_2$, and a slice weight α, the distance of $HeatF_1$, $HeatF_2$ can be denoted as

$$Dis(HeatF_1, HeatF_2) = \sum_k \alpha_k ||HeatF_{1,k} - HeatF_{2,k}||_1$$

which is the weighted sum of slices' L_1 distance. The α_k in this paper is $\dfrac{k}{Len(HeatF_{1,k})}$.

In the second step, HeatC decides the radius of the heat feature buckets based on a given radius parameter θ ($0 < \theta < 1$). We select m pairs of heat features extracted from the benchmark dataset. We then calculate their distances and sort these distances in ascending order. With the radius parameter θ, we choose the $\lfloor \theta m \rfloor$-th distance as the radius of the heat feature bucket. A bigger θ leads to a smaller radius, which means that the coverage targets, i.e., the heat feature buckets are finer-grained.

In the third step, Algorithm 2 finds the heat feature buckets based on the mean-shift algorithm. Algorithm 2 calculates the heat features of all samples in the benchmark dataset in line 3. The cluster center set *Buckets* and the processed feature set *Selected* are initialized in line 4 and line 5, respectively. Line 7 randomly selects one sample from the unprocessed features as a temporary cluster center (bucket center) until all samples are processed. Line 9 computes the distance between the temporary center and all features. Line 10 to line 15 find the features in the bucket of the temporary center (the distance between these features and the temporary center is less than the given bucket radius θ). Line 16 calculates the average of these features as the new center. If this new center is close to existing bucket centers or satisfies the convergence condition, line 18 to 20 adds the *candidate* and the *center* to the processed feature set and the bucket center set. Or rather, line 22 updates the *center* and Algorithm 2 starts a new loop from line 8 to line 24. Line 26 returns the result.

3.2   Test Adequacy Evaluation and Test Sample Selection

In this subsection, we present the second part of HeatC, i.e., the heat feature buckets based implementation of test adequacy evaluation and test sample selection.

Test adequacy evaluation of HeatC treats the heat feature buckets as the test targets. Given a benchmark data set and a test suite, HeatC calculates the heat feature buckets of the benchmark set and uses the test suite to cover these buckets. For a bucket b_i with center o_i and the radius r, if a test sample with feature s covers b_i, it must satisfy the following two conditions:

- For all uncovered buckets, s is closest to o_i.
- The distance between s and o_i is less than r.

Then we use the test samples which cannot cover any bucket to generate new heat feature buckets. The HeatC score can be defined as

$$HeatC_{score} = \frac{\nu + \mu}{\lambda + \mu}$$

where ν is the number of covered buckets from the benchmark dataset, μ is the number of newly generated buckets from the test suite, λ is the number of all buckets generated by the benchmark data set. The details of the test adequacy evaluation are shown in Algorithm 3.

In Algorithm 3, line 1 and line 2 declare the inputs and the output. Line 3 generates the bucket set B and the corresponding radius r of the benchmark data set. Line 4 extracts the heat feature F_T of the test data set. Line 5 initializes the tensor *InBucket* which records the test samples falling into the buckets in B. Line 6 calculates the distance matrix $BFDis$; each variable $BFDis[i, j]$ in $BFDis$ represents the distance between i-th bucket in B and j-th feature in F_T. Line 7 initializes the variable ν recording the number of covered buckets. For each row in $BFDis$, line 9 marks the samples falling into the buckets. Line 11

Algorithm 3. Algorithm for generating HeatC score

1: **Input:** benchmark data set D, test set T, neural network N, radius parameter θ
2: **Output:** $HeatC_{score}$
3: $B, r = \text{HeatB}(N,D,\theta)$
4: $F_T = \text{HeatF}(N,T)$
5: $InBucket = [\textbf{FALSE}]*\text{len(T)}$
6: $BFDis = \text{Dis}(B,F_T)$
7: $\nu = 0$
8: **for** i, d in enumerate($BFDis$) **do**
9:      $judge = (d < r)$
10:      **if** sum($judge$)> 0 **then**
11:          $j = \text{argmin}(d)$
12:          assign $+\infty$ to column j in $BFDis$
13:          $InBucket = InBucket \lor judge$
14:          $\nu + = 1$
15:      **end if**
16: **end for**
17: $B_{out} = \text{HeatB'}(N,T[\neg InBucket])$
18: $HeatC_{score} = \frac{\nu + |B_{out}|}{|B| + |B_{out}|}$
19: **Return** $HeatC_{score}$

---

selects the sample closet to $B[i]$; line 12 drops the feature having been used. Line 13 and 14 update the $InBucket$ and ν. Line 17 generates the buckets with the fixed radius for test samples out of B's buckets. Line 18 calculates the HashC score and Line 19 returns the result.

Test sample selection approach of HeatC is designed to select a given size test suite that is as adequate as possible. HeatC distributes the selected samples evenly among the test targets during selecting a small size test suite from a big unlabeled data set. In this way, the test suite can 1) enrich the features explored by the test suite, 2) prevent similar samples from wasting the places in the test suite. The workflow of HeatC's test sample selection is shown in Algorithm 4.

Algorithm 4 is introduced in detail as follows. Line 3 in Algorithm 4 contains a function $HeatB_S$ which generates the buckets of unlabeled data set D and returns the samples divided by these buckets. The list S consists of sample sets; the samples in each set fall into one bucket. Line 4 initializes the output test suite T. Line 5 to line 21 is a loop which selects the test samples one at a time. The variable m in line 5 represents the number of test samples to select. If m is greater than the number of buckets, line 6 to line 13 updates the m, pops one sample from each bucket and adds them to T, and finally removes the empty sets from S. Otherwise, line 14 to line 20 selects some buckets and adds their samples to T. It should be noted that our mean-shift based algorithm tends to put the adjacent buckets in adjacent positions in S. Thus, we select buckets at intervals of $\lfloor \frac{|B|}{m} \rfloor$ in S to make the selection more even. Line 22 returns the test suite T as the result.

Algorithm 4. Algorithm for test sample selection

1: **Input:** unlabeled data set D, neural network N, radius parameter θ, test suite size m
2: **Output:** test suite T
3: $S = HeatB_S(N,D,\theta)$
4: $T = \varnothing$
5: **while** $m > 0$ **do**
6:    **if** $m > |B|$ **then**
7:      $m\text{-}=|B|$
8:      **for** $bucket$ in S **do**
9:        $T.\text{add}(bucket.\text{pop}())$
10:        **if** $bucket = \varnothing$ **then**
11:          $S.\text{remove}(bucket)$
12:        **end if**
13:      **end for**
14:    **else**
15:      $step = \lfloor \frac{|B|}{m} \rfloor$
16:      **for** i in range(m) **do**
17:        $T.\text{add}(B[i * step].\text{pop}())$
18:      **end for**
19:      $m = 0$
20:    **end if**
21: **end while**
22: **Return** T

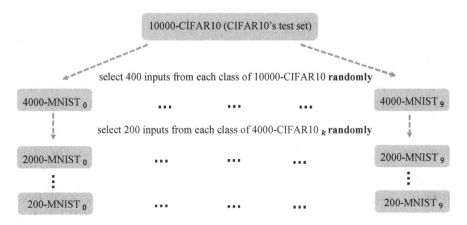

Fig. 3. The generation of test suites

4 Evaluation

In this section we compare HeatC with mainstream coverage criteria on two aspects:

– the sensibility in distinguishing test suites with different adequacies,

– the performance in selecting high-quality test suite from unlabeled dataset.

All the experiments are implemented on the Pytorch framework [12] and conducted on a GPU server. The server has 4 Xeon Gold 5118 2.30 GHz CPUs, 24 GB system memory, and 1 NVIDIA Titan XP GPU.

4.1   Experiment Design

We design two experiments. In ***Experiment 1***, we chose θ as 0.994 because we conducted multiple preliminary experiments ranging from 0.99 to 0.999. As θ increases, the time cost also increases, and we found that a granularity of 0.994 strikes a balance between evaluating effectiveness and time cost. In ***Experiment 2***, we selected θ as 0.99 because a coarser granularity of coverage criteria is beneficial for test case selection. This demonstrates the versatility of variable granularity for different tasks.

Experiment 1 compares HeatC with HashC, SC, NC, and KMNC. The hyperparameters of these coverage criteria are as follows:

– The activation threshold t of NC and HashC is set to 0.
– The k of KMNC is set to 4.
– The surprise metric of SC is L_2 and other parameters are the same as in [11]. SC analyzes the second to the last layer in DNNs.

We compare HeatC with HashC, KMNC, NC and SC by evaluating two series of synthetic test suites with different adequacies to show that HeatC is more sensitive. The comparison is deployed on five kinds of DNNs including LeNet-5, AlexNet, GoogLeNet, MobileNet, and ResNet18. All these DNNs are trained by Fashion-MNIST and CIFAR10. The two series of test suites are selected from the test sets of Fashion-MNIST and CIFAR10. For example, we first regard CIFAR10's test set as 10000-CIFAR10. The 4000-CIFAR10$_k$s select 400 inputs from each class of 10000-CIFAR10 randomly (CIFAR10 has ten classes), thus, 10000-CIFAR10 is the father of 4000-CIFAR10$_k$s. Then 2000-CIFAR10$_k$ selects 200 inputs from each class of its "father" 4000-CIFAR10$_k$. The other series of test suites are i-Fashion-MNISTs which are generated in the same way as i-CIFAR10s. These test sets' adequacies are different. The adequacies of i-CIFAR10$_k$s (i-Fashion-MNIST$_k$s) are in ascending order of i. For example, 4000-CIFAR10$_k$ is more adequate than 2000-CIFAR10$_k$, because 2000-CIFAR10$_k$ is a subset of 4000-CIFAR10$_k$. We take ten i-CIFAR10$_k$s' (i-Fashion-MNIST$_k$s') average coverage score to represent i-CIFAR10's (i-Fashion-MNIST's) score so as to eliminate the random error. The process for generating i-CIFAR10s, which is also the same process used for generating i-Fashion-MNIST, is illustrated in Fig. 3.

We use coverage criteria to assess the adequacy of different test suites, demonstrating the sensitivity of coverage criteria. An ideal sensitive coverage criterion should be able to give a lower score to test suites with lower adequacy, a higher score to test suites with higher adequacy, and provide as large a difference in

Table 1. Coverage scores of i-Fashion-MNISTs

		i-Fashion-MNISTs					
		200	500	1000	2000	4000	10000
HashC	AlexNet	0.0799	0.1355	0.1656	0.1866	0.3625	0.4318
HeatC		0.2574	0.3504	0.4322	0.5148	0.6113	0.7478
NC		0.9934	0.9959	0.9969	0.9978	0.9984	0.9987
KMNC		0.9878	0.9922	0.9943	0.9958	0.9970	0.9979
SC		0.1711	0.3447	0.5050	0.6449	0.7326	0.8250
HashC	GoogLeNet	0.2816	0.4076	0.4462	0.4639	0.9199	0.9594
HeatC		0.1431	0.2123	0.2842	0.3723	0.4896	0.6654
NC		0.9999	0.9999	1.0000	1.0000	1.0000	1.0000
KMNC		0.9986	0.9997	0.9999	0.9999	1.0000	1.0000
SC		0.1507	0.2767	0.3848	0.4935	0.5774	0.6630
HashC	LeNet-5	0.1766	0.2813	0.3311	0.3587	0.6685	0.7634
HeatC		0.2178	0.2862	0.3520	0.4257	0.5224	0.6382
NC		0.9859	0.9872	0.9884	0.9897	0.9906	0.9912
KMNC		0.9801	0.9843	0.9862	0.9875	0.9887	0.9898
SC		0.1708	0.3520	0.5398	0.7022	0.8181	0.9200
HashC	MobileNet	0.2972	0.4024	0.4399	0.4608	0.9103	0.9545
HeatC		0.1585	0.2239	0.2977	0.3778	0.4676	0.6307
NC		0.9999	1.0000	1.0000	1.0000	1.0000	1.0000
KMNC		0.9999	1.0000	1.0000	1.0000	1.0000	1.0000
SC		0.1535	0.2777	0.3615	0.4127	0.4541	0.4990
HashC	ResNet18	0.2407	0.3410	0.3834	0.4073	0.8018	0.8653
HeatC		0.1352	0.2238	0.3176	0.4130	0.5184	0.6552
NC		0.9997	0.9998	0.9999	0.9999	0.9999	1.0000
KMNC		0.9985	0.9994	0.9997	0.9998	0.9999	0.9999
SC		0.1530	0.2715	0.3585	0.4230	0.4660	0.5200

scores as possible between test suites with different adequacy levels to distinguish them.

Experiment 2 is designed for evaluating the performance of HeatC and mainstream coverage criteria in selecting high-quality test suites from unlabeled datasets. In this experiment, we use HeatC and other mainstream coverage criteria to select test suites based on different DNNs. All these test suites are selected from a synthetic unlabeled dataset which is generated as follows:

- Selecting 1000 source samples from the original dataset (e.g., the training set of Fashion-MNIST or CIFAR10).
- Applying data augmentation to the 1000 selected samples to get 10000 samples which form the synthetic unlabeled dataset. The data augmentation techniques include rotation, translation, cropping, adding noise, etc.

Table 2. Coverage scores of i-CIFAR10s

		i-CIFAR10s					
		200	500	1000	2000	4000	10000
HashC	AlexNet	0.3744	0.4762	0.4908	0.4955	0.9889	0.9966
HeatC		0.1486	0.2221	0.292	0.3823	0.4827	0.6265
NC		0.9965	0.9989	0.9995	0.9998	0.9999	1
KMNC		0.9999	1	1	1	1	1
SC		0.1609	0.3078	0.4244	0.5155	0.5767	0.642
HashC	GoogLeNet	0.3414	0.462	0.4836	0.4922	0.9787	0.9931
HeatC		0.1439	0.2662	0.3971	0.5468	0.6901	0.8153
NC		0.9998	0.9999	1	1	1	1
KMNC		0.9992	0.9997	0.9999	0.9999	1	1
SC		0.1248	0.2057	0.2745	0.3337	0.3758	0.418
HashC	LeNet-5	0.3138	0.4208	0.4583	0.4745	0.9371	0.978
HeatC		0.1166	0.1844	0.2519	0.3371	0.4426	0.5818
NC		0.9948	0.996	0.9968	0.9974	0.9979	0.9982
KMNC		0.9932	0.9945	0.9954	0.9962	0.9969	0.9975
SC		0.1511	0.267	0.355	0.4412	0.5304	0.6237
HashC	MobileNet	0.4262	0.4939	0.4992	0.4999	0.999	0.9999
HeatC		0.1383	0.2093	0.2881	0.3768	0.4783	0.6203
NC		1	1	1	1	1	1
KMNC		0.9998	1	1	1	1	1
SC		0.1291	0.2036	0.2488	0.2917	0.3364	0.394
HashC	ResNet18	0.312	0.4499	0.4784	0.4923	0.9724	0.9887
HeatC		0.1722	0.2611	0.3375	0.4292	0.5296	0.6852
NC		1	1	1	1	1	1
KMNC		0.999	0.9997	0.9999	1	1	1
SC		0.1334	0.2125	0.2711	0.3231	0.366	0.417

The distribution of samples in the synthetic unlabeled dataset is unreasonable, most of them are clustered around a few source samples. Such low-quality unlabeled datasets can easily arise in data acquisition due to laziness during photography (e.g. taking consecutive shots of the same target from a similar angle). The duty of coverage guided selection in this experiment is to select feature-rich and evenly distributed test suites. The selected test suites' sizes are 400. We also select test suites from each synthetic unlabeled dataset randomly as the baseline of *Experiment 2*.

Experiment 2 reuses the DNNs in *Experiment 1* and the compared coverage criteria are: HeatC, NC, KMNC, and TKNC. The hyper-parameters of NC and KMNC are the same as that in *Experiment 1*, the k of TKNC is set to 1.

4.2   Experiment Results

Experiment 1's evaluation results of i-Fashion-MNISTs and i-CIFAR10 are in Table 1 and 2, respectively.

From the table, we can observe that the assessment capabilities of NC and KMNC are quite limited. Many test suites receive scores close to 1, even though they vary significantly in their adequacy. Other coverage criteria ensure that coverage scores increase with adequacy and can distinguish between test suites with different levels of adequacy. To more directly evaluate which coverage criterion performs better in distinguishing test suites, we define the "sensitivity score" as follows.

Definition 2 (Sensitivity score). *A series of test suites $T_i s$' ($i = 0, 1, ..., N$) adequacies are in ascending order of i. Evaluating $T_i s$ by a coverage criteria $\mathcal{C}$ on a DNN $\mathcal{N}$, the $\mathcal{C}$ score of T_i can be denoted as s_i. The sensitivity score SS of $\mathcal{C}$ on T_i and $\mathcal{N}$ is defined as $SS = (s_N - s_0) * \sum_{i=1}^{N}(1 - (\frac{s_{i-1}}{s_i})^2).$*

Before the analysis of the evaluation results, we first review the sensitivity score. Sensitivity score measures the "increase" of each row in Table 1 and 2. In the case that the network and the data set under evaluation are the same, a coverage criteria with a higher "increase" in its corresponding row can separate the test suites with different adequacies more observably. For example, if s_i is larger than s_{i-1}, then $\frac{s_{i-1}}{s_i}$ will be smaller, and the final score will be higher. Additionally, to prevent the case that a large score caused by small differences, such as $s_i = 1e - 5$ and $s_{i-1} = 1e - 7$, we multiply the difference as a coefficient in front of the score. Thus the coverage criterion with higher sensitivity score is more sensitive in distinguishing test suites with different adequacies.

Table 3. Sensitivity scores of evaluated coverage criteria

	LeNet-5	AlexNet	GoogLeNet	ResNet18	MobileNet
			i-Fashion-MNIST		
NC	$6 * 10^{-5}$	$6 * 10^{-5}$	$2 * 10^{-8}$	$2 * 10^{-7}$	$2 * 10^{-8}$
KMNC	0.0002	0.0002	$4 * 10^{-6}$	$4 * 10^{-6}$	$2 * 10^{-8}$
HashC	1.1603	0.7831	1.0773	1.0668	0.9963
SC	**1.6639**	**1.3804**	1.0704	0.6472	0.5815
HeatC	0.7323	0.8439	**1.1936**	**1.1889**	**1.0127**
			i-CIFAR10		
NC	$2 * 10^{-5}$	$2 * 10^{-5}$	$8 * 10^{-8}$	0	0
KMNC	$3 * 10^{-5}$	$2 * 10^{-8}$	$1 * 10^{-6}$	$2 * 10^{-6}$	$8 * 10^{-8}$
HashC	0.9920	0.7614	0.8810	0.9925	0.5913
SC	0.9695	0.9223	0.5269	0.4928	0.4556
HeatC	**1.0919**	**1.0368**	**1.6024**	**1.0742**	**1.0777**

The sensitivity scores of all evaluated coverage criteria on *i*-Fashion-MNISTs and *i*-CIFAR10s are in Table 3 showing that HeatC performs better than NC, KMNC, SC, INC, and HashC on most DNNs and test suites. We sort the coverage criteria by their sensitivities, the result is: 1) HeatC, 2) HashC, 3) SC, 4) KMNC,

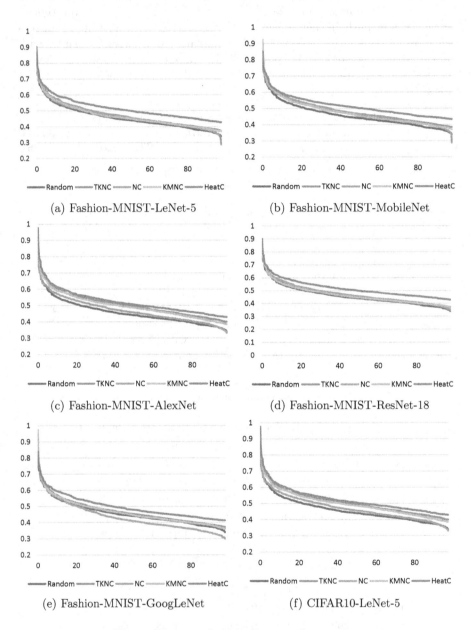

(a) Fashion-MNIST-LeNet-5

(b) Fashion-MNIST-MobileNet

(c) Fashion-MNIST-AlexNet

(d) Fashion-MNIST-ResNet-18

(e) Fashion-MNIST-GoogLeNet

(f) CIFAR10-LeNet-5

Fig. 4. Minimum feature-distance of test suites

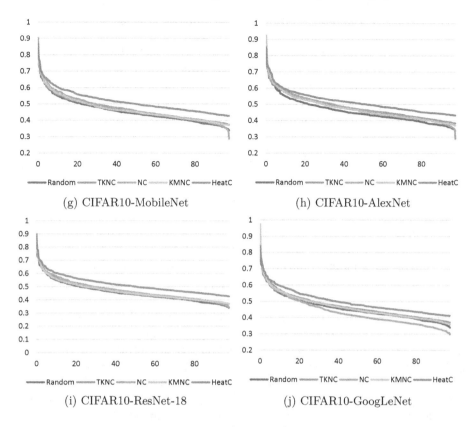

(g) CIFAR10-MobileNet

(h) CIFAR10-AlexNet

(i) CIFAR10-ResNet-18

(j) CIFAR10-GoogLeNet

Fig. 4. (*continued*)

5) NC. In addition, NC and KMNC are so easy to be satisfied, so that they cannot reflect the changes in test suites' adequacy when the score is close to 1. In conclusion, HeatC criteria are finer than other evaluated criteria.

Experiment 2's test suites are evaluated by the *top-k minimum feature distance* (TKMD) defined as follows.

$$M(T, k) = max_{T^k \subseteq T}(min_{x,y \in T^k (x \neq y)} D(x, y))$$

where T^k is the subset of the evaluated test suite satisfying $|T^k| = |T| * k\%$ and D is the perceptual similarity measurement LPIPS (Learned Perceptual Image Patch Similarity) [32]. The $T^{k'} = argmax_{T^k \subseteq T}(min_{x,y \in T^k (x \neq y)} D(x, y))$ denotes the most representative ($|T| * k\%$)-sample subset in T. Because the samples in $T^{k'}$ are far away from each other, and each of them can represent a region in the input space. The similarity measurements are designed to evaluate structured inputs' "perceptual distance", they can measure how similar are two pictures in a way coinciding with human judgment. In this experiment, we use the LPIPS to evaluate the feature distance between samples. Given two test suites T_1 and

Table 4. TKMD of evaluated coverage criteria

	LeNet-5	AlexNet	GoogLeNet	ResNet18	MobileNet
			i-Fashion-MNIST		
Random	0.2449	0.2192	0.2192	0.2192	0.2192
TKNC	0.2588	0.2413	0.2354	0.2361	0.2354
NC	0.2564	0.1803	0.2275	0.2277	0.2304
KMNC	0.2456	0.2388	0.2352	0.2400	0.2376
HeatC	**0.2652**	**0.2673**	**0.2388**	**0.2420**	**0.2429**
			i-CIFAR10		
Random	0.4573	0.4573	0.4573	0.4573	0.4573
TKNC	0.5070	0.4822	0.4711	0.4693	0.4689
HashC	0.4711	0.4810	0.4347	0.4738	0.4731
NC	0.4984	0.4749	0.4660	0.4656	0.4672
HeatC	**0.5232**	**0.5151**	**0.4992**	**0.5167**	**0.5153**

T_2, $M(T_1, k) > M(T_2, k)$ represents that the most representative ($|T| * k\%$)-sample subset in T_1 distributes more evenly than that of T_2 in perception. The comprehensive evaluation of test suites' TKMD is shown in Fig. 4. The subfigure name in Fig. 4 represents the source of test suites, e.g., Fig. 4a contains the test suites generated from Fashion-MNIST based on LeNet-5. The names of curves represent the generation methods, for example, the *Random* curves are the TKMD curves of test suites generated by random selection which is the baseline of *Experiment 2*. The ordinates denote the TKMD values, the abscissas represent the k of TKMD. It is obvious that the curves of HeatC generated test suites are higher than other curves.

A more brief conclusion of Fig. 4 is in Table 4. The data in Table 4 stands for "area under the TKMD curve", or rather, Table 4 measures the two-dimensional area underneath the TKMD curve of all test suites. The coverage criterion with a higher score in Table 4 can generate test suites distributing more reasonable. This experiment shows that HeatC is superior to other coverage criteria in selecting high-quality test suites.

5   Conclusion

To facilitate the use of coverage testing in different areas, we present a coverage criterion named HeatC which is a variable-grained DL coverage criterion. HeatC utilizes the activation mapping based test targets to combine the attention of the neural networks and the features of inputs. Guiding by the clustered test targets, HeatC can reflect the subtle behaviors of DNNs and adjust its own granularity. We also develop the test adequacy evaluation and test sample selection approaches for HeatC. Experiments show that HeatC performs better than existing mainstream coverage criteria in assessing the adequacy of test suites and selecting high-value test samples from the unlabeled dataset.

Acknowledgement. This research was sponsored by the National Natural Science Foundation of China under Grant No. 62172019, and CCF-Huawei Formal Verification Innovation Research Plan.

References

1. Chattopadhay, A., Sarkar, A., Howlader, P., Balasubramanian, V.N.: Grad-CAM++: generalized gradient-based visual explanations for deep convolutional networks. In: Proceedings of the 18th IEEE Winter Conference on Applications of Computer Vision, pp. 839–847. IEEE Computer Society (2018). https://doi.org/10.1109/WACV.2018.00097
2. Chen, J., Song, L., Wainwright, M.J., Jordan, M.I.: Learning to explain: an information-theoretic perspective on model interpretation. In: Proceedings of the 35th International Conference on Machine Learning, ICML 2018, pp. 1386–1418. PMLR 80. International Machine Learning Society (2018). https://doi.org/10.48550/arXiv.1802.07814
3. Desai, S., Ramaswamy, H.G.: Ablation-CAM: visual explanations for deep convolutional network via gradient-free localization. In: Proceedings of the 2020 IEEE Winter Conference on Applications of Computer Vision, pp. 972–980. IEEE (2020). https://doi.org/10.1109/WACV45572.2020.9093360
4. Dhillon, G.S., et al.: Stochastic activation pruning for robust adversarial defense. In: Proceedings of the 6th International Conference on Learning Representations. International Conference on Learning Representations (2018). https://doi.org/10.48550/arXiv.1803.01442
5. Feng, D., Harakeh, A., Waslander, S.L., Dietmayer, K.: A review and comparative study on probabilistic object detection in autonomous driving. IEEE Trans. Intell. Transp. Syst. **23**(8), 9961–9980 (2022). https://doi.org/10.1109/TITS.2021.3096854
6. Gehr, T., Mirman, M., Drachsler-Cohen, D., Tsankov, P., Chaudhuri, S., Vechev, M.T.: AI2: safety and robustness certification of neural networks with abstract interpretation. In: Proceedings of the 2018 IEEE Symposium on Security and Privacy, pp. 3–18. IEEE Computer Society (2018). https://doi.org/10.1109/SP.2018.00058
7. Gerasimou, S., Eniser, H.F., Sen, A., Cakan, A.: Importance-driven deep learning system testing. In: Proceedings of the 42nd International Conference on Software Engineering: Companion, pp. 322–323. IEEE (2020). https://doi.org/10.1145/3377812.3390793
8. Gerges, F., Boufadel, M.C., Bou-Zeid, E., Nassif, H., Wang, J.T.L.: A novel deep learning approach to the statistical downscaling of temperatures for monitoring climate change. In: Proceedings of the 6th International Conference on Machine Learning and Soft Computing, pp. 1–7. Advances in Intelligent Systems and Computing 887, ACM, Virtual, Online, China (2022)
9. Goodfellow, I.J., Shlens, J., Szegedy, C.: Explaining and harnessing adversarial examples. In: Proceedings of the 3rd International Conference on Learning Representations. International Conference on Learning Representations (2015). http://arxiv.org/abs/1412.6572

10. Guller, D.: Technical foundations of a DPLL-based SAT solver for propositional Godel logic. IEEE Trans. Fuzzy Syst. **26**(1), 84–100 (2018). https://doi.org/10.1109/TFUZZ.2016.2637374

11. Kim, J., Feldt, R., Yoo, S.: Guiding deep learning system testing using surprise adequacy. In: Proceedings of the 41st International Conference on Software Engineering, pp. 1039–1049. IEEE (2019). https://doi.org/10.1109/ICSE.2019.00108

12. Kim, S., Wimmer, H., Kim, J.: Analysis of deep learning libraries: Keras, Pytorch, and MXnet. In: Proceedings of the 20th IEEE/ACIS International Conference on Software Engineering Research, Management and Applications, pp. 54–62. IEEE (2022). https://doi.org/10.1109/SERA54885.2022.9806734

13. Krizhevsky, A., Hinton, G.: Learning multiple layers of features from tiny images. Technical report, pp. 32–33 (2009). https://www.cs.toronto.edu/kriz/learning-features-2009-TR.pdf

14. Kurakin, A., Goodfellow, I.J., Bengio, S.: Adversarial examples in the physical world. In: Proceedings of the 5th International Conference on Learning Representations. International Conference on Learning Representations (2019). https://openreview.net/forum?id=HJGU3Rodl

15. Lin, M., Chen, Q., Yan, S.: Network in network. In: Proceedings of the 2nd International Conference on Learning Representations. International Conference on Learning Representations (2014)

16. Ma, L., et al.: DeepCT: tomographic combinatorial testing for deep learning systems. In: Proceedings of the 26th IEEE International Conference on Software Analysis, Evolution and Reengineering, pp. 614–618. IEEE (2019). https://doi.org/10.1109/SANER.2019.8668044

17. Ma, L., et al.: DeepGauge: multi-granularity testing criteria for deep learning systems. In: Proceedings of the 33rd ACM/IEEE International Conference on Automated Software Engineering, pp. 120–131. ACM (2018). https://doi.org/10.1145/3238147.3238202

18. Mahendran, A., Vedaldi, A.: Understanding deep image representations by inverting them, pp. 5188–5196. IEEE Computer Society (2015). https://doi.org/10.1109/CVPR.2015.7299155

19. Omeiza, D., Speakman, S., Cintas, C., Weldemariam, K.: Smooth grad-CAM++: an enhanced inference level visualization technique for deep convolutional neural network models. CoRR abs/1908.01224 (2019). http://arxiv.org/abs/1908.01224

20. Pei, K., Cao, Y., Yang, J., Jana, S.: Towards practical verification of machine learning: the case of computer vision systems. CoRR abs/1712.01785 (2017). http://arxiv.org/abs/1712.01785

21. Pei, K., Cao, Y., Yang, J., Jana, S.: DeepXplore: automated whitebox testing of deep learning systems. In: Proceedings of the 26th ACM Symposium on Operating Systems Principles, pp. 1–18. ACM (2018). https://doi.org/10.1145/3132747.3132785

22. Poursaeed, O., Katsman, I., Gao, B., Belongie, S.: Generative adversarial perturbations, pp. 4422–4431. IEEE Computer Society (2018). https://doi.org/10.1109/CVPR.2018.00465

23. Razumovskaia, E., Glavas, G., Majewska, O., Ponti, E.M., Vulic, I.: Natural language processing for multilingual task-oriented dialogue. In: Proceedings of the 60th Annual Meeting of the Association for Computational Linguistics, pp. 44–50. Association for Computational Linguistics (2022). https://doi.org/10.18653/v1/2022.acl-tutorials.8

24. Salay, R., Czarnecki, K.: Using machine learning safely in automotive software: an assessment and adaption of software process requirements in ISO 26262. CoRR abs/1808.01614 (2018). http://arxiv.org/abs/1808.01614

25. Sekhon, J., Fleming, C.: Towards improved testing for deep learning. In: Proceedings of the 41st International Conference on Software Engineering, pp. 85–88. IEEE (2019). https://doi.org/10.1109/ICSE-NIER.2019.00030

26. Selvaraju, R.R., Cogswell, M., Das, A., Vedantam, R., Parikh, D., Batra, D.: Grad-CAM: visual explanations from deep networks via gradient-based localization. Int. J. Comput. Vis. **128**(2), 336–359 (2020). https://doi.org/10.1007/s11263-019-01228-7

27. Sun, W., Lu, Y., Sun, M.: Are coverage criteria meaningful metrics for DNNs? In: Proceedings of the 2021 International Joint Conference on Neural Networks, pp. 1–8. IEEE (2021). https://doi.org/10.1109/IJCNN52387.2021.9533987

28. Sun, Y., Huang, X., Kroening, D.: Testing deep neural networks. CoRR abs/1803.04792 (2018). http://arxiv.org/abs/1803.04792

29. Udeshi, S., Arora, P., Chattopadhyay, S.: Automated directed fairness testing. In: Proceedings of the 33rd ACM/IEEE International Conference on Automated Software Engineering, pp. 98–108. ACM (2018). https://doi.org/10.1145/3238147.3238165

30. Wang, H., et al.: Score-CAM: score-weighted visual explanations for convolutional neural networks. In: Proceedings of the 2020 IEEE/CVF Conference on Computer Vision and Pattern Recognition Workshops, pp. 111–119. IEEE (2020). https://doi.org/10.1109/CVPRW50498.2020.00020

31. Xiao, H., Rasul, K., Vollgraf, R.: Fashion MNIST: an MNIST-like dataset of 70,000 28×28 labeled fashion images (2017). https://github.com/zalandoresearch/fashion-mnist

32. Zhang, R., Isola, P., Efros, A.A., Shechtman, E., Wang, O.: The unreasonable effectiveness of deep features as a perceptual metric. In: Proceedings of the 31st IEEE Conference on Computer Vision and Pattern Recognition, pp. 586–595. IEEE Computer Society (2018). https://doi.org/10.1109/CVPR.2018.00068

33. Zhou, B., Khosla, A., Lapedriza, A., Oliva, A., Torralba, A.: Learning deep features for discriminative localization. In: Proceedings of the 29th IEEE Conference on Computer Vision and Pattern Recognition, pp. 2921–2929. IEEE Computer Society (2016). https://doi.org/10.1109/CVPR.2016.319

Formalization of Lambda Calculus with Explicit Names as a Nominal Reasoning Framework

Xinyi Wan and Qinxiang Cao$^{(\boxtimes)}$

Shanghai Jiao Tong University, Shanghai, China
wanxinyi@sjtu.edu.cn, caoqinxiang@gmail.com

Abstract. We formalize the metatheory of lambda calculus in Coq, in its classic form with explicit names. The formalization is founded upon an intuitive α-equivalence definition without substitution or name swapping. Furthermore, we provide structural and rule induction principles that encapsulate the Barendregt Variable Convention, enabling formal proofs mirroring informally-styled ones. These principles are leveraged to establish foundational results such as the Church-Rosser theorem. Demonstrating the framework's utility, we extend first-order logic with predicate definitions, ensuring its soundness through properties obtained from the metatheory by encoding propositions as lambda terms.

Keywords: Lambda Calculus · Nominal Syntax · First-Order Logic

1 Introduction

Formal reasoning about syntax with binders is notoriously cumbersome due to the intricacies arising from the various selections of bound variables, i.e. α-equivalence. In a paper-and-pencil setting, this issue is often avoided by identifying terms up to α-equivalence. When proofs involve binders, a common practice known as the *Barendregt Variable Convention* (BVC) is adopted. This convention assumes that binders are assigned fresh names that are distinct from the surrounding mathematical context. This practice simplifies the proof process, leading to elegant and straightforward informal proofs.

An illustration of this convention can be found in a widely used textbook [1, Page 28], where the author tries to prove the equation:

$$M[x \mapsto N][y \mapsto L] =_\alpha M[y \mapsto L][x \mapsto N[y \mapsto L]]. \qquad (1)$$

Here, M, N, L are lambda terms, x is a variable that does not occur freely in L, and $M[x \mapsto N]$ means the substitution of the free occurrences of x in M with N. The notation $=_a$ represents α-equivalence.

The proof is conducted through a structural induction on M. In the abstraction case, the author wrote:

H. Hermanns et al. (Eds.): SETTA 2023, LNCS 14464, pp. 262–278, 2024.
https://doi.org/10.1007/978-981-99-8664-4_15

CASE 2. $M = \lambda z.\ M_1$. By the variable convention we may assume $z \neq x, y$ and z is not free in N, L. Then by the induction hypothesis

$$
\begin{aligned}
(\lambda z.\ M_1)[x \mapsto N][y \mapsto L] &= \lambda z.\ M_1[x \mapsto N][y \mapsto L] \\
&= \lambda z.\ M_1[y \mapsto L][x \mapsto N[y \mapsto L]] \qquad (2) \\
&= (\lambda z.\ M_1)[y \mapsto L][x \mapsto N[y \mapsto L]]
\end{aligned}
$$

In the first step the binder z does not need renaming, as it is automatically treated as fresh according to the convention. This enables the direct application of the induction hypothesis in subsequent steps.

However, the justification of this convention does not arise spontaneously within a formal context. Structural induction, which necessitates case analysis on arbitrary binders rather than fresh ones, does not inherently support it. Therefore, a longstanding aspiration has been the development of a technique enabling proofs to be formalized in a manner similar to the one demonstrated above. In this paper we aim to formalize the metatheory of untyped lambda calculus with explicit names in Coq, and subsequently employ it as a framework for binder-related reasoning. In the second part, we demonstrate how specific entities (propositions in first-order logic) can be encoded as lambda terms, with properties concerning α-equivalence and substitution naturally derived from the established metatheory.

1.1 Related Work

Many approaches have been put forward to address formal treatment of binders, primarily categorized into three distinct approaches. The nameless approach, originating from De Brujin [6], involves encoding binders as numerical indicators of their positions. This technique has sparked further advancements, such as the locally nameless representation [2], leading to the development and utilization of automated libraries [12]. Nevertheless, a significant limitation of De Brujin indices lies in the substantial gap between the nameless representation and the classic syntax. As a consequence, considerable effort is required to transform informal proofs into proofs employing the nameless representation.

An alternative method is the higher-order abstract syntax (HOAS), wherein object-level binders are shallowly embedded through the employment of the meta-logic's binder, as presented in multiple formalizations [3,7,9]. This approach offers a light formalization, facilitated by the direct incorporation of binding mechanisms from the meta-logic. Nonetheless, since operations like substitution on object-level terms are fundamentally implemented at the meta-level, this formalization requires informal reasoning concerning meta-level operations to demonstrate the adequacy of the representation.

The nominal approach endeavors to retain the original syntax of binders (i.e. a variable parameter of the binding operator) and introduces induction principles applicable to α-equivalent terms, thereby enabling the direct utilization of BVC to emulate informal proofs. In an initial exploration [10], the manner in which equality embodies α-conversion is axiomatized and subsequently proved sound for De Brujin terms. A subsequent contribution establishes the nominal logic [11] as a framework for first-order languages featuring bindings, based on name swapping and permutation operations. This methodology is further refined within theorem provers, most notably by Urban in Isabelle/HOL [13–15]. This nominal syntax is also embraced in Copello et al.'s works [4,5], effectively formalizing theories related to untyped lambda calculus with a single category of names.

1.2 Our Contributions

Our study adopts the nominal-style methodology, but it distinguishes itself from preceding approaches. Current nominal techniques rely on the pivotal operation of name swapping. In contrast, we have discovered that the theory can be founded upon an intuitive definition of α-equivalence. Building upon this definition, we have formalized metatheories about untyped lambda calculus and introduced a Coq framework for nominal reasoning.

Furthermore, we introduce an α-structural induction principle for lambda terms and two novel rule induction principles for parallel reduction. These induction principles are designed to formally integrate BVC into the induction process. By leveraging these principles, we establish foundational outcomes, including the Church-Rosser theorem. Remarkably, the proofs of these outcomes elegantly mirror their informal counterparts.

Distinguishing our work from Copello et al.'s formalization [5], we support multiple categories for variables, thus enhancing its applicability, exemplified by an extended first-order logic featuring dynamically defined predicates in Sect. 4. Notably, our framework departs from certain operations like name swapping. Instead, our framework is exclusively parameterized based on variable name categories and a function for introducing fresh names. This design choice contributes to a more intuitive and straightforward usability.

The rest of this paper is organized as follows. In Sect. 2, we describe the syntax of lambda terms, introduce a definition for α-equialence and establish an α-structrual induction prnciple. Section 3 presents two rule induction principles and formalizes the Church-Rosser theorem. We show the framework's applicability in extending first-order logic with predicate definitions in Sect. 4. Finally, Sect. 5 concludes the paper.

2 Syntax and Alpha-Equivalence

2.1 Names

Variables within lambda terms ranges over a countable set of names, fixed as type $\mathbb{V}$ in this article. These variables can be categorized into distinct groups referred to as *sorts*, thereby facilitating binding across diverse entities. For instance, in second-order logic, this allows for the inclusion of both individual and set variables. Consequently, we establish an additional type, $\mathbb{VS}$, to describe these sorts and fix a function varsort of type $V \to VS$, assigning a specific sort to each individual name.

A key operation within α-equivalence involves the incorporation of a fresh binder, signifying a name not in the existing context. Consequently, this entails the requirement that $\forall x, y : V$, there exists a discriminating process: $\{x = y\} + \{x \neq y\}$.

Ultimately, the actual introduction of a fresh name is accomplished through the function newvar of type list $V \to VS \to V$. Provided with a list of names and a designated sort T, newvar yields a variable of sort T, ensuring its absence from the provided list.

In Coq, we employ a Module Type to encapsulate these fundamental requirements, establishing it as the cornerstone for subsequent developments. Users have the flexibility to instantiate this Module Type with various definitions satisfying the properties, allowing fine-grained control on names.

> Module Type Naming_module_type.
> Parameter C : Type.
> Parameter V: Type.
> Parameter VS: Type.
> Parameter varsort: $V \to VS$.
> Parameter newvar: list $V \to VS \to V$.
> Axiom var_eq_dec: $\forall v_1 v_2 : V, \{v_1 = v_2\} + \{v_1 \neq v_2\}$.
> Axiom constant_eq_dec: $\forall c_1 c_2 : C, \{c_1 = c_2\} + \{c_1 \neq c_2\}$.
> Axiom newvar_fresh: $\forall$(xs: list V) (T :VS), (newvar xs T) $\notin$ xs.
> Axiom newvar_sort: $\forall$(xs: list V) (T :VS), varsort(newvar xs T) $= T$.
> End Naming_module_type.

Fig. 1. The Module Type in Coq, C is the type for constants' names.

2.2   The Syntax of Lambda Calculus

The syntax of untyped lambda calculus is inductively defined as:

$$t ::= \text{Var } x \mid \text{Cons } c \mid \lambda x.t \mid t_1\ t_2, \tag{3}$$

where x ranges over V and c ranges over C. Free occurrences of a variable in a term is given by a recursive function.:

Definition 1 (Free Occurrence).

> *free_occur x(Var y) := if $x = y$ then 1 else 0*
> *free_occur x(Cons c) := 0*
> *free_occur x($t_1 t_2$) := free_occur x t_1 + free_occur x t_2*
> *free_occur x($\lambda s.t$) := if $x = s$ then 0 else free_occur x t,*

free_occur x t = 0 will be subsequently shortened to $x \notin$ FV(t), while free_occur x $t \neq 0$ will be $x \in$ FV(t). The function returns a natural number, a design choice made to accommodate potentially more subtle applications involving free occurrences. Returning a boolean would also suffice for the development presented in this paper.

2.3   Alpha Equivalence

The classic definition of α−equivalence is the least congruence relation achieved through the renaming of bound variables, i.e. $\lambda x.\ t =_a \lambda y.\ t[x \mapsto y]$. In this paper, we introduce a purely syntax-driven, intuitive and decidable definition of the α-equivalence relation. Notably, this definition does not involve any substitution or name swapping operations. The essence of this approach lies in the observation that when comparing terms like $\lambda x.\ t_1$ and $\lambda y.\ t_2$, one must recognize that the role of x in t_1 corresponds to the role of y in t_2. This realization prompts a subsequent examination of t_1 and t_2 under this established association between x and y. To encapsulate this linkage, a context may be maintained.

Definition 2 (Context). *A context Γ is a sequence of variable pairs that record the relationship between two binders, alongside a boolean value to indicate whether the correspondence is still "active".*

$$\Gamma : list\ (\mathbb{V} * \mathbb{V} * bool) ::= [\ ]\ |\ (x, y, b) :: \Gamma'. \tag{4}$$

Considering $\lambda xx.xz$ and $\lambda xy.yz$, when we assess the equivalence between $\lambda x.xz$ and $\lambda y.yz$, we observe that x on the left corresponds to x on the right. Consequently, a context (x, x, true) is established to record this correspondence. Delving deeper, when we explore the equivalence between xz and yz, we find that the binder x on the left aligns with y on the right. Therefore, a new correspondence, (x, y, true), should be added to the context. However, since x is already associated with x in the context, it should be deactivated by replacing (x, x, true) with (x, x, false). This results in the context $(x, y, \mathsf{true}) :: (x, x, \mathsf{false})$. Here is the definition of deactivating non-effective correspondence in a context:

Definition 3 (Deactivating non-effective correspondence in a context). *For variables x, y, m, n, and a boolean b, we define the deactivation of a pair of binders as follows:*

$$(m, n, b)\backslash(x, y) := (m, n, \mathsf{false}) \quad if\ x = m\ or\ n = y,$$
$$(m, n, b)\backslash(x, y) := (m, n, b) \quad\quad\quad\quad otherwise.$$

For a context Γ, this deactivation is performed on every pair of binders in it using the map *function.*

$$\Gamma\backslash(x, y) := map\ (fun\ (m, n, b) \Rightarrow (m, n, b)\backslash(x, y))\ \Gamma$$

This definition ensures that for any binder x, all of its original appearances on the corresponding projection (left if $\Gamma\backslash(x, \_)$ and right if $\Gamma\backslash(\_, x)$) in the context will be deactivated.

Then we may formalize the auxiliary α-equivalence relation augmented with a context:

Definition 4 (Alpha-Equivalence With Context).

$$\frac{}{\Gamma \vdash c \sim_a c} \; [\alpha_{\text{CONS}}]$$

$$\frac{(u, v, \text{true}) \in \Gamma}{\Gamma \vdash u \sim_a v} \; [\alpha_{\text{BIND}}] \qquad \frac{s \notin V(\Gamma)}{\Gamma \vdash s \sim_a s} \; [\alpha_{\text{FREE}}]$$

$$\frac{\Gamma \vdash M_1 \sim_a M_2 \qquad \Gamma \vdash N_1 \sim_a N_2}{\Gamma \vdash M_1 \, N_1 \sim_a M_2 \, N_2} \; [\alpha_{\text{APP}}]$$

$$\frac{\text{varsort}(x) = \text{varsort}(y) \qquad (x, y, \text{true}) :: (\Gamma \backslash (x, y)) \vdash M \sim_a N}{\Gamma \vdash \lambda x.\, M \sim_a \lambda y.\, N} \; [\alpha_{\text{ABS}}]$$

Definition 5 (Alpha-Equivalence). *When the context is empty, the preceding relation simplifies to the conventional α-equivalence.*

$$M =_a N \triangleq [\,] \vdash M \sim_a N. \tag{5}$$

The previous example involving $\lambda xx.xz$ and $\lambda xy.yz$ can now be formalized as shown in Fig. 2.

$$\frac{\dfrac{(x, y, \text{true}) \in (x, y, \text{true}) :: \dots}{(x, y, \text{true}) :: \dots \vdash x \sim_a y} \; [\alpha_{\text{BIND}}] \qquad \dfrac{z \notin V((x, y, \text{true}) :: (x, x, \text{false}))}{(x, y, \text{true}) :: (x, x, \text{false}) \vdash z \sim_a z} \; [\alpha_{\text{FREE}}]}{\dfrac{\dfrac{(x, y, \text{true}) :: (x, x, \text{false}) \vdash xz \sim_a yz}{(x, x, \text{true}) \vdash \lambda x.\, xz \sim_a \lambda y.\, yz} \; [\alpha_{\text{ABS}}]}{[\,] \vdash \lambda xx.\, xz \sim_\alpha \lambda xy.\, yz} \; [\alpha_{\text{ABS}}]} \; [\alpha_{\text{APP}}]$$

Fig. 2. Proof tree of $\lambda xx.\, xz =_a \lambda xy.yz$

To establish the equivalence between $\lambda xx.\, xz$ and $\lambda xy.\, yz$, we dive down through layers of binders by applying α_{ABS}. First the tuple (x, x, true) is introduced into the empty context. Then the tuple (x, y, true) is introduced into the context. The prior association of x with itself becomes redundant and is deactivated by $\Gamma \backslash (x, x)$. The operation $(x, y, \text{true}) \backslash (x, y)$ ensures that each distinct binder in the context on both sides is actively associated with exactly one binder on the other side at all times. In the atomic cases, $x \sim_a y$ since x and y are actively linked bound variables. Regarding variable z, which does not appear in any of the variables in the context, its presence must be a result of free occurrence. Here $V(\Gamma)$ represents all variables in a context. Therefore, it can solely be equivalent to itself.

The nature of this relation is evident in its top-down evaluation approach, wherein the context serves as a stack, recording the legitimate "renaming" of bound variables at each hierarchical level. It is straightforward to define an equivalent recursive function, thereby rendering this process decidable.

Lemma 1. $=_a$ *is an equivalence relation.*

Proof. Basic properties, such as equivalence, about $=_\alpha$ are proved by demonstrating a stronger version of $\sim_a$ through rule induction, provided the invariant property of the context during evaluation is correctly characterized. Consider transitivity as an example. During the simultaneous evaluation of $t_1 =_a t_2$, $t_2 =_a t_3$ and $t_1 =_a t_3$, the encountered binders will be recorded within three distinct contexts, obeying the following relation[1]:

$$\frac{\dfrac{}{\mathsf{trans\_ctx}\,[\,]\,[\,]\,[\,]} \qquad \mathsf{trans\_ctx}\ \Gamma_1\ \Gamma_2\ \Gamma_3}{\mathsf{trans\_ctx}\ (x,y,\_)::\Gamma_1 \quad (y,z,\_)::\Gamma_2 \quad (x,z,\_)::\Gamma_3}$$

Throughout the entire process, $\mathsf{trans\_ctx}$ will be preserved and we can now prove a stronger proposition: if $\Gamma_1 \vdash t_1 \sim_a t_2$, $\Gamma_2 \vdash t_2 \sim_a t_3$, and $\mathsf{trans\_ctx}\ \Gamma_1\ \Gamma_2\ \Gamma_3$, then $\Gamma_3 \vdash t_1 \sim_a t_3$. The proof is conducted through induction on $t_1 \sim_a t_2$, wherein we demonstrate two interesting cases:

- α_{BIND}. If $\Gamma_1 \vdash x \sim_a y$ because $(x,y,\mathrm{true}) \in \Gamma_1$, then $\Gamma_2 \vdash y \sim_a z$ can be established only by the α_{BIND} rule. This is because y occurs in Γ_1, thereby enforcing its presence in Γ_2 by the $\mathsf{trans\_ctx}$ relation. Subsequently, an additional induction on $\mathsf{trans\_ctx}$ will yield $(x,z,\mathrm{true}) \in \Gamma_3$, leading to $\Gamma_3 \vdash x \sim_a z$.
- α_{ABS}. If $\Gamma_1 \vdash \lambda x.\,t_1 \sim_a \lambda y.\,t_2$, $\Gamma_2 \vdash \lambda y.\,t_2 \sim_a \lambda z.\,t_3$. From the α_{ABS} rule, we know $(x,y,\mathrm{true}) :: \Gamma_1 \vdash t_1 \sim_a t_2$ and $(y,z,\mathrm{true}) :: \Gamma_2 \vdash t_2 \sim_a t_3$. As $(x,z,\mathrm{true}) :: \Gamma_3$ satisfies $\mathsf{trans\_ctx}$, we immediately derive from the induction hypothesis that $(x,z,\mathrm{true}) :: \Gamma_3 \vdash t_1 \sim_a t_3$, thus $\Gamma_3 \vdash \lambda x.\,t_1 \sim_a \lambda z.\,t_3$.

The proposition simplifies to the transitivity of $=_a$ when all three contexts are empty.

2.4   Substitution

We implement a parallel capture-avoiding substitution, enabling the simultaneous substitution of multiple variables. In the abstraction case, special care is taken to rename binders appropriately.

Definition 6 (Capture-Avoiding Substitution).
Subst_task is a list of variable and lambda term pairs, recording the variables to be substituted:

$$\sigma : subst\_task ::= [\,] \mid (x,t) :: \sigma. \tag{6}$$

---

[1] An additional constraint is that all "correct" contexts can only be obtained through the operation in the α_{ABS} rule. We assume it implicitly holds within this paper.

$$\_[\_ \mapsto \_] : term \rightarrow subst\_task \rightarrow term :=$$
$$c[\sigma] = c$$
$$x[x \mapsto t; ...] = t$$
$$y[x \mapsto t :: \sigma] = y[\sigma] \qquad\qquad\qquad if\ x \neq y,$$
$$(t_1\ t_2)[\sigma] = (t_1[\sigma])\ (t_2[\sigma])$$
$$(\lambda x.\ t)[\sigma] = \lambda x.(t[\sigma\backslash x]) \qquad\qquad if\ x \notin FV(\sigma\backslash x)$$
$$(\lambda x.\ t)[\sigma] = \lambda u.(t[x \mapsto u :: \sigma\backslash x]) \qquad if\ x \in FV(\sigma\backslash x).$$
$$where\ u = newvar([x; V(t); V(\sigma\backslash x)], varsort(x))$$

where $\sigma\backslash x$ means removing the substitution for x in subst_task σ and $V(\_)$ represents the list of all variable names present in the term t or subst_task σ. $FV(\sigma)$ represents all the variables freely occurring in the right projection of terms of a subst_task σ.

If the binder freely occurs in the substitution task, a fresh name with the same sort will be introduced to avoid capturing and this renaming process will be integrated into the task.

Substitution and α−equivalence can be related through the following lemmas:

Lemma 2 (Substitution is α−compatible).

$$M =_a N \Rightarrow M[\sigma] =_a N[\sigma].$$

Lemma 3 (Renaming keeps α−equivalence).

$$varsort(x) = varsort(y) \Rightarrow y \notin FV(t) \Rightarrow \lambda x.\ t =_a \lambda y.\ t[x \mapsto y].$$

These two lemmas are also established by proving a stronger version of $\sim_a$, facilitated by the introduction of a relation on contexts.

2.5   An Alpha-Structural Induction Principle

Lemma 3 demonstrates the alignment between our proposed definition of α-equivalence and the conventional definition. Building upon this, we proceed to provide a formalization of the *Barendregt Variable Convention* and derive an α−structural induction principle that exclusively requires proofs on fresh binders in the abstraction case.

Lemma 4 (Variable Convention). *Given any term t and a list of names xs, there exists a term t' such that $t =_a t'$ and any bound variable x in t' satisfies $x \notin xs$.*

Proof. Proven through structural induction on t, the significant case is abstraction. Consider $\lambda x.\ t$, the induction hypothesis permits the existence of $t' =_a t$ that meets the specified conditions. This leads to $\lambda x.\ t =_a \lambda x.\ t'$. Then we rename x to a fresh name y- a name that is not in xs and also not freely occurs in t', given by $newvar([xs; V(\lambda x.\ t)], varsort(x))$. By Lemma 3, we deduce $\lambda y.\ t'[x \mapsto y] =_a \lambda x.\ t$, thereby satisfying the requisite property.

This lemma enables us to formulate an α-structural induction principle parameterized by a list of names:

Theorem 1 (Alpha-Structural Induction).
Assume P: term$\to$ Prop is a predicate on lambda terms. Given a list of names xs, if the following five assertions hold:

1. P is $\alpha-compatible$: $\forall M =_a N, P\ M \Rightarrow P\ N$
2. $\forall x : \mathbb{V},\ P\ (\textit{Var } x)$.
3. $\forall c : \mathbb{C},\ P\ (\textit{Cons } x)$.
4. $\forall M\ N,\ P\ M \Rightarrow P\ N \Rightarrow P\ (M\ N)$.
5. $\forall x\ t,\ x \notin xs \Rightarrow P\ t \Rightarrow P\ (\lambda x.\ t)$.

then $\forall t : \textit{term}, P\ t$ holds.

Proof. To prove $P\ t$, utilizing assumption (1) and lemma 4, it suffices to demonstrate $P\ t'$ where $t =_a t'$ and all binders within t' are distinct from names in xs. A subsequent induction on t' immediately resolves the issue.

The assumption of α-compatibility states that the predicate remains invariant under α-equivalence, which is essential to ensure that binder renaming is sound. The name list xs typically includes the variables of other terms in the proof context. This choice effectively sidesteps binder renaming during substitution, so induction hypothesis can be directly applied in the abstraction case.

Following lemmas can be readily formalized through the the α-structural induction principle:

Lemma 5 (Communicativity of substitution). *If $x \neq y$ and $x \notin \mathsf{FV}(L)$, then*

$$M[x \mapsto N][y \mapsto L] =_\alpha M[y \mapsto L][x \mapsto N[y \mapsto L]].$$

Proof. The formal proof mirrors exactly the informal one in Sect. 1.

Lemma 6 (Substitution preserves α-equivalence).

$$M =_a M' \Rightarrow N =_a N' \Rightarrow M[x \mapsto N] =_a M'[x \mapsto N'].$$

3   The Church-Rosser Theorem

In this section, we extend the metatheory with the Church-Rosser theorem. The proof of this theorem largely follows the approach formulated by Tait and Martin-Lof [1], but revised to incorporate a formal treatment of α-equivalence.

Definition 7 (Beta Reduction). *β-reduction is the compatible closure of β-contraction, enabling one-step contraction, i.e. $(\lambda x.\ M)N \triangleright M[x \mapsto N]$, at any position within the term:*

$$\frac{}{(\lambda x.\ M)N \to_\beta M[x \mapsto N]}$$

$$\frac{M \to_\beta N}{L\, M \to_\beta L\, N} \qquad \frac{M \to_\beta N}{M\, L \to_\beta N\, L} \qquad \frac{M \to_\beta N}{\lambda x.\, M \ \to_\beta \lambda x.\, N}$$

The Church-Rosser theorem states its reflexive and transitive closure satisfies the diamond property (i.e. β-reduction is confluent):

If $M \to_\beta^* A$ and $M \to_\beta^* B$, then there exists N, such that $A \to_\beta^* N$ and $B \to_\beta^* N$ (Fig. 3).

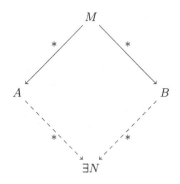

Fig. 3. The Church-Rosser theorem.

However, this statement is true only when α-equivalent terms are treated as identical. Due to the arbitrary reduction order allowed by β-reduction, distinct fresh names might be introduced among different reduction processes. Therefore, for a formal consideration of α-equivalence, the confluence property should be rephrased as follows:

Definition 8 (Confluence). *A relation is confluent means that for any two reduction orders, there exists reduction orders that converge to α-equivalent terms.*

$$\begin{aligned} \mathsf{confluence}(\to_\beta) \ := \ &\forall M\ A\ B,\ M \to_\beta^* A \Rightarrow M \to_\beta^* B \Rightarrow \\ &\exists N_A\ N_B, A \to_\beta^* N_A \wedge B \to_\beta^* N_B \wedge N_A =_\alpha N_B. \end{aligned} \tag{7}$$

The proof of this theorem relies on the so-called parallel-reduction $\twoheadrightarrow_1$:

Definition 9 (Parallel Reduction).

$$\frac{}{M \twoheadrightarrow_1 M}\ [\mathrm{P_{REFL}}] \qquad \frac{M \twoheadrightarrow_1 N}{\lambda x.\, M \twoheadrightarrow_1 \lambda x.\, N}\ [\mathrm{P_{ABS}}]$$

$$\frac{M \twoheadrightarrow_1 M' \qquad N \twoheadrightarrow_1 N'}{M\, N \twoheadrightarrow_1 M'\, N'}\ [\mathrm{P_{APP}}]$$

$$\frac{M \twoheadrightarrow_1 M' \qquad N \twoheadrightarrow_1 N'}{(\lambda x.\, M)\, N \twoheadrightarrow_1 M'[x \mapsto N']}\ [\mathrm{P_{CONTRACT}}]$$

3.1   Rule Induction Principles

We present two rule induction principles for parallel induction. These principles are implicitly employed within informal contexts. The first principle enhances the induction hypothesis to cover all terms with a smaller size. The specific definition of size is omitted here.

Theorem 2 (Size Rule Induction).
Assume P: term→ term → Prop is a relation on lambda terms. If the following four assertions hold:

1. $\forall M : term, P\ M\ M$
2. $\forall M\ M'$ *such that* $M \twoheadrightarrow_1 M'$,
   $(\forall L \twoheadrightarrow_1 L', size\ L \leq size\ M \Rightarrow P\ L\ L') \Rightarrow$
   $P\ (\lambda x.\ M)\ (\lambda x.\ M').$
3. $\forall M\ M'\ N\ N'$ *such that* $M \twoheadrightarrow_1 M'$, $N \twoheadrightarrow_1 N'$,
   $(\forall L \twoheadrightarrow_1 L', size\ L \leq size\ M \Rightarrow P\ L\ L') \Rightarrow$
   $(\forall L \twoheadrightarrow_1 L', size\ L \leq size\ N \Rightarrow P\ L\ L') \Rightarrow$
   $P\ (M\ N)\ (M'\ N').$
4. $\forall M\ M'\ N\ N'$ *such that* $M \twoheadrightarrow_1 M'$, $N \twoheadrightarrow_1 N'$, ,
   $(\forall L \twoheadrightarrow_1 L', size\ L \leq size\ M \Rightarrow P\ L\ L') \Rightarrow$
   $(\forall L \twoheadrightarrow_1 L', size\ L \leq size\ N \Rightarrow P\ L\ L') \Rightarrow$
   $P\ ((\lambda x.\ M)\ N)\ (M'[x \mapsto N']).$

then $\forall M\ N : term, M \twoheadrightarrow_1 N$ *implies* $P\ M\ N$.

Proof. Induction on the size of M establishes the theorem.

A more interesting problem is how to encode BVC into rule induction. Similar to the example presented in Sect. 1, it is assumed that the variable convention holds throughout the execution of rule induction within an informal context. To our knowledge, this problem has been explored in two existing studies [4,14], but both of them have to modify the definition of parallel reduction. In Copello et al.'s formalization [4], the $P_{CONTRACT}$ case directly integrates α-conversion, and rule induction is bypassed through α-structral induction on the first term of reduction. On the other hand, in Urban et al.'s study [14], BVC is directly incorporated into rule induction, but a freshness condition about x is added to the $P_{CONTRACT}$ case. Here we showcase how this induction can be achieved without the necessity of modifying parallel reduction. The induction principle relies on the observation that parallel reduction is modulo $\alpha-$equivalence (Fig. 4):

Lemma 7. *For any* $M \twoheadrightarrow_1 N$ *and* $M =_a M'$, *we can find* $M' \twoheadrightarrow_1 N'$ *and* $N =_a N'$.

Proof. Proved by size rule induction on $M \twoheadrightarrow_1 N$.

Now we begin to formulate the α-rule induction principle. First, we extend the concept of α-compatibility to relations:

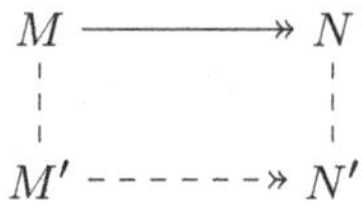

Fig. 4. Parallel reduction is modulo α−equivalence.

Definition 10 (Alpha-Compatible Relations).
A relation P:term→term→ *Prop is* α-compatible if

$$\forall M \ N, (\exists M' =_a M, N' =_a N, P \ M' \ N') \Rightarrow P \ M \ N. \tag{8}$$

Then the α-rule induction principle is as follows, parameterized by a name list xs:

Theorem 3 (Alpha Rule Induction).
Assume P: term→ term → *Prop is a relation on lambda terms and* xs *is a list of names. If the following five assertions hold:*

1. *P is* α−*compatible.*
2. $\forall M$: term, P M M.
3. $\forall M \ M'$ *such that* $M \twoheadrightarrow_1 M'$,
   $x \notin xs \Rightarrow P \ MM' \Rightarrow$
   $P \ (\lambda x. \ M) \ (\lambda x. \ M')$.
4. $\forall M \ M' \ N \ N'$ *such that* $M \twoheadrightarrow_1 M'$, $N \twoheadrightarrow_1 N'$,
   $P \ MM' \Rightarrow$
   $P \ NN' \Rightarrow$
   $P \ (M \ N) \ (M' \ N')$.
5. $\forall M \ M' \ N \ N'$ *such that* $M \twoheadrightarrow_1 M'$, $N \twoheadrightarrow_1 N'$,,
   $x \notin xs \Rightarrow$
   $P \ MM' \Rightarrow$
   $P \ NN' \Rightarrow$
   $P \ ((\lambda x. \ M) \ N) \ (M'[x \mapsto N'])$.

then $\forall M \ N$: term, $M \twoheadrightarrow_1 N$ *implies* P M N.

Proof. By assumption (1), we just need to find α−equivalent M' and N' that satisfies P M' N'. By Lemma 4, there exists $M' =_a M$ and binders of M' are not in xs. Then, employing Lemma 7, we establish the existence of $N' =_a N$ such that $M' \twoheadrightarrow_1 N'$. The goal now transforms into proving $M' \twoheadrightarrow_1 N' \Rightarrow$ P M' N', where M' only involve fresh binders. This problem can be resolved by conducting a standard rule induction on $M' \twoheadrightarrow_1 N'$ and subsequently applying assumptions (2)–(5). □

3.2   Proof of Church-Rosser

Armed with these two induction principles, the formal proof of the Church-Rosser theorem closely parallels the conventional informal proofs.

Lemma 8. (Substitutivity of $\twoheadrightarrow_1$).
If $M \twoheadrightarrow_1 M'$ and $N \twoheadrightarrow_1 N'$, then there exists L such that $M[x \mapsto N] \twoheadrightarrow_1 L$ and $L =_a M'[x \mapsto N']$.

Proof. Alpha-rule induction on $M \twoheadrightarrow_1 M'$, with xs including all variables in N and N'. The P_{REFL} case is addressed by another α-structural induction on M. Another intriguing scenario arises in the $P_{CONTRACT}$ case, where we want to show

$$\exists L, ((\lambda y.\ A)B)[x \mapsto N] \twoheadrightarrow_1 L \wedge L =_a A[y \mapsto B][x \mapsto N']. \tag{9}$$

As y is fresh, we have

$$((\lambda y.\ A)B)[x \mapsto N] = (\lambda y.\ A[x \mapsto N])(B[x \mapsto N])$$
$$\twoheadrightarrow_1 A[x \mapsto N'][y \mapsto B[x \mapsto N']] \quad \text{(Induction Hypothesis)}$$
$$=_a A[y \mapsto B][x \mapsto N']. \quad \text{(Lemma 5)}$$

Lemma 9. $\twoheadrightarrow_1$ *satisfies diamond property.*

Proof. Size rule induction is applied to $\twoheadrightarrow_1$. The proof is omitted here, and its informal equivalent can be found in the textbook [1], primarily based on Lemma 8. The α-rule induction is not required as no renaming situations are encountered.

Theorem 4 (Church-Rosser). $\rightarrow_\beta$ *is confluent.*

Proof. The diamond property is preserved through transitive closure, so $\twoheadrightarrow_1^+$ satisfies diamond property. By demonstrating the equivalence between $\twoheadrightarrow_1^+$ and $\rightarrow_\beta^*$, it can be established that $\rightarrow_\beta$ is confluent.

Corollary 1. *If $M \rightarrow_\beta^* A$, $M \rightarrow_\beta^* B$, with both A and B in β-normal form (i.e. they cannot undergo further $\rightarrow_\beta$ reduction), then $A =_a B$.*

Proof. By Church-Rosser, there exist $L_A =_a L_B$ such that $A \rightarrow_\beta^* L_A$ and $B \rightarrow_\beta^* L_B$. Given that both A and B are already in normal form, it follows that $A = L_A$ and $B = L_B$. We conclude that $A =_a B$.

4   Application: First-Order Logic Extended with Dynamically-Defined Predicates

Now, we explore how the formalized metatheory can serve as a framework to facilitate reasoning about nominal syntax with binders. We show that it is valid to extend the first-order language's syntax with a *let-in* constructor, allowing for arbitrary predicate definitions within a proposition. We will demonstrate that this new system is equivalent to the classical first-order language through a syntax transformation, fundamentally rooted in β-reduction.

We have previously formalized the ZFC axiomatic set theory in Coq using first-order logic (with rich connectives for educational usage):

Definition 11 (Terms And Propositions in ZFC).

$$t \; ::= \; \emptyset \mid \text{Var } x \mid \{t\} \mid t_1 \cap t_2 \mid t_1 \cup t_2.$$

$$P \; ::= \; t_1 = t_2 \mid t_1 \in t_2 \mid \neg P \mid P_1 \wedge P_2 \mid P_1 \vee P_2 \mid P_1 \rightarrow P_2 \mid P_1 \leftrightarrow P_2 \mid \forall x, \, P \mid \exists x, \, P$$

where $\emptyset$ is the constant symbol representing the empty set, and $\text{Var } x$ accepts a string to be utilized as a variable name. We have also developed the provability $\vdash P$ for propositions, including deduction rules for first-order logic and ZFC axioms. The rules can be found in a logic textbook [8].

To further enhance the usability, now we extend this syntax with a syntactic sugar for defining predicates, adding two constructors to propositions:

Definition 12 (Definition And Application of Predicates).

$$\textbf{\textit{let }} r(xs) := P \textbf{\textit{ in }} Q \mid r \; ts. \tag{10}$$

Here r ranges over the name for predicates, while xs and ts respectively denote lists of variable names and terms. $\textbf{\textit{let }} r(xs) := P \textbf{\textit{ in }} Q$ means we may define a new predicate named r, whose parameters are xs and definition is P. The newly defined predicate can then be applied to concrete terms in Q with the form of $r \; ts$[2]. To provide an example, the subset relation can be represented as follows:

$$\textbf{\textit{let }} \subseteq (x, y) := (\forall z, z \in x \rightarrow z \in y) \textbf{\textit{ in }} ... \subseteq (\emptyset, w)... \tag{11}$$

One may think that this approach is redundant, since symbols like $\subseteq$ can be defined as derived predicates or can be treated as a macro — in those approaches, it is not necessary to explicitly introduce the *let-in* syntax. However, it's crucial to recognize that this extension makes *let-in* an object-language component instead of a meta-language concept. That means, we can now formally reason about related syntactic transformation.

Accordingly, we add two deduction rules concerning predicate definition. To distinguish them from the original system, we use the subscript s to represent propositions and the deduction system with syntactic sugar.

$$\frac{\vdash_S \textbf{ let } r(l) := P_S \textbf{ in } Q_S}{\vdash_S Q_S[r \mapsto \lambda l.P_s]} \; [\text{Let}_{\text{ELIM}}]$$

$$\frac{\vdash_S \; Q_S[r \mapsto \lambda l.P_S]}{\vdash_S \textbf{ let } r(l) := P_S \textbf{ in } Q_S} \; [\text{Let}_{\text{INTRO}}]$$

These two rules describes the folding and unfolding predicate definitions. The unfolding of predicates at the predicate application case is

$$(r(t_1, ..., t_n))[r \mapsto \lambda l.P; ...] := P[l_1 \mapsto t_1; ...; l_n \mapsto t_n]. \tag{12}$$

Net we show that if $\vdash_S P_S$, by eliminating all predicate definitions, the proposition remains provable using the original deduction system.

---

[2] We require all propositions to be well-formed, i.e. propositions should not contain any freely-occurring predicates and all predicates are applied to correct number of terms as their definitions.

Definition 13 (Predicate Elimination).

$$elim \; (let \; r(xs) := P \; in \; Q) = (elim \; Q)[r \mapsto \lambda xs. \; elim \; P] \qquad (13)$$

To prove $\vdash_S P_S \Rightarrow \; \vdash elim \; P_S$, we require a property relating elimination and substitution. This is precisely where the formalized metatheory becomes crucial.

From the perspective of λ calculus, the act of binding a predicate definition to a proposition P corresponds to abstraction in λ calculus. Using Eq. 11 as an example, the operation of defining $\subseteq$ can be understood as:

$$(\lambda \subseteq . \underbrace{((\subseteq \; \emptyset) \; w))}_{\text{application } Q} (\lambda \underbrace{\;\; xy \;\;}_{\text{parameter}} \; l. \underbrace{\forall z.z \in x \to z \in y}_{\text{definition}} P) \qquad (14)$$

In proposition Q, $\subseteq$ is treated as a parameter, and it will be applied to $(\lambda xy. \; \forall z.z \in x \to z \in y)$. Performing one step of β-reduction on Eq. 14 will replace the $\subseteq$ symbol with its actual definition, resulting in:

$$((\lambda xy. \; \forall z.z \in x \to z \in y) \; \emptyset) \; w \to_\beta^* \; \forall z.z \in \emptyset \to z \in w, \qquad (15)$$

which is exactly the result of predicate elimination. If we can translate the proposition P_S into a lambda term, we can establish a connection between predicate elimination and β-reduction. This connection would enable us to apply the Church-Rosser theorem, obtaining favorable properties of elim directly.

The proofs in Sect. 2 and 3 have already been encapsulated in the verification module mentioned at the beginning. By providing the relevant parameters, one can automatically construct lambda terms of user-specified types and the corresponding Church-Rosser theorems. First, the types of variables in the propositions (V) and the types of predicates (R) are both based on the same String library in Coq. We unify them under type U, which serves as the uniform variable type $\mathbb{V}$ for lambda terms. Explicit variable sorts and the function sort can be readily provided, and constructing cases based on the constructors of U is straightforward. Subsequently, logic connectives, constants, and function symbols can be categorized into a constant type C, with each element corresponding to a symbol (denoted as $\forall$, etc.). It's easy to prove the properties required by Fig. 1 for these parameters.

Following this, we present the translation function from P_S to a lambda term. The lambda term corresponding to the proposition P is denoted as P^λ.

Definition 14 (Conversion to lambda terms).

$$(t_1 = t_2)^\lambda := \; = (t_1^\lambda \; t_2^\lambda)$$
$$(\neg P)^\lambda := \neg P^\lambda$$
$$(P_1 \wedge P_2)^\lambda := \wedge \; (P_1^\lambda \; P_2^\lambda)$$
$$(\forall x, P)^\lambda := \forall \; (\lambda x. \; P^\lambda)$$
$$(\exists x, P)^\lambda := \exists \; (\lambda x. \; P^\lambda)$$
$$(let \; r(l) := P \; in \; Q \;)^\lambda := (\lambda r. \; Q^\lambda) \; (\lambda l. P^\lambda).$$

The α-equivalence of propositions is defined to be the equivalence of their lambda terms. With this transformation, following lemmas can be proved:

Lemma 10. $P^\lambda \twoheadrightarrow_\beta^* (elim\ P)^\lambda.$

Lemma 11. $(elim\ P)^\lambda$ *is in β-normal form.*

Lemma 12 (Elimination and Substitution is Communicative).

$$elim\ (P)\ [x \mapsto t]\ =_\alpha\ elim\ (P[x \mapsto t]).$$

Proof. The lambda term forms of both propositions can be reached through multi-step reductions from $(\lambda x.P^\lambda)\ t^\lambda$. Further, utilizing Lemma 11, we know that both of these terms are β-normal forms. Therefore, by the corollary of Church-Rosser (Corollary 1), we can conclude that these two terms are α-equivalent, and translate the lambda term equivalence back to propositions.

Theorem 5 (Soundness of $\vdash_S$).

$$\vdash_S P_S \Rightarrow\ \vdash elim\ P_S.$$

Proof. Rule induction on $\vdash_S$. In the two cases concerning predicate definitions, we have $elim(\text{let}\ r(l) := P\ \text{in}\ Q)^\lambda =_\alpha elim(Q[r \mapsto \lambda l.P])^\lambda$ by Lemma 12. The case is then solved by the α-congruence rule in $\vdash$.

5   Conclusions

Formalizing informal proofs involving binders presents challenges. To address the problem, we have successfully formalized the metatheory of nominal lambda calculus within Coq, providing a framework for nominal reasoning with binders. Our work sets itself apart from existing approaches by avoiding the use of name swapping techniques. Instead, we introduce an intuitive α-equivalence definition and present several induction principles that encode the essence of the *Barendregt Variable Convention*. This enables formal proofs to closely mirror their informal counterparts. We introduce an α-rule induction for the original parallel reduction, an improvement from previous works that often required altering its definition [4,14]. Employing these principles, we seamlessly recreate the Church-Rosser theorem's proof by parallel reduction.

Our framework finds application in the formalization of ZFC set theory in first-order logic extended with predicate definitions. By transforming propositions into lambda terms, this operation can be explained as β-reduction. This facilitates the establishment of the soundness of the extended deduction system. Further research avenues could delve into systematically exploring the incorporation of BVC into rule induction, as well as the definition of α-recursion functions.

References

1. Barendregt, H.P., et al.: The lambda calculus, vol. 3. North-Holland Amsterdam (1984)
2. Charguéraud, A.: The locally nameless representation. J. Autom. Reason. **49**, 363–408 (2012)
3. Chlipala, A.: Parametric higher-order abstract syntax for mechanized semantics. In: Proceedings of the 13th ACM SIGPLAN International Conference on Functional Programming, pp. 143–156 (2008)
4. Copello, E., Szasz, N., Tasistro, Á.: Machine-checked proof of the Church-Rosser theorem for the lambda calculus using the Barendregt variable convention in constructive type theory. Electron. Notes Theor. Comput. Sci. **338**, 79–95 (2018)
5. Copello, E., Szasz, N., Tasistro, Á.: Formalization of metatheory of the lambda calculus in constructive type theory using the Barendregt variable convention. Math. Struct. Comput. Sci. **31**(3), 341–360 (2021)
6. De Bruijn, N.G.: Lambda calculus notation with nameless dummies, a tool for automatic formula manipulation, with application to the Church-Rosser theorem. In: Indagationes Mathematicae (Proceedings), vol. 75, pp. 381–392. Elsevier (1972)
7. Despeyroux, J., Felty, A., Hirschowitz, A.: Higher-order abstract syntax in Coq. In: Dezani-Ciancaglini, M., Plotkin, G. (eds.) TLCA 1995. LNCS, vol. 902, pp. 124–138. Springer, Heidelberg (1995). https://doi.org/10.1007/BFb0014049
8. Ebbinghaus, H.D., Flum, J., Thomas, W., Ferebee, A.S.: Mathematical Logic, vol. 1910. Springer, Heidelberg (1994). https://doi.org/10.1007/978-3-030-73839-6
9. Felty, A., Momigliano, A.: Hybrid: a definitional two-level approach to reasoning with higher-order abstract syntax. J. Autom. Reason. **48**(1), 43–105 (2012)
10. Gordon, A.D., Melham, T.: Five axioms of alpha-conversion. In: Goos, G., Hartmanis, J., van Leeuwen, J., von Wright, J., Grundy, J., Harrison, J. (eds.) TPHOLs 1996. LNCS, vol. 1125, pp. 173–190. Springer, Heidelberg (1996). https://doi.org/10.1007/BFb0105404
11. Pitts, A.M.: Nominal logic, a first order theory of names and binding. Inf. Comput. **186**(2), 165–193 (2003)
12. Stark, K., Schäfer, S., Kaiser, J.: Autosubst 2: reasoning with multi-sorted de bruijn terms and vector substitutions. In: Proceedings of the 8th ACM SIGPLAN International Conference on Certified Programs and Proofs, pp. 166–180 (2019)
13. Urban, C.: Nominal techniques in isabelle/hol. J. Autom. Reason. **40**, 327–356 (2008)
14. Urban, C., Berghofer, S., Norrish, M.: Barendregt's variable convention in rule inductions. In: Pfenning, F. (ed.) CADE 2007. LNCS (LNAI), vol. 4603, pp. 35–50. Springer, Heidelberg (2007). https://doi.org/10.1007/978-3-540-73595-3_4
15. Urban, C., Pitts, A.M., Gabbay, M.J.: Nominal unification. Theor. Comput. Sci. **323**(1–3), 473–497 (2004)

Vulnerability Report Analysis and Vulnerability Reproduction for Web Applications

Weiwei Wang[1] , Zidong Li[2], Feng You[2], and Ruilian Zhao[2]([✉])

[1] Beijing Institute of Petrochemical Technology, Beijing 102617, China
[2] Beijing University of Chemical Technology, Beijing 100029, China
rlzhao@mail.buct.edu.cn

Abstract. With the increasing complexity of Web applications, their security issues happen frequently. Vulnerability reports aim to document security issues of Web applications and assist in improving their security and quality. However, vulnerability reports are usually described in highly unstructured natural language, and the descriptions of vulnerabilities vary considerably. So automatically reproducing vulnerabilities from their reports is a challenging task. To this end, this paper proposes an approach to automatically comprehend vulnerability reports and reproduce vulnerabilities in Web applications. In order to automatically parse vulnerability reports of Web applications, a general syntactic dependency pattern is summarized from diverse vulnerability reports to guide the identification and extraction of key information in vulnerability reports. In particular, payloads in vulnerability reports exist mainly in the form of code fragments, unlike natural language. For this reason, a payload extraction rule is further designed. Moreover, considering that the descriptions of vulnerability reports and Web application are different but semantically similar, this paper uses semantic similarity to match the events of web application with the key information of the report, and then generates event sequences and corresponding test scripts to trigger the vulnerability, achieving vulnerability reproduction. To verify the effectiveness of our approach, we collect 400 vulnerability reports from more than 300 Web application projects and summarize syntactic dependency patterns. And 26 real vulnerability reports involving 23 open-source Web applications were used for experiments. The results show that our method can effectively extract critical information from vulnerability reports and generate feasible test scripts to reproduce vulnerabilities, reducing manual operations and improving the efficiency of vulnerability reproduction.

Keywords: web application testing · vulnerability report analysis · vulnerability reproduction · syntactic dependency pattern · test script

1 Introduction

With the rapid development of the Internet, Web applications have become popular in all aspects of social life. Meanwhile, the security of Web applications is increasingly important. According to the National Information Security Vulnerability Sharing Platform (CNVD) [5], a total of 1,764 security vulnerabilities were collected in July 2023, of which security vulnerabilities with respect to Web applications accounted for as many as 64%, seriously affecting the security of web applications. Hence, identifying and addressing vulnerabilities is urgently needed. If vulnerabilities found during testing or using can be reproduced, the causes of the vulnerabilities can be analyzed and repaired, thereby improving the quality and security of web applications.

A vulnerability report usually describes some key aspects of the vulnerability, which is critical to its reproduction and repair [2,3]. However, most vulnerability reports are currently written in natural language, and the descriptions of vulnerabilities vary a lot, so, it is difficult to automatically parse the reports and extract the key information involved in triggering vulnerabilities. At present, most existing studies on vulnerability reports focus on the identification of their structured information, such as the software name, the vendor, the type of vulnerability, and so on by using the named entity recognition or relationship extraction techniques [6,9,13]. But these techniques have difficulty in parsing a complex unstructured descriptions, such as the steps to trigger a vulnerability in the vulnerability report.

Furthermore, due to the imprecision and incompleteness of the vulnerability report itself [8], the vulnerability-triggering steps described in reports are not accurate enough. Meanwhile, modern Web applications involve a variety of GUI events. Thus, it is a challenge to map directly the vulnerability-triggering steps in reports to GUI events of actual Web applications [14], making it more difficult to reproduce a vulnerability automatically for web applications. To date, the existing vulnerability reproduction largely depends on manual experience and required the tester to have expertise in the security field, which makes the cost of vulnerability location and repair high.

Therefore, this paper proposes an approach to automatically reproduce vulnerabilities from vulnerability reports of Web applications, which involve both structured and unstructured information, and have various abstract descriptions. To parse the unstructured information of vulnerability reports, a general syntactic dependency pattern is summarized from diverse vulnerability reports of Web applications. In particular, there may exist some malicious codes, named attack payloads, in the unstructured part of reports, which refer to the specific data inputs or commands used to exploit a vulnerability. These attack payloads are usually illegal strings and mostly in the form of code fragments. Thus, to effectively obtain the attack payloads of vulnerability reports, corresponding attack payloads extraction rules are designed. On this basis, the critical information of triggering a vulnerability can be extracted from the reports automatically. Besides, considering that the description of vulnerability reports and Web applications are different but semantically similar, a test script generation method based on semantic similarity is proposed to realize vulnerability reproduction. To summarize syntactic dependency patterns of vulnerability reports, 400 reports from more than 300 Web application projects are collected and used. And to further verify the effectiveness of our approach, vulnerability analysis and reproduction experiments are conducted on 23 open-source Web applications involving

26 real vulnerability reports. The results show that our approach can effectively parse the vulnerability reports, and generate feasible test scripts to reproduce the vulnerabilities, improving the efficiency of vulnerability reproduction.

The main contributions are as follows:

1. An automatic vulnerability reports parsing approach is proposed to extract critical information that trigger vulnerabilities based on the syntactic dependency patterns summarized and attack payloads extraction rule.
2. A semantic similarity-based test script generation method is presented to reproduce vulnerabilities by correlating vulnerability-triggering steps in reports with GUI events in Web applications.
3. 400 vulnerability reports are collected for syntactic dependency patterns summarizing. And experiments are conducted on 26 vulnerability reports of 23 open-source Web applications. The results show that our approach can effectively analyze reports and reproduce vulnerabilities.

The rest of this paper is organized as follows: Sect. 2 introduces the related concepts and techniques, involving vulnerability report, natural language processing and test script for web applications. Section 3 describes our vulnerability report analysis and vulnerability reproduction approach. Section 4 conducts experiments on 26 vulnerability reports to validate the effectiveness of our approach. Finally, the paper concludes with a summary of the whole paper.

2   Basic Concepts and Related Techniques

This section introduces the components of vulnerability report of web applications, the NLP-related techniques, and test script, which are relevant to the work reported in this paper.

2.1   Vulnerability Report

Vulnerability reports are designed to record information, usually written in natural language, about vulnerabilities discovered by testers or users during their use of Web applications. Typically, it contains structured information, such as the title, date of found, exploit author, and so on, as well as unstructured information, such as vulnerability description, steps to reproduce the vulnerability, and so on. Figure 1 shows an example of a Stored Cross-Site Scripting (XSS) vulnerability report of a management system. From this example, we can see that the basic vulnerability information is described in the structural part marked with "#", while the steps that trigger the vulnerability are given in the unstructured part, documenting the user's interactions with Web applications when the vulnerability is exploited successfully. Moreover, some of the steps contain malicious code that can trigger a specific vulnerability, such as "><script>alert("XSS")</script> in step 5 in Fig. 1. The malicious code is generally named as the attack payload in vulnerability reports.

It is obvious that the critical information to reproduce vulnerabilities can be obtained from the unstructured part of vulnerability reports, especially the steps. Developers/testers can have some insight into the vulnerability by reading the report, getting the vulnerability-triggering steps, finding the corresponding GUI events of Web applications, triggering them step by step, and finally replicating the vulnerability. Thus, this paper focuses on the analysis of "Steps to Reproduce" to guide the automatic reproduction of the relevant vulnerability.

```
# Exploit Title: Student Study Center Management System v1.0 - Stored Cross-Site Scripting (XSS)
# Date of found: 12/05/2023
# Exploit Author: ....
... ...
# Software Link: https://phpgurukul.com/student-study-center-management-system-using-php-and-mysql/
# CVE: CVE-2023-33580
# CVE URL: https://cve.mitre.org/cgi-bin/cvename.cgi?name=CVE-2023-33580

Vulnerability Description -
    The Student Study Center Management System V1.0, developed by PHPGurukul....

Steps to Reproduce -
    The following steps demonstrate how to exploit the Stored XSS vulnerability in ...:
        1. Visit the Student Study Center Management System V1.0 application by accessing the URL:
           http://localhost/student-study-center-MS-PHP/sscms/index.php.
        2. Click on the "Admin" button to navigate to the admin login page.
        3. Login to the Admin account using the default credentials....
        4. Proceed to the Admin Profile page.
        5. Within the "Admin Name" field, inject the following XSS payload, enclosed in brackets:
           {"><script>alert("XSS")</script>}.
        6. Click on the "Submit" button.
        7. Refresh the page, and the injected payload will be executed.
```

Fig. 1. an example of a vulnerability report.

2.2   Natural Language Processing

Natural Language Processing (NLP) is an important area of artificial intelligence in the study of human-computer interaction. It aims to automatically analyze and understand natural language [12]. In order to parse vulnerability reports written in natural language, this paper will use lexical analysis techniques and dependency syntactic parsing techniques in NLP. Moreover, semantic similarity techniques will be also used to compare the operations in vulnerability reports and the events in Web applications.

Lexical Analysis. Lexical analysis techniques are a fundamental part of NLP, which are usually used to separate text into basic lexical units, such as words, punctuation marks, numbers, etc. It mainly consists of two important processes: tokenization and part-of-speech (POS) tagging.

Tokenization is the process of dividing a text into individual lexical units. Since English text usually uses Spaces to separate words, the simplest tokenizer only use spaces to split entire sentences. More complex tokenizers may also handle a text by other symbols such as parentheses, conjunctions, or word suffixes [10]. Besides, users can customize the tokenizer with other symbols.

In vulnerability reports of web applications, the attack payloads or URLs, in the "Steps to Reproduce" part, are different from the common text, which usually contain a long string of consecutive characters connected by special symbols. Thus, a custom tokenizer is needed for analyzing the steps sentence in the reports. *spaCy* [15], an open-source library for NLP, provides a variety of APIs for users to customize tokenizers. So, this paper adopts a customized *spaCy* to split steps information in reports into individual words or tokens.

POS tagging is the process of labeling each lexical unit, which can help to understand the grammatical or semantic role of every lexical unit in a sentence, such as nouns, verbs, adjectives, etc. There are many methods for part-of-speech tagging, such as grammar-based methods, statistic-based methods and deep learning methods. Since deep learning-baseds POS tagging have shown significant advantages over traditional approaches in capturing contextual information and handling out-of-vocabulary words, it is employed to tag the part-of-speech of steps information in vulnerability reports.

Dependency Syntactic Parsing. Dependency syntactic parsing is also an NLP technique that aims to analyze the grammatical structure of a sentence by identifying the syntactic relationships between words. Unlike traditional syntactic parsing techniques, dependency syntactic parsing not only focuses on the syntactic structure of a sentence, but also on the semantic relationships between words in the sentence.

Stanza [16] is an open-source Python NLP toolkit. Compared with other toolkits, *Stanza* can implement the POS tagging and accurate context-aware tagging based on deep learning techniques. At the same time, it incorporates a high-quality dependency parser that can analyze the syntactic structure of sentences and generate dependency parse trees, representing the relationships between words. It has been observed that the description of vulnerability reports often lacks certain sentence elements due to poor writing, while dependency syntactic parsing can infer elements by using the relationships among words. Thus, in this paper, *Stanza* is used for POS tagging and dependency parsing of vulnerability reports.

Semantic Similarity Calculation. Semantic similarity refers to the degree of similarity or relatedness between two pieces of text or concepts in terms of their meaning. Instead of relying solely on lexical or surface-level similarity, semantic similarity takes into account the contextual and conceptual similarity between words, phrases, or sentences.

One commonly used method to calculate the similarity between word groups is to convert words into vector representations and measure their similarity using cosine similarity. In this method, each word is represented as a vector in a high-dimensional space, with each dimensions capturing a different aspect of the word's meaning. The semantic similarity between word vectors is calculated by cosine similarity, where a larger value indicates that the two vectors are identical or very similar, while a value closer to zero suggests that the two vectors are orthogonal or dissimilar. Word2vec [17] are often used to converts text into vectors via neural networks. There are two main models in Word2vec, CBOW (Continuous Bag-of-Words) model and skip-grams model. The CBOW model predicts and analyses the current word from nearby contextual words, and the order of the contextual words does not affect the result. The skip-grams model predicts the context from the current word, with nearer words given more weight than more distant words. These two models have their advantages and disadvantages. Generally speaking, the CBOW model is faster, while skip-grams works better for less common words.

For vulnerability reports of web applications, it is a challenge that translates their step information into GUI events of Web applications because their lexical descriptions often differ greatly. But the semantics between steps and GUI events are similar. Therefore, they can be matched with the help of semantic similarity. Moreover, most of the words appearing in vulnerability reports are commonly used, so this paper employs the CBOW model to convert words into vectors to achieve higher efficiency.

2.3 Test Scripts and Testing Framework of Web Applications

For a web application, its test case consists of a sequence of events and the input values on the sequence. In order to automate the execution of test cases, test scripts need to be created to achieve automatic interaction with web page and their elements. And for most web applications, test scripts rely on DOM tree to locate elements and manipulate objects within the tree through a defined set of interactive functions. In that way, test cases can, for instance, automatically fill in and submit forms and click on hyperlinks [1,11]. That is to say, test scripts refer to a series of basic instructions, which can be executed under test automation frameworks to control the browser and interact with the web page and its elements. In fact, test cases are executed through test scripts under a test automation framework. Therefore, test scripts can reduce the workload of testers, and greatly improve the testing efficiency of Web applications [18].

Selenium is one of the most widely used test framework for Web applications, which can be used to drive browsers and manipulate page elements. For an event of Web applications, its test script in *Selenium* consists of a series of GUI atomic operations. Each atomic operation is represented as a triple <**Com, Tar, Val**>, where **Com** represents a GUI operation command, such as *click* and *input*; **Tar** remarks the target object of **Com**; and if the **Com** is an input command, **Val** is used to store user inputs; otherwise, the **Val** is empty. For example, a *login* event includes entering a username and password and clicking the login button. So, three atomic GUI operations are required in order to make this event executable. They are <*send_key, user, value1*>, <*send_key, pass, value2*> and <*click, //input[@value ='Login']*>, respectively. These atomic operations can be represented as test script in Selenium syntax, and the sample representations of these atomic operations of *Selenium* are shown in Table 1. This paper adopts *Selenium* to execute test cases of web applications.

Table 1. The sample representations of atomic operations in *Selenium*

event	Selenium atomic operations			Executable script(Python)
	Com	Tar	Val	
login	Send_key	user	admin	driver.find_element_by_name(user).send_keys("admin")
	Send_key	pass	123	driver.find_element_by_name(pass).send_keys("123")
	click	Xpath:(//input[@ value='Login'])	–	driver.find_element_by_xpath(":(//input[@value='Login'] ").click()

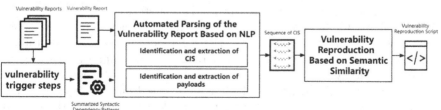

Fig. 2. Vulnerability reproduction from vulnerability report for Web applications

3 Vulnerability Report Analysis and Vulnerability Reproduction Approach for Web Applications

This section describes our vulnerability report analysis and vulnerability reproduction approach for Web applications in detail.

3.1 Overview

A vulnerability report of Web applications contains the steps to trigger the vulnerability. Generally, a step describes an action taken by users during interaction with the Web application, as well as information such as the object of the action, object type, and input values, known as **critical information of step**, abbreviated as **CIS**. The CIS can be expressed by a quadruple, i.e. <action, object, oType, input>, where oType stands for object type. Obviously, CIS is essential for reproducing a vulnerability.

In order to identify CISs in vulnerability reports, we first studied the way that users describe vulnerability-triggering steps and summarized them as syntactic dependency patterns. Then, syntactic reports are automatically analyzed according to the syntactic dependency patterns summarised, and their corresponding CISs are identified and extracted. Furthermore, the attack payloads, which are some malicious code written in the steps of vulnerability reports in order to trigger a specific vulnerability, are also identified and extracted. For a step with a payload, the payload is treated as the input value of corresponding action. As a result, a CIS sequence can be generated in the order of the corresponding steps. On this basis, the GUI events of Web applications associated with the sequence of CIS are identified based on their semantic similarity, and test scripts are constructed to reproduce the vulnerability in Web applications. The overall framework of vulnerability report analysis and vulnerability reproduction for web applications is shown in Fig. 2.

3.2   Syntactic Dependency Patterns Summarising from Vulnerability Reports

By analyzing real web applications and their vulnerability reports, we found that the core actions involved in web applications can be divided into five major categories, and the syntactic structure describing vulnerability-triggering steps is determined by the type of actions. We collected 400 vulnerability reports of more than 300 Web applications from Exploit-db, a vulnerability collection platform [7], and found that the verbs involved in the steps can be associated with one of the five action categories. Moreover, each type of action may correspond to multiple verbs in steps, and the concrete relationship is shown in Table 2. Therefore, for the collected vulnerability reports of web applications, we can identify and classify the verbs involved in their steps into different actions, and then analyze syntactic structures of these steps based on each type of action. Finally, they are summarized as syntactic dependency patterns of the steps of vulnerability reports.

In more detail, the description sentence of each step in the collected vulnerability reports is regarded as text, and tokenization and POS tagging are enforced on the text by automatic lexical analysis. Then, the verbs that indicate the actions are extracted and classified according to Table 2. After that, the syntactic structure of each step sentence is analyzed based on its type of action with the help of the dependency syntactic parsing technique. On the basis of the syntactic structures, the dependencies among the action and other critical information, including the objects of the action, the type of object and corresponding input are further resolved. These dependencies are then summarised to form dependency syntactic patterns for the steps of vulnerability reports. For example, for the action of "Click", it can be summarized that the object may be represented by a nominal/adjectival modifier or by a compound word of the type of the object. And the type of objects may be identified by the preposition of object, oblique nominal, adverbial modifier, and so on. Since the action of *Click* does not require input values, there are no input-related description involved in its pattern. So, the dependency syntactic pattern of "Click" action can be summarized as shown in the "click" row in Table 3, where *Nmod*, *Amod* and *Compound* stand for a nominal/adjectival modifier or a compound word, and *Pobj*, *Obl*, and *Advmod* indicate the preposition of object, oblique nominal, and adverbial modifier, respectively. For other types of action, similar generalizations can be made about their objects, object types, and input modifiers. As a result, the corresponding dependency syntactic patterns of the steps in the vulnerability reports are listed in Table 3, each consisting of multiple entries.

Therefore, the specific dependency syntactic patterns are summarised from each step sentence of collected vulnerability reports for web applications. And the summarised dependency syntactic patterns can be used for extracting critical information for vulnerability reproduction.

Table 2. Classification and Verbs in steps of vulnerability reports

Type of Action	Containing verbs
Jump	go,login,navigate,visit, triggered, using
Input	enter, type, add, write, paste, put, insert, fill
Use	use
Click	click
Change	change

3.3   Automated Parsing of Vulnerability Reports

For a vulnerability report, the CISs, i.e. <action, object, oType, input>, in its steps are essential to reproduce the vulnerability. Based on the dependency syntactic pattern summarised, the steps in the report are analyzed by lexical analysis and dependency syntactic parsing, and the corresponding CIS sequences are obtained, laying the foundation for vulnerability reproduction.

Table 3. Dependency syntactic patterns of different types of actions

Type of Action	Action objects	Type of Object	input values
Jump	Nmod, Amod	Obj, Parataxis, Obl	/
Input	Amod, Compound, Appos	Pobj, Obl	Dobj, Obj
Use	Amod, Compound	Pobj, Obl	Dobj, Obj
Click	Nmod, Amod, Compound	Pobj, Obl, Advmod	/
Change	Nmod, Amod	Obj	Obl

In addition, we note that some of vulnerability-triggering steps require an attack payload to be entered at a specified location. Unlike traditional natural language, the payload in vulnerability reports is usually an illegal string surrounded by quotation marks, mostly in the form of code fragments for attacking specific vulnerabilities. Thus, the forms of payloads needs to be analyzed and used for payload identification and extraction in this paper.

CIS Identification and Extraction. In order to obtain the sequence of CIS from a vulnerability report, the steps of triggering the vulnerability in the report should be first identified, and then theses steps sentences are parsed. It is observed that for vulnerability reports of web applications, the steps that trigger vulnerabilities generally start with the "Steps to Reproduce" keyword, so this paper uses string matching to locate the steps. Considering a single step in the reports may occupy multiple lines, this paper groups these lines into a text and treats it as one complete step.

As mentioned above, in a step sentence, its action is the most important and decides the syntactic structure of the step. So, the verb corresponding to the action is first identified by using lexical analysis. Specifically, tokenizer in lexical analysis is used to partition the sentence into separate lexical units, and part-of-speech tagging is used to mark each lexical unit with its lexicality. And the verbs in the step sentence are extracted and regarded as actions. Then, the object associated with the action, the object type and the input values are identified and extracted by using syntactic dependency parsing technique.

In particular, a single step sentence may contain multiple verbs. Thus, in addition to the root verb of the step sentence should be extracted as action, all verbs that have adverbial clause, conjunction or juxtapositions modifiers with the root verb should be also extracted as actions. The step sentence can be divided into intervals according to these verbs, and CIS should be extracted from each interval. If the sentence is not split, the accuracy of CIS extraction may be lower. For instance, if the step sentence *"click on the login button, enter username and password, click on the submit button"* is not separated, the CIS associated with the second *click* may overwrite the CIS of the first *click*, affecting the extraction accuracy of CISs from vulnerability reports.

Besides, when extracting the objects of actions, there may be case that a verb corresponds to multiple objects and inputs. So, this paper records these objects and inputs involved in a CIS in the form of a set. For example, in the sentence *"click on the 'save' and 'submit' button"*, the verb *click* is the root word of the sentence, namely the action of this step, and the action *click* corresponds to the *save* and *submit* objects. According to the syntactic dependency pattern, the *button* should be the type of the objects. And the dependency between *save* and *button* is compound, so *save* should be extracted as an object of the CIS; and the words *save* and *submit* are conjunction(Conj), so both *save* and *submit* should be added to the CIS as objects. Thus, the CIS of this sentence should be <click, [save,submit], [button], None>.

Payload Identification and Extraction. The payloads in vulnerability reports generally appear in two forms: 1) inside the steps; 2) under the heading of payload outside the steps. For the above two forms, we design two corresponding extraction rules.

For the form 1), the payloads are identified as follows. As mentioned above, the payload is a illegal string, mostly in the form of code fragments. As we know, standard tokenizer in lexical analysis would split the payload into multiple words, leading to errors in subsequent processing. Thus, this paper redesigns a custom tokenizer that can treat all the words involved in a payload as a whole, and then extracts the payload according to our syntactic dependency patterns summarized. It can be observed that attack payloads are usually enclosed in a pair of symbols such as parentheses, quotation marks, or square brackets. Thus, payloads in vulnerability reports can be matched by regular expressions. In order to accurately locate the payloads, this paper designs a set of regular expressions, as shown in Table 4, to identify the words involved in the payloads.

Concretely, the custom tokenizer first splits the step sentence into multiple words based on symbols or spaces in traditional way. Then, the location of the payload is identified by regular expression matching, and the related phrases involved in the payload are merged to form a complete payload. After that, the step sentence is parsed by using the syntactic dependency parsing. If the input value in CIS is the word *"payload"*, then the words that have a dependency on *"payload"* as adjectival modifier (Amod), appositional modifier (Appos), adverbial modifier (Advmod), or a compound are treated as the content of the payload.

Table 4. Regular expressions for extracting special case words in payload

Parentheses of payload	Regular expressions
"	'[^'|^]+[^']*[^'|^]+'
""	"[^"|^]+[^"]*[^"|^]+"
"	'[^'|^]+[^']*[^'|^]+'
()	([^(|^)]+)
{}	{[^(|^)]+}

For the form 2), that is, the payload is given under the heading "payload", whereas in a vulnerability report, the step sentence may only mention that a payload is to be entered at a certain location.

In this case, there are no words in the step sentence that have a dependency on the word "payload". Then, we will use "payload" as the keyword to search for the payload in full text. In addition, the URL of the homepage in vulnerability reports is similar to the payload. Thus, its identification is similar as that of the payloads.

In summary, for a vulnerability report, each of its step sentence is analyzed, and its CIS and the corresponding payload (if any) are determined. The CIS and payload in the same step are associated to form a complete CIS. Finally, these CISs are combined into a sequence in the order of the steps for reproducing the vulnerability.

3.4 Automatic Vulnerability Reproduction Based on Semantic Similarity Between CIS and Event of Web Application

To reproduce a vulnerability in a vulnerability report from a web application, a sequence of events on the Web application that corresponds to the CIS sequence of the report should be found. Although the CISs of the reports are syntactically different from the events of Web applications, they are semantically similar. So, we can match the object of CIS with the page element binding events according to their semantic similarity. To be specific, cosine similarity, a widely used measure of similarity, is used to calculate how similar an object in CIS is to the id or name attribute of a page element in a Web application. As a result, the event corresponding to the CIS can be obtained, and an executable test script for the event can be created and executed. Hence, the event sequence of the web application that matches the CIS sequence can be dynamically explored during web application execution, reproducing the vulnerability.

In more detail, starting from the home page of the Web application, the dynamic exploration process tries to match the GUI event sequence with the CIS sequence by their semantic similarity. That is, if there exists a page element similar to the current CIS, then an executable test script for the event binding that element is generated and executed to trigger the event, entering a new Web page. In this new page, its page element and the object of next CIS in the sequence is compared, and the element similar to the CIS is selected and triggered. Repeat the process above until all the CISs involved in the report have been traversed. In this case, it is believed that the event sequence triggered during the exploration of web application can reproduce the vulnerability.

The process of vulnerability reproduction is shown in Algorithm 1. Its inputs are the URL of a web application and the CIS sequence extracted from its corresponding vulnerability report. Specifically, it first does the initialization line (1–2) and then the html source code of the current page, starting from the home page of the Web application, is parsed with *BeautifulSoup* parser, a commonly used web application parser, and all web elements in this page are extracted (line 4). Then, the element with the greatest semantic similarity with the current CIS is found by matching the object in current CIS with the id or name of all page element in this page (line 5–9). Based on the matched element, the event binding this element is determined and the corresponding test script is created for the event (line 10–12). The script is executed to trigger the event, reaching a new web page (line 13). Considering that the page may not be fully loaded due to network reasons, if there are no elements on the page matching the current CIS, (that is, the semantic similarity is less than a threshold), the algorithm will wait for some time, such as 5 s, before continuing to search for elements related to the current CIS (line 16). If new page is loaded after waiting, indicating that new elements are generated, then we continue to find the elements matching the current CIS on the new loaded page (lines 17–18). Otherwise, we think the event for the current CIS is not found, and reproducing this vulnerability fails (line 20). When all CISs have been processed, the vulnerability can be triggered by executing the corresponding events via their test script, and the resulting test scripts are regarded as the vulnerability reproduction script.

Algorithm 1. Automatic vulnerability reproduction from a vulnerability report

---

Input: Web application URL; CIS sequence $CISs[]$
1: $TestScript[] = null, maxSim = 0, maxIdx = -1$ //Initialization
2: $Web.get(URL)$ //Loading the home page by the URL
3: **while** $i < CISs.size()$ **do**
4:     $element[] = ParseByBeautifulSoup(Web.page)$
5:     **while** $j < element.size()$ **do**
6:         $sim[j] = SemSim(CISs[i], element[j])$
7:         $maxSim = Max(maxSim, sim[j])$ //$maxSim$ records greatest similarity
8:         $maxIdx = Update(maxIdx, j)$ //$maxIdx$ records index of the element with greatest similarity with $CISs[i]$
9:     **end while**
10:     **if** $maxSim \geq Threshold$ **then**
11:         $script = generateScript(element[maxIdx])$
12:         $TestScript.add(script)$
13:         $Web.page\_source = execute(script)$ //Trigger the matched event and reach the new page
14:         $i++$ //Proceed to the next CIS
15:     **else**
16:         $NewPage = waitUntilLoaded()$ //Until the page are loaded completely
17:         **if** $NewPage \neq Web.page$ **then**
18:             $Web.page = NewPage, Continue$
19:         **else**
20:             $Break$ //The event for the current CIS is not found, break
21:         **end if**
22:     **end if**
23: **end while**

---

4   Experiment

This paper proposes an automatic vulnerability reports analysis and vulnerability reproduction approach for web application. In order to verify the effectiveness of this approach, real vulnerability reports, collected from vulnerability tracking platform, are analyzed, and vulnerability reproduction experiments are conducted on corresponding web applications. On this foundation, three research questions are raised to assess our approach.

RQ1. Can our automatic vulnerability report analysis method extract CIS sequences accurately?

RQ2. Is our attack payload extraction strategy effective?

RQ3. Can our vulnerability reproduction method generate test scripts to trigger vulnerabilities?

Table 5. Experimental subjects and classification

Category	No.	Name of Web Application	Number of reports
Pa	Pa-1	Loan Management System	1
	Pa-2	Simple Online College Entrance Exam System	1
	Pa-3	Hospitals Patient Records Management System	3
	Pa-4	Student Quarterly Grading System	1
	Pa-5	Simple Student Quarterly Result/Grade System	1
	Pa-6	Online DJ Booking Management System	1
	Pa-7	RATES SYSTEM	1
	Pa-8	Online Railway Reservation System	1
	Pa-9	Online Veterinary Appointment System	1
	Pa-10	Online Thesis Archiving System	1
	Pa-11	Online Enrollment Management System in PHP and PayPal	1
	Pa-12	Employee and Visitor Gate Pass Logging System	1
	Pa-13	Online Project Time Management System	1
	Pa-14	Online Diagnostic Lab Management System	1
	Pa-15	Hospitalss Patient Records Management System	1
	Pa-16	Gadget Works Online Ordering System	1
	Pa-17	COVID19 Testing Management System	2
	Pa-18	Simple Chatbot Application	1
	Pa-19	Online Employees Work From Home Attendance System 1.0	1
Re	Re-1	Young Entrepreneur E-Negosyo System	1
	Re-2	WordPress Plugin Wappointment	1
Thi	Thi-1	Cab Management System	1
	Thi-2	Online Diagnostic Lab Management System	1
Total			26

4.1 Experimental Subjects and Environment

In this paper, 400 vulnerability reports from over 300 projects in the vulnerability collection platform Exploit-db are selected, and the syntactic dependency patterns are summarised based on them. On this basis, 26 real vulnerability reports corresponding to 23 open source Web applications are analyzed and vulnerability reproduction experiments are carried out. According to their descriptions for triggering vulnerabilities, the reports can be divided into three categories. The first category of reports contains only Web page element operations in their step sentences, such as clicking buttons, entering information, and other GUI operations, denoted by Pa; The second category of reports contains request information in their step sentences, such as sending a request, represented by Re; The third category of reports contains third-party software operations in their step sentences, such as using burp suite [4] to intercept request information, denoted by Thi. Table 5 gives the vulnerability report classification, number and name.

In vulnerability report analysis experiments, all these three categories are used, while in vulnerability reproduction experiments, only Pa category is considered since Re and Thi categories require manual operations to construct test scripts for reproduction.

The experiments were carried out on a personal computer with a MacBook Pro (16-in, 2019), 2.3 GHz Intel Core i9 processor and 16 GB of running memory; the programming language is Python. Furthermore, a simple replication package containing experiment data is provided at Github, available at https://github.com/LiZD0424/ARV.

4.2   Analysis of Experimental Results

Results for RQ1. To evaluate whether our automatic vulnerability reports analysis method can extract CIS sequences accurately, this paper compares the CIS sequences extracted by our approach with those analyzed manually. Table 6 shows the total number of steps involved in the reports, where the steps refers to the intervals after processing, and each of them corresponds to one CIS. Further, the extraction accuracy of CIS sequence for each report is shown in this table, where extraction accuracy counts the proportion of CISs correctly parsed. As can be seen from the table, our method can successfully parse 23 vulnerability reports. And the average extraction accuracy of CIS sequences is 77%. This shows that our automatic parsing method for vulnerability reports is effective in identifying and extracting the critical information for triggering the vulnerabilities.

Table 6. CIS extraction accuracy of vulnerability report analysis

NO	Total number of steps	Steps of correct identification	The extraction accuracy
Pa-1	3	3	100%
Pa-2	3	3	100%
Pa-3	9	9	100%
Pa-4	3	3	100%
Pa-5	1	1	100%
Pa-6	5	3	60%
Pa-7	2	1	50%
Pa-8	3	1	33%
Pa-9	3	2	66%
Pa-10	3	2	66%
Pa-11	3	1	33%
Pa-12	4	2	50%
Pa-13	4	4	100%
Pa-14	4	2	50%
Pa-15	3	2	66%
Pa-16	5	5	100%
Pa-17	5	3	60%
Pa-18	5	4	80%
Pa-19	3	3	100%
Re-1	3	2	66%
Re-2	2	1	50%
Thi-1	5	5	100%
Thi-2	5	4	80%
Total	86	66	77%

It is worth noting that there are still errors when parsing some reports. Through analysis, we found that this is due to the non-standard writing of the steps in reports. For example, the sentence in report *Pa*-8 contains *"Navigate to 'Schedule'> go to 'Book' or 'Revervation Form' page using the following URL: http://localhost:8000/orrs/?page%20=reserve&sid=1"*. This step sentence uses the irregular symbol ' >', which resulted in the step not being divided into two intervals. Thus, it has an adverse impact on the CIS extraction results.

Results for RQ2. To answer whether our payload extraction method is effective, we performed payload extraction experiments on all vulnerability reports, except the reports corresponding to web application *Pa*-17 and *Re*-1 because they did not contain URL or payloads. The experiment results are shown in Table 7. For 26 vulnerability reports, there are 42 URLs and payloads in total. By using the traditional tokenizer, 42.9% of URLs and payloads are identified on average. By using the custom tokenizer, 66.7% of URLs and payloads are accurately identified. In other words, our payload extraction method can improve the extraction accuracy of payloads or URLs in vulnerability reports. In particular, the accuracy of payload extraction was increased by 55.48%.

Table 7. Effectiveness of URL and load identification

No.	Number of URLs or payloads	Accuracy of url or payload recognition	
		traditional tokenizer	custom tokenizer
Pa-1	2	50%	100%
Pa-2	2	50%	100%
Pa-3	3	100%	100%
Pa-4	2	50%	100%
Pa-5	1	100%	100%
Pa-6	3	100%	100%
Pa-7	2	0%	50%
Pa-8	2	0%	0%
Pa-9	2	50%	50%
Pa-10	3	0%	66%
Pa-11	1	0%	0%
Pa-12	2	0%	0%
Pa-13	1	100%	100%
Pa-14	2	0%	0%
Pa-15	2	0%	100%
Pa-16	1	100%	100%
Pa-17	3	33%	67%
Pa-18	/	/	/
Pa-19	2	50%	100%
Pa-1	/	/	/
Pa-2	1	0%	0%
Re-1	2	100%	100%
Re-2	3	33%	33%
Total	42	42.9%	66.7%

For the URLs and payloads that are not distinguished by our method, our analysis found that the main reason was due to the nonstandard description of steps in the vulnerability reports. For example, the sentence *"Create new user by adding the following payload in First Name and Last Name fields. <image src/onerror=prompt(document.cookie)>"* in the step of the vulnerability report *Pa*-14, the payload is written directly after the step sentence, neither as a component of the previous sentence nor with any marker to identify it as an payload. Another example is the sentence *"Login as admin to wp-admin portal, Go to Wappointment -- > Calendar (http://localhost/wordpress/wpadmin/admin.php?page=wappointment_calendar)"* in the vulnerability report *Pa*-2, this sentence is not standard due to the existence of symbol $'-->'$, which also has an impact on the extraction results.

Results for RQ3. Our automatic vulnerability reproduction focuses on the reports that contain only page elements operations (category *Pa*) and are correctly parsed. Based on the CIS sequence extracted from these reports, the executable events of the corresponding web application are explored to enable vulnerability reproduction. The results are shown in Table 8. We can see that among 11 reports, our method successfully reproduced 6 vulnerabilities, with a success rate of 55%.

Table 8. Vulnerability reproduction results

Web App No. - Report No	reproduction results
Pa-1-1	1
Pa-2-1	1
Pa-3-1	0
Pa-3-2	0
Pa-3-3	0
Pa-4-1	1
Pa-5-1	1
Pa-13-1	0
Pa-16-1	0
Pa-17-2	1
Pa-19-1	1

The main reasons why vulnerability reproduction fail can be summarized as follows: 1) The critical information in some vulnerability reports is missing, for example, the step information in the vulnerability report Pa-4 is "login as admin, click on setting", but the login username and password are not given in the report. 2) The id and class of Web page tags are artificially named, and sometimes they are not a meaningful word and do not appear in the standard corpus. These may lead to the inaccuracy of semantic similarity calculation, affecting vulnerability reproduction.

5 Conclusion

This paper proposes an automatic vulnerability report analysis and vulnerability reproduction approach for Web applications. First, the syntactic dependency patterns are analyzed and summarised the basis of 400 vulnerability reports from over 300 projects. Then, the CIS sequence from the reports are obtained by using lexical analysis and dependency syntactic parsing based on the dependency patterns summarised. At last, guided by the CIS sequence, the corresponding Web application is dynamically explored based on semantic similarity to get the events and associated test scripts to trigger vulnerabilities of Web applications. The experimental results show that the average extraction accuracy of CIS sequences in vulnerability report analysis is 77%. And 55% of the vulnerabilities are successfully reproduced. Therefore, our approach can handle vulnerability reports and reproduce vulnerabilities effectively.

References

1. Ahmad, T., Iqbal, J., Ashraf, A., Truscan, D., Porres, I.: Model-based testing using UML activity diagrams: a systematic mapping study. Comput. Sci. Rev. **33**, 98–112 (2019)
2. Bhuiyan, F.A., Shakya, R., Rahman, A.: Can we use software bug reports to identify vulnerability discovery strategies? In: Proceedings of the 7th Symposium on Hot Topics in the Science of Security, pp. 1–10 (2020)
3. Bhuiyan, F.A., Sharif, M.B., Rahman, A.: Security bug report usage for software vulnerability research: a systematic mapping study. IEEE Access **9**, 28471–28495 (2021)
4. (2022). https://portswigger.net/burp
5. (2022). https://www.cnvd.org.cn
6. Dong, Y., Guo, W., Chen, Y., Xing, X., Zhang, Y., Wang, G.: Towards the detection of inconsistencies in public security vulnerability reports. In: 28th USENIX Security Symposium (USENIX Security 2019), pp. 869–885 (2019)
7. (2022). https://www.exploit-db.com
8. Fazzini, M., Prammer, M., d'Amorim, M., Orso, A.: Automatically translating bug reports into test cases for mobile apps. In: Software Testing and Analysis (2018)
9. Feng, X., et al.: Understanding and securing device vulnerabilities through automated bug report analysis. In: SEC 2019: Proceedings of the 28th USENIX Conference on Security Symposium (2019)
10. Jin, Y.: Design of Japanese computer aided instruction system based on natural language processing. Tech. Autom. Appl. **40**(10), 52–55 (2021)
11. Leotta, M., Stocco, A., Ricca, F., Tonella, P.: Pesto: automated migration of dom-based web tests towards the visual approach. Softw. Test. Verif. Reliabil. **28**(4), e1665 (2018)

12. Li, R., Zhang, X., Li, C., et al.: Keyword extraction method for machine reading comprehension based on natural language processing. In: Journal of Physics: Conference Series, vol. 1955, no. 1, p. 012072 (2021)
13. Mu, D., et al.: Understanding the reproducibility of crowd-reported security vulnerabilities. In: 27th USENIX Security Symposium (USENIX Security 2018), pp. 919–936 (2018)
14. Ricca, F., Tonella, P.: Testing Processes of Web Applications. J. C. Baltzer AG Science Publishers (2002)
15. (2022). https://github.com/explosion/spaCy
16. (2022). https://github.com/stanfordnlp/stanza
17. (2022). https://github.com/danielfrg/word2vec
18. Yang, X., Qian, F., Liu, G.: Analysis of software automatic testing methods. China New Telecommun. **23**(10), 77–78 (2021)

Run-Time Assured Reinforcement Learning for Safe Spacecraft Rendezvous with Obstacle Avoidance

Yingmin Xiao[1,2], Zhibin Yang[1,2](✉), Yong Zhou[1,2], and Zhiqiu Huang[1,2]

[1] College of Computer Science and Technology, Nanjing University of Aeronautics and Astronautics, Nanjing 211106, China
yangzhibin168@163.com
[2] Key Laboratory of Safety-Critical Software, Ministry of Industry and Information Technology, Nanjing 211106, China

Abstract. Autonomous spacecraft rendezvous poses significant challenges in increasingly complex space missions. Recently, Reinforcement Learning (RL) has proven effective in the domain of spacecraft rendezvous, owing to its high performance in complex continuous control tasks and low online storage and computation cost. However, the lack of safety guarantees during the learning process restricts the application of RL to safety-critical control systems within real-world environments. To mitigate this challenge, we introduce a safe reinforcement learning framework with optimization-based Run-time Assurance (RTA) for spacecraft rendezvous, where the safety-critical constraints are enforced by Control Barrier Functions (CBFs). First, we formulate a discrete-time CBF to implement dynamic obstacle avoidance within uncertain environments, concurrently accounting for soft constraints of spacecraft including velocity, time, and fuel. Furthermore, we investigate the effect of RTA on reinforcement learning training performance in terms of training efficiency, satisfaction of safety constraints, control efficiency, task efficiency, and duration of training. Additionally, we evaluate our method through a spacecraft docking experiment conducted within a two-dimensional relative motion reference frame during proximity operations. Simulation and expanded test demonstrate the effectiveness of the proposed method, while our comprehensive framework employs RL algorithms for acquiring high-performance controllers and utilizes CBF-based controllers to guarantee safety.

Keywords: Run-time assurance · Safe reinforcement learning · Spacecraft rendezvous · Obstacle avoidance · Safety-critical system

Supported by National Natural Science Foundation of China (62072233) and Chinese Aeronautical Establishment (201919052002).

H. Hermanns et al. (Eds.): SETTA 2023, LNCS 14464, pp. 298–313, 2024.
https://doi.org/10.1007/978-981-99-8664-4_17

1 Introduction and Related Work

Spacecraft rendezvous refers to one spacecraft (the chaser) towards another (the target) from close proximity, with stringent limitations on the ultimate position, velocity, and attitude of the involved spacecraft. This process is fundamental for various on-orbit servicing missions, including tasks such as docking, maintenance, structural assembly, and formation flying. Given the escalating intricacy of space missions, the development of computationally efficient control strategies for spacecraft rendezvous presents a substantial challenge. Conventional optimal control approaches are computationally expensive, sensitive to the initial guess, not feasible for on-board real-time implementation, and usually limited by the simplifying assumptions (e.g., obstacles are static, no models for uncertainties and disturbance). Nevertheless, reinforcement learning which has demonstrated state-of-the-art results in numerous domains is appealing for solving control problems. RL shifts computational burden to offline training at design time by producing a static pre-trained Neural Network (NN) that is smaller and faster to compute online than other optimization algorithms. Although the training of a neural network controller requires a non-trivial length of time, obtaining a solution from a fully trained network occurs almost instantaneously.

Reinforcement learning is based on the idea of an agent learning a policy (i.e., controller) to choose actions to maximize long-term cumulative rewards. During the learning stage, the agent interacts with environment repeatedly by observing its state, executing an action based on current policy, receiving a reward, and modifying its policy to maximize its long-term rewards. RL has found successful application in continuous control tasks within the spacecraft rendezvous domain. For instance, Broida et al. investigated the use of RL for closed-loop control applied to satellite rendezvous missions [7]. Oestreich developed six-degree-of-freedom spacecraft docking maneuvers via RL [23]. In [14,16,19], RL has demonstrated successful usage in guiding autonomous spacecraft during proximity operations. Considering spacecraft constraints, Yang et al. developed a model-based reinforcement learning and neural-network-based policy compression approach for spacecraft rendezvous on resource-constrained embedded systems [29]. Scorsoglio et al. introduced a feedback guidance algorithm for near-rectilinear lunar orbits with path constraints based on actor-critic RL [26]. Nonetheless, while RL controllers exhibit excellent performance and consider certain spacecraft constraints in these endeavors, they cannot provide the same safety guarantees as traditional control. RL focuses on maximizing the long-term reward, and it may explore unsafe behaviors during its learning process, which limits the use of RL for safety-critical control systems. To achieve optimal results in terms of both performance and safety within safety-critical systems, an RL algorithm with safety guarantees becomes profoundly significant.

Safe RL refers to a process of policy learning that maximizes expected return while ensuring the satisfaction of some safety constraints [15]. Previous approaches to safe RL mainly fall into the categories of modifying the optimization criterion (i.e., reward shaping) or modifying the exploring process (i.e., RTA or shielding). Reward shaping aims to solve the constrained Markov Decision Process (MDP) with Lagrangian methods [1,28]. These methods tend to learn overly conservative policies or lack safety guarantees during learning - safety is only approximately guaranteed after a sufficient learning period. In contrast, RTA monitors unsafe behavior and intervenes with a backup safety controller to ensure safety of RL, achieved through various methods such as Lyapunov-based approaches [10,11], barrier functions [9,22], and formal verification utilizing model checking [3,8]. A limitation of these methods is that the creation of Lyapunov functions, barrier functions, or system automata relies on manual crafting, and synthesizing the backup safety controller or shielding is a non-trivial task.

In the field of spacecraft rendezvous, there is a dearth of research involving safe RL. Kyle Dunlap et al. conducted the most closely related prior work in this domain [13,17]. They explored 2-DOF RL using various forms of RTA to enforce a dynamic velocity constraint. However, there has been limited consideration given to obstacle constraints. Currently, there are over 21,000 pieces of debris larger than 10 cm being tracked in orbit around the Earth [20], and the mission environment for on-orbit servicing is becoming cluttered and full of uncertainty. Due to the possibility of potentially mission ending collisions, there is a need for the planning safe trajectories for safety-critical spacecraft. To address this issue, this paper introduces a novel approach to ensuring safe spacecraft rendezvous via run-time assured reinforcement learning, specifically aimed at obstacle avoidance within docking missions. The main contributions are as follows:

- We introduce a safe reinforcement learning framework with optimization-based run-time assurance for spacecraft rendezvous, where the safety-critical constraints are enforced by control barrier functions.
- We formulate a discrete-time CBF to implement dynamic obstacle avoidance within uncertain environments, where the obstacle constraints are assured during training phase, concurrently accounting for soft constraints of spacecraft including velocity, time, and fuel.
- Effect of RTA on reinforcement learning training performance is investigated in terms of training efficiency, satisfaction of safety constraints, control efficiency, task efficiency, and duration of training.
- Our method is evaluated through a spacecraft docking experiment conducted within a two-dimensional relative motion reference frame during proximity operations. Simulation and expanded test demonstrate the effectiveness of the proposed method, while our comprehensive framework employs RL algorithms for acquiring high-performance controllers and utilizes CBF-based controllers to guarantee safety.

This paper is organized as follows. In Sect. 2, we present the background of reinforcement learning and run-time assurance approaches. In Sect. 3, we introduce the relative motion dynamics of spacecraft and safety constraints in rendezvous missions. A discrete-time control barrier function is formulated for obstacle avoidance and run-time assured RL algorithm is discussed. In Sect. 4, we introduce experiments setup. We show the training results in Sect. 5, analyze the impact of RTA on RL training performance, and evaluate the proposed methods by simulation and expanded test. Section 6 provides concluding remarks.

2   Background

This section presents an introduction to RL and RTA. In the context of this study, RL is employed for training a neural network controller, while RTA is integrated with RL to ensure safety. This paper focuses on safety-critical control-affine dynamical systems, where $s \in S \subset \mathbb{R}^n$ denotes the state vector and $u \in U \subset \mathbb{R}^m$ denotes the control vector. The time evolution of the system is given by

$$s_{t+1} = f(s_t) + g(s_t) u_t, \tag{1}$$

where f and g compose a known nominal model of the dynamics.

2.1   Reinforcement Learning

The foundational framework of reinforcement learning is the Markov decision process $MDP = \langle S, A, T, r, \gamma \rangle$, where S is a set of states (i.e. state vectors), A is a set of actions (i.e. control vectors), $T : S \times A \rightarrow S$ is the transition function (i.e. system dynamic (1)), $r : S \times A \rightarrow \mathbb{R}$ is the reward function, and $\gamma \in (0, 1)$ is the discount factor. The goal of RL algorithms is to learn a policy $\pi : S \times A \rightarrow [0, 1]$ to maximize the expected cumulative discounted rewards in the process of interactions with the environment.

Let $J(\pi)$ denote expected cumulative discounted rewards of policy π:

$$J(\pi) = \mathbb{E}_{\tau \sim \pi} \left[\sum_{t=0}^{\infty} \gamma^t r_t \right], \tag{2}$$

where $\tau \sim \pi$ is a trajectory $\{s_0, a_0, r_0, s_1, a_1, r_1, ..., s_t, a_t, r_t, ...\}$ and the actions are sampled from policy $\pi(a|s)$. RL algorithms attempt to maximize $J(\pi)$ using various policy optimization methods, one of which is policy gradient methods including Deep Deterministic Policy Gradients (DDPG) [21], Proximal Policy Optimization (PPO) [25], and etc. Policy gradient methods estimate the gradient of $J(\pi)$ based on sampled trajectories and optimize the policy using gradient ascent. In practice, Policy gradient methods typically employ *actor-critic* architecture, where *actor* represents policy function $\pi(a|s)$ and *critic* represents value function V_π or action value function Q_π. V_π and Q_π are used to estimate the value of a state and an action, and are defined as below:

$$V_\pi(s_t) = \mathbb{E}_{a_t, s_{t+1}, a_{t+1}, ...} \left[\sum_{k=0}^{\infty} \gamma^k r_{t+k} \right], \tag{3}$$

$$Q_\pi(s_t, a_t) = \mathbb{E}_{s_{t+1}, a_{t+1}, ...} \left[\sum_{k=0}^{\infty} \gamma^k r_{t+k} \right], \tag{4}$$

where actions a_i are sample from distribution $a_i \sim \pi(a|s_i)$.

Proximal Policy Optimization. PPO is a policy gradient RL algorithm that uses two neural networks approximate the actor and the critic, which are parameterized as $\pi(a|s;\theta)$ and $V(s;\phi)$. The actor increases the probability of selecting actions if the resulting reward is better than the critic expected or decreases the action selection probability if the reward is less than expected.

PPO updates the critic network using the mean squared error and gradient descent method based on Eq. (3). To update the actor network, PPO optimizes the objective function incorporating a clipping function:

$$L^{CLIP}(\theta) = \hat{\mathbb{E}}_t\left[\min\left(R_t(\theta)\hat{A}_t, \text{clip}\left(R_t(\theta), 1-\varepsilon, 1+\varepsilon\right)\hat{A}_t\right)\right]. \tag{5}$$

Here $R_t(\theta)$ describes the difference between current policy π_θ and the old policy $\pi_{\theta_{\text{old}}}$, and is defined as

$$R_t(\theta) = \frac{\pi_\theta\left(a_t \mid s_t\right)}{\pi_{\theta_{\text{old}}}\left(a_t \mid s_t\right)}. \tag{6}$$

ϵ is a hyperparameter which roughly says how far away the new policy is allowed to go from the old. $\hat{A}_t$ is the estimate for the advantage function which is defined as the difference between the state value after taking an action and that before the action (λ is a hyperparameter between 0 and 1 to balance deviation and variance):

$$\hat{A}_t = \sum_{l=0}^{\infty}(\gamma\lambda)^l\left(r_{t+l} + \gamma V(s_{t+l+1}) - V(s_{t+l})\right). \tag{7}$$

In this research, we utilize PPO as it is one of the most advanced policy gradient algorithms in use today. Additionally, it is simple to implement, and well-suited for continuous control problems.

2.2   Run-Time Assurance

When dealing with RL, the complex nature of the NN-based control law often renders conventional offline verification techniques excessively difficult. In contrast, RTA techniques provide an online approach to prevent the NN controller to perform disastrous actions, where safety-critical requirements can be encoded in one or more monitors and enforced during learning and execution phases. RTA system is split into a performance-driven NN controller and a safety-driven RTA filter, which allows a designer to decouple performance objectives and safety guarantees. On one hand, RL agent learns performance goals through the reward function. On the other hand, RTA filter makes the agent respect significant properties including safety-critical requirements referred to as invariants.

Based on distinct intervention approaches, RTA can be classified into two categories: *switching-based* or *optimization based*. While switching-based RTA [24] is simple and relies on backup control designs, optimization-based RTA [5] is minimally invasive to the primary controller, where the intervention is smoother and more gradual than switching-based RTA. In this study, we employ optimization-based RTA aiming to ensure the safety while concurrently endeavoring to preserve the full performance of the primary NN controller. One possible implementation of a optimization-based RTA is constructed as

$$u(s, u_{NN}) = \text{argmin}_{u_b} \|u_{NN}(s) - u_b\|^2$$
$$\text{s.t.} BC_i(s, u_b) \geq 0, \forall i \in \{1, \ldots, M\} \tag{8}$$

where $BC_i(s, u_b)$ represents a set of M barrier constraints based on control barrier functions [4] used to enforce safety of the system.

Control Barrier Function. Assuming the dynamic system (1) is locally Lipschitz, inequality constraints $\varphi_i(s) : \mathbb{R}^n \to \mathbb{R}, \forall i \in \{1, ..., M\}$, can be used to define a set of M safety constraints, where the constraint is satisfied when $\varphi_i(s) \geq 0$. The *allowable* set $S_\varphi \subseteq S$, defined as the set of states where all constraints are satisfied, is then given by

$$S_\varphi := \{s \in S \mid \varphi_i(s) \geq 0, \forall i \in \{1, \ldots, M\}\}. \tag{9}$$

In order to ensure the safe operation of RTA systems, there is a need to define a stricter subset of states. By adhering to this stricter defined set, we avoid scenarios that can arise near the boundary of the allowable set, where no matter the action executed, the next state will be outside the allowable set. Therefore, we need limit safety to a *forward invariant* subset $S \subseteq S_\varphi$ referred to as the *safe* set, where

$$s_{t_0} \in S \implies s_t \in S, \forall t \geq t_0. \tag{10}$$

This set is *control invariant* if there exists a control law u that maintains its forward invariance subject to constraints.

We consider a set S_h defined as the superlevel set of a continuously differentiable function $h : \mathbb{R}^n \to \mathbb{R}$, yielding

$$S_h = \{s \in S \mid h(s) \geq 0\},$$
$$\partial S_h = \{s \in S \mid h(s) = 0\}, \tag{11}$$
$$\text{Int}S_h = \{s \in S \mid h(s) > 0\}.$$

Definition 1. *Let $S_h \subset \mathbb{R}^n$ be the superlevel set of a continuously differentiable function $h : \mathbb{R}^n \to \mathbb{R}$, then h is a control barrier function for the system (1) if there exists an extended class $\mathcal{K}_\infty$ function α such that for all $s \in S_h$,*

$$\sup_{u \in U}[L_f h(s) + L_g h(s)u] \geq -\alpha(h(s)) \tag{12}$$

Remark 1. L_f and L_g are Lie derivatives of f and g respectively (i.e. $\frac{\partial h(s)}{\partial s} \cdot f(s)$ and $\frac{\partial h(s)}{\partial s} \cdot g(s)$), and the extended class $\mathcal{K}_\infty$ function $\alpha : \mathbb{R} \to \mathbb{R}$ is a function that is strictly increasing and with $\alpha(0) = 0$. In this study, we let $\alpha(h(s)) = \eta h(s)$ where $\eta \in [0, 1]$ is a scalar and represents how strongly the barrier function "pushes" the state inwards within the safe set [9].

The existence of a CBF implies that there exists a controller such that the set S_h is forward invariant for system (1) [2,5]. In other words, if condition (12) is satisfied for all $s \in S_h$, then the set S_h is forward invariant. Therefore, we employ CBFs to construct barrier constraints of RTA filter, so that safety is certified. Consequently, the barrier constraint in optimization-based RTA (8) is then written as

$$
\begin{aligned}
BC(s, u) &= L_f h(s) + L_g h(s)u + \eta h(s) \\
&= \nabla h(s)(f(s) + g(s)u) + \eta h(s).
\end{aligned}
\tag{13}
$$

Again, $h(s)$ is a CBF with regard to safety-critical constraints of the system.

3 Safe Spacecraft Rendezvous

In the context of spacecraft rendezvous, an active spacecraft known as the "chaser" gradually approaches a passive "target" spacecraft, simulating docking within a linearized relative motion reference frame. Both spacecraft are considered rigid bodies and are represented as point-mass objects. Assumptions include the mass of spacecraft being markedly lower than that of Earth, negligible mass loss during maneuvers compared to the spacecraft mass, the target spacecraft existing in a circular orbit, and the distance between spacecraft being significantly shorter than their respective distances from Earth. This section discusses the relative motion dynamics, safety constraints, and applications of RTA for spacecraft rendezvous.

3.1 Relative Motion Dynamics

The location of the chaser with respect to the target is expressed in Hill's reference frame [18], where the origin is located at the mass center of the target. Here, we describe the problem with 2-dimensional dynamics. As shown in Fig. 1, the vector $\vec{x}$ points away from the center of the Earth and the vector $\vec{y}$ points in the direction of motion.

A first order approximation of the relative motion dynamics between the chaser and target spacecraft is given by the Clohessy-Wiltshire equations [12]:

$$
s_{t+1} = As_t + Bu_t,
\tag{14}
$$

where $s = [x, y, \dot{x}, \dot{y}]^T \in S = \mathbb{R}^4$ is the state vector, $u = [F_x, F_y]^T \in U = [-u_{max}, u_{max}]^2$ is the control vector, and

$$
A = \begin{bmatrix} 0 & 0 & 1 & 0 \\ 0 & 0 & 0 & 1 \\ 3n^2 & 0 & 0 & 2n \\ 0 & 0 & -2n & 0 \end{bmatrix}, \quad
B = \begin{bmatrix} 0 & 0 \\ 0 & 0 \\ 1/m & 0 \\ 0 & 1/m \end{bmatrix}.
\tag{15}
$$

Here $n = 0.001027$ rad/s is the spacecraft mean motion and $m = 12$ kg is the mass of the chaser. In this study, the chaser is initialized around the target with

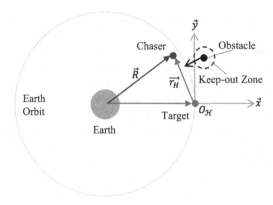

Fig. 1. Hill's reference frame centered on a target spacecraft.

the relative distance $\|r_H^{\rightarrow}\| = (x^2 + y^2)^{1/2} = 500$ m. The chaser successfully docks if $\|r_H^{\rightarrow}\|$ less than 0.5 m and the ultimate relative velocity $\|v_H\| = (\dot{x}^2 + \dot{y}^2)^{1/2}$ is less than 0.2 m/s.

3.2 Safety Constraints

The system is defined to be safe if the chaser never violates obstacle constraints. In this study, the obstacle moves in the environment with a random initial position and velocity, following the same dynamic equation as spacecraft except that the thrust terms are zero, as we assume the obstacle is unpowered. The chaser spacecraft can estimate relative position and velocity of the obstacle through sensors when the distance between them is less than d_{detect}, and is not allowed to enter a keep-out zone centered around the obstacle with a radius of d_{safe}.

To synthesize a safe controller, we formulate a quadratic barrier function for obstacle avoidance:

$$h(s) = (x - x_{ob})^2 + (y - y_{ob})^2 - (\sigma d_{safe})^2, \tag{16}$$

where x_{ob} and y_{ob} describe x/y-coordinate of the obstacle, and $\sigma \geq 1$ is a factor to expand warning zone for conservative safety. For the discrete-time system with $\triangle t = 1$ s, the barrier constraint is constructed as

$$\begin{aligned} BC(s_t, u) &= \nabla h(s)(f(s_t) + g(s_t)u) + \eta h(s_t) \\ &= h(s_{t+1}) - h(s_t) + \eta h(s_t) \\ &= h(s_{t+1}) - (1 - \eta)h(s_t). \end{aligned} \tag{17}$$

In realistic environments, spacecraft velocity and thrust are typically bounded. When velocity of the obstacle greatly exceeds that of the spacecraft, no forward invariant can meet safety constraints. This phenomenon arises due to specific states where the obstacle velocity is high and applying additional thrust does not prevent a significant reduction in the distance between the chaser and the obstacle. Therefore, this paper assumes that obstacle velocity on entering the detection range is similar to the chaser velocity. Concurrently, we employ factor σ as a hyperparameter in barrier function (16), which implies a warning zone that is larger than keep-out zone. Upon the chaser entries into the warning zone, endeavors should be made to promptly exit it.

Apart from the obstacle constraint, this paper also addresses soft constraints such as spacecraft velocity, time, and fuel, which are not obligatory during the training process due to obstacle avoidance. We consider the same velocity constraint as [13]: $\|\vec{v}_H\| \leq v_0 + v_1 \|\vec{r}_H\|$ where $v_0 = 0.2$ m/s and $v_1 = 2n$, which implies the chaser is expected to slow down as it approaches the target. Additionally, the rendezvous process is not expected to exceed a time limit of $1,800$ s or run out of fuel by using more than $1,500$ N of cumulative force, which is implemented by reward shaping (see details in Sect. 4).

3.3   Run-Time Assured RL Algorithm

For safe spacecraft rendezvous, we employ PPO algorithm with RTA to achieve a balance between the optimality and safety. Figure 2 illustrates the PPO learning framework incorporating a RTA filter in the training loop. Specifically, the state $s = (x, y, \dot{x}, \dot{y}, x_{ob}, y_{ob}, \dot{x}_{ob}, \dot{y}_{ob})$ is formed by concatenating the state vectors of the chaser and the obstacle. Within this framework, PPO utilizes sampled data to train a NN controller as introduced in Sect. 2.2, while the optimization-based filter is developed based on the methodology described by Eq. (8), and the barrier constraint is formulated using Eq. (16) and (17).

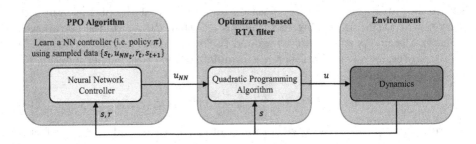

Fig. 2. PPO training process with an optimization-based RTA filter.

It is important to note that the optimization-based RTA filter generates a safe control action u, which might deviate from the desired action u_{NN} produced by the NN controller. During the integration of RTA into RL training, the safe action u provided to the environment does not contribute to training. Instead, the action u_{NN} from the NN controller is employed. This is critical for the effective training of the NN controller due to the on-policy nature of PPO algorithm. Consequently, the RL algorithm has no knowledge of when RTA is active, except through the reward function. In this study, we configure RTA in two modes: *RTA without punishment* and *RTA with punishment*. In situations where RTA does not intervene, both modes utilize the origin training data $\{s_t, u_{\mathrm{NN}t}, r_t, s_{t+1}\}$. However, when RTA intervenes, an additional punishment p is added to the reward associated with the latter mode, resulting in a transformation of the training data into $\{s_t, u_{\mathrm{NN}t}, r_t + p, s_{t+1}\}$.

4 Experiments

4.1 Spacecraft Rendezvous Environment

A custom reinforcement learning environment for spacecraft rendezvous is designed with the OpenAI Gym [6]. As mentioned above, the task succeeds if the chaser spacecraft satisfies $\|\vec{r_H}\| \leq 0.5\,\mathrm{m}$ with a velocity $\|v_H\| \leq 0.2\,\mathrm{m/s}$. The initial conditions are summarized in Table 1. The max thrust is $u_{max} = 1N$ and the radius of keep-out zone centered at the obstacle is $d_{safe} = 50$ m. An Euler integrator is employed to numerically advance the system dynamics. An episode within the environment will terminate under one of following several conditions: successful docking, collision of the chaser with the obstacle, traversal beyond the defined boundary, surpassing the time threshold of 1,800 s (i.e., steps), or depletion of fuel by using more than 1,500 N cumulative force. The termination criterion aims to restrict exploration to the more efficient rendezvous policies.

Table 1. Initial conditions

Items	Value
Position of the chaser	$x = 500\cos{(\pi/3)}$, $y = 500\sin{(\pi/3)}$
Velocity of the chaser	A random value $\|v_H\| \in [0, 1.2]$
Direction of the chaser	A random angle $\arctan{(\dot{y}/\dot{x})} \in [\pi, 1.5\pi]$
Position of the obstacle	A random value $x_{ob} \in [200, 300]$, $y_{ob} \in [200, 300]$
Velocity of the obstacle	A random value $\|v_{ob}\| \in [0, \mathrm{init}\,\|v_H\|]$
Direction of the obstacle	A random angle $\arctan{(\dot{y_{ob}}/\dot{x_{ob}})} \in [0, \pi]$
Boundaries	$x \in [-100, 600]$, $y \in [-100, 600]$

4.2 Reward Shaping

Reward shaping is one of the most critical work in the RL environment setup, which constructs and improves reward functions to encourage expected behaviors or punish the unexpected behaviors. In this spacecraft rendezvous environment, the reward function including *dense* rewards and *sparse* rewards is summarized in Table 2. Dense rewards are given at each time step of the simulation and sparse rewards are only given at the termination of the episode.

There are three different training cases in this research: No RTA, RTA without Punishment, and RTA with Punishment. No RTA case is a baseline, which encourages the spacecraft to adhere to safety constraints only by reward construction. However, this does not guarantee safety during training process. With RTA, barrier constraints can be used to ensure the spacecraft never enters an unsafe state. The distinction between no punishment case and punishment case is that small negative rewards are given to the latter case if RTA adjusts the desired action from the NN controller.

Table 2. Reward function

Dense rewards: all cases	
Proximity	$+0.002(\|r_H\|_{\text{old}} - \|r_H\|)$
$\|r_H\| \leq 1m$	$+0.1$
Sparse rewards: all cases	
$\|r_H\| \leq 0.5\,\text{m}$ and $\|v_H\| \leq 0.2\,\text{m/s}^2$	$+5$
$\|r_H\| \leq 0.5\,\text{m}$ but $\|v_H\| > 0.2\,\text{m/s}^2$	-0.001
Over max time/fuel	-1
Out of boundary	-1
Violation of obstacle	-1
Dense rewards: ONLY RTA with Punishment case	
RTA is active to intervene	-0.002

4.3 Hyperparameters

The algorithm used in this research is based on the PPO implementation from OpenAI SpinningUp. The actor and the critic of PPO are both implemented by full-connected neural networks with 2 hidden layers of 128 nodes each and *hyperbolic tangent* (tanh) activation functions. For optimization-based RTA, we employ IPOPT [27] to solve nonlinear quadratic programming problems. Hyperparameters used in PPO and RTA are summarized in Table 3.

Table 3. Hyperparameters setting for PPO training and RTA

HP Name	Value
Discount factor γ	0.99
Actor learning rate	$3e-4$
Critic learning rate	$1e-3$
Clip ratio ϵ in Eq. (5)	0.2
Gradient descent steps per epoch	80
Lambda λ in Eq. (7)	0.97
Epochs	60
Steps per epoch	36000
Factor σ in Eq. (16)	1.5
Barrier function scalar η in Eq. (17)	0.2

5 Results

In this section, we evaluate the training outcome and analyze RL performance in terms of training efficiency, satisfaction of safety constraints, control efficiency, task efficiency, and duration of training. Additionally, spacecraft rendezvous trajectories are simulated on both numeric calculation and rendering engine. Furthermore, we test different policies with or without RTA in expanded range.

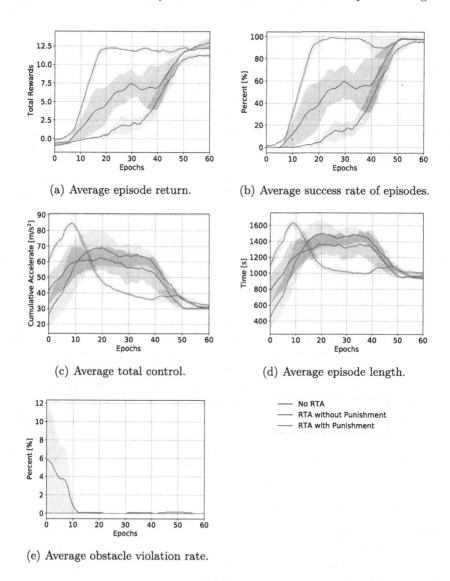

(a) Average episode return.

(b) Average success rate of episodes.

(c) Average total control.

(d) Average episode length.

(e) Average obstacle violation rate.

Fig. 3. Averaged training results.

5.1   Training Performance Analysis

Three different training cases are analyzed, each consisting of five trials with different random seeds: No RTA, RTA without Punishment, and RTA with Punishment. The random seeds are consistent for each training case. Figure 3 shows averaged training results of the five trials for each case over all epochs. The data are smoothed by averaging over a window of 10 epochs.

In this research, training efficiency is the time required to learn a successful policy measured as the first time it reaches 100% success. Figure 3(a) depicts the average episode return (i.e., accumulated discount rewards) during all epochs. It shows that RTA with Punishment rapidly converges near 20 epochs (720 thousand interactions), while No RTA or RTA without Punishment case converges to maximum return after 50 epochs. Figure 3(b) shows the average percentage of episodes that result in successful docking. We can see that the fastest time RTA with Punishment learns a successful policy is about 20 epochs, while the other two cases need 50 or more than 60 epochs. Therefore, RTA with Punishment has the best training efficiency in this spacecraft rendezvous environment. This advantage is likely because the RTA filter prevents an episode from being interrupted by the obstacle, and the small punishment helps the spacecraft learn safe behaviors more quickly, which could be beneficial to collecting complete and successful episodes as soon as possible.

Satisfaction of safety constraints is percent of constraint violation, which is shown in Fig. 3(e). Obviously, in two types of RTA cases, the spacecraft never crash the moving obstacle. During learning phase, it is inevitable to violate obstacle constraint in No RTA case though the violation rate gradually decreases to 0 as the interactions increase. This distinction shows the unique advantage of RTA approaches.

Control efficiency is measured by average cumulative accelerate (i.e., cumulative thrust divided by the mass), which is depicted by Fig. 3(c). All training cases effectively minimize fuel consumption by the conclusion of training. At the same time, task efficiency, which refers to the time required to complete the task measured by average episode length, has also decreased to about 1,000 timesteps for all cases, as shown in Fig. 3(d). Therefore, RTA with or without punishment has little impact on training performance in terms of control efficiency and task efficiency. As for duration of training which means the CPU time required to reach 60 epochs, RTA cases are slower than No RTA case in experiments due to their additional computation with the use of IPOPT solver.

5.2   Simulation and Expanded Test

We simulate a chaser spacecraft trajectory using the best trained policy of RTA with Punishment. Figure 4(a) shows the numeric simulation that the trajectory is smooth and almost straight. Figure 4(b) is a frame of rendering moving pictures within the custom spacecraft rendezvous environment, which is designed using OpenAI Gym built-in rendering functions to visualize how the policy is

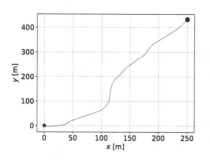

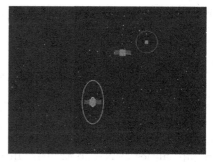

(a) Trajectory on numeric calculation.   (b) Rendering picture of spacecraft.

Fig. 4. Spacecraft rendezvous simulation.

performing. Both simulations demonstrate the effectiveness of run-time assured PPO algorithm for spacecraft rendezvous.

Once training is completed, the deterministic NN controller is a fixed. One common question is whether policies are adaptive for tasks they were not trained on and whether policies trained with the RTA filter are still effective in expanded test without RTA. Therefore, addition to simulations, we test different policies of all training cases within small dynamic noises in expanded range with or without RTA. In the training phase, the initial position of the chaser is stationary, as summarized in Table 1. In the test, it is uniformly sampled from a square area with the original initial position as the center and a side length of $100m$. We sample 100 test points randomly and compare the best policy (100% success rate in training phase) of each case. The results are shown in Table 4.

Table 4. Success rate for expanded test with or without RTA

Training policy	Test case	
	with RTA	without RTA
No RTA	96%	96%
RTA without Punishment	96%	92%
RTA with Punishment	97%	95%

The test results demonstrate generalization capabilities of the policies in all cases. As for the dependence of policies on RTA, the effect of RTA is negligible for the policy in No RTA training case, but noticeable for policies trained with RTA. Consequently, we recommend in engineering applications that when employing RTA during the training phase, its implementation during the deployment phase is advisable. In addition, RTA with Punishment demonstrates superiority over RTA without Punishment based on the aforementioned training performance analysis and expanded test results.

6   Conclusions

This paper introduced a run-time assured guidance approach with a focus on AI safety for RL-based spacecraft rendezvous. First, We formulated a discrete-time CBF to implement dynamic obstacle avoidance within uncertain environments, concurrently accounting for other constraints including velocity, time, and fuel by reward shaping. Furthermore, we explored the impact of RTA on RL and demonstrated its high training performance and safety. Finally, simulation and expanded test showed the effectiveness of the proposed method and generalization capabilities of NN controllers. In future work, we will expand this study to physical satellite systems under observation disturbances, and explore testing and verification methods for NN-based safety-critical heterogeneous systems when CBF is hard to construct.

References

1. Achiam, J., Held, D., Tamar, A., Abbeel, P.: Constrained policy optimization. In: International Conference on Machine Learning, pp. 22–31. PMLR (2017)
2. Agrawal, A., Sreenath, K.: Discrete control barrier functions for safety-critical control of discrete systems with application to bipedal robot navigation. In: Robotics: Science and Systems, vol. 13, pp. 1–10. Cambridge, MA, USA (2017)
3. Alshiekh, M., Bloem, R., Ehlers, R., Könighofer, B., Niekum, S., Topcu, U.: Safe reinforcement learning via shielding. In: Proceedings of the AAAI Conference on Artificial Intelligence, vol. 32 (2018)
4. Ames, A.D., Coogan, S., Egerstedt, M., Notomista, G., Sreenath, K., Tabuada, P.: Control barrier functions: theory and applications. In: 2019 18th European Control Conference (ECC), pp. 3420–3431. IEEE (2019)
5. Ames, A.D., Xu, X., Grizzle, J.W., Tabuada, P.: Control barrier function based quadratic programs for safety critical systems. IEEE Trans. Autom. Control **62**(8), 3861–3876 (2016)
6. Brockman, G., et al.: OpenAI gym. arXiv preprint arXiv:1606.01540 (2016)
7. Broida, J., Linares, R.: Spacecraft rendezvous guidance in cluttered environments via reinforcement learning. In: 29th AAS/AIAA Space Flight Mechanics Meeting, pp. 1–15. American Astronautical Society (2019)
8. Carr, S., Jansen, N., Junges, S., Topcu, U.: Safe reinforcement learning via shielding for pomdps. arXiv preprint (2022)
9. Cheng, R., Orosz, G., Murray, R.M., Burdick, J.W.: End-to-end safe reinforcement learning through barrier functions for safety-critical continuous control tasks. In: Proceedings of the AAAI Conference on Artificial Intelligence, vol. 33, pp. 3387–3395 (2019)
10. Chow, Y., Nachum, O., Duenez-Guzman, E., Ghavamzadeh, M.: A lyapunov-based approach to safe reinforcement learning. In: Advances in Neural Information Processing Systems, vol. 31 (2018)
11. Chow, Y., Nachum, O., Faust, A., Duenez-Guzman, E., Ghavamzadeh, M.: Lyapunov-based safe policy optimization for continuous control. arXiv preprint arXiv:1901.10031 (2019)
12. Clohessy, W., Wiltshire, R.: Terminal guidance system for satellite rendezvous. J. Aerosp. Sci. **27**(9), 653–658 (1960)

13. Dunlap, K., Mote, M., Delsing, K., Hobbs, K.L.: Run time assured reinforcement learning for safe satellite docking. J. Aerosp. Inf. Syst. **20**(1), 25–36 (2023)
14. Federici, L., Benedikter, B., Zavoli, A.: Deep learning techniques for autonomous spacecraft guidance during proximity operations. J. Spacecr. Rocket. **58**(6), 1774–1785 (2021)
15. Garcıa, J., Fernández, F.: A comprehensive survey on safe reinforcement learning. J. Mach. Learn. Res. **16**(1), 1437–1480 (2015)
16. Gaudet, B., Linares, R., Furfaro, R.: Adaptive guidance and integrated navigation with reinforcement meta-learning. Acta Astronaut. **169**, 180–190 (2020)
17. Hamilton, N., Dunlap, K., Johnson, T.T., Hobbs, K.L.: Ablation study of how run time assurance impacts the training and performance of reinforcement learning agents. In: 2023 IEEE 9th International Conference on Space Mission Challenges for Information Technology (SMC-IT), pp. 45–55. IEEE (2023)
18. Hill, G.W.: Researches in the lunar theory. Am. J. Math. **1**(1), 5–26 (1878)
19. Hovell, K., Ulrich, S.: On deep reinforcement learning for spacecraft guidance. In: AIAA Scitech 2020 Forum, p. 1600 (2020)
20. Jewison, C., Erwin, R.S., Saenz-Otero, A.: Model predictive control with ellipsoid obstacle constraints for spacecraft rendezvous. IFAC-PapersOnLine **48**(9), 257–262 (2015)
21. Lillicrap, T.P., et al.: Continuous control with deep reinforcement learning. arXiv preprint arXiv:1509.02971 (2015)
22. Ma, H., et al.: Model-based constrained reinforcement learning using generalized control barrier function. In: 2021 IEEE/RSJ International Conference on Intelligent Robots and Systems (IROS), pp. 4552–4559. IEEE (2021)
23. Oestreich, C.E., Linares, R., Gondhalekar, R.: Autonomous six-degree-of-freedom spacecraft docking maneuvers via reinforcement learning. arXiv preprint arXiv:2008.03215 (2020)
24. Rivera, J.G., Danylyszyn, A.A., Weinstock, C.B., Sha, L., Gagliardi, M.J.: An architectural description of the simplex architecture. Carnegie Mellon University, Pittsburg, Pennsylvania, Technical report, Software Engineering Institute (1996)
25. Schulman, J., Wolski, F., Dhariwal, P., Radford, A., Klimov, O.: Proximal policy optimization algorithms. arXiv preprint arXiv:1707.06347 (2017)
26. Scorsoglio, A., Furfaro, R., Linares, R., Massari, M.: Relative motion guidance for near-rectilinear lunar orbits with path constraints via actor-critic reinforcement learning. Adv. Space Res. **71**(1), 316–335 (2023)
27. Wächter, A., Biegler, L.T.: On the implementation of an interior-point filter line-search algorithm for large-scale nonlinear programming. Math. Program. **106**, 25–57 (2006)
28. Yang, L., et al.: Constrained update projection approach to safe policy optimization. Adv. Neural. Inf. Process. Syst. **35**, 9111–9124 (2022)
29. Yang, Z., et al.: Model-based reinforcement learning and neural-network-based policy compression for spacecraft rendezvous on resource-constrained embedded systems. IEEE Trans. Industr. Inf. **19**(1), 1107–1116 (2023)

An Abstract Domain of Linear Templates with Disjunctive Right-Hand-Side Intervals

Han Xu[1,3], Liqian Chen[1,2]([✉]), Guangsheng Fan[1,3], Banghu Yin[4]([✉]), and Ji Wang[1,3]

[1] College of Computer, National University of Defense Technology, Changsha 410073, China
{hanxu,guangshengfan,wj,lqchen}@nudt.edu.cn
[2] Hunan Key Laboratory of Software Engineering for Complex Systems, Changsha 410073, China
[3] HPCL, National University of Defense Technology, Changsha 410073, China
[4] College of Systems Engineering, National University of Defense Technology, Changsha 410073, China
bhyin@nudt.edu.cn

Abstract. Abstract interpretation provides a general framework for analyzing the value ranges of program variables while ensuring soundness. Abstract domains are at the core of the abstract interpretation framework, and the numerical abstract domains aiming at analyzing numerical properties have received extensive attention. The template constraint matrix domain (also called the template polyhedra domain) is widely used due to its configurable constraint matrix (describing limited but user-concerned linear relationships among variables) and its high efficiency. However, it cannot express non-convex properties that appear naturally due to the inherent disjunctive behaviors in a program. In this paper, we introduce a new abstract domain, namely the abstract domain of linear templates with disjunctive right-hand-side intervals, in the form of $\sum_i a_i x_i \in \bigvee_{j=0}^{p}[c_j, d_j]$ (where a_i's and p are configurable and fixed before conducting analysis). Experimental results of our prototype are encouraging: In practice, the new abstract domain can find interesting non-convex invariants that are out of the expressiveness of the classic template constraint matrix abstract domain.

Keywords: Abstract interpretation · Abstract domain · Template constraint matrix · Invariant

1 Introduction

The precision of program analysis based on abstract interpretation is largely dependent on the chosen abstract domain [8]. The polyhedra abstract domain [9] is currently one of the most expressive and widely used numerical abstract

© The Author(s), under exclusive license to Springer Nature Singapore Pte Ltd. 2024
H. Hermanns et al. (Eds.): SETTA 2023, LNCS 14464, pp. 314–330, 2024.
https://doi.org/10.1007/978-981-99-8664-4_18

domains. However, its applicability is severely limited by its worst-case exponential time and space complexity.

In order to reduce the complexity of the polyhedra abstract domain and at the same time derive practical linear invariants, Sankaranarayanan et al. [14,17] proposed the template constraint matrix (TCM) abstract domain (also called the template polyhedra domain). The domain representation of TCM polyhedra abstract domain is $Ax \leq b$, where the coefficient matrix A is predetermined before the analysis, x is a vector of variables appearing in the program environment, and the right-hand-side vector of constraint constants b is inferred automatically by the analysis [17]. The expression capability of TCM polyhedra abstract domain covers interval abstract domain [10] and the weakly relational linear abstract domains (e.g., octagonal abstract domain [15], octahedral abstract domain [7], etc.) commonly used in practical static analysis. Therefore, due to the representativeness of the TCM polyhedra abstract domain expressivity and its polynomial time complexity, the TCM polyhedra abstract domain has been receiving much attention from the academic community since its proposal.

However, like most current numerical abstract domains (e.g., interval abstract domain [10], octagonal abstract domain [15], etc.), the TCM abstract domain is based on a series of linear expressions, the corresponding geometric regions is convex, and therefore it can only express convex properties. In the actual analysis, the behavior of the program in the specific or collection semantics are generally non-convex. For example, "if-then-else" statements are often used in programs for case-by-case discussion. In addition, users are concerned about the non-convex numerical properties of a program, e.g., checking that a program does not have a "division-by-zero error" requires verifying a non-convex property such as "$x \neq 0$".

In this paper, we propose a novel method to combine the TCM abstract domain with fixed partitioning slots based powerset domain of intervals to design a new abstract domain, namely, an abstract domain of linear templates with disjunctive right-hand-side intervals (rhiTCM abstract domain). This domain aims to retain non-convex information of linear inequality relations among values of program variables, in the form of $Ax \in \bigvee_{i=0}^{p}[c_i, d_i]$ (where A is the preset template constraint matrix, x is the vector of variables in the program to be analyzed, c_i and d_i are vectors of constants, $\bigvee_{i=0}^{p}[c_i, d_i]$ are a disjunction of interval vectors based on fixed partitioning slots inferred by the analysis). To be more clear, each constraint in $Ax \in \bigvee_{i=0}^{p}[c_i, d_i]$ is formed as: $\sum_i a_i x_i \in [c_0, d_0] \vee [c_1, d_1] \vee \ldots \vee [c_p, d_p]$, where $a_i's$ together with p are fixed before analysis, and for each $i \in [0, p-1]$ it holds that $d_i \leq c_{i+1}$.

Motivating Example. In Fig. 1, we show a simple typical program that contains division in C language. This example involves non-convex (disjunctive) constraints that arise due to control-flow join. Specifically, at program line 10, the rhiTCM abstract domain is able to deduce that $x + y \in [-1, -1] \vee [1, 1]$, and as a result, the program can be deemed safe. In contrast, the classic TCM abstract domain infers that $x + y \in [-1, 1]$, leading to false alarms for division-by-zero errors.

```
1.  void main(){
2.      int r = cai_random();
3.      int x = cai_random();
4.      int y,z;
5.      if(r){
6.          y = -x-1;      /* x+y=1 */
7.      } else{
8.          y = -x+1;      /* x+y=-1 */
9.      }
10.     z = 1/(x+y);   /* division by x+y */
11. }
```

Fig. 1. Motivating Example

The new domain is more expressive than the classic TCM abstract domain and allows expressing certain non-convex (even unconnected) properties thanks to the expressiveness of the disjunctive right-hand-side intervals. We made a prototype implementation of the proposed abstract domain using rational numbers and interface it to the APRON [13] numerical abstract domain library. The preliminary experimental results of the prototype implementation are promising on example programs; the rhiTCM abstract domain can find linear invariants that are non-convex and out of the expressiveness of the conventional TCM polyhedra abstract domain in practice.

The rest of the paper is organized as follows. Section 2 describes some preliminaries. Section 3 presents the new proposed abstract domain of rhiTCM abstract domain. Section 4 presents our prototype implementation together with experimental results. Section 5 discusses some related work before Sect. 6 concludes.

2 Preliminaries

2.1 Fixed Partitioning Slots Based Powerset Domain of Intervals

We describe an abstract domain, namely, fixed partitioning slots based powerset domain of Intervals (FPSITVS). The main idea is to extract fixed partitioning points based on the value characteristics of variables in the program under analysis, and utilize these fixed partitioning points to divide the value space of variables. This approach aims to preserve more stable information regarding the range of variable values during program analysis. We use FP_SET to store the fixed partitioning points (FP_SET = $\{FP_1, FP_2, \ldots, FP_p\}$). Each fixed partitioning point $FP_i \in \mathbb{R}$ satisfies $FP_i < FP_{i+1}$.

Definition 1. FPSITVS$_p$ = $\{\bigvee_{i=0}^{p}[c_i, d_i] \mid for\ i \in [0, p-1], c_i \leq d_i \leq c_{i+1}, c_i, d_i \in \mathbb{R}\}$.

Let II $\in$ FPSITVS$_p$, which means that II is a disjunction of p disjoint intervals. The domain representation of fixed partitioning slots based powerset domain of intervals is $x \in [a_0, b_0] \vee [a_1, b_1] \vee \ldots \vee [a_p, b_p]$, where x is the variable in the program to be analysed, $[a_0, b_0] \subseteq [-\infty, FP_1]$, $[a_1, b_1] \subseteq$

$[FP_1, FP_2], \ldots, [a_p, b_p] \subseteq [FP_p, +\infty]$, $a_i, b_i \in \mathbb{R}$ is inferred by the analysis, FP_SET $= \{FP_1, FP_2 \ldots, FP_p\}$ is the preset configurable point set. It should be noted that p distinct fixed partitioning points correspond to $p + 1$ intervals. Let $\perp_{is}$ denote the bottom value of FPSITVS$_p$ ($\perp_{is} = \perp_{i0} \vee \perp_{i1} \vee \ldots \vee \perp_{ip}$) and let $\top_{is}$ denote the top value of FPSITVS$_p$ ($\top_{is} = [-\infty, FP_1] \vee [FP_1, FP_2] \vee \ldots \vee [FP_p, +\infty]$).

Domain Operations. Let $\mathrm{II} = [a_0, b_0] \vee [a_1, b_1] \vee \ldots \vee [a_p, b_p]$, $\mathrm{II}' = [a_0', b_0'] \vee [a_1', b_1'] \vee \ldots \vee [a_p', b_p']$. For simplicity, abbreviate the above expression as $\mathrm{II} = I_0 \vee I_1 \vee \ldots \vee I_p$, $\mathrm{II}' = I_0' \vee I_1' \vee \ldots \vee I_p'$. Let $\sqsubseteq_i, \sqcap_i, \sqcup_i$ respectively denote the abstract inclusion, meet, join operation in the classic interval domain [10].

- Inclusion test $\sqsubseteq_{is}$:
  $\mathrm{II} \sqsubseteq_{is} \mathrm{II}'$ iff $I_0 \sqsubseteq_i I_0' \wedge I_1 \sqsubseteq_i I_1' \wedge \ldots \wedge I_p \sqsubseteq_i I_p'$
- Meet $\sqcap_{is}$:
  $\mathrm{II} \sqcap_{is} \mathrm{II}' \triangleq I_0 \sqcap_i I_0' \vee I_1 \sqcap_i I_1' \vee \ldots \vee I_p \sqcap_i I_p'$
- Join $\sqcup_{is}$:
  $\mathrm{II} \sqcup_{is} \mathrm{II}' \triangleq I_0 \sqcup_i I_0' \vee I_1 \sqcup_i I_1' \vee \ldots \vee I_p \sqcup_i I_p'$

Extrapolations. Since the lattice of FPSITVS has infinite height, we need a widening operation for the FPSITVS abstract domain to guarantee the convergence of the analysis and a narrowing operation to reduce the precision loss caused by the widening operation. The symbol $\underline{I_i}$ represents the lower bound of interval I_i and the symbol $\overline{I_i}$ represents the upper bound of interval I_i.

- Widening operation (∇_{is}):
  $\mathrm{II} \nabla_{is} \mathrm{II}' \triangleq I_0'' \vee I_1'' \vee \ldots \vee I_p''$

$$
I_0'' = \begin{cases} I_0 & \text{if } I_0' = \perp_i \\ I_0' & \text{if } I_0 = \perp_i \\ [\underline{I_0} \leq \underline{I_0'} ? \underline{I_0} : -\infty, \overline{I_0} \geq \overline{I_0'} ? \overline{I_0} : FP_1] & \text{otherwise} \end{cases}
$$

when $0 < i < p$,

$$
I_i'' = \begin{cases} I_i & \text{if } I_i' = \perp_i \\ I_i' & \text{if } I_i = \perp_i \\ [\underline{I_i} \leq \underline{I_i'} ? \underline{I_i} : FP_i, \overline{I_i} \geq \overline{I_i'} ? \overline{I_i} : FP_{i+1}] & \text{otherwise} \end{cases}
$$

$$
I_p'' = \begin{cases} I_p & \text{if } I_p' = \perp_i \\ I_p' & \text{if } I_p = \perp_i \\ [\underline{I_p} \leq \underline{I_p'} ? \underline{I_p} : FP_p, \overline{I_p} \geq \overline{I_p'} ? \overline{I_p} : +\infty] & \text{otherwise} \end{cases}
$$

- Narrowing operation ($\triangle_{is}$):
  $$\text{II} \triangle_{is} \text{II}' \triangleq I_0'' \vee I_1'' \vee \ldots \vee I_p''$$

$$I_0'' = \begin{cases} I_0 & \text{if } I_0' = \bot_i \\ I_0' & \text{if } I_0 = \bot_i \\ [\underline{I_0} = -\infty \ ? \ \underline{I_0'} \ : \ \underline{I_0}, \overline{I_0} = FP_1 \ ? \ \overline{I_0'} \ : \ \overline{I_0}] & \text{otherwise} \end{cases}$$

when $0 < i < p$,

$$I_i'' = \begin{cases} I_i & \text{if } I_i' = \bot_i \\ I_i' & \text{if } I_i = \bot_i \\ [\underline{I_i} = FP_i \ ? \ \underline{I_i'} \ : \ \underline{I_i}, \overline{I_i} = FP_{i+1} \ ? \ \overline{I_i'} \ : \ \overline{I_i}] & \text{otherwise} \end{cases}$$

$$I_p'' = \begin{cases} I_p & \text{if } I_p' = \bot_i \\ I_p' & \text{if } I_p = \bot_i \\ [\underline{I_p} = FP_p \ ? \ \underline{I_p'} \ : \ \underline{I_p}, \overline{I_p} = +\infty \ ? \ \overline{I_p'} \ : \ \overline{I_p}] & \text{otherwise} \end{cases}$$

2.2 Mixed-Integer Linear Programming

Mixed-integer Linear Programming (MILP) problem is a type of linear programming problem where both the objective function and constraint conditions are linear equalities or inequalities. The variables in a MILP problem include both continuous and integer variables. Continuous variables can take any value within the real range, while integer variables can only take integer values. Due to the mixed nature of continuous and integer variables in the MILP problem, its optimal solution may exist in multiple local optimal solutions. The general form of a MILP problem can be expressed as:

$$\begin{aligned} \text{minimize (or maximize)} \quad & \boldsymbol{c}^T * \boldsymbol{x} + \boldsymbol{d}^T * \boldsymbol{y} \\ \text{subject to} \quad & A * \boldsymbol{x} + B * \boldsymbol{y} \leq \boldsymbol{b} \\ & \boldsymbol{x} \in \mathbb{R}^n \\ & \boldsymbol{y} \in \mathbb{Z}^m \end{aligned}$$

where $\boldsymbol{c}$ and $\boldsymbol{d}$ are given coefficient vectors, $\boldsymbol{x}$ represents the continuous variables, $\boldsymbol{y}$ represents the integer or boolean variables, A and B are known matrices, and $\boldsymbol{b}$ is the right-hand-side vector of constraints.

A MILP problem can have one of three results: (1) the problem has an optimal solution; (2) the problem is unbounded; (3) the problem is unfeasible.

2.3 Template Constraint Matrix Abstract Domain

The template constraint matrix abstract domain [17] is introduced by Sankaranarayanan et al. to characterize the linear constraints of variables under a given template constraint matrix: $A\boldsymbol{x} \leq \boldsymbol{b}$, where $A \in \mathbb{Q}^{m \times n}$ is an $m \times n$ matrix of coefficients (determined prior to the analysis), $\boldsymbol{x} \in \mathbb{Q}^{n \times 1}$ is an $n \times 1$ column vector (determined by the environment of the variables in the current analysis), and $\boldsymbol{b} \in \mathbb{Q}^{n \times 1}$ is a right-hand-side vector of constraints inferred by the analysis.

Figure 2 shows an instance of a template constraint matrix polyhedron. Assume that the program has two variables x and y, the template constraint matrix is A. In the TCM polyhedra abstract domain, $\boldsymbol{b}$ is obtained from the derivation of the matrix A during analysis.

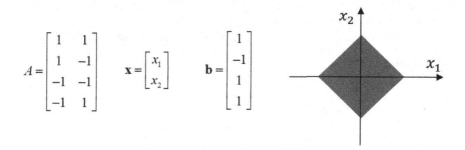

$$A = \begin{bmatrix} 1 & 1 \\ 1 & -1 \\ -1 & -1 \\ -1 & 1 \end{bmatrix} \quad \mathbf{x} = \begin{bmatrix} x_1 \\ x_2 \end{bmatrix} \quad \mathbf{b} = \begin{bmatrix} 1 \\ -1 \\ 1 \\ 1 \end{bmatrix}$$

Fig. 2. An Instance of TCM

3   An Abstract Domain of Linear Templates with Disjunctive Right-Hand-Side Intervals

In this section, we present a new abstract domain, namely the abstract domain of linear templates with disjunctive right-hand-side intervals (rhiTCM). The key idea is to use the fixed partitioning slots based powerset of intervals (FPSITVS) to express the right-hand value of linear templates constraints. It can be used to infer relationships of the form $\sum_k a_k x_k \in \Pi$ over program variables $x_k (k = 1, \ldots, n)$, where $a_k \in \mathbb{Q}$, $\Pi \in \text{FPSITVS}_p$ is automatically inferred by the analysis.

3.1   Domain Representation

The new abstract domain is used to infer relationships of the form $A\boldsymbol{x} \in \mathbf{\Pi}$, where $A \in \mathbb{Q}^{m \times n}$ is the preset template constraint matrix, $\boldsymbol{x} \in \mathbb{Q}^{n \times 1}$ is the vector of variables in the program to be analysed, $\mathbf{\Pi}$ is the vector of Π automatically inferred by the analysis ($\mathbf{\Pi}$ is composed of $\Pi^{m \times 1}$). For ease of understanding, we also write $A\boldsymbol{x} \in \mathbf{\Pi}$ as $\sum_k a_{ik} x_k \in \Pi_i$ (a_{ik} represents the element in the ith row and kth column of the matrix A, Π_i represents the element in the ith row of the vector $\mathbf{\Pi}$, $1 \le i \le m, 1 \le k \le n$).

Example 1. Consider a simple rhiTCM abstract domain representation as follows. Assume there are three variables x_1, x_2 and x_3.

$$A = \begin{bmatrix} 1 & 0 & 1 \\ 1 & -1 & 2 \\ 1 & 1 & 0 \\ 0 & 3 & -2 \\ 0 & 0 & -1 \end{bmatrix} \quad x = \begin{bmatrix} x_1 \\ x_2 \\ x_3 \end{bmatrix} \quad \text{representing constraints} \quad \begin{bmatrix} x_1 + x_3 & \in II_1 \\ x_1 - x_2 + 2x_3 & \in II_2 \\ x_1 + x_2 & \in II_3 \\ 3x_2 - 2x_3 & \in II_4 \\ -x_3 & \in II_5 \end{bmatrix}$$

Since the template matrix A remains unchanged during the analysis process, a vector **II** in the abstract domain rhiTCM represents the set of states described by the set of constraints $Ax \in$ **II**. The template constraint matrix is nonempty, i.e., $m > 0$, and the abstract domain contains m-dimensional vectors **II**.

Definition 2. *rhiTCM is defined as follows:*

$$rhiTCM \triangleq \begin{cases} \bot_{rhiTCM}, & \text{if } \exists II_i = \bot_{is} \\ \top_{rhiTCM}, & \text{if } \forall II_i = \top_{is} \\ Ax \in II & \text{otherwise} \end{cases}$$

where II_i is the element in the ith row of **II**. $\bot_{rhiTCM}$ is the bottom value of the rhiTCM abstract domain, representing this rhiTCM element is infeasible; $\top_{rhiTCM}$ is the top value of rhiTCM domain, representing the entire state space. Figure 3 presents a rhiTCM element.

$$A = \begin{bmatrix} 1 & 0 \\ 0 & 1 \\ 1 & -1 \\ 1 & 1 \end{bmatrix} \quad x = \begin{bmatrix} x_1 \\ x_2 \end{bmatrix} \quad II = \begin{bmatrix} [-2,0] \vee [0,2] \\ [-2,0] \vee [0,2] \\ [-2,-1] \vee [1,2] \\ [-2,-1] \vee [1,2] \end{bmatrix}$$

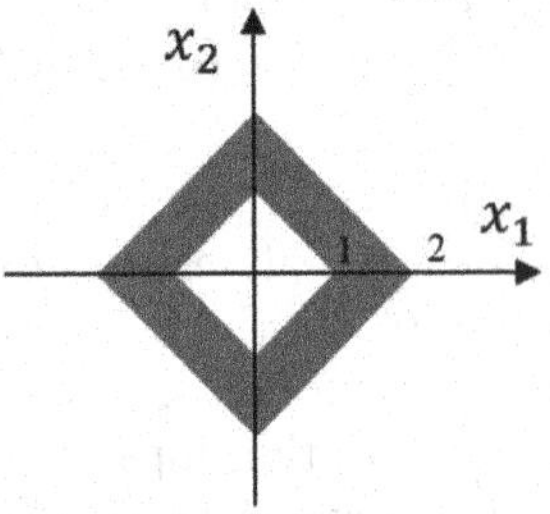

Fig. 3. A rhiTCM Element

3.2   Domain Operations

Now, we describe the design of most common domain operations required for static analysis over the rhiTCM abstract domain. Assume that there are n variables in the program to be analyzed ($x = [x_1, x_2, \ldots, x_n]^T$), and the template constraint matrix preset based on the program is A ($A \in \mathbb{Q}^{m \times n}$, representing matrix elements with a_{ij}, $i \in 1, 2, \ldots, m, j \in 1, 2, \ldots, n$). As mentioned earlier, the template constraint matrix for the domain representation corresponding to the abstract states of different program points in the rhiTCM abstract domain is the same, except for the constraint vector on the right side. Therefore, domain operations mainly act on the vector of II. Assuming there are currently two abstract states, their corresponding domain representations are $rhiTCM \triangleq A\boldsymbol{x} \in II$ and $rhiTCM' \triangleq A\boldsymbol{x} \in II'$, where $II = [II_1, II_2, \ldots, II_m]^T$ and $II' = [II'_1, II'_2, \ldots, II'_m]^T$.

Lattice Operations. The lattice operations include abstract inclusion, meet and join operation, represented by symbols $\sqsubseteq, \sqcap, \sqcup$ respectively. Let $\sqsubseteq_{is}, \sqcap_{is}, \sqcup_{is}$ respectively denote the abstract inclusion, meet, join operation in the FPSItvs abstract domain.

Inclusion Test. The inclusion test for rhiTCM abstract domain is implemented based on the inclusion test for vector II $(\preceq_{is})$.

Definition 3. *Inclusion test of vector* II $(\preceq_{is})$. *Let* $II = [II_1, II_2, \ldots, II_n]^T$, $II' = [II'_1, II'_2, \ldots, II'_n]^T$.

$$II \preceq_{is} II' \ iff \ \bigwedge_{i=1}^{n} (II_i \sqsubseteq_{is} II'_i)$$

For the rhiTCM abstract domain, $rhiTCM \sqsubseteq rhiTCM'$ implies the domain element of $rhiTCM$ is contained in $rhiTCM'$, which is geometrically equivalent to the graph corresponding to $rhiTCM$ is contained within the graph corresponding to $rhiTCM'$. With Definition 3, we define the inclusion test of rhiTCM abstract domain as follows:

$$rhiTCM \sqsubseteq rhiTCM' \ iff \ II \preceq_{is} II'.$$

Example 2. Assume $II = \begin{bmatrix} [-2, -2] \vee [2, 2] \\ [-3, -2] \vee [2, 3] \end{bmatrix}$, $II' = \begin{bmatrix} [-2, -1] \vee [1, 2] \\ [-3, -1] \vee [1, 3] \end{bmatrix}$ and $FP\_SET = \{0\}$. Note that:

$([-2, -2] \vee [2, 2] \sqsubseteq_{is} [-2, -1] \vee [1, 2]) \wedge ([-3, -2] \vee [2, 3] \sqsubseteq_{is} [-3, -1] \vee [1, 3])$,
thus $II \preceq_{is} II'$, $rhiTCM \sqsubseteq rhiTCM'$.

Meet. The meet operation of rhiTCM abstract domain is implemented based on the meet operation of vector II.

Definition 4. *Meet operation of vector* $II(\curlywedge_{is})$. *Let* $II = [II_1, II_2, \ldots, II_n]^T$, $II' = [II'_1, II'_2, \ldots, II'_n]^T$.

$$II \curlywedge_{is} II' \triangleq [II_1 \sqcap_{is} II'_1, \ldots, II_n \sqcap_{is} II'_n]^T$$

For the $rhiTCM$ abstract domain, $rhiTCM \sqcap rhiTCM'$ is geometrically equivalent to the part that exists simultaneously in both $rhiTCM$ and $rhiTCM'$. With Definition 4, we define the meet operation of $rhiTCM$ domain as follows:

$$rhiTCM \sqcap rhiTCM' \triangleq A\boldsymbol{x} \in (II \curlywedge_{is} II').$$

Join. The join operation of rhiTCM abstract domain is implemented based on the join operation of vector **II**.

Definition 5. *Join operation of vectors of* $\mathbf{II}(\curlyvee_{is})$*. Let* $\mathbf{II} = [II_1, II_2, \ldots, II_n]^T$*,* $\mathbf{II'} = [II'_1, II'_2, \ldots, II'_n]^T$*.*

$$\mathbf{II} \curlyvee_{is} \mathbf{II'} \triangleq [II_1 \sqcup_{is} II'_1, \ldots, II_n \sqcup_{is} II'_n]^T$$

For the rhiTCM abstract domain, $rhiTCM \sqcup rhiTCM'$ is geometrically equivalent to the part that envelope $rhiTCM$ and $rhiTCM'$. With Definition 5, we define the join operation of rhiTCM abstract domain as follows:

$$rhiTCM \sqcup rhiTCM' \triangleq Ax \in (\mathbf{II} \curlyvee_{is} \mathbf{II'}).$$

Example 3. Assume $\mathbf{II} = \begin{bmatrix} [-2,-2] \vee [2,2] \\ [-3,-2] \vee [2,3] \end{bmatrix}$, $\mathbf{II'} = \begin{bmatrix} [-2,-1] \vee [1,2] \\ [-3,-1] \vee [1,3] \end{bmatrix}$ and $FP\_SET = \{0\}$. We note that:

$$([-2,-2] \vee [2,2]) \sqcap_{is} ([-2,-1] \vee [1,2]) = [-2,-2] \vee [2,2],$$
$$([-3,-2] \vee [2,3]) \sqcap_{is} ([-3,-1] \vee [1,3]) = [-3,-2] \vee [2,3],$$
$$([-2,-2] \vee [2,2]) \sqcup_{is} ([-2,-1] \vee [1,2]) = [-2,-1] \vee [1,2],$$
$$([-3,-2] \vee [2,3]) \sqcup_{is} ([-3,-1] \vee [1,3]) = [-3,-1] \vee [1,3],$$

thus we can get:

$$rhiTCM \sqcap rhiTCM' \triangleq Ax \in (\mathbf{II} \curlywedge_{is} \mathbf{II'}) = Ax \in \begin{bmatrix} [-2,-2] \vee [2,2] \\ [-3,-2] \vee [2,3] \end{bmatrix},$$

$$rhiTCM \sqcup rhiTCM' \triangleq Ax \in (\mathbf{II} \curlyvee_{is} \mathbf{II'}) = Ax \in \begin{bmatrix} [-2,-1] \vee [1,2] \\ [-3,-1] \vee [1,3] \end{bmatrix}.$$

3.3 Extrapolations

The lattice of the rhiTCM abstract domain is of infinite height, and thus we need a widening operation to guarantee the convergence of the analysis. The widening operation of rhiTCM abstract domain is implemented based on the widening operation of vector **II**.

Definition 6. *Widening operation of vector* $\mathbf{II}$ (∇)*. Let* $\mathbf{II} = [II_1, II_2, \ldots, II_n]^T$*,* $\mathbf{II'} = [II'_1, II'_2, \ldots, II'_n]^T$*.*

$$\mathbf{II} \nabla \mathbf{II'} \triangleq [II_1 \nabla_{is} II'_1, \ldots, II_n \nabla_{is} II'_n]^T$$

The widening operation of rhiTCM abstract domain is as follows:

$$rhiTCM \nabla rhiTCM' \triangleq Ax \in (\mathbf{II} \nabla \mathbf{II'}).$$

The widening operation may result in substantial precision loss. To mitigate this, we utilize a narrowing operation to perform decreasing iterations once the widening iteration has converged, effectively reducing precision loss. Notably, this operation is capable of converging within a finite time. The implementation of the narrowing operation for the rhiTCM abstract domain is derived from the narrowing operation of vector II.

Definition 7. *Narrowing operation of vector II ($\triangle$).*

$$II \triangle II' \triangleq [II_1 \triangle_{is} II_1', \ldots, II_n \triangle_{is} II_n']^T$$

The narrowing operation of rhiTCM abstract domain is as follows:

$$rhiTCM \triangle rhiTCM' \triangleq A\boldsymbol{x} \in (II \triangle II').$$

Example 4. Assume $II = \begin{bmatrix} [-2,-2] \vee [2,2] \\ [-3,-2] \vee [2,3] \\ [-2,-2] \vee \perp_i \end{bmatrix}$, $II' = \begin{bmatrix} [-3,-2] \vee [2,3] \\ [-3,-1] \vee [1,3] \\ [-2,-2] \vee [2,2] \end{bmatrix}$ and

$FP\_SET = \{0\}$. Note that:

$$([-2,-2] \vee [2,2]) \nabla_{is} ([-3,-2] \vee [2,3]) = [-\infty,-2] \vee [2,+\infty],$$
$$([-3,-2] \vee [2,3]) \nabla_{is} ([-3,-1] \vee [1,3]) = [-3,0] \vee [0,3],$$
$$([-2,-2] \vee \perp_i) \nabla_{is} ([-2,-2] \vee [2,2]) = [-2,-2] \vee [2,2],$$

thus

$$rhiTCM \nabla rhiTCM' \triangleq A\boldsymbol{x} \in (II \nabla II') = A\boldsymbol{x} \in \begin{bmatrix} [-\infty,-2] \vee [2,+\infty] \\ [-3,0] \vee [0,3] \\ [-2,-2] \vee [2,2] \end{bmatrix},$$

Let $II'' = II \nabla II'$, $rhiTCM'' = rhiTCM \nabla rhiTCM'$, note that:

$$([-\infty,-2] \vee [2,+\infty]) \triangle_{is} ([-2,-2] \vee [2,2]) = [-2,-2] \vee [2,2],$$
$$([-3,0] \vee [0,3]) \triangle_{is} ([-3,-2] \vee [2,3]) = [-3,-2] \vee [2,3],$$
$$([-2,-2] \vee [2,2]) \triangle_{is} ([-2,-2] \vee \perp_i) = [-2,-2] \vee [2,2],$$

thus:

$$rhiTCM'' \triangle rhiTCM \triangleq A\boldsymbol{x} \in (II'' \triangle II) = A\boldsymbol{x} \in \begin{bmatrix} [-2,-2] \vee [2,2] \\ [-3,-2] \vee [2,3] \\ [-2,-2] \vee [2,2] \end{bmatrix}.$$

3.4   Transfer Functions

In program analysis based on abstract interpretation, an abstract environment is usually constructed for each program point, mapping the value of each program variable to a domain element on a specified abstract domain. Let $P^{\#}$ represent the abstract environment constructed by the rhiTCM abstract domain. Before introducing the test transfer function and the assignment transfer function of rhiTCM abstract domain, we introduce the MILP encoding of the rhiTCM abstract domain representation.

MILP Encoding. Note that the rhiTCM abstract domain representation $\sum_k a_{ik} x_k \in \mathrm{II}_i$ can be expressed in ordinary linear expressions as $(\sum_k a_{ik} x_k \geq c_{i1} \wedge \sum_k a_{ik} x_k \leq d_{i1}) \vee (\sum_k a_{ik} x_k \geq c_{i2} \wedge \sum_k a_{ik} x_k \leq d_{i2}) \vee \ldots \vee (\sum_k a_{ik} x_k \geq c_{i(p+1)} \wedge \sum_k a_{ik} x_k \leq d_{i(p+1)})$, where p is the number of fixed partitioning points. However, the expression cannot be directly solved using a LP (linear programming) solver because it contains the disjunction symbol "$\vee$". To tackle such problem, we typically introduce a significantly large number M and auxiliary binary decision variables (0–1 variables). This allows us to convert the linear programming problem, which contains disjunction symbols, into a mixed-integer linear programming problem. Thus, we can employ a mixed-integer linear programming solver to solve it.

We encode $(\sum_k a_{ik} x_k \geq c_{i1} \wedge \sum_k a_{ik} x_k \leq d_{i1}) \vee (\sum_k a_{ik} x_k \geq c_{i2} \wedge \sum_k a_{ik} x_k \leq d_{i2}) \vee \ldots \vee (\sum_k a_{ik} x_k \geq c_{ip} \wedge \sum_k a_{ik} x_k \leq d_{ip})$ as follows:

$$
\begin{cases}
\sum_k a_{ik} x_k \geq c_{i1} - M(1 - u_{i1}), & \sum_k a_{ik} x_k \leq d_{i1} + M(1 - u_{i1}) \\
\sum_k a_{ik} x_k \geq c_{i2} - M(1 - u_{i2}), & \sum_k a_{ik} x_k \leq d_{i2} + M(1 - u_{i2}) \\
\quad \vdots & \quad \vdots \\
\sum_k a_{ik} x_k \geq c_{ip} - M(1 - u_{ip}), & \sum_k a_{ik} x_k \leq d_{ip} + M(1 - u_{ip}) \\
\sum_j u_{ij} = 1 (u_{ij} \in \{0,1\}, 1 \leq j \leq p)
\end{cases}
$$

To simplify the treatment of the problem, we proceed to convert the constraints in the aforementioned linear system into the following form:

$$
\begin{cases}
\sum_k a_{ik} x_k + M u_{i1} \leq -c_{i1} + M, & \sum_k a_{ik} x_k + M u_{i1} \leq b_{i1} + M \\
\sum_k a_{ik} x_k + M u_{i2} \leq -c_{i2} + M, & \sum_k a_{ik} x_k + M u_{i2} \leq b_{i2} + M \\
\quad \vdots & \quad \vdots \\
\sum_k a_{ik} x_k + M u_{ip} \leq -c_{ip} + M, & \sum_k a_{ik} x_k + M u_{ip} \leq b_{ip} + M \\
\sum_j u_{ij} = 1 (u_{ij} \in \{0,1\}, 1 \leq j \leq p)
\end{cases}
$$

The above linear inequality system is a typical mixed-integer linear programming (MILP) problem, so we can directly call the MILP solver to solve the MILP problem. Nevertheless, when solving the MILP problem, it is important to note that the obtained results are limited to providing the maximum and minimum values of the objective function within the feasible domain. However, these extremal values might not reflect the desired outcome of the analysis. In order to tackle this problem, we introduce the fixed partitioning points information as additional sets of constraints into the existing MILP problem linear inequality system. Suppose the objective function is denoted as $\sum_j a_j x_j$. We sequentially introduce the constraints $\sum_j a_j x_j \leq FP_1$, $\sum_j a_j x_j \geq FP_1 \wedge \sum_j a_j x_j \leq FP_2$, $\ldots, \sum_j a_j x_j \geq FP_{p-1} \wedge \sum_j a_j x_j \leq FP_p$, $\sum_j a_j x_j \geq FP_p$ (FP_p is the last fixed partitioning point).

Therefore, in the process of calculating the extreme values of the objective function, we use an iterative method in which the information of the fixed partitioning points is introduced p times. This enables us to determine the extremum of the objective function across different fixed partitioning slots and consequently obtain the desired representation outcome. The aforementioned encoding and solving process is recorded as "$rhiTCM_{mip}$(objFun) s.t. Cons" in this paper, where objFun represents the objective function, and Cons represents the constraints to determine the extremes of the objective function.

Test Transfer Function. A linear conditional test based on precise arithmetic can be transformed into the form as $\sum_i w_i x_i \leq c$. For test transfer function $[\![\sum_i w_i x_i \leq c]\!]^{\#}(P^{\#})$, we simply combine constraint $\sum_i w_i x_i \leq c$ with the rhiTCM $P^{\#}(P^{\#} \triangleq A\boldsymbol{x} \in \mathbf{II})$ to obtain $P'^{\#}(P'^{\#} \triangleq P^{\#} \wedge \sum_i w_i x_i \leq c)$, and use $P'^{\#}$ as the constraint system, recalculate the new boundaries of the rhiTCM.

$$[\![\textstyle\sum_i w_i x_i \leq c]\!]^{\#}(P^{\#}) \triangleq \bigwedge_{i=1}^{m}\{\textstyle\sum_{k=1}^{n} a_{ik}x_k \in \mathbf{II}_i^* | \mathbf{II}_i^* \triangleq rhiTCM_{mip}(\textstyle\sum_{k=1}^{n} a_{ik}x_k)s.t.P'^{\#}\}.$$

Assignment Transfer Function. Assigning expression e to variable x_j is the assignment transfer function $[\![x_j := expr]\!]^{\#}(P^{\#})$. Firstly, we introduce a fresh variable x'_j to rewrite the assignment statement as $x'_j - expr = 0$. Then, add the new assignment statement to the $P^{\#}$ ($P^{\#} \triangleq A\boldsymbol{x} \in \mathbf{II}$) to get $P''^{\#}$ ($P''^{\#} \triangleq P^{\#} \wedge x'_j - expr = 0$). Finally, using $P''^{\#}$ as the constraint system, recalculate the new boundaries of the rhiTCM.

$$[\![x_j := expr]\!]^{\#}(P^{\#}) \triangleq \bigwedge_{i=1}^{m}\{\textstyle\sum_{k=1}^{j-1} a_{ik}x_k + a_{ij}x'_j + \textstyle\sum_{k=j+1}^{n} a_{ik} \in \mathbf{II}_i^* | \mathbf{II}_i^* \triangleq rhiTCM_{mip}(\textstyle\sum_{k=1}^{j-1} a_{ik}x_k + a_{ij}x'_j + \textstyle\sum_{k=j+1}^{n} a_{ik})s.t.P''^{\#}\}.$$

4   Implementation and Experiments

We have implemented our prototype domain rhiTCM based on Sect. 3 using multi-precision rational numbers. rhiTCM abstract domain is interfaced to the APRON numerical abstract domain library [13]. The linear programming problems that are involved in the rhiTCM abstract domain are solved using an exact arithmetic-based mixed-integer linear programming solver, which is provided by the PPL [3] library.

   To demonstrate the expressiveness of the rhiTCM abstract domain, we have firstly analyzed the program itv_pol5 shown in Fig. 4 taken from [5], along with the generated invariants. Program itv_pol5 in Fig. 4 consists two loops, increasing y in the inner loop and increasing x in the outer loop. In Fig. 4, "Polyhedra" is the classic polyhedra abstract domain [9] and "Interval Polyhedra" (itvPol) from [5] is an abstract domain can infer interval linear constraints over program variables (the domain representation is formed as $\sum_k [a_k, b_k]x_k \leq c$ and can express non-convex properties). "rhiTCM$_1$" and "rhiTCM$_2$" are rhiTCM abstract domain with different configurations. "rhiTCM$_1$": FP_SET = $\{0\}$, $A_1 = \begin{bmatrix} 1 & 0 \\ 0 & 1 \end{bmatrix}^T$;

"rhiTCM$_2$": FP_SET = $\{0\}$, $A_2 = \begin{bmatrix} 1 & 0 & 1 & 1 \\ 0 & 1 & 1 & -1 \end{bmatrix}^T$.

```
int main (){
    int x, y;
    x = 1;
    y = -20;
    while(x<=9){
    ① x = x + 1;
        while(y<=9){
            y = y + 1;
        }
    }②
    return 0;
}
```

Loc	Polyhedra	Interval Polyhedra	rhiTCM₁	rhiTCM₂
①	$y \geq -20$ $\wedge\, 1 \leq x \leq 9$	$y \geq -20$ $\wedge\, 1 \leq x \leq 9$ $\wedge -x + [0,1]y \leq -2$ $\wedge\, [-1,1]y \leq -10$	$x \in [1,9]$ $\wedge\, y \in [-20,-20] \vee [10,+\infty]$	$x \in [1,9]$ $\wedge\, y \in [-20,-20] \vee [10,+\infty]$ $\wedge\, x+y \in [-19,-19] \vee [12,+\infty]$ $\wedge\, x-y \in [-\infty,-1] \vee [21,21]$
②	$y \geq -20$ $\wedge\, x \geq 10$	$y \geq -20 \wedge x \geq 10$ $\wedge\, [-1,1]y \leq -10$	$x \in [10,+\infty]$ $\wedge\, y \in [-20,-20] \vee [10,+\infty]$	$x \in [10,31]$ $\wedge\, y \in [10,+\infty]$ $\wedge\, x+y \in [20,+\infty]$ $\wedge\, x-y \in [-\infty,0] \vee [0,21]$

Fig. 4. program itv_pol5 and the generated invariants

For program itv_pol5, at program point ②, polyhedra abstract domain can prove $y \geq -20$ (TCM abstract domain is the same), itvPol can prove that $-20 \leq y \leq -10 \vee y \geq 10$ (the invariants of itvpol come from [5]) while rhiTCM₁ can prove $y = -20 \vee y \geq 10$ which is more precise than itvPol. And rhiTCM₂ can prove $y \geq 10$. The results have shown that rhiTCM is more powerful on express non-convex properties than these compared abstract domains, and the expressiveness of rhiTCM can be improved with appropriate configurations on FP_SET and the template matrix.

To evaluate the precision and efficiency of rhiTCM further, we have conducted experiments to compare rhiTCM abstract domain with TCM polyhedra abstract domain. Table 1 shows the preliminary experimental results of comparing performance and resulting invariants on a selection of simple while widely used and representative programs. Program MotivEx is the motivating example presented in Sect. 1, programs itv_pol4, itv_pol5 come from [5], other programs are collected from the "loop-zilu", "loop-simple" and "locks" directory of SV-COMP2022, which are used for analysing programs involving disjunctive program behaviors.

The column "#var" gives the number of variables in the program. As experimental setup, for each program, the value of the widening delay parameter is set to 1. "#iter." gives the number of increasing iterations during the analysis.

Precision. The column "Precision" in Table 1 compares the invariants obtained. The symbol "⊏" indicates the invariants generated by rhiTCM is stronger (i.e.,

Table 1. Experimental results for benchmark examples

Program		TCM		rhiTCM		Invariant
name	#vars	#iter.	$t(ms)$	#iter.	$t(ms)$	TCM vs rhiTCM
MotivEx	4	0	4	0	4	⊏
itv_pol4	1	4	4	3	4	⊏
itv_pol5	2	4	16	5	44	⊏
nested_3.c	3	5	52	6	84	⊏
nested_4.c	4	6	140	7	200	⊏
benchmark31_disjunctive.c	2	3	44	3	60	=
benchmark44_disjunctive.c	2	3	100	3	144	=
test_locks_5.c	11	2	496	2	724	⊏
test_locks_6.c	13	2	908	2	1276	⊏
test_locks_7.c	15	2	1532	2	2080	⊏

more precise) than TCM, while "=" indicates the generated invariants are equivalent. The results in Table 1 show that rhiTCM can output stronger invariants than TCM in certain situations. One such situation is that $\sum_k a_{ik}x_k$ exhibits a discontinuous range of values. As the motivating example shown in Fig. 1, expression $x + y$ has two discontinuous possible values: 1 and -1. The rhiTCM can describe the values of $x + y$ as $x + y \in [-1, -1] \vee [1, 1]$ with the fixed partitioning points set FP_SET = $\{0\}$, while TCM describes the values of $x + y$ as $x + y \in [-1, 1]$ which is less precise than the former. Another situation arises when the assignment of variables within a loop can be enumerated. As the program itv_pol4, variable "x" is assigned a value of either 1 or -1 within the loop. At the loop header, the widening operation of rhiTCM (with FP_SET = $\{0\}$) is performed as: $([-1, -1]\nabla_i \perp_i) \vee (\perp_i \nabla[1, 1])$ and $([-1, -1]\nabla_i[-1, -1]) \vee ([1, 1]\nabla_i[1, 1])$, which results in $x \in [-1, -1] \vee [1, 1]$ while the widening operation of TCM is performed as: $[-1, -1]\nabla_i[1, 1]$ and $[-1, +\infty]\nabla_i[-1, -1]$, which results in $x \in [-1, +\infty]$.

Performance. All experiments are carried out on a virtual machine (using VirtualBox), with a guest OS of Ubuntu (4GB Memory), host OS of Windows 10, 16GB RAM and Intel Core i5 CPU 2.50 GHz. The column "t(ms)" presents the analysis time in milliseconds. Experimental time for each program is obtained by taking the average time of ten runnings. From Table 1, we can see that rhiTCM is less efficient than TCM. The size of matrix A and the number of the fixed partitioning points will affect the performance of rhiTCM. The smaller the size of matrix A and the fewer fixed partitioning points there are, the closer the performance of rhiTCM will be to the performance of TCM. In program MotivEx, there are two variables x, y. We set one linear constraint "$x + y$" in the template matrix with one fixed partitioning point "0" in the FP_SET. In this configuration, the analysis time of rhiTCM is almost the same as that of TCM.

5   Related Work

A variety of abstract domains have been designed for the analysis of non-convex properties. Allamigeon et al. [1] introduced max-plus polyhedra to infer min and max invariants over the program variables. Granger introduced congruence analysis [11], which can discover the properties like "the integer valued variable X is congruent to c modulo m", where c and m are automatically determined integers. Bagnara et al. proposed the abstract domain of grids [2], which is able to represent sets of equally spaced points and hyperplanes over an n-dimensional vector space. The domain is useful when program variables take distribution values. Chen et al. applied interval linear algebra to static analysis and introduced interval polyhedra [5] to infer and propagated interval linear constraints of the form $\sum_k [a_k, b_k] x_k \le c$.

To enhance numerical abstract domain with non-convex expressiveness, some work make use of special decision diagrams. Gurfinkel et al. proposed BOXES, which is implemented based on linear decision diagrams (LDDs) [12]. Gange et al. [16] extended the interval abstract domain based on range decision diagrams (RDDs), which can express more direct information about program variables and supports more precise abstract operations than LDD BOXES. Some work make use of mathematical functions that could express non-convex properties such as the absolute value function [4,6]. Sankaranarayanan et al. [18] proposed basic power set extensions of abstract domains. The power set extensions will cause exponential explosion problem.

The rhiTCM domain that we introduce in this paper is an extension of template constraint matrix domain, with the right-hand-side intervals to express certain disjunctive behaviors in a program, e.g., the right-hand value of linear expression may be discontinuous. The configurable finite fixed partitioning points restrict the number of the right-hand-side intervals, avoiding the exponential explosion problem.

6   Conclusion

In this paper, we propose a new abstract domain, namely, an abstract domain of linear templates with disjunctive right-hand-side intervals (rhiTCM abstract domain), to infer linear inequality relations among values of program variables in a program. The domain is in the form of $\sum_i a_i x_i \in \bigvee_{j=0}^{p} [c_j, d_j]$, where $a_i \in \mathbb{Q}$ is the variable coefficient specified in the preset template constraint matrix, x is the variables in the program to be analysed, $\bigvee_{j=0}^{p} [c_j, d_j]$ is the disjunctions of intervals based on fixed partitioning slots. The key idea is to employ the disjunctive intervals to get and retain discontinuous right-hand-side values of the template constraint thus can deal with non-convex behaviors in the program. We present the domain representation as well as domain operations designed for rhiTCM abstract domain. We have developed a prototype for the rhiTCM abstract domain using rational numbers and interface it to the APRON numerical abstract domain library. Experimental results are encouraging: The rhiTCM abstract domain can discover invariants that are non-convex and out of the expressiveness of the classic TCM abstract domain.

It remains for future work to test rhiTCM abstract domain on large realistic programs, and consider automatic methods to generate the template constraint matrix of the program to be analysed.

Acknowledgement. This work is supported by the National Key R&D Program of China (No. 2022YFA1005101), the National Natural Science Foundation of China (Nos. 62002363, 62102432), and the Natural Science Foundation of Hunan Province of China (No. 2021JJ40697).

References

1. Allamigeon, X., Gaubert, S., Goubault, É.: Inferring min and max invariants using max-plus polyhedra. In: Alpuente, M., Vidal, G. (eds.) SAS 2008. LNCS, vol. 5079, pp. 189–204. Springer, Heidelberg (2008). https://doi.org/10.1007/978-3-540-69166-2_13

2. Bagnara, R., Dobson, K., Hill, P.M., Mundell, M., Zaffanella, E.: Grids: a domain for analyzing the distribution of numerical values. In: Puebla, G. (ed.) LOPSTR 2006. LNCS, vol. 4407, pp. 219–235. Springer, Heidelberg (2007). https://doi.org/10.1007/978-3-540-71410-1_16

3. Bagnara, R., Hill, P.M., Zaffanella, E., Bagnara, A.: The parma polyhedra library. https://www.bugseng.com/ppl

4. Chen, L., Liu, J., Miné, A., Kapur, D., Wang, J.: An abstract domain to infer octagonal constraints with absolute value. In: Müller-Olm, M., Seidl, H. (eds.) SAS 2014. LNCS, vol. 8723, pp. 101–117. Springer, Cham (2014). https://doi.org/10.1007/978-3-319-10936-7_7

5. Chen, L., Miné, A., Wang, J., Cousot, P.: Interval polyhedra: an abstract domain to infer interval linear relationships. In: Palsberg, J., Su, Z. (eds.) SAS 2009. LNCS, vol. 5673, pp. 309–325. Springer, Heidelberg (2009). https://doi.org/10.1007/978-3-642-03237-0_21

6. Chen, L., Yin, B., Wei, D., Wang, J.: An abstract domain to infer linear absolute value equalities. In: Theoretical Aspects of Software Engineering, pp. 47–54 (2021)

7. Cortadella, R.C.: The octahedron abstract domain. Sci. Comput. Program. **64**, 115–139 (2007)

8. Cousot, P., Cousot, R.: Abstract interpretation: a unified lattice model for static analysis of programs by construction or approximation of fixpoints. In: Proceedings of the 4th ACM SIGACT-SIGPLAN Symposium on Principles of Programming Languages, pp. 238–252. Association for Computing Machinery (1977)

9. Cousot, P., Halbwachs, N.: Automatic discovery of linear restraints among variables of a program. In: ACM SIGPLAN-SIGACT Symposium on Principles of Programming Languages, pp. 84–96 (1978)

10. Golan, J.: Introduction to interval analysis. Comput. Rev. **51**(6), 336–337 (2010)

11. Granger, P.: Static analysis of arithmetical congruences. Int. J. Comput. Math. **30**(3–4), 165–190 (1989)

12. Gurfinkel, A., Chaki, S.: Boxes: a symbolic abstract domain of boxes. In: Cousot, R., Martel, M. (eds.) SAS 2010. LNCS, vol. 6337, pp. 287–303. Springer, Heidelberg (2010). https://doi.org/10.1007/978-3-642-15769-1_18

13. Jeannet, B., Miné, A.: APRON: a library of numerical abstract domains for static analysis. In: Bouajjani, A., Maler, O. (eds.) CAV 2009. LNCS, vol. 5643, pp. 661–667. Springer, Heidelberg (2009). https://doi.org/10.1007/978-3-642-02658-4_52

14. Sankaranarayanan, S., Sipma, H.B., Manna, Z.: Scalable analysis of linear systems using mathematical programming. In: Cousot, R. (ed.) VMCAI 2005. LNCS, vol. 3385, pp. 25–41. Springer, Heidelberg (2005). https://doi.org/10.1007/978-3-540-30579-8_2

15. Miné, A.: The octagon abstract domain. High.-Order Symb. Comput. **19**, 31–100 (2006)

16. Gange, G., Navas, J.A., Schachte, P., Søndergaard, H., Stuckey, P.J.: Disjunctive interval analysis. In: Drăgoi, C., Mukherjee, S., Namjoshi, K. (eds.) SAS 2021. LNCS, vol. 12913, pp. 144–165. Springer, Cham (2021). https://doi.org/10.1007/978-3-030-88806-0_7

17. Colón, M.A., Sankaranarayanan, S.: Generalizing the template polyhedral domain. In: Barthe, G. (ed.) ESOP 2011. LNCS, vol. 6602, pp. 176–195. Springer, Heidelberg (2011). https://doi.org/10.1007/978-3-642-19718-5_10

18. Sankaranarayanan, S., Ivančić, F., Shlyakhter, I., Gupta, A.: Static analysis in disjunctive numerical domains. In: Yi, K. (ed.) SAS 2006. LNCS, vol. 4134, pp. 3–17. Springer, Heidelberg (2006). https://doi.org/10.1007/11823230_2

Deducing Matching Strings
for Real-World Regular Expressions

Yixuan Yan[1,2], Weihao Su[1,2], Lixiao Zheng[3], Mengxi Wang[1,2],
Haiming Chen[1,2(✉)], Chengyao Peng[1,2], Rongchen Li[1,2], and Zixuan Chen[1,2]

[1] State Key Laboratory of Computer Science, Institute of Software,
Chinese Academy of Sciences, Beijing 100190, China
{yanyx,suwh,wangmx,chm,pengcy,lirc,chenzx}@ios.ac.cn
[2] University of Chinese Academy of Sciences, Beijing 101400, China
[3] College of Computer Science and Technology, Huaqiao University,
Xiamen, China

Abstract. Real-world regular expressions (regexes for short) have a
wide range of applications in software. However, the support for regexes
in test generation is insufficient. For example, existing works lack support
for some important features such as lookbehind, are not resilient to subtle
semantic differences (such as partial/full matching), fall short of Unicode
support, leading to loss of test coverage or missed bugs. To address these
challenges, in this paper, we propose a novel semantic model for comprehensively modeling the extended features in regexes, with an awareness
of different matching semantics (i.e. partial/full matching) and matching precedence (i.e. greedy/lazy matching). To the best of our knowledge,
this is the first attempt to consider partial/full matching semantics in
modeling and to support lookbehind. Leveraging this model we then
develop `PowerGen`, a tool for deducing matching strings for regexes, which
randomly generates matching strings from the input regex effectively. We
evaluate `PowerGen` against nine related state-of-the-art tools. The evaluation results show the high effectiveness and efficiency of `PowerGen`.

Keywords: regex · semantics · modeling · generation · matching
string

1   Introduction

As a versatile mechanism for pattern matching, searching, substituting, and
so on, real-world regular expressions (regexes for short) have become an
integral part of modern programming languages and software development,
with numerous applications across various fields [3,13,18,19,31,43]. Previous
research [12,18,53] has reported that regexes are utilized in 30–40% of Java,
JavaScript, and Python software.

Though popular, regexes can be difficult to comprehend and construct even
for proficient programmers, and error-prone, due to the intrinsic complexities

---

Y. Yan and W. Su—These authors contributed equally.
Zixuan Chen is currently employed at Kuaishou Technology.

H. Hermanns et al. (Eds.): SETTA 2023, LNCS 14464, pp. 331–350, 2024.
https://doi.org/10.1007/978-981-99-8664-4_19

of the syntax and semantics involved, resulting in tens of thousands of bug reports [13,27,30,31,44]. Therefore, it is crucial to offer automated techniques for test generation and bug finding within regexes. Producing matching strings for regexes is essential for many tasks, such as automated testing, verifying, and validating programs that utilize regexes. There have been numerous studies related to this problem using various techniques [14,25,26,28,29,42,50,52]. However, there are crucial concerns that have been either overlooked or inadequately addressed in the existing literature, limiting their utility. We classify these issues as follows.

Features Support. All existing works lack support for some important features. For example, none of the existing works support lookbehind, and only one work supports lookahead but with soundness errors (see Sect. 2.3). Regexes are featured with various extended features (or simply called features) such as lookarounds, capturing groups, and backreferences. An instance of a regex using a backreference is $(.^*)\backslash 1$, which defines a context-sensitive language $\{ww|w \in \Sigma^*\}$ where $\backslash 1$ is a backreference. In addition, if such an expression is also included in lookarounds, then those lookarounds effectively encode the intersection of context-sensitive languages [15]. These show that regexes are not limited to representing regular languages [1], and as a result, generating strings for regexes becomes more involved. For instance, in [15], the authors demonstrated that the emptiness problem of regular expressions with lookaheads and backreferences is undecidable. Thus, in many works, these features are often disregarded or imprecisely estimated. This lack of support can lead to, for instance, poor coverage or unrevealed bugs. Furthermore, based on our analysis of open-source projects for six programming languages (Java, Python, JavaScript, C#, PHP, Perl) which yielded 955,184 unique regexes, the average ratio of capturing group usage exceeds 38%, while the average percentage of lookarounds and backreferences is over 4%, while it approaches 10% in C#, thus those features are non-negligible. Similar observations for JavaScript were also reported by [29].

Subtle Semantic Differences. Regexes have different semantics which can result in different matching results. For example, there are partial and full matching functions for the regexes in most programming languages, which can lead to different matching results. For instance, the regex *node_modules(?=paradigm.*)* from practical project [19] matches *node_modulesparadigm* under a partial matching call, but is unsatisfiable under a full matching call. None of the existing works addressed the different matching semantics of regexes (such as partial/full matching), thus may lead to wrong results. As another example, backreference has different semantics in different programming languages. For instance, the regex $(?:(a)b)^?\backslash 1c$ can match c in JavaScript, but does not match c in Java, Python, PHP and C#. See more examples in Sect. 2.3.

Unicode Support. Supporting the Unicode Standard can be useful in the internationalization and localization of practical software. PCRE and POSIX standards for regexes defined several operators such as $\backslash uFFFF$, $[:word:]$ and $\backslash p\{L\}$ to represent Unicode code points, improving the usability of regexes. In modern mainstream regex engines and string constraint solvers [17,24,45], those operators are common. However, we found the existing tools show incomplete support for those features.

Various Kinds of Soundness Errors. We also found incorrect outputs generated by existing works, reflecting logic errors in their implementation which may be due to the intricacy of the syntax and semantics of regexes. See Sect. 2.3 for details.

To achieve the end, this paper proposes a novel semantic model for comprehensively modeling the extended features in regexes with the awareness of different matching semantics (i.e. partial/full matching) and matching precedence (i.e. greedy/lazy matching). Leveraging this model we then develop PowerGen, a tool for deducing matching strings for regexes. Specifically, PowerGen first rewrites the input regex by selecting the appropriate optimization rule based on the input programming language and rewrites the input regex based on the information of partial/full matching function. Then it uses Unicode automata to support a vast class of extended Unicode-related features. Next PowerGen selects the appropriate induction rules based on the input programming language to perform the top-down induction of the sub-expressions of the rewritten regex. Finally, PowerGen randomly generates matching strings according to the induction rules and stack compiled from the rewritten regex, which effectively identifies unsatisfiable cases.

We evaluate PowerGen by comparing PowerGen against nine state-of-the-art tools on publicly available datasets. Our evaluation demonstrates the high effectiveness and efficiency of PowerGen.

The contributions of this paper are listed as follows.

- We propose a novel semantic model for regexes, which comprehensively models the extended features, with the awareness of different matching semantics and matching precedence. To the best of our knowledge, it is the first one to consider partial/full matching semantics in modeling and supporting lookbehind.
- Based on our model, we develop PowerGen, a tool for deducing matching strings for regexes. To this end, we devise novel algorithms that randomly generate matching strings according to the input regex, which effectively identifies unsatisfiable cases.
- Evaluation shows the high effectiveness and efficiency of PowerGen.

2 Background

2.1 Regex

Let Σ be a finite alphabet of symbols and Σ^* be the set of all possible words (i.e. strings) over Σ, ε denotes the empty word and the empty set is denoted by $\varnothing$. For the definition of standard regular expressions we refer to [55].

Table 1. The Results from Each Tool for Examples in Practical Projects

No.	Regex	Egret	dk.brics	Mutrex	Generex	Exrex	Xeger (O'Connor)	Randexp.js	ExpoSE	Ostrich
#1	`^<(\S*?@@)>`	<@@>(✓)	-	-	-	<@>	<QrpwE~bd@>(✓)	-	<U + 00E7@>(✓)	<@>
#2	`\boldgnu\b.*\bformat\b`	oldgnu format(✓)	-	-	-	...8Uformat	oldgnuX...	oldgnuB...	error	oldgnuformat
#3	`(a)(b)(c)(d)(e)(f)(g)(h)(i)(j)(k)\11`	abcdefghijkk(✓)	-	-	-	abcdefghijkk(✓)	abcdefghijkk(✓)	abcdefghijk	unsat	-
#4	`(?<foo>xyz)(?<bar>\d*)abc\k<bar>`	xyz0abc0(✓)	-	-	-	xyz2375022abc2375022(✓)	xyz14369195abc14369195(✓)	error	error	-
#5	`^(?:(a\2)(b))*$`	-	-	-	-	-	-	ababbabbab...	ab(✓)	-
#6	`(?:()[0](?:(?:)[0])\1)|(?:()(?:(?:)))\2`	error	-	-	-	error	error	ε(✓)	unsat	-
#7	`^(?:(d)(a\2))*$`	error	-	-	-	error	error	dadaadaaa...	error	-
#8	`(a)(?=\1)\w*`	-	-	-	-	-	-	-	unsat	-

In practice, real-world regular expressions (regexes) are pervasive in diverse application scenarios. A regex over Σ is a well-formed parenthesized formula constructed by, besides using the constructs for standard regular expressions and character classes, as well as using the following operators (i) capturing group (E); (ii) named capturing group $(<name>E)$; (iii) non-capturing group $(?:E)$; (iv) lookarounds: positive lookahead $(?=E_1)E_2$, negative lookahead $(?!E_1)E_2$, positive lookbehind $E_1(?<=E_2)$, and negative lookbehind $E_1(?<!E_2)$; (v) anchors: word boundary $\backslash b$, non-word boundary $\backslash B$, start-of-line anchor $\hat{}$, and end-of-line anchor $\$$; (vi) greedy quantifiers: $E?$, E^*, E^+, and $E^{\{m,n\}}$; (vi) lazy quantifiers: $E^{??}$, $E^{*?}$, $E^{+?}$, and $E^{\{m,n\}?}$; (vii) backreference $\backslash i$ and (viii) named backreference $\backslash k<name>$, etc.

In addition, $E?$, E^*, E^+ and $E^{\{i\}}$ where $i \in \mathbb{N}$ are abbreviations of $E^{\{0,1\}}$, $E^{\{0,\infty\}}$, $E^{\{1,\infty\}}$ and $E^{\{i,i\}}$, respectively. $E_1^{\{m,\infty\}}$ is often simplified as $E_1^{\{m,\}}$. Following symbols (,), {, }, [,], $\hat{}$, $\$$, |, \, ., ?, * and + are escaped with the escape character \ in Σ. The *language* $L(E)$ of a regex E is the set of all strings accepted by E.

2.2 Research Problem

In this paper, we focus on the research problem of finding matching strings which depends on the partial/full matching semantics in regexes. We present related concepts below.

In most programming languages there are partial and full matching functions for the regexes (e.g. the `matches` and `find` functions in Java for full matching respectively partial matching). For a regex E, if it is used with the full matching function, then a string w is a **matching** string of E if $w \in L(E)$. If E is used with the partial matching function, then a string w is a **matching** string of E if $w \in L(.^*E.^*)$.

2.3 The Current Status of Existing String Generation Tools

We identified 9 state-of-the-art string generation tools for comparison which can be categorized into three groups: (1) string generation based on automata, including Egret [25], dk.brics [35], Mutrex [2] and Generex [54]; (2) string generation based on AST (Abstract Syntax Tree), including Exrex [49], Xeger (O'Connor) [37] and Randexp.js [22]; (3) string generation based on SMT (Satisfiability Modulo Theories) solvers, including ExpoSE [29], and Ostrich [14]. It

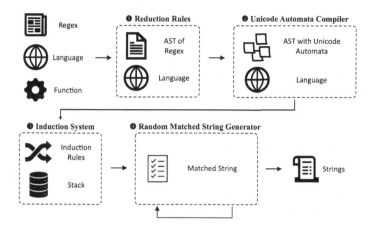

Fig. 1. The Framework of PowerGen

should be noticed that string constraint solvers do more work than string generators: they handle word equations and other more complicated string constraints like `ReplaceAll`.

We notice that, even under the features they claim to support, errors exist and are predominantly on features like lazy quantifier, word boundary, backreference. Examples[1] from practical projects [19] are listed in Table 1 with corresponding strings generated by each tool mentioned above, where the correct results are marked with "($\checkmark$)". In addition, "–" indicates that the tool does not support one or more features in the regex, *error* indicates run-time errors, and *unsat* indicates the tool determines that the regex cannot be satisfied with any input. It is evident that certain tools exhibit flawed handling of lazy quantifier, word boundary, backreference and lookaround. In the second example, the `.*` should be constrained to favor `\b`, but Exrex, Xeger (O'Connor), Randexp.js and Ostrich do not take that into account and gives wrong results, and Expose returns an error. For the third regex, Randexp.js and ExpoSE, yielding *abcdefghijk* and *unsat* respectively, fail to support more than 9 backreferences. In the case of the expression `^(?:(a\2)(b))+$` semantic differences arise between languages. JavaScript is capable of supporting backreferences preceding the corresponding capture group and generating the correct output, such as *ab*, *abab*. Nevertheless, Randexp.js fails to return the correct string. For the given example 6, the right node of the logical OR operator can accept an empty string. However, Egret, Exrex and Xeger('Connor) return an error and ExpoSE returns unsat. Moreover, none of them are capable of correctly handling a self-referenced backreference like example 7, or combining a backreference with lookaround as shown in example 8.

---

[1] To facilitate error identification, we simplify lengthy regexes by isolating the problematic fragment.

3   Overview

In this section, we provide an overview of our approach. Our method, depicted in Fig. 1, encompasses four main components: reduction rules, Unicode automata compiler, induction system, and random matching string generator. Initially, the **Reduction Rules** module takes the regex, the language, and a matching function to form an AST, addressing the semantic divergence between partial and full match calls. This simplified regex AST and language are then forwarded to the **Unicode Automata Compiler**, which develops automata to integrate the Unicode 15.0.0 standard into UTF-8 and compiles the AST leaves into the Unicode Automaton. The **Induction System** component, chosen based on the input language, converts the AST into induction rules and stack. Lastly, the **Random Matching String Generator** uses these induction rules and stack with capture information to generate matching strings. By iteratively executing the generation function, multiple matching strings are produced.

In the following section, we exemplify our approach by highlighting the intractable part of a regex $\Psi = (?:=(")^?[^;"\s]*\1)$ from Node.js version 18.16.0. The original regex is $^(?:<[^>]*>)(?:\s*;\s*[^;"\s]^+(?:=(")^?[^;"\s]*\1)^?)^*\$$, which is used to validate the Web Linking header within HTML documents. This validation process ensures that the input value is free from any syntactically invalid Uniform Resource Identifiers (URIs). A legal input of Ψ is $="style"$ and the backreference referred to the first capturing group $(")^?$ ensures the quotation marks " are matching, e.g. $= "style$ should be rejected by Ψ, but $= style$ is acceptable.

4   Modeling and String Generation Algorithms

In this section, we present the details of our model for regex semantics. First, we describe our extension of functions as a foundation for our model in Sect. 4.1. For optimizing the efficiency of our tool, we implemented some reduction rules in Sect. 4.2. Then, we introduce a new automaton model for effective representation and Boolean operations for Unicode character classes in Sect. 4.3. We provide the induction rules from the AST in Sect. 4.4. Finally, we give a brief account of the random generation algorithms in Sect. 4.5.

4.1   Extension of Functions to Regex

Among the basic functions to synthesize position automata [23], according to the nomenclature in [11], the output of *first, follow, last* functions are called *position sets*. Here we generalize the *nullable, first* and *last* functions to regexes by giving computation rules for operators of regexes, which is necessary for modeling regexes. Due to space limitation, the details of computation rules are shown in our complete version.[2] We also deploy these functions on tasks such as processing semantic of anchors and identification of unsatisfiable cases, as heuristics to avoid the algorithms that require exponential time [46].

---

[2] https://cdn.jsdelivr.net/npm/dataset2023/.

$$c_1|\ldots|c_n \Longrightarrow [c_1\text{-}c_n]$$

$$(?:E_1^{\{0,l\}})^{\{m,n\}} \Longrightarrow E_1^{\{0,l\times n\}}$$

$$(?\text{=}[cc_1])[cc_2] \Longrightarrow [[cc_1]\&\&[cc_2]]$$

$$[cc_1](?\text{<=}[cc_2]) \Longrightarrow [[cc_1]\&\&[cc_2]]$$

$$E_1|\ldots|E_n \Longrightarrow (?:E_1|\ldots|E_n)^{\{0,1\}}$$

$$[c_1c_2]|[c_1c_3] \Longrightarrow [c_1c_2c_3]$$

$$[[cc_1][^\wedge cc_1]] \Longrightarrow \text{.}$$

$$(?![cc_1])[cc_2] \Longrightarrow [[cc_1]\text{-}[cc_2]]$$

$$[cc_1](?\text{<!}[cc_2]) \Longrightarrow [[cc_1]\text{-}[cc_2]]$$

$$\underbrace{E_1\ldots E_1}_{k \text{ times}} \Longrightarrow E_1^{\{k\}}$$

Fig. 2. Reduction Rules for Regex

Definition 1. *For a regex E over Σ, we define the following functions:*

$$first(E) = \{a \mid aw \in L(E), a \in \Sigma, w \in \Sigma^*\} \tag{1}$$

$$last(E) = \{a \mid wa \in L(E), a \in \Sigma, w \in \Sigma^*\} \tag{2}$$

$$nullable(E) = \begin{cases} true, & if\ \varepsilon \in L(E) \\ false, & otherwise \end{cases} \tag{3}$$

The definitions effectively compute the possible prefix/suffix of length one from a regex, without a full traversal on the AST. For example, for $E = {^\wedge}\backslash b[{^\wedge}\backslash d]^{\{2,4\}}(?\text{<!}\backslash w)$, $first(E) = \{[a\text{-}zA\text{-}Z]\}$, $last(E) = \{[{^\wedge}\backslash w]\}$, $nullable(E) = false$. We also notice those functions for backreferences depends on the capturing information during the generation, which can not be soundly computed statically.

4.2 Reduction Rules for Regex

We implemented several reduction rules shown in Fig. 2 to optimize the efficiency of our tool. Some of these reduction rules above are derived from existing regex engines and practical tools. For instance, mechanic of $[c_1c_2]|[c_1c_3] \Longrightarrow [c_1c_2c_3]$ is also found in the C# regex library. The others provide significant help in terms of efficiency and precision. The reduction rules we show here are common among our language-dependent reduction rules according to their original engine implementation.

We handle the semantic differences of partial/full match calls in the reduction system. For tight relationships between function calls and anchors, we consider semantic equivalence reduction by appending $.^*$ in an unanchored prefix/suffix, and none when anchored under partial match call. We also consider the full matching semantic by appending $^\wedge$ and \$. Inside our algorithms, anchors are processed as empty characters with constraints and for the sake of succinctness, we support start-of-line/end-of-line anchors implicitly. For our running example Ψ, the ? and * operators are rewritten into $\{0,1\}$ and $\{0,\infty\}$, thus the output is $(?:=(")^{\{0,1\}}[^\wedge;"\backslash s]^{\{0,\infty\}}\backslash 1)$. However $E^\wedge$ and \$$E$ when E is not nullable will be considered *unsat* in the reduction system and directly return $\varnothing$.

4.3 Effective Representation of Unicode Character Classes

We build automata in a top-down manner to encode the Unicode 15.0.0 [51] standard into UTF-8 in Algorithm 1 and traverse the automata to generate acceptable strings in UTF-8 byte-by-byte. This structure makes string generation feasible in acceptable time. In situations when ASCII flags (e.g. re.A in Python) are enabled, our representation is simplified into ASCII ranges.

In Algorithm 1, each Unicode character sets c_i when transformed into UTF-8 encoding composed with several runes (ranges) c_i^j defined on a byte. After initialization, Algorithm 1 first checks whether the character class is $\varnothing$. If not, the algorithm iterates the Unicode ranges $c_1, c_2, .., c_r$ in the character class cc, initializes the current state $\mathcal{A}$ as the initial state $init$ and j as the height of each c_i.

Then Algorithm 1 checks whether $j \geq 0$ and whether there has been a transition with c_i^j from the current state $\mathcal{A}$ to a non-null state, if so make this state as the current state and substract j. If there is no such non-null state and $j \geq 0$, we build a new state $\mathcal{S}$, and mark a transition $\delta(\mathcal{A}, c_i^j)$ to $\mathcal{S}$, then take $\mathcal{S}$ as the current state and substract j. Finally, we mark the final states when $j = 0$.

The Unicode automaton allows us to support a vast class of Unicode-related extended features, which is a major factor of the high usability of our tool. The Unicode character classes effectively define an automaton of a finite language with more succinctness than those translated to standard regular expressions. The cost from Boolean operations among Unicode automata, including intersection [40], subset construction [41], has a major impact on the performance of our tool. To miti-

---

Algorithm 1: Unicode Automaton

Input: An Unicode character class
$cc = [c_1, c_2, ..., c_r]$
Output: Initial state $init$ of
Unicode automaton or $\varnothing$
otherwise

1   $init \leftarrow 0; \mathcal{F} \leftarrow \varnothing$;
2   **if** $cc = \varnothing$ **then**
3 | **return** $\varnothing$;
4   **for** $i \in 1...r$ **do**
5 | $\mathcal{A} \leftarrow init; j \leftarrow len(c_i)$;
6 | **while** $j \geq 0 \wedge \delta(\mathcal{A}, c_i^j) \neq \varnothing$ **do**
7 | | $\mathcal{A} \leftarrow \delta(\mathcal{A}, c_i^j); j \leftarrow j - 1$;
8 | **while** $j \geq 0$ **do**
9 | | $\delta(\mathcal{A}, c_i^j) \leftarrow \mathcal{S}; \mathcal{A} \leftarrow \mathcal{S}$;
10 | | $j \leftarrow j - 1$;
11 | **if** $\mathcal{A} \in \mathcal{F}$ **then**
12 | | $\mathcal{F} \leftarrow \mathcal{F} \cup \{\mathcal{A}\}$
13 | **else**
14 | | $\mathcal{F} \leftarrow \{\mathcal{A}\}$
15 **return** $init$;

---

gate the cost, we execute those algorithms lazily, e.g. for $[\hat{}; "\backslash s]$ in our running example Ψ, the complementation of $[; "\backslash s]$ is computed only if a character is to be generated from this character class, instead of pre-processing and rewritting them in advance [17], thus guarantee the efficiency. The other character classes in Ψ are also compiled into Unicode automata.

4.4 Induction System for Regex

To comprehensively model the semantics of extended operators and generate matching strings, we propose the induction system.

The induction rules are composed of *configurations* and logical constraints, where a triple (E, w, C) is called a configuration, where E is a regex, w is a variable representing strings that E defines, and C is a stack preserving the generated strings from the referenced subexpressions. To comprehensively model the semantics of regex operators, the extension of the basic functions defined in Sect. 4.1 is necessary for our induction system. Also the syntactic and semantic differences between dialects of regexes can hardly be negligible. To tackle this problem, we designed different induction rules for string generation, according to specified languages from the user. From the categorization in [5], we consider ε-semantics and $\varnothing$-semantics, and differentiate regex dialects in implementation details, e.g. $\backslash w$ is equal to $[a$-zA-$Z0$-$9\_]$ in Python mode and $[\backslash p\{L\}\backslash p\{Mn\}\backslash p\{Nd\}\backslash p\{Pc\}]$ in C# mode. The induction rules we show here are designed for JavaScript regexes. In our induction system, specialized induction rules for other dialects of regexes can also be found.

(CONCAT)
$$\frac{(E_1E_2, w_1w_2, C)}{(E_1, w_1, C)\ (E_2, w_2, C)}$$

(BACKREF)
$$\frac{(\backslash i, w, C)}{(\backslash i, w \leftarrow C_i, C)}$$

(ALTER)
$$\frac{(E_1|E_2, w_1w_2, C)}{(E_1, w_1, C) \vee (E_2, w_2, C)}$$

(POS-LA)
$$\frac{((?=E_1)E_2, w_1w_2, C)}{(E_1.^*, w_1, C) \wedge (E_2, w_1w_2, C)}$$

(GREEDY)
$$\frac{(E_1^{\{m,n\}}, w_1w_2...w_n, C)}{\bigwedge_{m<j\leq n}(E_1, w_j|\epsilon, C)\bigwedge_{0<i\leq m}(E_1, w_i, C)}$$

(NEG-LA)
$$\frac{((?!E_1)E_2, w_1w_2, C)}{(\neg(E_1.^*), w_1, C) \wedge (E_2, w_1w_2, C)}$$

(POS-LB)
$$\frac{(E_1(?<=E_2), w_1w_2, C)}{(E_1, w_1w_2, C) \wedge (.^*E_2, w_2, C)}$$

(LAZY)
$$\frac{(E_1^{\{m,n\}?}, w_1w_2...w_n, C)}{\bigwedge_{0<i\leq m}(E_1, w_i, C)\bigwedge_{m<j\leq n}(E_1, \epsilon|w_j, C)}$$

(NEG-LB)
$$\frac{(E_1(?<!E_2), w_1w_2, C)}{(E_1, w_1w_2, C) \wedge (\neg(.^*E_2), w_2, C)}$$

(CAPTURE)
$$\frac{((_nE_1)_n, w, C)}{\forall\backslash k, \backslash k \notin E_1 \wedge (E_1, w, C_n \leftarrow w)}$$

(WBOUND)
$$\frac{(E_1\backslash bE_2, w_1xyw_2, C)}{(E_1, w_1x, C)\wedge x\in last(E_1)\cap\backslash w\ (E_2, yw_2, C)\wedge y\in first(E_2)\cap\backslash W}$$
$$\vee\frac{(E_1\backslash bE_2, w_1xyw_2, C)}{(E_1, w_1x, C)\wedge x\in last(E_1)\cap\backslash W\ (E_2, yw_2, C)\wedge y\in first(E_2)\cap\backslash w}$$

(NON-WBOUND)
$$\frac{(E_1\backslash BE_2, w_1xyw_2, C)}{(E_1, w_1x, C)\wedge x\in last(E_1)\cap\backslash w\ (E_2, yw_2, C)\wedge y\in first(E_2)\cap\backslash w}$$
$$\vee\frac{(E_1\backslash BE_2, w_1xyw_2, C)}{(E_1, w_1x, C)\wedge x\in last(E_1)\cap\backslash W\ (E_2, yw_2, C)\wedge y\in first(E_2)\cap\backslash W}$$
$$\vee\frac{(E_1\backslash BE_2, w, C)}{(E_1, \epsilon, C)\wedge nullable(E_1)\ (E_2, \epsilon, C)\wedge nullable(E_2)}$$

The rules for standard operators are self-explanatory. For rule GREEDY, the original configuration unfolds this operator into a conjunction of series of configurations to generate strings separately. For rule LAZY, it makes the string that the expression matches as short as possible.

We constrain the expressive power of the regex in the rule CAPTURE as follows. When processing a Python/C# regex, we disallow backreferences to appear inside any referenced capturing group. And when the user specifies JavaScript regex for the input, the first assertion in the post-condition is canceled and the unassigned backreference is configured as ε by default. The configuration also pushes the generated string from its configuration into stack C for reference. As we do not rewrite quantifiers like in [29], the generated strings from the same capturing group will overwrite the stack of index i during generation. Notice that we do not present induction rule for non-capturing groups, since those are considered useless on AST as in regex engines like C#'s, and the unreferenced capture groups are considered non-capturing as in Java regex engine. Thus for those capturing groups not referenced within the regex, we treat them as non-capturing groups. For succinctness, the logic for named capturing groups is also contained in the rule CAPTURE.

In rule BACKREF, the configuration simply reads the context from the latest assigned value of the stack C_i into the string variable. For our running example Ψ, $last$ and $nullable$ will output $unknown$ and proceed to generate a character from $(")^?$, when the generation by the capturing group requires any of those functions from this exact capturing group, our algorithm returns $unknown$ to avoid non-termination. Once a character " is generated from the sub-regex $(")^?$, the above functions are considered decidable, i.e. $first(\Psi) = \{=\}$, $last(\Psi) = \{"\}$, $nullable(\Psi) = false$. Also, named backreferences are contained in this rule.

From ES2018 [20], lookbehinds are introduced into the standard. In the rules for lookarounds, take positive lookahead as an example, w_1 should belong to $E_1.^*$, w_1w_2 is generated from E_2, the result is the conjunction of two configurations, i.e. $(?=a)\backslash w^+$ can generate $abbbb$ even in full match mode. The most intractable case is when lookarounds are decorated by repetitions: the lookarounds also put limitations on each repeating subexpression adjacent to it, our induction system shows a natural advantage in handling these cases.

In rules WBOUND and NON-WBOUND, we categorize the situations by the $first$ and $last$ functions of subregexes. For instance, in regex `^\b(&|ab|c)`, & is not satisfiable. Thus we generate a character from $first((\&|ab|c))\cap\backslash w$ and prune the configuration of &. Also, the rules contain the case when the word-boundary appears at the start or end of the regex. And a Non-word boundary operator can generate ε when E_1 and E_2 are both nullable. If none of the situations are satisfied, the induction system will return $\varnothing$.

Furthermore, since the complement of a regular language requires exponential time [21,46], we also apply heuristics for identification of unsatisfiable cases. For $E_1(?<!E_2)$, if E_2 is $nullable$, the complement of E_2 is $\varnothing$, thus the regex is unsatisfiable. Similar strategies are applied to other zero-width assertions.

Back to running example Ψ, the result from applying induction rules is shown as below. Notice we simplified the induction process to improve readability.

$$\frac{\dfrac{((?:=(")^{\{0,1\}}[^\wedge;"\backslash s]^{\{0,\infty\}}\backslash1),w_1w_2w_3w_4,C)}{(=(")^{\{0,1\}}[^\wedge;"\backslash s]^{\{0,\infty\}}\backslash1,w_1w_2w_3w_4,C)}}{(=,w_1,C)\quad \underset{0<j\leq1}{\bigwedge}(("),w_2|\epsilon,C)\atop \underset{0<j\leq1}{\bigwedge}(",w_2|\epsilon,C_1\leftarrow w_2|\epsilon)\quad \dfrac{([^\wedge;"\backslash s]^{\{0,\infty\}},w_3^{0\ldots j},C)}{\underset{0<j\leq\infty}{\bigwedge}([^\wedge;"\backslash s],w_3^j|\epsilon,C)}\quad (\backslash1,w_4\leftarrow C_1,C)}$$

4.5   String Generation Algorithm

In this section, we introduce our algorithm `PowerGen`, which takes a regex, the corresponding language, and the matching function as inputs, and outputs matching strings.

Our algorithm first conducts a syntax check conforming to the regex syntax rules of the provided language, selects the corresponding reduction rules based on the language, and creates an AST. The reduction rules handle the semantic difference of partial/full match calls in the corresponding language. It then forwards the simplified regex AST and the language as input to the Unicode automata compiler. It develops automata to incorporate the Unicode 15.0.0 [51] standard into UTF-8 in Algorithm 1, and compiles the AST leaves into Unicode automata. Depending on the language, we choose the appropriate induction system. This system takes the AST as input and compiles it into induction rules with stack storage. Finally, our random matching string generator receives induction rules and stack information as input and produces a matching string as an output. The generator performs a top-down traversal on the induction rules to generate strings. All of the Boolean operations of induction rules are performed on Unicode automata in Sect. 4.3. If the induction system returns $\varnothing$, `PowerGen` outputs *unsat*. By running the generation function repetitively, multiple matching strings are produced, since our generation strategy is random. Returning to our running example, we can easily obtain random sentences from the string variable of the root configuration. One of the strings generated is `=":z2L@Q"`, while the "sound" modeling in [29] mistakenly returns `="`.

5 Evaluation

We implemented our algorithms in C++, and conducted experiments on a machine with 192-core Intel Xeon E7-8850 v2 2.30 GHz processors and 2048 GB of RAM, running Ubuntu 16.04.5 LTS. Our algorithm can generate matching strings in multiple languages, including Python, JavaScript, Java, PCRE2, and C#. Our empirical investigation aims to address the following research questions:

RQ1. When randomly generating strings, does accurate modeling of regexes improve string generation efficiency?

RQ2. Is our support for full matching and partial matching better than other tools, which only support one kind of matching semantics?

RQ3. How does our approach work in practical projects?

To address RQ1, we compare our approach with existing string-generation tools by evaluating our algorithm on publicly available datasets. We select representative examples to demonstrate the correctness of all the tools in generating strings according to their specified matching semantics, thus validating RQ2. Lastly, we assess the performance of our approach in comparison to other tools in practical projects to clarify RQ3.

5.1 Datasets

Our experiment was conducted on a benchmark from [19]. This benchmark contains 537,806 unique regexes extracted from 193,524 programs written in 8 programming languages, including JavaScript, Java, PHP, Python, Ruby, Go, Perl, and Rust. The unique regexes represent the set of expressions after removing duplications.

5.2 Tools for Comparison

We compared nine string generation tools (see Sect. 2.3). We ensured all tools were configured according to their original configurations as stated in their papers or documentation, respectively. Egret, dk.brics, Mutrex and Generex (extended on dk.brics) did not specify the regexes they supported in which programming language, so we classified them as Unspecific support. Meanwhile, Exrex and Xeger focused on Python regexes, and Randexp.js, ExpoSE and Ostrich specialized in JavaScript regexes. ExpoSE supports partial matching semantics, while the others support full matching semantics, as shown in Table 2.

Table 2. Language-Matching Calls-Features Support by String Generation Tools

Tools[a]	Egr	DK	Mut	Gen	Exr	Xeg	Rnd	Ost	Exp	PowerGen
Language	Unspecified				Python		JavaScript			Multi-Language
Matching Calls	Full								Partial	Full&Partial
Character Class	✓	✓	✓	✓	✓	✓	✓	✓	✓	✓
Greedy Quantifier	✓	✓	✓	✓	✓	✓	✓	✓	✓	✓
Lazy Quantifier	✓	✗	✗	✗	✓	✓	✗	✓	✓	✓
Unicode ($\backslash uxxxx$)	✗	✓	✓	✓	✓	✓	✓	✓	✓	✓
Capture/Non-Capturing Group	✓	✗	✗	✗	✓	✓	✓	✓	✓	✓
Input Start/End (^$)	✓	✗	✗	✗	✓	✓	✓	✓	✓	✓
Start/End-of-line Anchors	✓	✗	✗	✗	✓	✓	–	–	–	✓
Start/Reset match	✗	✗	✗	✗	–	–	–	–	–	✓
Word/Non-word Boundary	✓	✗	✗	✗	✓	✓	✓	✓	✓	✓
Lookahead	✗	✗	✗	✗	✗	✗	✗	✗	✓	✓
Lookbehind	✗	✗	✗	✗	✗	✗	✗	✗	✗	✓
Backreference	✓	✗	✗	✗	✓	✓	✓	✗	✓	✓
Ignore Case, Multi-line, Single-line Flags	✗	✗	✗	✗	✓	✓	✗	✗	✓	✓
Extended Flag	✗	✗	✗	✗	✓	✓	–	–	–	✓
Unicode Flag	✗	✗	✗	✗	✓	✓	✗	✗	✓	✓
Comment Group	✗	✗	✗	✗	✓	✓	–	–	–	✓

[a] abbreviations for each tool in this table, along with their respective definitions, are as follows: Egr (Egret), DK (dk.brics), Mut (Mutrex), Gen (Generex), Exr (Exrex), Xeg (Xeger (O'Connor)), Rnd (Randexp.js), Exp (ExpoSE), Ost (Ostrich)

5.3 Evaluation of Random String Generation

We compared the feature support for each tool. The results are presented in Table 2. The "–" in Table 2 indicates that the programming language specified by the tool lacks support for that feature, and the "✗" signifies that the corresponding tool does not support a feature. Our algorithm supports all the features listed earlier.

To begin with, we evaluate the impact of random generation. Through statistical analysis, the language-specific tools are based on the regexes of the Python or JavaScript languages. Therefore, in full matching comparisons, we evaluate each language-specific tool in its own language, and unspecific tools in both

Python and JavaScript. For partial matching comparisons, there is only one tool, ExpoSE, to compare with us. We filtered the dataset to ensure syntax correctness. We assess the accuracy rate and time of the tools, with results depicted in Table 3, where the full match validation are shown on the left and the JavaScript partial match validation on the right. The first line on the left is based on Python validation results, while the second line refers to JavaScript validation results (achieved by adding start and end-of-line anchors before and after the regex). The accuracy rate is defined as: $AccuracyRate = \frac{1}{|D|} \sum_{i=1}^{|D|} Match(r_i, s_i)$. In the given formulas, r_i denotes the i-th regex in the dataset D, where $|D|$ refers to the size of D. s_i denotes the string generated by r_i by the tool. $Match(r_i, s_i)$ represents the validation of string s_i using the language's matcher. It returns 1 for success and 0 for failure. It is noteworthy to mention that Ostrich, ExpoSE, and our approach perform checks for unsatisfiability. We classify regexes as unsatisfiable if all tools determine them to be either unsatisfiable or incorrect. The memory usage refers to the average maximum resident set size.

Table 3. Experimental Results of String Generation Tools under Specific Language

Matching calls	Full match							Partial match	
Tools	Egr	DK	Mut	Gen	Exr	Xeg	PowerGen	Exp	PowerGen
Accuracy (%)	90.90	39.94	40.54	38.87	92.33	92.71	**97.40**	77.84	**97.72**
Time (s)	0.154	0.489	3.346	0.610	0.146	0.159	**0.004**	53.14	**0.004**
Memory (KB)	13535	47522	109772	52020	11021	9652	**5835**	90132	**4975**
Tools	Egr	DK	Mut	Gen	Rnd	Ost	PowerGen		
Accuracy (%)	90.92	35.82	44.62	40.93	91.43	93.69	**97.71**		
Time (s)	0.153	0.471	3.354	0.599	0.172	8.540	**0.004**		
Memory (KB)	13522	47477	110737	52078	32418	138913	**4796**		

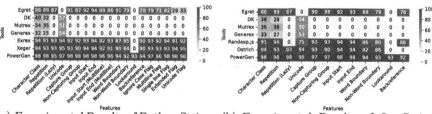

(a) Experimental Results of Python String Generation Tools on Feature Dataset

(b) Experimental Results of JavaScript String Generation Tools on Feature Dataset

Fig. 3. Experimental Results of String Generation Tools on Feature Dataset

The experimental results show that `PowerGen` achieves the highest accuracy in random string generators among state-of-the-art tools. In Python full matching validation, `PowerGen` achieved the highest accuracy of 97.40%, followed by Exrex and Xeger (O'Connor) with about 92%, and the worst performer was DK, Mutrex and Generex with about 40%. For JavaScript full matching validation, to be ranked according to accuracy, `PowerGen` achieved the highest percentage of 97.71%, followed by Randexp.js and Ostrich with about 92%, while DK, Mutrex and Generex achieved only 35.82%, 44.62% and 40.93% respectively. For JavaScript partial matching validation, `PowerGen` is about 20% higher than ExpoSE. Additionally, `PowerGen` generates correct results for all the examples mentioned in Sect. 2.3.

Regarding efficiency, in the full matching comparisons, the fastest among other tools is Exrex with 0.146 s, while our tool only takes 0.004 s, which has achieves a 36.5x speedup over Exrex. Moreover, our tool outperforms the slowest tool, Ostrich, by a factor of 2136. In the partial matching comparisons, we are up to ten thousand times faster than ExpoSE. We also expect our tool to be integrated into other softwares to improve their efficiency. Regarding memory usage, our memory usage is the least among tools in comparison.

To further analyze the experimental results, we then use the AST parsing tool to parse the regexes in the dataset and divide the dataset according to regex features. It should be noted that a regex can have multiple features thus can be split into multiple features categories. Due to the space limitation, we only present the comparison results under full matching calls. We calculate the accuracy rate for each feature and plot the Fig. 3(a) and 3(b) for Python and Javascript. The x-axis represents different features, the y-axis represents different tools, and the values indicate the accuracy rate.

The Fig. 3(a) and 3(b) indicate that our tool achieved the highest accuracy rate for each feature, where lookbehind is only supported by our tool. Among other tools that support Python regex syntax, their support for word boundary is relatively poor. Besides, for the tools that claim to support JavaScript regex syntax, their accuracy for word boundary, non-word boundary, and backreference achieves about 80%, and even 0% in some cases due to lack of support.

> **Summary to RQ1:** By better supporting features, in the full matching comparisons, our algorithm achieves the highest accuracy for both Python and JavaScript. Regarding efficiency, our tool is several dozen times faster than the fastest among existing tools. In the partial matching comparisons, Our accuracy is 20% higher than ExpoSE while being faster by a factor of ten-thousandth.

Table 4. The Results by Each Generator for Examples

Regex[a]	Possibly Acceptable Results		Tools										
	Full	Partial	Egr	DK	Mut	Gen	Exr	Xeg	Rnd	Ost	Exp	PowerGen	
			Full								Partial	Full	Partial
\b\$	unsat	a$	unsat	-	-	-	$	$	$	unsat	$	unsat	a$
\b\u0023	unsat	a#	unsat	-	-	-	$	$	$	unsat	$	unsat	a#
node_modules(?=paradigm.*) | (paradigm~gulp~watch)	paradigm~gupl-watch	node_modulesparadigmaaa	-	-	-	-	-	-	-	-	unsat	paradigm~gulp-watch	node_modulesparadigmaaa
"""(?=")	unsat	""""	-	-	-	-	-	-	-	-	unsat	unsat	""""
\n|(?=\?>)	\n	?>	-	-	-	-	-	-	-	-	unsat	\n	?>
$(?=a^{2,5})$\w	aa	aa	-	-	-	-	-	-	-	-	unsat	unsat	aa
$(?<=\d^{2,61})$	unsat	11	-	-	-	-	-	-	-	-	unsat	unsat	11
https:\/\/$(?=\w^{2,3})$.	unsat	https://aa	-	-	-	-	-	-	-	-	unsat	unsat	https://aa

[a] All the example regexes in this table are from [19]. We simplified some lengthy regexes for presentation.

5.4   Statistics for Full Matching and Partial Matching

The actual project library contains both full and partial matching capabilities. Unfortunately, the tools being compared only support one kind of matching semantics, which is inadequate for dealing with this situation. Furthermore, there are many logical errors in these tools regarding the semantics they claim to support. In this section, we analyse some representative examples from the dataset under full and partial matching calls in Table 4.

1. $\backslash b\backslash\$$

   Under full matching call, the regex above is unsatisfiable, while under partial matching it should return a string from $\backslash w\backslash$ $. Among those tools supporting full matching semantic, dk.brics, Mutrex and Generex lack support for word boundaries, Exrex, Xeger(O'Connor) and Randexp.js returns $, which is incorrect. ExpoSE's output $ is erroneous under partial match, while PowerGen is capable to find the correct results under both matching semantics.

2. $node\_modules(?=paradigm.^*)|(paradigm\text{-}gulp\text{-}watch)$

   Under full matching, $paradigm\text{-}gulp\text{-}watch$ is the matching string, while for partial matching, results from $node\_modulesparadigm.^*$ or $paradigm\text{-}gulp\text{-}watch$ are acceptable. Although ExpoSE claimed to support lookahead, it returned $unsat$, which is incorrect for both full and partial matching; PowerGen generates the correct answers under both cases.

3. $"""(?=")$

   For full matching, this regex is not satisfiable. In partial matching, lookaround requires that after matching three quotes, a quote must follow, resulting in the generation of four quotes. ExpoSE returns $unsat$, which is incorrect in the case of partial matching. In contrast, our result is accurate in both full and partial matching scenarios.

4. $(?=a^{\{2,5\}})\backslash w$

   For full matching, this regex is unsatisfiable. And under partial matching, a string aa is acceptable. ExpoSE returned $unsat$, which is wrong under partial matching, while our results are correct under both cases.

The other examples in the table are similar to four examples above.

> **Summary to RQ2:** By considering the distinctions between full matching and partial matching, our algorithm can generate correct strings for different semantics.

5.5　Results on Real Projects

Table 5. Examples in PyPI (Python) Project Library

FileName	Pattern	Matching calls	Egr	DK	Mut	Gen	Exr	Xeg	PowerGen
.../mcdre forged _plugin.py	$\backslash w^{\{1,16\}}$	full matching	–	–	–	–	–	–	7
	$(?<=\backslash u64027)$ $!!MCDR[\backslash w]^*$ $(?=\backslash u6402)$	partial matching	–	–	–	–	–	–	\u64027!!MC DR\u6402
.../conf igurati on.py	$[a\text{-}zA\text{-}Z0\text{-}9.\_\text{-}]^+@$ $[a\text{-}zA\text{-}Z0\text{-}9.\_\text{-}]^{\{2,\}}$ $\backslash.[a\text{-}z]^{\{2,4\}}$	partial matching	–	–	–	–	–	-	-@ddg.qq
	$[a\text{-}zA\text{-}Z0-9.\_\text{-}]^+@$ $[a\text{-}zA\text{-}Z0\text{-}9.\_\text{-}]^{\{2,\}}$ $\backslash.[a\text{-}z]^{\{2,4\}}$	full matching	evil@-.aaaa	---.aa	---.ab(✗)	error	rhxbe@9 c60bHn7...	g@HOZGmxj8 .meuy	_@kzz.dd
	$(?P<heures>\backslash d^+)[h:]$ $(?P<minutes>\backslash d^+).^{+7}$ $(?P<value>[a\text{-}zA\text{-}Z0\text{-}9\backslash.]^+)$	partial matching	–	–	–	–	-	-	001:77\ud90b \udf013
.../prep rocessi ng.py	$(?:(?<=\backslash s)\|(?<=\backslash W)\|$ $(?<=))(%\backslash w)\|(\backslash$ $\{.^*\ \backslash\})(?=\backslash s\|\backslash W\|\$)$	partial matching	–	–	–	–	–	–	%1
	$^\wedge\{.^{*7}\}\$$	full matching	ε	–	–	–	{bqs-$tx}	{}	{}

We inspected a large number of projects in PyPI [39], Maven [32], npm [36] and other project libraries, and found that many of them contain various matching calls within the same project. In Table 5 and 6, we present a few examples of this phenomenon. Similar to RQ1, we conducted experiments in languages supported by each tool. It can be seen that other tools give wrong results in most examples due to not supporting some features and/or the matching calls (indicated by –), run-time errors (indicated by *error*), or others (indicated by ✗). Our tool consistently produces the correct results thanks to considering different matching semantics and supporting a wider range of extended features.

> **Summary to RQ3:** Our approach is highly effective in real projects due to in-depth understanding of different matching semantics, as well as our comprehensive support for more extended features.

Table 6. Examples in Maven (Java) Project Library

FileName	Pattern	Matching calls	Egr	DK	Mut	Gen	PowerGen
.../JDBCUserStore Manager.java	$(\backslash*)\backslash1^+$	full matching	* * *	–	–	–	* * * *
	$(?<!\backslash\backslash)\backslash*$	partial matching	–	–	–	–	"*
.../Path.java	$/+$	partial matching	–	–	–	–	///
	$\backslash p\{Sc\}^+:$	full matching	–	error	error	error	$:
.../ImdbParser.java	$\backslash u00bb$	partial matching	–	–	–	–	\u00bb
	$(?i)Country.^*$	full matching	–	–	–	–	Country\udbb4\ude5c
.../OpSumIf.java	$.^*(?<!\sim)\backslash*.^*$	full matching	–	–	–	–	*
	$(?<!\sim)\backslash*$	partial matching	–	–	–	–	@*
	$(?<!\sim)\backslash?$	partial matching	–	–	–	–	?

6   Related Work

Matching Semantics and Extended Features. Leftmost-longest (POSIX-type) and Leftmost-greedy (PCRE-type) policies are two popular disambiguation strategies for regular expressions. However, POSIX implementations were found error-prone [16]. Okui and Suzuki [38] formalized leftmost-longest semantics and extended position automata [23] with leftmost-longest rule. Sulzmann and Lu extended Brzozowski's derivatives [7] to POSIX parsing problem [48]. Berglund et al. gave a formalization of Boost semantics for its combination of POSIX semantics and capturing groups [4]. Regular expressions with backreferences were first proposed by Aho in 90s [1]. Câmpeanu and colleagues gave rigorous formalisms and various properties [8–10] for regular expressions with backreferences. Recently Berglund and van der Merwe investigated theoretical aspects of regex with backreferences [5]. On the theoretical foundation for lookaheads, Miyazaki and Minamide [33] extended Brzozowski's derivatives [7] to lookaheads. Recently Berglund et al. [6] proposed a model based on Boolean Automata for regular expressions with lookaheads, and gave state complexity results. In 2022, Chida and Terauchi [15] gave the first formal study on regexes with both backreferences and lookaheads.

String Generation Toolkits. The Automaton Library [35] compiles a regex into an ϵ-NFA, and implements interfaces for random string generation. Egret [25] has a partial support for regexes to find inconsistency between regexes and specifications, it was found their tool lacks support for Unicode-related features. Reggae [26] supports string generation for regular expressions with intersection and complement operators; it also mentions that supporting lookarounds and boundaries is challenging. Veanes et al. [52] proposed Rex, which can be used for regular expression testing. Due to the cost of determinization on their proposed symbolic automata based on the construction of ϵ-NFAs, the string generation of Rex is not efficient. Loring et al. [29] claimed their model supports the complete regex language for ES6, but for lookarounds decorated by repetitions, ExpoSE seems to fail to give a correct result. Chen et al. [14] proposed a novel transducer model, namely PSST, to formalize the semantics of regex-dependent string functions, but backreference and lookarounds are still on their future work.

This paper and [47] both propose novel methods for modeling regexes. However, they develop different techniques because the problems they solve are different. The algorithmic differences are listed as follows: firstly our implementation is platform-independent based on induction rules instead of Z3 [34]. Secondly in [47] authors introduced the length constraint in modeling regex operators for checking satisfiability, which is insufficient to deduce fixed-length matched strings for generic purpose. Thirdly since the matching functions for regexes are ubiquitous in practical programs, for the first time we consider different matching semantics in modeling regexes for deducing matching strings. Also we constrained the expressive power of the input regex by induction rules to ensure the completeness of our algorithm within a fragment of the class of regexes, while in [47], authors introduced a CEGAR (counterexample-guided abstraction refinement) scheme which makes their algorithm incomplete.

7   Conclusion

We propose `PowerGen`, a tool for deducing matching strings for regexes. It is based on a novel semantic model for regexes, which comprehensively models the extended features, with the awareness of different matching semantics and matching precedence. The evaluation results demonstrate the high effectiveness and efficiency of our algorithms. We aim to develop methods to further deduce the shortest matching strings for regexes and thus get a more refined model for regex in the future.

Acknowledgements. The authors would like to thank the anonymous reviewers for their helpful comments and suggestions. Work supported by the Natural Science Foundation of Beijing, China (Grant No. 4232038) and the National Natural Science Foundation of China (Grant No. 62372439).

References

1. Aho, A.V.: Algorithms for finding patterns in strings. In: Handbook of Theoretical Computer Science, Volume A: Algorithms and Complexity, pp. 255–300. Elsevier and MIT Press (1990)
2. Arcaini, P., Gargantini, A., Riccobene, E.: MUTREX: a mutation-based generator of fault detecting strings for regular expressions. In: ICST Workshops 2017, pp. 87–96 (2017)
3. Bartoli, A., Lorenzo, A.D., Medvet, E., Tarlao, F.: Inference of regular expressions for text extraction from examples. IEEE Trans. Knowl. Data Eng. **28**(5), 1217–1230 (2016)
4. Berglund, M., Bester, W., van der Merwe, B.: Formalising boost POSIX regular expression matching. In: Fischer, B., Uustalu, T. (eds.) ICTAC 2018. LNCS, vol. 11187, pp. 99–115. Springer, Cham (2018). https://doi.org/10.1007/978-3-030-02508-3_6
5. Berglund, M., van der Merwe, B.: Re-examining regular expressions with backreferences. Theor. Comput. Sci. **940**, 66–80 (2023)
6. Berglund, M., van der Merwe, B., van Litsenborgh, S.: Regular expressions with lookahead. J. Univers. Comput. Sci. **27**(4), 324–340 (2021)
7. Brzozowski, J.A.: Derivatives of regular expressions. J. ACM **11**(4), 481–494 (1964)
8. Câmpeanu, C., Salomaa, K., Yu, S.: A formal study of practical regular expressions. Int. J. Found. Comput. Sci. **14**(6), 1007–1018 (2003)
9. Câmpeanu, C., Santean, N.: On the intersection of regex languages with regular languages. Theor. Comput. Sci. **410**(24–25), 2336–2344 (2009)
10. Câmpeanu, C., Yu, S.: Pattern expressions and pattern automata. Inf. Process. Lett. **92**(6), 267–274 (2004)

11. Caron, P., Champarnaud, J.-M., Mignot, L.: Partial derivatives of an extended regular expression. In: Dediu, A.-H., Inenaga, S., Martín-Vide, C. (eds.) LATA 2011. LNCS, vol. 6638, pp. 179–191. Springer, Heidelberg (2011). https://doi.org/10.1007/978-3-642-21254-3_13

12. Chapman, C., Stolee, K.T.: Exploring regular expression usage and context in python. In: ISSTA 2016, pp. 282–293 (2016)

13. Chapman, C., Wang, P., Stolee, K.T.: Exploring regular expression comprehension. In: ASE 2017, pp. 405–416 (2017)

14. Chen, T., Flores-Lamas, A., Hague, M., Han, Z., Hu, D., Kan, S., Lin, A.W., Rümmer, P., Wu, Z.: Solving string constraints with regex-dependent functions through transducers with priorities and variables. POPL 6, 1–31 (2022)

15. Chida, N., Terauchi, T.: On lookaheads in regular expressions with backreferences. In: FSCD 2022. LIPIcs, vol. 228, pp. 15:1–15:18 (2022)

16. Chris, K.: Regex posix - HaskellWiki. https://wiki.haskell.org/Regex_Posix

17. D'Antoni, L., Veanes, M.: Automata modulo theories. Commun. ACM 64, 86–95 (2021)

18. Davis, J.C., Coghlan, C.A., Servant, F., Lee, D.: The impact of regular expression denial of service (ReDoS) in practice: an empirical study at the ecosystem scale. In: ESEC/FSE 2018, pp. 246–256 (2018)

19. Davis, J.C., IV, L.G.M., Coghlan, C.A., Servant, F., Lee, D.: Why aren't regular expressions a lingua franca? An empirical study on the re-use and portability of regular expressions. In: ESEC/FSE 2019, pp. 443–454 (2019)

20. ECMA: ES2018. https://262.ecma-international.org/9.0

21. Ellul, K., Krawetz, B., Shallit, J.O., Wang, M.W.: Regular expressions: new results and open problems. J. Autom. Lang. Comb. 10(4), 407–437 (2005)

22. Fent: Randexp.js. https://github.com/fent/randexp.js

23. Glushkov, V.M.: The abstract theory of automata. Russ. Math. Surv. 16, 1–53 (1961)

24. Hooimeijer, P., Veanes, M.: An evaluation of automata algorithms for string analysis. In: Jhala, R., Schmidt, D. (eds.) VMCAI 2011. LNCS, vol. 6538, pp. 248–262. Springer, Heidelberg (2011). https://doi.org/10.1007/978-3-642-18275-4_18

25. Larson, E., Kirk, A.: Generating evil test strings for regular expressions. In: ICST 2016, pp. 309–319 (2016)

26. Li, N., Xie, T., Tillmann, N., de Halleux, J., Schulte, W.: Reggae: automated test generation for programs using complex regular expressions. In: ASE 2009, pp. 515–519 (2009)

27. Liu, X., Jiang, Y., Wu, D.: A lightweight framework for regular expression verification. In: HASE 2019, pp. 1–8 (2019)

28. Loring, B., Mitchell, D., Kinder, J.: ExpoSE: practical symbolic execution of standalone JavaScript. In: SPIN 2017, pp. 196–199 (2017)

29. Loring, B., Mitchell, D., Kinder, J.: Sound regular expression semantics for dynamic symbolic execution of javascript. In: PLDI 2019, pp. 425–438 (2019)

30. Luo, B., Feng, Y., Wang, Z., Huang, S., Yan, R., Zhao, D.: Marrying up regular expressions with neural networks: A case study for spoken language understanding. In: ACL 2018, pp. 2083–2093 (2018)

31. Michael, L.G., Donohue, J., Davis, J.C., Lee, D., Servant, F.: Regexes are hard: decision-making, difficulties, and risks in programming regular expressions. In: ASE 2019, pp. 415–426 (2019)

32. Miller, F.P., Vandome, A.F., McBrewster, J.: Apache maven (2010). https://repo1.maven.org/maven2/

33. Miyazaki, T., Minamide, Y.: Derivatives of regular expressions with lookahead. J. Inf. Process. **27**, 422–430 (2019)
34. de Moura, L., Bjørner, N.: Z3: an efficient SMT solver. In: Ramakrishnan, C.R., Rehof, J. (eds.) TACAS 2008. LNCS, vol. 4963, pp. 337–340. Springer, Heidelberg (2008). https://doi.org/10.1007/978-3-540-78800-3_24
35. Møller, A.: dk.brics.automaton. https://www.brics.dk/automaton/
36. npm Inc: npm. https://www.npmjs.com/
37. O'Connor, C.: Crdoconnor/xeger. https://github.com/crdoconnor/xeger
38. Okui, S., Suzuki, T.: Disambiguation in regular expression matching via position automata with augmented transitions. In: Domaratzki, M., Salomaa, K. (eds.) CIAA 2010. LNCS, vol. 6482, pp. 231–240. Springer, Heidelberg (2011). https://doi.org/10.1007/978-3-642-18098-9_25
39. Python Software Foundation: Python package index - pypi. https://pypi.org/
40. Rampersad, N., Shallit, J.: Detecting patterns in finite regular and context-free languages. Inf. Process. Lett. **110**(3), 108–112 (2010)
41. Salomaa, K., Yu, S.: NFA to DFA transformation for finite languages over arbitrary alphabets. J. Autom. Lang. Comb. **2**(3), 177–186 (1998)
42. Saxena, P., Akhawe, D., Hanna, S., Mao, F., McCamant, S., Song, D.: A symbolic execution framework for JavaScript. In: S&P 2010, pp. 513–528 (2010)
43. Shen, Y., Jiang, Y., Xu, C., Yu, P., Ma, X., Lu, J.: ReScue: crafting regular expression DoS attacks. In: ASE 2018, pp. 225–235 (2018)
44. Spishak, E., Dietl, W., Ernst, M.D.: A type system for regular expressions. In: FTfJP 2012, pp. 20–26 (2012)
45. Stanford, C., Veanes, M., Bjørner, N.: Symbolic Boolean derivatives for efficiently solving extended regular expression constraints. In: PLDI 2021, pp. 620–635 (2021)
46. Stockmeyer, L.J.: The complexity of decision problems in automata theory and logic. Ph.D. thesis, Massachusetts Institute of Technology, USA (1974)
47. Su, W., Chen, H., Li, R., Chen, Z.: Modeling regex operators for solving regex crossword puzzles. In: Hermanns, H., et al. (eds.) SETTA 2023, LNCS, vol. 14464, pp. 206–225. Springer, Cham (2023)
48. Sulzmann, M., Lu, K.Z.M.: POSIX regular expression parsing with derivatives. In: Codish, M., Sumii, E. (eds.) FLOPS 2014. LNCS, vol. 8475, pp. 203–220. Springer, Cham (2014). https://doi.org/10.1007/978-3-319-07151-0_13
49. Tauber, A.: EXREX. https://github.com/asciimoo/exrex
50. Trinh, M., Chu, D., Jaffar, J.: S3: a symbolic string solver for vulnerability detection in web applications. In: CCS 2014, pp. 1232–1243 (2014)
51. Unicode: Unicode 15.0.0. https://unicode.org/versions/Unicode15.0.0/
52. Veanes, M., de Halleux, P., Tillmann, N.: Rex: symbolic regular expression explorer. In: ICST 2010, pp. 498–507 (2010)
53. Wang, P., Stolee, K.T.: How well are regular expressions tested in the wild? In: ESEC/FSE 2018, pp. 668–678 (2018)
54. Youssef, M.: Generex. https://github.com/mifmif/Generex
55. Yu, S.: Regular languages. In: Handbook of Formal Languages, Vol. 1: Word, Language, Grammar, pp. 41–110 (1997)

Binary Level Concolic Execution on Windows with Rich Instrumentation Based Taint Analysis

Yixiao Yang, Chen Gao, Zhiqi Li, Yifan Wang, and Rui Wang[✉]

College of Information Engineering, Capital Normal University,
Beijing 100048, China
rwang04@163.com

Abstract. Windows programs are widely used. The effective testing of Windows applications can prevent financial losses. Currently, there are only a few tools that can test programs without source code on Windows. The state-of-art WinAFL tool suffers from the poor testing efficiency. Most of the other tools rely on analysing the source code on Linux. Concolic execution based on binary code is an efficient method to discover defects in program without source code. In this paper, we present WinTaintCE, which mainly uses Rich Instrument-based taint analysis technique for instruction refinement. The data in the input file of fuzzing tasks will be marked as the tainted source. All instructions that are flowing through tainted data will be extracted for symbolic execution. However, this step will overlook many instructions for calculating non tainted data. Thus, we innovatively propose Rich Instrument technology, which saves the values on all registers and memory addresses involved in an instruction to a trace file. During concolic execution based on that trace file, those saved values will be set directly for non tainted data in an instruction. Experimental results show that WinTaintCE can explore about 24%–130% more paths compared to WinAFL. Also, 96%–99% reduction in the number of instructions need to be analysed compared to existing binary analysis tools on Windows also proves the effectiveness of the methodology of this paper.

Keywords: software testing · binary testing · symbolic execution

1 Introduction

Windows applications are widely used in information systems, spanning various domains such as finance, healthcare, manufacturing, and more. Testing Windows programs is crucial as it can help prevent significant economic losses during the development phase. Due to commercial considerations, it is often impossible to access the source code of many software applications or development libraries for conducting gray-box or white-box testing. Concolic execution based on binary assembly code is an effective method for discovering program defects in the absence of source code. It typically starts by symbolizing some data within the program and collecting binary arithmetic and control instructions as constraint conditions. It then utilizes constraint solvers to systematically explore underlying code branches, aiming to traverse as many paths as possible within the binary program to uncover defects.

WinAFL [11] is one of the few tools available for testing binary Windows programs. It is built upon AFL to implement the core fuzzing loop, utilizes DynamoRIO for instrumentation and coverage measurement. WinAFL is based on fuzzing, the mutation operations of WinAFL are random. So the testing efficiency is low. Combining WinAFL with symbolic execution is a good idea. At present, there is no practical open source symbolic execution solution available that can be combined with fuzzing testing and can handle actual large binary programs on Windows. A large number of existing binary symbolic execution tools are targeted at Linux, such as KLEE [3], QSYM [32], S2E [4] or Sydr [30], all of which declare on their homepage that they can only run on Linux systems. There is currently no good support for Windows. KLEE relies on LLVM [16], although LLVM can run cross platforms, KLEE cannot run cross platforms. Similarly, there is Sydr, which relies on Triton [23], an open-source binary analysis framework. Although Sydr cannot run cross platforms, Triton can do so. It is worth noting that the Triton and the similar tool Miasm [24] libraries provide many functions for binary execution and analysis, but they cannot directly receive a binary file and perform symbolic execution.

Currently, performing symbolic execution [2,10,19] on binary Windows programs presents several challenges. On one hand, compiled binary programs contain a vast number of instructions, encompassing not only the code for the program's core logic but also the binary instructions from static and dynamic libraries. This results in low efficiency for symbolic analysis. In reality, many of these instructions are irrelevant for a single symbolic execution because they have no impact on constraint solving. Thus, there is a need to simplify the analysis by identifying and focusing on the instructions that are related to the constraint solving. On the other hand, when conducting dynamic symbolic execution on binary programs, a significant amount of memory and processor state information is analyzed, while data relevant to constraint solving is often scarce. Previous approaches have required retrieving the entire memory state, contributing to the inefficiency of symbolic execution. There are also numerous technical challenges, including the complexity of Windows system calls, necessitating hooking numerous file read and write operations. Furthermore, handling advanced instructions such as SIMD instructions presents additional difficulties.

To address these challenges and achieve more accurate and efficient testing of Windows programs, we propose a taint analysis technique based on Rich Instrument technology. We implement the open source testing tool WinTaintCE. The data in the input file of fuzzing tasks will be marked as the tainted source. All instructions that are flowing through tainted data will be extracted for symbolic execution. However, this step will overlook many instructions for calculating non tainted data. Thus, we innovatively propose Rich Instrument technology, which saves the values on all registers and memory addresses involved in an instruction to a trace file. During concolic execution based on that trace file, those saved values will be set directly for non tainted data in an instruction. We also evaluated WinTaintCE. First we compared the path discovery capability with WinAFL, and WinTaintCE could explore about 24%-130% more paths. Then we compared WinTaintCE with other formalised test case generation tools that run on Windows, and WinTaintCE can solve many complex models while CBMC and SLDV cannot. Not only that, we also separately evaluated our proposed Rich Instrumentation technology. This technique saves 96%-99% of the number of instructions to be analysed.

2   Background

This section introduces the background knowledge of existing symbolic tools on Windows and the drawbacks of the existing tools. Then, the motivations and the advantages of the proposed tool are introduced.

Existing Binary Symbolic Tools on Windows. Miasm [24] (Multi-Architecture Static and Dynamic Analysis Framework) is an open source binary analysis framework that can be used for static and dynamic analysis of binary files of various different architectures. Misam has a built-in symbolic execution engine, which can be used to analyze the execution path of binary files and find vulnerabilities. Triton is a dynamic binary analysis framework similar to Miasm. Both Triton and Miasm rely on a virtual simulation environment to do symbolic execution. This environment cannot handle system calls, thus, these two tools cannot directly load and run a binary. Users must do a lot of preparation work such as providing trace and memory data before invoking these two tools.

Advantage of the Proposed Tool. Although there exist many binary analysis frameworks on Windows, these tools only offer a virtual simulation environment and typically are employed only trivial and simple examples [14]. To analyze real world applications, many problems need to be solved. The first problem is how to observe file reads and writes at the Windows system call level to determine which are program inputs. The second problem is how to extract binary level machine state from the current program and set up a virtual environment to enable symbolic execution engine to run correctly. The third problem is how to handle the system calls which the analysis frameworks do not support. Because of the above mentioned engineering challenges and the lack of tool support for Windows, at present, there is no practical open source symbolic execution solution available on the Windows. On Linux, existing works dump the entire memory area of a running program and set up the virtual environment before the symbolic execution. Once a system call is encountered, the symbolic engine does not know what the system call is doing, the subsequent execution may produce wrong results. Besides, in all the memory area, there are many data related to the operating system which are unrelated to the logic of the program under test. Therefore, it is very time-consuming to process the entire memory data when simulating the execution environment. Thus, we propose Rich Instrument technology which can accurately analyze the memory and register information that each instruction relies on, and print them to trace to facilitate subsequent concolic execution. The memory data size of all our tainted instructions is about 1KB-5KB, and the data size of the entire memory is at least 10MB-10GB, which shows that our work can avoid a lot of extra overhead about setting up virtual memory environment.

Existing Binary Taint Analysis Methods on Windows. Currently, both the Triton and Miasm only support taint analysis based on symbolic execution engine in the virtual simulation environment. Users must dump the entire trace and memory to set up the virtual environment to do symbolic execution first, then to do taint analysis. The whole procedure is time consuming. Besides, once a system call is encountered, the engine may fail to do taint analysis as the behavior of a system call is unknown to the engine.

Advantage of the Proposed Taint Analysis Method. In order to reduce the overhead by allowing taint analysis to be carried out simultaneously with the program execution, the Rich Instrument based taint analysis is proposed in this paper. The Rich Instrument technique is to analyze every instruction to identify the memory or register dependency of an instruction. For Windows system call, the Rich Instrument technique monitors all system calls currently encountered and analyze their functionality to ensure the correctness of real-time taint analysis. Based on many engineering efforts, a fast and efficient real-time taint analysis method has been implemented.

3   Overall Framework

Figure 1 shows the various modules of the overall framework and their execution order. The dynamic taint analysis is carried out during program execution.

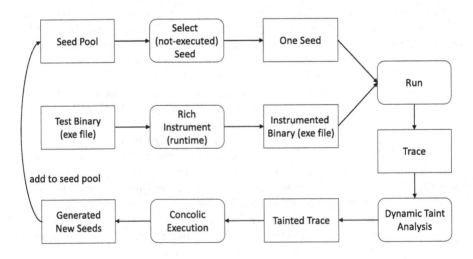

Fig. 1. Overall Framework

Before symbolic execution, the tested program will be instrumented. The task of the instrumentation program is to print the instruction execution procedure into a trace. Using the Rich Instrument technology proposed in this paper, the instrumentation not only prints information about the instruction itself, but also prints information about all registers and memory addresses associated with the instruction, as well as specific values on these registers and memory addresses. After the program is instrumented, the proposed framework selects a seed from the seed pool that has not been executed before, uses this seed as input to the instrumented program, executes the instrumented program, performs dynamic taint analysis and generates a reduced trace. The symbolic execution is performed on the reduced trace. Since the specific values are used during symbolic execution, this symbolic execution is actually a concolic execution. After symbolic execution, many new seeds will be generated, and these new seed files will be re-executed, recording all paths triggered by them. If a seed triggers a new path, it will be added to the seed pool, otherwise it will be discarded.

3.1 Rich Instrument

Traditional binary instrumentation typically only inserts a few binary instruction sequences before or after an instruction to achieve the goal of printing the opcode of the instruction or recording the binary code of the instruction. However, it is a complex task to print all the operand information, especially obtaining the stored values based on the operand type. Therefore, it is unrealistic to complete this task by inserting several binary instructions. So, we insert function calls before and after the instruction to be observed, and call self written functions to complete the task of recording operand values.

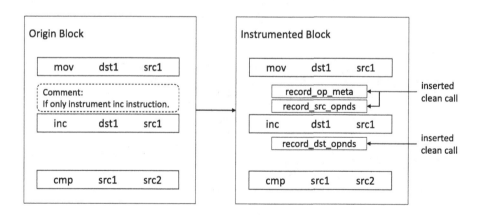

Fig. 2. Rich Instrument

As shown in Fig. 2, if only one instruction with opcode 'inc' needs to be instrumented, three functions are inserted before and after that instruction. Figure 3 shows the pseudo code implementation of three custom functions inserted in Fig. 2 with some complex operations explained with annotations. The binary instrumentation framework used in this paper is DynamoRIO. The pseudo code in Fig. 3 shows how to use DynamoRIO API to obtain information of instructions. The *get_opcode* API is to get the opcode of a binary instruction, *src_opnds* field refers to the source operands of an instruction, similarly, *dst_opnds* field refers to the destination operands of an instruction. The *type* field refers to the type of the operand which can be one of *reg* (register), *mem* (memory reference), *imm* (immediate number) or *pc* (jump address).

The binary instrumentation framework DynamoRIO used in this paper is a dynamic instrumentation framework that provides the ability to insert function calls before or after instructions. The inserted function calls are called Clean-Call. When Inserting a CleanCall, DynamoRIO will save the current execution status of the instrumented program, including all registers, stack pointer positions, and other information. In a CleanCall, the register information and the memory information including the stored values on registers or memory addresses of the instrumented program can be queried through the API provided by DynamoRIO. The function parameter type of the CleanCall can only be primitive type or pointer address (actually uint64_t type). In order to get the information of instrumented instruction in a CleanCall, we pass the memory address where the instruction is located as a parameter. In the CleanCall, DynamoRIO API is used to decode the binary form of an instruction located at the passed-in parameter into DynamoRIO objects. DynamoRIO API can also be used to query the register and memory address information. In CleanCall, it is allowed to write any C++code, so STL libraries and other complex libraries can be used. In fact, the taint analysis mentioned later can be directly implemented in a CleanCall.

```
void record_op_meta(instr_addr) {
    instr_info = decode(instr_addr);
    fprint(get_opcode(instr_info));
    fprint(get_eflags_usage(instr_info));
    fprint(get_predicate(instr_info));
}


void record_dst_opnds(instr_addr) {
    instr_info = decode(instr_addr);
    for (src_opnd : instr_info.dst_opnds) {
        // similar to record_src_opnds.
        // but record dst opnds.
    }
}
```

```
void record_src_opnds(instr_addr) {
    instr_info = decode(instr_addr);
    for (src_opnd : instr_info.src_opnds) {
        switch (src_opnd.type) {
            case reg:
                // fprint(src_opnd.reg_id and its value);
                break;
            case mem:
                // fprint (src_opnd.mem_addr and its value);
                break;
            case imm: fprint(src_opnd.imm); break;
            case pc: fprint(src_opnd.pc); break;
        }
    }
}
```

Fig. 3. Rich Instrument Pseudo Code

3.2   Dynamic Taint Analysis

The taint analysis is conducted on the instruction trace generated by Rich Instrument technology. All instructions satisfy the following form:

$$Opcode(, dst1)(, dst2)(, dst3)(, dst4)(, dst5)(, src1)(, src2)(, src3)(, src4)(, src5).$$

The contents in parentheses are operands that may exist. Most instructions only have one src operand and one dst operand. For example, the load instruction is an instruction that loads the value on a memory address into a register, its src operand is the memory address and its dst operand is the register. Instructions with no less than one target operands are generally data transfer instructions or arithmetic instructions. These data transfer instructions or arithmetic instructions are the key to taint analysis. Table 1 lists the commonly used instructions and the corresponding categories which may cause the taint propagation.

Table 1. Tainted Instructions

category	Instructions
data transfer	mov, cmovcc, movzx, movups, movss, cwde, cdq, ...
stack operation	push, pop, load, store
SIMD	vmovdqu, vinsertf128, punppcklbw, punpcklqdq, ...
arithmetic operation	add, sub, sbb, inc, dec, imul, cmpxchg, xchg, xadd, ...
logical operation	and, or, xor, xorps, psrldq, shl, shr, not, neg, ...
bit operation	bts, btr, bsf, bsr, rol, ror, sar, ...
string operation	movs, rep movs, ...

In computer architecture, A memory address can store one byte by default, a register can store many bytes. Each byte in a memory address or a register can be represented by a unique ID. For the byte in a memory address, the memory address itself can uniquely represent that byte. For the byte in a register, the register id and the byte offset from the beginning of the register can uniquely represent that byte. The granularity of the taint analysis implemented in this paper is byte, which means that this article will analyze which tainted bytes will taint a certain byte in an instruction.

At the beginning of taint analysis, a portion of data is firstly marked as tainted. We track the encountered kernel-level system call NtReadFile and mark the data read into memory as tainted. The function call or system call are also abstracted as a self-defined special instruction but this kind of instruction has no operands but just records the memory address of the file content read in and the length of the data read in. Each byte read in will be marked as tainted and put into a pool named as *tainted_byte_pool*.

For instructions that can cause taint propagation, it is necessary to check if their source operands has been tainted. If some bytes in source operands exist in *tainted_byte_pool*, that instruction and the corresponding operands containing the tainted bytes are tainted. Then, each byte of the destination operands affected by tainted bytes in source operands will be marked as tainted and put into *tainted_byte_pool*. The whole procedure is illustrated in the left part of Fig. 4, if each byte in the source operand of mov instruction is tainted, the corresponding byte in destination operand of mov instruction should also be tainted and added to *tainted_byte_pool*. In another situation, if an instruction causes taint propagation but its source operand is not tainted, its destination operand should be untainted and each byte in the destination operand should be removed in the *tainted_byte_pool*. The whole procedure is illustrated in the right part of Fig. 4, if each byte in the source operand of mov instruction is not tainted, the corresponding byte in destination operand of mov instruction should also be untainted and removed from *tainted_byte_pool*.

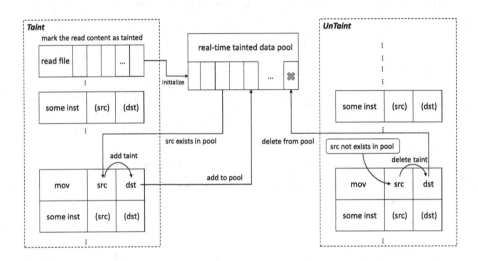

Fig. 4. Taint Analysis

In addition, some instructions do not directly cause explicit taint propagation, but they will read the Eflags register. If some tainted instructions modify the Eflags register, the modified flag bit of the Eflags register is taken as tainted and the instruction which reads the tainted bit of the Eflags register is taken as indirectly tainted. Figure 5 shows an example about the indirectly tainted instruction. The cmp instruction in Fig. 5 is used to compare the values of the first source operand (src1) and the second source operand (src2), and modifies the values of the ZF and SF flag bit in the Eflags register based on the comparison results. If the comparison result is that src1 and src2 are equal, the ZF flag bit is set to 0. Based on the value of ZF, the jz instruction in Fig. 5 determines whether to execute a jump. If ZF is 0, the jz instruction will cause the program to jump to the address indicated by the source operand of jz instruction. That is, whether the jz instruction performs the jump depends on the value of the

Eflags register written by the cmp instruction. If the source operands of the cmp instruction contain taint information, it is considered that the execution of the jz instruction is also affected by taint information and jz instruction is indirectly tainted. The indirectly tainted instructions such as jz or jne are important because these instructions perform the branch jump operations in binary programs and are commonly referred to as branch jump instructions. The binary symbolic execution framework Triton which will be described in the next subsection also depends on branch jump instructions to generate path constraints.

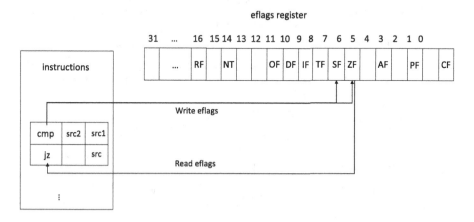

Fig. 5. Eflags Usage

Thus, for each of instructions in the original trace, we will check whether the instruction has directly operated on tainted data or is indirectly tainted as described above. If so, the directly or indirectly tainted instruction information including specific values of the operands of the instruction in the original trace will be retained and form a new sliced trace named as tainted trace. Note that, due to hardware compatibility design, registers with different bits have inclusion relationships. For example, AL register is of 8 bits, AX register is of 16 bits and AL is lower half part of AX register. Similarly, AX register is the lower half part of EAX register and EAX register is the lower half part of RAX register. If an operand is a register, in addition to storing the value of the register itself, it also needs to store the value of the largest register which contains that register. The value of the largest register will be used in symbolic execution in next subsection.

3.3 Dynamic Symbolic (Concolic) Execution

Triton is used to perform symbolic execution in this paper. Symbolic execution is a method of program analysis that uses abstract symbols instead of specific values as program inputs, simulates program execution, and generates program path constraint. Triton provides API to symbolize registers and memory addresses.

Once symbolize a byte, Triton will generate a symbolic variable and maintain a symbolic expression associated with the symbolic variable. Before simulating the execution of an instruction, it is necessary to use API provided by Triton to set specific values in the instruction operands. If the current instruction is a branch instruction, Triton provides API to collect symbolic expressions and combine symbol expressions into path constraints. Path constraints can be solved in Triton and the solution results are the possible values of abstract symbols.

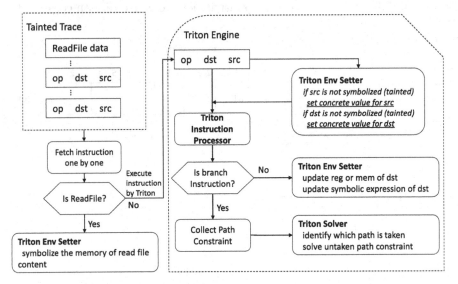

Fig. 6. Symbolic Execution

As shown in Fig. 6, the steps to perform symbolic execution in Triton are:

(1) Iterate each instruction, set up memory region for the bytes read by ReadFile instruction and mark them as tainted and symbolized.
(2) Set up values for operands of an instruction, if the operand is a register, if its largest register containing that register is not set before, also set the concrete value for the largest register.
(3) Processing the instruction in Triton.
(4) If the instruction is a branch instruction, collect constraints for each branch. Triton provides API to find those branches, and we need solve constraints for branches that are not executed.
(5) If it is not a branch instruction, Triton will automatically update the values and symbolic expressions of the destination operands of this instruction.

Taking the three instructions in the tainted trace as examples, the following will explain the process of symbolic execution in detail.

1. mov ECX, [EAX]
2. cmp ECX, 6
3. jne 0x62

Triton will iterate and execute these three instructions one by one. In the first mov instruction, value in the EAX register is considered as an address and this instruction will take 4 bytes of value from this address. Assume that this address is filled by ReadFile instruction and need to be symbolized. Use the API provided by Triton to set the value in the EAX and ECX register to their values in the tainted trace and symbolize the 4 bytes starting from the address [EAX]. The third jne instruction is a branch instruction, working similarly to the jz instruction mentioned earlier. If the value in ECX register is 6, the jump instruction (jne) will not be executed, otherwise, it will be executed. Triton treats branch instruction jne specially to generate and solve the path constraint to make the jne instruction execute or not execute.

4   Experiments

Implementations. This tool is an open source [31] Windows application which contains 12,000 lines of C++ code. The whole solution named as $WinTaintCE$ is divided into two sub-tools: $WinTaintCE$-$Trace$ and $WinTaintCE$-$Concolic$. The $WinTaintCE$-$Trace$ tool is implemented in 7000 lines of code containing the implementation of online taint analysis and rich trace logging. The trace generation tool $WinTaintCE$-$Trace$ uses DynamoRIO as the basic framework. $WinTaintCE$-$Concolic$ tool is implemented in 5000 lines of code containing the implementation of offline taint analysis and concolic execution based on tainted trace. The trace generation tool $WinTaintCE$-$Concolic$ uses Triton [23] as the basic framework. The whole solution $WinTaintCE$ is targeted at Windows and can handle Windows API and system calls at binary level.

The Design of Experiments. The experiments are divided into three parts. The first part is to verify the effectiveness of tools on real world Windows application fuzzing. The second part is to verify the effectiveness of tools with and without taint analysis. The third part is to verify the effectiveness of tools on traditional formal analysis problems such as model verification and testing. The organization of the experiments is as follows.

1 $WinTaintCE$ vs Windows Fuzzing Methods: Comparing the new paths found in real world Windows applications in binary form.
2 $WinTaintCE$ with and without Taint Analysis: Comparing the instructions need to be handled with and without taint analysis.
3 $WinTaintCE$ vs Traditional Formal Methods: Comparing the coverage and time in traditional formal problems such as model verification and testing.

4.1   The Experimental Setup

WinTaintCE Setting. The proposed WinTaintCE is a dynamic symbolic execution tool and it depends on actual program traces to do concolic execution. To make program traces more effective, inside WinTaintCE, there is a small random seed generator which is used to generate seeds of different lengths. That seed generator is adopted from WinAFL. Note that, in testing, only 5–10 seeds are generated from that generator. The rest seeds are generated through constraint-solving based on the traces generated from the 5–10 seeds. Once a seed is generated, that seed will be used as input for WinAFL, run to see how many new paths it can discover. In another words, we still use WinAFL to see how many paths the proposed tool can find. In 1 h testing, WinTaintCE only uses 45 min to do concolic execution, the rest 15 min are used by WinAFL to take all seeds generated by WinTaintCE as the initial seeds and run for 15 min to check the number of paths finally discovered.

WinAFL Setting. In experiments, WinAFL will run for 10 rounds from scratch. In all the 10 rounds, the maximum paths found will be retained. The initial seeds for each tested program are extracted from the test examples on WinLibs repository [9]. For each round, the WinAFL is configured to run for 1 h. In the experiment, the experiment results prove that after 1 h, it is difficult for WinAFL to discover new paths, and the number of paths increased very slowly. So, 1 h is enough to see the effectiveness of different tools.

CBMC Setting. CBMC is one of the baselines. It can test C programs. In this experiment, Simulink models are converted into C programs. In Simulink models, the model design is similar to the circuit design, the core logic basically does not include loops, but there is an outer loop that controls the number of executions of the core logic. Each execution of the loop requires corresponding input data to be provided. For comparison with formal methods, the Simulink models in benchmarks have set to loop only 5 times. In this experiment, when encountering loops, we directly set the outer loop bound in source code to 5, the loop bound will be determined at compile time, thus, CBMC will know how many times it should expand. The CBMC command is used as follows:

$$cbmc.exe\ test.c\ \ --cover\ branch\ \ --unwind\ 6\ \ --xml-ui \qquad (1)$$

Note that, we ensure the number of outer loops is 5, here the $--unwind$ 6 (unwind loops up to 6 times) option enables CBMC to fully expand all loops.

4.2   *WinTaintCE* vs Windows Fuzzing Methods

The Baselines. Sydr can only run on Linux but it mainly uses Triton. We implement WinTriton on Windows based on the proposed framework. The Win-Triton can be taken as the Triton which uses the full program trace and the static path exploration. WinAFL is another state-of-art baseline on Windows.

The Benchmark. Existing benchmark is in deep binding with Linux system. On Windows, the corresponding Windows version winlibs repository [9] contains projects such as win-libiconv, win-libtidy, win-libsodium or win-avif. The win-libfile is the commonly used c library for processing file on GitHub.

The Result. Table 2 shows the paths found in different libraries. In binary program, the libraries such as *memcpy_s* or *strcmp* used in the program are also taken into consideration, which means that the path computation also considers used libraries. From the result, the proposed WinTaintCE improves the found paths by at least 24%. The symbolic execution can cover many easy to cover branches very quickly while the fuzzing method gradually improve the found paths. One observation is that for a binary program, it will include many libiaries, for example, VCRUNTIME140.dll or NTDLL.dll. These libraries contain many branches which are pass checks. For symbol execution, covering these pass checks is easy while for fuzzing, passing these checks is difficult. This explains why the coverage increases fast for symbolic execution methods. WinTaintCE runs much faster than WinTriton because WinTaintCE only executes tainted instructions.

Table 2. Total Paths Found in 1 h

	Win-libfile	Win-avif	Win-libtidy	Win-libiconv	Win-libsodium
WinAFL	39	148	1442	93	16
WinTriton	789	153	1249	103	28
WinTaintCE	789	184	2970	214	269

Table 3 shows the paths found by WinAFL in different libraries at different times. As can be seen, within 1 h, the increment in the number of paths found by WinAFL was gradually decreasing. In most projects, WinAFL cannot find new paths after 30 min. This proves that 1 h is enough to compare the effectiveness of different tools.

Table 3. Paths Found for WinAFL at Different Times

	Win-libfile	Win-avif	Win-libtidy	Win-libiconv	Win-libsodium
5 mins	33	127	631	71	11
15 mins	35	130	778	93	14
30 mins	39	145	1126	93	16
50 mins	39	147	1410	93	16
60 mins	39	148	1442	93	16

4.3 *WinTaintCE* with and Without Taint Analysis

The Benchmark. The same benchmarks used in previous subsection are used here. In this subsection, the efficiency of taint analysis is illustrated here.

The Result. Table 4 shows the number of instructions before and after the taint analysis. As can be seen, the reduction in the number of instructions is very significant. In different binary programs, the reduction rate varies from 96% to 99%. Take win-libtidy as an example, If the taint analysis is not used, over 1 million instructions need to be executed and analyzed. After taint analysis, only 9000 instructions need to be analyzed. This improves the testing efficiency and constitutes one reason why WinTriton (uses static path exploration and full instruction trace) performs worse than WinTaintCE.

Table 4. Effectiveness of Taint Analysis.

	Win-libfile	Win-avif	Win-libtidy	Win-libiconv	Win-libsodium
Origin Instr Num	52397	78298	1012355	38273	299160
Tainted Instr Num	218	2801	9024	183	1528
Improvement	99.6%	96.4%	99.1%	99.5%	99.5%

4.4 *WinTaintCE* vs Traditional Formal Methods

The Baselines. One of the baselines is the Simulink Design Verifier (SLDV). Because SLDV [12] is a famous testing and verification tool which supports both the static analysis and dynamic analysis. Another baseline tool is an academic tool CBMC [5] which is a famous bounded model checking tool.

The Models in Benchmark. The Simulink models are used to compare *WinTaintCE* with traditional formal methods. The non-CI-CPS models [20,21] (i.e., RHB, AT, AFC) representing realistic CPS systems from domains including IoT, smart home and automobile are included in the benchmark. As the models contain state machines and continuous behaviors, Simulink Rapid Simulation Target is used to generate the code under testing, the generated code depends on Simulink library which is in binary form. In addition to non-CI-CPS models, we also include pure control logic models (i.e. NLGuidance, Euler321, BasicTwoTanks, EB, Regulator) in control fields such as fuel control, road control based on Euler distance and neural network guidance. These models are previously used in the Simulink verification survey [18]. The MHI1209 model is an industry model [6] from the Mitsubishi Heavy Industries (MHI) company.

Table 5. Effectiveness.

Condition & Decision Coverage			
Model	WinTaintCE	CBMC	SLDV
NLGuidance	69%	69%	38%
RHB	91%	0%	0%
Euler321	94%	94%	94%
BasicTwoTanks	100%	100%	96%
EB	98%	98%	93%
MHI1209	97%	0%	0%
AFC	71%	0%	0%
AT	82%	0%	0%
Regulator	75%	75%	64%

The Result. Table 5 shows the coverage values for WinTaintCE, CBMC and SLDV. CBMC and SLDV are run on source code but the proposed WinTaintCE is run on binary code. For complex non-CI-CPS models (RHB, MHI1209, etc.), the generated code relies on Simulink library (*.lib) binary files to perform integral calculus or run embedded S-Function and the symbolic executor SLDV or CBMC cannot handle those external binary libraries. That is why the coverage achieved by SLDV or CBMC is 0%. In the meanwhile, WinTaintCE performs significantly better than SLDV or CBMC. In other small or medium control logic models, WinTaintCE performs similarly as SLDV or CBMC. WinTaintCE can achieve similar results as those source code level symbolic execution tools.

5 Related Work

Dynamic symbolic execution (DSE) [2,10] has significant applications in computer security, such as fuzzing, vulnerability discovery, and reverse-engineering. For dynamic execution implementation, there are two mainstreams: one [19] is to log trace at first and then perform symbolic execution on the trace, and the other [17] is to do symbolic execution when the program is running. There are various ways to search for errors in programs: applying static analysis tools to source code [13] and binary code [1] manually during compilation, using dynamic analysis tools, and formal verification tools, among others. The fuzzing [7,22] technology and the dynamic symbolic execution [8] technology are widely used to detect errors [25,32].

In the field of embedded systems [26–29], researchers also face the problem about detecting errors. In large scale Simulink models, there may exist external dependencies, for example, models may depend on neural network libraries to handle image recognition issues. Most of the external libraries are in binary form. Traditional source code based testing techniques are no longer able to keep up with the development of existing model technologies, so there is an urgent need for improvement. A large amount of Simulink users use Windows as their operating systems. That is the why we propose the Windows concolic execution technology in this paper.

In recent years, Windows fuzzing [15] has attracted the attention of researchers. Existing technology is still based on coverage guided fuzzing not based on symbolic execution. Granting the ability to execute dynamic symbolic execution on the Windows operating system is an urgent issue that needs to be addressed. Although there already exist many tools for symbolic execution, the existing tools are mainly for Linux not for Windows. For dynamic symbolic execution, one basic rule is to dynamically run it and use concrete values to perform the symbolic execution. Obviously, on Linux, it is hard to run Windows application. The app will crash if there are many Windows system calls. Thus, it is necessary to implement a symbolic execution engine on Windows. As far as we know, the proposed tool $WinTaintCE$ in this paper is the first tool on Windows which can perform taint analysis and dynamic symbolic execution.

6 Conclusion

This paper proposes a dynamic symbolic execution solution on Windows platform and shows the effectiveness and efficiency of the proposed framework. To reduce the number of instructions to be analyzed from millions to thousands, the Rich Instrument and Taint Analysis techniques are proposed. The proposed tool can explore about 24%–130% more paths than state-of-art baselines and save 96%–99% of the number of instructions to be analysed. In the future, how to cover complex float branches and string hash related branches are two problems worth exploring and researching, and we will keep researching about the dynamic symbolic execution from the two mentioned aspects on Windows.

References

1. Aslanyan, H., Arutunian, M., Keropyan, G., Kurmangaleev, S., Vardanyan, V.: BinSide: static analysis framework for defects detection in binary code. In: 2020 Ivannikov Memorial Workshop (IVMEM), pp. 3–8. IEEE (2020)
2. Baldoni, R., Coppa, E., D'elia, D.C., Demetrescu, C., Finocchi, I.: A survey of symbolic execution techniques. ACM Comput. Surv. (CSUR) 51(3), 1–39 (2018)
3. Cadar, C., Dunbar, D., Engler, D.R.: KLEE: unassisted and automatic generation of high-coverage tests for complex systems programs. In: Usenix Conference on Operating Systems Design & Implementation (2009)
4. Chipounov, V., Kuznetsov, V., Candea, G.: S2E: a platform for in-vivo multi-path analysis of software systems. ACM SIGPLAN Not. 39(4), 265–278 (2012)
5. Clarke, E., Kroening, D., Lerda, F.: A tool for checking ANSI-C programs. In: Jensen, K., Podelski, A. (eds.) TACAS 2004. LNCS, vol. 2988, pp. 168–176. Springer, Heidelberg (2004). https://doi.org/10.1007/978-3-540-24730-2_15
6. Contributor, O.: Simulink benchmark. Web (2022). https://github.com/EmbedSystemTest/SimulinkTest
7. Fioraldi, A., Maier, D., Eißfeldt, H., Heuse, M.: {AFL++}: combining incremental steps of fuzzing research. In: 14th USENIX Workshop on Offensive Technologies (WOOT 20) (2020)
8. Gerasimov, A., et al.: Anxiety: a dynamic symbolic execution framework. In: 2017 Ivannikov ISPRAS Open Conference (ISPRAS), pp. 16–21. IEEE (2017)
9. Github Company: Winlibs (2023). https://github.com/winlibs
10. Godefroid, P., Levin, M.Y., Molnar, D.: SAGE: whitebox fuzzing for security testing: SAGE has had a remarkable impact at Microsoft. Queue 10(1), 20 (2012)
11. Google Company: Winafl (2023). https://github.com/googleprojectzero/winafl
12. Inc., M.: Simulink design verifier. Web (2022). https://nl.mathworks.com/products/simulink-design-verifier.html
13. Ivannikov, V., Belevantsev, A., Borodin, A., Ignatiev, V., Zhurikhin, D., Avetisyan, A.: Static analyzer SVACE for finding defects in a source program code. Program. Comput. Softw. 40, 265–275 (2014)
14. JonathanSalwan: Triton examples. Web (2023). https://github.com/JonathanSalwan/Triton/tree/master/src/examples/cpp
15. Jung, J., Tong, S., Hu, H., Lim, J., Kim, T.: WINNIE: fuzzing windows applications with harness synthesis and fast cloning. In: Network and Distributed System Security Symposium (2021)

16. Lattner, C.: LLVM: an infrastructure for multi-stage optimization (2003)
17. Molnar, D.A., Wagner, D., et al.: Catchconv: symbolic execution and run-time type inference for integer conversion errors. UC Berkeley EECS (2007)
18. Nejati, S., Gaaloul, K., Menghi, C., Briand, L.C., Foster, S., Wolfe, D.: Evaluating model testing and model checking for finding requirements violations in simulink models. In: Proceedings of the 2019 27th ACM Joint Meeting on European Software Engineering Conference and Symposium on the Foundations of Software Engineering, pp. 1015–1025 (2019)
19. Padaryan, V.A., Kaushan, V., Fedotov, A.: Automated exploit generation for stack buffer overflow vulnerabilities. Program. Comput. Softw. **41**, 373–380 (2015)
20. Roohi, N., Wang, Y., West, M., Dullerud, G.E., Viswanathan, M.: Statistical verification of the Toyota powertrain control verification benchmark. In: International Conference on Hybrid Systems: Computation and Control (2017)
21. Sankaranarayanan, S., Fainekos, G.: Simulating insulin infusion pump risks by *in-silico* modeling of the insulin-glucose regulatory system. In: Gilbert, D., Heiner, M. (eds.) CMSB 2012. LNCS, pp. 322–341. Springer, Heidelberg (2012). https://doi.org/10.1007/978-3-642-33636-2_19
22. Sargsyan, S., Hakobyan, J., Mehrabyan, M., Mishechkin, M., Akozin, V., Kurmangaleev, S.: ISP-fuzzer: extendable fuzzing framework. In: 2019 Ivannikov Memorial Workshop (IVMEM), pp. 68–71. IEEE (2019)
23. Saudel, F., Salwan, J.: Triton: a dynamic symbolic execution framework. In: Symposium sur la sécurité des Technologies de l'information et des Communications. pp. 31–54. SSTIC, Rennes, France (Jun 2015)
24. Security, C.I.: Miasm. Web (2023). https://github.com/cea-sec/miasm
25. Stephens, N., et al.: Driller: augmenting fuzzing through selective symbolic execution. In: NDSS, vol. 16, pp. 1–16 (2016)
26. Su, Z., et al.: Code synthesis for dataflow based embedded software design. IEEE Trans. Comput.-Aided Design Integr. Circuits Syst. **41**, 49–61 (2021)
27. Su, Z., et al.: MDD: a unified model-driven design framework for embedded control software. IEEE Trans. Comput. Aided Des. Integr. Circuits Syst. **41**(10), 3252–3265 (2022)
28. Su, Z., et al.: PHCG: optimizing simulink code generation for embedded system with SIMD instructions. IEEE Trans. Comput.-Aided Design Integr. Circuits Syst. **42**, 1072–1084 (2022)
29. Su, Z., et al.: STCG: state-aware test case generation for simulink models. In: 60th ACM/IEEE Design Automation Conference (DAC). ACM (2023)
30. Vishnyakov, A., et al.: Sydr: cutting edge dynamic symbolic execution. In: 2020 Ivannikov ISPRAS Open Conference (ISPRAS), pp. 46–54. IEEE (2020)
31. Yang, Y.: Wintaintce. Web (2023). https://github.com/GrowingCode/WinTaintCE-SETTA
32. Yun, I., Lee, S., Xu, M., Jang, Y., Kim, T.: QSYM: a practical concolic execution engine tailored for hybrid fuzzing. In: 27th USENIX Security Symposium (USENIX Security 2018), pp. 745–761 (2018)

Cheat-FlipIt: An Approach to Modeling and Perception of a Deceptive Opponent

Qian Yao[1,2], Xinli Xiong[1,2], and Yongjie Wang[1,2(✉)]

[1] College of Electronic Engineering, National University of Defense Technology,
Hefei 230037, China
{yaoqian21,xiongxinli_,wangyongjie17}@nudt.edu.cn
[2] Anhui Province Key Laboratory of Cyberspace Security Situation Awareness
and Evaluation, Hefei 230037, China

Abstract. The modeling of opponent deception in an intelligent game system is not sufficient. However, an opponent agent may launch deceptive actions to consume defense resources, such as feint. We focus on modeling a deceptive opponent. We extend the FlipIt game model and present Cheat-FlipIt model, in which the opponent agent may feint to flip the resources first, and then control the resources after a decay interval. The defense agent models and perceives the cheating behavior of the opponent agent. DQN has some shortcomings such as over-fitting and insufficient exploration, and is not suitable for opponent-deception environment. To address the problems of opponent-deception and non-stationary environment, we present NLD3QN, which incorporates Noisynet, LSTM, Dropout and Dueling Q-Network into the DQN. We further propose a series of cheat strategies of the opponent agent. The defense agent adopts NLD3QN to perceive the cheating behavior of opponents. The proposed approach are evaluated in the Cheat-FlipIt game environments. Experimental results performed on 1 vs. 1 games show that NLD3QN demonstrates superior performance to the baseline DQN. Confronted with a deceptive opponent, the winning rate of NLD3QN is 73.3%, while DQN's winning rate is 26.67%.

Keywords: Opponent modeling · FlipIt game · Reinforcement learning · Deceptive opponent

1 Introduction

Intelligent game technology provides a new solution for agents to make decisions in a game environment. In recent years, intelligent game has achieved great success [2,18,23], which relies on the organic combination of game theory and deep reinforcement learning paradigm. When there are opponent agents in a same environment, the environment will become a non-stationary system. The relationship between the agents may be cooperation, competition or hostility. In

---

X. Xiong—Equal contribution.

recent years, the issues of cooperation and competition have been widely studied. In fact, opponent agents may be bounded rational or deceptive to induce defense agents to make wrong decisions in the game process. The hostile and deceptive opponent agents have not been pay much attention.

However, with the development of artificial intelligence technology, the cost of opponent deception is lower. In this paper, we construct a Cheat-FlipIt model to simulate a scenario of opponent derception, which is an extension of the FlipIt game [21] model. In a FlipIt game, the defender and the opponent compete for controlling a sensitive resource, such as a private key, a database, etc. In fact, it's not easy to model the opponent deception, this paper considers a scenario of controlling sensitive resources and adopts the extended FlipIt game model. Cheat-FlipIt game model is a binary model, the sensitive resources can be controlled by defense agent or opponent agent. In the Cheat-FlipIt game model, the opponent agent may cheat to flip the resources first, and then control the resources after a decay interval. The cheating behavior of the opponent aims at confusing the defense agent and inducing it to make wrong decisions.

For solving the Cheat-FlipIt model, the traditional Nash equilibrium solution may not be obtained. This occurs because Nash equilibrium needs to find the global optimal solution, and its convergence conditions are not easily satisfied. Therefore, Deep reinforcement learning(DRL) is considered to find the near-optimal solution. DRL is a widely used approach to solve game models [11,27]. DRL combines reinforcement learning(RL) and deep learning(DL), and it has shown great performance in a wide variety of single-agent stationary settings. DQN [14] is a representative algorithm of DRL. However, DQN does not perform well in the non-stationary game environment, due to its shortcomings of over-fitting, over-estimation and insufficient exploration. The Cheat-FlipIt simulates a scenario where opponent agents may execute deceptive actions. It makes the game environment more non-stationary. DQN performs worse in such a scenario.

In the Cheat-FlipIt model, the defense agent needs to perceive opponent agent's intention explicitly or implicitly and model the opponent agent's behavior. Therefore, to solve the defects of DQN confronted with a deceptive opponent, we propose NLD3QN, which integrates **N**oisynet, **L**STM, **D**ropout, **D**ueling Q-Network and Constrained Q-Learning into **D**eep **Q**-Network. LSTM [7] can analyze historical interactive data, so as to identify opponent's deception behavior. Noisynet [5] improves the exploration ability of the defense agent. Dropout [19] solves the problem of over-fitting. Dueling Q-Network [24] has improved the decision-making ability. And Constrained Q-Learning [25] alleviates the problem of over-estimation. As a result, NLD3QN has improved its performance in many aspects. It can well identify opponent deception and adapt to the non-stationary game environment.

In conclusion, the deceptive action is introduced into the FlipIt game model, and the Cheat-FlipIt model is presented. And we propose a series of Cheat and Flip strategies of opponent agents, introduced in Sect. 3.3. NLD3QN improves the performance of DQN in many aspects and is used to solve the Cheat-FlipIt model. NLD3QN shows extraordinary superiority than DQN when confronted with a incompletely rational opponent agent. The method in this paper can be used to identify the cheating behavior of opponent agent, and can be applied to the field of intelligent robot confrontation. The contributions are summarized as follows:

- The cheating behavior of opponents are considered in the intelligent game model, and the Cheat-FlipIt model is proposed. The opponents may cheat to flip the resources first, and then control the resources after a decay interval. And we propose five Flip strategies: exp_decay, random_decay, gaussian_decay, fixed_decay and half_decay.
- The NLD3QN approach is proposed to solve the Cheat-FlipIt model, which integrates Noisynet, LSTM, Dropout, and Dueling Q -Network into Deep Q-Network. NLD3QN improves the performance in many aspects compared with DQN.
- We comprehensively evaluate NLD3QN in various Cheat-FlipIt scenarios. The experimental results demonstrated that NLD3QN shows extraordinary superiority when confronted with a deceptive opponent agent. The winning rate of defeating a deceptive opponent of NLD3QN is 73.3%, while DQN's winning rate is 26.67%.

The reminder of the paper is organized as follows. Section 2 introduces the related works about intelligent games, opponent modeling and deep reinforcement learning. Section 3 proposes the Cheat-FlipIt model. Section 4 introduces the architecture and implementation details of NLD3QN approach. Section 5 analyzes the experimental results. Section 6 summarizes the paper.

2   Related Work

Intelligent games depend on the organic combination of game theory and deep reinforcement learning paradigm. The key technologies in intelligent games are opponent modeling and deep reinforcement learning. Opponent modeling is used to deal with the problem of non-stationary game environment. Deep reinforcement learning is used to solve the intelligent game model, through the interaction between the agents and the environment.

Opponent modeling includes explicit and implicit modeling. Explicit modeling infers the opponent's intention directly by observing its behavior. DPIQN [10] adds a policy inferring module into DQN. Switching Agent Model (SAM) [3] identifies, tracks, and adjusts to the non-stationary agent. Yuxi et al. [13] makes a portrait of an opponent by using MADDPG in a competitive environment, and encodes the behavior of the opponent into a knowledge graph. Learning with Opponent-Learning Awareness(LOLA) [4] explicitly infers the other agents. Enhanced Rolling Horizon Evolution Algorithm (RHEA) [20] takes the historical information as training data, and the parameters of the opponent model are updated by online optimization. Self Other-Modeling [16] predicts the actions of the other agents and updates the learning agent's belief. Implicit modeling [1] tries to adopt a confrontational strategy without identifying the opponent's behavior. Deep Reinforcement Opponent Network (DRON) [9] encodes the observation of its opponent into DQN. Gleave et al. [6] presents that an agent can affect its opponent's observation through its actions and cause the opponent make a wrong decision.

The deceptive opponents have not been pay much attention in the existing game models. Macheng et al. [17] considers that an adversary agent may confuse the defense agent by adopting a deceptive policy, and proposes Soft Q-learning to achieve active perception. However, the modeling of opponent deception is not detailed enough.

RL is widely used to solve the game model. Lisa et al. [15] uses adaptive Q-Learning solving the FlipIt game. Laura et al. [8] uses DQN to solve the FlipIt game. However, the Q-Learning or classic DQN can't adapt to the non-stationary environment well when the opponent's strategy or game environment changes. Therefore, when an incompletely rational opponent agent launches a feint, DQN can't identify the opponent's deception and adopt correct defense strategies. Zhu et al. [27] adopts adaptive DQN for a non-stationary environment. However, the opponent adopts a fixed strategy in this work. In fact, the opponent's strategy may also be random, deceptive and unpredictable.

There are inevitable shortcomings when DQN solves the intelligent game model, such as over-fitting, insufficient exploration and over-estimation. During the training process, dropout technology randomly drops some units from the neural network. It breaks up the co-adaptations among specific hidden units, and is used to solve the over-fitting problem. To overcome the over-estimation problem, some methods [12,22] have been proposed. To strengthen the exploration ability, NoisyNet adds gaussian noise to the fully-connected layer. Dueling Q-Network splits the last layer of the neural network in state value function and advantage function. And then both streams are combined into a single output to estimate the Q-values. Constrained Q-Learning [25] takes a constrained mean value as the lower bounds of Q value, which is used to solve the over-estimation problem.

In conclusion, the existing game models without paying much attention in the deceptive opponents. How to perceive opponent's behavior and identify its cheating behavior is worth to research. RL is the mainstream method to solve the intelligent game. However, the RL algorithm has the defects of over-fitting [26], over-estimation and insufficient exploration, which can't adapt to the deceptive and uncertain game environment and can't infer the incompletely rational opponent agent's behavior.

3   Cheat-FlipIt Game Model

In this Section, the proposed Cheat-FlipIt game model are introduced. Section 3.1 introduces the assumptions of the Cheat-FlipIt game model. Section 3.2 presents the details of the Cheat-FlipIt model. Section 3.3 proposes the opponent's strategies.

3.1 Assumptions

The assumptions of Cheat-FlipIt game model are made as follows.

- Assuming that the opponent is not affected by the defense mechanism and launches an attack according to its strategy.
- Assuming that when the defense agent and the opponent control the resources at the same time, the defense agent controls the resources.
- Assuming that the defense agent can observe the opponent's cheat actions, but can't observe the flip actions. The flip actions need to be obtained by implicit reasoning based on historical interaction data.

3.2 Model

In a FlipIt game [21], the defender and the opponent compete for controlling a sensitive resource, such as a private key, a database, etc. In this paper, the opponent's deception behavior is integrated into the FlipIt game. We propose an extension of the FlipIt model, called Cheat-FlipIt. In this model, the opponent launches cheat actions in advance to confuse the defense agent, and then actually controls the resources after a decay interval. The Cheat-FlipIt game model is shown in Fig. 1.

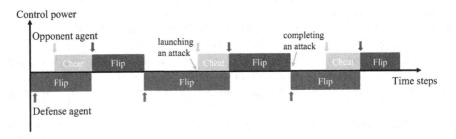

Fig. 1. illustration of Cheat-FlipIt game (Color figure online)

Here, the blue area represents the defense agent controls the resources currently, while the red area represents the opponent agent controls. There are Cheat and Flip strategies for the opponent in the Cheat-Flip model. Due to the cheat action of opponent agent is introduced, the light red area indicates the cheat attack (cheat strategy), which will be observed by defense agent. The dark red area is the real attack (flip strategy), which is partially observable for defense agent. The real attacks need to be obtained by implicit reasoning based on historical interaction data. If the player decides to flip, it will control the resource and spend the cost meanwhile.

In the Cheat-FlipIt game, $\mathcal{N}^d$ denotes a defense agent and $\mathcal{N}^o$ denotes an opponent agent. T^i_{LM} is the interval of time steps since the last move of the players $\mathcal{N}^i$. Defense agent $\mathcal{N}^d$ has full information of itself T^d_{LM}, but it only has cheat information of opponent T^o_{CH}. $\mathcal{N}^d$ perceives and reasons the strategy of the opponent π^{ρ^o} based on observed opponent's actions a^o_t. Where, ρ is a perceptual vector. The defense agent needs to identify the opponent's action a^o_t is cheat or flip. Then, $\mathcal{N}^d$ decides whether to control the resources according to the inferred information π^{ρ^o}. In the Cheat-FlipIt game process, the observation of $\mathcal{N}^d$ is affected by the joint actions of both sides. Cheat-FlipIt game model can be expressed as a 6-tuple $(\mathcal{N}, \mathcal{S}, \mathcal{A}, \tau, \mathcal{R}, \pi)$.

- $\mathcal{N} = \{\mathcal{N}^d, \mathcal{N}^o\}$ denotes the defense agent and opponent agent.
- $\mathcal{S} = \{s_1, s_2, \cdots, s_n\}$ represents the states observed by $\mathcal{N}^d$, expressed by $s_t = (T^d_{LM}, T^o_{CH} \mid \pi^{\rho^o}) \in \mathcal{S}$.
- $\mathcal{A} = \{\mathcal{A}^d, \mathcal{A}^o\}$ denotes the action space available to $\mathcal{N}^d$ and $\mathcal{N}^o$ in state $\mathcal{S}$ respectively, expressed as $a^d_t = \{flip, void\} \in \mathcal{A}^d$, $a^o_t = \{cheat, flip, void\} \in \mathcal{A}^o$.
- $\tau \{s, a^d, a^o, s'\}$ denotes the transferring probability to a state $s' \in S$ from the state $s \in S$ when $\mathcal{N}^d$ chooses a^d and $\mathcal{N}^o$ chooses a^o .
- $\mathcal{R} = \{\mathcal{R}^d, \mathcal{R}^o\}$, $\mathcal{R}^d$ and $\mathcal{R}^o$ represent the reward function of $\mathcal{N}^d$ and $\mathcal{N}^o$. The four circumstances are discussed as follows. (1) If a player does nothing, the rewards and costs are both zero. (2) If a player flips and $T^d_{LM} \leq T^o_{LM}$, it will not receive benefits b_{flip} but need to consume the cost c_{flip} instead, because the control power originally belongs to it. (3) If a player flips and $T^d_{LM} > T^o_{LM}$, the player regains control prower from its opponent $\mathcal{N}^o$. It will receive benefits b_{flip} and need to spend the costs c_{flip} meanwhile. (4) If the opponent decides to launch a feint, the cost and reward are both zero (assuming that the cheat cost can be ignored, it will only be consumed when the player controls the resource). In summary, r_t are expressed as follows.

$$
r_t = \begin{cases} 0 & if\ a_t\ =\ void \\ -c_{flip} & if\ a_t\ =\ flip\ and\ T^d_{LM} \leq T^o_{LM} \\ b_{flip} - c_{flip} & if\ a_t\ =\ flip\ and\ T^d_{LM} > T^o_{LM} \\ 0 & if\ a_t\ =\ cheat \end{cases} \tag{1}
$$

- $\pi = \{\pi^d, \pi^o\}$ represents the strategies adopted by $\mathcal{N}^d$ and $\mathcal{N}^o$ respectively. Opponent strategy π^o mainly includes cheat and flip strategy. $\mathcal{N}^d$ perceives and infers the opponent's strategy π^{ρ^o} by analyzing the historical interactive data. Then $\mathcal{N}^d$ executes π^d correspondingly.

An 1 vs. 1 scenario of the Cheat-FlipIt game is performed, including a defense agent $\mathcal{N}^d$ and an opponent agent $\mathcal{N}^o$. The Q function of $\mathcal{N}^d$ is expressed as

$$
Q(s, a \mid \pi^o) = \sum_{a^o} \pi^o(a^o \mid s) \sum_{s'} \tau\left(s, a^d, a^o, s'\right) \left[R(s, a^d, a^o, s') + \gamma E_{a'} \left[Q(s', a' \mid \pi^o)\right]\right] \tag{2}
$$

where, $\gamma \in [0, 1)$ denotes the discount factor. The Q-function is calculated by π^o to avoid the exponential increase in computation. The Cheat-FlipIt model is updated by batch gradient descent.

3.3 Opponent Strategies

The opponent agent's strategy is a double-driven attack, which means it can be divided into launching an attack (cheat) and completing an attack (flip). The opponent strategies enhance the concealment and deception of the attack, as shown in Table 1. The opponent agent does not control the resources immediately when launching an attack (cheat), and then controls the resources after a decay time (flip). The cheat strategy is a feint to consume the resources of the defense agent. The definitions of Cheat and Flip strategies are as follows.

Table 1. The Cheat and Flip strategies of opponent.

Flip	Cheat		
	Period	Uniform	Random period
exp_decay	Period+exp_decay	Uni+exp_decay	Ran_period+exp_decay
random_decay	Period+rand_decay	Uni+rand_decay	Ran_period+rand_decay
gaussian_decay	Period+gauss_decay	Uni+gauss_decay	Ran_period+gauss_decay
fixed_decay	Period+fixed_decay	Uni+fixed_decay	Ran_period+fixed_decay
half_decay	Period+half_decay	Uni+half_decay	Ran_period+half_decay

Definition 1. *Cheat strategy means that the opponent agent launches a feint to consume the resources of the defense agent, but actually does not control the resources.*

The cheat strategies adopted in this paper are period, uniform and random period strategy.

- **Period.** Period strategy means the opponent $\mathcal{N}^o$ flips with fixed δ time steps [21], represented by $st = \delta$. Where, st represents the interval of time steps of flipping.
- **Uniform.** Uniform strategy represents the opponent $\mathcal{N}^o$ flips with uniform u time steps, represented by $st = u$.
- **Random period.** A random factor $\zeta(|\zeta| < \delta)$ is introduced into Period strategy, represented by $st = \delta + \zeta$.

Definition 2. *Flip strategy means that the opponent agent actually controls the resources at a decay interval after launching a feint.*

The flip strategies adopted in this paper are exponential decay, random decay, gaussian decay, fixed decay and half decay.

- **Exponential decay.** The decay of time-inteval follows exponential distribution from feint attack to actually controlling resources.
- **Random decay.** The decay of time-inteval is random from feint attack to actually controlling resources.

- **Gaussian decay.** The decay of time-inteval follows gaussian distribution from feint attack to actually controlling resources.
- **Fixed decay.** The decay of time-inteval is a fixed value from feint attack to actually controlling resources.
- **Half decay.** The decay of time-inteval obeys the rule of half reduction from feint attack to actually controlling resources.

4   NLD3QN Approach

4.1   The Architecture of NLD3QN

Because of the influence of the opponent's deceptive strategy, the process of Cheat-FlipIt game is non-stationary, dynamic and uncertain. Thus, we propose NLD3QN to adapt to the Cheat-FlipIt game environment. NLD3QN aims at defending against the potentially deceptive opponent in a Cheat-FlipIt game environment. To solve the problems of opponent deception and non-stationary environment, NLD3QN combines NoisyNet, LSTM, Dropout, Dueling Q-Network and Constrained Q-Learning into DQN. NLD3QN improves performance in many ways and it can get a strategy that adapts to a non-stationary and deceptive environment. LSTM analyzes historical interactive data, identifies opponents' deception strategies, and reduces the probability of wrong decision-making of defense agents. The architecture of NLD3QN is shown in Fig. 2.

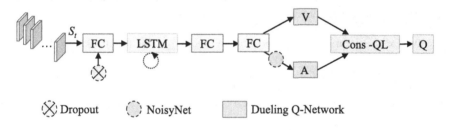

Fig. 2. The architecture of NLD3QN

NLD3QN is improved based on a three-layer fully connected network. There are 64 units in each layer. The first layer is directly connected with the observation space, and Dropout is used to prevent over-fitting. Then, a layer of LSTM with 64 units is added to process the historical interaction data and infer the opponent's deceptive strategy. Dueling Q-Network is divided into state value function V and action advantage function A after the third full connection layer. To enhance the exploratory ability of decision-making, NoisyNet is added before the action advantage function A. Finally, the two streams are merged into one stream, and then the Q value is calculated by Cons-QL.

In summary, the existing defects of DQN are over-fitting, over-estimation, insufficient exploration, etc. NLD3QN solves these classic problems. In addition, LSTM identifies the opponent's cheating behavior by analyzing historical interaction data. The components of NLD3QN are introduced as follows.

- NoisyNet adds the gaussian noise to the network to enhance the explore ability of the NLD3QN. The gassian noise is represented as $\xi \equiv (\mu + \sigma) \odot \epsilon$, where $(\mu + \sigma)$ are learnable parameter vectors, ϵ denotes a zero-mean noise.
- LSTM is a specific form of recursive neural network, which learns from the past interactive data to better analyze the deceptive strategy of the opponent agent.
- Dropout is used during the training process of NLD3QN to overcome the over-fitting problem. Owing to dropout training, NLD3QN is more suitable for the uncertain environment.
- Dueling Q-Network is adopted to improve the performance of NLD3QN. It splits the last layer of the neural network in two parts: the state-value function S and the advantage function A.
- Constrained Q-Learning(Cons-QL) adopts a constrained mean value as the lower bounds of Q value. It's used to solve the over-estimation problem.

4.2 The Training Procedure of NLD3QN

The training procedure of NLD3QN is shown in Algorithm 1.

Algorithm 1: The training procedure of NLD3QN.

---

1 Initialize replay memory M, Cheat-FlipIt simulator env, and observation s
2 Initialize evaluation network with random weights θ, dropout p, LSTM l, and noise ξ; target network with weights θ^-
3 Initialize the parameter of the advantage function α, the parameter of the state-value function β
4 **for** $t = 1$ *to* T **do**
5   Choose an action $a_d \leftarrow Q(s, a, \xi; \theta, \alpha, \beta, l)$
6   Take a^d in env and observe a^o, r, s'
7   Infer π^o is cheat or flip
8   Store transition $\tau\{s, a^d, a^o, s'\}$ in M
9   Sample minibatch of transition $\tau\{s_j, a_j^d, a_j^o, s_j'\}$ randomly from M
10   **for** $j = 1$ *to minibatch* **do**
11   **if** s_j' *is the terminal state* **then**
12               $Q(s_j, a_j^d | \pi^o) \leftarrow R(s_j, a_j^d, a_j^o, s_j')$
13   **end**
14           $Q(s_j, a_j^d \mid \pi^o) \leftarrow \sum_{a^o} \pi^o(a^o \mid s_j) \sum_{s'} \tau(s_j, a_j^d, a_j^o, s_j')$
             $[R(s_j, a_j^d, a_j^o, s_j') + \gamma E_{a'}[Q(s_j', a_j', \xi'; \theta^-, \alpha, \beta, l \mid \pi^o)]]$
15   Calculate Q value using Cons-QL $Q(s_j, a_j^d \mid \pi^o)$
16   Execute a gradient descent step to minimize the loss
             $\frac{1}{n}\sum_{i=1}^n (Q(s_j^d, a_j^d \mid \pi^o) - Q_E(s_j^d, a_j^d \mid \pi^o))^2$
17   **end**
18   Update the target network $\theta^- \leftarrow \theta$ every C steps
19 **end**

It is essential to infer opponents' intention from the past interactive data for defense agents. LSTM uses time series to analyze the input data, which can be adopted to analyze the deceptive behavior of the opponent. DRL interacts with the environment and makes sequential decisions without given prior information.

5 Experiments

The experiments are performed in a Cheat-FlipIt game simulator. Section 5.1 introduces the environmental settings. Section 5.2 describes the baseline algorithms. Section 5.3 analyzes the experimental results.

5.1 Environmental Settings

The series of experiments are conducted in a Cheat-FlipIt game simulator. The environmental parameters of the Cheat-FlipIt game are as follows. The cost of flipping equals 5, the reward of flipping equals 1, the numbers of episodes equal 10000, and the steps of one episode equal 200.

5.2 Baselines

In this section, the three baseline algorithms are introduced, including DQN, ND3QN and NRD3QN. Then we presents the hyperparameters used in this experiment.

- DQN [14]. DQN is an improved algorithm of Q-Learning, which uses deep neural network to solve Q value.
- ND3QN. It is an improved algorithm based on DQN, which integrates Noisynet, Dropout, Dueling Q-network and Cons-QL into DQN.
- NRD3QN. It is an improved algorithm based on ND3QN, which integrates RNN into ND3QN.

The components of the four algorithms are shown in Table 2.

Table 2. Components of four algorithms.

Components	NLD3QN	ND3QN	NRD3QN	DQN
Noisynet	✓	✓	✓	-
LSTM	✓	-	-	-
Dropout	✓	✓	✓	-
Dueling Q-network	✓	✓	✓	-
Cons-QL	✓	✓	✓	-
RNN	-	-	✓	-

- indicates that there are no values.

The hyperparameters of the four algorithms are as follows. buffer_size $= 2000$, batch_size $= 32$, learning rate $= 0.003$, $\tau = 0.003$, discount factor $\gamma = 0.99$, the frequency of update network $f = 5$, the probability of dropout $p = 0.05$.

5.3   Analysis of Experimental Results

Evaluation Index

- Last score. The average rewards of last 100 episodes received by $\mathcal{N}^d$ in 10000 episodes of the Cheat-FlipIt game.
- Winning rate. The number of times the defense agent wins in fifteen scenarios of opponent's combination strategies (the confidence interval is 95%).

Experimental Results. When the opponent adopts the cheat strategy of uniform and five strategies to control the resources, the comparison results of defense agent vs. opponent agent are shown in Figs. 3.

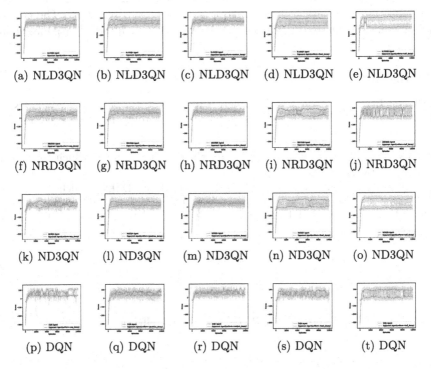

(a) NLD3QN   (b) NLD3QN   (c) NLD3QN   (d) NLD3QN   (e) NLD3QN

(f) NRD3QN   (g) NRD3QN   (h) NRD3QN   (i) NRD3QN   (j) NRD3QN

(k) ND3QN   (l) ND3QN   (m) ND3QN   (n) ND3QN   (o) ND3QN

(p) DQN   (q) DQN   (r) DQN   (s) DQN   (t) DQN

Fig. 3. Defense agent vs. opponent agent with cheat strategy of uniform. (a)(f)(k)(p) exp_decay; (b)(g)(l)(q) gaussian_decay; (c)(h)(m)(r) random_decay; (d)(i)(n)(s) fixed_decay; (e)(j)(o)(t) half_decay.

As can be seen from the Figs. 3, the agents of both sides tend to converge gradually after 1000 episodes of game and still fluctuate in a small range. It shows that the game process is non-stationary and will be affected by the opponent agent's strategy. When an opponent adopts a cheat strategy of uniform and various flip strategies, NLD3QN, NRD3QN and ND3QN all can beat their opponent, while DQN often loses to its opponent. Because of the over-fitting, over-estimating and insufficient-exploration of DQN. In addition, DQN can't learn the opponent's strategies from historical interactive data. While NLD3QN is integrated with LSTM, which can learn the opponent's deceptive strategies from historical interactive data. In terms of convergence, NLD3QN and ND3QN have better convergence, followed by NRD3QN, and DQN is the worst. This is because NLD3QN, NRD3QN and ND3QN are all integrated with Dropout technology, which can solve the problem of over-fitting. In terms of identifying the opponent's deception strategy, when the opponent flips with fixed or half decay, the defense agent has the best performance of identifying deception. When the opponent flips with exponential or gaussian decay, the performance of defense agent is moderate. When the opponent flips with random decay, the performance of defense agent is not very good. It indicates that the more randomized and dynamic the opponent's deception strategy is, the more difficult it is for the defense agent to identify the opponent's deception.

When the opponent adopts the cheat strategy of period and five strategies to control the resources, the comparison results are shown in Figs. 4.

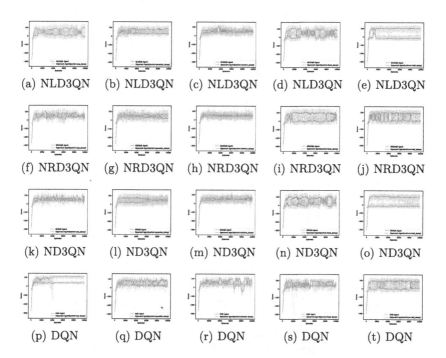

Fig. 4. Defense agent vs. opponent agent with cheat strategy of period. (a)(f)(k)(p) exp_decay; (b)(g)(l)(q) gaussian_decay; (c)(h)(m)(r) random_decay; (d)(i)(n)(s) fixed_decay; (e)(j)(o)(t) half_decay.

The winning rate of DQN is the lowest, and the convergence of DQN is the most unstable. Instead, the performance of NLD3QN, NRD3QN and ND3QN are better. As shown in Fig. 4 (a)(f)(k)(p), NLD3QN has the best ability to identify opponent deception, and it can continuously maintain its advantage over the opponent.

When the opponent adopts the cheat srategy of random period and above strategies to control the resources, the comparison results are shown in Figs. 5.

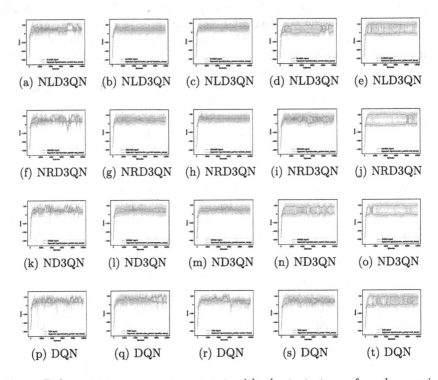

(a) NLD3QN   (b) NLD3QN   (c) NLD3QN   (d) NLD3QN   (e) NLD3QN

(f) NRD3QN   (g) NRD3QN   (h) NRD3QN   (i) NRD3QN   (j) NRD3QN

(k) ND3QN   (l) ND3QN   (m) ND3QN   (n) ND3QN   (o) ND3QN

(p) DQN   (q) DQN   (r) DQN   (s) DQN   (t) DQN

Fig. 5. Defense agent vs. opponent agent with cheat strategy of random period. (a)(f)(k)(p) exp_decay; (b)(g)(l)(q) gaussian_decay; (c)(h)(m)(r) random_decay; (d)(i)(n)(s) fixed_decay; (e)(j)(o)(t) half_decay.

Figures 5 show that when the opponent adopts exponential decay, gaussian decay or random decay strategies, the performance of identifying opponent deception is not very good. The performance of ND3QN is slightly better, the performance of NLD3QN and NRD3QN are moderate, and the performance of DQN is the worst. And the convergence of DQN is unstable and the winning rate of DQN is the lowest. When the opponent adopts fixed decay and half decay strategies to control the resources, the defense agent using these four algorithms can defeat the opponent. And the convergence of NLD3QN and ND3QN is more stable, followed by NRD3QN, and DQN is the worst. From the comprehensive Figs. 5, it can be concluded that when the opponent's deception strategy and control strategy are randomized, dynamic and uncertain, there is a higher requirement for the defense agent to identify deceptive behaviors of the opponent.

The all comparison results of the four algorithms are shown in Table 3. The data in the Table 3 is the last score of defense agent vs. opponent agent. In some cases, the average scores of both sides are unstable and the last score can't judge the outcome, represented by △. The criteria for judging the results are as follows. Firstly, the premise is that the defense agent should defeat the opponent agent; on this basis, the last scores of defense agents are compared. As can be seen from Table 3, the winning rate of NLD3QN is 73.33%, the winning rate of NRD3QN and ND3QN are 66.67%, while the winning rate of DQN is 26.67%. NLD3QN is more generalized and can adapt to more opponent deception strategies. this is because LSTM can analyze the historical interaction data to better learn the opponent's deception strategy. DQN can defeat the opponent when it adopts flip strategy of half decay. However, when the opponent adopts other strategies, DQN almost loses to the opponent. It indicates that the generalization of DQN is not satisfactory, and it is not suitable for other deception scenarios. When the flip strategy of the opponent agent adopts exponential decay and random decay, the four algorithms are all ineffective at identifying deception.

Table 3. Last score of the defense agent vs. opponent agent

Opponent	Winning rate			
	NLD3QN **73.33%**	NRD3QN 66.67%	ND3QN 66.67%	DQN 26.67%
period+exp_decay	94.69/4.71 ✓	32.56/49.99✗	52.51/80.84✗	36.29/110.21✗
period+rand_decay	42.09/45.86✗	53.55/42.20 ✓	33.61/62.09✗	55.50/65.20✗
period+gauss_decay	28.93/86.57✗	77.45/19.40 ✓	69.95/29.95 △	16.54/71.61 ✗
period+fixed_decay	82.14/13.86 ✓	74.96/22.69 ✓	97.41/-1.41 ✓	38.67/70.13 ✗
period+half_decay	82.09/19.81 ✓	113.48/-19.73 ✓	39.44/90.86✗	12.83/8.92 ✓
uniform+exp_decay	102.94/-14.54 ✓	82.46/22.24 ✓	48.78/49.92 ✓	36.63/110.37 ✗
uniform+rand_decay	48.20/44.20 ✓	47.20/51.55✗	68.67/29.23 ✓	30.21/101.09✗
uniform+gauss_decay	69.59/31.41 ✓	56.96/43.69 ✓	57.14/37.71 ✓	28.33/82.82 ✗
uniform+fixed_decay	91.76/2.14 ✓	87.58/7.67 ✓	69.13/23.47 ✓	58.31/31.09 ✓
uniform+half_decay	102.94/-14.54 ✓	94.02/-6.07 ✓	103.56/-19.21 ✓	90.92/2.98 ✓
ran_per+exp_decay	42.72/76.98✗	29.20/65.35✗	60.44/26.01 △	41.03/78.77✗
ran_per+rand_decay	40.00/58.85 ✗	46.65/52.60✗	58.11/34.49 ✓	35.23/47.72✗
ran_per+gauss_decay	64.60/34.50 ✓	69.64/22.96 ✓	67.59/27.91 ✓	30.24/104.56✗
ran_per+fixed_decay	84.61/5.44 ✓	54.13/70.12✗	91.64/-1.19 ✓	29.77/43.68✗
ran_per+half_decay	96.39/-9.64 ✓	99.04/-15.51 ✓	96.11/-13.76 ✓	86.36/5.74 ✓

✓ represents winning; ✗ represents losing; △ represents drawing.

The results of ablation experiment of ND3QN are shown in Table 4. Dropout technology has the greatest influence on winning rate. It shows that the opponent's deception strategy makes the environment more non-stationary, and dropout can prevent over-fitting and adapt to the non-stationary environment well. Dueling Q-network, Noisynet and Constrained Q-Learning are also helpful to improve the performance. Combining the results of Table 3, LSTM improves the winning rate and reward value of the defense agent.

Table 4. Ablation experiments of ND3QN.

Opponent	Winning rate			
	w-Dropout 20.00%	w-Dueling 73.33%	w-Noisynet 66.67%	w-Cons_QL 66.67%
period+exp_decay	12.78/53.67 ✗	31.11/75.54 ✗	3.11/46.79✗	52.51/80.84✗
period+rand_decay	34.30/112.20✗	60.05/41.25△	52.26/42.59△	33.61/62.09 ✗
period+gauss_decay	11.73/77.32 ✗	52.01/41.59 ✓	28.02/84.68 ✗	69.95/29.95 △
period+fixed_decay	35.27/108.33 ✗	77.34/45.01 ✓	84.16/6.79 ✓	97.41/-1.41 ✓
period+half_decay	78.94/26.41 ✓	103.35/-13.65 ✓	111.45/-15.90 ✓	39.44/90.86✗
uniform+exp_decay	59.40/52.05△	60.85/37.25 ✓	59.44/41.21 △	48.78/49.92 ✓
uniform+rand_decay	37.65/74.15✗	60.54/34.46 ✓	70.10/27.10 ✓	68.67/29.23 ✓
uniform+gauss_decay	38.88/83.22✗	58.38/39.77 ✓	64.39/36.91 ✓	57.14/37.71 ✓
uniform+fixed_decay	12.50/34.10 ✗	78.67/17.28 ✓	73.04/25.66 ✓	69.13/23.47 ✓
uniform+half_decay	60.88/44.52 ✓	100.80/-12.35 ✓	108.16/-21.06 ✓	103.56/-19.21 ✓
ran_per+exp_decay	35.05/110.95 ✗	45.49/40.96 △	57.66/37.84 ✓	43.12/86.98✗
ran_per+rand_decay	13.74/46.71✗	47.76/37.64 △	55.18/34.42 △	59.57/34.28 ✓
ran_per+gauss_decay	2.86/53.24 ✗	46.04/45.11 ✓	57.50/40.40 ✓	62.89/32.11 ✓
ran_per+fixed_decay	46.16/68.64 ✗	80.16/6.14 ✓	92.76/-6.21 ✓	89.23/-1.03 ✓
ran_per+half_decay	75.30/13.05 ✓	99.99/-13.94 ✓	97.22/-12.37 ✓	82.44/9.76 ✓

w is the abbreviation of without.

6   Conclusion

In this paper, we model a deceptive opponent and extend the FlipIt game model. We present Cheat-FlipIt model, in which the opponent agent may cheat to control the resources first, and then actually flip the resources after a decay interval. We further propose a variety of flip strategies of opponent agents. The defense agent needs to model and perceive the cheating behavior of the opponent agent. We present NLD3QN to solve the Cheat-FlipIt game model. To address the problems of opponent-deception and non-stationary environment, NLD3QN incorporates Noisynet, LSTM, Dropout, Dueling Q-Network and Constrained Q-Learning into DQN. Defense agent adopts NLD3QN to perceive and infer the cheating behavior of opponents. Moreover, we verify that NLD3QN is capable of dealing with opponent peeception by conducting experiments in 1 vs. 1 game scenarios. NLD3QN is superior to DQN when confronted with a deceptive opponent. The winning rate of NLD3QN is 73.3%, while DQN's winning rate is 26.67%. The method in this paper can be applied to the field of intelligent robot confrontation.

References

1. Bard, N., Johanson, M., Burch, N., Bowling, M.: Online implicit agent modelling. In: Proceedings of the 2013 International Conference on Autonomous Agents and Multi-Agent Systems, pp. 255–262 (2013)
2. Brown, N., Sandholm, T.: Superhuman AI for multiplayer poker. Science **365**(6456), 885–890 (2019)
3. Everett, R., Roberts, S.J.: Learning against non-stationary agents with opponent modelling and deep reinforcement learning. In: AAAI Spring Symposia (2018)
4. Foerster, J.N., Chen, R.Y., Al-Shedivat, M., Whiteson, S., Abbeel, P., Mordatch, I.: Learning with opponent-learning awareness. arXiv preprint arXiv:1709.04326 (2017)
5. Fortunato, M., et al.: Noisy networks for exploration. arXiv preprint arXiv:1706.10295 (2017)
6. Gleave, A., Dennis, M., Wild, C., Kant, N., Levine, S., Russell, S.: Adversarial policies: attacking deep reinforcement learning. arXiv preprint arXiv:1905.10615 (2019)
7. Graves, A.: Long Short-Term Memory. Supervised Sequence Labelling with Recurrent Neural Networks, pp. 37–45 (2012)
8. Greige, L., Chin, P.: Deep reinforcement learning for FlipIt security game. In: Benito, R.M., Cherifi, C., Cherifi, H., Moro, E., Rocha, L.M., Sales-Pardo, M. (eds.) COMPLEX NETWORKS 2021. Studies in Computational Intelligence, vol. 1072, pp. 831–843. Springer, Cham (2022). https://doi.org/10.1007/978-3-030-93409-5_68
9. He, H., Boyd-Graber, J., Kwok, K., Daumé III, H.: Opponent modeling in deep reinforcement learning. In: International Conference on Machine Learning, pp. 1804–1813. PMLR (2016)
10. Hong, Z.W., Su, S.Y., Shann, T.Y., Chang, Y.H., Lee, C.Y.: A deep policy inference q-network for multi-agent systems. arXiv preprint arXiv:1712.07893 (2017)
11. Hu, Y., Han, C., Li, H., Guo, T.: Modeling opponent learning in multiagent repeated games. Appl. Intell. **53**, 1–17 (2022)
12. Kumar, A., Zhou, A., Tucker, G., Levine, S.: Conservative q-learning for offline reinforcement learning. In: Advances in Neural Information Processing Systems, vol. 33, pp. 1179–1191 (2020)
13. Ma, Y., et al.: Opponent portrait for multiagent reinforcement learning in competitive environment. Int. J. Intell. Syst. **36**(12), 7461–7474 (2021)
14. Mnih, V., et al.: Human-level control through deep reinforcement learning. Nature **518**(7540), 529–533 (2015)
15. Oakley, L., Oprea, A.: QFlip?: an adaptive reinforcement learning strategy for the FlipIt security game. In: Alpcan, T., Vorobeychik, Y., Baras, J.S., Dán, G. (eds.) GameSec 2019. LNCS, vol. 11836, pp. 364–384. Springer, Cham (2019). https://doi.org/10.1007/978-3-030-32430-8_22
16. Raileanu, R., Denton, E., Szlam, A., Fergus, R.: Modeling others using oneself in multi-agent reinforcement learning. In: International Conference on Machine Learning, pp. 4257–4266. PMLR (2018)

17. Shen, M., How, J.P.: Active perception in adversarial scenarios using maximum entropy deep reinforcement learning. In: 2019 International Conference on Robotics and Automation (ICRA), pp. 3384–3390. IEEE (2019)
18. Silver, D., et al.: Mastering the game of go without human knowledge. Nature **550**(7676), 354–359 (2017)
19. Srivastava, N., Hinton, G., Krizhevsky, A., Sutskever, I., Salakhutdinov, R.: Dropout: a simple way to prevent neural networks from overfitting. J. Mach. Learn. Res. **15**(1), 1929–1958 (2014)
20. Tang, Z., Zhu, Y., Zhao, D., Lucas, S.M.: Enhanced rolling horizon evolution algorithm with opponent model learning. IEEE Trans. Games **15**, 5–15 (2020)
21. Van Dijk, M., Juels, A., Oprea, A., Rivest, R.L.: Flipit: the game of "stealthy takeover". J. Cryptol. **26**, 655–713 (2013)
22. Van Hasselt, H., Guez, A., Silver, D.: Deep reinforcement learning with double q-learning. In: Proceedings of the AAAI Conference on Artificial Intelligence, vol. 30 (2016)
23. Vinyals, O., et al.: Grandmaster level in StarCraft II using multi-agent reinforcement learning. Nature **575**(7782), 350–354 (2019)
24. Wang, Z., Schaul, T., Hessel, M., Hasselt, H., Lanctot, M., Freitas, N.: Dueling network architectures for deep reinforcement learning. In: International Conference on Machine Learning, pp. 1995–2003. PMLR (2016)
25. Yao, Q., Wang, Y., Xiong, X., Wang, P., Li, Y.: Adversarial decision-making for moving target defense: a multi-agent Markov game and reinforcement learning approach. Entropy **25**(4), 605 (2023)
26. Zhang, C., Vinyals, O., Munos, R., Bengio, S.: A study on overfitting in deep reinforcement learning. arXiv preprint arXiv:1804.06893 (2018)
27. Zhu, J., Wei, Y., Kang, Y., Jiang, X., Dullerud, G.E.: Adaptive deep reinforcement learning for non-stationary environments. Sci. China Inf. Sci. **65**(10), 202204 (2022)

Making an eBPF Virtual Machine Faster on Microcontrollers: Verified Optimization and Proof Simplification

Shenghao Yuan$^{(\boxtimes)}$ (iD), Benjamin Lion, Frédéric Besson(iD), and Jean-Pierre Talpin(iD)

Inria, Rennes, France
{shenghao.yuan,benjamin.lion,frederic.besson,jean-pierre.talpin}@inria.fr

Abstract. As a revolutionary kernel extension technology, Berkeley Packet Filters (BPF) has been applied for various operating systems from different domains, from servers (Linux's extended BPF) to microcontrollers (RIOT-OS rBPF). Previous works have formally proved the memory isolation property for the non-optimized rBPF virtual machine in the Coq proof assistant. In this paper, we introduce a verified optimization for rBPF, and highlight a novel proof approach for optimization correctness: a simplification process is first used to transform monadic models with option state to simplified non-monadic models with inline arguments; then the optimization correctness theorem is split into i) proving simplification correct and ii) proving the optimization correctness on simplified models. Our proof approach enjoys a fruitful proof simplification. Preliminary experiments demonstrate satisfying performance.

Keywords: BPF · Optimization · Verification · Monad Simplification

1 Introduction

One of the worst decision in software engineering is to compromise the correctness of the application in order to gain some runtime performance. As the saying goes, *premature optimization is the root of all evil*. The optimization of a program often comes with trade-off and good practices therefore advocate to first produce a modular and correct application, then looking for places to optimize.

This design strategy has been applied on the rBPF [19] virtual machine, whose correctness has been fully verified in the Coq proof assistant [3]. The correctness proof ensures that the interpreter is isolated: it will not allow rBPF instructions to modify memory regions in which it has insufficient permissions. The defensive function *check_mem* acts as a safeguard to enforce this requirement. The first proof of correctness in [18] defines a verified implementation of the *check_mem* function which checks every memory access at runtime against the list of all memory blocks, regions and permissions registered with the CompCert memory model of the virtual machine. As *check_mem* is often used by the interpreter (typically, every time a memory instruction is called), optimizing its implementation would obviously speed up execution. Since the rBPF instruction set

H. Hermanns et al. (Eds.): SETTA 2023, LNCS 14464, pp. 385–401, 2024.
https://doi.org/10.1007/978-981-99-8664-4_22

is used by operating systems for embedded devices and microcontrollers with low energy and resources, both correctness and performance are critical.

The interpreter has been formalized in Coq, candidates for optimization can be formally defined as a new implementation of the *check_mem* function and can be proved to preserve the semantics. The difficulty is to reason compositionally on the correctness of the interpreter with respect to the new *check_mem* function.

The formalization of the rBPF interpreter uses the native *check_mem* function, which is not optimized. For a given rBPF memory instruction, the *check_mem* function iterates over all memory regions, in sequence, to find whether the instruction points to a valid memory region. While such implementation is correct, the performance can be improved by changing the order in which *check_mem* iterates over the memory regions.

In this paper, we consider an alternative implementation of the *check_mem* function as a candidate for runtime optimization. When an rBPF memory instruction is executed for the first time, the *check_mem* function iterates sequentially over the memory regions until the accessed memory is reached, as the non-optimized *check_mem* does. The accessed memory region is stored in a cache, so that when the same instruction is called for a second time, the *check_mem* first looks at the cache before iterating over all the other memory regions.

We provide the following contributions. The first contribution is to prove that the new *check_mem* function is correct, *i.e.*, that the new interpreter performs the same behaviours as the non-optimized one. The main contribution is however the workflow employed to equally optimise and simplify these proofs, by the definition of a series of transformations on the monadic definition of the interpreter. The last contribution is to experimentally demonstrate that the new *check_mem* function is an optimization, by running benchmarks on the optimized and non-optimized interpreters.

The background material is presented in Sect. 2. The design choices for the new *check_mem* function are presented in Sect. 3, and the proof of correctness of the new interpreter is given in Sect. 4. Benchmarks are given in Sect. 5 and demonstrates that the new function is an optimization for the presented cases. Section 6 presents related works and Sect. 7 concludes.

2   Background

The CompCert Verified Compiler. CompCert is a C compiler, both programmed and proved correct in Coq, that generates efficient code for the ARM, PowerPC, RISC-V, and x86 processors. Two important CompCert concepts are used in this paper:

- A value $v \in val$ in CompCert can either be a 32-bit $Vint(i)$ or 64-bit $Vlong(i)$ integer, a pointer $Vptr(b, o)$ to a block b with offset o, a floating-point number or the undefined value $Vundef$.
- A CompCert memory m consists of a collection of separate blocks ($b \in block$) with a fixed size.

BPFs. Berkeley Packet Filters [11] (BPF) was designed originally for the purpose of network packet filtering. The Linux community adopted the concept of BPF and implemented eBPF (extended BPF) to run custom in-kernel VM code, for the untrusted kernel extension [6]. eBPF was then ported to micro-controllers, yielding RIOT-OS [2]'s specification: rBPF.

Both eBPF and rBPF take eBPF binary programs as input because the rBPF ISA is a subset of the eBPF one. The main difference is:

- eBPF depends on a sophisticated online verifier (*e.g.,* [7]) to guarantee security, *e.g.,* a binary eBPF program can not cause any memory leaks.
- As an MCU architecture cannot host such a large verifier, rBPF has a tiny verifier and adopts dynamic defensive strategies in its interpreter to ensure security. For instance, the rBPF interpreter only allows executing an rBPF memory instruction after the defensive function *chek_mem* checks this memory operation is valid at run-time. This requires rBPF users to additionally declare all memory regions used by their eBPF programs.

CertrBPF [18, 20] is a fully verified version of RIOT-OS rBPF that

- proves that rBPF isolates faults in the Coq proof assistant, and
- provides an end-to-end verification workflow to generate verified C programs from the CertrBPF specification in Gallina, the functional language embedded in the Coq proof assistant.

3   Design

This section introduces the *check_mem* optimization algorithm as well as the corresponding implementation.

3.1   High Level Intuition

Two scenarios for the optimized *check_mem* function are graphically depicted in Fig. 1. We detail the steps in each scenario.

The input binary, on the left of Fig. 1, contains two memory instructions, at location i and j. The list of memory regions are displayed next to the input binary array, and duplicated for readability (although, in practice, only one array of memory regions exists). The cache, in doted line, is initialized with 0.

When a memory instruction of the input binary is interpreted, the *check_mem* function is called. As the cache is initially empty, the optimized *check_mem* behaves, on the first call, as the non-optimized *check_mem* function and iterates sequentially over the memory regions to find if the instruction is valid. When the function finds the valid memory region (*e.g.,* mr_a for the i-th instruction and mr_b for the j-th instruction), the cache is updated with the index of that memory region (*e.g.,* a for the i-th instruction and b for the j-th instruction).

The second time that an instruction is interpreted, the optimized *check_mem* function behaves differently to the non-optimized *check_mem* function. The memory region that the cache points to is first checked. If that memory region is valid for the instruction, the cache keeps the reference, and we call such case a *cache hitting*. If not, all other memory regions are checked, in sequence, until one a valid one is found. The cache is updated with the new valid one (*e.g.*, the *j*-th memory instruction, on the second time, belongs to the memory region *mr_c*).

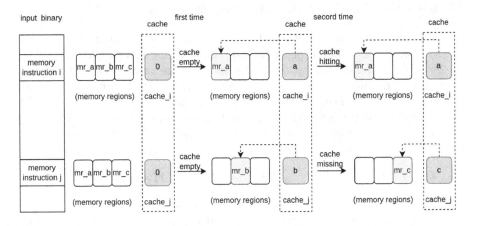

Fig. 1. check_mem optimization

3.2   Optimized check_mem Function

We fix *perm*, *chk*, *mrs*, *cache*, *addr*, and *pc*, to respectively denote a CompCert permission, a CompCert memory chunk (size of memory block to access), a list of memory regions, a cache where elements of the list are indexes in the list of memory region, a memory address, and a program counter. We also write $l[n \mapsto v]$ for updating the *n*-th element of list *l* with value *v*.

The new optimized *check_mem* (Algorithm 1) is explained as follows: it first checks if the cache is empty (line 2), if the cache is not empty, the algorithm calls the function *check_one_mem_region* to check if the memory address *addr* is within the history memory region with the index *cache[pc]* (line 3). If the result is valid which represents cache hitting, then the algorithm directly returns *true* and the old cache (line 7). The other two cases cache empty (line 9) and cache missing (line 5) are similar: performing the iteration of all memory regions by the recursive function *check_all_mrs* (line 10).

The iteration is from right to left which is implemented according to the argument *n* starting from the number of memory regions. When *n* arrives 0, representing that there is no valid pointers for all memory regions, the *check_all_mrs* function returns *false* and the old *cache* (line 12). *check_all_mrs* skips the region *cache_id* during the iteration (line 14). If *check_all_mrs* finds that the address *addr* is not within the current memory region indexed by *n*, it invokes the recursion to check the $(n-1)^{th}$ memory region (line 18). Otherwise, it returns *true* and the updated *cache* with the new memory region (line 20).

The function *check_one_mem_region* is used to calculate if the input address *addr* satisfies that the memory interval [*addr*, *addr* + *chk*) is in the range of the *id*-th memory region, it also checks alignment and permission of the interval.

Algorithm 1: The check_mem optimization algorithm

Data: (*perm* : *permission*), (*chk* : *memory_chunk*), (*mrs* :
    list memory_region), (*cache* : *list nat*), (*addr* : *val*), (*pc* : *int*)
Result: (*is_valid* : *bool*), (*new_cache* : *list nat*)
1 *check_mem* :
2 **if** *cache*[*pc*] ! = *null* **then**
3   *is_valid* ← *check_one_mem_region*(*mrs*[*cache*[*pc*]], *perm*, *chk*, *addr*) ;
4   **if** ! *is_valid* **then**
5   **return** *check_all_mrs*(*size*(*mrs*), *id*, *perm*, *chk*, *mrs*, *cache*, *addr*, *pc*);
         /* cache missing */
6   **else**
7   **return** (*true*, *cache*) ;   /* cache hitting */
8 **else**
9   **return** *check_all_mrs*(*size*(*mrs*), 0, *perm*, *chk*, *mrs*, *cache*, *addr*, *pc*) ;
     /* cache empty */

Data: (*n* : *nat*), (*cache_id* : *nat*), (*perm* : *permission*), (*chk* :
    memory_chunk), (*mrs* : *list memory_region*), (*cache* : *list nat*), (*addr* :
    val), (*pc* : *int*)
Result: (*is_valid* : *bool*), (*new_cache* : *list nat*)
10 *check_all_mrs* :
11 **if** *n* = 0 **then**
12   **return** (*false*, *cache*);
13 **else if** *n* = *cache_id* **then**
14   **return** *check_all_mrs*(*n* − 1, *cache_id*, *perm*, *chk*, *mrs*, *cache*, *addr*, *pc*);
15 **else**
16   *is_valid* ← *check_one_mem_region*(*mrs*[*n*], *perm*, *chk*, *addr*) ;
17   **if** ! *is_valid* **then**
18   **return** *check_all_mrs*(*n* − 1, *cache_id*, *perm*, *chk*, *mrs*, *cache*, *addr*, *pc*);
19   **else**
20   **return** (*true*, *cache*[*pc* ↦ *n*]);   /* cache updating */

3.3 Implementation

The Coq development reuses the CertrBPF Gallina specification which makes use of an option-state monad M to capture undefined behaviors (an option type has two cases: $\emptyset$ denoting failure and $\lfloor x \rfloor$ denoting success with result x) and memory-related side effects. We recall the definition of an option-state monad, for any value type A and state type *state*:

$$M\ state\ A := state \rightarrow \mathbf{option}(A \times state)$$

The optimized rBPF interpreter takes a new state that lifts the existing CertrBPF state with an additional field *cache*. We stipulate:

- *cache* represents a list of caches with the same length of the input rBPF binary list, *i.e.*, each memory instruction in the binary list has the same location as the corresponding cache in the *cache* list.
- the value of each cell of *cache* should be within range $[0, mrs\_num]$ where mrs_num is the number of memory regions. Initially, each *cache* cell is empty (0 by default), when it is updated with a *cache_id*, this cache points to the corresponding memory region with index $cache\_id - 1$.

Our new interpreter implementation introduces a flag '$opt\_flag : bool$': when users set the flag with $true$, the optimization is enabled. If $opt\_flag = false$, our specification is equivalent to the formally verified CertrBPF interpreter where *fuel* is for the termination of the interpreter (4096 by default) and *ctx_ptr* points to the start address of a special memory region of rBPF, named context, that is used to store all input values for rBPF programs. The bpf interpreter returns a value from an option-state monad with *val* the type of the bpf interpreter status:

$$bpf\_interp \ (opt\_flag : \ bool) \ (fuel : \ nat) \ (ctx\_ptr : \ val) : \ M \ state \ val.$$

Benefiting from the CertrBPF workflow [18], an executable C program could be automatically extracted from our Gallina model.

4   Proof

The monadic definition of the rBPF interpreter is such that every sub function of the interpreter is a monadic function defined over the same state. The benefit of having a monadic model is that the binding operator of the monad composes the value and threads the state over each function. For instance, given $f_1 : A \to M \ state \ B$ and $f_2 : B \to M \ state \ C$, then the composition is simply the binding of f_1 and f_2, written as $do \ x \leftarrow f_1; f_2$. The drawback, however, is that every function is defined over the same option-state monad with a global state. As a consequence, if the global state changes (*e.g.*, due to an optimization), all invariants have to be proved again. More details are given in Subsect. 4.1.

Alternatively, each function of the model can be defined over the projection of the state that the function modifies. For instance, if the function f_1 only modifies the substate s of the state *state*, the projection f_1' has the new signature $f_1' : A \times s \to (B \times s)$. The benefit of such approach is that if the global state *state* is modified (*e.g.*, due to an optimization), but the modification is not in s, then the invariant of f_1' still hold, without additional proof. The drawback, however, is that composition of f_1' and f_2' (for some projection of f_2) is no longer as simple as the monadic binding as the signatures may not coincide. We call *simplification* the transformation that takes a function defined over an option-state monad and returns the projected function as detailed above.

Our strategy is then the following. We keep the monadic model for design, as monadic composition makes specification easier. We use the *simplification* transformation, as detailed in Subsect. 4.2, on the rBPF interpreter with optimization, and prove the correctness of the *check_mem* optimization. Last, we prove that the simplification is correct with the equivalence proof in Subsect. 4.3.

4.1   Challenge

Following the workflow of CertrBPF, our new proof model adopts the monadic form with an option *state* monad M. The standard refinement proof adopted by CompCert and CertrBPF is to prove the theorem *optimization_correctness* that the two models (non-optimized and optimized) preserve a proper forward simulation relation.

The simulation relation $match\_states \subseteq state \times state$ is straightforward: the equality between all other fields in two states, except for the *cache*.

$$match\_states(st_1,\ st_2) \stackrel{def}{=} \bigwedge \begin{cases} st_1.pc = st_2.pc \\ st_1.flag = st_2.flag \\ \dots \end{cases}$$

```
Theorem optimization_correctness: ...
  (Hsim: match_states st1 st2)
  (Hinterp: bpf_interp false fuel input_v st1 = ⌊(res, st1')⌋),
  ∃ st2',
    bpf_interp true fuel input_v st2 = ⌊(res, st2')⌋ /\
    match_states st1' st2'.
```

Theorem *optimization_correctness* only considers the case when the monadic interpreter returns successfully because the existing isolation proof [18] guarantees the monadic CertrBPF interpreter (*i.e.*, *opt_flag = false*) never crashes.

We illustrate the challenge of directly proving the correctness of the optimization within our monadic model and present our solution in the next section.

We first introduce the function tree of our Gallina model because the proof process of the theorem follows this tree structure. We highlight four nodes of the function tree, as depicted in Fig. 2:

- bpf_interp: The top function of our new CertrBPF model;
- step: It interprets single rBPF instruction with an initial state, and results a new state;
- upd_reg: The leaf node that updates the register map field of the global monad state;
- check_mem: The key function where the *opt_flag = true* branch enables the *check_mem* optimization. We underline that the optimized case and the non-optimized one return different states as the former can modify the cache field of the global state.

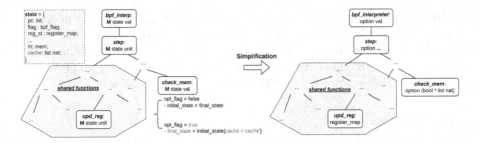

Fig. 2. Function tree of the optimized interpreter. Left is the monadic model with the global state. Right is our simplified model. The grey region includes the shared functions whose simulation proofs can be eliminated on the right side.

To complete this standard state-based refinement proof, it then requires a forward simulation proof of each node in Fig. 2. The main reason is that all monadic functions in the tree share the same global state and check_mem has different effects on this state, depending on the optimization flag *opt_flag*. The existing experience from CertrBPF has shown evidence that this way is quite complex and spends a lot of time proving many trivial but very detailed lemmas.

There are several potential ways that may tackle the challenge.

- *dependent type*: CertrBPF adopts 'implementation-proof-separation' way that this proof model doesn't contain any proof invariant. We could try to re-implement CertrBPF by embedding some invariant in a dependent-type form, and it may simplify the final simulation proof.
- *monadic laws*: Our proof model is monadic, therefore we could consider proof based on monadic laws. Similar to monad transformer in Haskell, we define monad projection and injection, along with the related laws, in order to declare the side-effect on the global state of each sub functions *e.g.*, upd_reg and check_mem.

Our solution is much more direct: we forget the monadic structure, and replace the global state with proper inline arguments, by a so-called *simplification* process. It results in a fruitful proof simplification of the final theorem: we omit the simulation proof of most shared functions since they have the exactly same behavior in both optimized and non-optimized models.

4.2   Simplification

The *simplification* is to

- replace the global state with the *essential* local parameters derived from fields of the state;
- replace the monad along with monad operations to the normal Gallina functions, and

– simplify the simulation relation (match_states) to the equivalence between outputs of models, in our cases, they are the non-optimized model and the *check_mem* optimized model.

As depicted in Fig. 3, the *simplification* process consists of four steps:

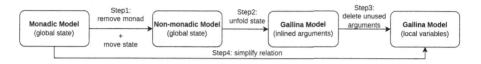

Fig. 3. The simplification process.

$$f\ (\_ : a):\ M\ state\ b$$

$(step1) \quad \Rightarrow f_1\ (\_ : a)\ (\_ : state): option\ (b \times state)$

$(step2) \quad \Rightarrow f_2\ (\_ : a)\ (\_ : t_1)\ (\_ : t_2)\ \ldots\ (\_ : t_n): option\ (b \times t_1 \times t_2 \times \ldots \times t_n)$

$(step3) \quad \Rightarrow f_3\ (\_ : a)\ (\_ : t_j)\ (\_ : t_j)\ \ldots: option\ (b \times t_i \times t_j \times \ldots)$

$(step4) \quad (f, f^{opt}) \in R \Rightarrow (f_3, f_3^{opt}) \in R_{simpl}$

Step 1: Remove Monad Along with Standard (and Non-standard) Monad Operations. We unfold our option state monad M and its operations, then we move the initial state to an argument for readability: this syntax-level transformation doesn't modify the semantics of Gallina programs.

Step 2: Replace the Global State with Inline Arguments. Assume the global *state* contains several fields with the signature $t_1 \times t_2 \times \ldots \times t_n$, we construct a new function by:

1. unfold the initial state as a list of arguments with types t_1, t_2, $\ldots$,t_n, and
2. replace the final state with the projection of all its components.

Step 3: Bottom-Up Delete Unused Arguments and Outputs. According to the function tree of our monadic model, we remove all unused arguments and reduce fields of outputs starting from leaf nodes. Only modified components allow to output and their types are reserved in the type signature.

For instance, the initial monadic functions (see comments) and the final simplified versions of **upd_reg**, **step**, and **bpf_interpreter** are shown as follows:

– **upd_reg** only modifies the register map *regmap* field in the global state, therefore we only reserve this type in the input and output.
– **step** takes most fields of the monadic state, except for the bpf flag, because we only execute *step* when the interpreter status is normal. **step** returns a new pc (affected by *Branch* instructions), a new register map (modified by most instructions, *e.g.*, alu), a new CompCert memory (because of *Store*

instructions), a bpf flag (produced by *e.g.*, div-by-zero, etc.), and a new cache (updated by the *check_mem* optimization). Some fields are not returned, such as the binary instruction list l, the input binary size *len* and the memory region list *mrs*, which naturally represents they are unchanged by step.

- bpf_interpreter takes all components of the global state as parameters and returns the final result if successful.

```
(**r Definition upd_reg  (r: reg)  (v: val)  : M state unit := ...  *)
Definition upd_reg (r: reg) (v: val) (rs: regmap): regmap := ...

(**r Definition step  (opt_flag: bool)  : M state unit := ...  *)
Definition step (opt_flag: bool) (pc: int) (cache: list nat)
   (l: list int64) (len: nat) (rs: regmap) (mrs_num: nat)
   (mrs: MyMemRegionsType) (m: mem):
     option (int * regmap * mem * bpf_flag * list nat) := ...
 match ins with
 | Alu  ... => match step_alu ... with
                | ∅ => ∅
                | ⌊(rs', f)⌋  => ⌊(pc, rs', m, f, cache)⌋
                end
   ...
(**r Definition bpf_interpreter  (fuel: nat)  (ctx_ptr: val)
     (opt_flag: bool): M state val := ...  *)
Definition bpf_interpreter (opt_flag: bool) (fuel: nat) (ctx_ptr: val)
   (pc: int) (cache: list nat) (l: list int64) (len: nat)
   (rs: regmap) (mrs_num: nat) (mrs: MyMemRegionsType) (m: mem):
     option (val * int * regmap * mem * bpf_flag * list nat) := ...
```

Step 4: Simplify the Simulation Relation. Since the simplified model doesn't have any states, the simulation relation R can be equivalently replaced by a much simpler and more intuitive input-output relation R_{simpl}: the simulation relation of a pair of initial states of function f and f^{opt} is transformed into an input relation that the simplified f_3 and f_3^{opt} have the same input value of simplified arguments; the simulation of finial state is also translated into the relation that f_3 and f_3^{opt} have the same value for simplified output fields.

For example, the lemma *step_preserves_simulation_relation* declares an input-output relation derived from *match_states*.

- *input*: The initial simulation relation is replaced by the constraint that all inline input arguments (pc, register map, CompCert memory, and bpf flag) must be identical for the optimized function ($opt\_flag = true$) and the non-optimized one.
- *output*: The final simulation relation is expressed as two parts:
  - *Explication*: all fields that are used in *match_states* also exist in the output should be identical, *e.g.*, the new pc value pc'.
  - *Implication*: all fields that do not appear in the output are unmodified, *e.g.*, the read-only memory region list *mrs*.

```
Lemma step_preserves_simulation_relation: ...
   (Hstep: step false pc cache l len rs mrs_num mrs m = ⌊(pc', rs', m',
   ↪ f', cache'⌋),
   ∃ cache1,
      step true pc cache l len rs mrs_num mrs m = ⌊(pc', rs', m', f',
      ↪ cache1)⌋.
```

Last, the construction of the final state is replaced by finding a new *cache*.

4.3   Equivalence Proof

This section mainly discusses two theorems:

- *The simplification is correct* (Theorem 1): prove the equivalence between the initial monadic models and the simplified models;
- *The check_mem optimization is correct* (Theorem 2): prove that the non-optimized model and the optimized model are equivalent.

Theorem 1 (Simplification Correctness). *Assume the monadic interpreter* bpf_interp *takes initial state st1 and successfully outputs result res and final state st2, the simplified version* bpf_interpreter *passes all fields of st1 as arguments, it returns the same result.*

```
Theorem simplification_correctness: ...
   (Hinterp: bpf_interp opt_flag fuel ctx_ptr st1 = ⌊(res, st2)⌋),
      bpf_interpreter opt_flag fuel ctx_ptr (pc_loc st1) (cache st1)
      (ins st1) (ins_len st1) (regs_st st1) (mrs_num st1)
      (bpf_mrs st1) (bpf_m st1) =
         ⌊(res, pc_loc st2, regs_st st2, bpf_m st2, flag st2, cache
         ↪ st2)⌋.
```

Proof. The key part is that the monadic *check_mem* function may modify the global state, therefore a related lemma is proved to show this function has no effect on all other fields that are used by all consequent monadic functions.

Theorem 2 (Optimization Correctness). *Assume the simplified rBPF interpreter accepts the same arguments, the one disabling the* check_mem *optimization returns the same result as another enabling the optimization.*

```
Theorem optimization_correctness_simpl: ...
   (Hmem_disjoint: memory_regions_disjoint mrs_num mrs m0)
   (Hcache_inv: cache_inv cache l mrs_num)
   (Hinterp: bpf_interpreter false ... = ⌊(res, pc, rs, m, f, cache)⌋),
   ∃ cache1,
      bpf_interpreter true ... = ⌊(res, pc, rs, m, f, cache1)⌋.
```

This theorem requires two assumptions:

- the user declared memory regions mrs are disjoint: there is no overlap between any two memory regions. This one is directly derived from the memory invariant of the original isolation proof.
- Due to the new field $cache$, an additional invariant is used to formalize the stipulation mentioned in Subsect. 3.3 for proving Theorem 2: $cache\_inv$ specifies the length of the cache list and the valid range of each element in the list.

Proof. We first case analysis on rBPF instructions, the proof of the non-memory instructions is trivial because both non-optimized and optimized models execute identical behaviors. The memory instruction cases are non-trivial because the $check\_mem$ function of two models has different behaviors: the optimized model may update $cache$. Therefore we prove an important lemma $check\_mem\_preserves\_simulation\_relation$ that indicates two models return the same result pointer ptr but different $caches$.

```
Lemma check_mem_preserves_simulation_relation: ...
   (Hcheck: check_mem false mrs_num ... = Some (ptr, cache')),
   ∃ cache1,
     check_mem true mrs_num ...  = Some (ptr, cache1).
```

Next, the $check\_mem$ lemma proof consists of three cases of the cache in the optimized model:

- *cache not exists* ($cache\_id = 0$): This is the simplest case which represents the cache is empty and the optimized model performs the normal memory checking as same as the non-optimized version, the only difference is that once it finds a valid pointer, it updates the cache with the corresponding memory region index before output. In this case, the proof is trivial.
- *cache exists* ($cache\_id \neq 0$): the optimized model observes the cache is not empty, there are two cases,
  - *cache missing*: The input address is not valid in the corresponding memory region of $cache\_id$, therefore the optimized model performs the normal memory checking as same as the non-optimized version but skips the memory region $cache\_id$ (Algorithm 1: line 16–17). This case proves by induction on the number of memory regions mrs_num and returns a new cache.
  - *cache hitting*: The proof is also by induction on mrs_num, and this case doesn't modify the cache because the input address is valid in the corresponding memory region of $cache\_id$. The proof requires that the non-optimized version is also (and only) valid in this memory region where we use the assumption that memory regions are disjoint.

5   Evaluation

Our experimental objects are the original non-verified rBPF interpreter (*i.e.,* vanilla-rBPF), CertrBPF, and the optimized CertrBPF. Our measurements focus on the memory requirements of the virtual machines and the instruction execution throughput.

5.1   Experimental Evaluation Setup

Our experiments are performed on a *nrf52840dk* support board which uses an Arm Cortex-M4 microcontroller, a popular 32-bit architecture (arm-v7m). The code is compiled using the Arm GNU toolchain version 12.2. The compilation is using level 2 optimization enabled and the following GCC options:

- `-foptimize-sibling-calls`: optimize all tail-recursive calls and in turn, bound the stack usage;
- `-fwrapv`, `-fwrapv-pointer`: both signed and pointer arithmetic wrap around according to the two's-complement encoding;
- `-fno-strict-aliasing`: there is no aliasing assumption.

The last three options are passed for the purpose of avoiding a possible mismatch between the CompCert semantics and the GCC semantics.

5.2   Memory Footprint

We first evaluate the memory footprint of the CertrBPF interpreter and the CertrBPF-opt implementation, compared to vanilla-rBPF. We measure i) *Flash size*: all read-only data, including the actual code; ii) *Stack*: the approximate RAM used for stack space.

Table 1. Memory footprint of rBPF engines

Size	Vanilla-rBPF	CertrBPF	CertrBPF (opt)
Flash	2018 B	**1502 B**	2114 B
Stack	356 B	**68 B**	96 B

We compare the required memory by the different implementations in Table 1. In terms of Flash, the *check_mem* optimized CertrBPF increases the footprint because of the additional cache field, compared to CertrBPF, but this optimized version is comparable with Vanilla-rBPF. In terms of Stack, both CertrBPF and optimized CertrBPF have less stack usage, compared to Vanilla-rBPF. One reason is that Vanilla-rBPF has an extra call module that occupies approximately 108 B.

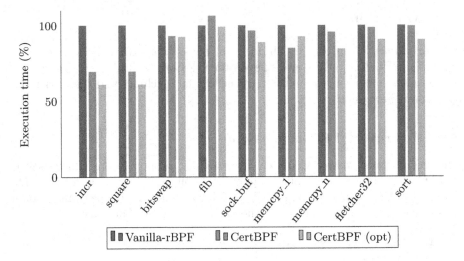

Fig. 4. Performance of runtime (optimized) CertBPF generated code relative to Vanilla-rBPF generated code on a Arm Cortex-M4 processor. Shorter is better. The baseline, in blue, is Vanilla-rBPF without optimizations. The optimization is in green. (Color figure online)

5.3 Experiments

We evaluate the performance of actual benchmarks using CertrBPF (enable and disable the *check_mem* optimization):

- The first four benchmarks test pure computation tasks mainly consisting of rBPF `alu` operations and one extra *exit* instruction (for the purpose of validating the rBPF verifier). These results are averaged over 1000 runs to guarantee accuracy.
- Then, we select three special cases with more memory operations but fewer `alu32` operations: the classical BPF socket buffer read/write, memory copies only 1 element (average over 1000 times), and memory copies many elements.
- Finally, we benchmark the performance of actual IoT data processing using the Fletcher32 algorithm or a sort algorithm.

Summary. As shown in Fig. 4, the optimized CertrBPF speedups most of the benchmarks, compared to the original CertrBPF.

For the first four benchmarks, the possible reason for the performance improvement of the optimized CertrBPF may be that GCC with optimizations changes the layout of the final binary forms generated from the source C rBPF interpreters because of the additional cache-related functions. Therefore, the evaluation result produces slight difference, *e.g.*, incr in CertrBPF is 5.750 µs, and incr in CertrBPF (opt) is 5.376 µs.

We observe that the optimized CertrBPF is slower than the original CertrBPF in the case of *memcpy_1*, but still faster than Vanilla-rBPF. This slow-down is caused by copying only one element: it takes the additional expense to update cache but then exits before benefiting from any acceleration of cache. The benchmark *memcpy_n* (n = 60) shows the optimized version enjoys speedup due to the extra cache. This behavior is also visible in our data processing benchmarks.

Discussion. We could image the worst case of the optimized CertrBPF: one rBPF program frequently switches one pointer to different memory regions, and it results in a lot of cache updating but never cache hitting. For this worst case, users should disable the *check_mem* optimization, another alternative is to design an advanced rBPF verifier that adopts static analysis techniques to determine whether the optimization should be enable or not.

6 Related Work

Monadification. Many existing research works on lifting non-monadic functions into a monadic form, *i.e.,* monadification, for quite various purposes: Martin et al. [5] describe an algorithm to automatically transform non-monadic programs into monadic form for structuring and modularizing functional programs. Simon et al. [17] present a framework in Isabelle/HOL for automatic memoization of recursive functions which uses monadification to produce immediate representation of recursive functions with the state monad. Akira et al. [14] consider the formally-verified transformation from Coq to low-level C code, they propose a monadification algorithm that inserts proper monads into programs for the preservation of critical properties, *e.g.,* absence of overflows.

The simplification presented in this paper is the opposite operation of monadification by forgetting the monadic structure and localizing the global state as proper arguments. This choice makes us benefit from a fruitful proof simplification: most shared functions between the optimized model and the non-optimized one are free of proof.

To the best of our knowledge, the closest related work is AutoCorres [8,9]. AutoCorres is a formally verified tool that abstracts monadic C representations (deep embedding in Isabelle/HOL) into shallow embedding forms in Isabelle/HOL. One of its steps, named 'local variable lifting', translates a monadic C representation into a simplified monadic representation where local variables are lifted out of the program's global state. AutoCorres and our simplification differ in the following ways:

- AutoCorres considers a verified transformation between two monadic representations, while our method targets the non-monadic form; and
- AutoCorres provides an automatic proof for this lifting step, whereas we handle our simplification process manually.

Verified Optimization. There has been a good deal of work on proving the correctness of optimizing transformations for various functional languages, such as CompCert [10], CakeML [12], and CertiCoq [1]. In the context of BPF, Linux eBPF adopts JIT techniques as well as many modern JIT-related optimizations to accelerate the execution time of eBPF programs. However, existing formal verification research [13,15,16] on eBPF JITs primarily focuses on the correctness of the JITs compilation instead of verified optimizations.

When turning to RIOT-OS rBPF, both the unverified Vanilla-rBPF and verified CertrBPF consider fewer (verified) optimizations. To address it, this paper presents a verified *check_mem* optimization for rBPF.

7   Conclusion and Future Work

This paper presents a verified optimization algorithm for the formally verified CertrBPF virtual machine, and introduces a simplification process from monadic functions to non-monadic form for the purpose of simplify the proof that the optimization is correct. The algorithm implementation and proofs of our optimized virtual machine are formalized in Coq and are available on the repository [4].

Next step, we aim at: i) designing an algorithm, similar to AutoCorres, for the automatic simplification of monadic programs; ii) exploring a monadic framework in Coq to prove the correctness of optimized programs in a monad form: we plan a monadic state transformer to only modify state without changing monad, by reusing the existing monad transformer technique.

References

1. Anand, A., et al.: CertiCoq: a verified compiler for Coq. In: CoqPL, Paris, France (2017)
2. Baccelli, E., et al.: RIOT: an open source operating system for low-end embedded devices in the IoT. IoT-J **5**(6), 4428–4440 (2018)
3. Bertot, Y., Castéran, P.: Interactive Theorem Proving and Program Development: Coq'Art: The Calculus of Inductive Constructions. Springer, Heidelberg (2013)
4. CertrBPFOpt: a verified optimization of CertrBPF (2023). https://gitlab.inria.fr/syuan/certrbpfopt
5. Erwig, M., Ren, D.: Monadification of functional programs. Sci. Comput. Program. **52**(1), 101–129 (2004). https://doi.org/10.1016/j.scico.2004.03.004
6. Fleming, M.: A Thorough Introduction to eBPF (2017)
7. Gershuni, E., et al.: Simple and precise static analysis of untrusted Linux kernel extensions. In: Proceedings of the 40th ACM SIGPLAN Conference on Programming Language Design and Implementation, PLDI 2019, New York, NY, USA, pp. 1069–1084. Association for Computing Machinery (2019). https://doi.org/10.1145/3314221.3314590
8. Greenaway, D.: Automated proof-producing abstraction of C code. Ph.D. thesis, UNSW Sydney (2014)
9. Greenaway, D., Lim, J., Andronick, J., Klein, G.: Don't sweat the small stuff: formal verification of c code without the pain. In: Proceedings of the 35th ACM SIGPLAN Conference on Programming Language Design and Implementation, PLDI 2014, New York, NY, USA, pp. 429–439. Association for Computing Machinery (2014). https://doi.org/10.1145/2594291.2594296

10. Leroy, X.: Formal verification of a realistic compiler. Commun. ACM **52**(7), 107–115 (2009)
11. McCanne, S., Jacobson, V.: The BSD packet filter: a new architecture for user-level packet capture. In: USENIX Winter Conference, San Diego, California, USA, vol. 46, pp. 259–270. USENIX (1993)
12. Myreen, M.O., Owens, S.: Proof-producing synthesis of ml from higher-order logic. In: Proceedings of the 17th ACM SIGPLAN International Conference on Functional Programming, ICFP 2012, New York, NY, USA, pp. 115–126. Association for Computing Machinery (2012). https://doi.org/10.1145/2364527.2364545
13. Nelson, L., Geffen, J.V., Torlak, E., Wang, X.: Specification and verification in the field: applying formal methods to BPF just-in-time compilers in the Linux kernel. In: 14th USENIX Symposium on Operating Systems Design and Implementation (OSDI 2020), pp. 41–61. USENIX Association, USA, November 2020. https://www.usenix.org/conference/osdi20/presentation/nelson
14. Tanaka, A., Affeldt, R., Garrigue, J.: Safe low-level code generation in Coq using monomorphization and monadification. J. Inf. Process. **26**, 54–72 (2018). https://api.semanticscholar.org/CorpusID:4571133
15. Van Geffen, J., Nelson, L., Dillig, I., Wang, X., Torlak, E.: Synthesizing JIT compilers for in-kernel DSLs. In: Lahiri, S.K., Wang, C. (eds.) CAV 2020. LNCS, vol. 12225, pp. 564–586. Springer, Cham (2020). https://doi.org/10.1007/978-3-030-53291-8_29
16. Wang, X., Lazar, D., Zeldovich, N., Chlipala, A., Tatlock, Z.: Jitk: a trustworthy in-kernel interpreter infrastructure. In: 11th USENIX Symposium on Operating Systems Design and Implementation (OSDI 2014), Broomfield, CO, pp. 33–47. USENIX Association, October 2014. https://www.usenix.org/conference/osdi14/technical-sessions/presentation/wang_xi
17. Wimmer, S., Hu, S., Nipkow, T.: Verified memoization and dynamic programming. In: International Conference on Interactive Theorem Proving (2018). https://api.semanticscholar.org/CorpusID:14004609
18. Yuan, S., Besson, F., Talpin, J.P., Hym, S., Zandberg, K., Baccelli, E.: End-to-end mechanized proof of an eBPF virtual machine for micro-controllers. In: Shoham, S., Vizel, Y. (eds.) CAV 2022. LNCS, vol. 13372, pp. 293–316. Springer, Cham (2022). https://doi.org/10.1007/978-3-031-13188-2_15
19. Zandberg, K., Baccelli, E.: Minimal virtual machines on IoT microcontrollers: the case of Berkeley Packet Filters with rBPF. In: PEMWN, pp. 1–6. IEEE, Berlin/Virtual, Germany (2020)
20. Zandberg, K., Baccelli, E., Yuan, S., Besson, F., Talpin, J.P.: Femto-containers: lightweight virtualization and fault isolation for small software functions on low-power IoT microcontrollers. In: Proceedings of the 23rd ACM/IFIP International Middleware Conference, Middleware 2022, New York, NY, USA, pp. 161–173. Association for Computing Machinery (2022). https://doi.org/10.1145/3528535.3565242

An Optimized Solution for Highly Contended Transactional Workloads

Chunxi Zhang[1(✉)], Shuyan Zhang[2], Ting Chen[2], Rong Zhang[2], and Kai Liu[1]

[1] Shanghai Stock Exchange, Shanghai 200000, China
{chxzhang,kliu}@sse.com.cn
[2] East China Normal University, Shanghai 200000, China
{shyzhang,tingc,rzhang}@dase.ecnu.edu.cn

Abstract. High contention frequently explodes in E-commerce scenario when promotions are held. However, modern multi-core main-memory databases cannot achieve ideal performance under high contention. Transactions contending for the same resources must be executed serially in traditional architecture to guarantee correctness, which severely chokes database management systems. In this paper, we propose to optimize the transaction processing scheme for highly contended E-commerce workloads. First, we analyze the characteristics of these workloads in detail. Second, we design to filter ineffective operations at IO layer instead of sending them to executing layer, considering the limited number of items involved in the promotion. Third, we make out a homogeneous operation merging scheme to share database execution resources, e.g., locks, and improve parallelization. We implement a prototype, FILMER, to demonstrate our idea. FILMER launches *filtering* and *merging* for contended transactions to make full use of system resources and improve parallelization. Extensive experiments show that *filtering* and *merging* improve the throughput by up to 1.95× and 2.55× respectively.

Keywords: transaction processing · concurrency control · high contention

1 Introduction

Large-scale transaction processing is increasingly critical in emerging businesses, especially E-commerce. One of the most representative applications is the promotional activities widely expected by global customers, running on some special on Alibaba's platform. Alibaba processes up to 491,000 transactions per second during the promotion [8]. As the backbone of the transactional business, database management systems (DBMSs) face increasing pressure, which requires it to have the ability to handle intensive workloads with the characteristics of high concurrency and serious skews.

During the promotion, lots of users read (R) or write (W) the same inventory at the same time, resulting in transactions rush to access the same item. The

H. Hermanns et al. (Eds.): SETTA 2023, LNCS 14464, pp. 402–418, 2024.
https://doi.org/10.1007/978-981-99-8664-4_23

remaining ineffective operations will greatly waste system resources. Besides, severe conflicts caused by R-W, W-R, or W-W operations and high concurrency bring a lot of data contention, which drags down the latency or leads to a large number of request timeouts. Contention processing is one of the most costly actions in relational DBMS. Optimistic concurrency control protocol (OCC) exhibits poor performance due to frequent rollback under high contention [6]; Even if the concurrency control protocol is optimized [16,20], contention caused by W-W conflicts cannot be relieved, which leads to low parallelism among transactions [11].

Fortunately, E-commerce applications have weak requirements for database consistency [5]. Many methods can be used to mitigate the contention for data from read operations. One of the representative ways is to use Read/Write Separation architecture (RW-Sep), by separating the reads and writes to different servers. In E-commerce, high contention is mainly caused by the write operations for stock reduction, because every sale transaction needs to subtract the stocks. In order to improve the performance of DBMSs, the traffic is usually intercepted by queuing [12] the requests at the service layer. But this solution highly couples with the business. Once the business changes, the service layer code also needs to be modified.

In this paper, we design and implement FILMER, a prototype system, to handle E-commerce workloads with intensive contention. Compared with traditional processing scheme, FILMER optimizes transaction processing at different levels of database implementation. First, at IO layer, FILMER records failed operations to filter the subsequent ineffective operations and avoids resource wasting at the execution layer. Second, at the execution layer, we propose to merge homogeneous operations, which can make conflicting writes share the same write lock. This enables the transactions the operations belong to can be executed in parallel and reduces the number of data modifications. Lastly, FILMER implements the architecture of binding workers to a logical data partition to further relieve central lock contention [13]. To the best of our knowledge, FILMER is the first work to filter ineffective traffic in DBMSs, and the first to propose a strategy to share resources among write operations. Experiments show that ineffective traffic filtering and homogeneous operation merging can lead up to 1.95x and 2.55x increase in throughput, respectively.

2   Preliminaries and Overview

In this section, we first analyze the characteristics of workloads in E-commerce scenario. Then, we identify the difficulties when dealing with these workloads and propose an optimized transaction processing scheme. Finally, we give an overview of our design in FILMER.

2.1   Characteristics of E-Commerce Workloads

When an E-commerce business starts a promotion, the price of items will be reduced within a specified time, which greatly increases the probability of customers rushing for items at the same time, and the best-selling items are quickly sold out. Accordingly, we summarize the characteristics of these workloads into the following three points:

High Contention. Customers snap up items in a short time, and thus the concurrency of transactions is very high. Lots of transactions request to read or write the same tuple in database due to the relatively small number of items involved in promotions, resulting in a high conflict rate of operations.

Definition 1. *Homogeneous Operations shall satisfy the following three conditions:*

(1) They are UPDATE operations generated from the same SQL template.
(2) They only add or subtract a constant from the attribute value(s).
(3) They access the same tuple.

Numerous Homogeneous Operations. Homogeneous operation is defined in Definition 1. In Example 1, two users want to buy the item $pk = 3$ in inventory R by operations $O1$ and $O2$, both of which have the same *SQL Template* "*UPDATE R SET c = c - ? WHERE pk = ? AND c ≥ ?;*" and reduce the stock of the same item c.

Example 1.

$O1$: UPDATE R SET c = c - 1 WHERE pk = 3 AND c ≥ 1;
$O2$: UPDATE R SET c = c - 2 WHERE pk = 3 AND c ≥ 2;

Since items involved in a promotion usually cover a very small portion of the whole stock and lots of customers rush for the popular items, there will be a large number of such homogeneous operations, e.g., $O1$ and $O2$, contending for the same tuples, e.g., $pk = 3$.

Numerous Ineffective Operations. Since the quantity of each item for promotion is limited, the items may have been sold out when many purchase requests arrive at the database. A lot of operations that still try to reduce the number of sold-out items are doomed to fail. We call these operations *ineffective operations*. If RW-Sep architecture is adopted or a cache is built at the service layer, inconsistency read to the sold-out items will attract more ineffective operations to DBMS and aggravating the waste of system resources.

2.2 Optimized Scheme

Traditionally, DBMS allocates one worker thread to each transaction. Since each thread manages different transactions, contention between threads for shared data resources inevitably arise when transactions are executed concurrently. A study in Dora [13] proves that contention in central lock manager can become a system bottleneck. In order to mitigate the contention pressure introduced to the lock manager, we implement the transaction access model by logically binding threads to data partitions, that is data on the same partition can only be accessed by a unique thread. The lock table for data changes from global to local, which significantly reduces the contention of global resources.

Because operations on the same data are handed over to the same thread, the thread-to-data model provides an opportunity to merge homogeneous operations and share locks among different transactions. For example, $O1\_2$ is generated for $O1$ and $O2$ in Example 1. $O1\_2$: *UPDATE R SET c = c - 3 WHERE pk = 3 AND c $\geq$ 3*; In this way, transactions that would otherwise have to be executed serially can be executed in parallel without changing the transaction semantics, which greatly increases the concurrency among transactions and multiple data updates can be reduced to one. In addition, we build an ineffective operation recognizer by introducing a *filter table* to filter numerous ineffective operations in workloads, identify them at the IO layer and return *fail* immediately, so as to reduce the waste of system resources as much as possible.

2.3   System Overview

FILMER is a prototype implemented as an in-memory database to improve processing performance with intensive contention. Since OCC always suffer poor performance due to frequent aborts under intensive contention, FILMER adopts a pessimistic protocol, two-phase locking (or 2PL) [2], for its concurrency control. For simplicity, we implement a single-versioned 2PL in FILMER, which is enough to demonstrate our idea. Retaining more data versions does not help resolve *W-W* conflicts.

The overall architecture and the workflow of FILMER are shown in Fig. 1. The operations sent by a client reach **IO Manager** (*IOM*) first. *IOM* consists of a filter and a dispatcher. filter identifies the ineffective operations, and returns *fail* to the client directly; otherwise, the operations will be handed over to dispatcher for subsequent processing. dispatcher is responsible for two tasks. One is to dispatch the general CRUD operations, i.e., *insert, delete, select* and *update*, to the corresponding worker based on the primary keys of the data to be accessed. The other one is to pass transaction operations, i.e., *begin, commit*, or *rollback*, to **Transaction Manager** (*TM*).

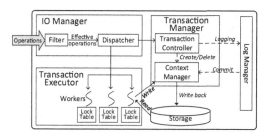

Fig. 1. The Overall Architecture and Workflow of FILMER

In **Transaction Executor** (*TE*), data is divided into disjoint logical partitions according to primary keys. Each partition is managed by a different worker and each worker maintains its own local lock table. The worker thread fetches a set of homogeneous operations at a time, and locks the data to be accessed using a local lock table. Operations that are unable to obtain the lock will be placed in waiting queue and be executed after the lock is released. If the operation locks data successfully, the worker will read the required data from the storage first, and then record updated results in transaction context. Our execution strategy guarantees that the worker can merge all the homogeneous operations that have arrived and execute them together. Different operations of the same transaction are likely to be executed by different threads, but all the information of a transaction will be stored in its transaction context.

The transaction controller chooses different execution methods for different transaction operations. For a *begin* (resp., *abort*) operation, it only needs to create (resp., delete) the context of the corresponding transaction. For a *commit* operation, it notifies the **Log Manager** (*LM*) to write the redo log. After the log is persisted, *LM* sends a commit message to context manager. At this point, a transaction is actually completed. *IOM* replies to the client that the transaction has been committed. At the same time context manager processes the messages one by one, writing updates in the transaction context to the storage.

All threads in *IOM, TM* and *TE*, are executed in a non-blocking style, which helps to avoid frequent context switching in kernels.

3   Ineffective Operations Filtering

In order to avoid unnecessary resource contention, we choose to filter ineffective operations at *IOM*, the entrance of the whole system. In this section, we first give a method to identify ineffective operations, then elaborate the entire filtering process.

Definition 2. *If a single-point UPDATE operation U intends to subtract a positive number from current value of attribute α, and the integrity constraint on α requires it to belong to a left-closed interval, then U is a **Count-Constraint Update (CC-Update)** and α is a **constraint-attribute** of U.*

Definition 3. *If an UPDATE operation U intends to add a positive number to current value of attribute α, then U is a **Count-Supplement Update (CS-Update)**, and α is a **constraint-attribute** of U.*

Algorithm 1. Identify CC-Update and CS-Update

Input: UPDATE operation s
Output: the category of s
1: array $\Psi \leftarrow$ expressions split by "," after "SET" in s
2: array $\Omega \leftarrow$ predicates split by "AND" after "WHERE" in s
3: $n \leftarrow$ the number of tuples that s attempts to modify
4: **for all** expression e **in** Ψ **do**
5:      $\alpha \leftarrow$ attribute that e attempts to modify
6:      **if** $n=1$ **and** e is to subtract a positive number from α **then**
7:          **for all** predicate p **in** Ω **do**
8:              **if** p has the form "$\alpha \geq$ constant" **then**
9:                  **return** 1
10:              **end if**
11:          **end for**
12:      **else if** e is to add a positive number to α **then**
13:          **return** 2
14:      **end if**
15: **end for**
16: **return** 0

3.1 Ineffective Operation Identification

During promotion, UPDATE operations have a high probability of being ineffective as declared in Sect. 2. We define two kinds of updates for our problem as in Definition 2–3. A stock reducing operation is a typical *CC-Update* because the quantity of items is required to be a positive integer. In contrast, a re-stocking operation is a *CS-Update*. Usually, although the items have been sold out, there will still be a lot of updates trying to reduce the numbers, i.e., *CC-Updates*, which become ineffective inevitably. Obviously, the same *CC-Update* can only be performed a limited number of times if no *CS-Update* with the same constraint-attribute is launched. In order to efficiently identify ineffective operations and save system overhead, our filtering behavior is only aimed at *CC-Update*.

We describe the details of identifying *CC-Update* and *CS-Update* in Algorithm 1. For an update s, we initialize array Ψ and Ω to record its expressions and predicates respectively, then calculate n, the number of tuples that s attempts to modify (Line 1 to 3). For each expression, if $n = 1$ and it subtracts a positive number from attribute α, we check whether there is an integrity constraint on α in the predicate, and if so, it is a *CC-Update* (Line 6 to 11). Otherwise, if the expression adds a positive number to α, it is a *CS-Update* (Line 12 to 14). In other cases, we return 0, i.e., other types. The time complexity of the algorithm is $O(EP)$, where E and P are the number of expressions and predicates.

We design a **Filter Table** to record ineffective updates so as to determine if a *CC-Update* is still effective. Each entry in the table is defined by a triple as $< Table\ name, Primary\ key, Column\ id >$. *Table name* and *Primary key* specify the tuple that U is trying to modify, and *Column id* refers to the *constraint-attribute* of U. If a *CC-Update* U is found to be ineffective, its operation information will be in the filter table. If a *CC-Update* has more than one *constraint-attributes*, we will add multiple entries in filter table.

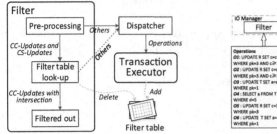

Fig. 2. Filtering Procedure

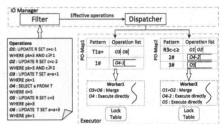

Fig. 3. Merging Procedure

3.2   Filtering Procedure

The whole filtering process is shown in Fig. 2. As mentioned before, requests sent by clients first arrive at *IOM*. *IOM* compiles the operations and obtain the primary keys of the tuples it about to access according to its predicate. If the location predicate is not based on primary keys, we need first locate the keys. For example, if it is based on the secondary index, we need to first access the secondary index to get the values of corresponding primary keys. If the operation is an UPDATE, we use Algorithm 1 to determine the specific type of operation. If it is a *CC-Update* or *CS-Update*, then its $<$ *Table name, Primary key, Column id* $>$ will be extracted, probably more than one, for comparison with the entries in the filter table. If they are found to have a intersection, there are two cases:

1) For a *CC-Update*, an ineffective operation is found. *IOM* filters out the operations and returns *fail* directly to the client.

2) For a *CS-Update*, *IOM* deletes the intersecting entries from the filter table and dispatch the operation since a *CS-Update* is likely to make the *CC-Update* with the same constraint-attribute no longer ineffective.

For all other cases, operations will be dispatched to *TE* directly according to their primary key values. When a *CC-Update* fails because of violating the integrity constraint on a constrain-attribute, *TE* inserts new entries into filter table.

Filter table is a concurrent data structure that needs to be accessed by multiple threads. Since *IOM* needs to do checking for each *CC-Update* or *CS-Update* in filter table, filter table is frequently read, but it is only written when adding or deleting entries in or from it. Therefore, we use copy-on-write technology [17] to implement it. In a high contention scenario, filter table is usually small and only used for popular items that have been sold out, and thus the copying cost is little.

Theorem 1. *The filtering behavior does not affect the conflict-serializability of transactions.*

Proof.

(1) If no operation is filtered in transaction T, then all operations are executed in DBMS normally.
(2) If an operation in transaction T is filtered, it means that the operation failed. Because of the atomicity of transactions, T will be aborted eventually as if it never happened.

Accordingly, filtering will not affect transaction conflict-serializability in DBMS.

4   Homogeneous Operations Merging

In this section, we introduce the key ideas of operation merging, and discuss the details of the whole merging procedure.

4.1   Design of Merging

If we want to merge operations, we should first screen out the candidate operations that may have homogeneous companions. For an operation, if it does not satisfy the following two conditions, it can not be merged:

1) It is an UPDATE operation;
2) It only adds or subtracts a constant from the attribute value(s).

For such an operation, we simply assign it a unique string as its pattern, and then put it together with the pattern into PO-Map (Pattern-Operation Map), such as $O5$ with its pattern "3#" in Fig. 3. Otherwise, for a mergeable operation candidate, we construct its unique pattern using its pivotal information which includes the tables it accesses, the primary key value of the tuple to be accessed, the attributes it attempts to modify and the corresponding arithmetic operators, the attributes and relational operators in condition predicates. Then we put the mergeable candidate into PO-Map with the pattern as shown in Fig. 3. After doing this, operations with the same pattern are homogeneous. For example, in Fig. 3, $O1$ and $O2$ have the same pattern "R3c-c≥" which means they both access the tuple with $pk = 3$ on table R, do subtraction on attribute c, and both require c to be greater than or equal to a certain value.

The second concern is how to merge operations in a candidate list. The processing of assignment expression after *set* is quite simple. We only need to add or subtract a constant value from the attribute. In Fig. 3, "set $a = a+1$" and "set $a = a+3$" in $O3$ and $O6$ are merged into "set $a = a+4$". In contrast, the merging of predicates is a little complicated. We classify the predicates in an operation into two categories: **location predicates** and **condition predicates**. Location predicates refer to the predicates used to access the index, which determine the location of the target tuples. Since homogeneous operations access the same tuple, their location predicates must be equal and have been used in pre-processing. Thus, there is no need to merge them. Besides location predicates, we call all the other predicates in SQL statements condition predicates, which are used to further check - whether the tuples found by location predicates meet some additional conditions. The merging of condition predicates needs to be configured according to the logic of the application. The easiest way is to take the intersection, such as merging "$c \geq 1$" and "$c \geq 2$" in $O1$ and $O2$ into "$c \geq 2$". However, if the two operations perform the reduction of the quantity of a item when the item is in stock, it is obvious that the merged operation generated by the above merging method do not conform to the semantics of the original operations. In this scenario, we can accumulate the values after the relational operators, i.e., "$c \geq 3$". Currently, we only support these two ways of predicate merging. However, predicates in OLTP workloads are not complex and usually only appear in the form of "*column op constant*", and thus it is not difficult to specify how they are merged based on application logic.

4.2 Merging Procedure

In *TE*, each thread is responsible for a logical data partition and maintains its PO-Map locally. As mentioned in Sect. 3.2, the operations that arrive at dispatcher are pre-processed, that is, we already know the primary key values of the tuples to be accessed. If an operation has more than one target tuple, dispatcher splits it to ensure that the operation dispatched to the thread need not access other data partitions. Each target tuple corresponds to a sub-operation. After splitting, all operations are single-point queries based on primary keys, and the pattern of an operation is calculated by dispatcher as mentioned in Sect. 3.2. For example, in Fig. 3, the attribute d in $O4$ has a secondary key, the filter pre-processes $O4$ by using the predicate "$d = 5$" to find the corresponding primary key values. In this case, we assume that $O4$ has two target tuples with primary key values of 1 and 2, thus the dispatcher splits $O4$ into two sub-operations, namely *O4-1: SELECT a FROM T WHERE pk=1* and *O4-2: SELECT a FROM T WHERE pk=3*. Then, according to the primary key, the corresponding worker thread is assigned and the operation is put into the operation list located by the pattern in PO-Map of the thread. In Fig. 3, *worker*1 and *worker*2 are assigned to operations which access the tuple with $pk = 1$ and tuple with $pk = 3$ respectively. If PO-Map does not have the pattern, dispatcher insert a new entry for it.

The worker fetches one entry from its PO-Map at a time. If there is more than one operation in its operation list, we merge the operations with the approaches mentioned in Sect. 4.1. For example, in Fig. 3, $O1$ and $O2$ are merged to "*UPDATE R SET c = c - 3 WHERE pk = 3 AND c ≥ 3*", $O3$ and $O6$ are merged to "*UPDATE T SET a = a + 4 WHERE pk = 1*". Data lock is needed before an operation is executed. Like traditional write locks, a write lock requested by a merged operation is not compatible with other write or read locks. However, in order to guarantee the serializability of transactions, merged write locks are shared by multiple transactions, and no transaction is allowed to reenter the lock, even though it seems that some merged transactions have already taken possession of the lock. Therefore, we need to ensure that in the transaction to which a mergeable operation belongs, no other operation that accesses the same data as the mergeable operation, otherwise a deadlock will occur. In addition, if there is only one operation in the list, we lock the data and do execution directly, such as $O5$, $O4$-1 and $O4$-2 in Fig. 3. If the merged operation fails the predicate check, TE will take it apart again and execute them one by one.

At this stage, all updates to data are localized. Updates are written back to the storage when the transaction is committed. When a transaction is executed, the locks it requests and the updates are recorded in its context. For updates made by merged operations, they only need to be recorded in the context of one transaction. This method reduces the number of times transactions operate the memory. However, if a transaction that has been merged aborts, in order to assure the atomicity of transactions, we must abort all the transactions that have been merged with it, which are recorded in *merging set*. Besides, transactions in the same merging set must also be committed at the same time, so as to avoid partial fail among transactions. We can configure the merge granularity to ensure the performance considering partial rolling back.

Discussion About Serializability. Supposing n UPDATE operations are merged executed, we treat the n transactions to which these operations belong as a big transaction BT. In schedule S, it involves m BTs. According to $2PL$, S is conflict-equivalent to a serial schedule in which m BTs are executed one by one. In a BT, there is no conflict between operations other than those involved in the merging, otherwise a deadlock will happen. Merged operations are essentially exchangeable according to the additive commutative law although they are conflicting. Therefore, the individual transactions that make up a BT can be regarded as executed in any serial order. Therefore, our scheduling is always serializable.

5   Evaluation

Settings. FILMER is deployed on a single server, which is equipped with 2 Intel Xeon Gold 6126 @ 2.60 GHz CPUs, 256 GB memory, 8 TB HDD disk configured in RAID-5. Each CPU has 12 physical cores and 24 logical cores, and enables hyperthreading. We choose two open source DBMSs for comparison, i.e., MySQL(v5.7.27) and PostgreSQL(v10.10), and the number of connection is set to 20 defaultedly for the best performance under high conflict.

Workloads. Traditional benchmarks, e.g., TPC-C [4] or SmallBank [1], neither simulate contention situation nor control the contention intensity. We use

PeakBench [21], a benchmark based on Alibaba "11· 11" promotion, to evaluate the performance of our design. Our experiments take two transactions from PeakBench, i.e., *Submit Order* and *Select Order*, as write transaction and read transaction respectively to demonstrate the effects of *filtering* and *merging*. *Submit Order* is to reduce the stock, which generates the most contention during promotion. *Select Order* has three read statements to check the information of an order submitted by a specified customer.

Default Configuration. Zipf parameter α is to control the conflict rate. We set α to 2 to simulate a high-conflict workload. The concurrency factor representing the degree of concurrency is set to 50 for high concurrency. The higher the value of α and the concurrency factor, the more intensive the contention are. The number of workers in **Transaction Executor** (TE) and **IO Manager** (IOM) are set to 2 and 4 respectively. The isolation level is serializable. *Submit Order* is used in following experiments if not specified.

5.1   Micro Exploration of *Filtering and* Merging

We launch two sets of experiments to explore the effect of *Filtering* and *Merging* on the performance of DBMS under different application scenarios.

Influence of *Filtering* We turn off *merging* to show the effectiveness of *filtering*.

In Fig. 4, it shows the change of throughput and latency of FILMER by switching on (*filter-on*) or off (*filter-off*) *filtering*. The stock level of each item is $300K$. *Success filter-on* (resp., *failure filter-off*) represents the performance of successful (resp., failed) transactions with *filter-on* (resp.,*filter-off*). In Fig. 4(a), we can see that at the beginning, the quantity of items is sufficient. Thus, the throughput of failed transactions is 0 and using *filtering* or not has almost no obvious influence on performance. From the 15th second, some items are sold out, resulting in the occurrence of failed transactions. At this time, if *filter-on*, the throughput of successful transactions is better than that with *filter-off*, and the latency in Fig. 4(b) increases instantaneously for multiple threads suddenly update or read the filter table at the moment. Subsequently, the throughput of failed transactions rises along with the number of sold-out items. Finally, *filter-on* achieves 1.5x higher throughput than *filter-off*. On the whole, as the filtering of ineffective operations saves the resources of workers, the processing efficiency of successful transactions is also improved.

In Fig. 5 we demonstrate the performance of traditional DBMSs, MySQL and PostgreSQL, in handling the same workloads as used in Fig. 4. we can see that the performance of MySQL is relatively stable compared to PostgreSQL. When items are not sold out, the performance of MySQL is better than that of PostgreSQL, owning to the advantages of the lock-based concurrency control in MySQL in handling high-conflict workloads. Once there are items sold out, MySQL has lower throughput for both successful and failed transactions than PostgreSQL. PostgreSQL has a higher efficiency in handling ineffective operations. As is shown in Fig. 5(b), the latency of handling of failed transactions in PostgreSQL is only about 13% of that in MySQL. It is because of the optimistic mechanism in PostgreSQL, which avoids lock waiting for ineffective operations. FILMER takes the advantages of both MySQL and PostgreSQL, using $2PL$ when processing successful transactions, and filtering ineffective operations to avoid waiting for locks. For PostgreSQL, the failure throughput is at most about 2× higher than that of the success throughput; however, for FILMER, it can be up to 5× if *filter-on*. *Filtering* is effective to tackle with failed transactions.

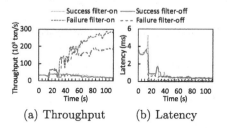

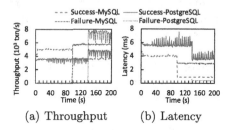

(a) Throughput   (b) Latency   (a) Throughput   (b) Latency

Fig. 4. Performance Fluctuation with *Merge-off* on FILMER.

Fig. 5. Performance Fluctuation on MySQL and PostgreSQL

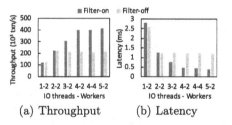

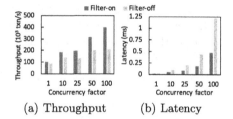

(a) Throughput   (b) Latency   (a) Throughput   (b) Latency

Fig. 6. Scalability of *IOM* to Handle Ineffective Operations with *Merge-off*.

Fig. 7. Performance of FILMER under High Conflict with *Merge-off*.

In Fig. 6, we generate even harsher scenario by setting concurrency factor to 100. The inventory of each item is set to 0. In this scenario, there is only throughput for failed transactions. We illustrate the throughput and latency by varying the number of IO threads and workers. The first 4 sets of experiments are all conducted with the number of workers set to 2, and the number of IO threads increases from 1 to 4. When the number of IO threads is only 1, *IOM* is the bottleneck. At this time *filtering* make *IOM* more busy for its additional computing task, which leads to slightly lower performance. When the number of IO threads increase from 2, the throughput and latency will not change significantly under *filter-off*. The reason is that the ineffective transactions contend with each other, and must be executed serially, which makes *TE* a bottleneck. In such a case, even when we double the number of workers (4-4 in Fig. 4), the performance remains unchanged. When the number of IO threads increases from 1 to 4, *filter-on* performance increases proportionally. This is because IO threads can deal with ineffective operations in parallel without locking serially under *filter-on*. When the number of IO threads changes to 5, *TE* becomes the bottleneck due to effective conflicting read operations still need to be processed serially by the same worker, and thus the performance can not be further improved. Finally, the throughput of *filter-on* is 1.95 times of that of *filter-off*. In short, when DBMS handles workloads with high contention, increasing the number of threads of *TE* does not always improve performance, but filtering ineffective operations in advance can greatly improve the scalability of DBMS.

In Fig. 7, the inventory of each item is also set to 0 for exploring the performance of *filtering* under high conflict with different concurrency factor. The larger the concurrency factor is, the more transactions need to be processed simultaneously. When the concurrency factor increases, the throughput keeps increasing and *filter-on* has an obvious dominance over *filter-off*. Especially, when concurrency factor increases from 50 to 100, throughput changes gently if *filter-off*. Even worse, the latency of *filter-off* increases much higher than that of *filter-on*. Overall, *filtering* reduces the process of ineffective operations in DBMS, which makes the performance significantly better.

Influence of *Merging*. In this part, we switch off *filtering* to show the effectiveness of *merging*. The number of each item is set to $100M$ to ensure that all the transactions can be successfully submitted.

In Fig. 8, we change α to observe the impact of different conflict rate on performance. If $\alpha = 0$, i.e., items are accessed evenly, merging improve the throughput of FILMER at the cost of higher latency. Since the workload of each worker is balanced, there are fewer operations that can be merged at one time. Moreover, the *merging* process is time-consuming. Hence, the latency is higher when *merge-on*. When α increases to 1, *merging* is obvious better in both throughput and latency. When α is 2.5, *merge-on* is about 2.4× better in throughput than that of *merge-off* with only 40% latency. If the merged big transactions are contending for resources, they still need to be executed serially. Therefore, when contention grows, the performance deteriorate even if *merge-on*. Comparing the throughput for $\alpha = 2.5$ and $\alpha = 0$, the damping for FILMER with *merge-on*, MySQL and PostgreSQL are about $45\%, 86\%$ and 77%, respectively. It can be seen that *merging* is effective in processing high-conflict transactions.

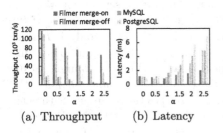

(a) Throughput   (b) Latency

Fig. 8. The Influence of Conflict Rate on FILMER with *Filter-off*.

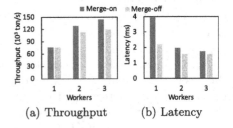

(a) Throughput   (b) Latency

Fig. 9. *Merging* Scalability on Different Number of Workers with *Filter-off*.

In Fig. 9, we test the scalability of *merging*. We set $\alpha = 0$ because TE obviously cannot scale under high conflict rate. In order to fill up the workers as evenly as possible, we set the number of IO threads and concurrency factor to 6 and 100, respectively. As a single worker thread can only perform each operation serially, even if the homogeneous operations are merged, the transactions cannot be executed in parallel. Moreover, the commit time of the merged transactions is decided by the latest transaction submitted involved in merging. Therefore, when the number of workers is 1, the throughput of the two are similar and the latency of *merge-on* is much higher. When the number of workers increases, conflicting transactions can be executed in parallel after merging, which decreases the latency. Even with the lowest conflict rate, the advantage of *merging* is obvious. The scalability of FILMER's processing of homogeneous operations is not ideal, because lots of logs need to be written to disk when a bunch of *Submit Order* submitted, which becomes a bottleneck.

In Fig. 10, we illustrate performance in throughput and latency by changing concurrency factor from 1 to 100. Since a transaction needs to wait for all the conflicting transactions that arrived before to be processed before it can be executed, increasing concurrency in a traditional DBMS will not increase the throughput, but will only allow the system to store more transaction context and build a longer wait queue. When *merge-off*, increasing concurrency does not increase the throughput, but only makes the latency higher. On the other hand, when we merge homogeneous operations, the larger the concurrency factor is, the more operations can be executed in one merge. The throughput can be up to 2.55× higher than that of *merge-off*. Meanwhile, as the transaction processing efficiency is improved as a whole, the latency is also reduced. When the concurrency factor is 100, the latency of *merge-on* is only 44% of that of *merge-off*.

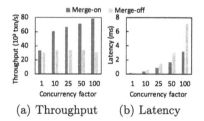 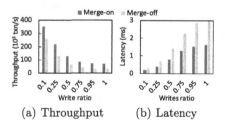

(a) Throughput   (b) Latency   (a) Throughput   (b) Latency

Fig. 10. Performance of FILMER under High Conflict with *Filter-off*.

Fig. 11. *Merging* Performance by Adjusting of Transaction Ratios with *Filter-off*.

We adjust the ratio between reads and writes in Fig. 11, by using *Submit Order* and *Select Order* as the test workloads. The write ratio in Fig. 11 refers to the proportion of *Submit Order* in workloads. From the results, we can see that even if the write ratio is extremely low (only 10%) in high-concurrency and high-contention scenario, the throughput increases by 34%, and the latency decreases by 31% with *merge-on*. With the increasing of writes, the advantage of *merge-on* becomes more and more obvious. When the write ratio is 1, the throughput of *merge-on* is 2× higher than that of *merge-off*, but the latency increases only 54%. We can conclude that in the highly contended workloads, *merging* can improve system performance by optimizing the processing of write transactions.

5.2 Macro Evaluation of FILMER

To further observe the mutual influence of *filtering* and *merging*, we turn on *merging* to test the change of performance over time when the number of items is insufficient in Fig. 12. All other settings are the same as Fig. 4. Before the 6th second, the items are enough, there are no failed transactions, and the throughput and latency of *filter-on* and *filter-off* are the same. Compared with Fig. 4, the occurrence of failed transactions is earlier, because *merging* improves throughput. At the 6th second, the performance of successful transactions under *filter-on* suddenly deteriorates for a short period, and the latency is higher than the peak latency in Fig. 4. In addition to the multi-threads read and write to the filter table, this is also affected by the split of the merged operation. When a merged operation generated from multiple homogeneous operations executes unsuccessfully, the *TE* will split them again into single operations to execute one by one. When there are sold-out items that have not been inserted into the filter table, some merged operations will fail. This process affects the performance of the system, resulting in unsatisfactory performance of successful and failed transactions under *filter-off* in the subsequent period. When *filter-off*, a large quantity of ineffective operations flood into *TE*, so that the merged operation splitting continues to occur, occupying system resources, and then all transaction processing slows down. By contrast, when *filter-on*, it will mitigate splitting effectively. Therefore, *merging* had better be used together with *filtering*.

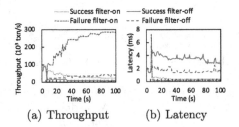

(a) Throughput   (b) Latency

Fig. 12. Overall Performance with *Merging* and *Filtering*.

6   Related Work

Recently, great efforts have been put to improve the performance of DBMSs when dealing with highly contended workloads. Two design principles are proposed by Orthrus [16]. One is to arrange special threads to manage concurrency control (CC). Each CC thread is responsible for a disjoint subset of the database objects to avoid data movement and reduce synchronization overhead. The other one is to grant locks to transactions in a consistent order to avoid deadlocks. Contention-aware lock scheduling algorithm [19] improves lock-based protocols by capturing the contention and the dependencies among concurrent transactions. Its algorithm preferentially grants locks to transactions that block many others. Our work does not focus on locking scheduling, and this algorithm complements our work. MOCC [20] introduces locking mechanism in OCC. When a transaction accesses data with high temperature, it needs to acquire a lock to reduce the rollback rate of transactions. None of these work have targeted the optimization of homogeneous operations or ineffective operations in highly contented E-commerce workloads.

Workload sharing has been studied for a long time. Multi Query Optimization (MQO) [18] executes a subquery only once no matter how many times the subquery appears in an OLAP query. This method only supports sharing resources in a single query, provided there are multiple similar subqueries in the query. MQJoin [9] and CJOIN [3] use pipelining to share resource in joins. But joins are not common in OLTP workloads. Strife [14] uses a dynamic partitioning approach that allows contention transactions to be executed without concurrency control, but this makes the system limited, even on the same physical machine can produce distributed transactions. SharedDB [7] and BatchDB [10] take OLTP workloads into consideration. SharedDB batches queries and compiles them into a big plan. Different queries share operators. BatchDB separates OLTP replica and OLAP replica, and resources can be shared among OLAP queries. The focus of these research is to deal with OLAP queries. OLTPShare [15] is the closest to our work, which proposes to merge statements in OLTP workloads to adapt to high loaded scenarios. However, it only merges single-point read-only statements instead of writes. Moreover, OLTPShare requires that the statement to be merged must be the only statement in its transaction, which is not required by FILMER.

7   Conclusion

This paper designs an efficient transaction processing scheme for highly contended E-commerce workloads, and implements the prototype system FILMER to verify the effectiveness of the scheme. FILMER logically binds threads to data, sets a filter at IO layer to intercept ineffective operations, and merges homogeneous operations in transaction executor. By *filtering*, it saves the system resources, improves the scalability of transaction processing. *Merging* increases the parallelism of transaction processing, reduces the number of data modification, and finally improves the performance of DBMS. Combining of *filtering* and *merging* will get better performance.

References

1. Alomari, M., Cahill, M., Fekete, A., Rohm, U.: The cost of serializability on platforms that use snapshot isolation. In: ICDE, pp. 576–585. IEEE (2008)
2. Bernstein, P.A., Hadzilacos, V., Goodman, N.: Concurrency Control and Recovery in Database Systems. Addison-Wesley, Boston (1987)
3. Candea, G., Polyzotis, N., Vingralek, R.: Predictable performance and high query concurrency for data analytics. VLDB **20**(2), 227–248 (2011)
4. Council, T.P.P.: TPC-C benchmark (1992). https://www.tpc.org/tpcc/
5. DeCandia, G., et al.: Dynamo: Amazon's highly available key-value store. In: SOSP, pp. 205–220 (2007)
6. Faleiro, J.M., Abadi, D.J.: Rethinking serializable multiversion concurrency control. VLDB **8**(11), 1190–1201 (2015)
7. Giannikis, G., Alonso, G., Kossmann, D.: SharedDB: killing one thousand queries with one stone. VLDB **5**(6), 526–537 (2012)
8. Huang, G., et al.: X-Engine: an optimized storage engine for large-scale e-commerce transaction processing. In: SIGMOD, pp. 651–665 (2019)
9. Makreshanski, D., Giannikis, G., Alonso, G., Kossmann, D.: MQJoin: efficient shared execution of main-memory joins. VLDB **9**(6), 480–491 (2016)
10. Makreshanski, D., Giceva, J., Barthels, C., Alonso, G.: BatchDB: efficient isolated execution of hybrid OLTP+OLAP workloads for interactive applications. In: SIGMOD, pp. 37–50 (2017)
11. Narula, N., Cutler, C., Kohler, E., Morris, R.: Phase reconciliation for contended in-memory transactions. In: OSDI, pp. 511–524 (2014)
12. Oracle: Oracle Database 12c: Advanced Queuing Whitepaper (2015)
13. Pandis, I., Johnson, R., Hardavellas, N., Ailamaki, A.: Data-oriented transaction execution. VLDB **3**(1–2), 928–939 (2010)
14. Prasaad, G., Cheung, A., Suciu, D.: Handling highly contended OLTP workloads using fast dynamic partitioning. In: International Conference on Management of Data, SIGMOD/PODS 2020 (2020)
15. Rehrmann, R., Binnig, C., Böhm, A., Kim, K., Lehner, W., Rizk, A.: OLTPshare: the case for sharing in OLTP workloads. VLDB **11**(12), 1769–1780 (2018)
16. Ren, K., Faleiro, J.M., Abadi, D.J.: Design principles for scaling multi-core OLTP under high contention. In: SIGMOD, pp. 1583–1598 (2016)
17. Rodeh, O.: B-trees, shadowing, and clones. TOS **3**(4), 2 (2008)
18. Sellis, T.K.: Multiple-query optimization. TODS **13**(1), 23–52 (1988)
19. Tian, B., Huang, J., Mozafari, B., Schoenebeck, G.: Contention-aware lock scheduling for transactional databases. VLDB **11**(5), 648–662 (2018)
20. Wang, T., Kimura, H.: Mostly-optimistic concurrency control for highly contended dynamic workloads on a thousand cores. VLDB **10**(2), 49–60 (2016)
21. Zhang, C., Li, Y., Zhang, R., Qian, W., Zhou, A.: Benchmarking on intensive transaction processing. Front. Comp. Sci. **14**(5), 1–18 (2020)

DeepTD: Diversity-Guided Deep Neural Network Test Generation

Jin Zhu[1], Chuanqi Tao[1,2,3,4]([✉]), Hongjing Guo[1], and Yue Ju[1]

[1] College of Computer Science and Technology, Nanjing University of Aeronautics and Astronautics, Nanjing, China
{taochuanqi,guohongjing,juyue}@nuaa.edu.cn
[2] Ministry Key Laboratory for Safety-Critical Software Development and Verification, Nanjing, China
[3] State Key Laboratory for Novel Software Technology, Nanjing, China
[4] Collaborative Innovation Center of Novel Software Technology and Industrialization, Nanjing, China

Abstract. Coverage-guided Fuzz Testing (CGF) techniques have been applied to deep neural network (DNN) testing in recent years, generating a significant number of test samples to uncover inherent defects in DNN models. However, the effectiveness of CGF techniques that utilize structured coverage metrics as coverage criteria is currently being questioned. A few unstructured coverage metrics, such as surprise adequacy, only take into account the diversity of the test samples against the training set, while ignoring the diversity of the test samples themselves. In addition to this, the existing surprise adequacy metrics have some limitations in their applications. Therefore, this paper proposes DeepTD, a diversity-guided deep neural networks test generation method. Firstly, DeepTD selects high-loss test samples from each class on average, ensuring these test seeds possess a strong ability to reveal model errors. Then, DeepTD transforms these test seeds to enhance the diversity of the generated samples. Finally, Cluster-based Surprise Adequacy is designed to guide the generation of test samples. To evaluate the effectiveness of DeepTD, six DNN models are selected as subjects, covering two well-known image datasets. Experimental results demonstrate that the Cluster-based Surprise Adequacy outperforms the two existing metrics not only in computational efficiency but also in discovering more model defects. What's more, the test samples generated by DeepTD are on average 6.04% and 3.24% more effective for model retraining in MNIST and CIFAR10 compared to baseline methods, respectively.

Keywords: Coverage-guided fuzz testing · Deep neural network · Test samples diversity · Test generation

1 Introduction

With the rapid development of artificial intelligence technology, more and more deep neural network (DNN) models are deployed in intelligent software systems

H. Hermanns et al. (Eds.): SETTA 2023, LNCS 14464, pp. 419–433, 2024.
https://doi.org/10.1007/978-981-99-8664-4_24

and widely used in industrial production, social life, etc. However, the problems of reliability, safety, and robustness of DNN models are becoming more and more prominent, especially in safety-related fields, such as autonomous driving [2] and medical imaging [22], which may cause serious consequences in case of failure. Therefore, how to guarantee the quality of DNN models is a crucial issue.

Unlike traditional software testing, DNN is essentially a mathematical model that fits the intrinsic laws of the data in an approximate way, and it is impossible to show the execution logic of each step like traditional software. The current effective way to test DNN models is to expose the intrinsic defects of DNN models through a large amount of test data. Therefore, designing effective test sample generation methods for DNN models is a hot research topic in the field of DNN testing in recent years. Coverage-guided Fuzz testing has demonstrated a strong error-revealing capability in traditional software, and is able to utilize limited test data to automatically generate a large amount of test data with high coverage. Therefore, the CGF method is also applied to test sample generation for DNN models [16,23,26].

The coverage criterion is one of the most important parts of the CGF methods. A well-designed coverage criterion can effectively guide DNN test sample generation. Most current methods use structured metrics as coverage criterion, but their effectiveness has been questioned. Whereas some unstructured coverage metrics, such as test sample diversity, have been demonstrated to be effective in guiding DNN testing [1,8]. Kim et al. [8] referred to the diversity of test samples with respect to the training set as surprise adequacy, and proposed two surprise adequacy metrics, Likelihood-based Surprise Adequacy (LSA) and Distance-based Surprise Adequacy (DSA). The higher the surprise adequacy value, the greater the difference between the test samples and the training samples, and the more likely to reveal the hidden errors of the DNN model. Zohreh et al. [1] took into account the diversity of the test samples themselves, and proposed three metrics for the diversity of the test samples, namely Geometric Diversity, Normalized Compression Distance, and Standard Deviation. The experiments proved that the three diversity metrics can effectively guide the testing of DNN models.

Although the above two methods consider the diversity of test samples, they only consider one aspect of it, which is obviously not comprehensive enough. Therefore, in connection with the above definition of diversity of test samples, this paper gives the following more complete description of the diversity of test samples. The diversity of the test sample is not only reflected in its own diversity, but also in the fact that it is also more diverse compared to the training set. What's more, the above two surprise metrics are cumbersome and restrictive in their computation. LSA requires the feature matrix of the training set to be non-singular during the computation process, and DSA needs to traverse the samples of the whole training set for every computation, which limit the application of the two surprise metrics in real environments. In addition to this, seed selection is a key step in the CGF technique, but most of the existing methods use a randomized strategy to screen the seed samples, ignoring the ability of the seed samples to reveal model errors.

To address the above problems, this paper proposes a diversity-guided test sample generation method for deep neural networks (DeepTD). Firstly, DeepTD selects test samples with high loss values from each class of samples as test seeds on average, which ensures that the test seeds have high error-revealing ability and the generated test samples cover all classes. Then, DeepTD transforms the test seeds to enhance the diversity of test samples in the same class. Second, DeepTD designs Cluster-based Surprise Adequacy to address the problems with the two surprise indicators. In this paper, we conduct an experiment evaluation of DeepTD on 2 classical deep learning datasets and the corresponding 6 models. The experiment results show that DeepTD generates more diverse test samples compared to DLFuzz and RobOT. In terms of guiding model retraining, DeepTD is on average 6.04% more effective for model retraining on MNIST compared to the baseline method, and 3.24% more effective on CIFAR10.

The main contributions of the paper are as follows:

- This paper proposes a seed selection strategy based on loss values and takes into account the classes of seeds. Some of the samples with high loss values in each class are selected as test seeds on average in the test set, which improves the error-revealing ability of the seeds.
- The paper summarizes the diversity of test samples proposed in existing research, gives a more complete description of the diversity of the test sample. The diversity of test samples is reflected not only in the samples themselves but also in their contrast with training samples.
- Guided by the diversity of test samples in two aspects, this paper proposes to transform the seeds as well as to design Cluster-based Surprise Adequacy which are more effective than the existing surprise adequacy metrics.
- Experiments on 2 public image datasets and 6 DNN models in this paper demonstrate that the test samples generated by DeepTD can effectively guide model retraining, and compared with the existing methods, DeepTD can achieve up to 15.97%, 9.38%, 10.22%, 6.22%, 20.69%, and 29.59% retraining effect on 6 models.

The remainder of this paper is organized as follows. Section 2 provides an overview of the relevant basic concepts. Section 3 describes DeepTD in detail. Section 4 presents the experimental settings for our study and discusses the experimental results for the research questions. Section 5 shows the threats to validity for DeepTD. Section 6 provides an overview of related work, and finally, Sect. 7 concludes the paper.

2 Background

2.1 Deep Neural Networks

A deep neural network typically consists of three layers: the input layer, hidden layer, and output layer, each containing numerous neurons [12]. Weight and bias parameters are set between these layers. Training a neural network is essentially learning these parameters that allow the neural network to fit the patterns inherent in the data. The input layer specifies the input format, the hidden layer extracts the input features, and the output layer produces the prediction result. According to the prediction results, the deep neural network can be divided into two categories: the prediction results are discrete values, the classification model, and the prediction results are continuous values, the regression model.

2.2   Coverage-Guide Fuzz Testing for DNN

Coverage-guide Fuzz testing (CGF) is an essential testing technique in traditional software that has been applied to DNN testing in recent years because of its reliability and effectiveness. This technique uses a coverage criterion as a feedback to perform specific mutations on a given test seed to generate new test samples with maximum coverage and maximum possible exposure of model errors. The CGF testing technique consists of four main parts, seed selection, seed mutation, coverage analysis and test result determination.

Seed Selection: Seed selection is mainly reflected in two aspects: 1) what strategy is adopted to select some samples from the data set to build a seed queue; 2) what strategy is adopted to select seeds from the seed queue for mutation.

Seed Mutation: Seed mutation is the core of CGF technique. It mainly includes the use of domain knowledge [24], white noise [3], adversarial generative networks [27], etc. to design mutation strategies, and at the same time limit the degree of mutation so that the mutated data and the original seed have semantic invariance.

Coverage Analysis: This part mainly uses the test adequacy criterion [8,13,14] of DNN to analyse the execution of the DNN model by the mutated seeds and then extracts valuable information. This information determines whether to add the mutated seed to the seed queue and to guide the seed mutation.

Test Result Determination: This part mainly determines whether the prediction result of DNN on mutated seeds passes or not. Since the decision logic of DNN model is closed to testers, it is generally unknown whether the prediction result of DNN model meets the expectation or not, which is also the difficult point of DNN testing. Currently differential testing [19] and metamorphic testing [21] are the main methods to solve DNN testing oracles.

3   Approach

The main structure of DeepTD is shown as Fig. 1. Firstly, samples with high loss value are selected from the test set to construct a seed queue according to the category, and then the brightness and saturation of each seed sample in the seed queue are randomly transformed. Next, we will maximize the error behavior of the model and Cluster-based Surprise Adequacy (CSA) of the sample as the joint optimization objective, use the gradient ascending algorithm to calculate the gradient of the objective function, and add the gradient to the seed as a

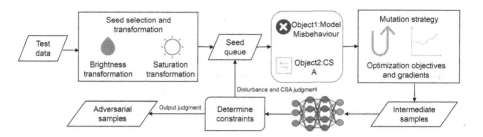

Fig. 1. Overview of DeepTD

disturbance to generate intermediate samples. Finally, it determines whether the intermediate samples satisfy the constraints, which determines whether the intermediate samples are added to the seed queue or become new generated samples.

3.1 Seed Selection and Transformations

Diverse test samples can improve the ability of fuzz testing to explore the internality of DNN models, and can reveal as many errors as possible that cannot be exposed by the original test set. As the basis of fuzz testing, seed samples have a profound impact on the diversity of generated samples. According to the labels of the seed samples, DeepTD selects the samples with high loss values in each class of test samples on average. The higher the loss value of a sample, the more likely it is to reveal errors in the model. Although the average selection of each class of samples ensures that the classes of seed samples are more diverse, but in order to improve the diversity of the same class of samples, the seed samples also need to be transformed.

In order to get closer to the different states of the samples in the real environment, DeepTD chooses to transform the brightness and saturation of the samples. The brightness and saturation of the sample will change with illumination, distance and other factors in the real environment, which are the two most common transformations. To achieve this, DeepTD uses the built-in brightness and saturation transformation functions in the tensorflow framework [17], as shown below:

Tensorflow.image.random_brightness(image,max_delta,seed=None),image represents the input image sample, max_delta indicates that the function randomly adjusts the brightness of the image between [-max_delta, max_delta]. DeepTD sets max_delta = 0.3.

Tensorflow.image.random_contrast(image, the lower and upper, seed, seed = None), image input images of samples, lower and upper denote that the function randomly adjusts the contrast of the image between [lower, upper]. DeepTD sets lower and upper to 0.3, 1, respectively.

3.2 Cluster-Based Surprise Adequacy

As a manifestation of diversity, the more surprise the test sample, the more diverse it is compared to the training set, and the higher the likelihood of triggering model errors. In order to measure the surprise of test samples, DeepTD designs a Cluster-based Surprise Adequacy (CSA). Compared with DSA and LSA proposed by the literature [8], the calculation process of CSA is more concise and efficient.

Let D be a DNN model and x be a input. For an input x, $D(x)$ represents the output of the model, and $D_i(x)$ represents the output of ith layer of the model. X represents the training set. According to the training label, X is divided into k sets $\{X_1, X_2, ..., X_j, ..., X_k(1 << j << k)\}$, k denotes the number of classes. For each training sample x in X_j, we can obtain $D_i(x)$, and all $D_i(x)$ constitute the output feature set X'_j. Then X'_j is divided into n clusters using K-Means [6], with n determined by the Silhouette Coefficient [20], and the cluster centers are $\{C_1^j, C_2^j, ..., C_h^j, ..., C_n^j(1 << h << n)\}$. For a test input t in the test set T, the output feature $D_i(t)$ is obtained. Based on its class label y, we use the corresponding the already trained K-Means to determine the cluster it belongs to and get its cluster center C_h^j. The csa of test input t is calculated as follows:

$$csa = \left\| D_i(t) - C_h^j \right\|_2 \tag{1}$$

CSA evaluates the surprise of a test sample primarily by measuring the distance of the test sample from the cluster center of the cluster in which it is located. The further the test sample is from the cluster center, the more surprise the test sample is. This distance is measured by the 2-norm.

3.3 Test Samples Generation

DeepTD uses a gradient ascent algorithm to maximize the objective loss function, solves for the gradient, and then attaches the gradient as a perturbation to the seed samples to generate test samples. The objective function is defined as follows:

$$obj = \sum_{i=1}^{k} p(c_i) - p(c) + \lambda \times csa \tag{2}$$

Where given a sample, the probability vector distribution of the DNN model at the softmax layer can be denoted as $(p(c_1), p(c_2), ..., p(c_n))$, each component is the probability that the model predicted sample belongs to each class. $p(c)$ denotes the largest probability value in the probability vector, and c is its corresponding class label. $c_i(1 << i << k)$ denotes one of the k class labels with the largest predicted probability other than c. In this paper, k is set to 5. The first half of the objective function aims to make the generated test samples cross the decision boundaries of the DNN model, so that the model will happen the misclassification behavior. The second half maximizes the surprise adequacy of the generated samples, making the generated samples more diverse relative to

---

Algorithm 1. Seed Mutation

Input: tested model D, seed queue *seed_queue*, seed labels *lables*, training set *train_set*, learning rate lr, iteration times *iter_times*

Output: adversarial test samples *adv_samples*

 1: Initialization: *adv_samples* $= \emptyset$
 2: $D\_con \leftarrow$ construct_contrast_model()
 3: **while** *seed* in $seed_queue$ **do**
 4:    *seed_list* $= [seed]$
 5:    $c\_ori = labels[seed]$
 6:    **while** len(*seed_list* > 0) **do**
 7:       $x = $ *seed_list*.pop()
 8:       $c, c\_topk = D$.predict(x)
 9:       $csa = $ cal_CSA($x, D, train\_set$)
10:       $obj = $ sum(c_topk) - c $+ \lambda \times csa$
11:       $grads = \partial obj / \partial x$
12:       **while** *iter* in range(*iter_times*) **do**
13:          $perb = $ processing($grads$)
14:          $x' = x + perb \times lr$
15:          $dis = $ dis_constraint(x, x')
16:          **if** $csa\_max < csa$ and $dis < \varepsilon$ **then**
17:             *seed_list*.append(x')
18:          **end if**
19:          $c' = D$.predict(x')
20:          **if** c' != c_ori **then**
21:             *adv_samples*.append((x', c_ori))
22:          **end if**
23:       **end while**
24:    **end while**
25: **end while**

---

the training samples. Algorithm 1 shows the process of seed sample mutation. The algorithm takes tested model D, the seed queue *seed_queue*, the seed sample labels *labels*, the training set *train_set*, and the pre-set learning rate lr and iteration times *iter_times* as inputs. The algorithm outputs the generated adversarial sample *adv_samples*. *seed_list* is used to store the intermediate samples generated from each seed. The algorithm first extracts the seed samples from the seed queue as well as the corresponding labels and stores the seed samples in *seed_list* (line 2–4). Then for each sample in *seed_list*, compute the maximum predicted probability c, the top k predicted probabilities c_topk below c, and the Cluster-based Surprise Adequacy csa. Bring them into the objective function to calculate the gradient $grads$ with respect to the sample x (line 6–10). The derived gradient $grads$ are further processed to generate a perturbation $perb$, which is multiplied by the learning rate lr and added to the seed sample x to generate an intermediate sample x' (line 12–13). Based on whether the surprise value can be boosted or not and the distance constraint between the samples, it is decided whether the intermediate samples should be retained for the next iteration to generate the test samples. dis_constraint() is used to compute the

Euclidean distance between the samples (line 14–18). If the generated intermediate sample is predicted by the model to be inconsistent with the original label, it indicates that the sample is an adversarial test sample and is added to *adv_samples* along with the true label (line 19–21). The above is a one iteration process and after many iterations, more adversarial test samples are generated.

The total number of seed samples set by the algorithm is 200, the learning rate is 0.1, the number of iterations is 5, and the distance threshold is 0.05. The objective function weight is set to 1, with larger values indicating that the algorithm prefers generating samples that enhance surprise adequacy.

4   Experiments

The experiment is implemented based on the following frameworks, Tensorflow 2.5.0 and Keras 2.4.3. We develop and evaluate on a computer with a 12th generation Intel(R) Core(TM) i7-12700F 2.10 GHz, 32 GB RAM, an NVIDIA GTX 3080 GPU, and Windows 11 as the host operating system.

4.1   Dataset and Models

The experiment utilizes MNIST [9] and the models LeNet-1, LeNet-4, LeNet-5 [10], CIFAR10 and the models ResNet-20, ResNet-32, ResNet-44 [7] as the objects of study. MNIST is an image dataset of handwritten numerals (0 9). The CIFAR10 dataset contains images of 10 types of real-world objects (birds, airplanes, etc.). See Table 1 for specific details.

Table 1. Details of the DNN models and datasets

Dataset	Model	Parameters	Layers	Accuracy
MNIST	LeNet-1	7206	8	0.9855
	LeNet-4	69362	9	0.9897
	LeNet-5	107786	10	0.9908
CIFAR10	ResNet20	274442	73	0.9046
	ResNet32	470218	115	0.9113
	ResNet44	665994	157	0.9147

4.2   Evaluation Metrics and Baselines

Mistake-n denotes the number of misclassified samples in the first n priority samples screened to assess whether the surprise adequacy metrics are able to detect more misbehaviour in the model. Standard Deviation (STD) [1], Likelihood-based Surprise Coverage Score (LSC) and Distance-based Surprise Coverage

Score (DSC) [8] are used as metrics for assessing the diversity of the test set. STD is used to assess the diversity of the test samples with respect to the test samples of the same class. To get the diversity of the whole test set, we define STD_{total}, calculated as follows:

$$STD_{total} = \sum_{i=0}^{n} STD_i \div n \qquad (3)$$

STD_i denotes the STD value for each class of samples in the test set, and n denotes the number of classes. Larger STD_{total} indicate more diverse samples of the same class. DSC and LSC are used to assess the diversity of the test samples relative to the training samples of the same class. Accuracy (ACC) is used to determine whether the generated samples are able to guide model retraining. The baseline methods used in this experiment are DLFuzz [5] and RoBot [25], details of which are given in Sect. 6.

Table 2. Effectiveness and efficiency results of CSA, DSA and LSA on six models

Models	Methods	Time	Mistake-100	Mistake-200	Mistake-300	Mistake-500	Mistake-1000
LeNet-1	DSA	76	2	4	6	15	22
	LSA	3	2	4	5	5	13
	CSA	1	28	44	60	82	110
LeNet-4	DSA	76	1	3	3	5	9
	LSA	3	0	1	1	4	8
	CSA	1	23	41	54	68	84
LeNet-5	DSA	76	1	3	6	8	11
	LSA	3	1	4	4	8	13
	CSA	1	37	59	71	79	88
ResNet-20	DSA	70	12	21	32	49	95
	LSA	7	8	21	31	44	82
	CSA	2	58	110	154	232	402
ResNet-32	DSA	74	12	20	33	54	96
	LSA	9	11	17	29	44	78
	CSA	2	74	134	190	292	479
ResNet-44	DSA	74	13	25	30	47	90
	LSA	13	6	19	27	50	92
	CSA	2	71	136	181	262	427

4.3   Research Questions and Results

RQ1: Is CSA more efficient compared to DSA and LSA calculations, and can it detect more misbehaviour of the model?
To evaluate the efficiency of the computation of different metrics, we measure the time consumed to compute the surprise adequacy of all test samples in the test set on different models. Then, based on the surprise adequacy of the test

samples, we prioritise the test samples. The higher the surprise adequacy, the higher the priority of the test samples. Some of the high priority test samples are then selected to determine whether the model has more misbehaviour. The evaluation indicators use Mistake-n,n are taken as 100, 200, 300, 500, 1000, respectively.

The experimental results are shown in Table 2. In terms of computational efficiency, the average time consumed by CSA on the LeNet series of models is 1 s, the average time consumed on the ResNet series of models is 2 s, and the overall average is 1.5 s. The average time consumed by DSA on the LeNet series of models is 76 s, and the average time consumed on the ResNet series of models is 72.6 s, and the overall average is 74.3 s. The average time consumed by LSA on the LeNet series model is 3 s, on the ResNet series model is 2 s, and the overall average is 2.5 s. From the results, CSA takes the least time, followed by LSA, with an average of only 1 s more compared to CSA. DSA takes the most time on average, which is approximately 49 times as much as CSA and 30 times as much as LSA. The computational time consumed by DSA is further prolonged when computing larger test sets. This also limits the use of DSA in large-scale datasets. In terms of revealing the misbehaviour of the models, the number of misclassified samples screened by CSA on the six models about Mistake-100, Mistake-200, Mistake-300, Mistake-500, Mistake-1000 are on average 48, 87, 118, 169, 265, respectively, and for DSA are 6, 12, 18, 29, 53, LSA is 4, 11, 16, 25, 47 respectively. In the case of screening the same number of priority samples, CSA discovers 4 to 7 times more misclassified samples than DSA and 5 to 10 times more than LSA. This is strong evidence that CSA has a greater ability to detect model misbehaviour.

Result of RQ1: Compared with the already existing two surprise adequacy metrics, DSA and LSA, CSA is not only more computationally efficient, but also can discover more erroneous behaviours of the model.

RQ2: Are the test samples generated by the DeepTD method more diverse?

To answer RQ2, 1000 samples are randomly selected from the test samples generated by DeepTD and other baseline methods, and then STD_{total}, LSC, and LSC are calculated to evaluate the diversity of these samples.

Figure 2 show the diversity results of test samples generated by all methods on MNIST. It is clear from Fig. 2 that DeepTD is significantly higher than the other two methods in the three metrics of diversity. Considering the average diversity in the three models, DeepTD is 0.8254, 0.3213, 0.1407 for STD_{total}, DSC and LSC, respectively, 0.4181, 0.254, 0.0803 for RobOT, respectively and 0.7612, 0.1853, 0.0913 for DLFuzz, respectively. On STD_{total}, DeepTD is nearly twice as high compared to the RobOT method. On CIFAR10, DeepTD is higher than the other two methods in STD_{total} and DSC, but lower than DLFuzz in LSC. As can be seen in Fig. 3, DeepTD, although performing slightly worse in terms of LSC, still has an overall advantage in all three metrics.

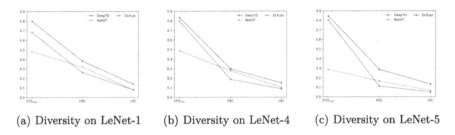

(a) Diversity on LeNet-1   (b) Diversity on LeNet-4   (c) Diversity on LeNet-5

Fig. 2. Evaluation results of diversity of test samples generated by different methods on MNIST

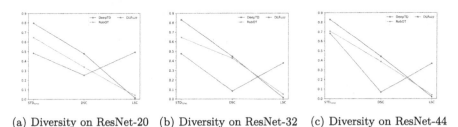

(a) Diversity on ResNet-20   (b) Diversity on ResNet-32   (c) Diversity on ResNet-44

Fig. 3. Evaluation results of diversity of test samples generated by different methods on CIFAR10

Result of RQ2: The test samples generated by the DeepTD method show high diversity on both MNIST and CIFAR10 compared to the baseline method, proving that DeepTD can generate more diverse test samples.

RQ3: Can the test samples generated by DeepTD guide model retraining?

In order to answer RQ3, this section uses PGD [15], FGSM [4] adversarial samples generation methods to generate adversarial samples, which are mixed with the test set to construct the mixed test set. Then from the generated test samples, 500, 1000, 1500 samples are randomly selected and mixed with the training set to retrain the model and observe whether the model's accuracy is improved under the mixed test set.

Table 3 shows the number of samples generated by each method on different models and the effect of retraining on Sample-n. Sample-n denotes the new training set of n generated samples mixed with the original training set. In terms of the number of generated samples, DeepTD generates more test samples compared to all other baseline methods except LeNet-1. In terms of the effect of retraining, on MNIST, DeepTD is 0.32% to 15.5% more effective in retraining the model on LeNet-1, LeNet-4, and LeNet-5 compared to the other baseline methods, with an average of 6.04%. On CIFAR10, DeepTD on ResNet-20, ResNet-32, and ResNet-44 outperforms the other baseline methods by 0.88% to 7.91%, with an average of 3.24%. On randomly selecting 500 samples for LeNet-5 retraining, DeepTD

Table 3. The effect of retraining models with test samples generated by different methods

DataSets	Methods	Samples	PGD + Original Test Set			FGSM + Original Test Set		
			Sample-500	Sample-1000	Sample-1500	Sample-500	Sample-1000	Sample-1500
Lenet-1	DeepTD	2489	**2.99%**	**7.03%**	**13.93%**	**10.23%**	**15.78%**	**15.97%**
	RobOT	3025	0.05%	0.11%	0	0.51%	0.28%	0.68%
	DLFuzz	2241	0.33%	0.40%	0.26%	2.12%	2.15%	2.30%
Lenet-4	DeepTD	2486	**0.91%**	**3.69%**	**5.60%**	**6.96%**	**9.18%**	**9.38%**
	RobOT	2303	0.10%	0.01%	0.06%	1.09%	1.14%	1.19%
	DLFuzz	1896	0.25%	0.24%	0.35%	4.09%	4.62%	4.54%
Lenet-5	DeepTD	2422	0.48%	**3.34%**	**5.75%**	7.51%	**9.06%**	**10.22%**
	RobOT	1752	0.11%	0.07%	0.07%	1.53%	1.55%	1.54%
	DLFuzz	1863	**0.58%**	0.58%	0.74%	**8.00%**	8.74%	8.06%
Resnet-20	DeepTD	3551	**4.46%**	**5.21%**	**6.22%**	**2.54%**	**3.34%**	**3.55%**
	RobOT	3441	2.75%	3.30%	2.62%	1.30%	1.08%	0.98%
	DLFuzz	1973	3.14%	3.57%	3.88%	0.94%	1.02%	1.15%
Resnet-32	DeepTD	3505	**26.54%**	**28.71%**	**30.69%**	**25.78%**	**26.73%**	**27.37%**
	RobOT	2889	21.52%	22.95%	22.78%	21.46%	22.74%	22.36%
	DLFuzz	1923	24.61%	25.19%	26.20%	24.10%	24.23%	24.47%
Resnet-44	DeepTD	3440	**26.07%**	**28.16%**	**29.59%**	**24.51%**	**26.02%**	**27.12%**
	RobOT	2435	22.15%	22.81%	22.85%	21.47%	21.62%	22.26%
	DLFuzz	1968	24.59%	25.35%	26.19%	23.63%	23.71%	23.59%

is slightly lower than DLFuzz, but in addition, the contribution of the samples generated by DeepTD to model retraining is better than DLFuzz and RobOT methods.

Result of RQ3: In summary, both the number of samples generated and the improvement in model retraining demonstrate that the test samples generated by DeepTD are capable of guiding model retraining to improve model robustness.

5   Threats to Validity

Internal. This is mainly reflected in the implementation of the DeepTD method, the implementation of the comparison method, and the implementation of the code for analysing and evaluating the experimental results. In addition, the code implementation used for the analysis and evaluation of the experimental results was carefully checked to ensure that the results are error-free.

External. The threat mainly comes from the deep learning dataset used in this paper and the DNN model to be tested. To verify the effectiveness of DeepTD, our work adopts two well-known datasets and six models of different sizes, structures, and complexity. What's more, DeepTD also used adversarial generation methods to construct mixed test sets. Due to the joint optimization goal designed by DeepTD being only applicable to classification models, this paper only conducts experiments on test samples generation on classification models in the image field. How DeepTD can be applied to regression models as well as larger scale datasets is part of our future work.

6   Related Work

6.1   Test Coverage Criteria for DNN

The test adequacy of software is a key indicator for evaluating and guaranteeing the quality of software, and traditional software testing has formed a set of relatively mature test adequacy metrics, such as branch coverage, conditional coverage, MC/DC coverage, etc. However, the composition mechanism and operation theory of DNN models are different from those of traditional software, so it is difficult to apply the test coverage criteria for traditional software to DNN models directly. Researchers have proposed structural and unstructural test coverage criteria for DNN models to evaluate the adequacy of testing.

The structural coverage criterion quantifies the degree to which the internal structure of a DNN model is covered by the test dataset. Pei et al. [18] proposed the first white-box test coverage criterion for DNNs, neuron coverage, which quantifies the ratio of the number of neurons activated in the test samples to the total number of neurons in the DNN. Ma et al. [14] defined multi-granularity coverage criterion for DNNs at the neuron level and network level, including K-multipartite region neuron coverage, neuron boundary coverage, Top-K neuron coverage, and so on from the perspectives of output distribution, sequence of active neurons, and so on.

The current unstructured coverage criterion mainly refers to surprise coverage. Kim et al. [8] proposed two kinds of surprise adequacy indicators from the perspective of the diversity of test samples to training samples, and then designed the surprise coverage criterion on this basis.

6.2   Test Samples Generation for DNN

Coverage-guide Fuzz testing, as an important part of DNN testing, aims to use a small number of valid test samples as seeds to generate a large number of test samples that do not meet the model expectations and cover the model boundary regions as much as possible. Pei et al. first proposed a neuron coverage criterion, which was then combined with differential testing aimed at maximising the difference in output results of different DNN models and neuron coverage to generate test samples. Guo et al. [5] proposed the DLFuzz method to maximize neuron coverage and model prediction differences between the original and mutated samples, while defining four neuron selection strategies to select neurons that are more likely to improve coverage. Lee et al. [11] proposed an adaptive neuron selection strategy, which utilizes the static and dynamic characteristics of the neurons during the generation of test samples to automatically select the appropriate neurons. Zhang et al. [28] proposed the CAGFuzz method, which uses neuron coverage as a guide to generate test samples using adversarial neural networks. Wang et al. [25] proposed the RobOT method from the perspective of model robustness, which can guide the selection or generation of test samples to improve the robustness of the model.

7   Conclusion

In this paper, we propose DeepTD, a diversity-guided deep neutral network test generation method. The method makes some changes in two key aspects of CGF-seed selection and seed mutation. On seed selection, guided by enhancing the diversity of test samples to the same class of test samples, the samples with high loss values in the test set are selected evenly by class, and brightness and saturation transformations are applied. On seed mutation, guided by enhancing the diversity of test samples to the same class of training samples, Cluster-based Surprise Adequacy is proposed to guide test sample generation. Experiments on 2 image datasets and 6 DNN models demonstrate the effectiveness of DeepTD. In the future, the DeepTD method will be improved to be used on regression models and more complex datasets.

Acknowledgment. This work is supported by the National Natural Science Foundation of China (No. 62202223), the Natural Science Foundation of Jiangsu Province (No. BK20220881), the Open Fund of the State Key Laboratory for Novel Software Technology (No. KFKT2021B32), the Fundamental Research Funds for the Central Universities (No. NT2022027) and the Postgraduate Research Practice Innovation Program of NUAA (No. xcxjh20221613).

References

1. Aghababaeyan, Z., Abdellatif, M., Briand, L., Ramesh, S., Bagherzadeh, M.: Black-box testing of deep neural networks through test case diversity. IEEE Trans. Softw. Eng. (2023)
2. Chen, C., Seff, A., Kornhauser, A., Xiao, J.: Deepdriving: learning affordance for direct perception in autonomous driving. In: Proceedings of the IEEE International Conference on Computer Vision, pp. 2722–2730 (2015)
3. Du, X., Xie, X., Li, Y., Ma, L., Zhao, J., Liu, Y.: Deepcruiser: automated guided testing for stateful deep learning systems. arXiv preprint arXiv:1812.05339 (2018)
4. Goodfellow, I.J., Shlens, J., Szegedy, C.: Explaining and harnessing adversarial examples. arXiv preprint arXiv:1412.6572 (2014)
5. Guo, J., Jiang, Y., Zhao, Y., Chen, Q., Sun, J.: DLFuzz: differential fuzzing testing of deep learning systems. In: Proceedings of the 2018 26th ACM Joint Meeting on European Software Engineering Conference and Symposium on the Foundations of Software Engineering, pp. 739–743 (2018)
6. Hartigan, J.A., Wong, M.A.: Algorithm AS 136: a k-means clustering algorithm. J. Roy. Stat. Soc. Ser. C (Appl. Stat.) **28**(1), 100–108 (1979)
7. He, K., Zhang, X., Ren, S., Sun, J.: Deep residual learning for image recognition. In: Proceedings of the IEEE Conference on Computer Vision and Pattern Recognition, pp. 770–778 (2016)
8. Kim, J., Feldt, R., Yoo, S.: Guiding deep learning system testing using surprise adequacy. In: 2019 IEEE/ACM 41st International Conference on Software Engineering (ICSE), pp. 1039–1049. IEEE (2019)
9. LeCun, Y.: The MNIST database of handwritten digits (1998). https://yann.lecun.com/exdb/mnist/
10. LeCun, Y., Bottou, L., Bengio, Y., Haffner, P.: Gradient-based learning applied to document recognition. Proc. IEEE **86**(11), 2278–2324 (1998)

11. Lee, S., Cha, S., Lee, D., Oh, H.: Effective white-box testing of deep neural networks with adaptive neuron-selection strategy. In: Proceedings of the 29th ACM SIGSOFT International Symposium on Software Testing and Analysis, pp. 165–176 (2020)
12. Liu, W., Wang, Z., Liu, X., Zeng, N., Liu, Y., Alsaadi, F.E.: A survey of deep neural network architectures and their applications. Neurocomputing **234**, 11–26 (2017)
13. Ma, L., et al.: DeepCT: tomographic combinatorial testing for deep learning systems. In: 2019 IEEE 26th International Conference on Software Analysis, Evolution and Reengineering (SANER), pp. 614–618. IEEE (2019)
14. Ma, L., et al.: DeepGauge: multi-granularity testing criteria for deep learning systems. In: Proceedings of the 33rd ACM/IEEE International Conference on Automated Software Engineering, pp. 120–131 (2018)
15. Madry, A., Makelov, A., Schmidt, L., Tsipras, D., Vladu, A.: Towards deep learning models resistant to adversarial attacks. arXiv preprint arXiv:1706.06083 (2017)
16. Odena, A., Olsson, C., Andersen, D., Goodfellow, I.: TensorFuzz: debugging neural networks with coverage-guided fuzzing. In: International Conference on Machine Learning, pp. 4901–4911. PMLR (2019)
17. Pang, B., Nijkamp, E., Wu, Y.N.: Deep learning with tensorflow: a review. J. Educ. Behav. Stat. **45**(2), 227–248 (2020)
18. Pei, K., Cao, Y., Yang, J., Jana, S.: DeepXplore: automated whitebox testing of deep learning systems. In: proceedings of the 26th Symposium on Operating Systems Principles, pp. 1–18 (2017)
19. Riccio, V., Jahangirova, G., Stocco, A., Humbatova, N., Weiss, M., Tonella, P.: Testing machine learning based systems: a systematic mapping. Empir. Softw. Eng. **25**, 5193–5254 (2020)
20. Rousseeuw, P.J.: Silhouettes: a graphical aid to the interpretation and validation of cluster analysis. J. Comput. Appl. Math. **20**, 53–65 (1987)
21. Segura, S., Fraser, G., Sanchez, A.B., Ruiz-Cortés, A.: A survey on metamorphic testing. IEEE Trans. Softw. Eng. **42**(9), 805–824 (2016)
22. Shen, D., Wu, G., Suk, H.I.: Deep learning in medical image analysis. Ann. Rev. Biomed. Eng. **19**, 221–248 (2017)
23. Tao, C., Tao, Y., Guo, H., Huang, Z., Sun, X.: DLRegion: coverage-guided fuzz testing of deep neural networks with region-based neuron selection strategies. Inf. Softw. Technol., 107266 (2023)
24. Tian, Y., Pei, K., Jana, S., Ray, B.: DeepTest: automated testing of deep-neural-network-driven autonomous cars. In: Proceedings of the 40th International Conference on Software Engineering, pp. 303–314 (2018)
25. Wang, J., et al.: Robot: robustness-oriented testing for deep learning systems. In: 2021 IEEE/ACM 43rd International Conference on Software Engineering (ICSE), pp. 300–311. IEEE (2021)
26. Xie, X., et al.: DeepHunter: a coverage-guided fuzz testing framework for deep neural networks. In: Proceedings of the 28th ACM SIGSOFT International Symposium on Software Testing and Analysis, pp. 146–157 (2019)
27. Zhang, P., Dai, Q., Ji, S.: Condition-guided adversarial generative testing for deep learning systems. In: 2019 IEEE International Conference on Artificial Intelligence Testing (AITest), pp. 71–72. IEEE (2019)
28. Zhang, P., Ren, B., Dong, H., Dai, Q.: CAGFuzz: coverage-guided adversarial generative fuzzing testing for image-based deep learning systems. IEEE Trans. Softw. Eng. **48**(11), 4630–4646 (2021)

Author Index

Printed in the United States
by Baker & Taylor Publisher Services